Product Design and Manufacturing

SEVENTH EDITION

A.K. CHITALE
Academic Advisor
Govindram Seksaria Institute of Management and Research
Indore

R.C. GUPTA
Professor and Head
Department of Industrial and Production Engineering
Shri Govindram Seksaria Institute of Technology and Science
Indore

PHI Learning Private Limited
Delhi-110092
2026

In fond memory of ***Shri Asoke K. Ghosh*** *(October 1942 – February 2024), Founder Chairman and Managing Director of PHI Learning, whose vision endlessly inspires.*

The Legacy Continues. . . .

Published by Pushpita Ghosh, PHI Learning Private Limited, Rimjhim House, 111, Patparganj Industrial Estate, Delhi-110092 and Printed by Multi Colour Services, 92, DSIDC Sheds, Okhla Industrial Area, Phase-I, New Delhi-110020.

₹995.00

PRODUCT DESIGN AND MANUFACTURING, Seventh Edition
A.K. Chitale and R.C. Gupta

ISBN-978-93-91818-72-2 (Print Book)
ISBN-978-93-91818-66-1 (e-Book)

The export rights of the book are vested solely with the publisher.

Contents

Preface *xiii*
Preface to the Sixth Edition *xv*
Preface to the Fifth Edition *xvii*

1. INTRODUCTION TO PRODUCT DESIGN: ASIMOW'S MODEL 1–29

1.1 Definition of Product Design *1*
1.2 Design by Evolution *1*
1.3 Design by Innovation *2*
1.4 Essential Factors of Product Design *2*
1.5 Production–Consumption Cycle *5*
1.6 Flow and Value Addition in the Production–Consumption Cycle *6*
1.7 The Morphology of Design (The Seven Phases) *7*
1.7.1 Phase I—Feasibility Study *7*
1.7.2 Phase II—Preliminary Design *8*
1.7.3 Phase III—Detailed Design *8*
1.7.4 Phase IV—Planning the Production Process *9*
1.7.5 Phase V—Planning for Distribution *9*
1.7.6 Phase VI—Planning for Consumption *10*
1.7.7 Phase VII—Planning for Retirement *10*
1.8 Primary Design Phases and Flowcharting—The 25 Steps *11*
1.8.1 Phase I—Feasibility Study *12*
1.8.2 Phase II—The Preliminary Design *14*
1.8.3 Phase III—Detailed Design *16*
1.9 Role of Allowance, Process Capability, and Tolerance in Detailed Design and Assembly *18*
1.9.1 Allowance (*A*) *18*
1.9.2 Process Capability (*P*) *18*
1.9.3 Tolerance (*T*) *18*
1.9.4 Types of Fits *19*
1.9.5 Selection of Fit *19*
1.9.6 Specific Principles *20*
1.10 Summary of Detailed Design Phase *21*

Review Questions *21*
References *29*

2. PRODUCT DESIGN PRACTICE AND INDUSTRY 30–62

2.1 Introduction *30*
2.2 Product Strategies *30*
2.2.1 Pricing Strategy for Product *30*
2.2.2 Product Quality Strategy *30*
2.2.3 Product Luxuriousness Strategy *31*
2.2.4 Product Utility Strategy *31*

2.3 Time to Market *31*
2.4 Analysis of the Product *32*
2.4.1 Product and Market *32*
2.4.2 The Product Characteristics *34*
2.5 The Three S's *37*
2.6 Standardization *38*
2.7 Renard Series (Preferred Numbers) *39*
2.8 Simplification *40*
2.9 The Designer and His Role *42*
2.10 The Designer: Myth and Reality *42*
2.11 The Industrial Design Organization *43*
2.12 Basic Design Considerations *43*
2.13 Problems Faced by Industrial Designer *45*
2.14 Procedure Adopted by Industrial Designers *45*
2.15 Types of Models Designed by Industrial Designers *46*
2.16 What the Designer Contributes *47*
2.17 Role of Aesthetics in Product Design *47*
2.17.1 Analysis of Product Aesthetics *47*
2.17.2 Basic Form Elements *48*
2.17.3 Integrating Basic Form Elements *49*
2.17.4 Product Message *53*
2.18 Functional Design Practice *54*
2.18.1 Biasing *54*
2.18.2 Cascading or Stage Formation *55*
2.18.3 Regeneration *55*
2.18.4 Avoiding Redundancy *56*
2.18.5 Compatibility and Matching Considerations in Product Design *56*

Review Questions *57*
References *62*

3. STRENGTH CONSIDERATION IN PRODUCT DESIGN.. 63–75

3.1 Principal Stress Trajectories (Force-Flow Lines) *63*
3.2 Balanced Design *65*
3.2.1 Analysis of Stresses during the Bending of a Curved Beam *67*
3.3 Criteria and Objectives of Design *70*
3.3.1 Strength Based Design *70*
3.3.2 Rigidity Based Design *71*
3.3.3 Impact Based Design *71*
3.4 Material Toughness: Resilience *71*
3.5 Designing for Uniform Strength *72*
3.6 Tension Vis-a-Vis Compression *74*

Review Questions *75*
References *75*

4. DESIGN FOR STIFFNESS AND RIGIDITY.. 76–99

4.1 Pure Struts and Pure Columns *76*
4.2 Structure Involving both Tension and Compression Members *76*
4.3 Mapping of Principal Stresses *76*
4.4 Buckling and Instability *77*
4.5 Theory of Long Columns *78*
4.5.1 Critical Load for Columns: Derivation of Formula *79*
4.5.2 Practical Considerations *80*
4.5.3 Stiffening of Columns *81*

4.6 Hollow Columns *81*
 4.6.1 Effect of Length and Thickness on Failure Modes *81*
 4.6.2 Practical Design Approach *82*
4.7 Plastic Design *83*
 4.7.1 Plastic Deformation *83*
 4.7.2 Elastic and Plastic Behaviour of Beams *83*
 4.7.3 Advantages and Disadvantages of Plastic Design *84*
4.8 Practical Ideas for Material Saving in Design *84*
 4.8.1 Slimming Down *85*
 4.8.2 Achieving Balance through Reinforcement *85*
 4.8.3 Cardboard Model of Plate Structures *85*
 4.8.4 Soap Film Analogy of Torsional Shear Stresses 86
4.9 Ribs, Corrugations, Laminates and Membranes *88*
 4.9.1 Stiff Skins *89*
 4.9.2 Sandwiches and Laminates *94*
 4.9.3 Membrane Structures *95*

Review Questions *96*
References *99*

5. PRODUCTION PROCESSES.. 100–166

5.1 Introduction *100*
5.2 Primary Processes *101*
 5.2.1 Casting Process *101*
 5.2.2 Forming Process *115*
 5.2.3 Joining Processes *128*
5.3 Welding Processes *132*
 5.3.1 Arc Welding *132*
 5.3.2 Tungsten Inert Gas (TIG) *136*
 5.3.3 MIG Arc Welding *137*
 5.3.4 Resistance Welding *137*
 5.3.5 Oxy-Acetylene Welding *139*
5.4 Machining Process *140*
 5.4.1 Shaping and Planing *141*
 5.4.2 Turning *142*
 5.4.3 Drilling *142*
 5.4.4 Milling *143*
 5.4.5 Grinding *143*
 5.4.6 Chip Formation Mechanism *143*
 5.4.7 Analysis of Metal Cutting Process *144*
 5.4.8 Analysis of Grinding Process *149*
 5.4.9 Machinability *150*
 5.4.10 Economics of Metal Cutting *151*
 5.4.11 The Tool Material *154*
 5.4.12 Cutting Fluids *155*
 5.4.13 Friction at Chip-Tool Interface *156*
5.5 Microfinishing Operations *157*
 5.5.1 Lapping *157*
 5.5.2 Honing *157*
 5.5.3 Superfinishing *157*
5.6 Non-traditional Machining Processes *158*
 5.6.1 Abrasive Jet Machining (AJM) *158*
 5.6.2 Ultrasonic Machining (USM) *159*
 5.6.3 Electrochemical Machining (ECM) *159*

5.6.4 Electric Discharge Machining (EDM) *160*
5.6.5 Electron Beam Machining (EBM) *160*
5.6.6 Laser Beam Machining (LBM) *161*

Review Questions *161*
References *166*

6. DESIGN FOR PRODUCTION: METAL PARTS 167–188

6.1 Producibility Requirements in the Design of Machine Components *167*
6.2 Forging Design *168*
6.3 Pressed Components Design *171*
6.4 Casting Design *173*
6.5 Design for Machining Ease *176*
6.6 The Role of Process Engineer *180*
6.7 Ease of Location and Clamping *180*
6.8 Some Additional Aspects of Production Design *182*
6.9 Die Casting and Special Castings *182*
6.10 Design of Powder Metallurgical Parts *183*
6.11 Expanded Metals and Wire Forms *184*
6.11.1 Expanded Metals *185*
6.11.2 Wire Forms *186*

Review Questions *187*
References *188*

7. MATERIAL PROCESSING OF PLASTICS, RUBBER, GLASS AND CERAMICS 189–224

7.1 Plastics *189*
7.1.1 Some Definitions *190*
7.2 Concepts in Chemistry of Plastics *190*
7.2.1 Types of Polymerization *190*
7.2.2 Effect of Heating on Thermoplastic *192*
7.2.3 Cross-Linked Polymers *193*
7.2.4 Thermosetting Polymers *193*
7.3 Properties of Plastics *195*
7.4 Classification of Plastics *196*
7.5 Phenol Formaldehyde and Urea Formaldehyde Resin Products *196*
7.6 Compression Moulding *197*
7.7 Transfer Moulding *198*
7.8 Injection Moulding *199*
7.9 High-Pressure Laminates *201*
7.10 Reinforced Plastic Moulding or Low-Pressure Laminating *202*
7.11 Forming and Drawing of Plastic Sheets *204*
7.12 Design of Plastic Parts *205*
7.13 Natural Rubber *206*
7.13.1 Vulcanization of Rubber *207*
7.14 Artificial Rubber *207*
7.15 Engineering Properties of Rubber *209*
7.16 Glass *210*
7.16.1 Glassy State *210*
7.16.2 The Glass Making Oxides *211*
7.17 The Functions of the Glass-Making Oxides *213*
7.18 Manufacture of Glass *213*
7.19 Ceramics *215*

Review Questions 216
References 224

8. DESIGNING WITH PLASTICS, RUBBER, CERAMICS AND WOOD....................... 225–247

8.1 Approach to Design with Plastics 225
8.2 Plastic Bush Bearings 226
8.3 Gears in Plastic 227
8.3.1 Moulded Plastic Gear: Manufacturing Technique 228
8.4 Fasteners in Plastic 228
8.4.1 Design Creativity with Hinges 228
8.5 Rubber Parts 229
8.5.1 Production Processes for Rubber 230
8.5.2 Popular Rubber Products 230
8.6 Design Recommendations for Rubber Parts 231
8.6.1 Gating 231
8.6.2 Holes 231
8.6.3 Wall Thickness 232
8.6.4 Undercuts 232
8.6.5 Screw Threads 233
8.6.6 Inserts 233
8.6.7 Draft 233
8.6.8 Corners 234
8.6.9 Flash 235
8.6.10 Parting Line 235
8.6.11 Venting 235
8.6.12 Surface Texture 236
8.6.13 Shrinkage 236
8.7 Distortion in Rubber 236
8.8 Dimensional Effects 237
8.9 Tolerances 237
8.10 Ceramics and Glass Parts 238
8.10.1 Properties of Ceramics and Glass 238
8.11 Production Design Factors for Ceramic Parts 239
8.11.1 Problems of Manufacture of Ceramic Parts 239
8.12 Special Considerations for Design of Glass Parts 243
8.13 Dimensional Factors and Tolerances 244
8.13.1 Ceramic Parts 244
8.13.2 Glass Parts 244
8.14 Wood 244
8.14.1 Some Engineering Properties of Wood 244
8.14.2 Wood-based Composite Materials 245
8.14.3 Joinery in Woodwork 245

Review Questions 246
References 247

9. OPTIMIZATION IN DESIGN... 248–263

9.1 Introduction 248
9.2 Siddal's Classification of Design Approaches 249
9.3 Optimization by Differential Calculus 250
9.4 Lagrange Multipliers 251
9.5 Linear Programming (Simplex Method) 252
9.5.1 Inequality Constraints 253

9.5.2 Simplex Method: Maximization *253*
9.6 Geometric Programming *256*
9.7 Johnson's Method of Optimum Design *260*
Review Questions *261*
References *263*

10. ECONOMIC FACTORS INFLUENCING DESIGN 264–283
10.1 Product Value *264*
10.2 Design for Safety, Reliability and Environmental Considerations *265*
10.2.1 Design for Safety *266*
10.2.2 Mistake Proofing *266*
10.2.3 Factor of Safety and Reliability *267*
10.2.4 Design for Reliability *269*
10.3 Manufacturing Operations in Relation to Design *271*
10.4 Economic Analysis *274*
10.5 Profit and Competitiveness *274*
10.6 Break-Even Analysis *276*
10.6.1 Conventional Break-Even Chart Approach *276*
10.6.2 Profit-Volume Chart Approach *279*
10.6.3 Multiproduct Profit-Volume Chart *280*
10.7 Economics of a New Product Design (Samuel Eilon Model) *281*
Review Questions *282*
Reference *283*

11. HUMAN ENGINEERING CONSIDERATIONS IN PRODUCT DESIGN 284–307
11.1 Introduction *284*
11.2 Human Being as Applicator of Forces *284*
11.3 Anthropometry: Man as Occupant of Space *287*
11.4 The Design of Controls *291*
11.5 The Design of Displays *294*
11.6 Man/Machine Information Exchange *296*
11.7 Workplace Layout from Ergonomic Considerations *298*
11.8 Noise *300*
11.8.1 Measurement of Noise *300*
11.8.2 Precautions against Noise *300*
11.9 Heating and Ventilating *301*
11.9.1 Standard for Industrial Thermal Comfort *301*
11.9.2 Air Conditioning *303*
11.9.3 Heating Methods *303*
11.10 Lighting *303*
11.10.1 Measurement and Amount of Light *304*
11.10.2 Types of Electric Lamps *304*
11.10.3 Glare *305*
11.11 Concluding Remarks *305*
Review Questions *306*
References *307*

12. VALUE ENGINEERING AND PRODUCT DESIGN 308–339
12.1 Introduction *308*
12.2 Historical Perspective *308*
12.3 What is Value? *309*
12.4 Nature and Measurement of Value *309*
12.5 Maximum Value *310*

12.6 Normal Degree of Value 310
12.7 Importance of Value 310
12.8 The Value Analysis Job Plan 311
12.9 Creativity 313
12.9.1 The Creative Process 313
12.9.2 Blocks to Creativity 314
12.9.3 Factors Conducive to Creativity 314
12.9.4 Creative Techniques 315
12.10 Steps to Problem-Solving and Value Analysis 319
12.11 Value Analysis Tests 320
12.11.1 Details of Value Analysis Tests 321
12.12 Value Engineering Idea Generation Check-list 322
12.13 Cost Reduction through Value Engineering Case Study on Tap Switch Control Assembly 323
12.13.1 The Problem 323
12.13.2 The Objective 324
12.13.3 The Team 324
12.13.4 The Methodology 324
12.13.5 Benefits of Value Engineering 328
12.14 Material and Process Selection in Value Engineering 331
12.14.1 The Problem 331
12.14.2 Design, Material, Process and Supplier Decisions 332
12.14.3 Product Parameters 333
12.14.4 Process Selection 333
12.14.5 Process Selection Parameters 334
12.14.6 Material Selection 334
12.14.7 Material Selection Parameters 335
12.14.8 Multivariable Chart 336
12.14.9 Organizing for Material and Process Selection 337
Review Questions 337
References 339

13. ROLE OF COMPUTER IN PRODUCT DESIGN, MANUFACTURING AND MANAGEMENT 340–392
13.1 CAD/CAM: Some Definitions 340
13.2 Product Cycle and CAD/CAM 340
13.3 Role of Computer in Manufacturing 341
13.4 Role of Computer in Design Process 342
13.4.1 Geometric Modelling 342
13.4.2 Engineering Analysis 346
13.4.3 Design Review and Evaluation 347
13.4.4 Automated Drafting 347
13.5 Creation of a Manufacturing Database 348
13.6 Computer Integrated Manufacturing 349
13.6.1 CIM: Definition 350
13.6.2 Integrating Product Design, Manufacturing and Production Control 350
13.6.3 Benefits of CIM 351
13.6.4 Installing CIM 351
13.6.5 Database Development in CIM 351
13.7 Communication Networks 352
13.8 Group Technology 355
13.8.1 Reasons for Adopting Group Technology 355
13.8.2 Benefits of Group Technology 355

13.8.3 Obstacles to the Application of Group Technology *357*
13.8.4 Classification and Coding of Parts *357*
13.8.5 Concept of a Composite Part *358*
13.9 Production Flow Analysis (PFA) *358*
13.10 Computer-Aided Process Planning (CAPP) *359*
13.10.1 Benefits of CAPP *360*
13.10.2 Types of CAPP *360*
13.11 Material Requirement Planning (MRP) *361*
13.12 Moving Towards Total Automation: Role of Artificial Intelligence *361*
13.12.1 Expert Systems *362*
13.12.2 Artificial Vision *362*
13.12.3 Robots with AI *362*
13.13 Flexible Manufacturing Systems *362*
13.13.1 Elements of Flexible Manufacturing System (FMS) *364*
13.13.2 Flexible Manufacturing Cells *367*
13.14 Just-in-Time (JIT) Manufacturing *368*
13.14.1 Introduction to JIT *368*
13.14.2 Just-in-Time and Product Design *370*

APPENDIX *371*
Review Questions *377*
References *392*

14. MODERN APPROACHES TO PRODUCT DESIGN 393–406

14.1 Concurrent Design *393*
14.1.1 The Design Team *393*
14.1.2 Benefits from Concurrent Design Approach *395*
14.2 Quality Function Deployment (QFD) *395*
14.3 Rapid Prototyping *398*
14.3.1 Principle of Rapid Prototyping *399*
14.3.2 Rapid Prototyping Technologies *399*

Review Questions *400*
References *406*

15. QUALITY ASSURANCE IN PRODUCT DESIGN AND MANUFACTURING 407–464

15.1 Evolution of Quality Concepts and Applications *407*
15.2 Quality and Design Spiral *408*
15.3 Theory of Sampling Inspection *409*
15.3.1 Single Sampling Plans *409*
15.3.2 The Operating Characteristic Curve *409*
15.3.3 The AQL (Acceptable Quality Level) and LTPD (Lot Tolerance Proportion Defective) *410*
15.3.4 The AOQ Curve and the AOQL *411*
15.3.5 Average Total Inspection (ATI) *413*
15.3.6 Double Sampling Plan *413*
15.3.7 Multiple Sample Plans *415*
15.3.8 Sequential Sampling Plans *418*
15.3.9 Practical Method of Selecting a Sampling Plan *420*
15.3.10 Sampling Plan for Variables *421*
15.4 Control Charts and In-Process Monitoring of Quality *423*
15.4.1 Introduction *423*
15.4.2 Control Charts *424*

15.4.3 Discussion on Variability in a Constant Cause System *425*
15.4.4 Procedure in Quality Control *426*
15.4.5 Theory of Control Charts *427*
15.4.6 Significance of $\overline{X}$ and R Charts *430*
15.4.7 Control Chart for Defective: *np* Chart: Comparison with $\overline{X}$ and R Charts *430*
15.4.8 Control Chart for Number of Defectives c per Unit: Areas of Application *431*
15.4.9 Control Chart for p (a special case of *np* chart when n varies) *432*
15.4.10 Cusum Chart *433*
15.5 Quality of Performance: Reliability and Allied Topics *434*
15.5.1 Failure Pattern of Equipment *434*
15.5.2 Reliability *435*
15.5.3 Models of Reliability *435*
15.5.4 Numerical Example *438*
15.5.5 Determination of System Reliability from Subsystem or Component Reliability *439*
15.5.6 Repairable System Reliability Analysis *441*
15.5.7 Failure Modes and Effects Analysis and Fault Tree Analysis *442*
15.5.8 Failure Modes and Effects Criticality Analysis (FMECA) *443*
15.6 Taguchi Method of Robust Design of Products *444*
15.7 Six Sigma Quality Concepts *449*
15.7.1 Statistical Background *449*
15.7.2 Six Sigma Relationships *450*
15.7.3 Procedure to Work Out Operating Sigma Level of a Process *450*
15.7.4 Rolled Throughput Yield *452*
15.7.5 Advantage of Yield and Allied Calculations *453*
15.7.6 Normalized Yield and Z-Value for Benchmarking *453*
15.7.7 Design for Six Sigma (DFSS) *453*
15.7.8 Cost Benefits and Leveraging through Better Design *453*
15.7.9 Relationship between C_P and C_{PK} Values *455*
15.7.10 Implementation of Six Sigma *455*
15.7.11 The Twelve MAIC Objectives *456*
15.7.12 Future Avenues *457*
Review Questions *460*
References *463*

16. NEW PRODUCT DEVELOPMENT AND PRODUCT MANAGEMENT 465–505
16.1 What is a Product? *465*
16.2 Defining Product by Nature of Demand *465*
16.3 New Product Strategy *466*
16.4 Product Classification *467*
16.5 Product Development and Product Management *468*
16.5.1 The Product Life Cycle *469*
16.5.2 Booz, Allen, Hamilton New Product Development Process *470*
16.6 New Product Development *473*
16.6.1 New Product Development Process *473*
16.7 Models Utilized in Various Phases of New Product Development *485*
16.7.1 Similarity/Dissimilarity Analysis Applied to Comparison of Product Concepts *485*
16.7.2 A-T-A-R Model Applied to Financial Analysis in Business Worthiness Phase *486*

16.7.3 Expected Commercial Value Approach *486*
16.7.4 House of Quality for Converting Voice of Customer to Technical Specifications *487*
16.8 Managing Product Life Cycle *488*
16.8.1 Various Stages of Product Life Cycle *489*
16.8.2 Utilizing the Product Life Cycle Concept: Yoram Wind's Analysis *492*
16.8.3 Product Life Cycle and Marketing Strategy *496*
16.8.4 Product Life Cycle Extensions *498*
16.8.5 Product Life Cycle and Profitability *498*
16.9 Diffusion Models: Models of First Purchase *499*
16.10 Concluding Remarks *503*
Review Questions *504*
References *505*

17. DESIGN FOR ENVIRONMENT 506–517
17.1 Various Stages of Total Life Cycle Materials *506*
17.1.1 Life Cycle Assessment *507*
17.2 Eco-Indicator 95 *508*
17.2.1 Eco-Indicator 95 Method *508*
17.3 Eco-Indicator 95 Worksheet *511*
Review Questions *517*
References *517*

Question Bank* *519–539
Appendix A Limits, Fits and Toleranes* *541–549
Appendix B Introduction to Part Programming in G and M Codes* *550–555
Appendix C Aesthetics in Industrial Design* *556–561
Appendix D Application of Bernoulli's Laws to Casting System* *562–576
Appendix E Some Physical Metallurgical Aspects of Ferrous and Non-ferrous Metals* *577–591
Appendix F Example of Applying Autodesk AutoCAD for Solid Modeling an Object Given the Orthographic Views* *592–597
Index* *599–608

Preface

It is gratifying to note that the sixth edition has been well-received by the teachers and students alike. The authors felt the need to enhance its contents further to make the new book more contemporary considering recent increased focus on CAD/CAM and required updates in the chapter on Design for Environment. Further, it was felt necessary to cover the syllabi of some universities which introduced the subject of design at BE level. For the ME students, it was needed to incorporate the details of Product Lifecycle Management. This has been done in the chapter on New Product Development which is analogous to Product Lifecycle Management.

In this edition the main highlight is the provision of Answer Key. It pertains to all the 17 Chapters of the book. In the section on Review Questions of every chapter it has been indicated how to locate the answer to every question. The Section number, Page number and Figure number to find answer to every specific question has been provided in all the 17 Chapters.

An Appendix F has been introduced to explain use of Autodesk AutoCAD Software for Solid Modelling. This procedure has been used by Design Professionals across the World. In addition to the above, several changes have been made in this edition to keep pace with new developments in the field of Product Design after 2015. A Question Bank has been developed which contains Answers to 51 questions based on the syllabi of various universities where concepts in engineering design have been introduced right at the first year level. A new chapter on New Product Development highlighting its similarity to the recent focus on Product Lifecycle Management has been introduced. Likewise the chapter on 'Design for Environment' has been redrafted to make it contemporary. We hope that the students and teachers will find the New Edition useful to meet the requirement of latest syllabi of the subject offered by various universities.

The Authors are thankful to Mr. Ankur Gupta of CAD/CAM laboratory of Shri Govindram Seksaria Institute of Technology and Science, Indore for his assistance during the preparation of the present Edition. Finally the Authors are thankful to Editorial and Production teams for their support. Authors also wish to thank Mr V. Balamurugan, General Manager–Sales for helping the authors during the course of preparation of the manuscript of the book.

A.K. Chitale
R.C. Gupta

Preface to the Sixth Edition

It is gratifying to note that the earlier Edition of the book has been well accepted by the readers. However, based on the feedback received from the readers, the following areas of Product Design and Manufacturing have been explained in more detail in this edition.

(i) A discussion on limits, fits and tolerances with their applications are discussed in Appendix A.
(ii) Use of G and M codes for part programming with illustrative examples are discussed in Appendix B.
(iii) Advanced concepts in Aesthetics are explained in Appendix C.

In the Sixth Edition we have introduced two more Appendices as under:

(iv) Application of Bernoulli's Equations of fluid Mechanics to efficient Casting design covered in Appendix D.
(v) Some Physical Metallurgical Aspects of ferrous and non-ferrous metals have been discussed in Appendix E.

It is hoped that the above Appendices D and E will help students and teachers to have a deep knowledge and solid grounding of Foundry Engineering and Metallurgy.

The authors are thankful to Editorial, Production and Marketing Executives of PHI Learning for providing support to the authors.

A.K. Chitale
R.C. Gupta

Preface to the Fifth Edition

The first printing of this book was undertaken in 1995. The authors were inspired to write on Product Design and Manufacturing because the AMIE had introduced a paper on the subject, common to 10 branches of Engineering. At that time, no authentic book covering the syllabus of Product Design and Manufacturing existed, barring one or two books that were available more or less in the form of guide books to enable the AMIE students to jump the hurdle of the tough AMIE exams. Apart from this, there emerged Institutes of Design such as the National Institute of Design, Ahmedabad and similar Industrial Design Centres at the Indian Institute of Technology (IIT) Delhi and the IIT Bombay. The concept of product design that emerged differed from purely technical (mechanical design, electrical design or civil engineering) design. The need for a qualified designer well-versed with a range of product designs was also felt by the Industry. A well-balanced treatment of the subject demanded inputs from morphology of the design process with inputs from strength and stiffness analysis, aesthetics, ergonomics, design for manufacturing ease and cost effectiveness, apart from reliability and durability and other considerations.

The Fifth Edition is a revised and enlarged version of the previous edition. We have included some chapters and sections and updated the material, which should benefit the readers considerably. Chapter 1 begins with a definition of design as a process of conversion of ideas into concrete reality. The difference between design by evolution and design by innovation is explained. The chapter further discusses the seven phases of morphology of design process as proposed by the design philosopher Morris Asimov. Next, the three primary design phases, namely Feasibility analysis, Preliminary analysis and Detailed analysis, are developed by considering the 25 steps with input, output and decision box at each step.

Chapter 2 then discusses product design as practised by industry, focusing on product strategies, relationship between design, production and marketing, product characteristics, standardization and variety reduction. Further, the role of a designer: myth and reality, various types of models used by the designer, aesthetics, including form elements and product message and functional design practice, are discussed. The review questions of this chapter focus on functional design, production design, design for transportation, design for maintenance and ergonomic design, types of design work, such as adaptive design, variant design, creative design, configuration design and modular design explaining their characteristics.

Chapter 3 covers the strength aspects of design using an approach deviating from classical strength of materials (which makes excessive use of mathematical models). Here, concepts such as force flow lines and trajectories to represent principal stresses are used.

Chapter 4 on stiffness based design uses analogies and physical models proposed by design philosophers like Euler, Prandtl and others to recommend material saving approaches. The chapter develops formulae for ribbed plates, corrugated plates and membrane structures. These designs are rarely available in standard textbooks on applied mechanics even though industry makes profitable use of such material-saving approaches. Practising design engineers will find this chapter quite useful.

Chapter 5 on production processes gives a detailed fundamental approach to several primary processes such as casting processes of various types. Forging, extruding and joining processes are also dealt with in detail to guide a designer to effectively use it. The scope of metal cutting and abrasive processes has been enlarged in this edition of the book. A brief description of non-traditional machining is also given to guide the designer in contributing to effective process planning.

Chapter 6 on design for production focuses on the desirable design aspects for forged components, pressed components, machining, powder metallurgy, expanded metals, and wire forms. The details of this chapter should provide a guideline for a process engineer who is a connecting link between a designer and a production engineer.

Chapter 7 discusses the material science aspect, processing aspect, and the design aspects of plastics, rubber, glass and ceramics. These non-metallic materials considerably extend the repertoire of a designer. In several cases, metals cannot replace the above group of materials. In the review questions, details of design with fibre-reinforced plastics as well as metallic composites are also included which can be useful to a practising designer.

Chapter 8 gives design recommendations with plastics, rubber, ceramics and wood.

Chapter 9 on optimization in design focuses on empirical and mathematical approaches such as linear programming, geometric programming, the calculus approach, and Johnson's method of optimal design. In this chapter a reliability based design is also taken up as an example.

Chapter 10 deals with economic factors of design and gives recommendation on how profit can be achieved through increasing the price or expanding the market or reducing the cost. This chapter also discusses other aspects such as safety, mistake-proofing, reliability and estimation of break-even point using conventional approach and P/V chart approach for single and multiple product situations.

Chapter 11 on human engineering considerations in product design deals with the well-known branch of Ergonomics, with special emphasis on a human being as occupant of space, as a reader of display, an applicator of force, and as a controller of machines. Detailed discussions on anthropometry, seating design, displays and controls, man/machine information exchange are given along with the rights and wrongs of display design, and the relationship between control and display. In the present enlarged edition, workplace layout design, noise, heating and ventilation, thermal comfort, air conditioning, heating methods, lighting, effect of glare, etc. have been added taking into account their effect on human productivity.

Chapter 12 explains the concept of the **value of a product**. Value is defined as the ratio of benefit provided by a product divided by the cost of the product. The chapter explains various aspects of value engineering and value analysis of any product. A value analysis job plan proposed by its founder Lawrence Miles and others such as Mudge, Fallon, Dell' Isola and General Services Administration is also included.

The various steps of value analysis given by Miles, which include information analysis, creativity, judgment, are discussed in detail. Other tools of value analysis such as cost-worth approach, checklisting, product and process analysis and multivariable chart developed by M. Vasant Rao of NITIE are included in this chapter. A case study as per the value analysis job plan is also discussed to highlight the application of the theory. In the review questions to this chapter, the use of multivariable chart and the use of FAST (Functional Analysis System Technique) diagram for an overhead projector are taken up.

Chapter 13 highlights the role of computer in Product Design, Manufacturing and Management. The concepts of CAD, CAM, CIM, Group Technology, Computer Aided Process planning of variant and generative types are also discussed. Then the evolution of robotics and artificial intelligence are dealt with. Finally, flexible manufacturing centre, FM cell, and an FM system are discussed. In the review questions to this chapter, an example on FMS for hobbing and broaching a gear is given. This section also contains a numerical example illustrating the use of FEM for a stepped bar with axial load. Further, an example using NC machining with APT language and the EIA system approach using a punched tape is provided. The working of open loop and closed loop NC systems is also explained. Other aspects of automation covered in the review questions of this chapter are: Robots, AGV, AS/RS and programmable logic controller studied at the introductory level.

Chapter 14 on modern approaches to product design covers concurrent design, quality function deployment (because it is a step by step approach to customer driven design) and various rapid prototyping methods.

Chapter 15 on quality assurance in product design contains an introduction to quality evolution and is followed by theory and application of sampling plans, quality control charts, reliability and allied topics such as FMEA and fault tolerance analysis. The coverage of this topic is fortified with many numerical examples.

Chapter 16 on new product development and product management deals with pre-market and marketing phases of a new product. The pre-market phases deal with seven phases of new product development, i.e. idea generation, idea screening, concept development, business analysis, prototype development, test marketing, and product launching. The marketing phases are concerned with that part of product life cycle which involves product introduction, growth, maturity and decline. These aspects are covered in the chapter with descriptive and mathematical models.

Chapter 17 contains design for environment. With the passage of time, the pressure on industry to produce eco-friendly products has increased. Noting this trend, we had introduced a chapter on Design for Environment (DFE) in the Fourth Edition itself.

We received some feedback from students indicating the need for inclusion of certain materials to enhance the utility of the book:

- **End of chapter review questions** so that the readers have a better understanding of the subject.
- More information on **metal machining** as well as **micro-machining processes**.
- They also highlighted the need for covering in detail the topic of Welding Processes considering its importance.
- The need was felt for additional input for the topic of Human Factors in Engineering so as to include the design of work place, effect of noise, light and glare, heat and humidity on human operators.

Besides the above feedback from the students, the authors also observed certain changes in the syllabi of AMIE and some proactive universities which necessitated the inclusion of topics such as Fibre Reinforced Plastics and Ceramics.

This updated and enlarged edition takes into account the changes that have taken place ever since the previous edition was published. Most of the requirements of the students and the proactive universities have now been taken care of.

We wish to thank the Publishers, PHI Learning and the members of the editorial and production team, particularly Mr. K.C. Devasia, Senior Editor; Mr. Arvind Pahwa, General Manger Production; and Mr. Pankaj Manohar, Assistant Production Manager, for the support provided by them.

Any suggestions for further improvement of the book will be warmly appreciated.

A.K. Chitale
R.C. Gupta

Chapter 1

Introduction to Product Design
Asimow's Model

1.1 DEFINITION OF PRODUCT DESIGN

Product design deals with conversion of ideas into reality and, as in other forms of human activity, aims at fulfilling human needs.

A designer does not usually produce the goods or services which immediately satisfy consumer's needs. Rather, he produces the prototype which is used as a sample for reproducing the particular goods or services as many times as required. A design may be of a pattern on upholstery or of a dress in the world of fashion. If the producer believes that a sufficient number of customers will be satisfied by the product, then mass production of the item or service may be taken up by the production department. In the course of production, an error made by the producer in manufacturing an item may lead to its rejection; but an error in design, which will be repeated in all products, may lead to an economic misadventure of enormous proportions. The designer's responsibility is therefore serious.

1.2 DESIGN BY EVOLUTION

In the past, designs used to evolve over long spans of time. The leisurely pace of technological change reduced the risk of making major errors. The circumstances rarely demanded analytical capabilities of the designer. This was *design by evolution*. Development of the bicycle from its crank operated version to its present day chain and sprocket version over a period of about a century is a typical example of design by evolution.

The disadvantages of evolutionary design are:

Unsuitability for mass production. An evolved design is rather crude and is more oriented towards design by masses for Production by masses (Gandhian philosophy) rather than mass production. It is acceptable at village level but unacceptable at urban level.

Difficulty in modification. A design by evolution is shaped by demands of time. On the other hand, design by invention and creative process uses sophisticated tools and techniques such as CAD (Computer-Aided Design) workstation. The CAD workstation helps to generate a large number of design alternatives within minutes.

Inability to tap new technologies. A new technology can result in a totally new design based on a different working principle as compared with evolutionary design which relies heavily on small modifications in an existing design. It is well known that the new technology has made artisans and craftsmen of certain categories redundant.

1.3 DESIGN BY INNOVATION

Following a scientific discovery, a new body of technical knowledge develops rapidly; the proper use of this discovery may result in an almost complete deviation from past practice. Every skill, which the designer or the design team can muster in analysis and synthesis, is instrumental in a totally novel design. Examples of design by innovation are:

1. Invention of laser beam which has brought about a revolution in medical and engineering fields. Laser based tools have made surgical knife in medicine and gas cutting in engineering obsolete.
2. Invention of solid state electronic devices resulting in miniaturization of electronic products, which has made vacuum tubes obsolete.

1.4 ESSENTIAL FACTORS OF PRODUCT DESIGN

(i) **Need.** A design must be in response to individual or social needs, which can be satisfied by the technological status of the times when the design is to be prepared.

(ii) **Physical realizability.** A design should be convertible into material goods or services, i.e., it must be physically realizable. The technique for determining the physical realizability is termed, design tree approach (Figure 1.1(a)). In this approach, the success of a design concept depends on the success of its subproblems, say Q_1 and Q_2. Let D_{11}, D_{12}, ... represent alternative solutions of Q_1 and D_{21}, D_{22} represent alternative solutions of Q_2, and so forth. The probability equations are:

$$P(D) = P(Q_1)\,P(Q_2) \tag{1.1}$$

$$P(Q_1) = P(D_{11} \text{ or } D_{12}) = P(D_{11}) + P(D_{12}) - P(D_{11})P(D_{12}) \tag{1.2}$$

$$P(Q_2) = P(D_{21} \text{ or } D_{22}) = P(D_{21}) + P(D_{22}) - P(D_{21})P(P_{22}) \tag{1.3}$$

The probability values of D_{11}, D_{12}, D_{21}, and D_{22} should be estimated from practical considerations. An example of development of device for combating automobile head-on-crash is also illustrated in Figure 1.1(b).

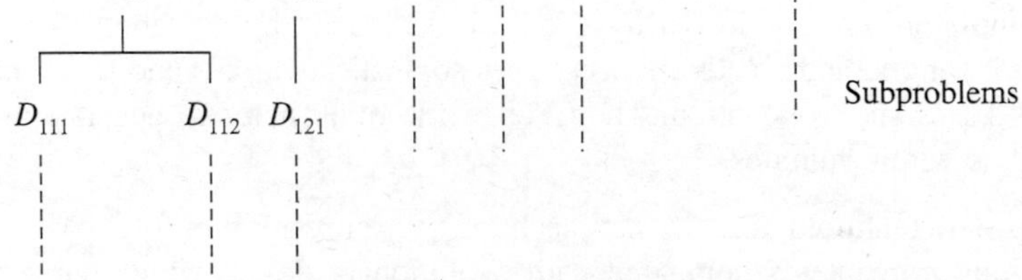

(a) Design tree for a design concept D

FIGURE 1.1 Contd.

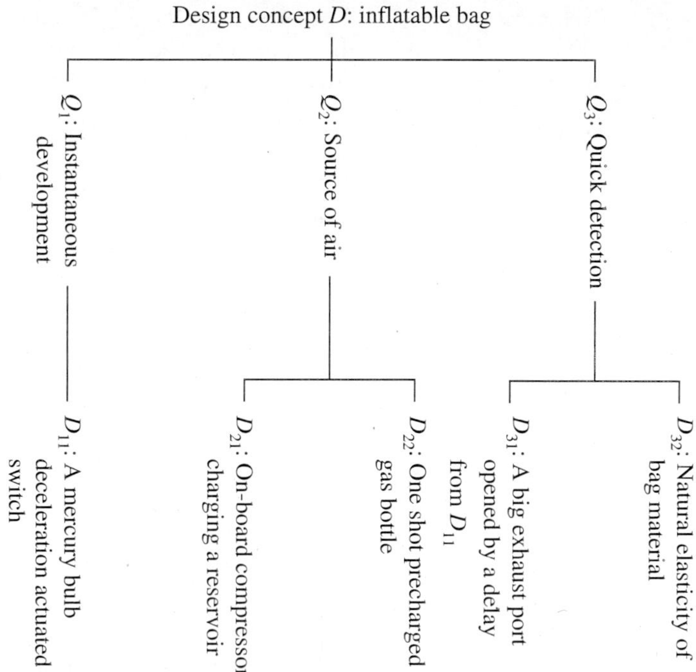

(b) Design tree for protection device in automobile head on crash

FIGURE 1.1 Determination of physical realizability through use of design tree.

(iii) **Economic worthwhileness.** The goods or services, described by a design, must have a utility to the consumer which equals or exceeds the sum of the total costs of making it available to him. For example, a bulb with luminous intensity 3 and life 4 on a ten-point scale has a lower utility than a bulb with luminous intensity 2.5 and life 5.

(iv) **Financial feasibility.** The operations of designing, producing and distributing the goods must be financially supportable, i.e., a design project should be capable for being funded by suitable agencies or people. The method for assessment of financial feasibility could be 'Net present value' which states that the present worth of cash flows in the project when added up during the useful life of the product should be greater than the initial investment for the project.

(v) **Optimality.** The choice of a design concept must be optimal amongst the available alternatives; the selection of the chosen design concept must be optimal among all possible design proposals. Optimal design, in theory, strives to achieve the best or singular point derived by calculus methods. In the context of optimization under constraints for mechanical strength, minimum weight and minimum cost are usually taken up as criteria for optimization.

(vi) **Design criterion.** Optimality must be established relative to a design criterion which represents the designer's compromise among possibly conflicting value judgements which include those of the consumer, the producer, the distributor, and his own. In Chapter 9, the concept of optimum design under constraints has been discussed.

(vii) **Morphology.** Design is progression from the abstract to the concrete. This gives a chronologically horizontal structure to a design project. The three phases of design proposed by Asimow [1] are: Feasibility study phase, preliminary design phase, and detailed design phase, as indicated in Figure 1.2.

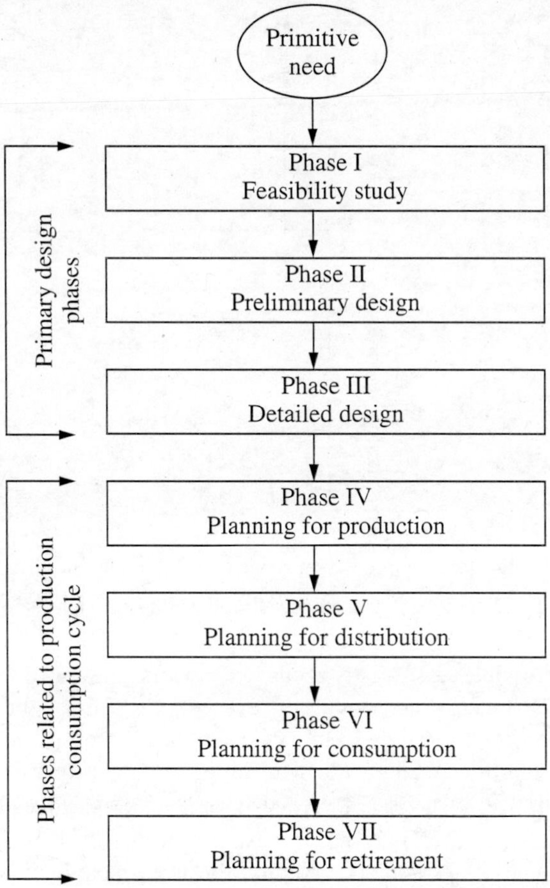

FIGURE 1.2 Morphology of design process.

(viii) **Design process.** Design is an iterative problem-solving process. This gives a vertical structure to each design phase. The iterative nature of design is owing to feedback from existing design and improvement with further information in the form of technological, financial and creativity inputs. This is indicated in Figure 1.3.

(ix) **Subproblems.** During the process of solution of a design problem, a sublayer of subproblems appears; the solution of the original problem is dependent on the solution of the subproblems. The "Design Tree" of Figure1.1 reveals the concept of subproblems.

(x) **Reduction of uncertainty.** Design is derived after processing of information that results in a transition from uncertainty, about the success or failure of a design towards certainty. Each step in design morphology from step (i) to step (x) enhances the level of confidence of the designer.

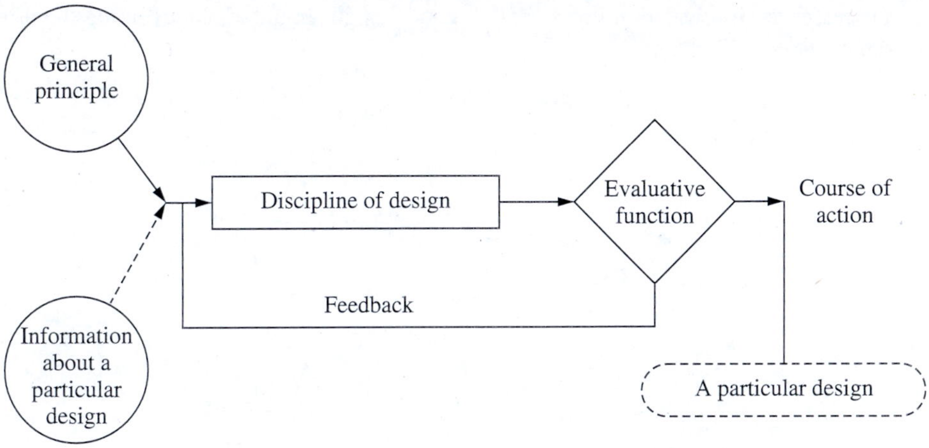

FIGURE 1.3 Iterative nature of design process.

(xi) **Economic worth of evidence.** Information gathering and processing have a cost that must be balanced by the worth of the evidence, which affects the success or failure of the design. Authentic information should be gathered to make the design project a success. Today, information is regarded as a resource which is as valuable as money, manpower and material.

(xii) **Bases for decision.** A design project is terminated when it is obvious that its failure calls for its abandonment. It is continued when confidence in an available design solution is high enough to indicate the commitment of resources necessary for the next phase.

(xiii) **Minimum commitment.** In the solution of a design problem at any stage of the process, commitments which will fix future design decisions must not be made beyond what is necessary to execute the immediate solution. This will allow maximum freedom in finding solutions to subproblems at the lower levels of design. A model of design problem, subproblems, etc. is developed through a *design tree* (see Figure 1.1).

(xiv) **Communication.** A design is a description of an object and prescription for its production; it will exist to the extent it is expressed in the available modes of communication. The best way to communicate a design is through drawings, which is the universal language of designers. Three-dimensional renderings or cut-away views help to explain the design to the sponsor or user of the design. The present day impact of computer aided modelling and drafting has resulted in very effective communication between the designer and the sponsor.

1.5 PRODUCTION–CONSUMPTION CYCLE

The production–consumption cycle, one of the main features of the socio-ecological systems, consists of four processes:

1. Production
2. Distribution
3. Consumption
4. Recovery or disposal.

The processes are illustrated in Figure 1.4. A good design should aim at avoiding the production of undesirable.

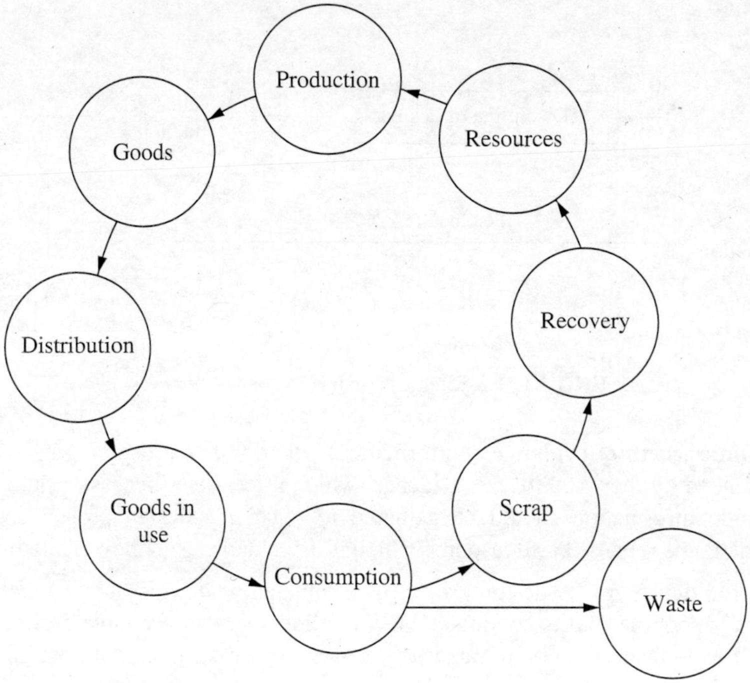

FIGURE 1.4 Production–consumption cycle.

1.6 FLOW AND VALUE ADDITION IN THE PRODUCTION–CONSUMPTION CYCLE

So far we have focussed our attention on the flow or travel of physical objects in the production–consumption cycle. But two other sets of more abstract objects flow through the cycle also—value addition and information—which are now discussed.

(i) **Value addition.** Consider a particular product. We begin the cycle with some resources. These may be raw materials, energy, amortizable production facilities, and human effort. Some amount of these economic factors is required to produce one unit of product. Associated with this amount is a value, generally measurable in rupees and usually called the cost of production. The emerging product also has a value measured in rupees and determined by the forces in the market place. The difference between output and input values, called *gross profit*, provides an economic driving force which motivates the enterprise. Another measure of value is the ratio between the value of output and the cost of input. Similarly, there is an augmentation of value through the process of distribution, accompanied by an augmentation in value as measured in rupees, arising from a more favourable time and location for marketing. The consumer pays the price, but he does so because the product has a greater worth to him than the purchase price. At this point, we lose our objective measure of value. We can only hypothesize a subjective measure of value which economists have called "utility". The lack of an objective measure poses serious conceptual difficulties, and is a recurring problem in product design: First, because of the designers' concern with setting values on the consumption process and, second, because all design decisions are based on logically organizable information coupled with intuition and judgement in decision making. When we deal with the element of judgement, as with the estimates of utility, we treat subjective measures of value. However, we have to seek out the best tools with which to cope with such measures.

(ii) **Information.** The second set of objects is concerned with information which plays a major role in engineering design because design is essentially a process of gathering and organizing information. The latent information, available at the effort and cost of gathering it at each point in the cycle, is of great importance because it is utilized for the redesign of products, or for the design of new products. Of equal importance is the information about components, materials, processes, environments, and specifications. The task of maintaining the store of information in a useful fashion is a formidable task. The volume of new technical data generated each year is tremendous. The gathering, organizing, updating, storing and retrieving of such data are very large and very important. It has been proposed that a few design-data-processing centres be established in the country at strategic locations. These proposed centres would be accessible to design offices throughout the country through communication networks. The information will become available on presentation of the properly coded queries to the computers. TIFAC (Technology Information Forecasting Assessment Council) of the Government of India at New Delhi has plans to have such information storage and linking.

1.7 THE MORPHOLOGY OF DESIGN (THE SEVEN PHASES)

The morphology of design refers to the study of the chronological structure of design projects. It is defined by the phases (see Figure 1.2) and their constituent steps. The various steps involved in the design phases will be discussed in detail in the following sections. Of the seven phases, the first three phases belong to design, and the remaining four phases belong to production, distribution, consumption, and retirement.

1.7.1 Phase I—Feasibility Study

A design project begins with a feasibility study; the purpose is to achieve a set of useful solutions to the design problem. Sometimes, a design group is assigned a project for which a design concept has already been fixed. This implies one of the three possibilities:

1. A feasibility study has been previously done.
2. The design department has so much experience with the particular design problem that further study is superfluous.
3. The top management, by omitting the feasibility study, is proceeding on unsupported intuition.

The first step in the study is to demonstrate whether the original need, which was presumed to be valid, does indeed have current existence or strong evidence of latent existence. The second step is to explore the design problem generated by the need and to identify its elements such as parameters, constraints, and major design criteria. Third, an effort has to be made to seek a number of feasible solutions to the problem. Fourth, the potentially useful solutions are sorted out from the feasible set in three steps on the basis of physical realizability, economic worthwhileness, and financial feasibility. Finally, the completed study indicates whether a current or a potential need exists, what the design problem is, and whether useful solutions can be found. It investigates the feasibility of the proposed project. Computer aided modelling is very useful in generating alternative designs from which the best can be selected.

1.7.2 Phase II—Preliminary Design

The preliminary design phase starts with the set of useful solutions which were developed in the feasibility study. The purpose of preliminary design is to establish which of the preferred alternatives is the best design concept. Each of the alternative solutions is subjected to quantitative analysis until evidence suggests either that the particular solution is inferior to some of the others, or that it is superior to all the others. The surviving solution is tentatively accepted for closer examination. Synthesis studies are initiated for establishing to a first approximation the fineness of the range within which the major design parameters of the system must be controlled. Further studies investigate the tolerances in the characteristics of major components and critical materials which will be required to ensure mutual compatibility and proper fit into the system. Other studies examine the extent to which perturbations of environmental or internal forces will affect the stability of the system. Sophisticated methods such as the finite element method are used now-a-days to carry out design analysis of components, with a view to finding critical areas of stress concentration. Photoelastic studies are also of great help in accurate stress analysis.

Next, project type studies are undertaken to know as to how the solution will be feasible in future. The socio-economic conditions, such as consumers' tastes, competitors' offerings or availability of critical raw materials may change; the state of technology may advance and, eventually, corrosion, fatigue, and deterioration of performance may set in. Time will almost certainly erode the quality of the product. The question is: how fast? The rate of obsolescence or wear must be accounted for. The critical aspects of the design must be put to test in order to validate the design concept and to provide essential information for its subsequent phases.

1.7.3 Phase III—Detailed Design

The detailed design phase begins with the concept evolved in the preliminary design. Its purpose is to furnish the engineering description of a tested and producible design. Up to this point the design project is characterized by great flexibility. Major changes in concept could be accommodated without great financial losses. In the first two phases such flexibility is essential, because they are exploratory in nature, seeking to reveal an adequate range of possible solutions. In the third phase, however, either exploration on a large scale must come to an end or a final decision for a particular design concept must be made.

With the design concept in mind and the preliminary synthesis information at hand, a provisional synthesis is accomplished. It is developed as a master layout. With this as a basis, the detailed design or specification of components is carried forward. From time to time, exigencies in the detailed work at the component level may dictate changes in the master layout; therefore, it has a provisional status. As the paper design progresses, experimental design is initiated. Experimental models are constructed to check out untried ideas which are not suitable to final simulation or analysis. Components, partial prototypes and, finally, complete prototypes are tested as the need for information arises. This information, gathered from the testing programs, provides a basis for redesign and refinement until an engineering description of a proven design is accomplished.

1.7.4 Phase IV—Planning the Production Process

The above-mentioned three phases were particularly in the area of engineering design; much of the responsibility for phase 4 will be shared with other areas of management. A new battery of skills, those of tool design and production engineering, come into play. The original project group, however, may continue in its role of leadership. Often, the decision to produce involves an enormous economic commitment. The level of confidence in the success of the product must be very high to support a positive decision. The decision itself must be made at the top level of management. The evidences on which the engineer responsible for the design project bases his confidence must be communicated in a condensed, but fully revealing form to the top management. The designer's confidence will have to be shared by the top management who will re-evaluate this confidence, using additional information on financial capability, business conditions, etc., before arriving at a final decision.

The production planning phase involves many steps which will vary in form and detail according to the particular industry. The following shortened list is typical of the mass production industries:

1. Detailed process planning is required for every part, subassembly and the final assembly. The information is usually displayed on process sheets, one for each part of subassembly. The process sheet contains a sequential list of operations which must be performed to produce the part. It specifies the raw material, clarifies special instructions, and indicates the tools and machines required. This step is particularly important, because design features that lead to difficulties in production are revealed. Such difficulties should have been minimized earlier by timely consultations between product designers and tool designers. Similarly, questions about materials should have been resolved by consultation with metallurgists.
2. Design of tools and fixtures: This design work proceeds generally from the information developed in the operations analysis on the process sheets.
3. Planning, specifying or designing new production and plant facilities.
4. Planning the quality control system.
5. Planning for production personnel: Job-specifications are developed, standard times are determined, and labour costs estimated.
6. Planning for production control: Work schedules and inventory controls are evolved. Standard costs for labour, materials, and services are established and integrated with the accounting system.
7. Planning the information-flow system: The information necessary for transmission of instructions and provision of feedback for control is determined. Appropriate forms and records are designed and integrated with computers when available. Flow patterns and routines are established.
8. Financial planning: Usually, large sums of money are required to initiate production of a new product. The source of the financing must be carefully established, and the means and rate of recovering the capital determined.

1.7.5 Phase V—Planning for Distribution

Production is the first process in the production–consumption cycle. The second is *distribution*. Although the product designer may not be directly involved in planning for distribution, he will often find that the problems of distribution have an important impact on the original design of the product. The purpose of this phase is to plan an effective and flexible system of distribution of the designed goods. The short list we now give is indicative of the planning for distribution.

(i) **Designing the packaging of the product.** The outer shape of the product may be influenced by the need to effect economy in transportation costs. Individual and special packaging may be needed to secure protection from shock and weather. Special strapping and palletizing may be needed to facilitate handling.

(ii) **Planning the warehousing systems.** The economically favourable locations for warehouse are determined and the warehousing facilities are designed.

(iii) **Planning the promotional activity.** Technical sales brochures based on design information and test data may have to be developed.

(iv) **Designing the product for conditions arising in distribution.** Such factors as shelf-life, attractive display and final conditioning, before delivery to the consumer, may affect the design of the product. There may be need for enough flexibility in the design to allow for special modifications to suit customers' needs or for further adding available optional features as required by the customer, or for modular additions to the system to enlarge its capacity.

1.7.6 Phase VI—Planning for Consumption

Consumption is the third process in the production–consumption cycle. Its influence on design is profound because it pervades all phases. As a process, it occurs naturally after distribution. As a phase, in the time-pattern of the design project, most of the processes of consumption must be anticipated in the early stages of design in order to have a timely impact. Therefore, it is for the most part a diffused phase concerned with consumers needs and utilities, and mingled with and attached to the earlier phases. It is set up separately only to emphasize some of the special contributions which it makes in addition to its more general and pervading influences. This separate status as phase does not imply that consideration, even of the steps enumerated here as belonging to the consumption phase, is to be deferred until this late stage; in fact, after, the contrary is true. The purpose of this phase is to incorporate in the design, adequate service features and to provide a rational basis for product improvement and redesign. Design for consumption must consider the following factors:

1. Design for maintenance
2. Design for reliability
3. Design for safety
4. Design for convenience in use (taking into account human factors)
5. Design for aesthetic features
6. Design for operational economy
7. Design for adequate duration of services
8. Obtain service data that can provide a basis for product improvement, for next-generation designs, and for the design of different, but related products.

1.7.7 Phase VII—Planning for Retirement

The fourth process in the production–consumption cycle is the disposal of the retired product. For large and semi-permanent installations, the mere removal may pose difficult engineering problems, as for example, the demolition of a tall building closely surrounded by buildings on either side.

Sometimes, an old structure or design must be replaced with new one with minimum disruption of normal operation.

What determines as to when an economic commodity in use (e.g. a consumer's product, a commercial or industrial device, or a private or public system) has reached an age at which it should be retired? This is one of the principal questions raised by a study of engineering economy. If the article in use is worn to the point at which it can no longer render adequate service, then the need for replacement is clear. However, the same fast pace of technology which compels the designer also accelerates the aging process of goods in use. It is a hallmark of our times that goods in use are retired more frequently because of technical obsolescence than for physical deterioration. Changes in fashions, often deliberately cultivated by industry, also produce their share of casualties. In the design of soft goods, such as clothing, exploiting fashion changes is an accepted practice, since the value of such goods lies in their aesthetic appeal.

To the product designer, the question whether to design for physical deterioration or for technical obsolescence is of fundamental importance. Ideally, the system should be designed so that it wears out physically as it becomes technically obsolete; then no extra cost would be incurred for providing for a longer than useful life. But usually, the elements of design that contribute to a longer life are also essential to adequate reliability and maintenance; thus a full compromise between obsolescence and wearout is generally not possible. These aspects of design need further study.

What values are available when a product reaches a terminal point of service and how do these values influence design? The latter question is the concern of the retirement phase in design. The purpose of this phase is to take into account the problems associated with retiring and disposing of a product. Designing for retirement, according to Asimow, must consider the following aspects:

1. Designing to reduce the rate of obsolescence by taking into account the anticipated effects of technical developments.
2. Designing physical life to match anticipated service life.
3. Designing for several levels of use so that when service life at higher level of use is terminated, the product will be adaptable for further use with a less demanding level.
4. Designing the product so that reusable materials and long-lived components can be recovered. Modularity in design can be contemplated, instead of integrated designs.
5. Examining and testing of service-terminated products in the laboratory to obtain useful design information.

In summary, although the first three design phases, forming a primary set, are the principal concern of the design group, the remaining four, which constitute a secondary set, arising from the production–consumption cycle, have such a great impact on the design that they must be considered in detail.

1.8 PRIMARY DESIGN PHASES AND FLOWCHARTING—THE 25 STEPS

Morris Asimow, the design philosopher, has proposed three phases of design:

1. Feasibility study
2. Preliminary design
3. Detailed design phase.

These will be discussed in detail now. Asimow [1] represented his model as a flow chart (Figure 1.5) with a circle indicating information input, a rectangle indicating step in design process, a decision box as a rhombus, and a rounded box as an output. Output from an earlier step, together with additional information, results in activating a subsequent design process and its accompanying output which acts as an output to a decision box. This cycle continues from top to bottom in a zig-zag repetitive manner. Feasibility study has six steps, preliminary design has 10 steps, and detailed design has nine steps, making a total of 25 steps. These are indicated in Figure 1.5.

1.8.1 Phase I—Feasibility Study

Step 1: The need—Establishing its economic existence. The starting point of a design project is a hypothetical need which may have been observed currently on the socio-economic scene. It may be worded in the form of a primitive need statement; or it may have been elaborated into a sophisticated and authenticated statement based on market and consumer studies. The need may not yet exist, but there may be evidence that it is latent, and that it may arise when economic means for its satisfaction become available. The need may be suggested by a technical breakthrough which motivates its exploitation through product for social good. In whatever way the need has been perceived, its economic existence, latent or current, must be established with sufficient confidence to justify the commitment of the funds necessary to explore the feasibility of developed means satisfying it. By economic existence of a need, we mean that individuals, institutions or society will recognize the need and will pay the price of the product which can satisfy the need. The product may be available in the market for a purchase price and there could be a number of firms supplying the product. The importance of establishing the need can hardly be overestimated. Too often, an organization will go in for a project and develop a base while ending up in financial failure because the assumed need was imaginary and disappeared in the light of reality. Primitive need statement contains a vague description of what is required. It does not point out the way a design should be made. It only states the sponsor's need in a general statement. For example, a primitive's need statement for an electronic fire alarm could be "A gadget to accurately and precisely sense the rise of temperature in the building above 80°C and have a sound system to alarm or warn inhabitants of such an occurrence." Note that in the primitive need statement, nowhere is a mention of "Electronic" or "Fire" made. Primitive statements enable the generation of more ideas than specific statements.

Intuitive knowledge about people, their habits and lifestyles and their behaviour in the socio-economic system, may be combined with specific information obtained by market research to provide the information necessary for making a need analysis. After performing the need analysis, a decision must be made about the validity of the economic worthwhileness of the need. If it is favourable, the results of this step are summarized in a set of specifications of desired outputs which the product or system must be capable of producing in order to satisfy the need. As stated earlier, the need statement should not immediately converge to suggest a single design but should be primitive or general and encourage multiple solutions and idea generation.

Step 2: The design problem—Identification and formulation. The information available comes from the results of the preceding step, particularly the specifications of desired outputs, and from relevant technical knowledge about environments, resources and the general engineering principle. With this information, an activity analysis is performed whereby the design problem is given a technical formulation. The question which must be asked before this step may be considered complete, is: Is the resulting engineering statement of the problem sufficiently relevant and adequate to commit the ensuing steps to the design? New information is constantly developed by the design work itself which previously was either overlooked or unknown. This new information changes the confidence levels on which prior decisions were made. If the deterioration in confidence is enough to destroy the basis for a particular decision, the decision-maker will demand that the affected steps

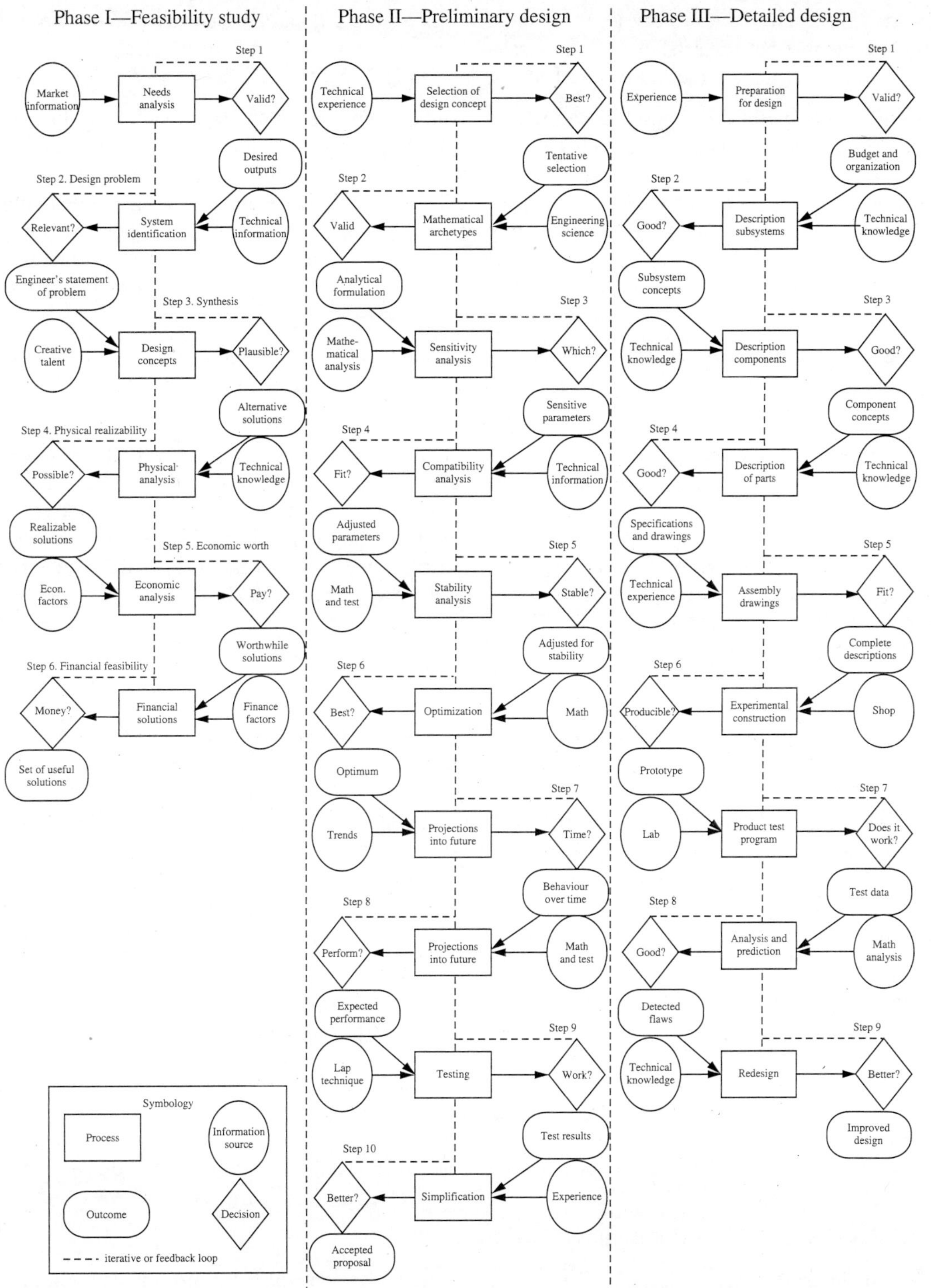

FIGURE 1.5 Asimow's model on morphology of design process.

be reworked until the necessary level of confidence is restored. It can be seen from Figure 1.5 that this results in feedback as shown by the dashed line starting at the vertex of the decision box and the dashed line joining the vertical dashed line indicating a feedback channel.

Step 3: The synthesis of possible solutions. Synthesis implies combining or bringing different ideas to produce an integrated whole. This is the which characterizes, more than anything else, the project as a design undertaking. This requires innovative and creative effort. Creativity is therefore an essential ingredient for product design. In the context of design, we offer the following as a definition of creativity: "A talent for discovering a combination of principles, materials or components, which are especially suitable as solutions to the problem in hand". For example, design systems that may reduce the fatality of a car crash could be among others: (a) seat belt, (b) collapsible steering rod, and (c) air cushion.

Step 4: Physical realizability. The problem is whether it is possible to accomplish such a practical physical embodiment, as is suggested by the concept. The designer can visualize the elements and results of a new concept. (The concept of design tree has already been explained.)

Step 5: Economic worthwhileness. No object is a proper subject of product design, if it is unable to pass the test of economic worthwhileness. Literally, this means that the object of the design must be "... of sufficient value to repay off effort." Value has meaning which is singularly personal; it depends on the evaluator, his viewpoint, and the prevailing circumstances. The only objective measure is in the market place. When this instrument of measure can be applied, the results can be quantitatively expressed in terms of money. Indirect tools, highly sophisticated and difficult to apply, must be used for their measure. Utility is a good measure of economic worthwhileness of a product. Repeating the earlier example, on a comparative basis, a bulb with 4 units life (on a 10-point scale) and luminous intensity 3 units has a higher utility than a bulb with 5 units life and luminous intensity 2.5 units.

It is of interest to note the different values set a producer and a consumer attach to a product. The producer must acquire the requisite resources of raw materials, energy, capital, and manpower. These he can obtain in the open market; therefore, their value of acquisition can be determined objectively. The final product, after its completion, by transforming the input resources, is returned to the market place. Again, the value can be determined, and the input-output values compared. If the flux of values through the production process has occasioned an augmentation of value sufficient to induce its continuance, the process is deemed to be economically worthwhile. The extension to the distributor follows in the same manner. The consumer attaches value to a product because it meets some of his needs.

Step 6: Financial feasibility. Sometimes it happens that a project, meritorious from every point of view, and of great economic worth, cannot be realized because it is difficult to mobilize resources for its implementation.

The last three steps are like sieves. Through the first sieve only those solutions are passed which are physically realizable; through the second, only those possessing economic worthwhileness for producer, distributor and consumer; and through the third, only those that are financially feasible. The set of useful solutions comprises the ones passing successfully through each of the three sieves.

1.8.2 Phase II—The Preliminary Design

The preliminary design is intended to establish an overall concept for the project, which will serve as a guide for the detailed design. An evolution of the design concept is carried forward far enough so that a decision can be made about committing for the next phase. The preliminary design phase is shown diagrammatically in Figure 1.5. Optimization is the main objective in this phase.

Step 1: Selection of the design concept. In the set of useful solutions developed in the feasibility study, the most promising one must be identified. The design concept is selected on the basis of utility. Factors such as reliability, safety, cost, and user friendliness are given consideration and the design concept with the highest point rating qualifies as the best concept.

Step 2: Formulation of mathematical model. Design proceeds from the abstract to the concrete. We do this by describing the idea in words, in graphic illustrations, and in mathematical equations. Mathematical models enable useful software to be developed so that the design can be optimized on a computer.

Step 3: Sensitivity analysis. We visualize a system as being described in the form of equations or a mathematical model involving the design parameters and the input and output variables. We would like to know how sensitive the performance of the system is to the adjustment of several design parameters. Those which critically affect the performance must be carefully adjusted, whereas others which are less critical can be adapted to suit convenience. In recent years, Taguchi the Japanese pioneer of quality control, has been advocating the concept of robust design. According to his philosophy, the design parameters, which, on changing, result in a large change in undesirable output from the system, should be deleted. Identification of such parameters is possible through factorial design of experiments.

Step 4: Compatibility analysis. A system or a complicated device can be thought of as an object which is itself a combination of objects on the next lower order of complexity. In the case of a complex system such objects would be referred to as sub-systems.

Compatibility may involve straightforward considerations such as geometrical tolerance or chemical tolerance. More difficult problems of compatibility arise when interacting co-members must have matching operating characteristics, as when one member is in series with another so that the outputs of one are the inputs of the other. One example of this aspect of compatibility is electric motor and pump combination.

Step 5: Stability analysis. Systems and devices that engineers design are often exposed to a dynamic environment. For example, a building is apparently a stable and static structure, but an earthquake may apply an impulsive displacement to the foundation, resulting in a catastrophe.

A designer would like the systems he designs to have an inherent stability so that uncommon perturbations in the environment or accidental large inputs or loads will not cause catastrophic failures or malfunctions.

Step 6: Formal optimization. Till now we have not tried to fix all the major design parameters at definite and singular values. However, for the design to advance, the parameters must receive specific design values. Among all the feasible combinations of parameter values (i.e., combinations which satisfy all the design constraints and therefore could be expected to work), there is one superior to all others, viz. the optimum combination. The process for finding this destination is called optimization. In mechanical design, R.C. Johnson-developed in 1979 a method of optimum design (MOD) subject to constraints. It is called Johnson's MOD and is discussed in some detail in Chapter 9 on Optimization.

Step 7: Projections into the future. We may now pose two main questions: the first is on the socio-economic environment that will exist when the product comes into actual use, and the second refers to the race against technical obsolescence. The development period for a product should not be so large that by the time it comes in the market, the competitor would have launched a superior product. The other aspect of the future projections is the expected useful 'shelf life' of the product.

Step 8: Prediction of system behaviour. A system must function in an acceptable manner throughout a reasonable service life. The desired outputs must be produced over a span of time as well as at the start when the system is new.

Step 9: Testing the design concept. The proof of a design is in the use of the product. Evolutionary design waits for the evidence and allows time to pass for its utility to be revealed. A novel design cannot wait because it relies much more on innovation. Innovation must speed ahead; otherwise, it will be overtaken by the next wave of new technology. The new design concept can be tested with a scale model or through computer simulation.

Step 10: Simplification of design. As a design moves through various steps, the original concept becomes more complicated. The simple and the obvious are hard to achieve. One of the most important questions for the designer to ask is whether the projected solution is the simplest.

The detailed design to be discussed now onwards carries the overall design concept, developed in its preliminary stage, to the final hardware. To do so, the overall concept must be brought to a state of design that is clearly physically realizable. This state is achieved by finally constructing a prototype from a full set of design instructions; testing it and making the necessary revisions in both prototype and design instructions until the system or device are satisfactory for production, distribution and consumption.

1.8.3 Phase III—Detailed Design

Step 1: Preparation for design. In order to go ahead we need budgetary approvals and a strong design team. The commitment to proceed is not final because relatively close estimates of time and money are needed, prior to the design. For practical reasons, it is only the top management who, having the responsibility for the final economic success of the project, can make the decision to suspend the project, or to approve the necessary budgets. The art and science of estimation is very important. One must make use of costing data such as provided by Trucks [2] and Wilson [3].

Step 2: Overall design of subsystems. In the preliminary design, we are concerned with the overall concepts; subsystems are examined only to evaluate the quality of the overall system concept. Subsequently, each subsystem must be looked at as an individual entity. Compatibility of one subsystem with the other also needs to be verified.

Finally, a provisional master layout is prepared for each subsystem which translates the results of the subsystem designs into drawings. These master layouts become the basis for developing the design of the components.

Step 3: Overall design of components. The work which is required for the overall design of components is practically a repetition of what has been indicated for the subsystems. Just as the system comprises several subsystems, so the subsystems usually comprise a certain number of components, which are developed in the same way as the subsystem. But as we move down to successively lower levels in the design project, the objects we deal with become progressively less abstract and the problem of ultimate hardware becomes urgent. Some of the components can even be purchased as complete assemblies of hardware. A set of ball bearings is a typical example of bought-out items.

As in the case of the subsystem, the results of the component designs are covered in provisional master layouts which form the basis for the detailed design of parts.

Step 4: Detailed design of parts. Parts are the elementary pieces from which components are assembled. It is here in the work of designing parts that we come to grip with the concrete realities of hardware. In the design of subsystems or components, a large number of relatively minor questions about achieving physical realization are allowed to go unanswered because we feel very sure that answers will come from sources of immediately accessible knowledge and from available experience in the technology when the actual parts are being designed. When a part is being designed, no questions pertaining to its design may remain unanswered; no ambiguities about its shape, its material, or its surface treatment should interfere with the instructions for its manufacture. We have come to the place, on the long path from the abstract to the concrete, from the concept of the system or device to the physical embodiment where the final transition is made, where the idea merges into physical reality. Today, great progress is being made in part design, particularly through sophisticated methods such as photoelasticity and the finite element methods. The latter are covered in Chapter 13.

Step 5: Preparation of assembly drawings. After the constituent parts have been designed, the form of a component can be fixed. The provisional layout of the component can now be replaced by tentative final assembly drawings. In producing the assembly drawings, cases of incompatibility and oversight in the compatibility analyses will generally be revealed. The affected parts are suitably modified.

After the component assemblies are prepared, the corresponding assembly drawings for the subsystems can be drafted. Again, incompatibilities and misfits of various kinds may be revealed, and these are corrected by the usual iterative process. Finally, the final assembly for the system is similarly undertaken. Computer-aided Design and Drafting is the latest practice in computerized drafting.

Step 6: Experimental construction. With the completed drawings at hand, the prototype shop can undertake to build the first full-scale prototypes. Sometimes, the first prototype is also the end-product.

When the prototypes have to serve an experimental purpose, greater freedom in revision is permissible, but change for the sake of change is undesirable.

Step 7: Product test program. The programs can be enormously expensive and, if improperly planned, yield insufficient evidence for or against the design. They provide scant information on which suitable revisions can be based. Factorial experiments provide a very effective method of testing with low cost. In this method, the independent variables are changed between their high limit and low limit. The effect of such change on the response variable (or the main design objective) is determined. Interested readers can refer to Cochran and Cox [4], and Davies [5], and others, for detailed literature on response surface methodology.

Step 8: Analysis and prediction. With the notes and records of the experimental construction and the data and other general observations of the test program, preparation for revision or redesign can begin, if necessary.

Step 9: Redesign. The analysis and prediction of performance are the prelude to redesign. If the experimental construction and the test program have not found the design inadequate, the work of redesign may be just that of minor revision. If major flaws and shortcomings have been exposed, then the work of redesign may reach major proportions, and entirely new concepts may have to be sought for major components and even for subsystems.

1.9 ROLE OF ALLOWANCE, PROCESS CAPABILITY, AND TOLERANCE IN DETAILED DESIGN AND ASSEMBLY

1.9.1 Allowance (*A*)

Allowance is the difference of dimension between a female member and a male member of the assembly. A practical example of a male member would be a shaft, and its corresponding female member would be a hole. The concept of allowance is illustrated in Figure 1.6(a). If the allowance is positive, the type of fit is termed a *clearance fit*; if the allowance is negative, the type of fit is termed an *interference fit*; if the allowance has a very small positive value or a very small negative value, it is called a transition fit. The various types of fits are described in Section 1.9.4.

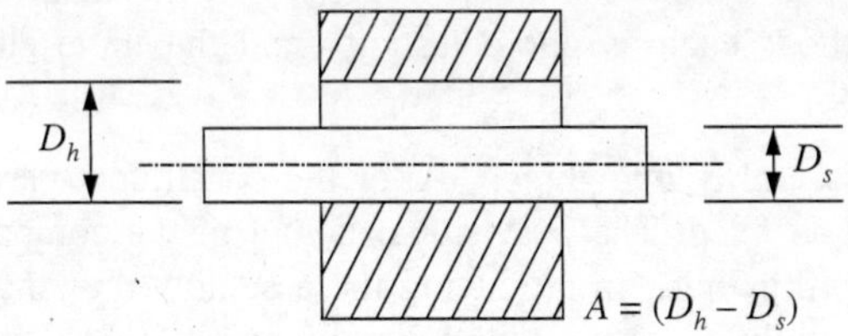

FIGURE 1.6(a) Concept of allowance in a shaft-hole combination.

1.9.2 Process Capability (*P*)

A production process which is set up to produce a certain dimension (*D*) of a part will not be able to produce all parts to the set-up dimension. There will always be a few oversized parts with dimension D_{max} and a few undersized parts with dimension D_{min}. The difference between D_{max} and D_{min} is termed *process capability*. A precise production process such as grinding will have a narrower band width ($D_{max} - D_{min}$) as compared with a less precise production process such as, say, rough turning on lathe. Referring to Figure 1.6(b), a frequency distribution curve of machine cut parts follows a bell-shaped normal distribution curve.

1.9.3 Tolerance (*T*)

The product designer is aware that a process set up at a size *D* will occasionally produce pieces, which are either oversized or undersized. For this reason, a designer always specifies a part dimension ($D + T/2$), where *T* is the tolerance prescribed by the designer. In order to avoid the production of defective parts, the tolerance *T* should be matched to the process capability *P* such that *P* is less than *T*. The usual ratio of *T*/*P* is 2. This ratio is termed *relative precision index*. Figure 1.6(b) indicates the relationship between *P* and *T*.

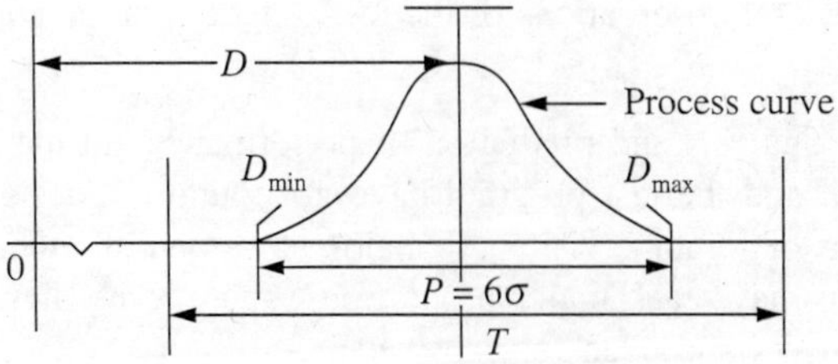

FIGURE 1.6(b) Tolerance and process capability.

1.9.4 Types of Fits

Taking the example of the assembly of a shaft and hole, the allowance A is the difference of dimensions D_h and D_s (see Figure 1.6(a)). A designer usually starts with an ideal allowance between a shaft and a hole.

(i) **Clearance fit.** For a bearing, allowance is positive, i.e. $(D_h - D_x)$ = positive. This is called clearance, and this type of fit is called a clearance fit. The designer visualizes the clearance fit for successful operation of a bearing in which the shaft and hole are separated by a film of lubricant.

(ii) **Interference fit.** In the case of a press fit, a designer recommends a negative clearance so that $(D_h - D_s)$ = negative. This type of fit is called interference fit. A practical example of this is a bush fitted in a housing bore.

(iii) **Snug fit and transition fit.** A third type of fit is called the snug fit which has $(D_h - D_s)$ = zero (small positive value or a small negative value in practice). Such a fit is useful for location of a component having a bore with a pin. It is termed *transition fit*. Figure 1.7(a) illustrates the designer's concept of a clearance fit. This will be discussed in detail now from Figure 1.7(b), it may be observed that due to the inability of a process to produce an exact dimension, it becomes essential for the designer to specify certain permissible variation, T which is more than the process capability P. This permissible variation has to be indicated on any realistic detailed drawing. Figure 1.7(b) shows the shaft hole combination of Figure 1.7(a) modified to take care of tolerance for the production of the shaft and the hole. Figure 1.7(c) illustrates a conventional diagram of fits.

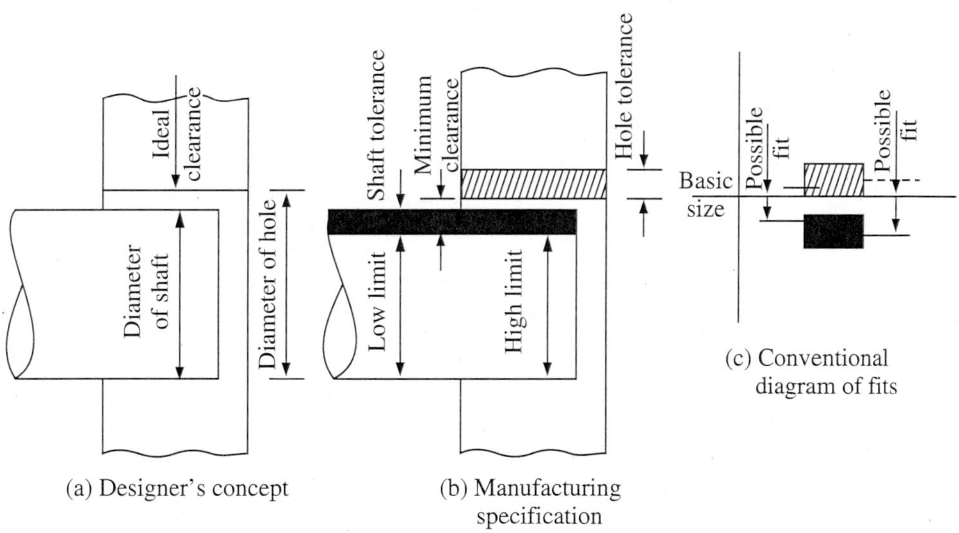

FIGURE 1.7 Fundamentals of a limit system.

1.9.5 Selection of Fit

A designer's concept of fit, manufacturing specifications for a fit, and conventional diagrams of fit are shown in Figure 1.7(a)–(c), respectively.

A fit can be obtained by a combination of two apparently independent variables:

1. Tolerance grades, 18 in Number: IT-1 to IT-18.
2. Fundamental deviation, FD, denoted by lower case letters such as c, d, e, etc. for shafts and capital letter *H* for holes.

However, due to designer's intent to standardize and effect variety reduction and the types of fit, only a few preferred combinations are adopted in practice. One typical example followed by BS4500 is illustrated in Figure 1.8.

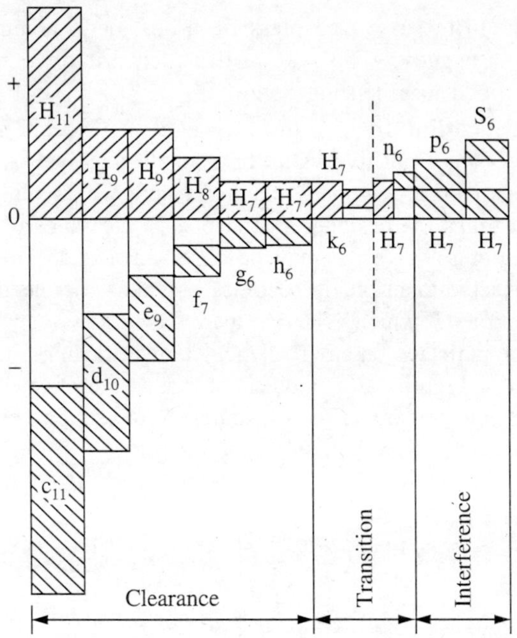

FIGURE 1.8 Preferred combinations of fits.

1.9.6 Specific Principles

1. Tolerance need not be assigned to atmospheric surfaces. For such surfaces, finish should be good enough to prevent corrosion and ill effects of pollutants. However, for journal bearing type design, a positive clearance is desirable.
2. For a location fit such as pulley on a shaft (where subsequently a key shall be driven in), a location fit or a transition fit is essential.
3. A situation where one component has to be rigidly fitted to another, an interference fit or a press fit is recommended. An example of such a fit is fitting a gear on a shaft for transmission of power.
4. From process engineering point of view, tolerance grades IT-1 to IT-6 are obtained by lapping, honing, microfinishing and precision grinding.
5. Tolerance grades IT-7 and IT-8 represent finished turning and semifinished turning, whereas grade IT-9 is rough turning. All tolerances above grade IT-9 belong to various primary processes such as rolling, casting, forging, etc.

1.10 SUMMARY OF DETAILED DESIGN PHASE

We have seen that the detailed designs, involving large commitments for design work, require careful preparation of capital budgets and time schedules. This is the first step. Top management, in the light of these estimates, must decide whether to continue with the design project. If the decision is favourable, then a project organization must be developed.

The second and third steps involving the overall designs of subsystems and components are similar in many ways to the preliminary design. In the fourth step, the detailed design of parts is undertaken, and followed in the fifth step by the preparation of assemblies for the components and subsystems.

In the sixth and seventh steps, the prototype is built and tested. The difficulties encountered in both of the operations, constructing and testing, become the subjects of analysis in the eighth step. Also, performance is predicted under conditions of customers operation, and any shortcomings, evident or anticipated, are included in the difficulties.

The final step is the making of revisions. A major problem to be tackled is that the design as a whole should be least affected. Small revisions can start a chain of consequences which could destroy the originality of the earlier design.

Finally, the iterative character of design work should be noted. After the revisions have been made in the redesign step, building of new prototypes and subsequent testing may follow, again leading to further revisions. A successful project is, however, highly convergent so that only a few iterations are required to reach a final solution. The high rate of convergence stems from the high confidence levels which are required in critical decisions.

REVIEW QUESTIONS

1. What are the seven phases of the morphology of design process ? What is the difference between Primary phases and Secondary phases? P4 (vii) P7 Sec.1.7
2. What is meant by physical realizability? Explain taking example of inflatable air bag used in automobiles to protect the driver of an automobile from a head-on crash. What are the factors for a successful design? P2 & P3
3. If the probabilities estimated by the designer for the design concept, as shown in Figure 1.1(b), are given, calculate the probability of a successful design for physical realizability.

   [Probabilities of protection in automobile head-on crash: Assume the data as below. This data is based upon designer's subjective estimates.

   $$P(D_{11}) = 0.95,\ P(D_{22}) = 0.92$$

   $$P(D_{21}) = 0.60,\ P(D_{32}) = 0.50,\ P\left(\frac{D_{31}}{D_{11}}\right) = 0.95$$

   Solution

   Now we have, $P(Q_1) = P(D_{11}) = 0.95$

   $$\begin{aligned} P(Q_2) &= P(D_{21} \text{ or } D_{22}) \\ &= 0.60 + 0.92 - (0.60)\,(0.92) \\ &= 0.97 \end{aligned}$$

$$P(Q_3) = P(D_{31}) + P(D_{32}) - P(D_{31})\, P(D_{32})$$

But $$P\left(\frac{D_{31}}{D_{11}}\right) P(D_{11})$$

$$= 0.95 \times 0.95 = 0.9$$

$$P(Q_3) = 0.9 + 0.5 - 0.9 \times 0.5 = 0.95$$

Now $$P(D) = P(Q_1)\, P(Q_2)\, P(Q_3)$$

$$= 0.95 \times 0.97 \times 0.95 = 0.87$$

Hence, the physical realizability of the design concept is 87%.]

4. How is the economic worth or utility of alternative designs compared? Illustrate through examples.

[Ans: Economic feasibility

The economic feasibility of a design is best measured by its utility factor.

As an example: If two electric bulbs have the following data on illuminating ability and life, both represented on a 10-point scale:

Bulb	*Illumination*	*Life*
A	7	3.5
B	8	3

Bulb *A* has total utility $U_A = 7 + 3.5 = 10.5$

Bulb *B* has total utility $U_B = 8 + 3 = 11$

Thus, bulb *B* is of more utility. Cost factor alone is not a measure of economic worth.

One of the recent trends in evaluation of alternate designs is based upon determining geometric mean rather than arithmetic addition of arithmetic mean.

Example From alternative CD deck designs *A*, *B*, *C*, evaluate the best. Data are given in table below:

	Rating		
Product design	1	2	3
A	8	10	₹ 100
B	9	8	₹ 120
C	7	9	₹ 90
Weightage	$W_1 = 3$	$W_2 = 1$	$W_3 = 2$

It is tempting to multiply each design by weightage and determines $E(U)$. But, this is theoretically incorrect. For example, an object weighing 100 lbs is two times as heavy as one weighing 50 lbs. But, a room at 120°F is not twice as hot as a room at 60°F. Therefore, arithmetic addition is not logical.

$$U_A = (8)^3\,(10)^1\left(\frac{1}{100}\right)^2 = 0.512$$

$$U_B = (9)^3\,(8)^1\left(\frac{1}{120}\right)^2 = 0.405$$

$$U_C = (7)^3(9)^1\left(\frac{1}{90}\right)^2 = 0.381$$

Thus, design *A* has higher utility factor than *B* or *C*.

For checking the economic worthwhileness and for determining rational cost of a product, various cost components such as direct material, direct labour, indirect material, indirect labour, factory overhead, administrative overheads, and selling expense are to be worked out. To this cost, the profit margin is to be added to give the total selling price of the product.]

5. Which of the following designs are 'design by evolution'?

(i) A power tiller used in farming *Design by evolution*

(ii) The pitcher made by a potter *Design by evolution*

(iii) The bullock cart *Design by evolution*

(iv) The electric shaver *Design by innovation.*

Explain your answer with supportive arguments.

6. How does design by evolution differ from 'design by innovation'? Explain with suitable examples. Sec. 1.2 and 1.3.

7. What is meant by design through creative routes? What are the desirable qualities of a creative designer?

[**Ans: Design through creative routes**

Creativity is a subject of research by psychologists. It is true that some persons are more creative than others. They can generate more useful ideas than others. However, even an average person can be creative, if he cultivates and sharpens his wits. A positive and sunny frame of mind is a must. Alger and Hayes have given the following phases of creative design:

(i) Establishment of familiarity with the problem.

(ii) Soaking the mind with the problem.

(iii) Try various combinations.

(iv) Permitting 'incubation' of the problem in the conscious and subconscious mind.

(v) 'Illumination' is the stage when a solution obtained.

(vi) 'Recording' the solution and further refinement of solution.

Desirable qualities of a creative designer are:

He should be:

- Open and perceptive.
- Free from fixity of mind.

- Enthusiastic with a positive frame of mind and motivated.
- Imaginative and apply fantasy.
- Able to synthesize various combinations to arrive at the design.
- Risk taker.
- Knowledgeable.
- Capable of converting ideas into practice.]

8. What are modelling and simulation? How is a scale model tested?

[**Ans: Modelling and simulation**

A model is an idealization of reality. Once a model is developed and experimentation on the model is carried out, it is possible to understand the real world problem. Broadly speaking, models can be divided into various types as shown in Figure 1.9.

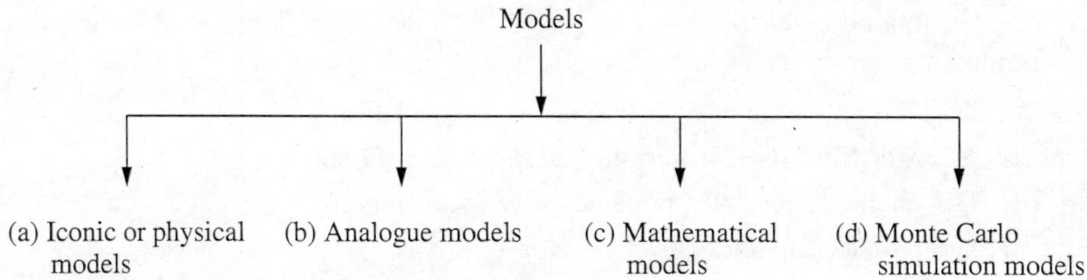

FIGURE 1.9 Types of models.

(a) *Iconic* or *physical models* are physical representations of the product. In product design, the various types of physical models are:

1. **Scale models.** A scale model is often reduced scale version of the real product. It should satisfy the conditions of geometric similarity with the actual product. It should also be dynamically similar to the real product in certain cases. This concept of dynamic similarity is very common in fluid mechanics, heat transfer, etc. Dynamic similarity is explained later on.
2. **Mock-ups.** A mock-up is used in case of outer bodies, cabinets of items with aesthetic value. For example, before finalizing the shape of a TV cabinet, a plaster of Paris or cheap wooden model mock-up is prepared to see the visual effect.
3. **Clay models.** Special hard wax like clay is used in shaping up products like automobile shapes, etc. in industry.
4. **Prototype.** It is a full-scale working model of the product to verify its performance.

   Modern practice is to use the CAD system to develop physical models. A technique called *rapid prototyping* cuts the models with a laser beam side by side with the generation of the CAD model on computer screen.

(b) **Analogue models.** Certain systems of mechanical type like spring-mass-damper are analogous to electric circuits of R–L–C type. However, an electrical system can be manipulated more efficiently than a corresponding mechanical system. Analogy of such type is used for design optimization and determination of sensitivity and stability.

(c) **Mathematical models.** Mathematical models of physical systems and management systems have attained great importance with the development of computer. Computer software is being developed in design using finite element techniques for stress determination in loaded machine members. On the other hand, material requirement planning (MRP) systems help in economic and efficient running of production systems.

(d) **Monte Carlo Simulation method.** In probabilistic systems of stochastic nature, *random numbers* are used to generate random demands for products, random delivery lead times in inventory problems; random interval times (A_t) and service times (S_t) in queuing systems, etc. Details of Monte Carlo simulation can be referred to in any text-book of operations research.

Examples of scale models calculations

Assume that a plastic model has modulus of elasticity $E_m = 2.76 \times 10^6$ N/mm^2 to represent product of steel $E_P = 200 \times 10^6$ N/MN^2. If a steel part is loaded with 500 kg in actual practice, what should be the load on plastic part with given properties. The model has scale factor 1:10, $s = 0.1$.

Solution

$$\text{The load on the model} = 50,000\frac{2.76 \times 10^6}{200 \times 10^6} \times (0.1)^2$$

$$= 6.9 \text{ kg}$$

Illustration of dynamic similarity

In dynamic similarity, the forces acting on the model and prototype are in a fixed ratio. This was shown in the earlier example. Taking example from fluid mechanics;

$$\text{Inertia force} = \text{Mass} \times \text{Acceleration}$$

$$(F_i) = \rho L^3 \frac{L}{T^2} = (\rho L^2 v^2)$$

$$\text{Viscous force } (F_v) = \tau L^2 = \mu \frac{du}{dy} \times L^2$$

$$= \mu \frac{v}{L} \times L^2 = (\mu v L)$$

where v is velocity, ρ is density, τ is shear stress and μ is viscosity.

The Reynolds number (N_R) which is ratio of (F_i) and (F_r) is ($\rho Lv/\mu$).

In wind tunnel testing of scale models or hydraulic machines, the value of (N_R) for model should be same as would be experienced by the actual product.]

9. What are qualifying design concepts and test programmes for products?

[**Ans: Qualifying design concept and test programs for products**

Testing is used to demonstrate the adequacy of a product or design. Testing is an important means of showing what a product or design can do because it gives direct and tangible results. Tests are used to investigate ideas, check the feasibility or concept, and demonstrate compliance with a specific requirement. Various types of tests to qualify design concepts are:

1. **Scale model test (carried out on reduced size part).** Used to evaluate new concepts, gain insights and determine feasibility. Wind tunnel tests are examples of this test.
2. **Development tests.** These are used for verifying design concept and follow the iterative process, i.e. learning from failure and building on successes. This leads to improved design.
3. **Prototype test (performed on full-size, preproduction items).** These tests are carried out to investigate the workability of design prior to taking up large scale or mass production. Prototypes resemble final design and represent the output from the design and development efforts. Loading is done beyond design values to demonstrate the design capability and to verify the correctness of the design and analyse methods. These are called *accelerated tests*.
4. **Proof tests.** Several of advanced prototype items are tested to examine the degree of variability and also to identify the failure modes and weak lines in the design. These provide important data for verification of design. Certain diodes and electronic items are tested between –30°C to + 60°C.
5. **Acceptance tests.** Non-destructive tests conducted on final product to demonstrate that the product meets the design requirement within expected operating range. This test is a direct effort to verify the design.

   Lathes and other machine tools are subjected to accuracy tests and performance tests. The latter are dynamic in nature.
6. **Model test.** In this case, a specified number of test articles are subjected to a rigorous series of tests to demonstrate the adequacy of the design. It is common practice for customer to withhold approval for production, pending the successful outcome of a model test. Reliability and life testing are well known in research. Any flaw noted in performance of the design is analyzed (step 8 of detailed design-phase III) and redesign (step 9) is the last step of detailed design.]

10. 'Design is an iterative process'. Explain the statement in the light of Asimow's model.

11. What is meant by activity analysis? What is the role of activity analysis in the development of specifications and standards of performance?

[**Ans: Standards of performance**

In contrast with specifications, standards of performance are set of broad requirements that cover the field of (1) reliability level, (2) safety, (3) ease of use, (4) adaptability under various environments, (5) ease of maintenance and (6) costs.

In each of the above cases, the minimum level of performance is very important even though it does not directly come under the domain of specification.

Some of the standards of performance may be akin to specification. For examples, the reliability for an aircraft could be desired at 0.99999..., whereas the cost of a chair could be constrained at ₹ 100. There is, in fact, no clear line of demarcation which separates specification from standard of performance.

Another standard of performance is that the product should not have any ill effects on the ecological balance of our planet.

Environment factors

Special precaution has to be taken by the designer while designing equipment which is to work in aggressive environment, such as one containing gases and suspensions which attack the material of which the product is made.

Further, the environment in which the product is to operate, e.g. extremes of temperature and altitude are also to be considered. For example, the volumetric efficiency of an engine suffers at high altitude and suitable blowing arrangements to keep desirable air fuel ratio is a must. Similarly, radiator of a motor vehicle should be more efficient and well designed. Asimow has explained how inputs, both desirable inputs such as fuel and undesirable input such as shock, vibration, environmental factors and desirable output, e.g. pollutants guide a designer in analysis and development of good products. Figure 1.10 shows 'activity analysis' and its role in development of specifications and tolerances.

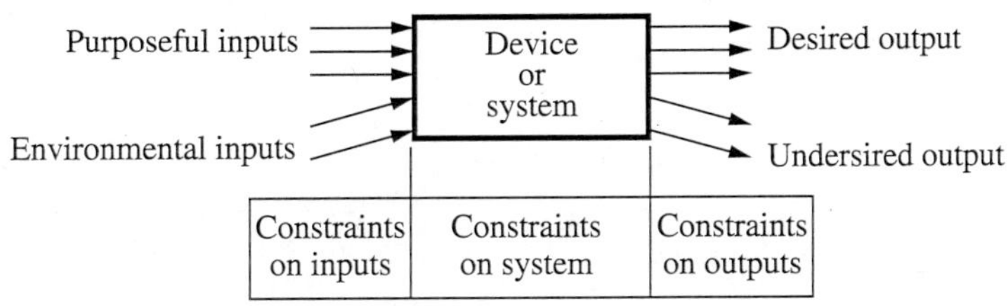

FIGURE 1.10 Activity analysis (leads to the formulation of the design problem).

A checklist of specification and standards of performance is as under:

I. *Preliminary need statement*

II. *Desired output*
   (a) Overload capacity
   (b) Reliability
   (c) Safety and unacceptable failure modes
   (d) Adaptability
   (e) Maintenance
   (f) Cost
   (g) Effects of physical environment (pollution)

III. *Environment factor*
   (a) Ambient temperature
   (b) Ambient pressure
   (c) Humidity
   (d) Vibration levels
   (e) Noise levels
   (f) Any other

IV. *Resources and constraints*

(a) Constraints on design: Time, budget and facilities

(b) Constraints on production: Number required, machines and processes, labour skills and financial status of manufacturer

(c) Constraints on operation: Maintenance facilities and operator skill

12. Through a diagram gives an example of clearance fit, transition fit and interference fit. In what situations each of the following fits is recommended?

(i) H_7p_6 (ii) H_7f_6 (iii) H_7j_6

[**Ans:** See Sections 1.9.5 and 1.9.6 along with Figure 1.11.]

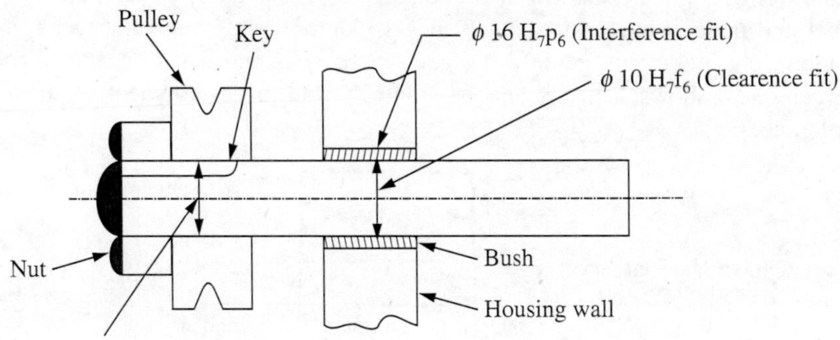

FIGURE 1.11 A drawing showing various fits.

13. Explain through an example the design for assembly.

[**Ans: Design rules for manufacturing and ease of assembly**

1. Design for a minimum number of parts.
2. Develop a modular design.
3. Minimize part variations.
4. Design parts to be multifunctional.
5. Design parts to be multiuse.
6. Design parts for ease of fabrication.
7. Avoid non-standard fasteners.
8. Minimize assembly direction; preferably top down.
9. Maximize compliance in parts; make assembly easy through, leads tapers.
10. Evaluate assembly sequence for efficiency.
11. Improve component accessibility.
12. Avoid flexible component as they are difficult in automated assembly.
13. Allow for maximum in tolerance of parts.
14. Use known vendors and suppliers.
15. Use parts at derated values of stress for increased reliability.
16. Minimize sub-assemblies.

17. Use new technology only when necessary.
18. Emphasise standardization.
19. Use the simplest operations with known capability.
20. Design components for symmetry from end to end and about axis of insertion.]

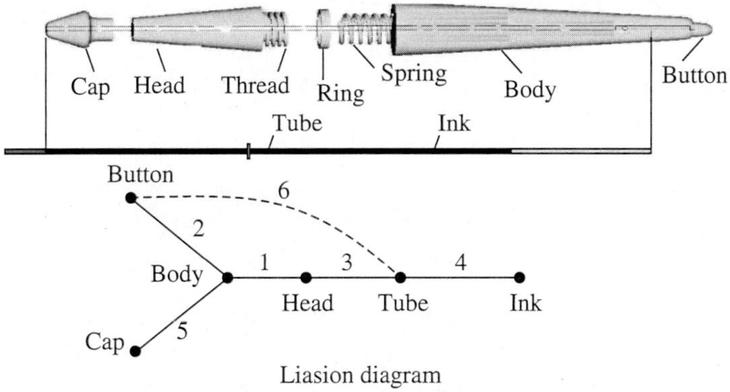

FIGURE 1.12 Ball point pen assembly.

Liaison diagram is a graphical representation of connections between assembled parts of a product.

REFERENCES

[1] Asimow, M., *Fundamentals of Engineering Design*, Prentice-Hall, Englewood Cliffs, New Jersey, 1962.

[2] Trucks, F., *Design for Manufacturing, Society of Manufacturing Engineers*, Dearborn (Michigan), 1987.

[3] Wilson, F.W., *Manufacturing Planning and Estimating Handbook*, ASTME, Dearborn (Michigan), 1963.

[4] Cochran, W.G. and Cox D.L., *Design of Experiments*, McGraw-Hill, New York, 1975.

[5] Davies, O.L., *Design of Experiments for Optimal Conditions, McGraw-Hill,* New York, 1970.

Chapter 2

Product Design Practice and Industry

2.1 INTRODUCTION

Product development and design is closely linked with industrial activity and production. When a new product is planned, the designer has to bear in mind the available resources of the plant and the possible impact of the firm having to acquire, modify or substitute existing machines and equipment or buy various components from other suppliers. It is therefore obvious that product development and design is at the core of the development and growth of the production centre and its departments. Thus, product design is one of the fundamental elements of management policy. Eilon [1] has emphasized the close relation between product development and production planning and control.

2.2 PRODUCT STRATEGIES

What is the product strategy of an organization, and how does it affect the design of the product? Surveys in industry, by use of questionnaires and interaction with executives of manufacturing firms, have revealed that there is no such common policy for all organizations.

2.2.1 Pricing Strategy for Product

As an example of pricing strategy, one large chain of departmental stores aims at offering commodities to the public at a minimum price, whatever be the quality. In fact, one may be quite sure that articles bought at this stores cannot be obtained cheaper or even at the same price elsewhere. The company bases this policy on the assumption that the type of goods it offers need not have a very long life and that, if sold cheaply enough, the volume of sales is likely to be very large, so that even a very marginal profit per unit will lead to substantial gains. This strategy is termed *pricing strategy*.

2.2.2 Product Quality Strategy

Other manufacturers (e.g. the aircraft industry and many precision instrument makers) define their aim as *high quality*, whatever be the cost. The Chairman of Bajaj Auto Ltd. has recently expressed that for his company, product quality is the secret of success for over the last three decades. The high quality is manifested in minimal maintenance, high reliability and ergonomic superiority of the Bajaj scooter for Indian conditions. Similarly, *LML Vespa* and *Kinetic Honda* have been able to capture substantial market share due to their superior product quality.

2.2.3 Product Luxuriousness Strategy

In same cases, luxury and comfort are the prime considerations that cost becomes secondary, e.g., Rolls Royce. However, in others, precision and prestige play an important part, for instance, Mercedes, BMW and Toyota. The manufacturers of these automobiles produce luxurious models (of course, Toyota has several popular models besides the luxury models), but the number produced is not very large, and in spite of the high price of the finished product, the firm cannot expect to get high profits from this line of production alone.

2.2.4 Product Utility Strategy

Other automobile firms like Maruti motors aim at large volume production of a low-priced car that will compete with more expensive models (Esteem) by having some of their successful and popular features and innovations. Most companies, however, say they aim at striking a satisfactory balance between very high quality and a reasonable price. Others go further and try to improve this balance in favour of the customer, by improving quality and leaving the price unchanged or by improving production methods and offering the same quality at a reduced price.

2.3 TIME TO MARKET

The importance of product development and design for long-range planning by management is further emphasized by the amount of time that elapses from the inception of the idea for the new design until production starts. Some surveys in industry, reported by Eilon [1], revealed remarkable figures for this "incubation" period or time to market:

Automobile bodies	2 years
Automobile engines	4–7 years
Radios and television sets	6–12 months
Specialized welding equipment	6 months
Telecommunications equipment	4 years
Aircraft	10–15 years
Household equipment	2 years
Metal-cutting equipment	4–5 years
Shipbuilding (depending on size of vessels; Special shipbuilding design may be developed over several years)	6–12 months
Fashion	Several weeks

In defence projects, where development and design take somewhat long time, because of the complexity of the problems involved, some design may become "obsolete" even before their production has begun, as new models are being developed at the Computer-Aided Design workstations and in the testing laboratories by competitors at a very fast rate.

2.4 ANALYSIS OF THE PRODUCT

Many factors have to be analyzed in relation to development and design factors which vary in character and complexity, and factors related to different fields in production and industrial engineering. Some of these may be grouped as follows:

1. Marketing aspect
2. Product characteristics:
   (a) Functional aspect
   (b) Operational aspect
   (c) Durability and dependability aspects
   (d) Aesthetic aspect
3. Economic analysis:
   (a) Profit consideration
   (b) Effect of standardization, simplification and specialization
   (c) Break-even analysis
4. Production aspects

Aspects 3 and 4, i.e., Economic analysis and Production aspects are considered in Chapters 6 and 10 respectively in the book.

All these factors are interrelated and each presents many issues that have to be carefully considered, as indicated by Figure 2.1. Market research may guide product designers in their work to improve existing products or to develop new ones. The design and its characteristics have to undergo an economic analysis and must be researched in the light of available production facilities and techniques. A costing analysis is naturally dependent on the sales volume; hence, the proposed design has to be re-evaluated by market research so that a sales projection can be done. This expected sales volume provides the basis for a further study from the production methods aspect, and the economic analysis has to be rechecked and perhaps modified. Thus, product development and design is an excellent example of interdependence of a multitude of factors that have to be unified and integrated into a final composition.

2.4.1 Product and Market

First, it is necessary to establish that the proposed product will fulfil a demand in the market, what it is supposed to do, and the services it can offer are both desirable and acceptable. If no consumption is expected, it is futile to go ahead with product design.

The demand for the product in the market may already exist, and its volume can then be assessed by market research and sales figures for similar products. Demand can also be created with the introduction of a new product, either by filling in a gap in the market or by offering new attributes, such as novelty, form and shape, or some other specific quality. The volume of such a demand is more difficult to forecast. Market research is a useful tool in these cases, but experience and sound judgement are required to evaluate and apply the results of such research, and in some cases, a certain amount of speculation cannot be avoided.

The volume of demand is a function of several factors, such as trends, cyclic effects, seasonal effects, etc., some of which are closely related to local conditions and are sometimes difficult to define or measure. It is, therefore, essential for an enterprise to keep in touch with the market and "feel" its trends, especially when this market is remote and different in character from the local one.

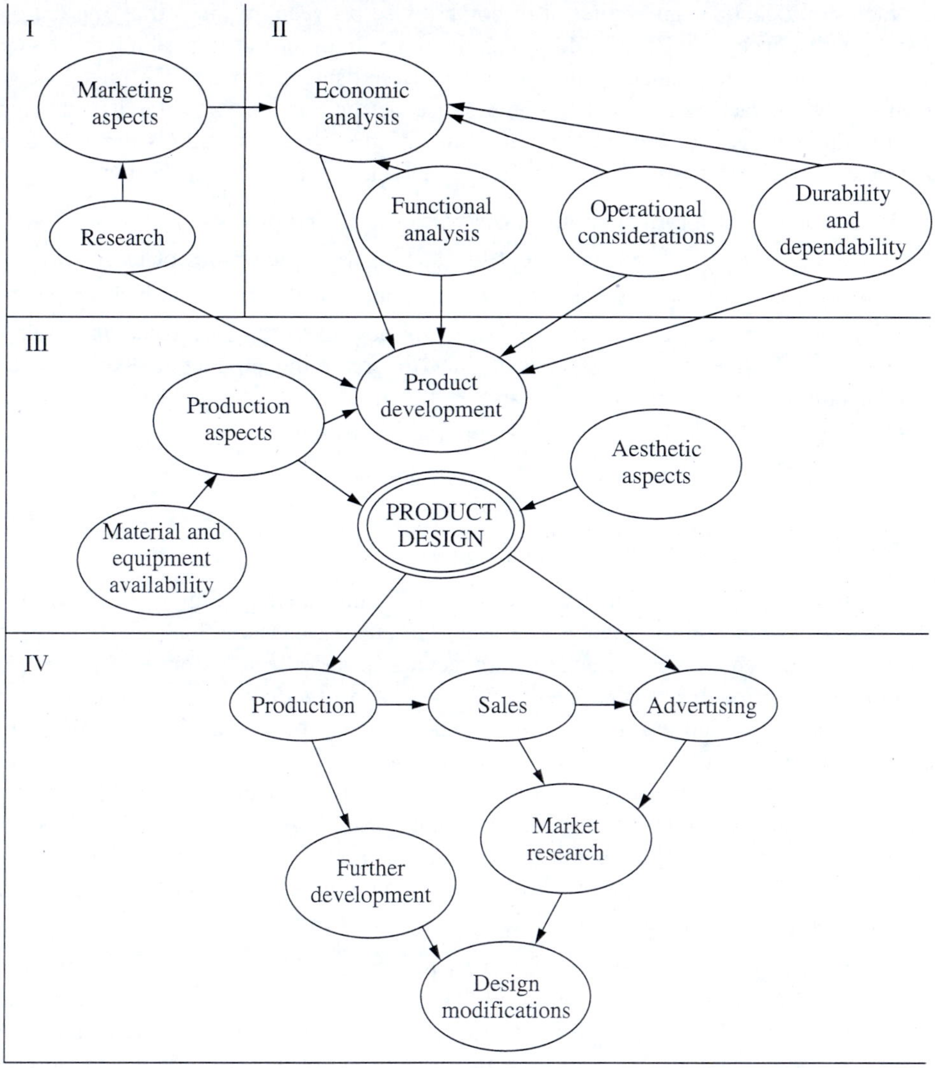

FIGURE 2.1 Various relationships in design, production and marketing.

This is of particular importance to firms depending on export trade for the distribution of their products.

Another relevant question related to product design is: Should the customer get what he wants or should he be served with what he needs? Basically, this is an economic question. If the management wants to achieve maximum satisfaction and sets itself as a target to supply the customer with what he wants, it may be faced with the possibility of having to produce an infinite variety of models to suit every taste. On the other hand, if the management was to ignore the customer's wishes or to maintain that he does not really know what he wants and should therefore be told what is good for him, the designer's task would become far more simpler, but the sales department would have to face an unpredictable market. The decision in such cases is difficult.

In practice, product design is a result of compromise between infinite variety on the one hand and the designer's concept of the ideal design on the other. In order to try to selling this compromise to potential customers, the management opts for an advertising campaign, the policy of which is dependent on the characteristics of the "compromise design" and on how far it conforms to, or differs from, the expressed desires of the market to which such a campaign is directed. Generally, the main objective of advertising is to expand the market, this being achieved by:

1. Providing general information about the existence of the product
2. Providing technical information about its functional characteristics or utility
3. Drawing the customer's attention to those attributes of the product which he wants
4. Winning the undecided customer by exhibiting possible attractions (such as colour, design, novelty and price) that may persuade him to prefer the product to the one offered by competitors
5. Creating demand among a passive population of customers
6. Educating the customer, or telling him what he should want

2.4.2 The Product Characteristics

The various relationships in design have already been illustrated in Figure 2.1. Now it can be seen how market research starts driving the 'design-production-consumption' cycle. Needs analysis generates functional requirement which in turn generates specification for product development. Apart from the functional aspects, other aspects, termed *standards of performance,* e.g., cost durability, dependability and ergonomics, are essential inputs to product development. Production design which considers incorporation of production into the design is another important aspect of design and development. Aesthetics or considerations of product appearance usually enter product design at a later stage rather than at the development stage. After the product design is complete, the subsequent steps are prototype production and later on, batch or mass production. The next step involves the actual selling of the product to the appropriate market. From the market, the feedback loop too needs analysis is complete.

(i) **Functional aspect.** When the marketing possibilities have been explored, the functional scope of the product has to be carefully analyzed and properly defined. Sometimes, functional aspects are multiple, and usage of the product can be left to the customer's choice. A steam iron is a case in point. The additional function of dampening the cloth when required, prior to or during ironing, is incorporated in the steam iron, the main functions of which is to iron the cloth. The customer can decide whether and when to exploit this characteristic of the apparatus.

There is a trend to offer functional versatility of the product, thereby increasing the range of applications and sometimes combining several tools in one. A mixer, for example, allows for a large number of attachments to be added for a variety of duties. It is labelled as a "kitchen machine" to enhance its positioning. Basically, the mixer housing contains a power unit and a speed regulator, but it has to be so designed as to serve all the attachments, and the customer has to decide and define for himself the functional scope to be compatible with his needs, his taste and his pocket. Again, household power-tool sets are designed on very much the same principle: The hand drill such as Wolf Cubmaster is the basic unit, and with attachments, it can become a table drill, a lathe, a grinder, etc. Versatility of production machinery may quite often result in substantial savings in production shopfloor space and capital expenditure, and this may become one of the fundamental factors affecting design policy. Another example of versatility in design is seen in multifunctional modular office furniture designed by furniture designers.

(ii) **Operational aspect (Ergonomic considerations).** After determining the functional aspect, the operational aspect has to be considered. Not only must the product function properly, it must be easy to handle and easy to operate. Sometimes, it has to be adaptable to various operational conditions, and very often it is subjected to varying degrees of skill of potential operators. The designer's problem becomes all the more critical with the rising trend for increased versatility because this characteristic implies using basic attachments as elements for building suitable combinations for specific purposes. This requires a certain amount of operator intelligence and skill, which increases with the complexity of the machine. The scarcity of skill is a constraint in this respect on the product designer.

The "start" stage before the proper operation and the "cleanup" time (including cleaning) should be carefully analyzed with respect to the expected skill of the operator. Too often, one finds highly efficient gadgets (e.g., in the field of household equipment) that are capable of performing an operation in a fraction of the time normally required but which involve such complicated preparations or such lengthy cleaning and "put away" subsequent operations, that the ratio of net machine time to overall machine time becomes too insignificant. The beneficial features attributed to the gadget in such cases are rather debatable.

Versatility of equipment should also be analyzed in the case of multiple chucks which should be a 'quick change chuck'. Especially, when subsequent operations are to be carried out with the aid of different attachments, the designer should always bear in mind the time required for an operator to perform the changeover and should ensure that the changeover time is in reasonable proportion to the operation time.

(iii) **Ease of maintenance and durability.** There are two factors closely related to the selection of materials and class of workmanship and hence to the design of the product and the economical analysis of its cost. Quality is not always a simple characteristic to define, but durability and dependability are two factors that often determine quality and have to be carefully considered by the designer. Durability is defined mainly by the length of the service life or endurance of the product under given, working conditions, but a measure of the product capability to idle or withstand storage is also often considered in assessing durability. Selection of good materials alone does not guarantee the durability of a product. The actual service life of a match or a rocket motor may be rather limited, but that does not mean that materials for these articles may be of low quality. An additional criterion, therefore, has to be considered, that of reliability, or the capability of the product to do its job. In the case of matches, for instance, reliability may be related to the number of sticks in a box, and while the manufacturer is eager to reduce this number to a minimum, he need not choose the very best raw materials to ensure that not even one match will fail. Dependability of rocket motors, however, may be more rigidly defined, and quality materials are chosen in spite of the short active life envisaged for them in some applications. The standard of performance and specifications of different products should be assessed with caution.

Another aspect of durability is that of *maintenance and repair.* The amount of repair and preventive maintenance required for some products is closely related to quality and design policy. This is of particular importance when the equipment is supposed to operate continuously and when any repair involves a loss of running time.

(iv) **Aesthetic aspect.** In what way does the appearance of a product affect its design? In most cases where the functional scope, durability and dependability have already been defined, the aesthetics aspect is mainly concerned with moulding the final shape around the basic skeleton. This moulding of shape may very often be severely limited in scope, and what finally emerges is sometimes termed a *junctional shape.* The view that functional shape is necessarily divorced from aesthetics is well illustrated by bridges, locomotives, or machines of the late 19th or early 20th century.

However, a study of the gradual changes in shape of these objects in the past few decades should convince us that there has been an increasing recognition of the role of aesthetics in design. This is perhaps partly due to man's aesthetic taste being reconciled to accepting these objects as an integral part, of the landscape or everyday life, thereby leading to a modification of the original attitude that these freaks are hopelessly ugly and should be discarded.

Functional shape is a concept in its own right among designers. Those who believe in functional shape argue that compatibility of function with shape is logical and should therefore be accentuated and exploited, rather than covered up. A standard lamp is first and foremost a lamp and not a butterfly, and there is nothing wrong with its looking like a lamp. This approach is illustrated in Figure 2.1. In this approach, the aesthetic aspects are examined at the design stage, after all the other aspects of the proposed product have been analyzed.

In some cases, however, plastic moulding of shape may have financial implications; for instance, when special materials have to be used or added to those basically required from the functional point of view or when additional processes are involved. Such cases will require careful cost analysis of the aesthetic aspects. In some cases, aesthetics is the governing factor in design and completely dominates it. This is especially true for many consumer goods or fashion goods. In the case of these goods, both variety and rate of design change are very high; Arthur D. Little Inc., USA classifies such products as *turbulent products.*

Whereas styling is a dominant factor in product design, it is often used as a means to create demand. In such products, appearance is the sole reason for purchase of the product. Changes in fashion and taste, evolution of form, and the introduction of new ideas quickly replace previous designs. If the market is turbulent and eager to discard outdated designs in favour of new ones, styling becomes a race against time, a race that determines the saleability of the product. Eilon [1] recommends the following techniques to enhance aesthetic appeal in product design:

1. *Use of special materials, either for the parts of the housing or as additional decorations.* Notable is the use of chromium strips, plastics, wood, glass and fabrics for the purpose.
2. *Use of colour, either natural colour of the material or colour provided by paints, platings, spraying, or even lighting.* Composition and contrast of colours are of great importance to the industrial designer in creating a design with convenient operational and aesthetic characteristics.
3. *Texture supplements colour, either by appropriate treatment of the given surfaces or coatings.* Surface finish and requirements of brightness as determined by styling may in turn affect the production processes in the finishing stages. Matt finish, mirror finish, and mottled finish are examples of surface finish varieties which are in vogue.
4. *Shape denoted by outer contours and similarity to familiar objects.* Shape can be exploited to accentuate particular features, to create a sense of spaciousness or illusions of size, richness and dependability.

5. *Use of line to break the form.* It is also used for the purpose of emphasizing parts of it, or to give a sense of continuity, graciousness and attainability.
6. *Scaling the product, either to a blown-up size or to a small size* (modelling). This creates novelty and a sense of completeness. The success of styling of some popular small automobiles in Europe may be partly due to the designer's talent in creating a feeling of stillness having the full-size version, with all its features.
7. *Packaging, especially for small items, novelty and attractiveness of packaging are often transferred in the mind of the customer.* In extreme cases, packaging may assume an appreciable portion of the total production costs and become the centre of the design project.

Aesthetic moulding, especially when governed by selection of material, colour, texture and sometimes even line, has great economic advantages, since great variety can be achieved at a comparatively low cost. The basic product remains the same, and variety is obtained by finishing processes alone. Henry Ford's maxim that the customer may choose any colour he likes, provided it is black, is no longer valid. Modern production control techniques allow for a vast number of combination of colours and textures to be offered with little difficulty. Customers are willing to pay more for design with special aesthetic features as demanded by them. Strangely, this holds true even for instrumentation and control panel.

Aesthetics has been fully recognized as an integral part of design, and no good designer can afford to ignore its implications, its tools and its benefits. The role of aesthetics in product design is of great importance and has been covered in Section 2.17.

2.5 THE THREE S's

The three S's refer to standardization, simplification, and specialization—three related subjects which are at the root of any economic analysis of product design. The three S's can be defined as follows: *Standardization* is the process of defining and applying the "conditions" necessary to ensure that a given range of requirements can normally be met with a minimum of variety and in a reproducible and economic manner on the basis of the best current techniques. Reduction is the essence of standardization: The effect of variety reduction on production and set-up times is shown in Figure 2.2. It has attained so much importance that ISO 9000 system of International Standards has now become

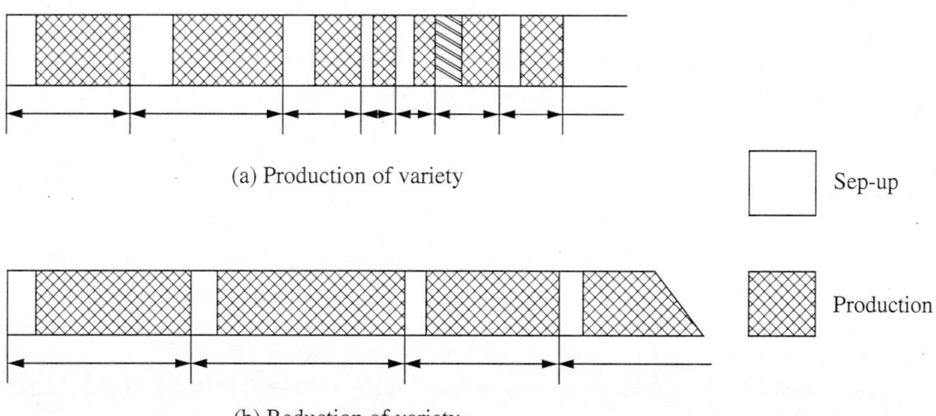

(a) Production of variety

(b) Reduction of variety

FIGURE 2.2 Effect of simplification and variety reduction on set-up and production cycle times.

a synonym for quality and prestige. Several industries are aiming at achieving this standard to be able to compete globally. The reader is advised to study special literature on Quality Management for detailed information on ISO 9000.

Simplification is the process of reducing the number of types of products within a definite range. It is also an attempt to reduce variety.

Specialization is the process whereby particular firms concentrate on the manufacture of a limited number of products or types of products. Specialization often is a result of one's aim to monopolize the market.

The three processes are usually linked together and develop as a logical sequence. From a wide range of requirements it is first necessary to sort out the essential features, define them, and then work out in a scientific manner the minimum variety required to meet these essentials. This is a process of standardization, and it is mainly an engineering process. Within a given range, whether covered by standards or not, a process of simplification can be carried out with a view to reducing the variety of products or materials that are produced or purchased. This is both an economic and an engineering process, and specialization is one of its natural outcomes.

2.6 STANDARDIZATION

Standardization covers a wide field of activity. These activities include:

1. Physical dimension and tolerances of components within a defined range.
2. Rating of machines or equipment (in units of energy, temperature, current, speed, etc.).
3. Specification of physical and chemical properties of materials.
4. Methods of testing characteristics or performances.
5. Methods of installation to comply with minimum precautionary measures and convenience of use.

The first three categories relate to limitation of the number of sizes or grades and some aspects of quality, one of the important aims being interchangeability of components or assemblies. Adherence to standards of raw materials is one of the fundamentals of product design since any deviation from the standards in this respect may cause a substantial increase in the cost of materials. Industry is rich with examples in which the designer specifies "special" materials whereas the standard grades can do just as well.

Standardization and interchangeability impose certain limitations on the designer and demand high skill and effort in planning. It is easy enough when designing a new component to decide that no standard really meets the special requirements of the case in hand and that a part has to be specified. What designers seem to forget is that one of the purposes of standards is to provide solutions to relieve them of the task of having to solve afresh some basic problem, and thereby allow them more time to concentrate on the broader aspects of the design.

Another prerequisite of interchangeability is the precision required in the manufacturing process in order to obtain production within the specified tolerances. This implies that production control has to be tightened so that any deviation from the given standards will be immediately noticed and appropriate action can be taken to avoid the process getting out of control.

Standardization has, however, many advantages, some of which may be briefly listed now:

1. Reduction of material waste and obsolescence
2. Concentration of effort in manufacturing: hence, simplification and specialization

3. Reduction in inventories, both of materials, and semifinished and finished products
4. Reduction in book-keeping and other paperwork
5. Lowering the grades of skill required in manufacture and assembly
6. Reduction in price: hence expansion of the market
7. Reduction in repair and maintenance costs.

2.7 RENARD SERIES (PREFERRED NUMBERS)

According to the American Standards Association, *preferred numbers* are defined as "a series of numbers selected to be used for standardization purposes in preference to other numbers. Their use will lead to simplified practice and they should, therefore, be employed whenever possible for individual standard sizes and ratings, or for a series thereof," in applications relating to important or characteristic linear dimensions (such as diameters and lengths) or specifications as areas, volumes, weights, and capacities; ratings of machinery and apparatus.

The problem of selecting preferred numbers was first tackled by the French engineer Col. Charles Renard in 1870 and, therefore, the series is sometimes referred to as the Renard series. Renard was an officer in the French Army and was faced with the problem of 425 different sizes of cables which were in use in his unit. He recognized that the process of standardization consisted of two problems: to define the number of terms in the series and to determine the method by which these sizes should be preferred to others.

Colonel Renard suggested the use of a combination of geometrical progression as well as multiples of ten (decimal series) as a guide for selection, and this system has indeed been adopted in standardization to cover the given ranges satisfactorily.

Suppose a manufacturer wants to produce containers having between 10 and 100 gallons capacity. In selecting the type of series he can choose any of the following four series:

A 5-series, i.e., covering the range of 10 to 100 in 5 steps
A 10-series, i.e., covering the range of 10 to 100 in 10 steps
A 20-series, i.e., covering the range of 10 to 100 in 20 steps
A 40-series, i.e., covering the range of 10 to 100 in 40 steps.

The need for more terms in a series (having fewer steps than those obtained in the 40-series) is very rare in practice, but when such a need arises, it is possible to use the 80-series. If a manufacturer decides to adopt the 5-series, his capacity ratings according to the geometric progression series will be:

First size 10 (given)

$$\left.\begin{array}{l}\text{Second size } 10 \times q \\ \text{Third size } 10 \times q^2 \\ \text{Fourth size } 10 \times q^3 \\ \text{Fifth size } 10 \times q^4\end{array}\right\} \text{5 steps (given)}$$

Sixth size $10 \times q^5 = 100$

Hence,

$$q^5 = 10 \quad \therefore \quad q \Rightarrow (10)^{1/5} = 1.585$$

The calculated sizes would be:

First size 10.00, i.e. select 10
Second size 15.85, i.e. select 16
Third size 25.12, i.e. select 25
Fourth size 39.82, i.e. select 40
Fifth size 63.11, i.e. select 63
Sixth size 100.00, i.e. select 100

} 5 steps

Similarly, the step size of the other series can be determined for:

5-series: $q = \sqrt[5]{10} = 1.5849$ or a step increase by about 60%

10-series: $q = \sqrt[10]{10} = 1.2589$ or a step increase by about 25%

20-series: $q = \sqrt[20]{10} = 1.1220$ or a step increase by about 12%

5-series: $q = \sqrt[40]{10} = 1.0593$ or a step increase by about 6%

The basic preferred numbers for all these series, as suggested by the International System, are shown in Table 2.1, where the given rounded numbers do not depart from the theoretical calculations by more than 1.3 per cent. The 5-series is given in column *A*. To obtain the 10 series, column E should be added; hence, the series would read: 10, 12.5, 16, 20, 25, etc. Similarly, for the 20-series, read 10, 11.2, 12.5, 14, 16 and so on.

TABLE 2.1 Basic preferred numbers (10 to 100)

Columns	*A*	*B*	*C*	*D*	*E*	*F*	*G*	*H*
	10	10.6	11.2	11.8	12.5	13.2	14	15
	16	17	18	19	20	21.2	22.4	23.6
	25	26.5	28	30	31.5	33.5	35.5	37.5
	40	42.5	45	47.5	50	53	56	60
	63	67	71	75	80	85	90	95
	...							
	100							

5 series (60% steps)—column *A*
10 series (25% steps)—column *A*, *E*
20 series (12% steps)—column *A*, *C*, *E*, *G*
40 series (6% steps)—column *A*, *B*, *C*, *D*, *E*, *F*, *G*, *H*.

2.8 SIMPLIFICATION

Simplification is a constant source of disagreement between the marketing department and the production personnel. A production engineer prefers little variety, minimum set-up, and long runs (see Figure 2.2). Simplification enables the production department to improve planning, achieve higher rates of production and machine utilization, and simplify control procedures. The salesman, on the other hand, strives to satisfy the customer by giving him a choice or by offering him the nearest to what he wants. The pros and cons of simplification are given in the following tabular representation:

Pro-Simplification	*Pro-Variety*
Reduce inventories of materials and finished products. Reduce investment on plant and equipment. Save storage space. Simplify planning and production methods. Simplify inspection and control. Reduce required technical personnel. Reduce sales price. Shorten or eliminate order queues.	Satisfy a wide range of demand. Enable better contact with the market to study its tastes and requirements. Avoid losing orders for more saleable products because the customer directs all his orders to other vendors. Create demand.

Perhaps, the last point in favour of variety deserves further clarification. Some sales people claim that variety encourages consumption and that, especially where consumer goods are concerned, the psychological effect of plenty creates demand. Further, market research by some firms seems to suggest that in some cases similar products tend to capture roughly the same portion of a given market. The prospects of increasing total demand on the one hand and the firm's portion of the market on the other may have been the main causes for boosting variety to the extent found nowadays in industry. From the customer's point of view, this is a very unsatisfactory state of affairs. A flood of variety pleases the customer, who ceases in many cases to appreciate the fine distinction between similar products and has either to make a haphazard choice or to invest effort, time and study (and quite often money) to enable him to make an intelligent choice.

This is undesirable for the firm as well. Apart from missing all the advantages listed above, when simplification is applied, an analysis of the market sometimes shows that variety has long exceeded the saturation point and that an increase in variety will not even be noticed in the market.

Also, the division of the market between a large number of products (in fact, too large) makes each portion so small that prices have to be kept at high levels to avoid losses.

When a great variety exists, a sales analysis can be made to establish the saleability of the products. When the accumulated sales income is plotted against die number of products offered for sale, it is often revealed that a comparatively small number of products contributes substantially to the total sales (Figure 2.3). This is sometimes referred to in industry as the "25% to 75%" relationship because in many cases it was found that 25% of the products brought in 75% of the income, although in some extreme cases, studies revealed as small as 10 to 90% relationships. This leads to unnecessary drain of the firm's efforts, which should be directed to promote the more profitable products. A more desirable situation is when responsibility for income is more evenly distributed between products, i.e., when the curve is "flat" as the lower curve in Figure 2.3 shows, which is achieved through reduction of variety.

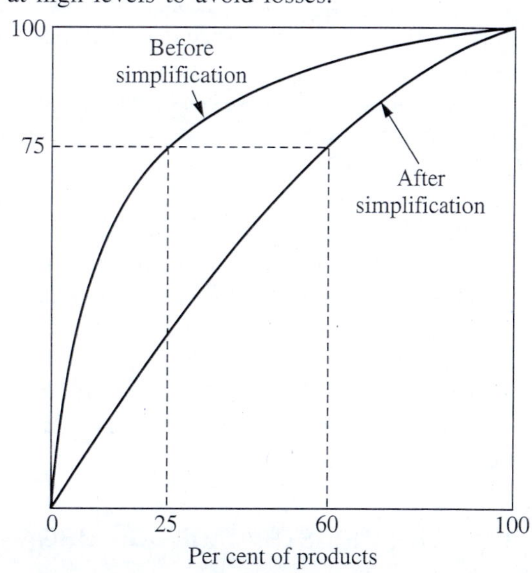

FIGURE 2.3 Effect of simplification on Pareto diagram (ABC diagram).

2.9 THE DESIGNER AND HIS ROLE

An industrial designer should realize that the appearance of a product is one of the major reasons for its sales appeal. Hence, it is more realistic to know that sales, engineering manufacturing and quality are all equally important factors, and that the right combination of these elements properly blended makes the perfect product—a "perfect product" being that which enjoys the greatest percentage of industry sales and brings a fair profit to the manufacturer.

It should be emphasized at the outset that the designer's main objective is to make money for his employer (and in turn, of course, for himself). Since industrial design is a comparatively new profession and not completely understood by everyone, we will try to answer four basic questions: What is industrial design? Who are industrial designers? How do they work? What do they accomplish?

Of these questions, the first is certainly the simplest. Industrial design has been briefly and well defined by the Illinois Institute of Technology as "The art and science of increasing the beauty and value of mass-produced products." To answer the other questions, we have to discuss in little more detail.

2.10 THE DESIGNER: MYTH AND REALITY

There was a time, not too long ago, when the industrial designer was portrayed as a temperamental artist, complete with flowing smock, beret, long cigarette holder, and foreign-make sports car (customized, of course, by himself). He was supposed to be highly sensitive to colour and form, but unable to tell a die casting from a metal stamping and was proud of it. He arrived, according to the popular image, with his portfolio of impressive airbrush renderings showing the transformation of the particular product from a study of engineered form into a teardrop, streamlined, jet-propelled gadget. All of this immediately impressed the President of the company—who by the way, was his sole contact. In the next scene, his designs were turned over to the company's engineers, who immediately cursed them in chorus, filed them, and proceeded as before. This was once the general impression. The picture has changed now.

In contrast, the typical designer of today is one who has graduated from one of the many good schools that offer a four-year course in industrial design: the NID, Ahmedabad; Industrial Design Centre (IDC) Bombay; Industrial Design and Development Centre (IDDC), Delhi; J.J. School, Bombay, at National level and Pratt Institute; Georgia Tech.; Syracuse University; The Philadelphia Museum School of Art; The University of Cincinnati; or the Rhode Island School of Art, all in the United States of America. In all these schools, they teach drafting and detailing, model making, design research, production planning, market analysis, basic science and engineering, and mass-production techniques. Through the cooperation of industry, they make numerous plant visits and work on actual design problems. Some of the graduates after finishing their studies, join an independent design firm or company-operated design department. The Indian scenario today indicates that more than 50% designers start their own studios and consultancies instead of joining a company.

2.11 THE INDUSTRIAL DESIGN ORGANIZATION

Before we can consider how the designer works, we should have some notion of the design group's position in the structure of company. At XYZ Corporation, USA for example, the designer reports directly to the Vice President and the General Manager of the division.

Some firms have a five-year planning committee in each division. This committee consists of the General Manager and representatives of the product planning, engineering product design, manufacturing cost and accounting and purchasing functions. It evaluates and defines the program for the items which are to be produced in the five-year period. All the departments represented feed ideas and recommendations to the group for evaluation. This is a continuous process, and the program is kept flexible to meet changing technical knowledge and market conditions. When the program has been agreed upon, it is time for the operating people to put the ideas into concrete form.

A team of design, engineering and manufacturing personnel is now formed to carry the program up to the stage of production. Gone are the days when the engineering department closed its doors until it had the product completely ready for tooling, then called in the designers to select the colour and apply some trim and nameplate. It is the "We Design—You Produce Approach" in which design and production activities are insulated by a barrier of indifference.

In some firms, the Product Design Department is divided into two groups—one responsible for the design of the product for one or two years, and the other responsible for three years and beyond. This is also true of the Engineering Department. If engineering and design activity are not divided in this way, there will never be any constructive effort on advanced products. As long as the same group is responsible for both production design and product planning, it will be continually "putting out fires" and will never have time to study new-product ideas. Under such conditions, the company may catch up with its competitors soon enough, but when it does, it will almost certainly find that the competitors are already far ahead of it because they have been working on new products. No matter what the size of the company, it is most important to designate someone to plan for the future.

2.12 BASIC DESIGN CONSIDERATIONS

Let us assume that a five-year product plan has been established. There are still major factors which the designer must consider before he puts pencil to sketch pad:

1. Convenience of use
2. Maintenance
3. Costs
4. Sales
5. Appearance.

These factors have already been considered earlier in this chapter in product analysis. Some of these are discussed once again in brief.

(i) **Convenience of use.** No matter what the product is, convenience is of primary importance. Whether the customer or user is a housewife with a hair-dryer or an engineer driving a limousine, it is the designer's primary objective to make the product desirable through its utility. In determining the proper approach, he has several sources from which he may seek assistance. These sources are now described.

1. It is always possible for marketing research people to find out what the customer dislikes about the company's previous models. Returned warranty cards and field reports from dealers and sates representatives are good sources of information.

2. Customer surveys may be conducted by making working models and pre-testing potential users. This is, of course, a costly method, whose value is sometimes questionable. Both the automobile industry, through its experimental car models, and appliance manufacturers, through their "kitchens of the future", use this approach to elicit public reaction.
3. The least costly and the most commonly used approach is common sense.

(ii) **Maintenance.** Ease of maintenance and life of parts are important factors. It is the customer who ultimately benefits from proper consideration in this area, and the designer must be careful to resist the temptation of designing primarily to please the service personnel. It cannot be repeated too often that the customer must always come first in the designer's thinking.

(iii) **Cost.** Although cost certainly cannot be ignored, it should not be the overriding consideration in all cases. The lowest-priced item does not necessarily out-sell the highest-priced, as the automobile industry offers ample evidence.

If the only consideration was cost, we would still be using the hand crank handle instead of the automatic starter, and the manual shift instead of the automatic transmission. Here again, it is the customer who must ultimately decide how much the product is worth.

(iv) **Sales.** We must know the volume of sales anticipated, the competition that will be encountered, what the competitors are offering, and what we plan to offer. With regard to sales, it will be better to remember that maximum efficiency and good performance do not necessarily help in selling the product.

Again, as an example, the first automatic washing machines did not wash clothes as clean as the wringer-type, yet they were sold in great quantity. A good number of men use electric razors, even though these razors cannot give as good a shave as the safety razors. Like all the rest, people prefer convenience; and this seems to be the overriding consideration in the motivation of most sales today.

(v) **Appearance.** Appearance should not be underestimated, for it determines the whole "character" of the product. It should reflect pride of ownership, the function served, high product quality and value, and the reputation of the maker. Figure 2.4 shows role of appearance for various products.

Great ↑ Jewellery
Cloths
Furniture
Domestic appliances
Radio, TV, Tape recorders
Office machines
Machine tools
Contractors plant
Electrical equipment
Engines
Valves
Nil | Nails, screws

FIGURE 2.4 Significance of appearance.

2.13 PROBLEMS FACED BY INDUSTRIAL DESIGNER

The industrial designer is faced with three basic types of design problems:

1. *Minor tooling with minor functional contributions.* This is a "face lift" type of design problem. It is a low-cost approach to a "new look" and a difficult job not relished by designers.
2. *Major tooling with minor functional contributions.* Here, the exterior form takes on a new appearance, although the function of the product basically remains the same.
3. *Major tooling with major functional contributions.* The combination of washer dryer, colour television and Philco's Ionitron air conditioner is example of this type of design problem.

2.14 PROCEDURE ADOPTED BY INDUSTRIAL DESIGNERS

Knowing the type of design problem being considered, the designer can now proceed. Quite briefly, the various stages of design are:

1. Rough sketches and colour renderings
2. Detail drawings (full size)
3. Three-dimensional models in clay, plaster, wood, metal or plastic (all actual materials to be finally specified). These models are evaluated, improved and revised. New models are made and then presented to management for evaluation and approval.

Through all these design stages, the design group work very closely with the engineering staff. Several versions of the final product will be carried along in the early stages, but these will be narrowed down as the programme progresses. In many cases, two and possibly three widely diverse designs may be presented for management's approval. Management should not be asked whether or not it personally prefers the red or the maroon nameplate, the round or the elongated handle; it is, after all, the customer who is to be pleased. Management should have confidence in the design specialists it has employed to make such decisions. Designers should be satisfying not the management but the market.

Good designers are in constant touch with all aspects of art and industry, through publications, visits, technical meetings, seminars, panel discussions and the like. In this way, they keep abreast of new techniques, materials, finishes, and processes as they appear in the market. They watch closely the trends in the allied fields of architecture, fine arts, and craft. And speaking of trends, they are responsible for establishing many by themselves. Every new trend, after all, had to be started by someone who was not satisfied with the established way. The industrial designers probably the most dissatisfied person in industry today, because he does not consider the existing product is ultimate in quality on designs. We should be thankful that this is so, for as soon as we say, "This is the ultimate", we have stopped progressing. Once a new product actually appears, no matter how well it may impress others, it is not unusual to find its designer lacking in enthusiasm, simply because he has thought of half a dozen new and better ways to make it. Dissatisfaction is probably the only thing that brings changes in the design business.

2.15 TYPES OF MODELS DESIGNED BY INDUSTRIAL DESIGNERS

The types of models usually met with in the development of the product or a line of products are: Clay studies, mock-ups, scale models, and prototypes. These are now briefly described.

(i) **Clay studies.** These are made full size or to a smaller scale by the designer himself, not his understudy. These are valuable in the study of form relationships, e.g. Is the base too small for the superstructure of subtitles, of curvature and camber, of size, of radii and fillets, and so on? Though primarily intended for form analysis, these can be of great help later in discussions with tool and die engineers in the final stages of the project.

(ii) **Mock-ups.** This is a proven and old technique in model-making. It involves making a false model to simulate the real product or prototypes. It is made in wood or plaster instead of, say, cast iron or plastics. The mock-up has to be painted in suitable metallic or other paint to create an impression of the actual future product. There is a trend nowadays of designing for ease of operation, i.e., ergonomic design. The person who is to use the product is looked upon as an object needing space, user of physical effort, sensor or observer and finally, controller of the product. The latest trends in mock-ups simulate human mannequins on the CAD terminal and determine "Space requirement envelope" of the dummy, check up how man and machine fit, and carry out a stress analysis on the dummy, should an accident occur. These methods help build better and user friendly designs through interactive computer graphics and animation. The latest trend in "mock-up" is to use CAD instead of plaster of paris or wood mock-ups (see Chapter 13).

(iii) **Scale models.** These are favoured when a material, which can take a very good finish is available, this is not possible in clay modelling. Plaster is the commonest material for scale models.

(iv) **Prototypes.** It is a full-size model of the real product, but is seldom made by the designer. Before going into large-scale production of any major product, an operating or working model has to be built, exact in every minute detail, inside and outside. Prototypes are costly in terms of labour but are essential before going for mass production. Nowadays, computer simulation is widely used for testing a final design. A prototype is still the best technique to improve the level of confidence of the designer for new products.

Rapid Prototyping. Since the middle of the last decade, a silent revolution has been taking place in the field of manufacturing. As a result, a host of new manufacturing techniques has been developed using which it is possible to produce a solid object with the required shape, size, and accuracy directly from its computer model. Though at present such techniques of direct shape-generation are being applied primarily for rapid prototype development, it is firmly believed by many that the age-old concepts and methods will gradually be replaced by these techniques in the actual manufacture of shaped articles and components as also spare part production. Most of the generative manufacturing machines, commonly known as rapid prototyping machines, are still in the developing stage. A few such as stereolithography, selective laser sintering, solid ground curing, fused deposition modelling, and laminated object manufacturing are now commercially available and are being used by many industries for rapid prototyping.

2.16 WHAT THE DESIGNER CONTRIBUTES

The industrial designer helps increase sales by increasing the product's appeal to the consumer, Designers like Lee Iacocca have brought the Chrysler Corporation out of the woods through pure eye appeal, and the Ford Motor Company has declared that it will allow the designer to retool completely every year to the tune of some 200 million dollars. Every major manufacturer employs the services of the industrial designer. He has become a vital part of the team.

As the industrial designer is constantly dissatisfied with the "approved solution", he constantly motivates every one in the organisation to explore another approach to find a better way. Who profits by this? Everyone: the consumer, the company, and the entire workforce.

2.17 ROLE OF AESTHETICS IN PRODUCT DESIGN

Considering the importance of *aesthetics,* which is sometimes used interchangeably with industrial design, this section is devoted to further analytical treatment of aesthetics.

2.17.1 Analysis of Product Aesthetics

The appearance of a product is the *total visual effect* produced by structure, form, material, dimension and surface finish (including colour). Form refers to the profile of the product. In composite products, structure implies combined effect produced by positioning of adjacent forms in deriving the final product. Appearance can only be judged subjectively and there is no yardstick for expressing it objectively.

Referring to Figure 2.4, from the stand point of product design, the visual appeal of objects like jewellery is very important. On the other hand, items such as screws, nails, and ferrules have sheer functional value and negligible aesthetic value. A clear-cut definition of beauty is very difficult. Some individuals admire strict geometric forms. Others prefer bright and gaudy colours. While it is very difficult to define beauty, it is possible to assign the cause of ugliness in a product. For example, a discordant, shoddy, incomplete product can be immediately labelled as 'ugly'. As far as the parameters which decide whether a product is beautiful or ugly, it is possible to list them. Unity and order are most essential for a product to be classed as aesthetic (Figure 2.5).

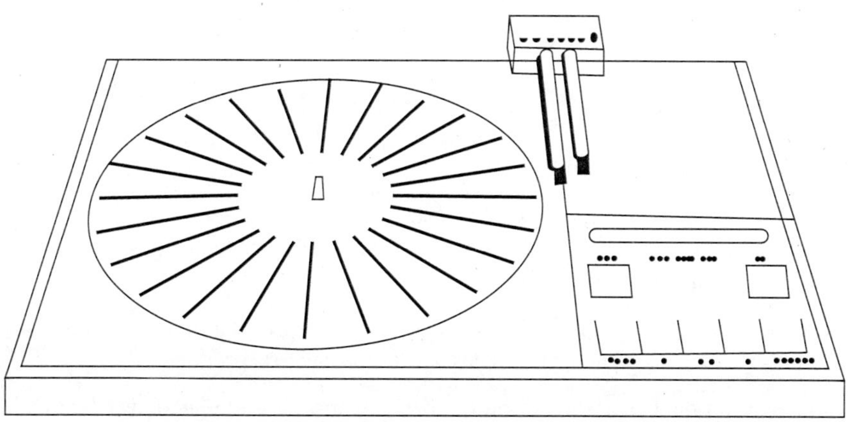

FIGURE 2.5 Aesthetic product characterized by unity and order.

(i) **Unity.** A product must appear as a finished, complete unit, and its separate elements and details harmonized in a logical way. There must be no elements that appear as if they are superfluous and cause surprise. It will also 'offend' the eye if the product has some part missing.

(ii) **Order.** Order refers to repetition of patterns with a suitable break of monotony.

2.17.2 Basic Form Elements

The majority of industrial products are composed of a number of elements of simple geometrical form.

Every well-designed product is characterized by a number of form elements, which together make up the final outer form. These form elements help give the product its final appearance.

The form elements encountered most frequently are the cube, the cylinder, the sphere, the pyramid, the cone and the ellipsoid or parts of these (see Figure 2.6). The box and the cylinder are the most frequently used shapes. The majority of products consist of lines and planes at right angles to each other. Several reasons for the orthogonal shape of objects may be stated.

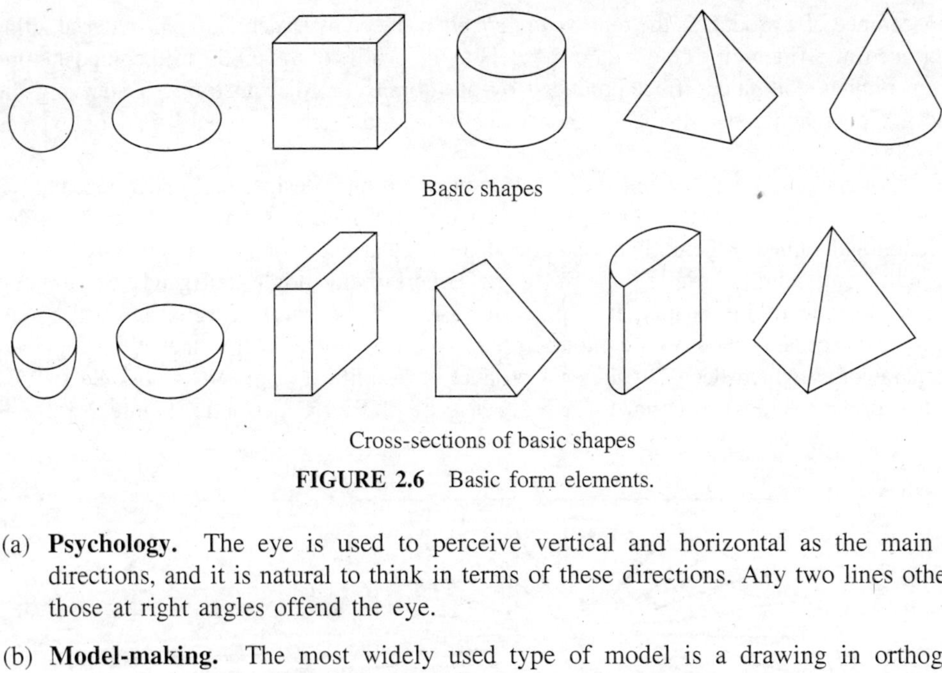

FIGURE 2.6 Basic form elements.

(a) **Psychology.** The eye is used to perceive vertical and horizontal as the main visual directions, and it is natural to think in terms of these directions. Any two lines other than those at right angles offend the eye.

(b) **Model-making.** The most widely used type of model is a drawing in orthographic projections. In this system of projection, the easiest objects to sketch are those which consist of planes parallel to the projection planes.

(c) **Ease of production.** From the point of view of ease of production for casting, forging, machining, etc., faces at right angles are the easiest to produce.

If a number of products are studied on the basis of the form elements, we see that they consist of the basic shapes. Figure 2.7 shows this for a number of small components.

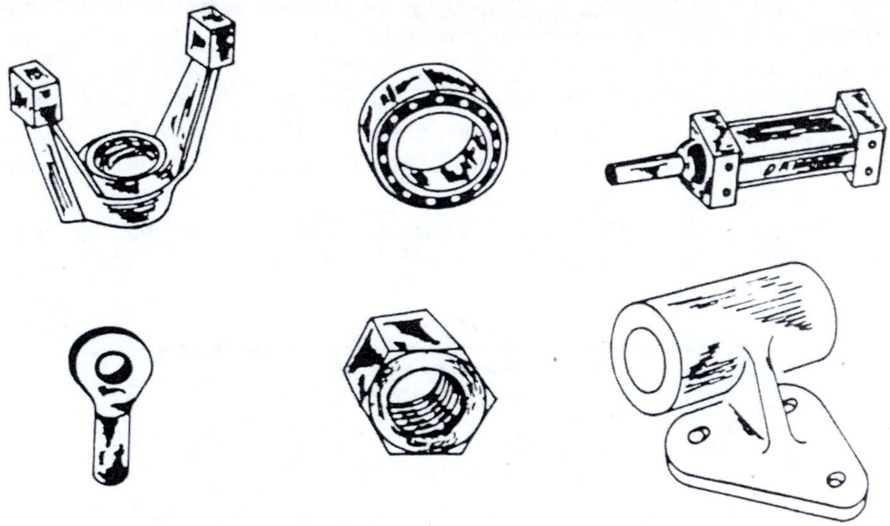

FIGURE 2.7 Incorporation of basic shapes in products.

It may be pointed out that it is not enough to simply emphasize the importance of the idea of basic form elements considered in isolation. The designer must realize that the correct integration and merging of the form elements are essential to the appearance of the composite product. In the following section, we discuss as to what happens when several form elements are put together, and what can be done to achieve a harmonious result.

2.17.3 Integrating Basic Form Elements

(i) **Balance.** Let us examine two isolated form elements and attempt at combining them. If the form elements are moved towards each other, it is noticed that, at a certain distance, they seem to belong together to form a group (see Figure 2.8).

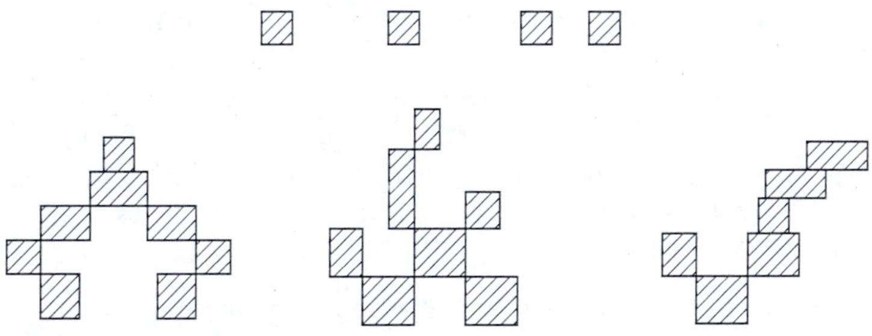

FIGURE 2.8 Symmetry, balance and group effect in aesthetics.

The idea of group formation is fundamental to our visual perception. If we study a number of elements in a group, we see that they interact with each other apart from just appearing to be together. It will be felt that the elements are visually in balance.

A visual balance may be achieved by symmetry, or it may be asymmetrical. In the latter case, the component elements have to be arranged in relation to each other in such a way that unity seems to exist.

If a group of form elements is not in balance, they may offend the eye. A designer must guard against cases where the total form is very nearly but not exactly symmetrical. A good guideline is that the form must be either symmetrical or sufficiently asymmetrical deliberately and not simply lopsided.

Figures 2.9 and 2.10 provide examples of visual balance on the front of two meters. Figure 2.11 shows a vacuum pump in visual imbalance. Figure 2.12 illustrates visually balanced vertical drill.

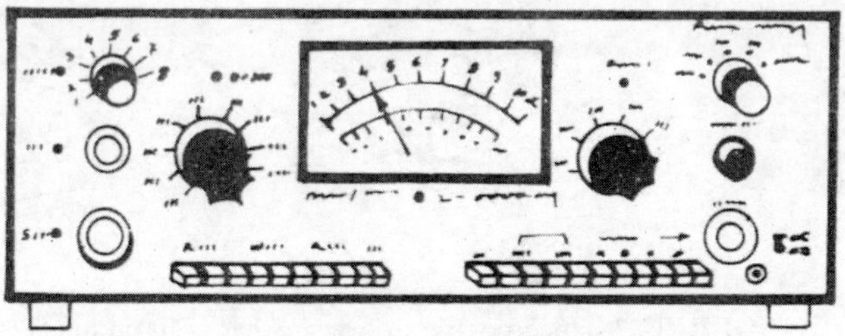

FIGURE 2.9 Visual appeal through symmetry.

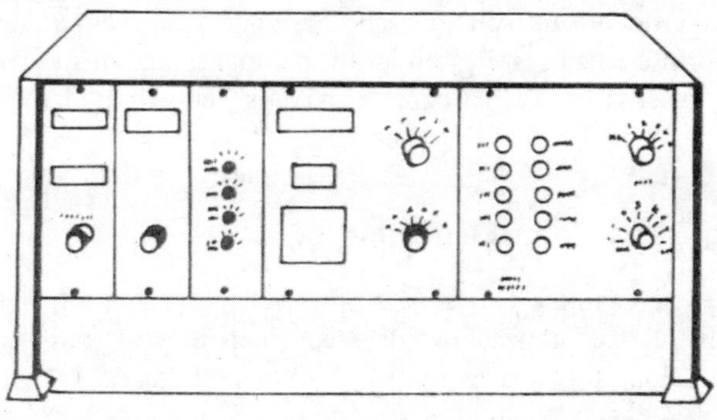

FIGURE 2.10 Visual appeal through deliberate imbalance.

(ii) **Elegance and rhythm.** Rhythm based on varying the direction of distinct angle of the elements can also be a powerful tool in providing a dynamic effect on the product. In the cars shown in Figure 2.13, the shape of windows and doors gives rise to the system of lines which they form. The arrangement, shape and angle of the lines together form a pleasing and aesthetic rhythm which varies for different cars.

(iii) **Proportion.** One of the most important parameters that conveys the overall impression is the proportion of the object. From the times of Euclid, man has always been interested in discovering the connection between proportion and beauty. There are examples of ideal measurements for physically attractive human body *dimensions.* The Golden Section, which is a mathematically determined ratio between two lines A and B, is defined by.

$$\frac{A}{B} = \frac{B}{A - B}$$

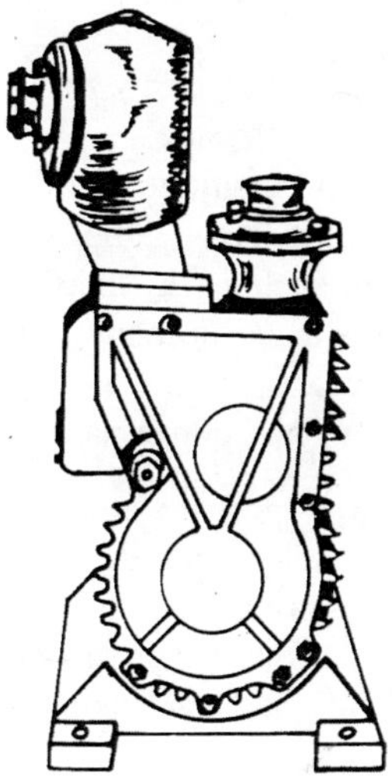

FIGURE 2.11 Compressor with visual appeal through deliberate imbalance.

FIGURE 2.12 Vertical drill with visual appeal through balance.

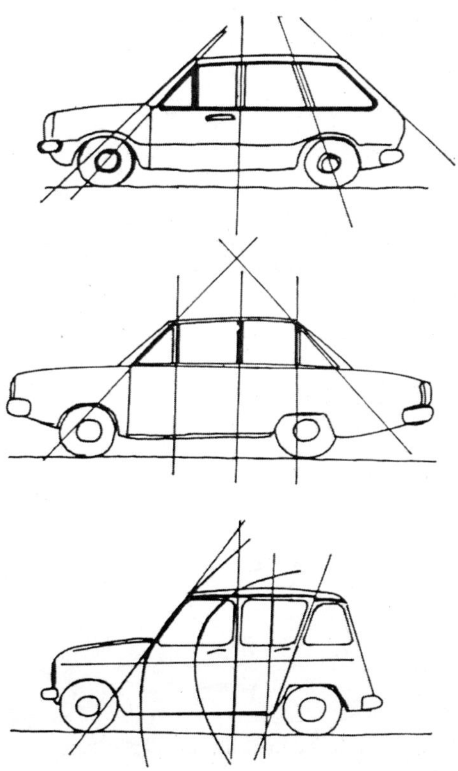

FIGURE 2.13 Automobile body designs illustrating rhythm and lack of rhythm.

This gives:

$$\frac{A}{B} = \frac{1}{2}(1+\sqrt{5}) = 1.618$$

A rectangle with this ratio between its sides is characterized by being divisible into a square and another rectangle with the same ratio between its sides.

Ratios, such as 2:3, 3:5, and 6:8, are close approximations to the Golden Section. These proportions are applied in a many areas. For instance, textbooks on photography advice placing the most important part of the picture in such a way that it divides the sides in the ratio 2:3 or 3:5. These proportions may be recognized in many products. Architects frequently utilize the Golden Section in building design.

Using modules to divide an area into sections, e.g., on control panels, is a convenient way of fitting elements of different sizes as a whole, aesthetically.

(iv) **Inclined planes and lines.** Occasionally, when form elements are put together, totally unexpected visual effects will arise. The visual impression obtained when looking at a unit is not just the sum of the impressions from the elements. Synergistic effect is very common in combining form elements. Visual effect produced by lines and planes at a certain angle produce an aesthetically desirable effect.

The qualities of unity and order depend on the run of the lines and planes. One therefore usually tries to give the prominent lines in the product the same character, e.g. straight lines, curves and lines at a certain angle (see Figure 2.14). Continuity in the run of the individual lines is also significant.

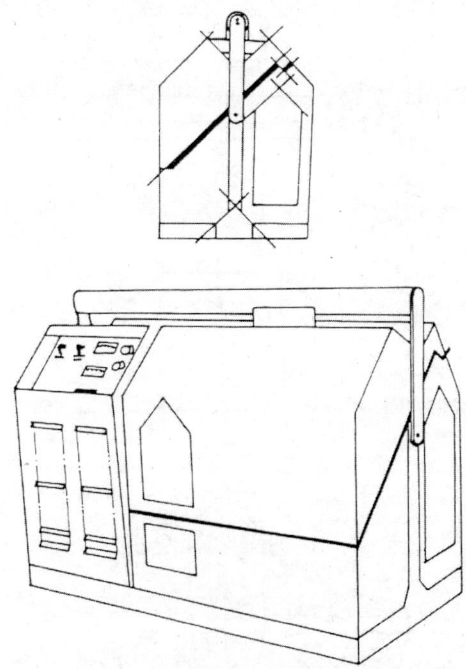

FIGURE 2.14 Use of inclined lines and planes for aesthetic appeal.

(v) **Joints.** Joints between form elements can give rise to both production and visual problems. If two planes or edges meet tightly with an uncovered dividing line, it will often demand un-reasonable accuracy and parallelism. From a visual point of view, a designer adopts two strategies for joints.

(a) The elements are so designed that the joint on the whole is unnoticed.

(b) The joint is emphasized and deliberately used as part of the form characteristic of the product.

2.17.4 Product Message

Every product is like a live object and conveys a message to the onlooker.

(i) **Lightness.** One quality that can be emphasized through the form is lightness. Figure 2.15 shows two situations where an object seems to have been made lighter.

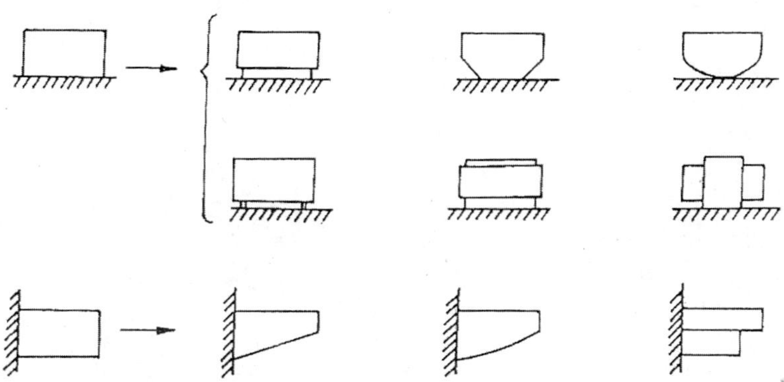

FIGURE 2.15 Strategies in form design to convey message of light weight.

(ii) **Stability and weight.** The means that can be used to express stability and weight through the form aim at placing the centre of gravity in the lowest feasible position. Heavy curves are useful to convey such an effect.

Slopping lines. A single slopping line expresses instability, white two lines leaning towards each other convey a message of high degree of stability, as shown in Figure 2.16(a). Figure 2.16(b) demonstrates how bodies with slightly concave sides appear heavier as compared to bodies with convex sides. Figure 2.16(a) gives examples of various ways in which these two effects can be employed to stress the stability of a box-shaped body. In some of the examples, the form is divided into two form elements which give greater freedom in choosing proportion.

Products which are heavy and solid can be shaped such that this message is conveyed in their form. Figure 2.16(b) shows some machines that convey stability and strength.

(iii) **Speed.** A message of speed can be conveyed by a product design made up of slopping lines that meet at a point; this has associations with an arrow. It is therefore possible to convey the message of movement by using slopping lines at a relatively slight angle to the direction of movement (see Figure 2.17). The movement may be further emphasized by pointing lines in the direction of movement, as we know from 'speed stripes' which are painted on some cars and railway carriages, etc.

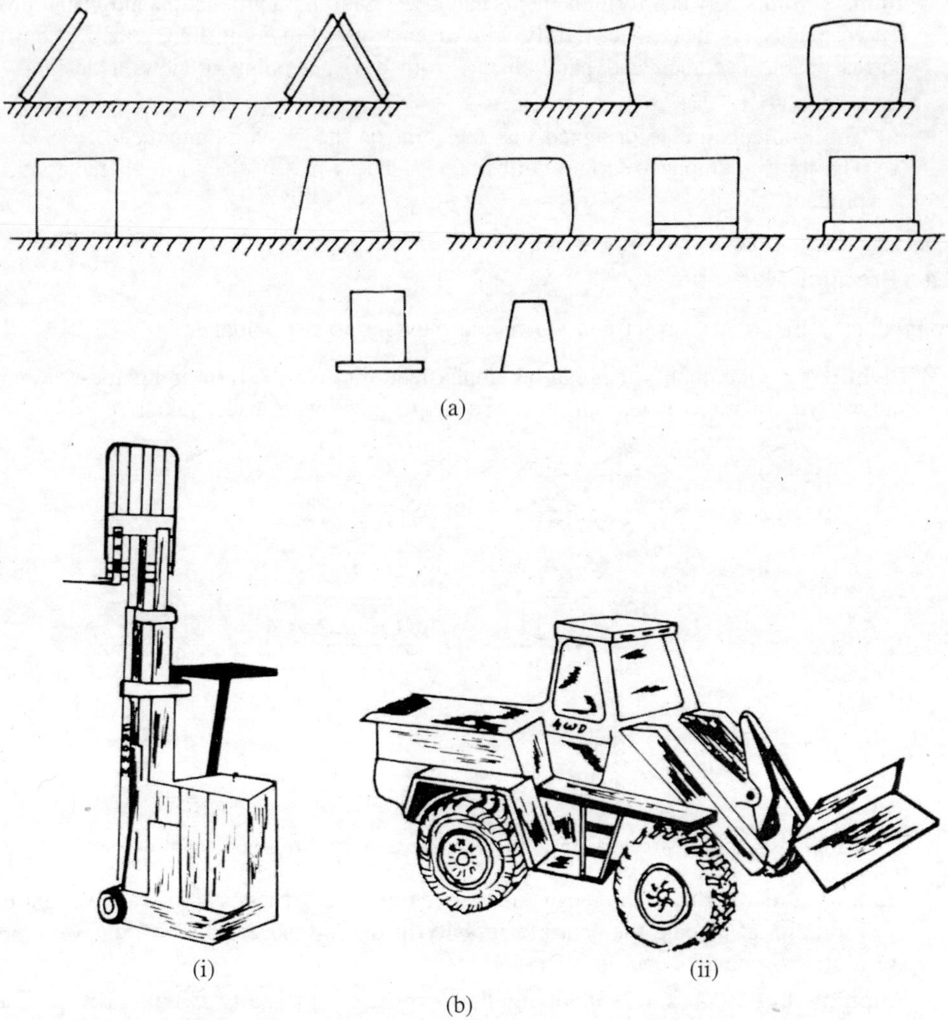

FIGURE 2.16 Strategies to convey the message of stability in products.

2.18 FUNCTIONAL DESIGN PRACTICE

Apart from aesthetics which play a key role in enhancing the appearance of consumer products, functional design is very important in designing engineering products. Certain strategies used by product designers for engineering products are now discussed.

2.18.1 Biasing

Biasing comprises prestressing members of machine parts at no load in such a way that when actual external loads are imposed during working, the resultant stress in the member becomes zero. The spokes of a bicycle wheel are put in tension and the air pressure introduces hoop tension in the

FIGURE 2.17 Products conveying message of speed.

walls of tube and tyre. Under actual loading, which is compressive in nature, the resultant stresses in the spokes and tube walls tend to zero or very small in magnitude.

2.18.2 Cascading or Stage Formation

Use of multiple blades in fans, multiple stages in pumps and compressors are examples, where use of multiple elements results in greater output from the machine.

2.18.3 Regeneration

Regeneration (Figure 2.16) is based on the principle, "Never waste anything of value". Examples of effective regeneration are: use of exhaust gases for preheating of incoming fuel, application of waste heat in heat exchangers for preheating incoming fluid, etc. An interesting example of effective utilization of heat energy is in the tunnel kiln for the manufacture of ceramic parts. As can be seen from Figure 2.18, the cold air blown in form the exit end of the trolley containing fired ceramic ware, is preheated and passes through the mid-section of the tunnel where it acquires a high temperature owing to heat of oil firing. The hot air from mid-section leaves at the point where the trolley containing 'green' ceramic ware enters the kiln. This facilitates drying of ceramic ware at entrance. The strategy of opposing direction of air and trolley results in a very favourable temperature profile for the production of ceramic products.

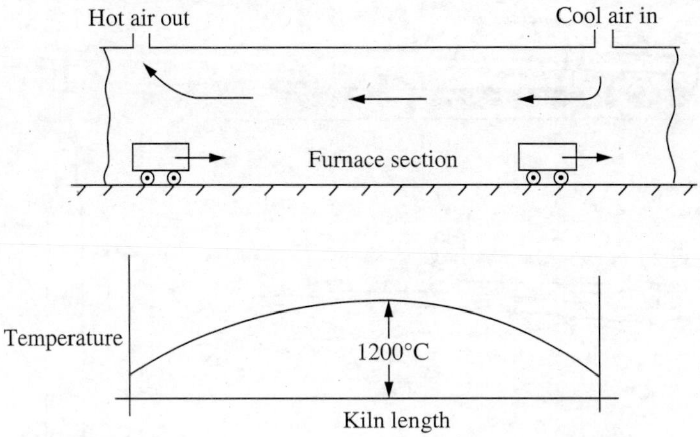

FIGURE 2.18 Principle of regeneration applied in kiln design.

2.18.4 Avoiding Redundancy

Designers employ the Kinematic design principle of avoiding redundancy. This is particularly useful in designing structures and mechanisms. In a structure, the number of members should be exactly the same as the number of members essential for fulfilling the functional requirement. An example is that of a stool. A three-legged stool is very stable because three points of support are provided, which completely define a unique plane surface. Such a stool is stable even on a rough plane. A four-legged stool can be stable only on a perfectly flat surface. Wireform garden chairs should attempt to provide three points of contact. However, furniture designers insist upon four legs for chairs and tables for reasons of aesthetics and load bearing considerations. Mechanisms and machines should contain the minimum number of parts or links to be accurate and precise. Redundant members reduce the reliability and functional efficiency apart from being clumsy in appearance.

2.18.5 Compatibility and Matching Considerations in Product Design

Many design systems include a power developing device—a motor, an engine or a human being. At the load end, are seen a power absorbing device, a pump, a propeller, etc. It is essential to determine an *operating point* for a design system for which both the power developing device and the power absorbing device will work. If a unique point is not obtained, the system will fail to function and is deemed to be incompatible. A designer's role is to determine the correct operating point. For this purpose, characteristic curves of power developing and power absorbing devices should be known or modelled.

Example.

(a) *Bicycle rider and bicycle.* The graphs in Figure 2.19 show the force that can be comfortably produced by the rider at the rear wheel. At low speed, a high torque/force at the rear wheel can be produced. This value of torque reduces as the speed increases. Graph 2 shows the road resistance vs. speed which is mainly a function of road material, road condition, and tyre material. On gradient, the road resistance is greater. Intersection of graphs 1 and 2 explains how a rider will have to apply greater torque/force to go up a gradient. Points *A* and *B* are the operating points.

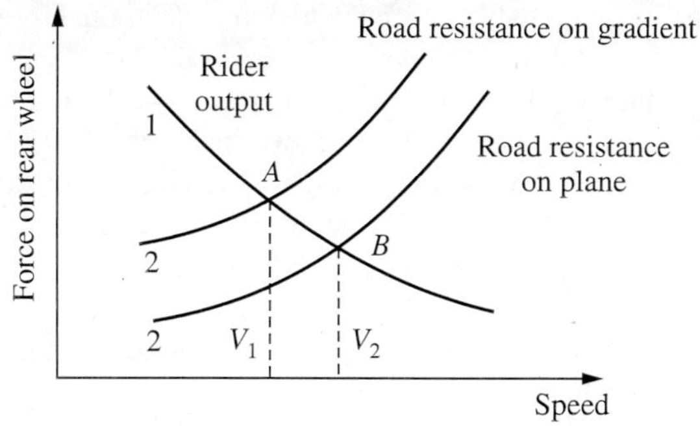

FIGURE 2.19 Load and effort graphs as a function of speed for bicycle rider.

(b) In a ship driven by gas turbines, efficient speeds of the propeller may be one-hundredth of the turbine. Propellers displace a large mass of sea water at a low speed. Turbines are driven by high velocity gases of products of combustion of fuel. Thus, between turbine shaft and propeller shaft, a suitable gearing will have to be provided to reduce the speed of the propeller. The gearing will help achieve compatibility between the turbine and the propeller.

These two examples are due to French [2].

REVIEW QUESTIONS

1. List the various product design strategies. Sec.2.2, P 30, 31
2. How is product design related with the customer and the market in general. Sec. 2.4.1
3. Explain various relationships between design, production and marketing through a flow chart. Figure 2.1, P 33
4. Explain the following terms: (i) Functional design, (ii) Production design, (iii) Design for transportation, (iv) Maintainability based design, (v) Ergonomic design.

   [**Ans: Functional design**

   Design of a product for performing its function effectively depends upon application of appropriate branches of engineering. For examples, a good design of a centrifugal pump—the impeller, the spiral casing and the suction and delivery ends depends heavily upon a sound knowledge of fluid mechanics. Functional design of pump is in effect a hydraulic design. Likewise, an engine cylinder and piston are designed based on the laws of thermal engineering—gas dynamics, combustion, heat transfer, etc.

   Machine elements such as gears, screws, levers, bearings, etc. are designed from the standpoint of strength wear, fatigue, etc. A sound stress and strength analysis, preferably with modern techniques of 'Finite Element Method', should help arriving at the pertinent dimensions.

   Production design or design for manufacturability

   A product design should be such that it should be easily producible by the production process. Design for production or manufacturability is a topic of importance in product design.

Every part of a product which is designed for functional requirement has also to be designed for ease of production. For example, a part to be produced by casting should be such that during solidification of the molten metal in the mould no such stresses should be induced as to cause cracks or distortion of the part. A pulley with curved arms is preferred to a pulley with straight arms. This is because during solidification of the rim, which is of heavier section and occurs in the end, stresses are induced in the arms. Curved arms take up the stresses and straighten up a little. They do not undergo tearing during solidification.

Production development and design should consider whether geometrically a design has a good compatibility with material and production process for making a producible design. A typical example given earlier is that of a pulley in which curved arms are provided so that during production there are no casting problems and high tensile stresses being set up in the arms during casting solidification are prevented. Therefore, it is always suggested to take care of production process involved in manufacturing the required product in designing the product.

Designing for transportation

Special features should be provided in design for ease of transportation. A design which is of everyday observation is the welded ring fitted on top of a cooking gas cylinder to enable its being lifted and moved from one place to other. Modular designs and compact design help simplifying transportation (Figure 2.20).

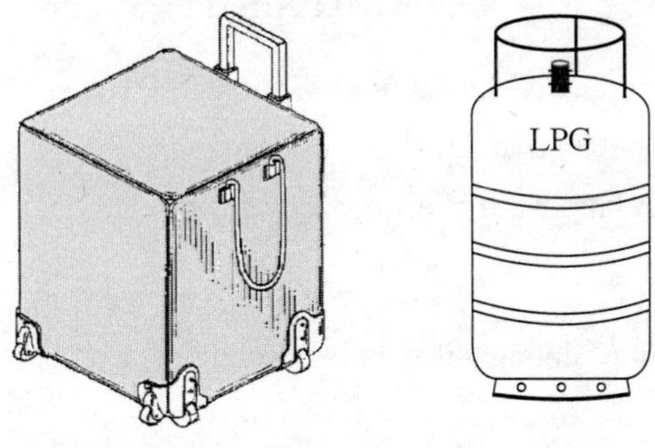

FIGURE 2.20 Design for transportation.

Design for maintenance or maintainability-based design

A product should be so designed that, it should be assembled and disassembled with ease. There should be increased use of fasteners like quick action hand nuts, levers, etc. The Japanese make minimum use of full turn screw and nut assembly. Instead, quick action clamps are provided on Japanese designs. Easy access to cleaning and maintenance should start right at the preliminary design stage. Diagnostic key points should be provided on machines where a light should indicate occurrence of fault at any critical spot. Machines with intricate electronic circuitry like modem machine tools have such diagnostic points. Large castings are made with a horizontal parting line or horizontal split casting. This enables cleaning up the machine after removing the upper half of the split casing without disturbing the horizontal gear shaft from it bearings (Figure 2.21).

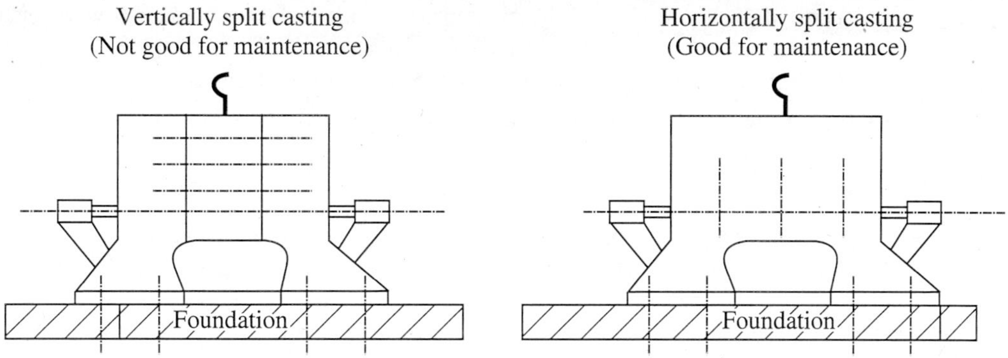

FIGURE 2.21 Design for maintainability (gearbox assembly).

Ergonomic design or product design for human use

Ergonomic designs: Until recently, products were designed with technical feasibility and cost as main criteria. The difficulty in operation and control of cars, aircrafts and other devices of previous generations was at the root of many accidents. Limited visibility, difficult to read for unsafe operation and at times loss of life.

Designing products and machines to adapt them to human characteristics is the domain of *ergonomics*. Ergonomics has experiences impressive growth since World War II.]

5. Explain the term 'industrial standardization'. What is Renard series and how does it help a designer in fixing the sizes, capacities, horsepower, etc. of products? Sec. 2.6; P 38, 39, 40

6. What is meant by 'simplification' in design? Explain with an example. Sec. 2.8; P 40, 41, 42

7. What are the points which favour simplification? What are advantages of variety in products owing to line extension? P 41

8. Design combines 'art' with 'technology'. Explain.

9. Explain the basic form elements: balance, elegance and rhythm, proportion and golden section. Use of inclined planes and lines. Sec. 2.17.2

10. How the concept of 'single point perspective' is exploited in automobile body design? Figure. 2.13

11. What is a product message? How are lightness, speed, stability conveyed in products? Illustrate through examples. Sec. 2.17.4; P 53–54

12. Explain the following terms:

(i) Adaptive design, (ii) Variant design, (iii) Creative design, (iv) Configuration design and (v) Modular design.

[**Ans: Type of design work**

In terms of level of intellectual effort and creativity, there are mainly following three types of design work:

1. **Adaptive design.** This design requires only minor modification usually in size alone. The level of creativity needed is negligible because only adaptation of existing design is essential. Some authors call it adaptive design even if the changes are more but original design concept is same.

2. **Variant design.** This is a design approach followed by companies who wish to serve product variety to satisfy varying customer tastes. For examples, Hero Honda: CD 100, CD Deluxe, Passion and Splendor are variant designs.
3. **Creative design.** The most demanding design effort and creativity is needed when a totally new product is to be designed.

Some other nomenclatures in design are as below:

Configuration design. Configuration design helps in synthesis, analysis and choice of best combination of parts. In the detailed design phase (Section 1.8.3) Step 5 is to verify that the different components and subassemblies fit very well to form the final product. Configuration design is represented in the form of special assembly drawings to 'prove' the success (or failure) of the assembly. Configuration design differs from detail design in the sense that layout drawing are made in configuration drawings. They cannot be used for the preparation of process planning. Detailed drawings in orthographic projections are essential for fixing operations essential to produce final product. Concept of obtaining various configuration for computers is often cited as example of configuration design.

Modular design. The use of 'modules' or building blocks for assembling and producing a variety of products is termed *modular design*. It will be recalled how furniture companies enable the production of a wide range of racks, etc. as end products by assembly of different modules. The advantage of modular design over integral design is lower inventory, better flexibility, lower cost, etc.]

13. Explain design organization. Explain organization chart for design department.

[**Ans: Organization of design group**

The role of design engineer in a design department can be seen from the chart. In a small department, all the personnel may be busy in all aspects of design work. In a larger department, senior personnel will spend more time in management tasks. Likewise, staff could be specialized in specific design areas. The term 'design engineer' is reserved for persons capable of working independently and creatively. Less qualified staff may be designated as assistants, draftsman, technicians, etc. For small projects, the entire task of design, Production and sales may be performed by the design engineer. For larger projects, a designer plays the role of team member. The relationship between design department with customer on one side and marketing, production, finance within the organization is important for the success of a product.

Organization of staff in design engineering department (Figure 2.22).]

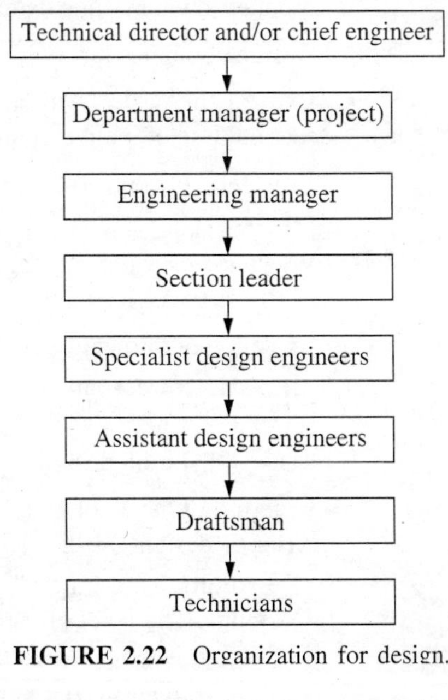

FIGURE 2.22 Organization for design.

14. Explain how a design is communicated by the designer to head of the design group?

[**Ans: Communicating the design**

1. *Nature of communication.* Once the design is complete and the designer has come up with some novel concepts and a cost estimate which promises a good profit, it becomes essential that colleagues, subordinates and superiors are made aware of the success story.
2. *Technical report.* The quality of a technical report enables the reader to perceive about the quality of design work done. Written report is more useful than a spoken word. Technical persons are known to be better writers than orators. Referring to the communication model (Figure 2.23) the sources is the 'mind' of the writer. The process of encoding consists of translating the idea from mind to words on a paper. The channel is the pile of papers. Decoding depends upon the readers' ability to understand the message. Final receiver is the 'mind' of the readers. It is essential to know the audience before a written report is submitted.

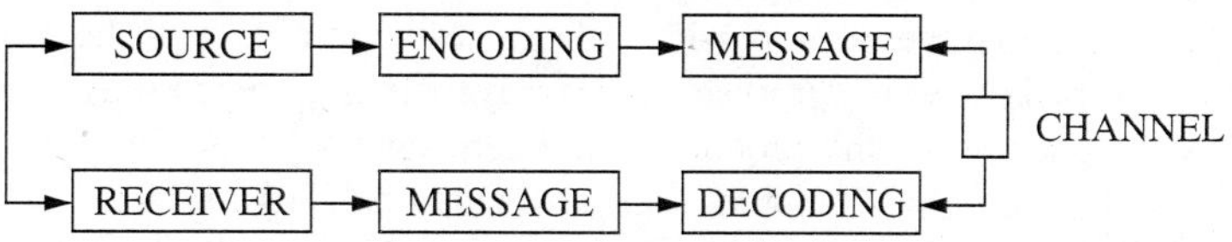

FIGURE 2.23 Transmission of message in design communication.

Memorandum report. A memorandum report is written to a specific group on a specific subject. It contains: data (to, from), subject, introduction (why the study was carried out), discussion (includes data and its analysis), conclusions (including recommendation), memo, reports are short (one to three pages).

3. *Formal technical reports.* The details of a formal technical report are:
   - Covering letter (letter of transmittal)
   - Summary (with conclusions)
   - Introduction
   - Experimental procedure
   - Discussion of results
   - Conclusions
   - References
   - Appendix
   - Tables and figures

   How to write a good report?

   The word, POWER indicating P–Plan the writing, O–outline the report, W–write, E–Edit, R–Rewrite, in writing a good report.
4. *Oral presentations.* Oral communication has several special features: personal impact, impact of visual aids, importance of tone, gesture and emphasis. A quick feedback is characteristic of oral presentations. The logic and sequence of matter presented are more important in oral presentation than in written reports. Noise is a drawback of oral communication.
5. *Visual aids* are important part of any talk of technical nature. Good visual aids increase idea retention by 50%.

For small informal talks up to 10–12 people, handouts of data, charts and outline are useful. For larger group, up to 200, transparencies with an overhead projector (OHP) or computer projectors are useful aids. Computer LCD projector is preferred by large audiences.

Certain other factors concerning visual aids are:

- Limit slides to less than one per minute.
- Each slide should contain one idea.
- Slides with maximum of three curves and 30 words are acceptable.
- The slide sequence should be properly planned with title in the beginning, matter in the intermediate slides and summary in the last slides.
- Avoid leaving on the screen, a slide which is explained and replace with a blank slide. This enables the audience to focus attention upon the talk.

6. *Design presentations through models and perspective drawings.* The sponsor of a project is always presented with a cut-away perspective drawing of the product so that he may get a proper idea of the aesthetic aspect of the product. Industrial designers make use of airbrush (like spray painting) renderings to highlight the colours and shading of the product. In modern context, the computer with colour graphics is a great help in making such presentations (Figure 2.24).

FIGURE 2.24 Design for stability—scale model.

15. Explain the following strategies used by product designers in 'functional design practice':
(i) Biasing, (ii) Cascading, (iii) Regeneration, (iv) Avoidance of redundancy, (v) Compatibility.

Give suitable examples. Sec. 2.18 P 54–P57

REFERENCES

[1] Eilon, S., *Elements of Production, Planning and Control* (Macmillan, London, 1962), 3rd ed. reprinted by Universal Publishing Corporation, Bombay, 1991.

[2] French, M., *Innovation in Design,* McGraw-Hill, New York, 1992.

Chapter 3

Strength Consideration in Product Design

3.1 PRINCIPAL STRESS TRAJECTORIES (FORCE-FLOW LINES)

Machines are made to transmit forces such that effective work can be done. The ability of a particular machine element to carry external load is its strength. The punch shown in Figure 3.1 is a device that directs and focusses forces to a point. Lines of force can be imagined to flow from the hammer to the end of the punch. They pass along the length of the punch and come out at the tip. The concentration of lines of force represents the stress. Thus, the stress is low at the upper end where the area is large. The stress is very large at the tip where the area approaches zero. The stress at any section perpendicular to the lines of force has to be less than the yield strength of the material to avoid failure. Thus,

$$\text{Stress } \sigma = \text{force/area}$$

where,

$$\text{Stress } \sigma < \text{yield strength } S_y$$

FIGURE 3.1 Flow of force-flow lines through a punch.

In pure compression and pure, tension applications, the forces flow smoothly and straight through the part. The force carried by a punch is purely compressive, and the force existing in a fishing rod is purely tensile. Components carrying pure compressive force or pure tensile force are quite efficient in utilizing the strength of the material. If the force flows in curves, there is usually bending applied to the member. Maximum shear stresses exist in planes at 45° to the lines of force. In Strength of Materials terminology, force flow lines are termed *principal stress trajectories.*

Figure 3.2 illustrates the various stresses in different parts of a C-clamp. In zone A, there is pure compression. In zone B, there is bending and axial tension. In zone C, the force flows from the curved beam into the screw. The forces produce compression in zone D, similar to that in zone A.

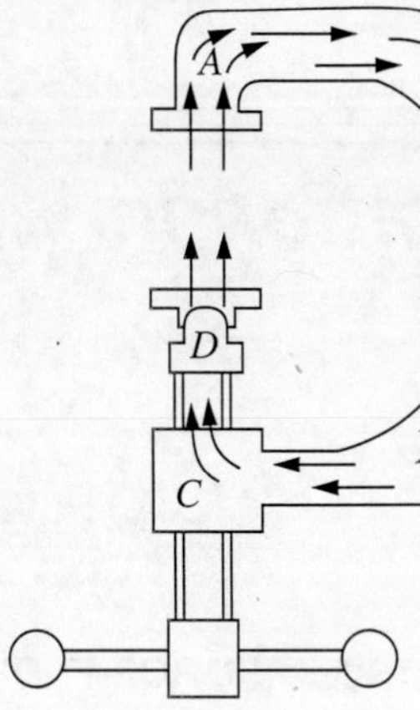

FIGURE 3.2 Force-flow lines through a C clamp.

The C-clamp can fail by compressive yielding in zone A, bending failure in zone B, shear failure of screw threads in zone C, and compressive yielding in zone D. There should be enough strength to prevent each mode of failure. The force-flow concept is very useful in identifying areas of high stress and potential failure.

To support a load with the least amount of material, lines of force should be allowed to flow directly between points of external forces. Direct lines of force do not cause any bending and result in the shortest physical length of a load-carrying member. The two chairs in Figure 3.3 illustrate this point. Figure 3.3(a) depicts the chair design and Figure 3.3(b) illustrates force flow. The chair with direct force-flow is more efficient than the chair with curved force-flow. Force-flow visualization is a good technique for understanding how force is transmitted through components and assemblies. According to Ullman [1], 'Treat forces like a fluid that flows in and out of the interface through a path of least resistance through the component." Label flow lines for major types of stress: tension (*T*), compression (*C*), shear (*S*), and bending (*B*). Bending can be decomposed into tension and compression; and shear must occur between tension and compression on a flow line. The example of a bolted assembly as in Figure 3.4(a) illustrates this concept with clarity. Figures 3.4(b), (c) and (d) illustrate the force flow lines in flange, bolt and nuts, respectively. Figure 3.4(e) shows the overall force flow in the joint.

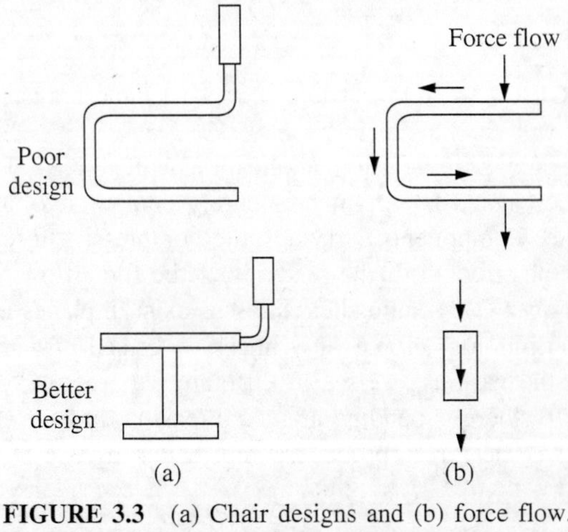

FIGURE 3.3 (a) Chair designs and (b) force flow.

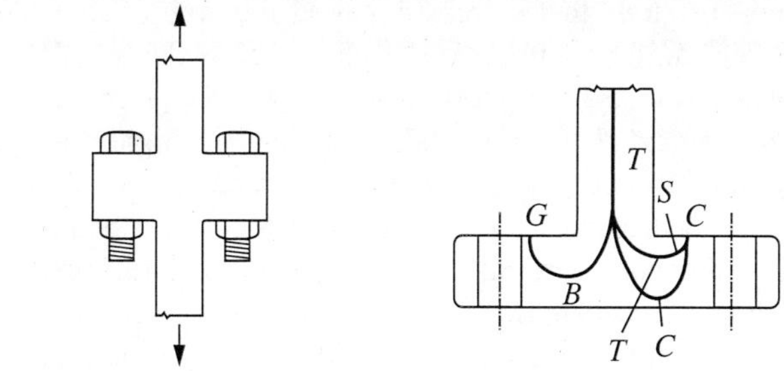

(a) Flanged joint under load (b) Force flow in flange

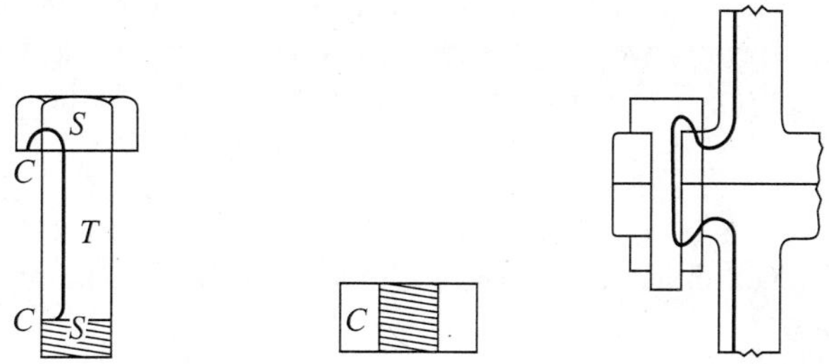

(c) Force flow in bolt (d) Force flow in nut (e) Force flow through left-half portion of flanged joint

FIGURE 3.4 Development of force-flow lines through a flanged joint.

Budynas states that "The fluid flow analogy can be extended to the study of stress concentration effects such as [those] due to holes in a plate". Referring to Figure 3.5(a), the velocity of a fluid through a channel across a circular submerged body indicates the velocity pattern. A thin rectangular plate with a hole, subjected to tension, indicates stress concentration effects similar to the velocity profile where 'velocity' and 'stress' are analogous. Improvement in the situation shown in the figure is possible by making the hole 'elliptical' instead of circular as in Figure 3.5(b). Another, and better alternative, is indicated in Figure 3.5(c) where the plate has two small holes drilled mean the larger hole.

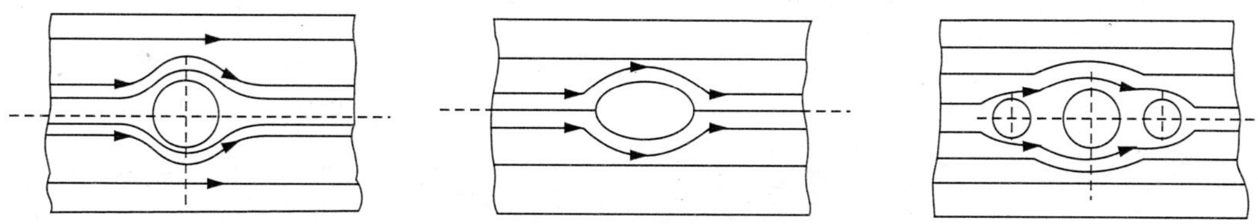

(a) Plate with circular hole (b) Plate with elliptical hole (c) Plate with three holes for streamlining force flow

FIGURE 3.5 Force-flow lines through plates with holes.

3.2 BALANCED DESIGN

In order to prevent failure, the strength of a member has to be greater than the induced stress in the member. However, a member with excessive strength wastes material. Such a member is "overdesigned". The ratio of strength to stress is called the *safety factor.* As far as possible, the safety factor should be kept uniform throughout each machine element for a balanced design.

The component of a machine having the lowest safety factor is the critical element. For the C-clamp in Figure 3.2, the critical element is *B* because it has the highest bending moment. Doubling or tripling the strength at cross-sections *A*, *C* or *D* will not improve the clamp as a whole. A balanced design without excessive overstrength would result if the safety factor for every component in the machine were the same. Balancing strength between sections *C* and *D* results in a simplified rule: the thickness of a nut should be about twice the diameter of the screw.

Figure 3.6 shows two cantilever beams, both of which have the highest bending moments at the fixed ends, which are the critical elements of the beams. If the stresses at the fixed ends are less than the strength of the material, the beams will not fail. Due to their smaller stresses, other elements in the uniform beam have larger safety factors than the critical element. The uniform beam is, therefore, not balanced in stress and strength. The width of the tapered beam decreases correspondingly with the bending moment which decreases linearly from the fixed end to the point of application of the force. The tapered beam, with uniform safety factors, is thus a balanced design. Both the cantilever beams have the same sectional area at the fixed end. They can bear the same maximum external load. Yet, the tapered beam has only half the volume of the uniform beam and results in material saving.

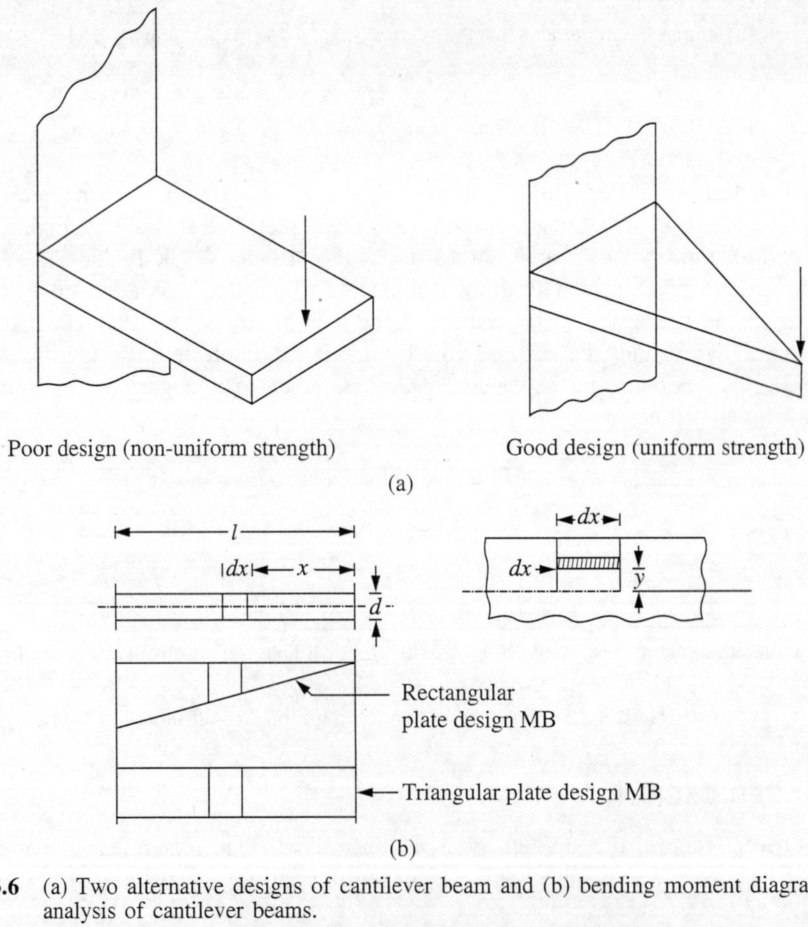

FIGURE 3.6 (a) Two alternative designs of cantilever beam and (b) bending moment diagram and stress analysis of cantilever beams.

The punch shown in Figure 3.1 has a uniform load, but a decreasing sectional area. A balanced design would call for increasing the yield strength of the material towards the tip. This is usually achieved in practice by heat-treating the tip of the punch.

$$\text{Stress } \sigma = F/A$$

$$\text{Safety factor SF} = S_y/\sigma$$

$$S_y = (\text{SF} \cdot \sigma) = (\text{SF})F/A$$

where the external force F and the safety factor SF are held constant. For a balanced design, the yield strength S_y should be made inversely proportional to the sectional area A. This is achieved by suitable heat treatment.

The tensile strength of cast iron is one-fourth of its compressive strength. To compensate for this, cast-iron beams should have extra webbing on the tension side.

3.2.1 Analysis of Stresses during the Bending of a Curved Beam

When a curved beam is subjected to a bending moment as shown in Figure 3.7(a), the outermost fibre undergoes a tensile strain (e_1) and the innermost fibre undergoes a compressive strain (e_2). The equation for strain is:

$$e_1 = \delta/AB = \delta/(R + t)\theta \qquad \text{(Tensile)}$$

$$e_2 = \delta/CD = \delta/R\theta \qquad \text{(Compressive)}$$

It should be noted that

$$e_1 < e_2, \text{ and}$$

$$e_1/e_2 = (R)/(R + t)$$

The corresponding stresses are

$$\sigma_1 = Ee_1 \qquad \text{(Tensile)}$$

$$\delta_2 = Ee_2 \qquad \text{(Compressive)}$$

A brief examination will show that σ_1 is less than σ_2 because $e_1 < e_2$. The stress distribution across the section is indicated in Figure 3.7(a).

Curved beams of uniform symmetrical cross-section such as rectangle and circle show stress concentration at the inner fibres owing to higher values of induced stress. It can be proved that the stress distribution is hyperbolic. A balanced design of curved beam should provide more material at the inner fibres to combat this curvature effect in curved beams represented by the hole, the vice and the press machine frame as shown in Figure 3.7(b).

The geometry of the curved beam (Figure 3.6) demands unequal tensile and compressive stresses in the beam unless extra webbing is used. The stress distribution in the curved beam is hyperbolic, and the stress is higher at the inside radius. A solution could be to shift the neutral axis towards the inside radius by using a T-section or a channel section with extra webs on the inside radius.

Toughened glass is obtained by a special heat treatment of glass. The glass to be toughened is heated as shown in Figure 3.8(a). It undergoes an elongation as illustrated in Figure 3.8(b). During the cooling cycle, Figure 3.8(c) and (d), the upper and the lower layers shrink first, while the central layer cools and shortens in the end. Due to this differential cooling, the central layer pulls the outer fibres and subjects them to compressive stress above and below the neutral axis. This residual compressive stress makes the glass tough and stronger against externally applied loads.

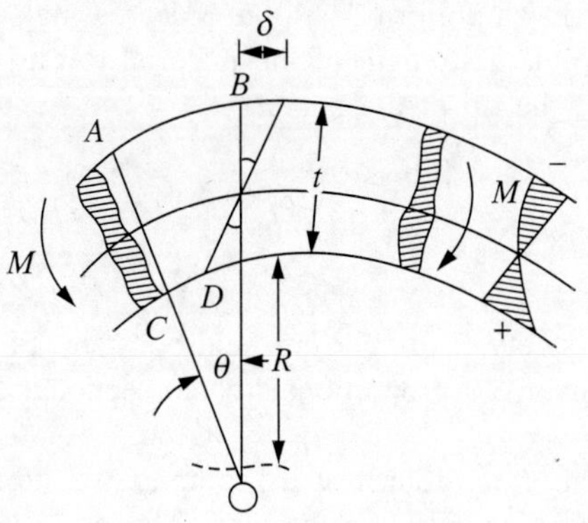

(a)

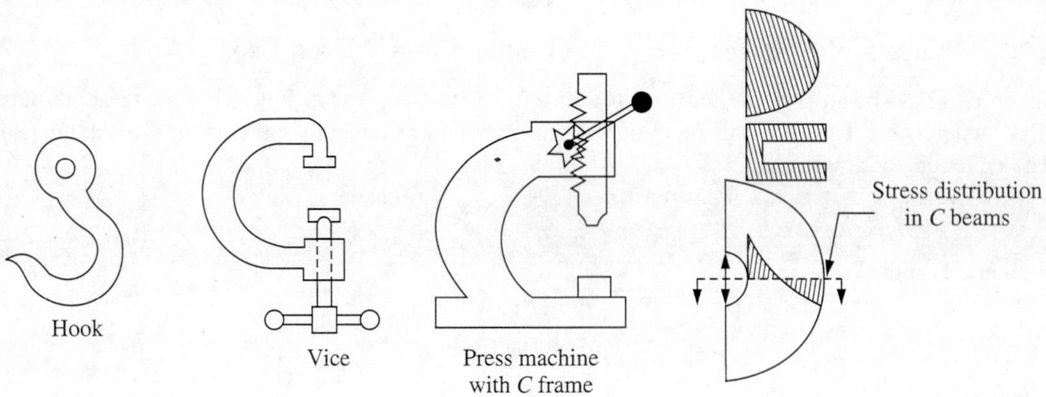

(b)

FIGURE 3.7 (a) Illustration of the theory of curved beams and (b) stress distribution across the cross-section of a curved C beam.

A quenched and toughened glass plate can support four times the bending load than that of the regular glass plate. Figure 3.8(e) shows the reason behind this. Glass is five times stronger in compression than in tension, and practically all failures of glass plates in bending are due to tensile fractures. Quenching produces residual compressive stresses on both top and bottom surfaces of the glass plate. When an external bending load is applied to the glass plate, the residual compressive stress is subtracted from the tensile stress caused by the external load, thus suppressing the fracture.

The gear and pinion have equal forces on their teeth as shown in Figure 3.9, because of their action and reaction relationship. However, the pinion teeth have higher stresses because of their thinner profiles due to undercut provided on them. The pinion teeth are also more vulnerable to fatigue failure, because the pinion has higher rotational speed. The pinion teeth are, therefore, more frequently loaded. If the gear and the pinion are made with the same material and the same accuracy, the pinion will always fail first. Cost reduction can be realized by using slightly less strong material for the gear, such that both the gear and the pinion have the same safety factor. A typical gear set may have a cast-iron gear and a steel pinion. In a worm and worm wheel pair, the worm is made of steel, whereas the worm wheel is made of gunmetal for equal wear for both the elements. In a crown wheel and pinion pair (used in the rear wheel transmission of a car), the pinion is made more wear resistant, so as to achieve a balanced design.

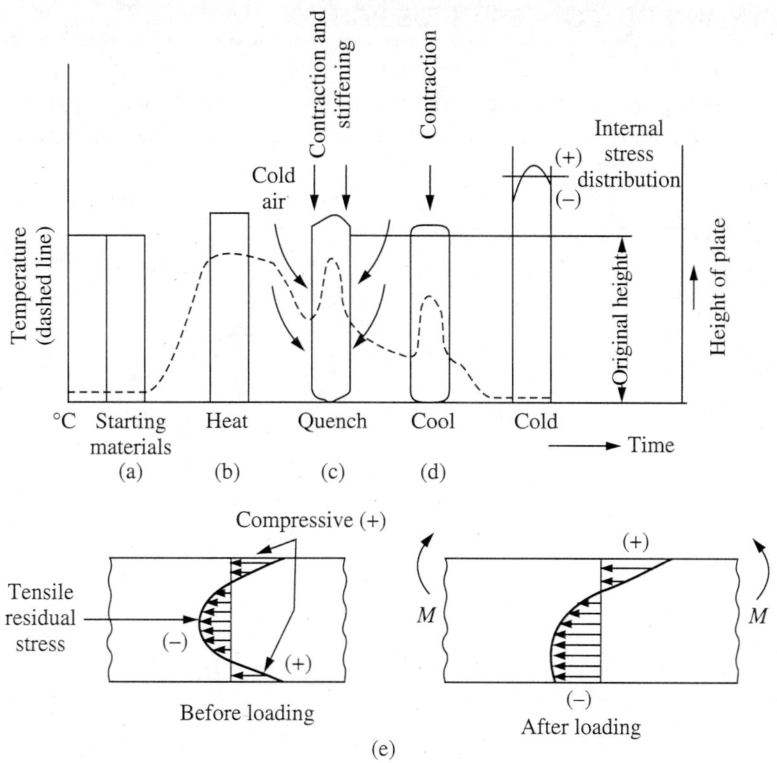

FIGURE 3.8 Heat treatment cycle and development of initial stresses in toughened glass.

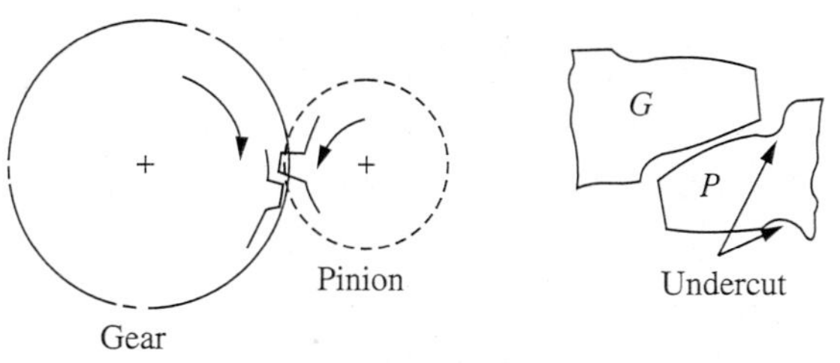

FIGURE 3.9 Balanced design for gear and pinion teeth.

In a gear train, the motor is usually a high-speed low-torque driver. The input torque from the motor is progressively increased through the gear train to the output shaft. Figure 3.10 shows an increase in the face width and the circular pitch of the gears. The diameters of the shafts are also increased to keep the balance of strength.

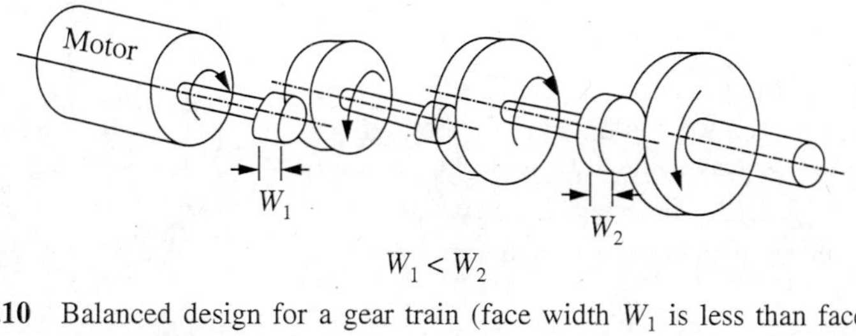

FIGURE 3.10 Balanced design for a gear train (face width W_1 is less than face width W_2).

3.3 CRITERIA AND OBJECTIVES OF DESIGN

A system that cannot perform its design objective is said to have failed. Failure does not imply fracture. A fuse is designed to protect electric circuits from being overloaded. If the fuse does not burn in case of an overload, it is a failure. Thus, an overdesigned fuse not only wastes material, but also loads to failure of its function.

A micrometer is a metrological instrument and is designed to measure accurately. It would be a failure if the deflection in the measuring arm was excessive. There is no fracture or destruction associated with such failures. Structurally, a C-clamp and a micrometer are similar (Figure 3.11). The former is designed for strength and the latter is designed for stiffness. The following subsections discuss four common types of design strategies outlined by Chow [2].

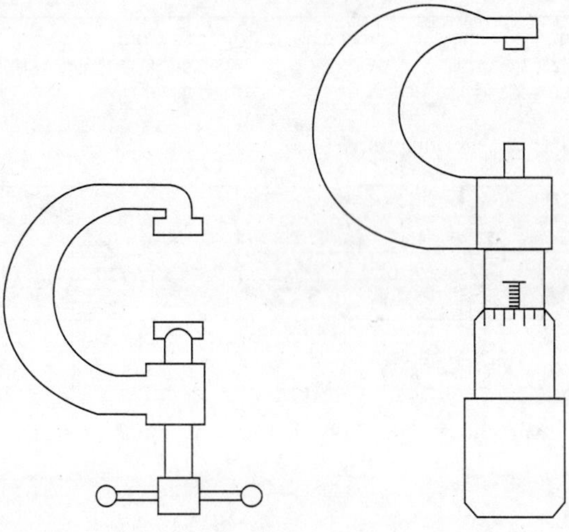

(a) Mechanical vise (b) Micrometer

FIGURE 3.11 Different design objectives for two practical C-shaped designs.

3.3.1 Strength Based Design

Design for strength is the same as design against yielding and fracture. The criterion is that the strength of the material must be larger than the induced stress, σ, any-where in the machine, especially in the critical elements.

$$\text{To prevent yielding, } S_y > \sigma$$

$$\text{To prevent fracture, } S_{ult} > \sigma$$

where S_y is the yield strength and S_{ult} is the ultimate strength. S_{ult} is greater than S_y and can be obtained from tensile test. Figure 3.12 shows S_y and S_{ult} on a stress–strain diagram. Ductile materials usually fail by yielding. Brittle materials usually fail by fracture.

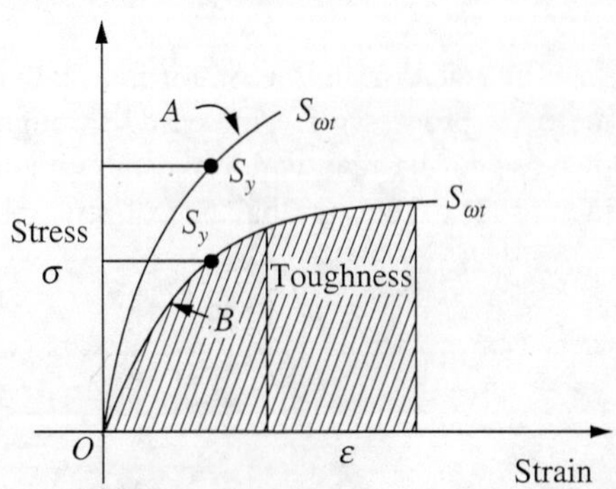

FIGURE 3.12 Stress–strain diagrams for materials *A* and *B*.

3.3.2 Rigidity Based Design

This design criterion is usually applied in machine tool design and instrument design. The stress level involved is very low and there is no danger of failing by fracture. Cast iron is used extensively in machine tools because of a high modulus-to-strength ratio. Rigidity in structures is important in the prevention of vibration. It is an important factor in the design of consumer products. Note that this factor favours the use of low-strength, high-modulus materials.

3.3.3 Impact Based Design

An impact is a load applied suddenly on an object. Impacts can create momentary peak stresses and subsequent vibrations in the impacted bodies. Drinking glasses or ceramic ware will seldom fail under ordinary static loads. However, they will chip or fracture under local or overall impact. Impact is likely to be the most severe load on an object. That is why high-impact styrene has completely replaced crystal styrene in many applications. Impact design and shock proofing are most important in the case of automobile bumpers, automobile safety devices, power tools, watches, electrical and electronic products. Impact is also the foremost factor in designing boxes and containers for packaging.

In an impact situation, the controlling characteristic of a structure is the product of strength and deflection, i.e., its energy storage capacity, termed as *resilience* in literature on strength of materials. A specification for impact strength could be: "The object has to survive drops in all directions from a height of 1 m onto a concrete floor".

If you hit a hammer hard on a steel anvil, the impact force can be as high as 3200 kg. Applying the same impacting action on a soft object will cause an impact force of about 10 to 20 pounds. The difference in the impact force is due to the fact that a soft object will 'give', and thus absorb the impact energy over a longer distance. As the steel anvil will not 'give', the impact energy has to be absorbed over a very small distance (such as 0.05 cm.), which results in a huge force. Impact energy equals one-half the product of the maximum force and maximum deflection:

$$\text{Impact energy} = 1/2\ F_{\max}\ \delta_{max}$$

$$\text{For soft objects, } 80 \text{ cm-kg} = 1/2 \times 32 \text{ kg} \times 5 \text{ cm}$$

$$\text{For the anvil, } 80 \text{ cm-kg} = 1/2 \times 3200 \text{ kg} \times 0.05 \text{ cm}$$

where the 80 cm-kg is a reasonable estimate of the kinetic energy in the hammer immediately before impact.

3.4 MATERIAL TOUGHNESS: RESILIENCE

The energy that a unit volume of material absorbs is the area under the stress–strain curve. The elastic part of this energy capacity is called the modulus of resilience, R, which is mathematically equal to 1/2 $[(S_y)^2/E]$. The energy capacity up to the fracture point of a material is the toughness. Material A shown in Figure 3.12 has a high yield strength and a high ultimate strength. However, it is not as tough as material B because of its smaller strain in fracture. Material B has a larger elongation at fracture and, thus, a higher energy absorption capacity. High-impact styrene is made by adding low-strength ingredients (plasticizers) to crystal styrene. The purpose of this is to increase the elongation at fracture at a small expense of the ultimate strength. The material becomes noticeably softer (i.e., with a smaller elastic modulus, E). Quenched or cold-worked metallic parts are often annealed to increase ductility and impact strength. Annealing in a controlled elevated temperature allows for increased molecular orientation and increased grain size. Impact strength is an important factor in choosing composite materials. As an example, adding microglass beads to plastics will increase the ultimate strength and decrease the elongation. The toughness of the material may be lowered. This composite material would not be suitable for an application where impact strength is needed.

An impact with more energy than the toughness of the material causes fracture. It is found that materials usually are stronger, if the duration of the load is short. Hence, the impact toughness may be a bit larger than the static toughness obtained from a static stress–strain curve.

3.5 DESIGNING FOR UNIFORM STRENGTH

Uniform distribution is usually the ideal stress distribution. In such a case, the design is balanced and the material is fully utilized. The threaded rods shown in Figure 3.13(a) are limited by the strength at the threads. The rod in Figure 3.13(b) is stronger in impact and consumes less material. Since the rod in Figure 3.13(b) has a slimmer shank, it stretches more on impact. This elasticity lowers the peak force in a manner similar to that in the example of the pillow and anvil.

(a) Good design

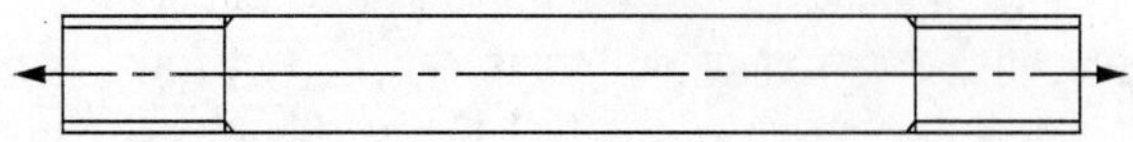

(b) Poor design

FIGURE 3.13 Two alternative designs of studs.

If the stress is really uniform, the energy capacity of the object is equal to the toughness of the material multiplied by volume. In most practical situations, end connections and geometric arrangements prevent perfectly uniform stress distributions. Both cantilever beams shown in Figure 3.6 have equal static strengths. The uniform cantilever beam can absorb energy which equals (1/9) the modulus of resilience of the material, i.e.,

$$(1/9)\ (S_y^2)/2E$$

As compared with ($S_y^2/2E$) for a bar in pure tension, the tapered cantilever can absorb 1/3 the modulus of resilience of the material, i.e.,

$$(1/3)\ (S_y^2)/2E$$

We now give the derivation of formulae for strain energy modulus of cantilever beams (refer Figure 3.6(b)).

(a) Cantilever beam of rectangular plan shape:

$$dU = (S_{xy})^2 \frac{1}{2E} dv$$

$$dU = \left[S_y \frac{y}{d} \frac{x}{l} \right]^2 \frac{1}{2E} dx\, dy$$

where $S_{xy} = [S_y(y/d) \cdot (x/l)]$ is the induced stress at a point distant x from free end and distant y from neutral axis of the cantilever beam. The stress S_{xy} varies with x as well as y according to a triangular distribution, as shown in Figure 3.6(b)

d = half-depth of rectangular cross-section
l = width of cantilever beam (assuming unity)
L = length of beam
dv = volume of element of length dx, thickness dy, and width unity

The integration should be carried out for half-depth of the beam, and volume of beam above neutral axis should be considered for algebraic simplicity. Hence,

$$U = \frac{S_y^2}{2E}\frac{(dl)}{9} = \frac{1}{9}\frac{S_y^2}{2E}\text{(volume)}$$

(b) Cantilever beam of triangular plan shape:

$$dU = (S_{xy})^2 \frac{1}{2E} dv$$

$$dU = \left[S_y \frac{y}{d}\right]^2 \frac{1}{2E}\left(dx\, dy \frac{x}{l}\right)$$

In the cantilever beam of triangular plan shape, the stress distribution does not vary in magnitude along the x-direction, but it increases from zero value at the neutral axis to its maximum value at the outer fibre, distant d from neutral axis. Therefore,

$$U = \frac{1}{2E} S_y^2 \frac{dl}{6} = \frac{1}{2E} S_y^2 \frac{1}{3}\left[\frac{dl}{2}\right]$$

$$U = \frac{1}{2E} S_y^2 \frac{1}{3} \text{ (volume of the beam)}$$

The volume of a triangular beam of length l, depth d, and width unity = $ld/2$

The tapered cantilever utilizes only 33% of its material energy capacity because of the non-uniform stress distribution across the section. The stress is zero at the neutral axis of bending. Further improvements can be made by changing the cross-section to an I-section or a channel section.

To obtain a uniform stress distribution, stress concentration should be avoided, and 100% of the material should be subjected to the highest level of stress.

The static tensile strength of regular and high-impact stud shown in Figure 3.13 is the same because the critical area in both is at the root of the screw threads.

$$F = S_y(A_r/K_t)$$

where

A_r = root area
K_t = stress concentration factor
S_y = yield strength of material

With the sectional area of the shank reduced to A_r/K_t, the stud becomes more resilient as a whole. A slender member, if properly designed, is tougher than a bulky member.

3.6 TENSION VIS-A-VIS COMPRESSION

Structures with members in pure tension or in pure compression utilize the material most efficiently, see Chow[2].

A suspension bridge or 'Laxman Jhula' supports weight by tension in the steel cables (Figure 3.14). An arch bridge supports weight by compression in the material. Sometimes, a designer has to choose between using a tension or a compression member. In this case, the material strength, the geometric stability, and the fatigue strength in each member have to be considered.

Many materials are stronger in compression. Glass rods and concrete bars will fail in tension if bending loads are applied. The ratio of compressive strength to tensile strength is: 3.5, for cast iron; 5 for glass; and 10 for concrete. Noticeable exceptions are materials with oriented grain or molecular structures such as steel cables, nylon fibres, natural fibres, and glass fibres. Such materials are stronger in tension than in compression.

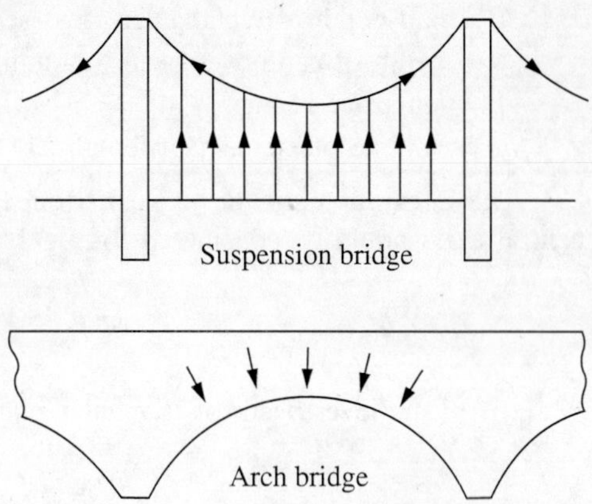

FIGURE 3.14 Purely tensile and purely compressive structures.

Stability is the major advantage of tension members. A slightly curved member will straighten out under a tensile load. Compression members are unstable and may buckle. Long members are unstable and may buckle. The stability of long and slender compression members depends on the elastic modulus, E, rather than on the material yield strength, S_y. As far as stability goes, high-strength steel members are not superior to low-strength steel members.

A concave end-plate for pressure cylinder experiences compressive stresses and may fail due to buckling (Figure 3.15(a)). A convex end-plate is under tensile stress and may fail if the material in the plate has a low tensile strength. Therefore, a steel end-plate should be made convex. If cast iron is used, the concave shape is preferable as shown in Figure 3.15(b). The choice of the shape depends on the strength-to-stiffness (elastic modulus, E) ratio of the material. The same logic can be applied to a dam or a bridge.

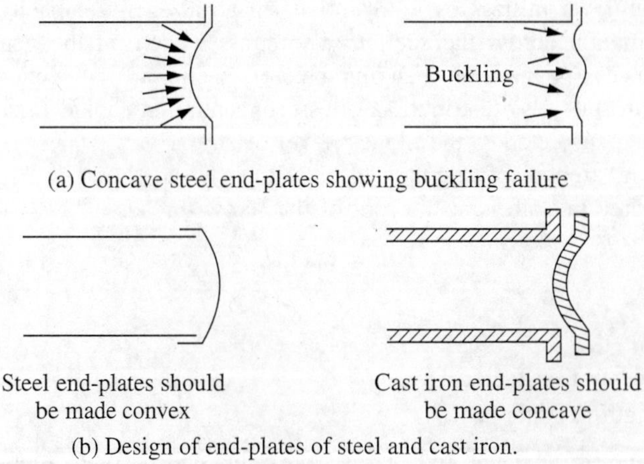

(a) Concave steel end-plates showing buckling failure

(b) Design of end-plates of steel and cast iron.

FIGURE 3.15 Design of end-plates of steel and cast iron.

REVIEW QUESTIONS

1. What are the principle stress trajectories? How the principles of force-flow lines help in arriving a good chair design? Sec.3.1 P 63, 64, 65 Figure 3.3
2. What is a balanced designed? Why is the material of a worm wheel selected as brass while for a worm, steel is used? Sec.3.2 P 65 to 69
3. Power is to be transmitted from a high speed motor to a line-shaft through a gear train. Why is the face width of the gear is increased progressively from driving gear to driven gears? Figure 3.9, 3.10
4. What is a fluid flow analogy used to simulate force flow lines? In a flanged joint subjected to tension mark the zones of tension, compression, bending and shear. Figure 3.4
5. Why a curved beam has section which is unsymmetrical with respect to neutral axis? What steps are taken to equalize the force above and below neutral axis in case of curved beams? Sec.3.2.1 Figure 3.7
6. How is toughened glass pre-stressed to make it impact resistant and stronger in bending? Sec. 3.8 P68, 69
7. How are: strength-based design, impact-based design and rigidity-based design achieved? Sec.3.3.1, 3.3.2, 3.3.3
8. What is meant by designing for uniform strength? Give any two examples: one from machine design and one from structural design. Sec. 3.5 P 72–73
9. Give two examples of designs utilizing members in pure tension and pure compression. Sec. 3.6 P 74

REFERENCES

[1] Ullmann, D., *The Mechanical Design Process*, McGraw-Hill, New York, 1992.

[2] Chow, W.W., *Cost Reduction in Product Design*, Van Nostrand Reinhold, New York, 1978.

Chapter 4

Design for Stiffness and Rigidity

Several concepts for efficient design from the point of view of strength have been discussed in Chapter 3. In this chapter, we indicate some practical ways to obtain greater strength while using less material. Techniques of increasing rigidity can be useful while utilizing materials such as plastics, compositors and other newly developed materials.

4.1 PURE STRUTS AND PURE COLUMNS

A structure composed of only tension members or only compression members needs less material than one containing both tension and compression members. Choice of material in such cases becomes simple, resulting in economy. The presence of a bending moment necessitates design improvement and sophisticated methods of stress and strength analysis. French [1] has stated a law discovered by Leonhard Euler, a famous German scientist: "In a structure containing tension and compression members, the difference in volume of material in tension and volume of material in compression is a constant". Now, if a structure has no compression members but only tension members, the material requirement in such a structure will be minimum.

4.2 STRUCTURE INVOLVING BOTH TENSION AND COMPRESSION MEMBERS

When tensile members are orthogonal (perpendicular) to compressive members, the forces in these members will not cancel each other. As the loading conditions change, the optimum configuration changes. Figure 4.1 shows two structures which are both superior under a specific load. Sensitivity analysis can be used to determine the range of loads where an optimum structure remains best.

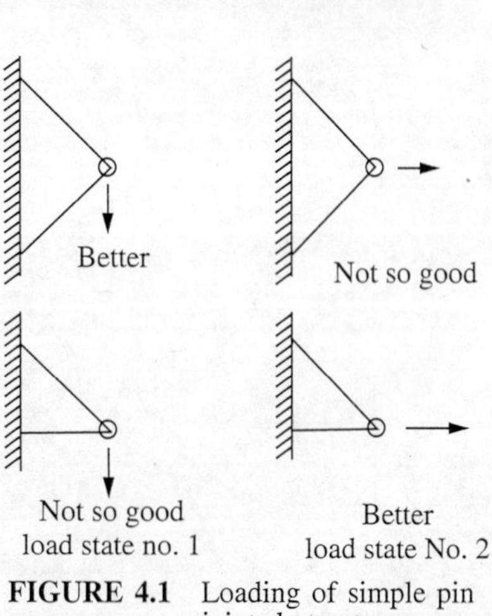

FIGURE 4.1 Loading of simple pin jointed structures.

4.3 MAPPING OF PRINCIPAL STRESSES

A Michell strain field is a map of the directions of principal strains over the design space for a set of externally applied forces. A structure with all members in the direction of the strain field is potentially the most efficient structure. Intuitively, when the member is in the direction of the strain field, there is either pure compression or pure tension.

The Michell strain field for a wheel under torsion between the hub and the rim is shown in Figure 4.2. This concept is easily applied to a plastic gear (Figure 4.3). The torsion induces pure compression in curved areas with no bending action, which is desirable.

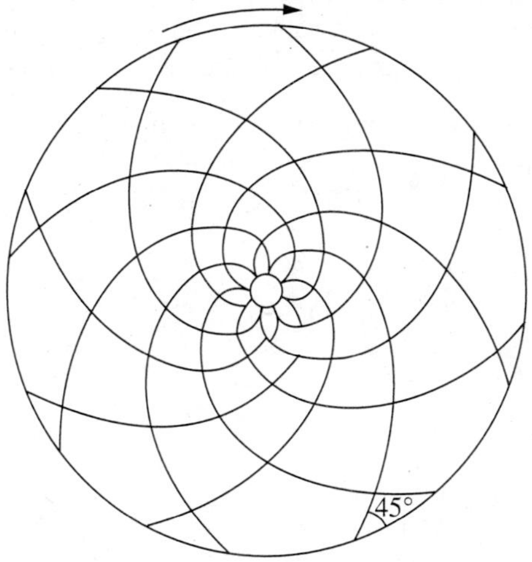

FIGURE 4.2 Michell strain field for disc in torsion.

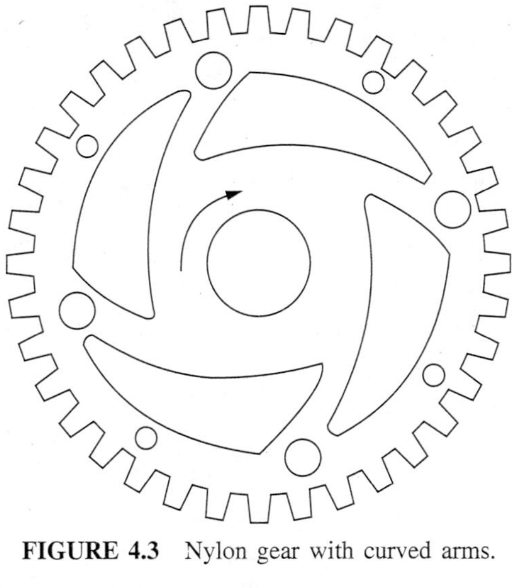

FIGURE 4.3 Nylon gear with curved arms.

4.4 BUCKLING AND INSTABILITY

The bending strength of a beam can be augmented by increasing its depth and decreasing its thickness. Is a beam which is very deep and thin, strong enough? No. Though such a beam would not easily fail by stress failure, it would easily buckle. Buckling is a failure due to insufficient stiffness and instability. Thin and slender structures are prone to buckling. In practice, thin sections are often used to get more efficient structures. Buckling is usually the dominant criterion for designs with a high strength-to-weight ratio. The same is true for a torsional member. By replacing a solid rod with tube, material utilization in carrying the torsional load is increased. However, such a design strategy is constrained by buckling failure.

An example of compression buckling is illustrated in Figure 4.4(a). Figure 4.4(b) shows local buckling for thin tubing under torsion. The cause of buckling is insufficient stiffness. Preventive measures to act as guidelines to designers are summarized as follows:

1. Use a more rigid material with a higher Young's modulus, E and a higher shear modulus, G.
2. Use a low-strength material (lower S_y) such that yielding, rather than buckling, becomes dominant and suppresses buckling. High-strength materials will definitely fail in buckling because they will not yield.

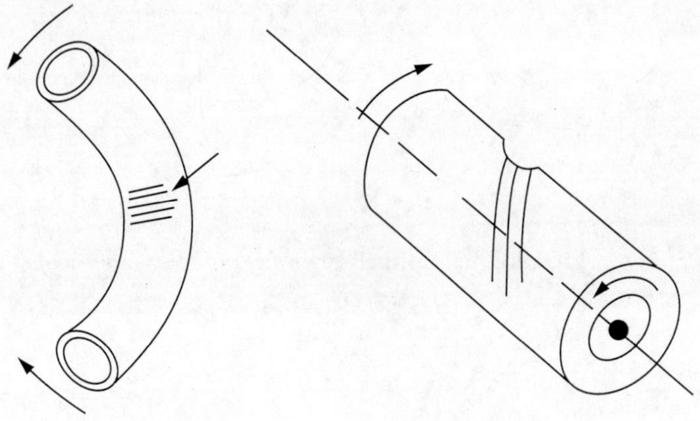

(a) Bending induced wrinkles (b) Torsion induced wrinkles

FIGURE 4.4 Buckling of tube in bending and torsion.

3. Increase the thickness of the wall. A small diameter tubing with a thick wall of ductile material is less likely to buckle under bending.
4. Apply material to prevent lateral deflection. This method is very effective against the buckling modes shown in Figure 4.5.
5. Use stiffeners such as ribs, corrugations, honeycombs and surface textures to prevent local buckling. Ribs can be used to prevent the buckling of compression and tension webs of beams.
6. Use a filler such as sand, paraffin wax or resin when a thin-wall tubing has to be bent. The filler will stiffen the walls and create hydrostatic pressure during bending. After the bending, the filler can be melted, reclaimed and reused. For bending thin plates, fibre glass can be used to sandwich the plate. These stiffeners, which are temporarily clamped on both sides of the plate, spring back to a straight shape when released.

4.5 THEORY OF LONG COLUMNS

For a beam subjected to end moments, M, its stiffness K is given by

$$K = M/\delta$$

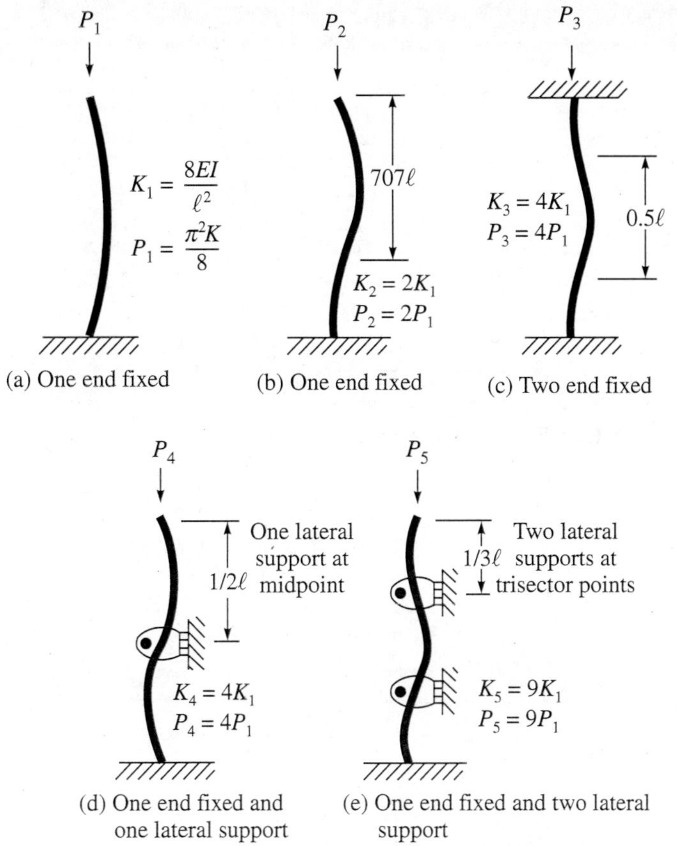

FIGURE 4.5 Illustration of how adding end constraints and lateral supports increases stiffness owing to decrease in effective bending length.

From the geometry of circular arc of radius R and chord sag δ (see Figure 4.6), we have

$$K = (M/\delta) = (8EI/l^2) \text{ (in-lb/in)}$$

Since buckling is due to insufficient stiffness, Euler's equation for the buckling load is directly related to the stiffness defined above.

4.5.1 Critical Load for Columns: Derivation of Formula

As can be seen from Figure 4.6, with both ends free, the following equation is applicable:

$$Py = -EI/(d^2y/dx^2)$$

Setting $(P/EI)^{1/2} = C$, the differential equation is

$$\frac{d^2y}{dx^2} + C^2y = 0$$

A general solution is

$$y = A\cos Cx + B\sin Cx$$

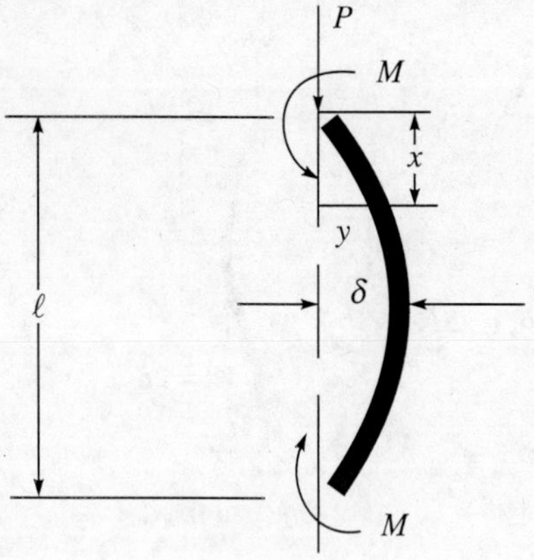

FIGURE 4.6 Euler's model for buckling of long columns.

Hence, with the conditions: at $x = 0$, $y = 0$; and at $x = l$, $y = 0$, we have:

$$B \sin Cl = 0$$

or

$$Cl = n\pi; \quad \text{at } n = 1$$

$$Cl = \pi$$

from which we get:

$$P = \frac{\pi^2 EI}{l^2} = \frac{\pi^2 k}{8}$$

The maximum load without buckling is:

$$P_{cr} = \frac{\pi^2 EI}{l^2} = \frac{\pi^2 k}{8}$$

The allowable stress (load/cross-sectional area) is:

$$\sigma_{\text{allowable}} = P_{\text{cr}}/\text{area} = \pi^2 E/(l/r)^2$$

where

r = radius of gyration of the section area $Ar^2 = I$,

l = length of the member

(l/r) = slenderness ratio

4.5.2 Practical Considerations

A column which is flexible in bending has a low buckling strength, irrespective of material yield strength. Further, Euler's equation predicts infinite strength against buckling for extremely short columns. Euler's equation is not applicable when the column becomes short. The column strength can be broken down into four sections:

1. For very short columns, allowable stress = S_y.

2. For intermediate length columns (with slenderness ratio between 10 and approximately 120), Johnson's parabolic formula, which is empirical in nature, is applicable. According to Johnson's formula:

$$\text{Allowable stress} = S_y - S_y^2(l/r)^2/(4\pi^2 E)$$

3. For long columns (slenderness ratio between 120 and 200), Euler's equation is applicable:

$$\text{Allowable stress} = \pi^2 E/(l/r)^2$$

4. For very long columns (slenderness ratio > 200), the column is practically useless. Still, its strength can be predicted accurately by Euler's equation. If the slenderness ratio is over 120, the buckling is elastic and the column has postbuckling strength as illustrated in Figure 4.7.

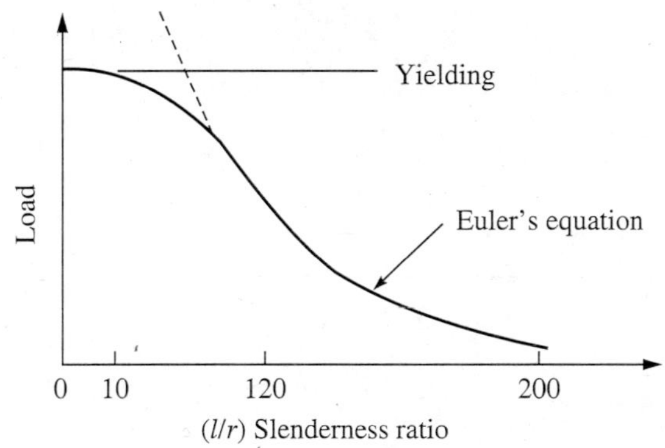

FIGURE 4.7 Plot between load carrying capacity of column vs. slenderness ratio.

4.5.3 Stiffening of Columns

A column can be made stiffer by adding lateral supports. The buckling strength depends on the effective curvature of the beam. Figure 4.5 shows how additional end constraints and lateral supports change the effective bending length, curvature and stiffness and, thus, the allowable load. Buckling cannot occur when lateral deflection is avoided. Euler's equation $P_{cr} = \pi^2 EI/l^2$ for a column with both ends free is modified, if the constraints are changed and 'equivalent length' is substituted in the basic formula. Figure 4.5 indicates how the effective length of a column is reduced due to providing lateral supports at various points.

4.6 HOLLOW COLUMNS

Product designers prefer and recommend tubular hollow column due to the material saving effect achieved in comparison with solid rod-type columns. For the same amount of material, a hollow column has greater outside radius (r_o) and strength against buckling than a solid rod. It should, however, be noted that a tubular column, when subjected to axial loading, is prone to local yielding as well as generalized yielding when the induced stress (S) in the tube wall equals the yield stress S_y.

4.6.1 Effect of Length and Thickness on Failure Modes

For the most efficient design, the column tube thickness could be selected so that two modes of failure are equally likely. The three failure modes are: (i) Elastic buckling due to long column effect; (ii) Local yielding (Euler typed); and (iii) Generalized yielding.

Figure 4.8 is plotted between tube thickness t and tube length l (per unit radius r_o). A failure curve divides the design space (l/r_o) into two distinct parts. The domain above the failure curve indicates buckling through column action. The domain below the failure curve shows state of yielding divided by a vertical line at $t = t_{cr}$, the zone on the right being local yielding and the zone on the left being general yielding.

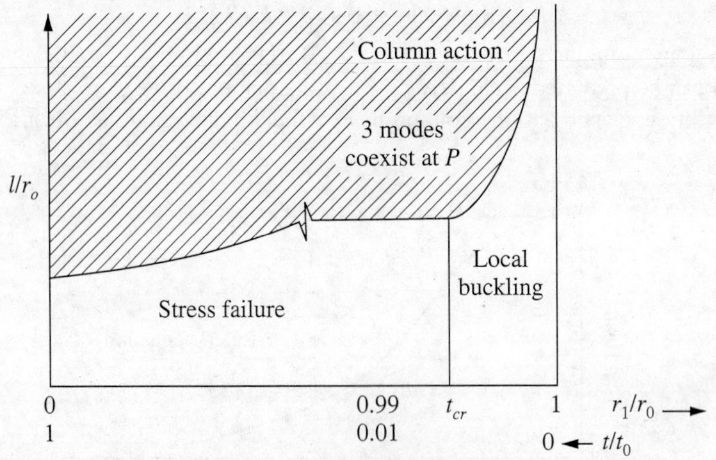

FIGURE 4.8 Various modes of failure of hollow columns.

4.6.2 Practical Design Approach

From practical considerations, standardization makes it possible to select only a specific tube thickness (t) for a certain tube outside radius (r_o). Marshek and Rosenberg* have recommended the following two-point approach to design of columns:

1. Calculate the thickness t_{cr} from the formula:

$$t_{cr} = \frac{r_o}{12.5 + \dfrac{E}{S_y}\dfrac{0.577}{\sqrt{1-\nu^2}}}$$

where,

E = Young's modulus
S_y = yieldstress
ν = Poisson's ratio

2. Compare the value of t_{cr} with selected tube thickness (t). Calculate the length of column, l, by the length formulae given now.

Length formulae

(i) If the value of t_{cr} is less than the selected thickness t, the following formula for length of column is applicable

*K.M. Marshek and M.A. Rosenberg, Designing lightweight frames, *Machine Design*, May 15, 1975, p. 88.

Formula I: $$l = \frac{r_o \pi}{2} \sqrt{\frac{E}{S_y}\left[1+\left(\frac{r_1}{r_o}\right)^2\right]}$$

(ii) The above case of t greater than t_{cr} is most common.

In rare cases if t is less than t_{cr}, the following approximate formula is used:

Formula II: $$l = \frac{r_o \pi}{2} \sqrt{[3(1-v^2)]^{1/2}} \sqrt{\frac{2}{[1-(r_1/r_o)]}}$$

Illustrative example. Calculate the length of a hollow column with outside radius r_o = 50 mm, $E = 2.1 \times 10^6$, S_y = 2800 kg/cm^2.

Solution. Adopt a tube with thickness t = 0.5 mm and r_o = 50 mm. Now,

$$t_{cr} = \frac{r_o}{112.5 + \frac{E}{S_y}\frac{0.577}{\sqrt{1-v^2}}} = \frac{50}{12.5 + \left(\frac{2,100,000}{2800}\right)\frac{0.577}{0.95}} = 0.11 \text{ mm}$$

because t_{cr} = 0.11 mm is less than the selected value t = 0.5, formula I for calculating the length of column is utilized. Hence,

$$l = \frac{r_o \pi}{2} \sqrt{\frac{E}{S_y}\left[1+\left(\frac{r_i}{r_o}\right)^2\right]} = \frac{50\pi}{2} \sqrt{\frac{2,100,000}{2800}\left[1+\left(\frac{49.5}{50}\right)^2\right]} = 3026 \text{ mm}$$

In rare instances, t_{cr} is greater than t. In such a situation, formula II for calculating l is utilized.

4.7 PLASTIC DESIGN

4.7.1 Plastic Deformation

Ductile materials can undergo plastic deformation without failure. Figure 4.9 shows that the stress–strain curve reaches a plateau where the stress remains constant with plastic strains. Consider a notched bar with a stress concentration effect with factor c. If the material is brittle, failure may occur when the average stress is $1/c$ (the material strength). The bar will fail when the average stress is equal to the material yield strength. In the design of bolt-joints, once the allowable stress in one of the bolts is exceeded, there will be plastic deformation (or slipping) and stress redistribution in all the bolts of the joint.

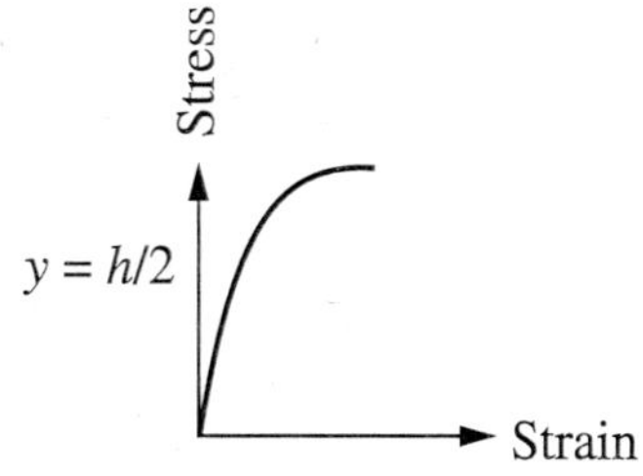

FIGURE 4.9 Stress–strain curve.

4.7.2 Elastic and Plastic Behaviour of Beams

A beam has higher stresses at the top and bottom surfaces and very low stresses near the neutral axis. Since the stress is non-uniform, local yielding does not represent the collapse of the entire beam. The ratio of the moment, M_p (which causes full yielding) to the moment, M_y (which in turn causes initial yielding) is the shape factor. As can be seen from Figure 4.10.

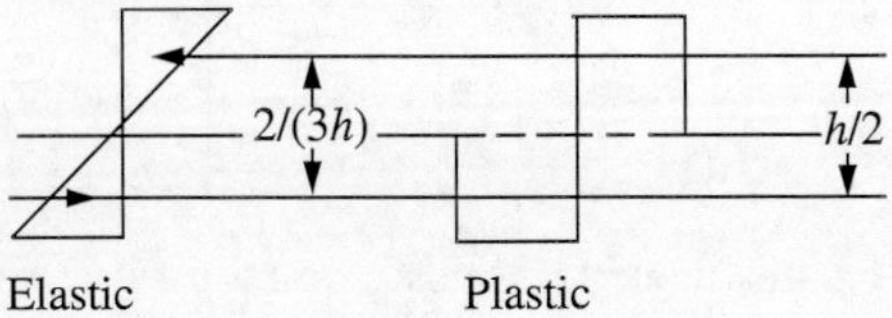

FIGURE 4.10 Stress distribution across the cross-section of beam.

$$\text{The plastic moment } M_p = F \cdot r = S_y\,(A/2)r$$
$$= S_y\,(bh/2)\,h/2$$
$$= S_y\,bh^2/4$$

$$\text{For elastic bending, } S_y = M_y C/I = M_y(h/2)/I$$

$$\text{Maximum elastic moment } M_y = S_y I/(h/2) = S_y\,bh^2/6$$

Therefore,

$$\text{Shape factor} = (M_p/M_y) = 1.5$$

4.7.3 Advantages and Disadvantages of Plastic Design

The basic assumption in the above discussion is that the material is perfectly plastic. For any amount of strain larger than the elastic limit, the stress is equal to the yield stress (Figure 4.11). Real materials work-harden, and the stress can get larger as the amount of plastic strain increases. This work-hardening will increase the collapse strength and make our calculations still safe. Real materials also will not satisfy the indefinite yielding of perfectly plastic material. Fracture may occur with real materials because of finite yielding and imposes a constraint on widespread use of plastic design for less ductile materials.

The theory of plastic design predicts the collapse strength of a structure. This will not be applicable in situations where the structure collapses in buckling, or fails due to too large a deflection.

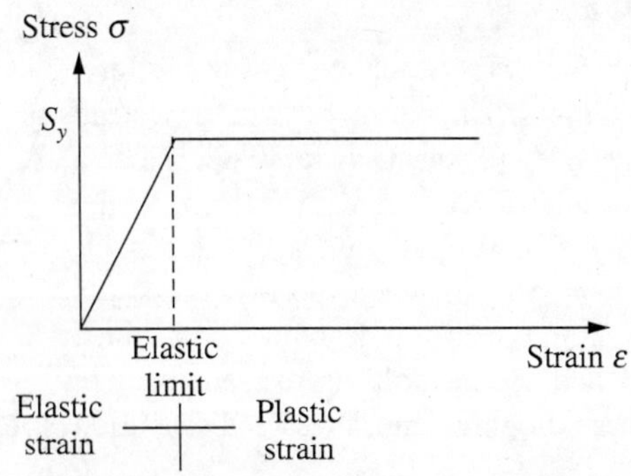

FIGURE 4.11 Stress–strain of elastic ideally plastic material.

4.8 PRACTICAL IDEAS FOR MATERIAL SAVING IN DESIGN

Very rarely can any product be developed completely on an analytical basis. Judgment and the designer's personal choice add a touch of "originality". In this section, we present several practical concepts concerning strength and weight. Each concept should be viewed as a special interpretation or application of the general theories.

4.8.1 Slimming Down

Slimming down or carve-out means "shave material from where it is not needed". A good designer can see through the part and visualize the flow of forces. He can cut holes or thin down sections where there is little flow of force. Experimentally, if many samples of an existing product are available, holes can be made and material can be removed in suspected low-stress areas. The original and modified samples will be tested for failure, and their strength-to-weight ratios will be compared. The one with the highest strength-to-weight ratio is the most efficient. This structure does not have to be the strongest. If the strength of the most efficient design is lower than the required strength, its shape should be retained.

4.8.2 Achieving Balance through Reinforcement

Reinforcement means "patching up" the weak spots. Through such an operation, a balanced design, in which there are no weak spots or every section has the same safety factor, can be obtained. Even though reinforcement can be achieved by adding webs of the same material, more often composite materials are used to take advantage of the strengths of different materials. A material which is weak in tension (e.g., concrete or plastic) may be strengthened by steel, glass or carbon fibres. The stiffer material will carry most of the force. The reinforcing material should be stiffer than the reinforced material (the matrix). A typical relationship for fibre and plastic is shown in Figure 4.12. The uniaxial tensile strength and modulus are in-between the values for the fibre and the plastic. The fracture strain is about the same as that for the fibre. The fibre-reinforced plastic is stronger and more rigid than the matrix, but may not increase resistance to impact. Since concrete is weak in tension, steel bars are embedded at places of high tension to strengthen concrete.

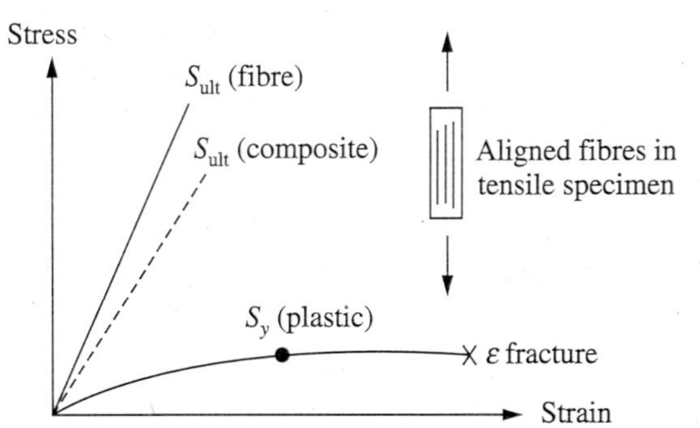

FIGURE 4.12 Stress–strain diagrams for fibre, plastic and composite.

4.8.3 Cardboard Model of Plate Structures

Cardboard models can be used to show the relative deflections and stress distribution in steel plate structure. Failure modes, weak spots and stress concentrations can be estimated by simulation. Since paper models are inexpensive, such an experimental method is very useful. Deflections are especially easy to observe because of the flexibility of paper material.

It has long been observed by designers that a box frame with diagonal braces (see Figure 4.13(a)) has exceptional torsional rigidity. Stiffness in lathe beds provides a typical example of diagonal bracing. Figure 4.13(b) shows that torsion creates shear stresses along the horizontal and vertical lines on the surface of the cylinder. Maximum compressive stress occurs along right-hand helices and maximum tensile stresses occur along left hand helices on the cylinder. When the braces in Figure 4.13(a) make an angle of 45° with the sides, the braces are subjected to in-plane bending. The behaviour of various members of the frames can be evaluated simply by cutting them or replacing them with more flexible members.

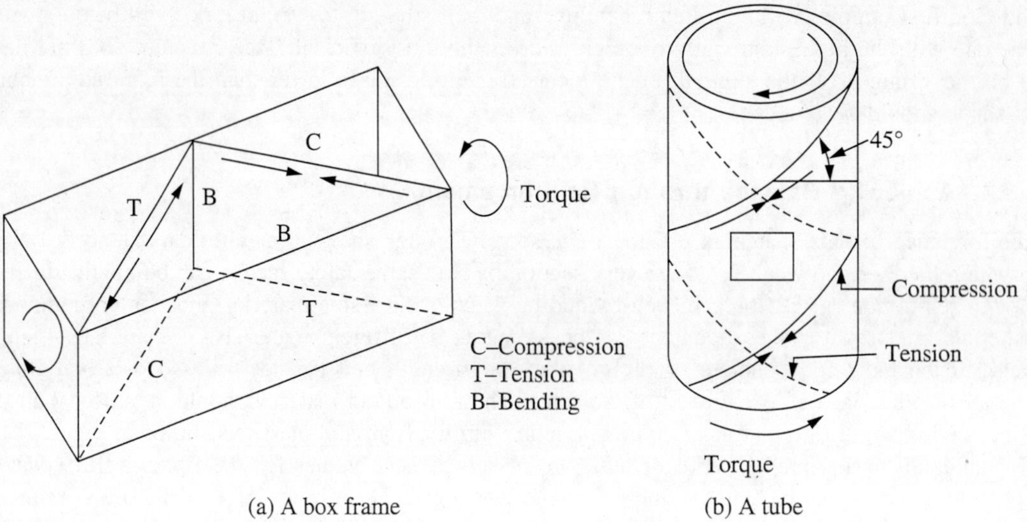

FIGURE 4.13 Torsion of a box frame and a tube.

4.8.4 Soap Film Analogy of Torsional Shear Stresses

The following discussion is based on research done by Agrawal [2].

The stresses in a cylindrical member under a torsional load are easy to visualize (Figure 4.13(b)). Fortunately, most torsional members, such as shafts and pulleys, are indeed circular in cross-section. If the section is non-circular, the stress distribution is so complex that most designers lose conceptual feel. During a practical study of the behaviour of a split tube (roll pin) under torsion, it is seen that a transverse plane which is initially flat becomes warped (Figure 4.14).

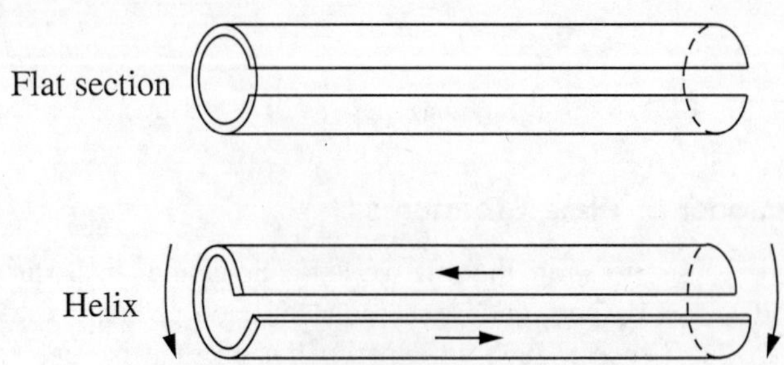

FIGURE 4.14 Torsion of a split tube.

The membrane analogy first stated by Ludwig Prandtl (1903), in Germany is based on the similarity of the stress function (ϕ) and the height function Z as shown in Figure 4.15(a). The cross-section of the member is replaced by a wire frame, which is an exact duplicate of the circumferential contour of the section. The wire frame is covered by membrane. Pressure is applied to one side of the membrane so that a dome is formed. The maximum slope of the membrane at a point represents the shear stress at that point. In twisting of shells, the protruding convex corners carry very little shear stresses, whereas sharp internal and external corners should be avoided because of stress concentration. The centre of a circle or the middle of a narrow web is location of zero slope and zero stress. The directions of the shear stresses in the cross-section are contour lines (constant z-lines) on the membrane. The volume under the membrane is proportional to the torsional strength of the member. The analogy is extended to torque and direction of shear stress in Figures 4.15(b) and 4.15(c), respectively.

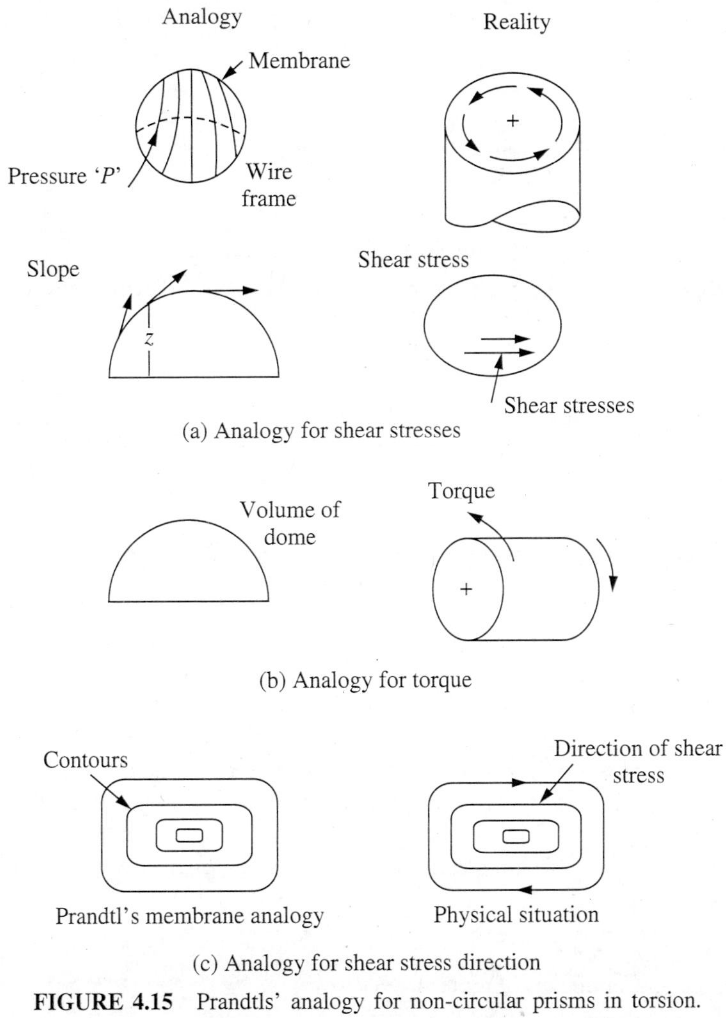

FIGURE 4.15 Prandtls' analogy for non-circular prisms in torsion.

Figure 4.16 shows that sections which are open (with a split on the circumference) are much weaker than closed sections, the volume under the dome increases greatly if the section is generally round or closed. Agrawal [2] states: "To increase strength, increase the volume of the analog bubble". If the section is an open shape, such as a thin blade, an I-section, T-section or U-section or a Z-section, then the torsional strength is proportional to the product of the sectional area, *A,* and the web thickness *t.* This implies that the shape of the section is rather unimportant.

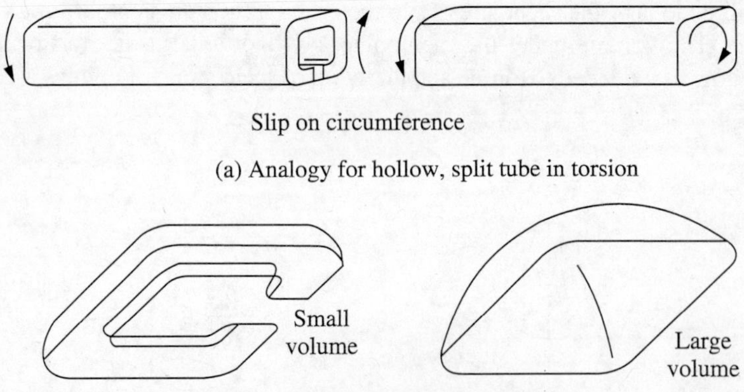

(a) Analogy for hollow, split tube in torsion

(b) Analogy for solid shaft in torsion

FIGURE 4.16 Analogy for torsion of hollow and solid non-circular sections.

If the section is hollow instead of solid, the loss in strength is very small. The internal hole can be represented by the thin weightless plate which is cemented to the membrane. Because of this plate, the hollowed area has a zero slope and no stress. The web adds nothing to the torsional strength because it bisects an internal hollow space. The membrane model of the web is flat, and the volume under the dome remains constant regardless of the presence of the web.

4.9 RIBS, CORRUGATIONS, LAMINATES AND MEMBRANES

Chow [3] has carried out a thorough analysis in this field. Often, designers can draw inspiration from nature to analyse or develop designs. Trusses, beams and frames are components of skeleton structures. They resemble bones, with which vertebrates support loads. Insects do not have bones: they support loads with stiff skins. The fact that an ant can carry objects several times its weight shows that stiff-skin structures can be very efficient. Bridges, trusses, cranes and bicycles are examples of skeleton structures. On the other hand, shells, pressure vessels, space vehicles and ocean vessels are examples of stiff-skin structures. Manufacturing methods such as wire-forming are well adapted to producing skeleton structures. Blow-moulding and rotation-moulding produce stiff-skin structures. Four classes of lightweight design concepts are discussed in this section:

1. Stiff skins (Figure 4.17)
2. Sandwiches and laminates (Figure 4.18)
3. Tension skins (Figure 4.19)
4. Textured materials.

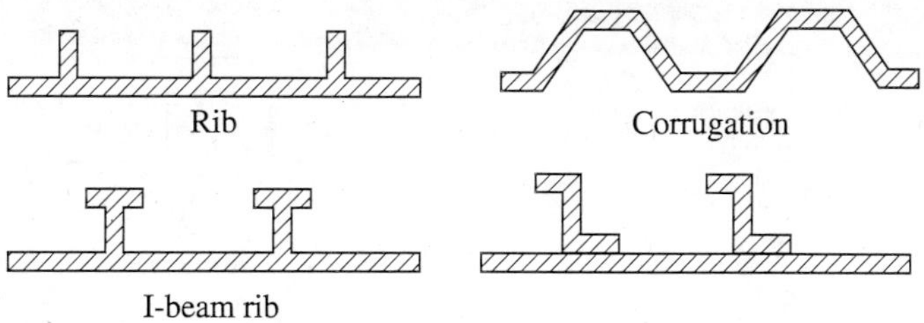

FIGURE 4.17 Designs of ribs, corrugations, and laminations.

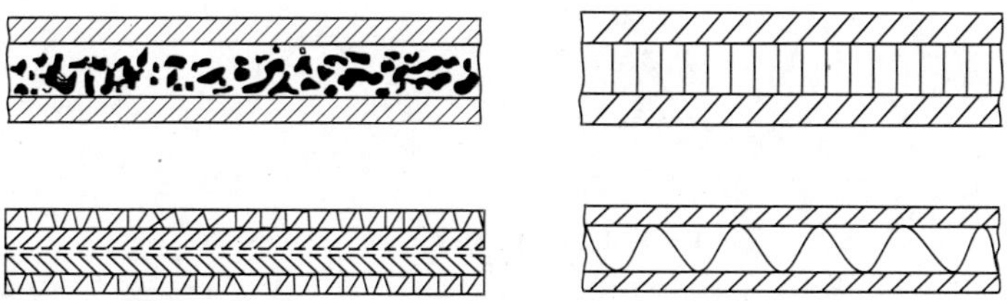

FIGURE 4.18 Designs of sandwiches and laminations.

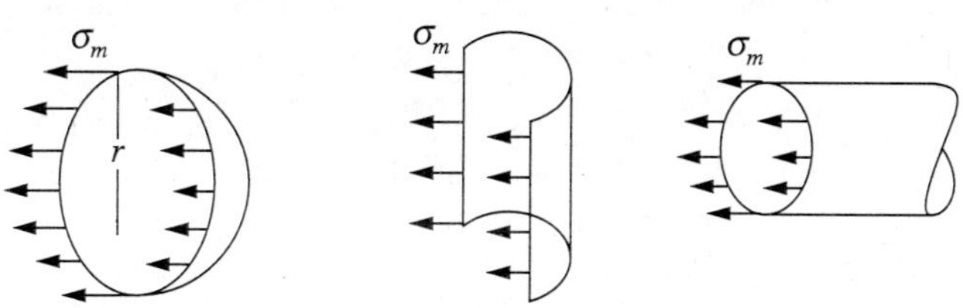

(a) Spherical (b) Cylindrical (c) Cylindrical

FIGURE 4.19 Loading of membrane structures.

4.9.1 Stiff Skins

Stiffening is the design strategy for preventing buckling, which is the common mode of failure of thin shells. It is achieved by adding ribs and corrugations. The ribs and corrugations bear the bending moments and forces better than flat plates (see Figures 4.20 and 4.21). The following is a description

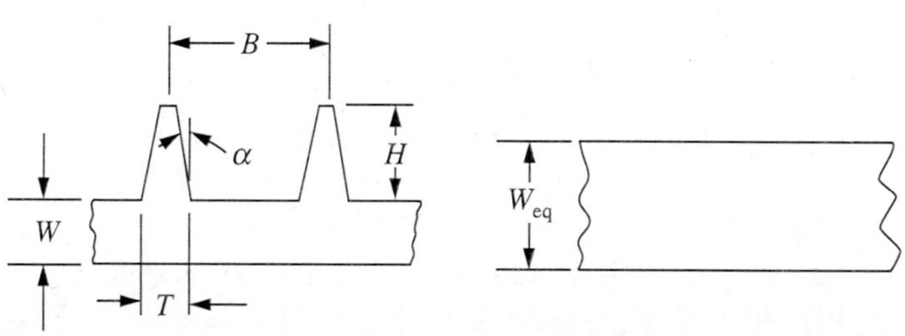

(a) Ribbed wall (b) Flat wall with equivalent strength (or stiffness)

FIGURE 4.20 Dimensions of ribbed plate and equivalent flat plate.

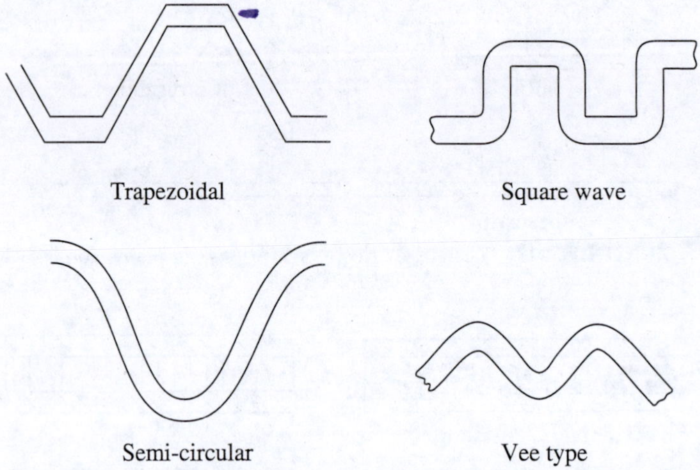

FIGURE 4.21 Corrugation designs.

of rib design and corrugation design. Such a design analysis is based on elastic bending, assuming no buckling and no plastic deformation. Formulae for rib design and corrugations are explained in the end. The strengthening and stiffening effects of ribs and corrugations are attributed to the *increased distance of material from the neutral axis of bending.*

(i) **Rib design.** Usually, the rib thickness T is less than the thickness of the wall, W, to avoid shrinkage marks (Figure 4.20). For low-shrinkage material, thickness is $(3/4)W$, and a 1° draft is provided for the ribs. For high-shrinkage material, a combination of thickness and $(1/2W)$ draft is more appropriate.

Analysis. From the equation $(M/I) = (\sigma/C)$ used widely in bending analysis, we have:

$$M = [I/C]\sigma$$

The bending strength of a beam is proportional to its section modulus (I/C), where C is the distance from the neutral axis to the tip of the rib which is the first point to yield because it is farthest from the neutral axis. If the part is made of a material which is weak in tension (e.g. plastic, cast iron or glass), the skin should be subjected to tension and the ribs to compression. As an example, if the wall is a part of a pressurized housing, the ribs should be on the side with higher pressure. The bending stiffness of a beam is proportional to its moment of inertia, I. This is clear from the following equation:

$$M/I = (E/R) \quad \text{or} \quad R = (EI/M)$$

where R is the radius of curvature of bend and is proportional to stiffness. Thus, the greater the moment of inertia, the more the stiffness. The above formulae are useful in calculating the strengthening factor and stiffness factor due to ribs.

1. The strengthening factor is the ratio of the strength before adding the ribs to the strength after adding the ribs:

$$\text{Strengthening factor} = \frac{(I/c), \text{ with ribs}}{(I/c), \text{ without ribs}} \doteq W_{eq}^2/W^2$$

2. The stiffening factor is the ratio of stiffness before and after adding the ribs:

$$\text{Stiffening factor} = \frac{I\ (\text{with ribs})}{I\ (\text{without ribs})}$$

Since the section modulus (I/c) increases with the square of the wall thickness, a flat wall of thickness, W_{eq}, is equivalent in strength to a ribbed wall of thickness, W:

$$W_{eq}\ \text{strength} = W\sqrt{\text{strengthening factor}}$$

$$\text{Material saving} = [W_{eq} - (W_t + t)]/W_{eq}$$

$$1 - \frac{W+t}{W_{eq}} = 1 - \frac{1+t}{W_{eq}/W}$$

i.e.,

$$\text{Saving in material} = 1 - \frac{1 + \text{rib material}}{\sqrt{\text{strengthening factor}}}$$

Similarly, savings in material can be realized by using ribbed plates, instead of flat plates, if stiffness is the main design criterion. The stiffness of a plate depends on I, which increases by the cube of the thickness. The flat wall equivalent in stiffness to the ribbed wall would have a thickness W_{eq}:

$$W_{eq} = W\ (\text{stiffening factor})^{1/3}$$

$$\text{Saving} = [W_{eq} - (W + t)]/W_{eq} = 1 - [(W + t)/W_{eq}]$$

i.e.,

$$\text{Saving in material} = 1 - \frac{1 + \text{rib material}}{(\text{stiffening factor})^{1/3}}$$

Diagonal ribs. The strengthening and stiffening effects of the ribs are only for bending in the plane of the ribs. For two-directional bending, such as that in the wall of a fluid container, cross (diagonal) ribs are needed. The saving in material then becomes:

$$\text{Equivalent strength saving in material} = 1 - \frac{1 + 2\ (\text{rib material})}{\sqrt{\text{strengthening factor}}}$$

Since double the amount of material is used in cross ribbing,

$$\text{Equivalent stiffness saving material} = 1 - \frac{1 + 2\ (\text{rib material})}{(\text{stiffening factor})^{1/3}}$$

The ribbing needed to produce a plate strong in all directions is the triangular isogrid. With this type of ribbing, the load is distributed among all ribs regardless of the direction of bending.

Total strengthening factor = strengthening factor × $(W^2/W^2_{original}) \times (E_{ribbed}/E_{original})$

For equivalent strength, the total strengthening factor should be equal to 1.

Total stiffening factor = stiffening factor × $(W/W_{original})^3 \times (E_{ribbed}/E_{original})$

For equivalent stiffness, the total stiffening factor should be equal to 1.

Besides the straight-sided ribs, I-beam ribs can further increase the strength-to-weight ratio. I-beam can be produced by machining or investment casting. One-directional I-beam ribs can be produced by extrusion.

(ii) **Corrugation design.** Corrugating is a method for strengthening and stiffening in which a flat sheet is curved into waves to increase the moment of inertia, *I*. Figure 4.21 shows corrugations obtained by moulding, drawing (pressing) and rolling bending. For the drawn corrugation, the web is thinner than the crest because the material stretches during drawing. The sheet maintains the same overall dimension before and after corrugating. The rolled corrugation causes reduction in the overall length of the sheet, but maintains a uniform thickness at the web. A drawn corrugated sheet has a higher strength-to-weight ratio than the rolled type because of the thinner webs. The corrugated material is stronger and stiffer only in the direction of the corrugation. Roofing of asbestos cement is a familiar example of corrugation design.

(iii) **Development of formulae for strength and stiffness of ribbed section corrugations**

(a) *Rib sections.* Chow [3] has given the following approach for determining moment of inertia of a ribbed section: A ribbed section consists usually of two sections: (i) a rectangular section and (ii) a trapezoidal section. Moment of inertia of these two types of sections is given in standard books on Strength of Materials and Applied Mechanics. These can be combined by applying the Theorem of Parallel Axis to determine the moment of inertia of a ribbed section. The theorem of parallel axis is mathematically expressed as:

$$I_{xx} = I_{gg} + AY^2$$

where I_{xx} is the moment of inertia of a section about the *xx*-axis, I_{gg} is the moment of inertia about an axis parallel to *xx*, but passing through the CG, *Y* is the centroidal distance from the *xx*-axis and *A* is the area of cross-section.

Rectangular section: From Figure 4.22

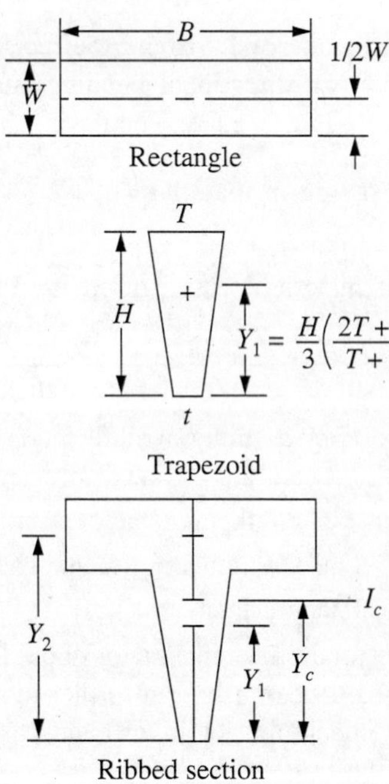

FIGURE 4.22 Ribbed section and its rectangular and trapezoidal elements.

$I_r = BW^3/12;\quad A_r = BW$

$I_t = (H^3/36)\,(T^2 + 4Tt + t^2)/(T + t);\quad A_t = (H/2)\,(t + T);\quad Y_1 = [(H/3)\,(2T + t)]/(t + T)$

$Y_2 = H + W/2;\quad Y_c = (A_tY_1 + A_r \times Y_2)/(A_t + A_r);\quad I_c = I_t + A_t\,(Y_c - Y_1)^2 + I_r + A_r\,(Y_c - Y_2)^2$

$$\text{Stiffening factor} = (I_c/I_r)$$

$$\text{Strengthening factor} = (I_c/Y_c)/I_r/(W/2)$$

Stiffness and strength of corrugations

Trapezoidal corrugation. The moment of inertia, I, is derived for a pressed (drawn) corrugation as shown in Figure 4.23.

$$\text{Rectangular portion } I_F = FT^3/12,\ A_F = FT$$

$$\text{Parallelogram shaped web } I_w = (TW/12)\,(T^2 + H^2)$$

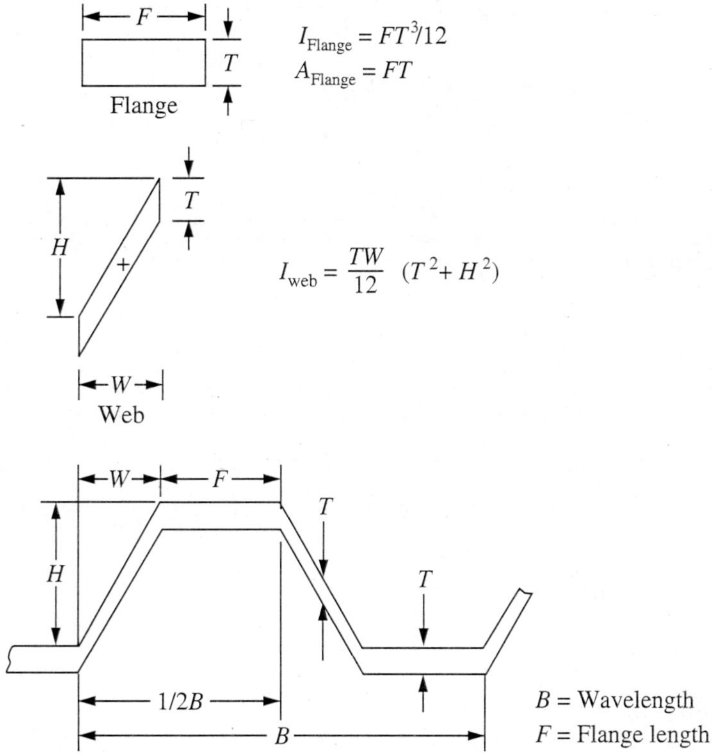

FIGURE 4.23 Trapezoidal corrugation and its rectangular and parallelogram shaped elements.

If B is the wavelength, F the flange length,

$$I_{\text{corr}} = 2[I_f + A_f\,(H/2)^2 + I_w],\quad I_{\text{flat plate}} = BT^3/12$$

$$\text{Stiffening factor} = (I_{\text{corr}}/I_{\text{flat plate}})$$

Similarly, adopting

$$C_{\text{corr}} = (H + T)/2,\ C_{\text{flat plate}} = (T/2),$$

We get,

$$\text{Strength factor} = (I_c/C_{\text{corr}})/(I_F/C_F)$$

Illustrative examples

(i) **Ribbed plate.** A typical ribbed plate is shown in Figure 4.22; determine the stiffness factor and strength factor as a consequence of the provision of the rib. Assume the data for calculation as:

$$B = 4,\ W = 1,\ T = t = 0.75,\ H = 2$$

Solution. Referring to 4.22 and neglecting the effect of draft angle, we have, on application of various formulae, the equations:

$$I_r = 1/3,\ A_r = 4,\ I_t = \frac{2^3}{12}\frac{3}{4} = 0.5,\ A_t = 1.5$$

$$Y_1 = 1,\ Y_2, = 2.5,\ Y_c = \frac{A_r Y_2 + A_t Y_1}{A_r + A_t} = \frac{4 \times 2.5 + 1.5 \times 1}{4 + 1.5} \approx 2$$

$$I_c = I_r + I_t + A_t(Y_c - Y_1)^2 + A_r(Y_c - Y_2)^2$$

$$= 0.33 + 0.50 + 1.5 + 1.0 = 3.33$$

$$\text{Stiffness factor} = I_c/I_r = 3.33/0.33 = 10$$

$$\text{Strength factor} = \frac{I/C_c}{I_r/C_r} = \frac{I}{I_r} \times \frac{C_r}{C_c} = 10 \times \frac{1}{2 \times 2} = 2.5$$

(ii) **Corrugation with 65° angle.** Referring to the corrugation in Figure 4.23, assume: $F = 6$, $T = 1$, $W = 2$, $B = 16$. Then,

$$I_f = 6/12 = 0.5, \quad A_f = 6, \quad I_{\text{web}} = (2/12)(1 + 16) = 2.83$$

$$I_c = 2[0.5 + 6 \times 4 + 2.83] = 54.66$$

$$I_f = 16/12 = 1.33;\ \text{Stiffness factor} = 54.66/1.33 = \boxed{42}$$

Thus,

$$\text{Strength factor} = \left(\frac{I_c}{I_f} \times \frac{C_f}{C_c}\right) = \frac{42 \times 1}{2 \times 2.25} = \boxed{9.3}$$

4.9.2 Sandwiches and Laminates

Laminates are made to take advantage of a combination of material properties. The following may be obtained from lamination: (a) A higher strength-to-weight ratio, (b) corrosion resistance, (c) fireproofing, (d) reflective and decorative surfaces, (e) sound damping, (f) friction properties, (g) thermal conductance or resistance, and (h) electrical properties. Laminates of plastics and glass produce unbreakable glass. Laminates of plastic on photographs give scratch protection. The directional properties of wood are eliminated in plywood. Stainless steel pots and pans are laminated with copper to increase conductivity. Aluminum pans are coated with Teflon to reduce food sticking in non-sticking frying pans. A sandwich is a three-layer laminate consisting of two strong top plates and a relatively weaker, lighter core. From strength of materials standpoint, *a sandwich is like an I-beam:* the top plates carry most of the bending stresses and the core takes the bending shear and supports the faceplates against crushing caused by loads normal to the face. Several types of sandwiches are shown in Figure 4.18.

4.9.3 Membrane Structures

An inflated membrane structure is a tension skin enclosing a volume of compressed fluid. Provided that the skin is strong enough, the stiffness and the collapse strength of the structure increase, if the internal volume is maximum for the amount of skin area. Because of this, the structures generally have spherical surfaces and rounded edges and corners. Examples of inflated structures are life rafts and automobile safety air bags which prevent smashing of the head on collision, air cushions, etc.

A membrane is flexible and has only tension strength in the plane of the material. It has neither compression strength nor bending strength. Because a membrane is very thin, stresses are measured as force per unit length, instead of the standard practice of force per unit sectional area. Note the analogy with surface tension phenomenon in liquids. When an external load is applied to an inflated structure, the volume of the structure decreases. The external work is absorbed in the form of increased pressure in the fluid and tension in the membrane.

"In the case of air cushions, the body weight is supported by fluid pressures in the cushion and by membrane tension." This is shown in Figure 4.24. The mathematical equation for equilibrium of a spherical membrane is:

$$\sigma_m \cdot 2\pi r = \pi r^2 P$$

where P is internal fluid pressure and σ_m is the membrane stress in kg/unit length or $\sigma_m = (Pr/2)$ (see Figure 4.19(a)). If σ_t is the tensile stress in the membrane and t is the thickness of the membrane, then

$$\sigma_t \times t = \sigma_m = Pr/2$$

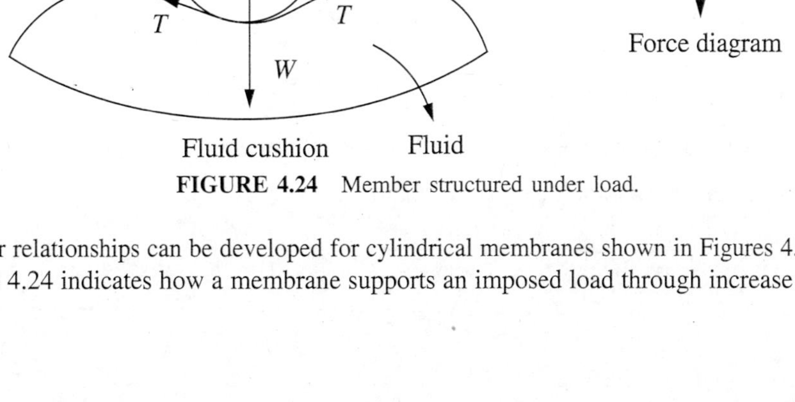

FIGURE 4.24 Member structured under load.

Similar relationships can be developed for cylindrical membranes shown in Figures 4.19(b) and (c).

Figure 4.24 indicates how a membrane supports an imposed load through increase in membrane tension.

REVIEW QUESTIONS

1. What is a Michael strainfield? How is this concept utilized in designing a Nylon gear? Sec 4.3; P 76, 77

2. What are the measures taken to use long columns as machine members?

[**Ans:** The Euler's formula for long columns is given by:

$$P = \frac{n\pi^2 EI}{\ell^2}$$

where P is buckling load, E is the Young's modulus, I is moment of inertia, l is length of the column, and n has values as under:

$$\begin{aligned} n &= 1 \text{ (for both ends hinged)} \\ &= 0.25 \text{ (for one end fixed, one end free)} \\ &= 2 \text{ (for one end hinged, one end fixed)} \\ &= 4 \text{ (for both ends fixed)} \end{aligned}$$

For most materials, long columns with slenderness ratio 120–200 cannot be used as design members for structures.]

3. What are the implications of providing lateral support at:
   (i) mid point
   (ii) two lateral supports at 2/3 length.

Compare with sketches the equivalence between effect of end conditions with lateral support (Figure 4.25).

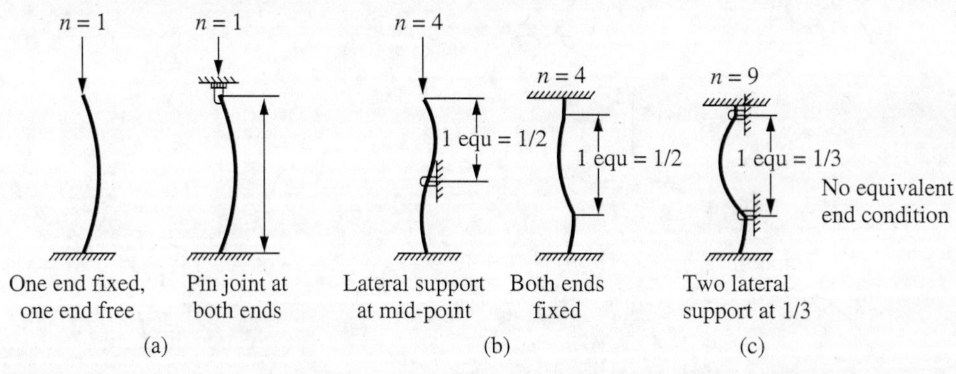

FIGURE 4.25 Equivalence of laterally supported columns with columns having different end conditions.

4. What is Rankine–Gordon's empirical formula? Explain its application.

[**Ans:** Rankine–Gordon empirical relation is:

$$P_c = \frac{\sigma_c A}{1 + a\left(\frac{\ell}{k}\right)^2}$$

where ℓ/k is slenderness ratio; ℓ is length of column and k is radius for circular cross-section (Table 4.1).

TABLE 4.1 Values of constant a for steel and cast iron

Material	*Both ends hinged*	*Both ends fixed*	*One end fixed and one end hinged*
Steel	$\frac{1}{6250}$	$\frac{1}{25000}$	$\frac{1.25}{25000}$
Cast iron	$\frac{1}{1250}$	$\frac{1}{5000}$	$\frac{1.95}{5000}$

Rankine–Gordon's empirical relation covers short columns to long columns. It has been found to give good feasible solutions.]

5. Calculate the length of a hollow column with outside radius
   r_0 = 50 mm, $E = 2.1 \times 10^6$, S_y = 2000 kg/cm^2. P 83 illustrative Example
6. What is plastic design of a beam? Calculate the shape factor as a result of plasticity based approach. P 83 Sec.4.7.1, 4.7.2
7. Explain the applications of providing ribs, corrugations, laminates and membranes in product design. Sec. 4.9 P 88, 89
8. How provision of ribs increases the stiffness and strength of a plate? P 89–P 94
9. Calculate the material saving in a ribbed plate of dimensions as shown:
   $B = 4$, $W = 1$, $T = t = 0.75$, $H = 2$. The calculated values of $I_r = 1/3$, $I_c = 3.33$

$$\text{Strength factor} = \frac{I_c}{I_r} \times \frac{C_r}{C_c} = \frac{3.33}{1/3} \times \frac{1}{2 \times 2} = 2.5$$

$$\text{Stiffness factor} = \frac{I_c}{I_r} = \frac{3.33}{1/3} = 10$$

where I_r is moment of inertia of rectangular section and I_c is moment of inertia of combined section.

Solution

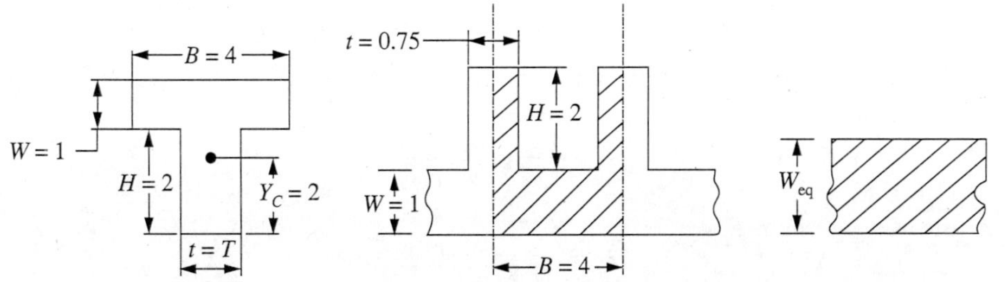

(a) Ribbed section (b) One wavelength of rib section (c) Equivalent plate

FIGURE 4.26 Ribbed section details.

$$\text{With strength as design criteria} = \left[\frac{w_{eq} - (\text{Plate material} + \text{rib material})}{W_{eq}}\right]$$

$$\text{Material saving} = 1 - \frac{W + \text{Rib material}}{w_{eq}}$$

$$= 1 - \frac{1 + (\text{Rib material/plate material})}{(W_{eq}/W)}$$

$$= \left(1 - \frac{1 + (\text{Rib material/plate material})}{\sqrt{\text{Strengthing factor}}}\right)$$

$$\text{Material saving with strength criteria} = \left(1 - \frac{1 + (0.75 \times 2)/(1 \times 4)}{\sqrt{2.5}}\right) = 1 - \frac{1 + (1.5/4)}{\sqrt{2.5}}$$

$$= 1 - \frac{1.375}{1.58} = 1 - 0.87 = 0.13 \text{ or } 13\% \text{ saving}$$

$$\text{Material saving with stiffness criteria} = \left(1 - \frac{1.375}{\sqrt{10}}\right)$$

$$= 1 - 0.435 = 0.56 \text{ or } 56\% \text{ saving}$$

10. Calculate the material saving by use of corrugation of trapezoidal shape, given the following data:

$$I_{corrugation} = 54.66$$

Wavelength $B = 16$, flange thickness $t = 1$

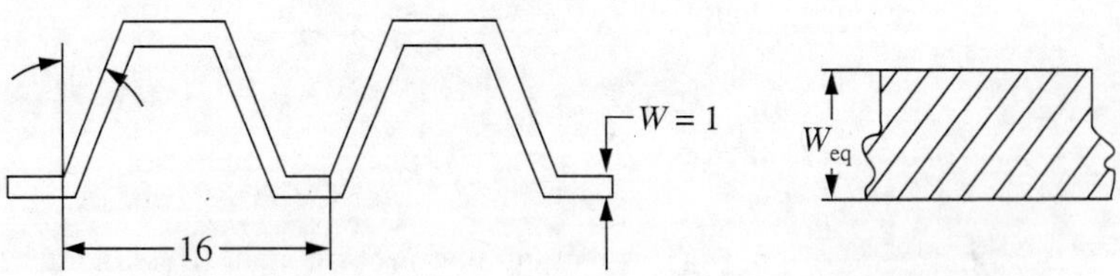

FIGURE 4.27 Corrugated plate and equivalent flat plate.

Solution If W_{eq} is the thickness of a flat plate of which the moment of inertia equals that of the corrugation, we have:

$$\frac{BW_{eq}^3}{12} = 54.66$$

Since wavelength $B = 16$

$$W_{eq}^3 = \frac{12 \times 54.66}{16} = 41$$

or $$W_{eq} = 3.4$$

∴ $$\text{Material saving} = \frac{W_{eq} - W}{W_{eq}} = \frac{3.4 - 1}{3.4} = \frac{2.4}{3.4} = 0.705$$

Thus, there is 70% saving of material if stiffness criteria are used.

If strength criteria are used $W_{eq}^2 = 54$ and $W_{eq} = 6.4$

$$\text{Material saving} = \left(\frac{6.4 - 1}{6.4}\right) = \frac{5.4}{6.4} = 0.843$$

Thus, material saving = 84.3%

11. Calculate the membrane stress induced in an air bag when a load of 100 kg is applied on it. Assume the bag as ellipsoidal approximated by a sphere of radius (r) 600 mm and thickness (t) 2 mm.

Solution The various formulae are

$$\sigma_m = \frac{Pr}{2} \qquad (1)$$

$$\sigma_t = \sigma_m/t \qquad (2)$$

Inserting the values of:

$$P = 100 \text{ kg}, \; r = 600 \text{ mm and } t = 2 \text{ mm}$$

$$\sigma_t = \frac{Pr}{2t} = \frac{100 \times 600}{2 \times 2} = 15{,}000 \text{ kg/mm}^2$$

$$\text{Membrane stress } \sigma_m = (\sigma_t \times t) = 15{,}000 \times 2$$

$$= (30{,}000) \text{ kg/mm}$$

The membranes are very strong in tension but do not have bending strength owing to their flexibility.

REFERENCES

[1] French, M., *Innovation in Design*, McGraw-Hill, New York, 1992.

[2] Agrawal, H.N., A Simple Way to Visualize Torsional Stress, *Machine Design*, pp. 98–101, September 1975.

[3] Chow, W.W., *Cost Reduction in Product Design,* Van Nostrand Reinhold, New York, 1978.

Chapter 5

Production Processes

5.1 INTRODUCTION

Since the dawn of civilization, man has been engaged in converting natural resources into useful products. The entire field of engineering is mainly concerned with this. Of all the subdisciplines of engineering, production is perhaps most vital because it involves the conversion of raw material into the final product.

The industrial revolution was a major turning point in the history of mankind, which set in motion the battle for abundance. The world today is totally dependent on science and technology, and the nations are classified according to their degree of industrialization. Since manufacturing plays a vital role in extracting wealth from the earth, it is quite easy to realize the importance of manufacturing. In spite of this, production engineering has received very little attention from scientists and engineers. This probably is due to the empirical nature of the production activity and its heavy dependence on empirical relations, experience, and trial and error methods. But, no branch of science and technology can progress fast enough with trial and error methods and thumb rules. Throughout the world market today, there is a continuous struggle for cheaper production with better quality. This can be achieved only through optimal utilization of both material and human resources. Besides, with the advancement in technology, the manufacturing engineers are facing challenging problems requiring development of newer and better methods of production. The required rate of growth in production cannot be achieved through trial and error; a scientific approach is necessary. This has attracted the attention of scientists and engineers, and production has now become a science which was not the case earlier.

The conversion of resource into raw materials is normally done by two subdisciplines of engineering: mining and metallurgy. The real shaping starts from the stage a material is available in raw form. Changing a raw material into a final product generally involves various processes. The major processes a component undergoes before it is converted into a final product are:

1. Casting: primary and secondary forming
2. Machining
3. Joining: assembly and finishing

A material is often subjected to primary forming for producing standard shapes such as those of rods, bars and sheets. However, it may also undergo secondary forming, and this is performed when the objective is to obtain a shape other than the standard shapes.

The three engineering activities that require an understanding of the production processes are (i) designing, (ii) production, and (iii) development of new techniques. At the design stage, manufacturing considerations have to be taken into account, not only for producing the part in the most economical manner, but also for imparting to the part some required properties such as strength and hardness. Besides, in the production shop, a successful engineer must have a thorough understanding of the subject if he has to select and implement the right processes. The selection of the important process parameters is extremely important to achieve success in manufacturing. The third type of activity is development of new manufacturing processes and modification of the existing technology. It has already been mentioned that the production engineers are facing more and more challenging problems, and often such problems cannot be solved with the help of existing conventional methods. Thus, a variety of new processes have evolved during the last two decades. This group of production processes is generally known as *non-conventional* or *new technology.*

Unlike the fundamental subjects in science and engineering, the subject dealing with the production processes is interdisciplinary in nature. Therefore, understanding the science underlying the processes is not simple, since generally the situations are not governed by theoretical models. However, many important generalized conclusions can be drawn with the help of simple models. The same information would otherwise require a large number of experiments or considerable experience.

5.2 PRIMARY PROCESSES

A study of production processes is essential because of the close relationship between process, material and conveniently producible shape or design. Specific product geometries or configurations are feasible for every production process. For this reason, an outline of various processes is taken up first.

5.2.1 Casting Process

In the casting process (Figure 5.1), the material is first liquefied by properly heating it in a suitable furnace. Then the liquid is poured in a mould cavity where it solidifies. Subsequently, the product is taken out of the mould cavity, trimmed and cleaned. A successful casting operation has to focus on the following areas:

1. Preparation of pattern and mould
2. Melting and pouring liquefied metal
3. Solidification and further cooling to room temperature

(i) **Pattern.** A pattern is a replica of the part to be cast and is used in developing the mould cavity. Patterns are made of wood or metal. The mould cavity is the negative of the desired product and contains secondary cavities for pouring and channelling the liquid material into the main cavity.

(ii) **Flask.** It is a sided frame in which a sand mould is made. If the mould is made in, say, two parts, the top portion is termed as *cope,* and the bottom one as *drag.*

(iii) **Core.** A core is usually a piece of a specific sand which rests on core prints in the mould cavity. It is used to produce hollow castings.

(iv) **Greensand mould.** The material for a greensand mould is a mixture of sand, clay, water, organic additives, e.g., wood flour and coal. Ratio is 70–85% sand, 10–20% clay, 3–6% water, and 1–6% additives.

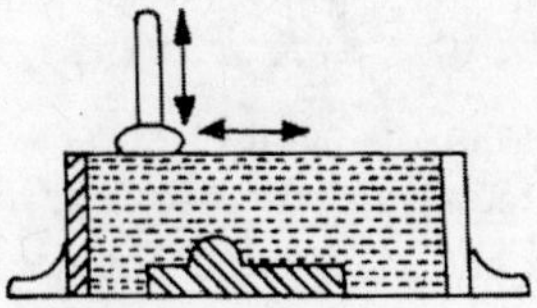

(a) Ramming of sand in drag

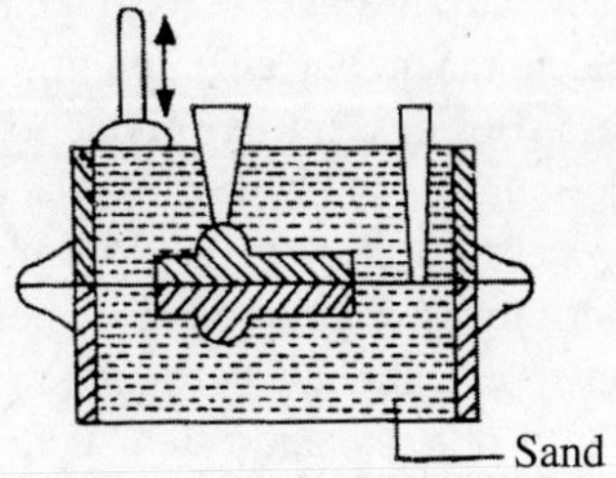

(b) Ramming of sand in cope with sprue and rise in pin position

(c) Drag and cope positions prior to pattern removal

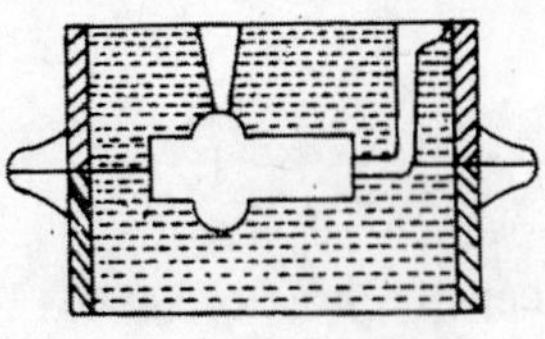

(d) Mould ready for pouring after pattern removal and assembly of drag and cope

FIGURE 5.1 Sand casting steps.

(v) **Dry sand moulding.** As already mentioned, green sand moulds contain up to 7% water, depending on the type and percentage of the binding material. Therefore, this type of mould can be used only for smaller castings with thin walls, since large casting with thick walls would heat the mould, resulting in vaporization of water. This would, in turn, lead to bubbles in the castings. For this reason, moulds for large castings should be dried after they are made in the same way as greensand moulds. The drying operation is carried out in ovens at a temperature ranging from 300 to 650°F (150 to 350°C) for 8 to 48 h, depending upon the type and amount of binder used.

(vi) **Core sand moulding.** When the mould is too big to fit in an oven, moulds are made by assembling several pieces of sand cores. Consequently, patterns are not required and core boxes are employed instead, to make the different sand cores necessary for constructing the mould. Since core-sand mixture (which has superior moulding properties) is used, a very good quality and dimensional accuracy of the casting is obtained.

(vii) **Cement bonded sand moulds.** A mixture of silica sand containing 8–12% cement and 4–6% water is used. When making the mould, the cement-bonded sand mixture must be allowed to harden first, before the pattern is withdrawn. The mould obtained is then allowed to cure for about 3–5 days. Large castings with intricate shapes, accurate dimensions and smooth surfaces are usually produced by this method. The only shortcoming being the long time required for the moulding process.

(viii) **Carbon dioxide process for moulding.** Silica sand is mixed with a binder consisting of 6% solution of sodium silicate (water glass). After the mould is rammed, CO_2 is blown through the sand mixture. As a result, the gel of silica bonds the sand grains together, and no drying is needed. Since the moulds are allowed to harden while the pattern is in position, higher dimensional accuracy of moulds is obtained.

(ix) **Plaster moulds.** A plaster mould is appropriate for casting silver, gold, magnesium, copper and aluminum alloys. The moulding material is a mixture of fine silica sand, asbestos and Plaster of Paris which is used as a binder. Water is added to the mixture until a creamy slurry is obtained, which is then used in moulding. The drying process should be very slow to avoid cracking of the mould.

(x) **Loam moulds.** The loam mould is used for very large jobs. The basic shape of the desired mould is constructed with bricks and mortar (just like a brick house). A loam mixture is used as a moulding material to obtain the desired intricacies of a mould. Templates, sweeps and the like are employed in the moulding process. The loam mixture used in moulding consists of 50% or more loam, with the rest being mainly silica sand. Loam moulds must be thoroughly dried before pouring the molten metal.

(xi) **Shell moulding.** It is a process in which, a thin mould is made around a heated metallic pattern plate. The moulding material is a mixture of dry, fine silica sand (clay content should be kept very low), and 3–8% of a thermosetting resin like phenol formaldehyde or urea-formaldehyde. Conventional dry mixing techniques are used for obtaining the moulding mixture. Specially prepared resin coated sands are also used (see Figure 5.2).

When the moulding mixture drops on to the pattern plate, which is heated to a temperature of 35 to 700°F (18 to 375°C), a shell of about 6 mm thickness is formed. In order to cure the shell completely, it must be heated to 440 to 650°F (230 to 350°C) for about 1–3 min. The shell is then released from the pattern plate by ejector pins. To prevent sticking of the baked shell (sometimes called a biscuit) to the pattern plate, a silicone release agent is applied to the latter before the moulding mixture drops on to it. Figure 5.2 shows a typical sequence used in shell moulding.

Shell moulding is suitable for mass production of thin walled, grey cast iron (and aluminum alloy) castings having a maximum weight between 35 and 45 pounds (15 to 20 kg). However, castings weighing up to 1000 pounds can be made by shell moulding on an individual basis. The advantages of shell moulding include good surface finish, fewer restrictions on casting design, besides rendering itself suitable for automation.

(xii) **Ceramic moulds.** The moulding material is actually a slurry consisting of refractory grains, ceramic binder, water, alcohol and an agent to adjust the pH value. The slurry is poured around the permanent pattern and is allowed to harden before the pattern is withdrawn. Next, the mould is left to dry for some time and then is fired to gain strength. In fact, ceramic moulds are usually preheated before pouring the molten metal. For this reason, they are suitable for casting high pouring temperature alloys. Excellent surface finish and very close tolerances of the castings are among the advantages of this moulding process. Apparently, this leads to the elimination of the machining operations which are usually performed on castings. Therefore, ceramic moulds are certainly advantageous when casting precious or difficult to machine metals as well as for castings with great intricacies.

(xiii) **Precision moulding (investment moulding).** Precision moulding is used when castings with intricate shapes, good dimensional accuracy and very smooth surfaces are required. The process is especially advantageous for high melting, point alloys as well as for those metals which are difficult to machine. It is also most suitable for producing small castings

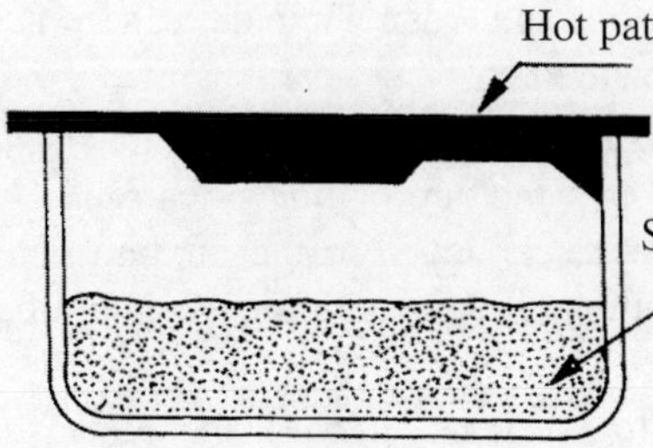

(a) A heated metal pattern is clamped over a box containing sand mixed with thermosetting resin.

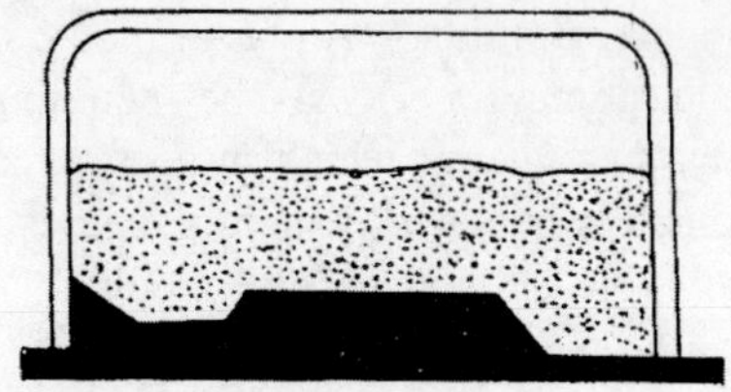

(b) Box and pattern are inverted for a short time. Heat in the pattern gives an initial set to resin next to pattern.

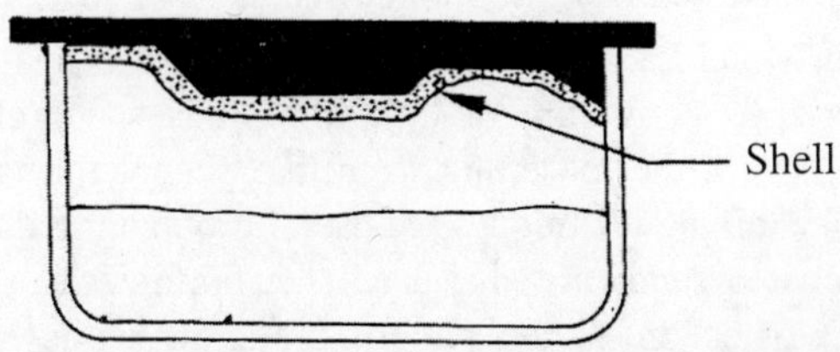

(c) When box and pattern are righted, shell of resin bonded sand are retained on pattern surface while unaffected sand falls into box.

(d) The shell on the pattern is placed in an oven and "heat threated" to thoroughly set the resin. The temperature of the oven and the time required to give the shell its final set varies with resin and other factors.

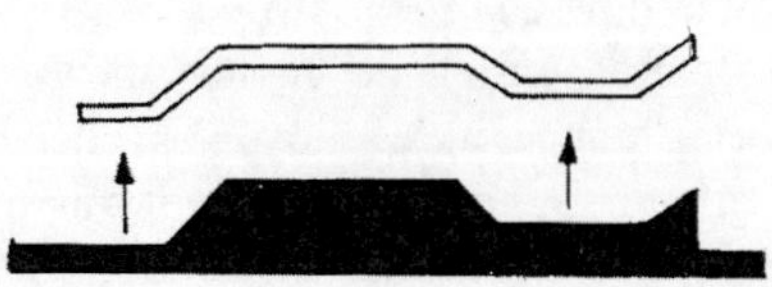

(e) The shell is ejected from the pattern usually by ejector pins built into pattern.

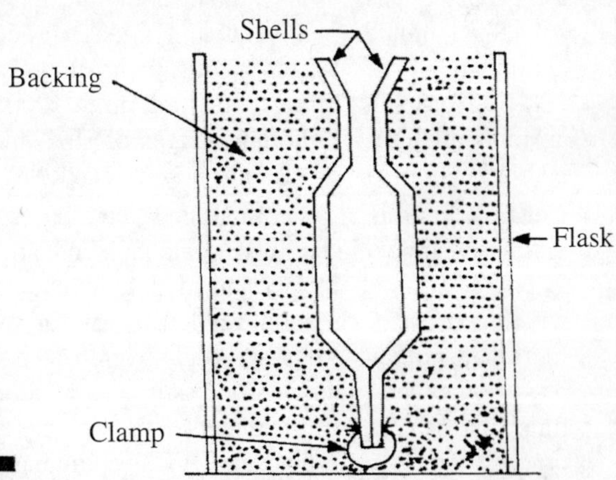

(f) Two shells are assembled with clamps and supported in a flask with metal shot or other backing material. The shell mould is now ready to receive molten metal.

FIGURE 5.2 Shell moulding steps.

having intricate shapes as shown in Figure 5.3, which shows a group of investment castings. A non-permanent pattern, which is usually made of wax, must be prepared for each casting. Therefore, the process is sometimes referred to as lost-wax process. Generally, the precision moulding process involves the following steps:

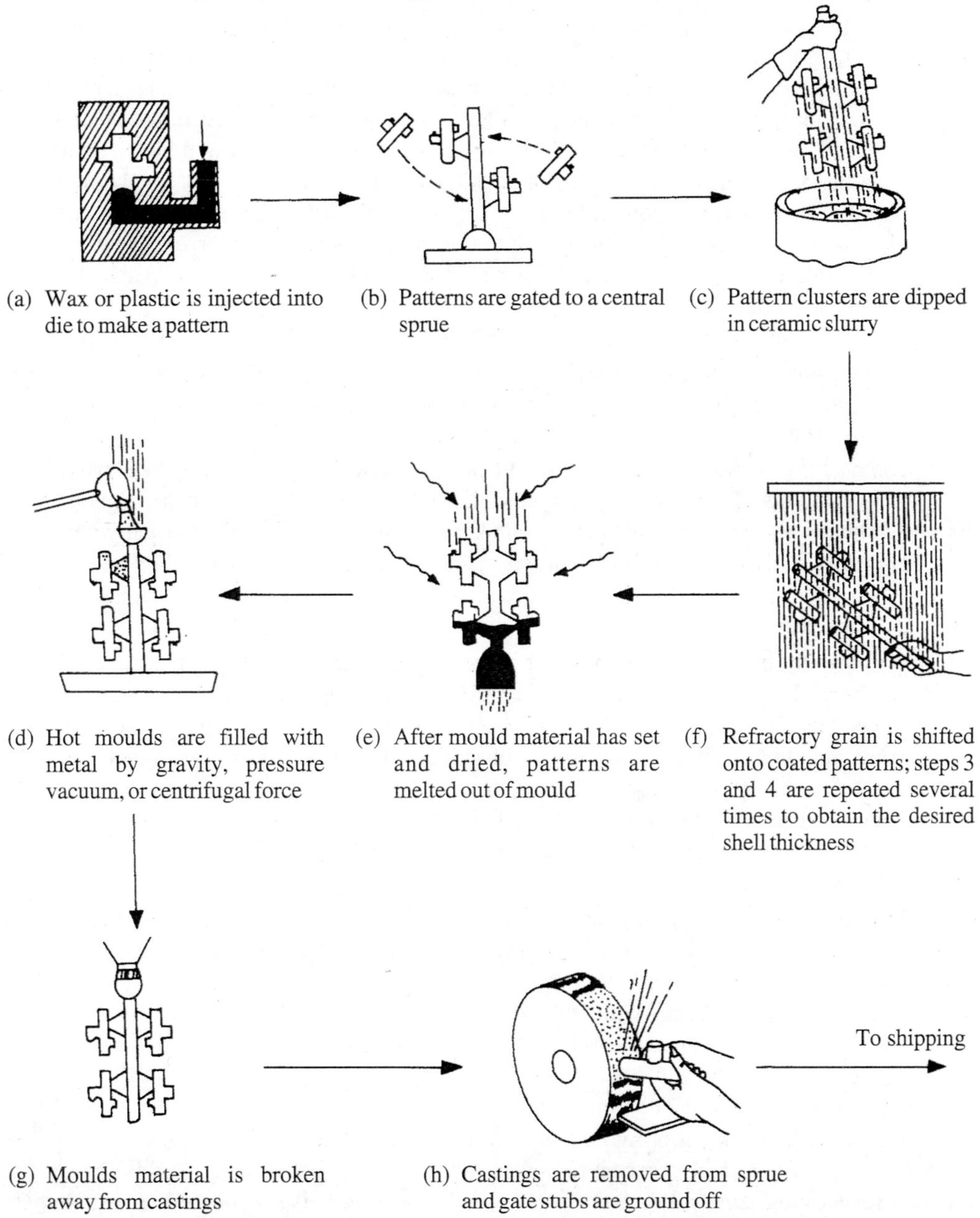

FIGURE 5.3 Lost-wax process.

1. A heat-disposable pattern, together with its gating system, is prepared by injecting wax of plastic into a die cavity.
2. A pattern assembly which is composed of a number of identical patterns is made. Patterns are attached to a runner bar made of wax of plastic, in much the same manner as leaves are attached to branches. A ceramic pouring cup is also attached to the top of the pattern assembly which is sometimes referred to as the tree or cluster.
3. The tree is then invested by separately dipping it into a ceramic slurry, which is composed of silica flour suspended in a solution of ethyl silicate, and then sprinkling it with very fine silica sand. This enables a self-supporting ceramic shell mould of about 6 mm in thickness to be formed all around the wax assembly. Alternatively, a thin ceramic coating is obtained first (precoating); then a cluster is placed in a flask and thick slurry is poured around it as a backup material.
4. The pattern assembly is then baked in an oven or steam autoclave to melt out the wax (or plastic). Hence the dimensions of the mould cavity precisely match those of the desired product.
5. The resulting shell mould is fired at a temperature ranging between 1600 and 1800°F, in order to eliminate all traces of wax and to gain reasonable strength.
6. The molten metal is poured into the mould while the latter is still hot and a cluster of castings is obtained.

Today, the lost-wax process is used in manufacturing larger objects, like cylinder heads and camshafts. The modern process, which is known as the lost-foam method, involves employing a styrofoam replica of the finished product, which is then coated with refractory material and located in a box, where sand is moulded around it by vibratory compaction. When the molten metal is finally poured into the mould, the styrofoam vaporizes, allowing the molten metal to replace it.

(xiv) **Graphite moulds.** Graphite is used in making moulds to receive alloys such as titanium, which can be poured only into inert moulds. The casting process must be performed in a vacuum to eliminate any possibility of contaminating the metal. The graphite moulds can be made either by machining a block of graphite to create the desired mould cavity or by compacting a graphite base aggregate around the pattern and then sintering the obtained mould at a temperature 1800 to 2000°F in reducing atmosphere (see Chapter 6). In fact, graphite mould liners have found widespread industrial applications in the centrifugal casting of brass and bronze.

(xv) **Permanent moulds.** A permanent mould can be used repeatedly for producing casting of the same form and dimension. Permanent moulds are usually made of steel or grey cast iron. Each mould is generally made of two or more pieces, which are assembled together by fitting and clamping. Although the different parts of the mould can be cast to their rough contours, subsequent machining and finishing operations are necessary to eliminate the possibility of sticking of the casting to the mould. Simple cores made of metal are frequently used. When complex cores are required, they are made (usually) of sand or plaster, and the mould is said to be semi-permanent.

Different metals and alloys can be successfully cast in permanent moulds. They include aluminum, magnesium, zinc, lead, copper alloys and cast iron. It is obvious that the mould should be preheated to an appropriate temperature, prior to casting. In fact, the mould operating temperature, which depends on the metal to be cast, is a very important factor in successful permanent mould casting.

Based on the foregoing discussion, we expect the mould life to be dependent on a number of interrelated factors, including the mould material, the metal to be cast, and the operating temperature of the mould. Nevertheless, it can be stated that the life of a permanent mould is about 100,000 pourings or more when casting zinc, magnesium or aluminum alloys, and not more than 20,000 pourings for copper alloys.

Classification of casting according to the metal to be cast. When classified according to the metal to be cast, castings are either ferrous or non-ferrous. The ferrous casting includes cast steels and the family of cast irons, whereas the non-ferrous casting includes all other metals such as aluminium, copper, magnesium, titanium and their alloys. Each of these metals and alloys is melted in a particular type of foundry furnace, which may not be appropriate for melting other metals and alloys. Also, moulding method and material, as well as fluxes, degassers and additives depend on the metal to be cast. Therefore, this classification method is popular in foundry practice. The following is a brief discussion of each of these cast alloys.

(i) **Ferrous metal.** Cast steel is smelted in open-hearth furnaces, converters, electric arc furnaces and electric induction furnaces. It can be either plain-carbon, low alloy or high alloy steel. However, plain carbon casting steel is by far the most commonly produced type. As compared with cast iron, steel certainly has poorer casting properties, namely, higher melting point, higher shrinkage and poor fluidity. Steel is also more susceptible to hot and cold cracks after the casting process. Therefore, cast steel is mostly subjected to heat treatment to relieve the internal stresses and improve mechanical properties.

In order to control the oxygen content of molten steels, either aluminium, silicon or manganese is used as a deoxidizer. Aluminium is the most commonly used of these elements because of its availability, low cost, and effectiveness.

There is a major difference between cast steel and the wrought product. This involves the presence of a 'skin' of thin layer, just below the surface of a casting, where scales, oxides and impurities are concentrated. Also, that layer may be chemically or structurally different from the base metal. Therefore, it has to be removed by machining in a single deep cut, which is achieved through reducing the cutting speed to half of the conventionally recommended value.

Grey cast iron is characterized by the presence of free graphite flakes, when its microstructure is examined under the microscope. This kind of microstructure is, in fact, responsible for the superior properties possessed by grey cast iron. For instance, this dispersion of graphite flakes acts as a lubricant during machining of grey cast iron, thus eliminating the need for matching lubricants and coolants. As compared with any other ferrous cast alloys, grey cast iron certainly possesses superior machinability. The presence of these graphite flakes enables absorbing of vibrations that characterize grey cast iron. The compressive strength is better—normally four times its tensile strength. Grey cast iron finds widespread applications, mainly because of its two properties: for machine tool beds and the like. On the other hand, it has some disadvantages such as its low tensile strength, brittleness and poor weldability. Nevertheless, it has the lowest casting temperature, least shrinkage, and the best castability of all cast ferrous alloys.

The cupola is the most widely used foundry furnace for producing and melting grey cast iron. The chemical composition, microstructure, as also the properties of the obtained casting are determined by the constituents of the charge of the cupola furnace. Therefore, the composition and properties of the grey cast iron are controlled by changing the percentages of the charge constituents and by adding inoculants and alloying elements. Commonly used inoculants include calcium silicate, ferro silicon and ferro manganese. An inoculant is added to the molten metal (either in cupola spout or the ladle) and usually amounts to 0.1–0.5% of the molten iron by weight. It acts as a deoxidizer and hinders the growth of precipitated graphite flakes. It is also important to remember as a product designer that the properties of grey cast iron are also dependent on the dimensions (in fact, the thickness of the walls) of that product because the cooling rate is adversely affected by the cross-section of the casting. Actually, the cooling rate is high for small castings with thin walls, sometimes yielding white cast iron. For this reason, grey cast iron must be specified by the strength of critical cross-sections.

(ii) **White cast iron.** When the molten cast iron alloy is rapidly chilled after being poured into the mould cavity, dissolved carbon does not have enough time to precipitate in the form of flakes. Instead, it remains chemically combined with iron in the form of cementite. This material is primarily responsible for the white crystalline appearance of a fractured surface of white cast iron. Cementite is also responsible for high hardness, extreme brittleness, and excellent wear resistance of such cast iron. Industrial applications of white cast iron include components subjected to abrasion. Sometimes grey cast iron can be chilled to produce a surface layer of white cast iron in order to combine to advantageous properties of the two types of cast iron. In such a case, the product metal is usually referred to as chilled cast iron.

(iii) **Ductile cast iron.** Ductile cast iron is also called *nodular cast iron* and spheroidal graphite cast iron. It is obtained by adding small amounts of magnesium to a very pure molten alloy of grey iron that has been subjected to desulphurization. Sometimes, a small quantity of cerium is also added to prevent the harmful effects of impurities like aluminium, titanium and lead. The presence of magnesium and cerium causes the graphite to precipitate during solidification of the molten alloy in the form of small spheroids, rather thin flakes, as in the case of grey cast iron. This microstructural change results in marked increase in ductility, strength, toughness and stiffness of ductile iron, as compared with such properties of grey cast iron, because the stress concentration effect of a flake is far higher than that of a spheroid (remember what you learned in fracture mechanics). Ductile cast iron is used for making machine parts like axles, brackets, levers, crank shaft housing, die pads and die shoes.

(iv) **Compacted graphite cast iron.** Compacted graphite cast iron falls between grey and ductile cast irons, both in its microstructure and mechanical properties. The free graphite in this type of iron takes the form of short, blunt and interconnected flakes. The mechanical properties of compacted graphite cast iron are superior to those of grey cast iron but are inferior to those of ductile cast iron. The thermal conductivity and damping capacity of compacted graphite cast iron approach those of grey cast iron. Compacted graphite cast iron has some applications in the manufacture of diesel engines.

(v) **Malleable cast iron.** Malleable cast iron is obtained in two stages: by heat treatment and graphitizations. Heat treatment of white cast iron with appropriate chemical combination: The hard white cast iron becomes malleable after heat treatment due to microstructural changes. The combined carbon separates as free graphite, which takes the form of nodules. Since the raw material for producing malleable cast iron is actually white cast iron, there are always limitations on casting design. Large cross-sections and thick walls are not permitted, since it is difficult to produce a white cast iron part with these geometric characteristics.

There are two basic types of malleable cast iron: pearlitic and ferritic (black heart). Although the starting alloy for both types is the same (white cast iron), the heat treatment cycle and the atmosphere of the heat-treating furnace are different in each case. Furnaces with oxidizing atmospheres are employed for producing pearlitic malleable cast iron, whereas furnaces with neutral atmospheres are used for producing ferritic malleable cast iron. When we compare the properties of these two types, we find that the ferritic grade normally has higher ductility and better machinability, but lower strength and hardness. Pearlitic grades can, however, be subjected to further surface hardening where the depth of the hardened layer can be controlled.

Figure 5.4 shows the heat-treating sequence for producing malleable cast iron, which is usually referred to as the malleabilizing cycle. As can be seen from the figure, the malleabilizing cycle includes two stages. In the first stage, the casting is slowly heated to a temperature of about 1700°F and kept at that temperature for about 30 hours. The second step involves decreasing the temperature very slowly at the rate of 5 to 9°F per hour from a temperature of about 1450°F to a temperature of 1200°F, where the process ends and the casting is taken out of furnace. The whole malleabilizing cycle takes normally about 60 hours.

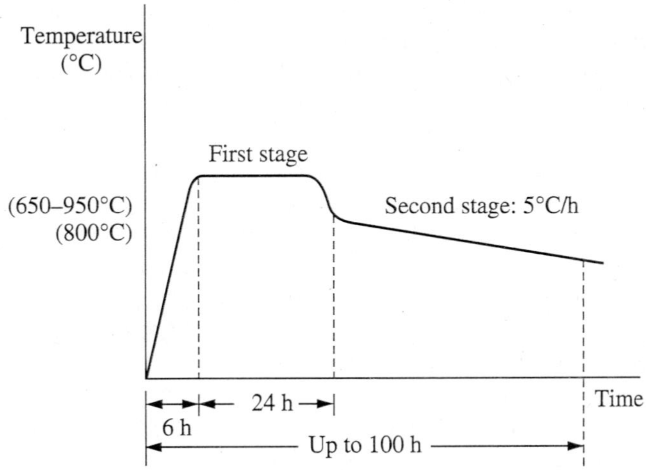

FIGURE 5.4 Heat treatment cycle.

Malleable cast iron is normally selected when the engineering application requires good machinability and ductility. Excellent castability and high toughness are other properties that make malleable cast iron suitable for flanges, pipe fitting and valve parts for pressure service at elevated temperature, steering-gear housings, mounting brackets, compressors, crankshafts and hubs, and the like.

(vi) **Alloyed cast iron.** Alloying elements like chromium, nickel, molybdenum are added to cast iron to manipulate the microstructure of the alloy. The goal is to improve the mechanical properties of the casting and to impart some special properties to it, like wear resistance, corrosion resistance and heat resistance. A typical example of the alloyed cast iron is the white cast iron containing nickel and chromium, which is used for corrosion resistant (and abrasion-resistant) applications like water pump housings and grinding balls (in a ball mill).

(vii) **Non-ferrous metals.** Cast aluminium and its alloys continue to gain wider industrial applications, especially in the automotive and electronic industries because of its distinct strength-to-weight ratio and high electrical conductivity. Alloying elements can be added to aluminium to improve its mechanical properties and metallurgical characteristics. Silicon, magnesium, zinc, tin and copper are the elements most commonly alloyed with aluminium. In fact, most metallic elements can be alloyed with aluminium, but commercial and industrial applications are limited to those just mentioned.

The real advantage of aluminium is that it can be cast by almost all casting processes. Nevertheless, the common methods for casting aluminium include die casting, gravity casting (in sand and permanent moulds) and investment casting.

The presence of hydrogen, when melting aluminium, always results in unsound castings. Typical sources of hydrogen are furnace atmosphere and charged metal. When the furnace has a reducing atmosphere because of incomplete combustion of fuel, carbon monoxide and hydrogen are generated and absorbed by the molten metal. The presence of contaminants like moisture, oil or grease which are chemically stable at elevated temperature can also liberate hydrogen. Unfortunately, hydrogen is highly soluble in molten aluminium, but has limited solubility in solidified aluminium. Therefore, any hydrogen absorbed by the molten metal is liberated or expelled during solidification to form porosity that may vary in shape and size. Hydrogen may also react with (and reduce) metallic oxide to form water vapour which again causes porosity. Hydrogen must be completely removed from molten aluminium before casting. This is achieved by using appropriate degassers—chlorine and nitrogen are considered to be traditional degassers for aluminium. Either of these is blown through molten aluminium to eliminate any hydrogen. However, since chlorine is toxic and nitrogen is not that efficient, organic chloride fluxing compounds (chlorinated hydrocarbons) are added to generate chloride within the melt. They are commercially available in different forms such as blocks, powders and tablets. The most commonly used fluxing degasser is perhaps hexachloroethane. Another source of problems, when casting aluminium, is iron which dissolves readily in molten aluminium. Therefore, care must be taken to spray (or cover) iron lades and all iron surfaces that come into direct contact with the molten aluminium with ceramic coating. This extends the service life of the iron tools used and enables one to obtain sound castings.

The most important cast aluminium alloys are those containing silicon. These serve to improve castability, reduce thermal expansion, and increase wear resistance of aluminium. Small additions of magnesium make these alloys heat-treatable, thus enabling controlling of the final properties of casting. Aluminium-silicon alloys (with 1–5% silicon) are used in making automobile parts, e.g., pistons and aerospace components.

Aluminium-copper alloys are characterized by their very high tensile strength to weight ratio. They are, therefore, mainly used for manufacturing of premium quality aerospace parts. Nevertheless, these alloys have poorer castability than aluminium-silicon alloys. Also, the amount of the copper constituent, in excess of 12%, makes the alloy brittle. Copper additions of up to 5% are normally used and result in improved high temperature properties and machinability.

Additions of magnesium to aluminium result in improved corrosion resistance and machinability, higher strength and attractive appearance of the casting, when anodized. However, aluminium-magnesium alloys are generally difficult to cast. Zinc alloys have good machinability and moderately high strength. But these alloys are generally prone to hot cracking and have poor castability and high shrinkage. Therefore, zinc is used with aluminium in combination with other alloying elements and is employed in such cases for promoting very high strength. Aluminium tin alloys are used where high load carrying capacity and fatigue strength are required. Therefore, they are used for making bearings and bushings.

(viii) **Cast copper alloys.** The melting temperatures of cast copper alloys are far higher than those of aluminium, zinc or magnesium alloys. Cast copper alloys can be grouped according to their composition into four groups:

1. Pure copper and high copper alloys
2. Brasses, i.e., alloys including zinc as the principal alloying element
3. Bronzes, i.e., alloys including tin as the principal alloying element
4. Nickel silvers, including copper-nickel alloys and copper-nickel-zinc alloys

Cast copper alloys are melted in crucible furnaces, open flame furnaces, induction furnaces or indirect arc furnaces. The selection of a furnace depends on the type of alloy to be melted as well as the purity and quantity required. In melting pure copper, high copper alloys, bronzes or nickel silvers, precaution must be taken to prevent contamination of the molten metal with hydrogen. It is recommended that the atmosphere of the furnace be slightly oxidizing and a covering flux be used. Prior to casting, however, the molten metal should be deoxidized. For this, phosphorus, in the form of phosphorus copper flux, should be added. On the other hand, brass is usually not susceptible to hydrogen porosity. The problem associated with melting brass is the vaporization and oxidation of zinc. As a remedy, the atmosphere of the furnace should be slightly reducing. Also, a covering flux should be used to prevent vaporization of zinc; then the deoxidizing flux (like phosphorus copper) is added immediately prior to pouring. The applications of the cast copper alloys include pipe fitting, ornaments, propeller hubs and blades, steam valves and bearings.

(ix) **Zinc alloys.** The family of zinc alloys is characterized by low melting temperature. Zinc alloys also possess good fluidity. Therefore, they can be produced in thin section by submerged hot chamber die casting. Alloying elements include aluminium, copper, and magnesium.

(x) **Magnesium alloys.** The main characteristic of magnesium is its low density which is lower than that of any other commercial metal. The potential of magnesium is good, since it constitutes a sensible percentage of sea water. Most of the disadvantages and limitations of magnesium can be eliminated by alloying. Magnesium alloys are usually cast in permanent moulds.

Design considerations for casting. A product designer who selects casting as the primary manufacturing process should make a design not only to serve the function (by being capable of withstanding the loads and the environmental conditions to which it is going to be subjected during its service life), but also to facilitate or favour the casting process. The following are some design considerations and guidelines.

1. *Promote directional solidification when designing the mould.* The riser should be properly dimensioned and located to promote solidification of the casting towards riser. In other words, the presence of large sections or heat masses in locations distant from the risers should be avoided and good rising practice, which has been previously discussed, should be followed. Failure to do so may result in shrinkage cavities, porosity or cracks in those large sections distant from the risers.
2. *Avoid the shortcomings of columnar solidification.* Dendrites often start to form on the cold surface of the mould and then grow to form a columnar casting structure. This almost always results in planes of weakness at sharp corners, as illustrated in Figure 5.5(a). Therefore, rounding of the edges is necessary to eliminate the development of planes of weakness as shown in Figure 5.5(b).

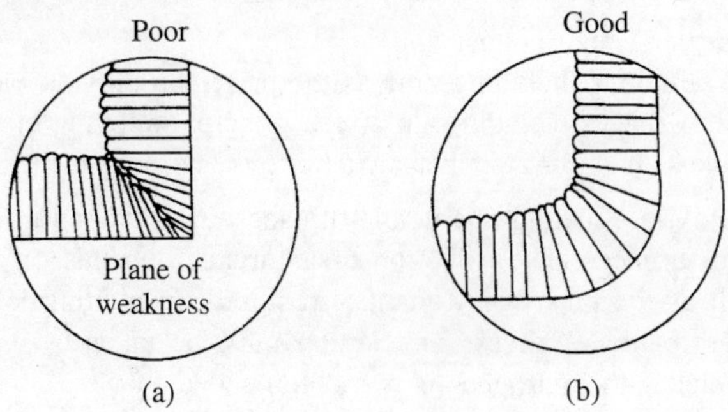

FIGURE 5.5 Good and poor design practice for casting.

3. *Avoid hot spots.* Certain shapes, because of their effect on the rate of heat dissipation during solidification, tend to promote the formation of the shrinkage cavities. This is always the case at any particular location where the rate of solidification is slower than that at the surrounding regions of the casting. The rate of solidification (and the rate of heat dissipation, to start with) is slower at locations having a low ratio of surface area to volume. Such locations are usually referred to as *hot spots* of the foundry practice. Unless precaution is taken during the desired phase, hot spots as also shrinkage cavities are likely to occur at the L, T, V, Y and + junctions. Shrinkage cavities can be avoided by modifying the design. Also, it is always advisable to avoid abrupt changes in sections and to use taper, together with generous radii, to join thin-to-heavy section as shown in Figure 5.6.

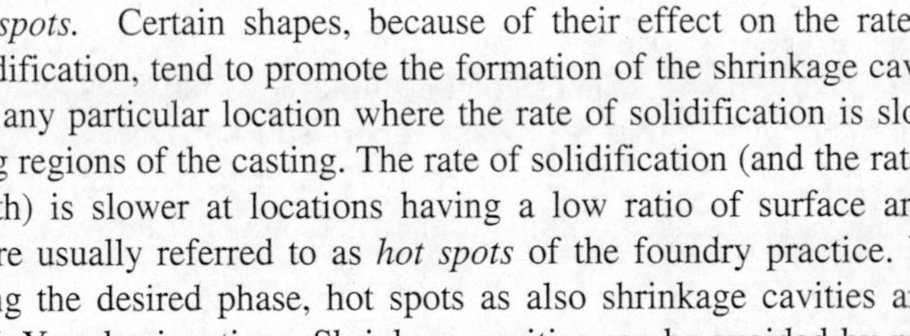

FIGURE 5.6 Gradual change in section as design recommendations.

4. *Avoid the causes of hot tears.* Hot tears are casting defects caused by tensile stresses as a result of restraining a part of the casting. Figure 5.7(a) indicates a casting design that would promote hot tears, whereas Figure 5.7(b) shows a recommended design that would eliminate the formation of hot tears.

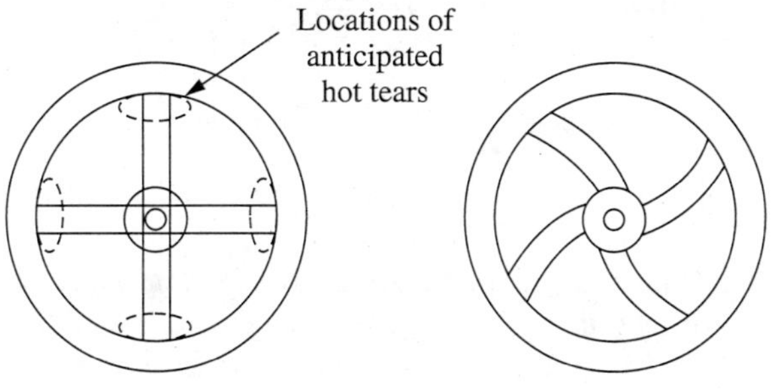

(a) Poor design (b) Good design

FIGURE 5.7 Formation of hot tears and their remedy.

Ensure easy pattern drawing: It is important that the pattern can be easily withdrawn from the mould. Undercuts, protruding bosses (especially if their axes do not fall within the parting plane), and the like should be avoided.

Classification of casting according to solidification and further cooling to room temperature

(i) **Gravity die casting.** In gravity die casting, permanent mould is used. The liquid metal is poured into a non-expandable mould under the force of gravity. The process is normally used for cast iron and, occasionally, for non-ferrous castings. The mould is made of heat resistant cast iron and is provided with fins on its other surface for efficient air cooling. The inner surface of the mould cavity is sprayed with an oil-carbon-silica mixture before each pouring.

(ii) **Die casting.** In the die casting process, unlike in gravity casting, the liquid metal is forced into the mould cavity under high pressure. The process is used for casting a low melting temperature material, e.g., aluminium and zinc alloys. The mould, normally called a die, is made in two halves (see Figure 5.8), of which one is fixed and the other moving. Medium carbon, low alloy tool steel is the most common die material. The die is cooled by water for effective casting. This also increases the die life. The process is referred to as a hot chamber (Figure 5.9) or a cold chamber (Figure 5.8) process, depending on whether the melting

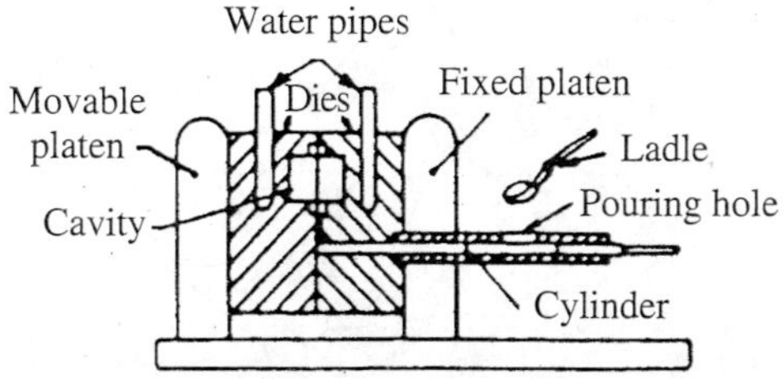

FIGURE 5.8 Cold chamber die casting.

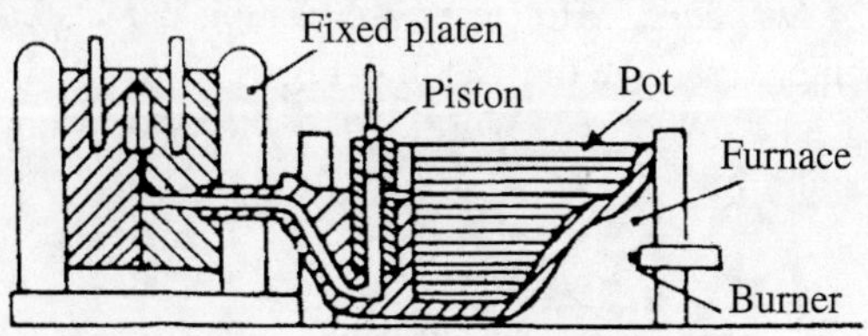

FIGURE 5.9 Hot chamber die casting.

furnace is an integral part of the mould. Since the liquid metal is forced into the die with higher external pressure, sections which are very much thinner, can be cast by this process. The process, when applied to a plastic casting, is called *injection moulding* (see Figure 5.10). For moulding of thermosetting plastics, the granules are heated in a separate chamber and transferred through gating to the mould casting. This is termed as *transfer moulding.*

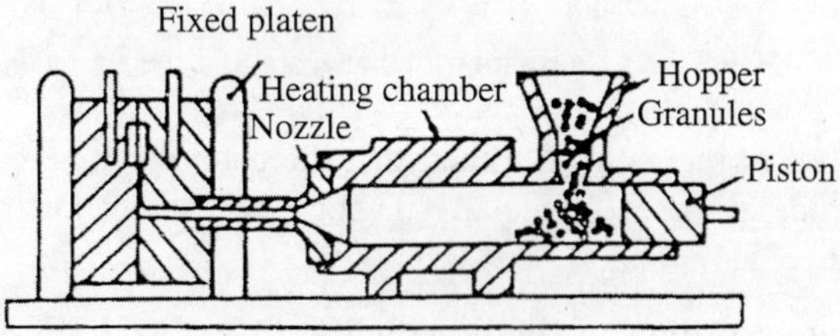

FIGURE 5.10 Injection moulding.

(iii) **Centrifugal casting.** The centrifugal casting process is normally carried out in a permanent mould which is rotated during the solidification of the casting, as illustrated in Figure 5.11. For producing a hollow part, the axis of rotation is placed at the centre of the desired casting. The speed of rotation is maintained high so as to produce a centripetal acceleration of the order of 60 g to 75 g. The centrifugal action segregates the less dense non-metallic inclusions near the centre of rotation. It should be noted that the casting of hollow parts needs no core in this process. Solid parts can also be cast by this process by placing the entire mould cavity on one side of the axis of rotation. The castings produced by this method are very dense. By having several mould cavities, more than one casting can be made simultaneously.

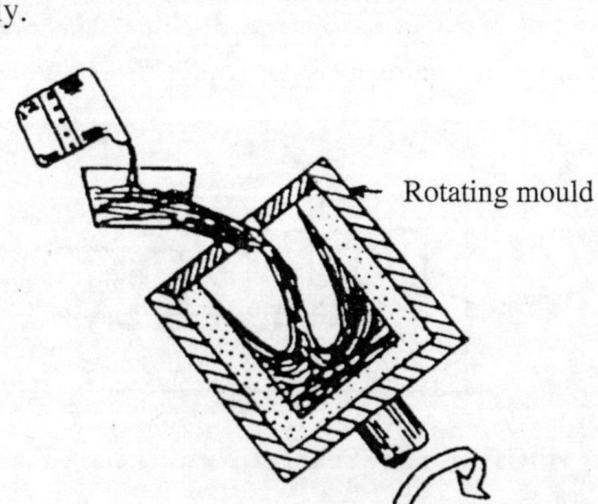

FIGURE 5.11 Centrifugal casting.

5.2.2 Forming Process

Forming can be defined as a process in which the desired size and shape are obtained through the plastic deformation of a material. The stresses induced during the process are greater than the yield strength, but less than the fracture strength of the material. The type of loading may be tensile, compressive, bending or shearing or a combination of these. This is a very economical process as the desired shape, size and finish can be obtained without any significant loss of material. Moreover, a part of the input energy is utilized in improving the strength of the product through strain hardening.

Analysis of metal forming mechanics. During the process of metal forming, a material is deformed inelastically. Considering a tensile test specimen, let l_1 be the initial gauge length. During the process of plastic flow and necking, the gauge length changes its value continuously. However, considering discrete steps of gauge length l_1, l_2, l_3, ..., we can write:

$$\text{Total strain } \varepsilon = (dl_1/l_1) + (dl_2/l_2) + (dl_3/l_3) + \cdots$$

Therefore,

$$\varepsilon = \int_{l_i}^{l_f} (dl/l) = \ln(l_f/l_i)$$

where,

$$l_f = \text{final length}, \qquad l_i = \text{initial length}$$

Since the volume V is constant, the equation can be written on volume constancy, as:

$$V = l_i A_i = l_f A_f \qquad \text{or} \qquad (l_f/l_i) = (A_i/A_f)$$

Thus,

$$\text{Total strain} = \text{true strain} = \varepsilon = \ln(A_i/A_f)$$

The work done per unit volume in homogeneous deformation is:

$$W = (\text{True stress} \times \text{True strain}) = (\sigma_{av} \times \ln(A_i/A_f))$$

If the effects of internal friction due to internal metallic shearing at shear or slip planes is not accounted and external friction is also not considered, the above formula can be applied to problems such as extrusion or wire drawing. In extrusion, considering ram pressure, p and area = 1. The work done per unit volume of material for a displacement of the billet by unit distance = $(p \times 1)$ = $\sigma_{av} \ln(A_i/A_f)$.

As a result of metal working research, Rao and Johnson [2], and some others have found that

$$p = 2K[a + b \ln(A_1/A_2)]$$

where a = 0.7, a factor that accounts for redundant work or internal metallic shear, and b = 1.5, a factor that accounts for friction between billet and the container wall.

(i) **Slab method of metal working analysis.** In the slab method, a thin slab of thickness (dx) of material being plastically deformed is considered. Two conditions are applied to the material in the slab.

1. Conditions of equilibrium are fulfilled. That is, the summation of all forces in the x-direction is zero; $\Sigma F_x = 0$.

2. The slab is in a fully plastic state. That is the difference of principal stresses acting in two mutually perpendicular directions on the slab equals twice the yield shear stress of the slab material. This is also called the condition of plasticity.

Figure 5.12 indicates the problem of drawing of a sheet of half thickness (h_b) to a reduction resulting in half thickness (h_a) with a back tension σ_b applied to the sheet. Consider only the upper half above the centre line.

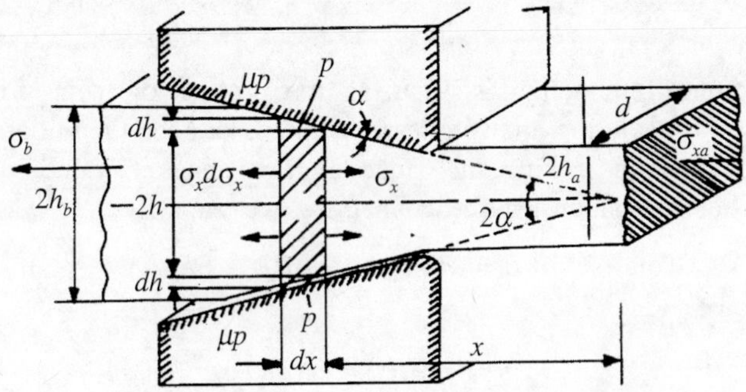

FIGURE 5.12 Slab method of metal working.

(ii) **Condition of equilibrium.** For equilibrium along the x-axis,

$$(\sigma_x + d\sigma_x)(h + dh) - \sigma_x \times h + p\,(dx/\cos\alpha)(\sin\alpha) + \mu p\,(dx/\cos\alpha)\cos\alpha = 0$$

where

$$h = xt_g\,\alpha, \quad (dh) = (dx\,t_g\alpha) \tag{5.1}$$

Therefore,

$$\sigma_x dh + hd\sigma_x + p\,dh + \mu p\,dh\cot\alpha = 0 \tag{5.2}$$

B is put equal to ($\mu\cot\alpha$) in the subsequent calculations.

(iii) **Condition of plasticity.** Now, we can utilize the condition of plasticity to eliminate p from Eq. (5.2). Then,

$$[\sigma_x + p] = 2K = S \tag{5.3}$$

where K is the shear flow stress and S is the direct yield stress. Substituting in Eq. (5.2) and arranging, we get,

$$\frac{d\sigma_x}{\sigma_x + (S - \sigma_x)(1 + B)} = -\frac{dh}{h}$$

or

$$\frac{d\sigma_x}{B\sigma_x - S(1 + B)} = -\frac{dh}{h}$$

or

$$[1/B]\ln[B\sigma_x - S(1 + B)] = \ln(h) + C \tag{5.4}$$

To evaluate the constant of integration, we apply the boundary condition that $h = h_b$, $\sigma_x = \sigma_b$. Therefore,

$$C = 1/B\ln\,[B\sigma_b - S(1 + B)\} - \ln(h_b) \tag{5.5}$$

Substituting from Eq. (5.5) into Eq. (5.4), we get

$$1/B\ln[B\sigma_x - S(1 + B)] = \ln(h) + 1/B\ln[B\sigma_b - S(1 + B)\} - \ln(h_b)$$

$$\ln[B\sigma_x - S(1 + B)] = \ln[(h/h_b)^B\,\{B\sigma_b - S(1 + B)\}]$$

Taking antilog, we get:

$$[B\sigma_x - S(1 + B)] = (h/h_b)^B\,[B\sigma_b - S(1 + B)]$$

Dividing throughout by SB, we get

$$\left[\frac{\sigma_x}{S} - \frac{1+B}{B}\right] = (h/h_b)^B \left[\frac{\sigma_b}{S} - \frac{1+B}{B}\right]$$

Therefore,

$$\frac{\sigma_x}{S} = \frac{1+B}{B}\left[1 - \left(\frac{h}{h_b}\right)^B\right] + \left(\frac{h}{h_b}\right)^B \left[\frac{\sigma_b}{S}\right] \tag{5.6}$$

To calculate the value of front tension, put $\sigma_x = \sigma_{xa}$ and $h = h_a$ in Eq. (5.6). Then we have

$$\frac{\sigma_x}{S} = \frac{1+B}{B}\left[1 - \left(\frac{h_a}{h_b}\right)^B\right] + \left(\frac{h_a}{h_b}\right)^B \left[\frac{\sigma_b}{S}\right] \tag{5.7}$$

Without backpull, Eq. (5.7) reduces to

$$\boxed{\frac{\sigma_{xa}}{S} = \frac{1+B}{B}[1 - (h_b/h_b)^B} \tag{5.8}$$

(iv) **Particular cases.** Equation 5.8 is very important and can be utilized to develop analogous expressions for rod drawing, tube drawing etc., if (h_a/h_b) is regarded as an area ratio. For example, in the case of rod drawing or wire drawing,

$$\frac{\sigma_{xa}}{S} = \frac{1+B}{B}[1 - (D_a/D_b)^{2B}]$$

Note that the area of rod is proportional to the square of diameter. For tube drawing.

$$\frac{\sigma_{xa}}{S} = \frac{1+B}{B}[1 - (D_a/D_b)^{B}]$$

Note that the area of tube annulus is proportional to $D \times h$.

Note. It can be proved that in the case of extrusion,

$$\frac{\sigma_{xa}}{S} = \frac{1+B}{B}[1 - (h_b/h_a)^{B}]$$

To facilitate further understanding of the topic, an illustrative example is taken up.

Example. Determine the power required to draw wire from 12.5 mm to 10 mm in diameter at 100 m/min. $\mu = 0.1$, $\alpha = 4°$, $S = 2K = 30$ kg/mm^2. Also calculate the maximum reduction possible.

Solution

$$D_a = 10,\ D_b = 12.5,\ B = \mu \cot\alpha = (1.43),\ 2K = 30 \text{ kg/mm}^2$$

$$\frac{\sigma_{xa}}{S} = \frac{1+B}{B}[1 - (D_a/D_b)^{2B}]$$

$$\frac{\sigma_{xa}}{30} = \frac{1+1.43}{1.43}[1-(10/12.5)^{2.86}] = 0.8012$$

$$\sigma_{xa} = 30 \times 0.8012 = 24.03 \text{ kg/mm}^2$$

$$\text{Draw force} = (\pi/4)\, D_a \sigma_{xa} = (\pi/4) \times 100 \times 24.03 = 1886 \text{ kg}$$

$$\text{Power required} = [1886 \times 100] \text{ kg m/min} = 41.92 \text{ HP}$$

To obtain the maximum reduction, putting $\sigma_{xa} = S$, we have

$$\frac{\sigma_{xa}}{S} = 1 = \frac{2.43}{1.43}\left[1-\left(\frac{D_a}{D_b}\right)^{2.86}\right] \qquad \therefore \qquad \left(\frac{D_a}{D_b}\right) = 0.735$$

The earlier magnitude of reduction was 0.8, while the tensile stress, σ_{xa} was 24.03 kg/mm^2.

Forming processes: Practical details. The forming process can be grouped under two broad categories: (i) cold forming and (ii) hot forming. If the working temperature is higher than the recrystallization temperature of the material, then the process is called *hot forming*. Otherwise, the process is termed *cold forming*. The flow stress behaviour of a material is entirely different above and below its recrystallization temperature. During hot working, a large amount of plastic deformation can be imparted without significant strain hardening which renders the material brittle. The frictional characteristics of the two forming processes are also entirely different, e.g., the coefficient of friction in cold the forming is generally of the order of 0.1, whereas the coefficient of friction in hot forming can be as high as 0.6. Further, hot forming lowers the material strength, so that a machine with a reasonable capacity can be used even for a product having large dimensions. The typical forming processes are:

- Rolling
- Forging
- Drawing
- Deep drawing
- Bending
- Extrusion
- Punching and blanking

For a better understanding of the mechanics of various forming operations, we shall briefly discuss each of these processes. Two other common production processes, namely, punching and blanking, though not classified under the forming processes, will also be briefly considered, because of their similarity to the forming processes.

(i) **Rolling.** In this process, the job is drawn by means of friction though a regulated opening between two power-driven rolls (Figure 5.13). The shape and size of the product are decided by the gap between the rolls and their contours. This is a very useful process for the production of sheet metal and various common sections, e.g., rail, channel, angle and round.

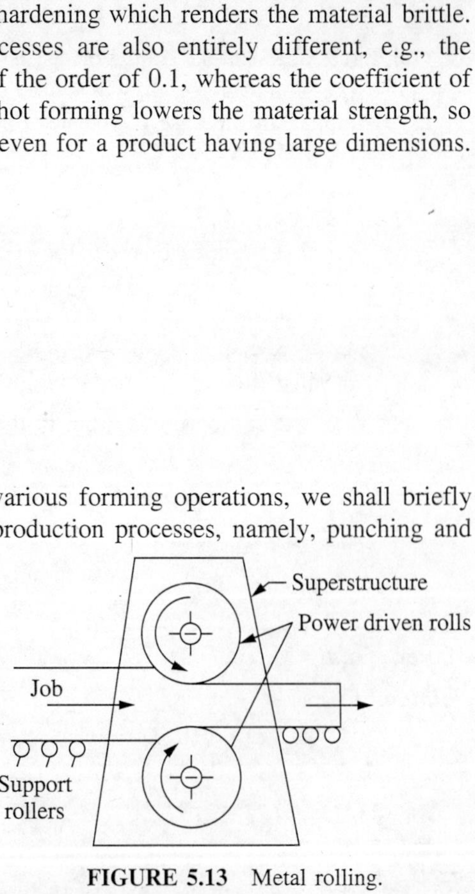

FIGURE 5.13 Metal rolling.

(ii) **Forging.** In forging, the material is squeezed between two or more dies to alter its shape and size. Depending on the situation, the dies may be open (Figure 5.14(a)) or closed (Figure 5.14(b)).

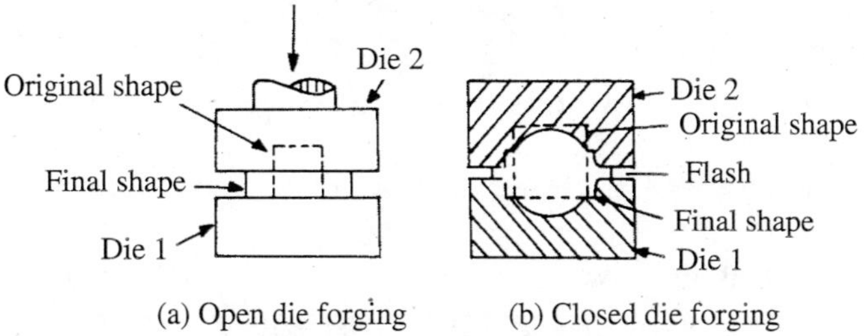

FIGURE 5.14 Metal forging.

(iii) **Drawing.** In this process, the cross-section of a wire or that of a bar or tube is reduced by pulling the workpiece through the conical orifice of a die. Figure 5.15 represents the operation schematically. When more reduction is required, it may be necessary to perform the operation in several passes.

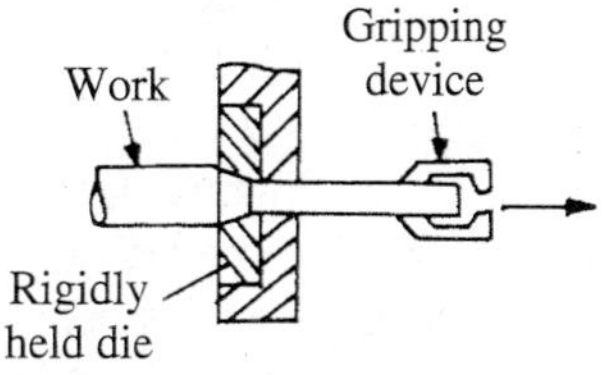

FIGURE 5.15 Wire drawing.

(iv) **Deep drawing.** In deep drawing, a cup-shaped product is obtained from a flat sheet metal with the help of punch and die. Figure 5.16 shows the operation schematically. The sheet metal is held over the die by means of a blank holder to avoid defects in the product.

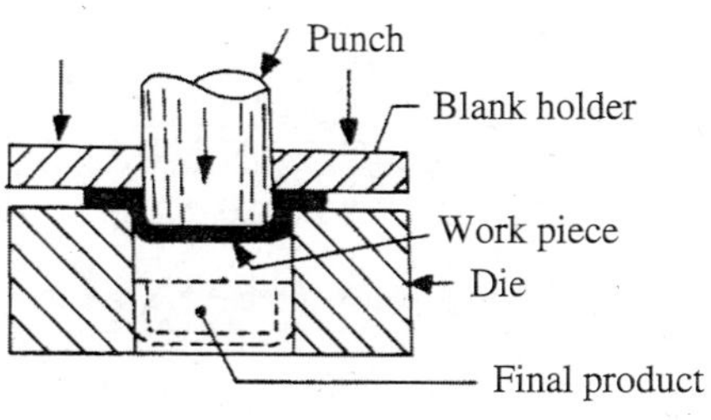

FIGURE 5.16 Sheet metal drawing.

(v) **Bending.** As the name implies, this is a process of bending a metal sheet plastically to obtain in desired shape. This is achieved by a set of suitably designed punch and die. A typical process is shown schematically in Figure 5.17.

(vi) **Extrusion.** This is a process which is basically similar to the closed die forging. However, in this operation, the work piece is compressed in a closed space, forcing the material to flow out through a suitable opening, called a die (Figure 5.18). In this process, only the shapes with constant cross-section (die outlet cross-section) can be produced.

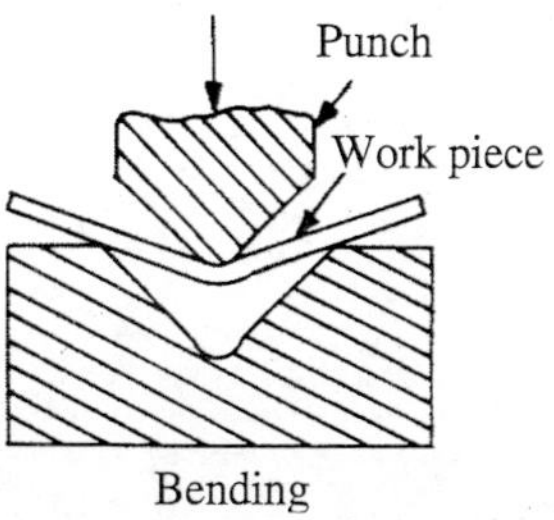

FIGURE 5.17 Sheet metal bending.

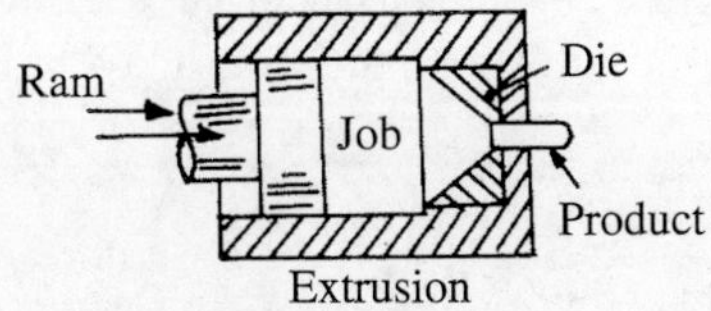

FIGURE 5.18 Forward extrusion.

Apart from the foregoing processes, there are various other forming operations which we shall take up later.

(vii) **Punching and blanking.** As we have already noted, the punching and blanking processes cannot, strictly speaking, be grouped under the forming operations. In these processes, a finite volume from a sheet metal is removed by using a die and punch. If the final product happens to be the removed portion, then the operation is termed as *blanking*. On the other hand, if the pierced sheet metal is the final product, then the operation is called *punching*. Since the basic mechanics of material removal is the same in both the operations, we shall discuss these under a single heading, namely, punching.

Figure 5.19 shows a simple punching operation. As in deep drawing, the job holders are used to prevent any distortion and to provide a support. It should be noted that the punch and die cones are not provided with any radius (unlike in the deep drawing operation) as the objective in this process is to cause a rupture of the material. A clearance c is provided between the punch and the die. Hence, the die diameter $d_d = d_p + 2c$, where d_p is the diameter of the punch.

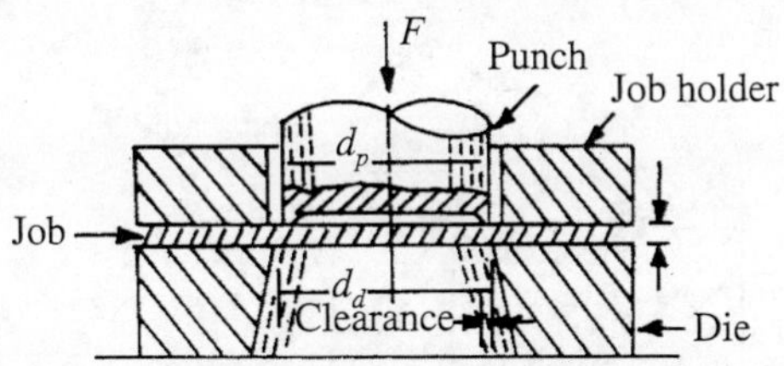

FIGURE 5.19 Punching.

Design considerations for metal forming

(i) **Extrusion.** Extrusion is a process with high potential. It can be performed in hot or cold conditions. In forward extrusion, the billet is required to move forward, resulting in large frictional loss and high punch load. The container is also subjected to high radial stresses. The foregoing difficulties can be overcome by backward extrusion where the billet remains stationary, as shown in Figure 5.20. The load is independent of the billet length.

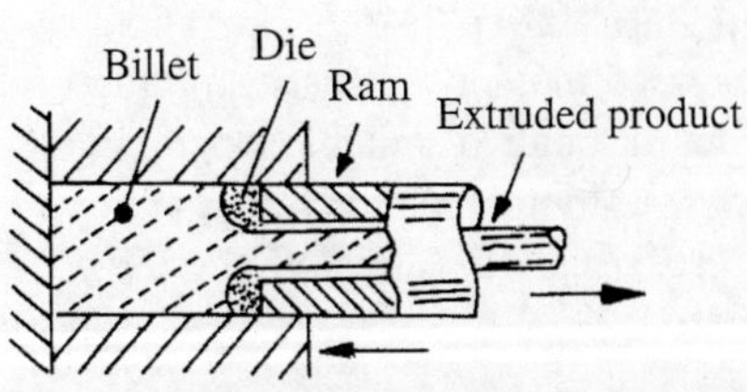

FIGURE 5.20 Reverse extrusion.

(a) *Impact extrusion.* This process is eminently suited for making thin walled cans. The process is limited to soft and ductile materials and performed under cold conditions see Figure 5.21.

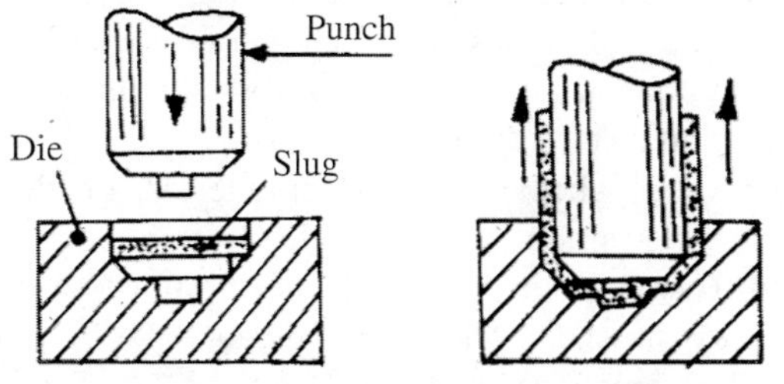

FIGURE 5.21 Impact extrusion.

(b) *Conventional extrusions.* When making parts that have constant cross-sections, the extrusion process is usually more economical and faster than machining, casting or fabricating the shapes by welding (or riveting). Also, the designer of the extruded section is relatively free to put the metal where he wants. Nevertheless, there are some design guidelines that must be taken into consideration when designing an extruded section.

1. The circle size, i.e., the diameter of the smallest circle that will enclose the extruded cross-section, can be 31 in. when extruding light metals.
2. Solid shapes are the easiest to extrude. Semi-hollow and hollow shapes are more difficult to extrude, especially if they have thin walls or include abrupt changes in wall thickness.
3. Wall thickness must be kept uniform. If not, all transitions must be streamlined by generous radii at the thick-thin junctions.
4. Sharp corners at the root of a die tongue should be avoided when extruding semi-hollow sections.
5. A complicated section should be broken into a group of simpler sections, which are assembled after separate extrusion processes. In such a case, the sections should be designed to simplify assembly, for example, they should fit, hook or snap together. Screw slots or slots to receive other tightening materials, such as plastic, may also be provided.

(c) *Aluminum impact extrusion.* In order to obtain good designs of aluminum impact extrusions, all factors associated with and affecting the process must be taken into account. Examples are alloy selection, tool design, and lubrication. This is added to the general consideration of mechanical design. The following are some basic guidelines and design examples:

1. Use alloys that apply in the desired case and have the lowest strength.
2. An impact extrusion should be symmetrical around the punch.
3. Threads, cuts, projections and so on are made by subjecting the impact extrusions to further processing.
4. For reverse extrusions, the ratio of maximum length to internal diameter must not exceed eight, to avoid failure of long punches.
5. A small outer corner radius must be provided for a reverse extrusion. On the contrary, the inner corner radius must be kept as small as possible.

6. The thickness of the bottom near the wall must be 15 per cent more than the thickness of the wall itself, to prevent shear failure.
7. The inside bottom should not be wholly flat. To avoid the possibility of the punch skidding on the billet, only 80 per cent of it at the most can be flat.
8. External and internal bosses are permitted, provided they are coaxial with the part. However, the diameter of the internal boss should not be more than one-fourth of the internal diameter of the shell.
9. Longitudinal ribs, whether external or internal, on the full length of the impact extrusion are permitted. They should preferably be located in a symmetrical distribution. However, the height of each rib must not exceed double the thickness of the wall of the shell. The main function of ribs is to provide stiffness to the wall of shells. Sometimes, they are also used for other reasons, such as to provide locations for drilling and tapping (to assemble the part), to enhance cooling by radiation, and to provide an appropriate gripping surface.
10. An impact extrusion can have a wall with varying thickness along its length, i.e., it can be multiple-diameter part. However, internal steps near the top of the product should be avoided, since they cause excessive loading and wear of the punch.
11. Remember that it is sometimes impossible to obtain the desired shape directly by impacting. However, an impact extrusion can be considered as an intermediate product, which can be subjected to further working or secondary operations like machining, flange upsetting, nosing, and necking or ironing.

(ii) **Forging process: Detailed design consideration.** The basic requirements of a forging die have been outlined by El Wakil [3]. They are as follows:

1. To ease the metal flow around the comers, for which a proper fillet radius should be provided. This also prevents excessive wear of the dies.
2. As in moulding patterns, a suitable taper and draft should be given to vertical surfaces. This enables easy removal of job from the die.
3. For the semi-finishing or blocker die, the depth of the cavity should be more than the component thickness.
4. For the finishing die, gutter should be provided for flow of excess material available from the earlier (blocker) step (see Figure 5.22(a)).

Fundamentals of closed-die forging design: Detailed design considerations. There is a wide variety of forged products with respect to size, shape and properties. For this reason, it is both advisable and advantageous for the product designer to consider forging in the early stages of planning the processes for manufacturing new products. The forging design is influenced not only by its function and the properties of the material being processed, but also by the kind, capabilities and shortcomings of the production equipment available in the manufacturing facilities. Therefore, it is impossible to discuss in detail all considerations arising from the infinite combinations of the various factors. Nevertheless, some general guidelines apply in all cases and should be strictly adhered to, if a successful and sound forging is to be obtained. The following are some recommended forging design principles.

(i) **Parting line.** The plane of separation between the upper and lower halves of a closed die set is called the *parting line*. It can be straight—horizontal or inclined. The parting line can also be irregular, including more than one plane. It must be designated on all forging drawings, since it affects the initial cost and wear of the forging die, the grain flow which, in turn, affects the mechanical properties of the forging and, finally, the trimming procedure and/or subsequent machining operations on the finished part. The following are some considerations for determining the shape and position of the parting line:

1. The parting line should usually pass through the maximum periphery of the forging. This is mainly because it is always easier to spread the metal laterally than to force it to fill deep, narrow die impressions as indicated in Figure 5.22(b).

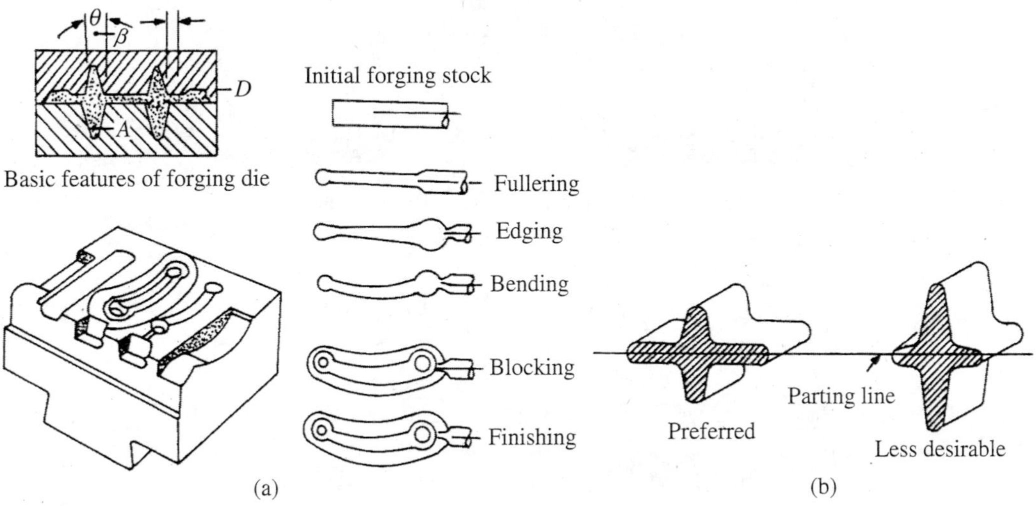

FIGURE 5.22 (a) Forging process and forging die and (b) Good and less desirable component shapes.

2. It is always advantageous, whenever possible, to try to simplify the die construction, if the design is to end up with flat-sided forgings. This will markedly reduce the die cost, since machining is limited to the lower die half. Also, the possibility of mismatch between die halves is eliminated (see Figure 5.23).

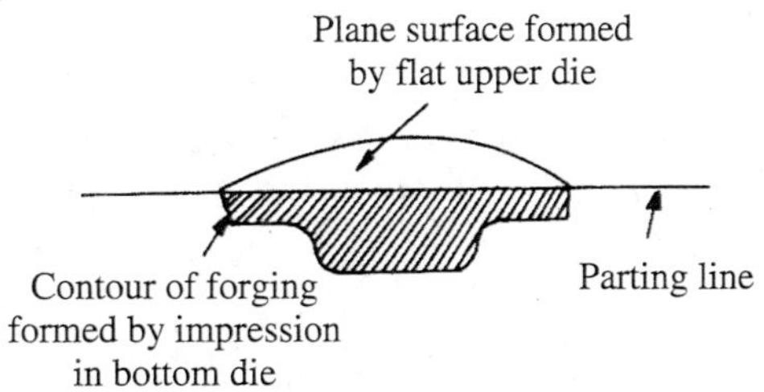

FIGURE 5.23 Flat top forged product.

3. If an inclined parting line has to exist, it is generally recommended to limit the inclination so that it does not exceed 70°. This is because inclined flashes may create problems in trimming and subsequent machining.
4. A parting line should be located in such a manner as to promote alignment of the fibrous macrostructure to fulfill the strength requirement of a forging. Since excess

metal flows out of the die cavity into the gutter as the process proceeds, mislocating the parting line will probably result in irregularities. We can see this clearly in Figure 5.24 which indicates the fibrous macrostructure resulting from different locations for the parting line.

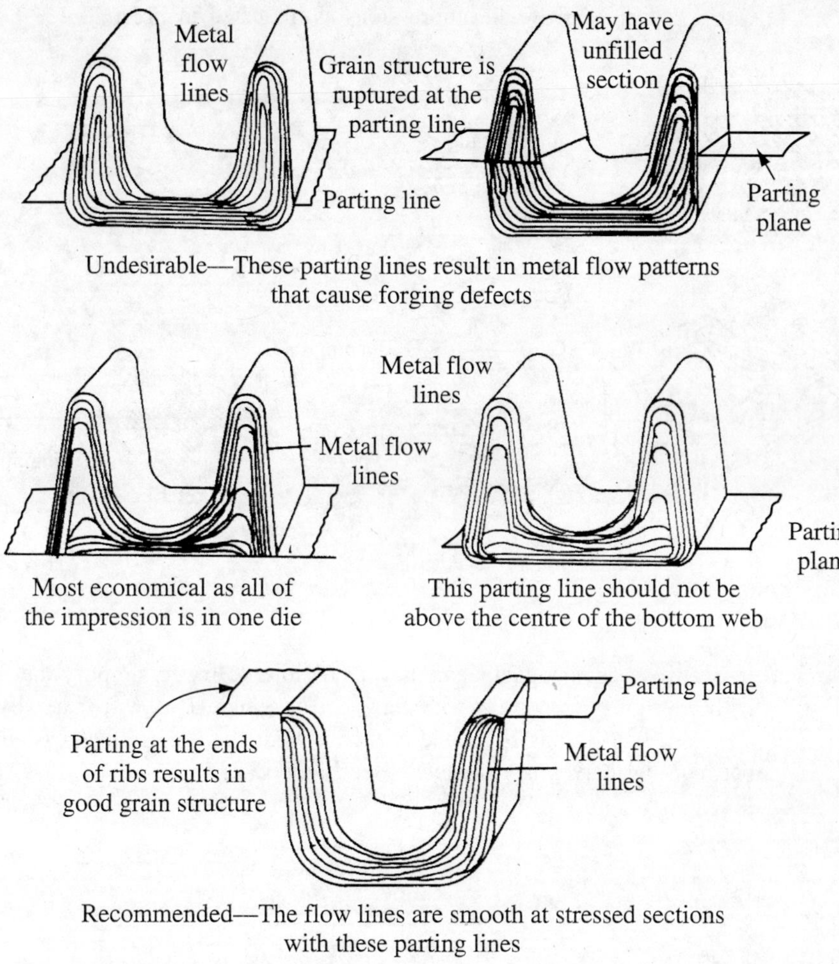

FIGURE 5.24 Selection of parting line to encourage unbroken grain flow lines.

5. When the forging comprises a web enclosed by ribs, as illustrated in Figure 5.25, the parting line should preferably pass through the centre-line of the web. It is also preferable with respect to the alignment of fibres, to have the parting line either at the top or at the bottom surfaces. However, the desirable location usually creates manufacturing problems and is not used, unless the direction of the fibrous macrostructure is critical.
6. If an irregular parting line has to exist, avoid side thrust of the die, which would cause the die halves to shift away from each other sideways, resulting in match errors. Figure 5.25 indicates the problem of side thrust accompanying irregular parting lines as well as two suggested solutions.

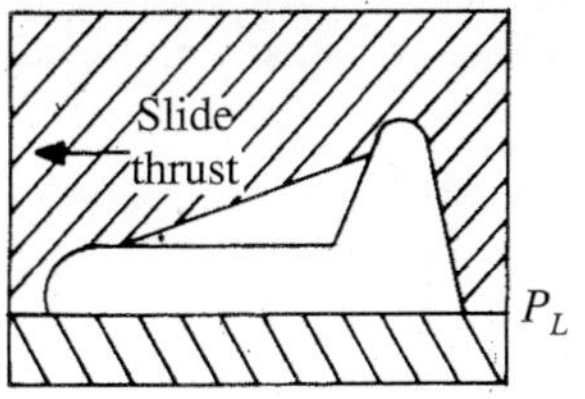

(a) Impractical: Slide thrust causes mismatch

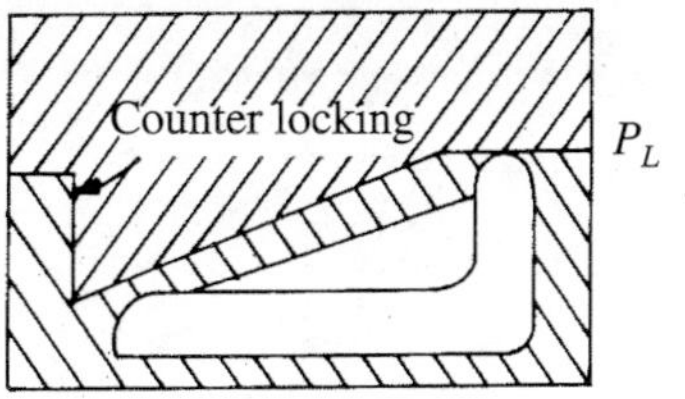

(b) Not recommended: Dies with counterlock difficult to produce and maintain

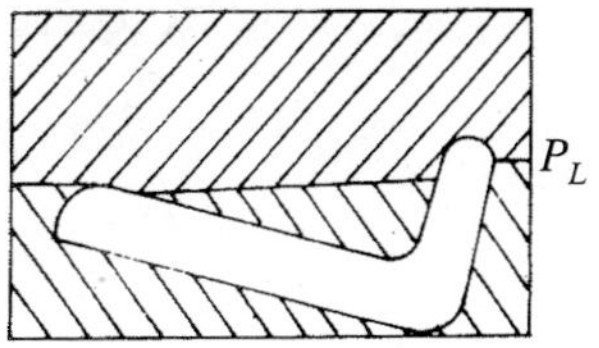

(c) Preferred: Incline the forging with respect to forging plane

FIGURE 5.25 Elimination of side thrust in closed-impression forgings.

(ii) **Draft.** Draft refers to the taper given to internal and external sides of a closed-die forging and is expressed as an angle from the direction of the forging stroke. Draft is required on the vast majority for forgings to avoid production difficulties, to aid in achieving the desired metal flow, and to allow easy removal of the forging from the die cavity. It is obvious that the smaller the draft angle, the more difficult it is to remove the forging out of the die. For this reason, draft angles of less than 5° are not permitted if the part is to be produced by drop forging (remember that there is no ejector to push the part out). Standard draft angles are 7°, 5°, 3°, 1° and 0°. A draft angle of 3° is usually used for metal having good forgeability, such as aluminium and magnesium, whereas draft angles of 5° and 7° are used for steel, titanium, and the like. It is a recommended practice to use a constant draft all over the periphery of the forging. It is also common to apply a smaller draft angle on the outside periphery than on the inside one. This is justified because the outside surface will shrink away from the surface of the die cavity as a result of the part cooling down, thus facilitating the removal of the forging. The following are some useful examples and guidelines:

1. When designing the product, try to make use of the natural draft inherent in some shapes, such as circular and diamond-shaped surfaces as shown in Figure 5.26.

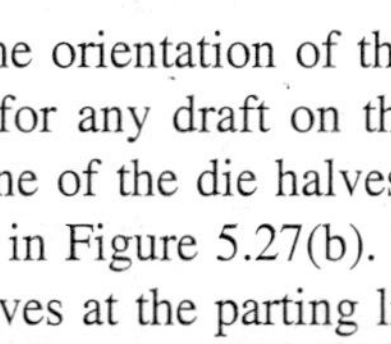

FIGURE 5.26 Natural draft as a result of part shape.

2. In some cases, changing the orientation of the die cavity may result in a natural draft, thus eliminating the need for any draft on the surfaces (see Figure 5.27(a)).
3. Sometimes, the cavity in one of the die halves (e.g., the upper) is shallower than that in the other half as illustrated in Figure 5.27(b). This may create problems in matching the contours of the two die halves at the parting line. The first method involves keeping the draft the same, as in the lower cavity, but increasing the dimension of the upper surface of the cavity. This results in an increase in weight and is limited to smaller cavities. The second method is based on keeping the draft constant in both halves by introducing a 'pad', whose height varies between 0.06 in. (1.5 mm) and 0.5 in. (12.7 mm), depending

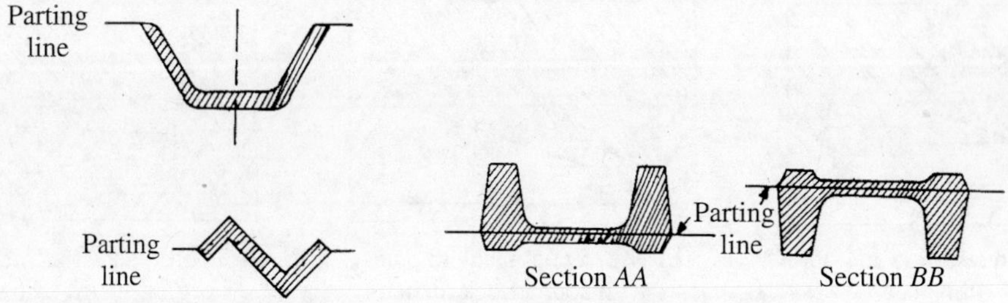

(a) Suitable part orientation to obtain draft

(b) Matching draft

FIGURE 5.27

on the size of the forging. The third method, which is more common, is to provide greater draft on the shallower die cavity; this is usually referred to as matching draft.

(iii) **Ribs.** A rib is a thin part of the forging which is normal to the forging plane (or slightly inclined to that normal). It is obvious that the optimized lighter weight of a forging requires reduction in the thickness of long rib. The higher the forging pressure, the more difficult it is to obtain a sound rib. It is actually a common practice to keep the height-to-thickness ratio of a rib below 6, preferably at 4. The choice of a value for this ratio does depend on many factors such as the kind of metal being processed and the forging geometry; i.e., the location of the rib, the location of the parting line, and the fillet radii. Figures 5.28 and 5.29 indicate the desired rib design as well as limitations imposed on possible alternatives.

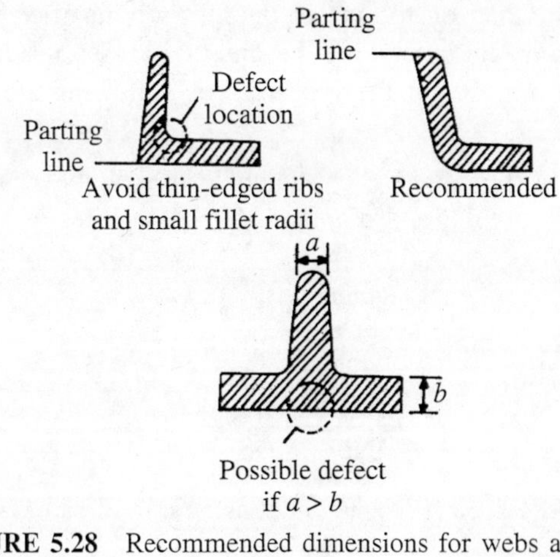

FIGURE 5.28 Recommended dimensions for webs and ribs.

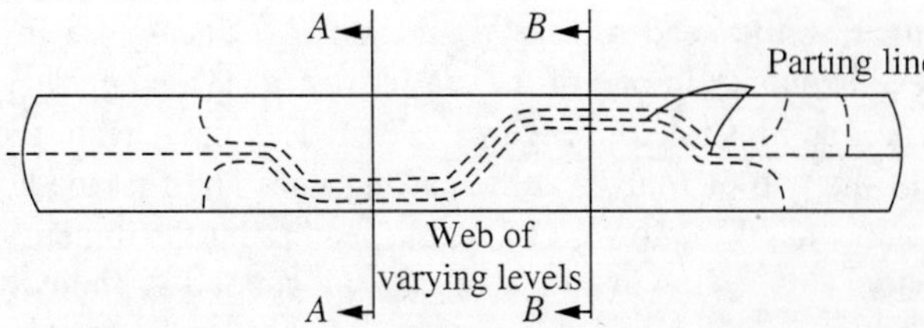

FIGURE 5.29 Choosing parting line to pass through webs.

(iv) **Webs.** A web is a thin part of the forging passing through or parallel to the forging plane (see Figure 5.30). Although it is always preferable to keep the thickness of a web at the minimum, there are practical limits to that. The minimum thickness of webs depends on the kind of material being worked (actually on its forging temperature range), the size of forging (expressed as the net area of metal at the parting line), and the average width. Also, for steels and other metals having poor forgeability than aluminium, it is advisable to increase the values for web thickness. Thin webs may cause unfilled sections, warp in heat treatment, and require additional straightening operations. They even cool faster than the rest of the forging after the forging process, resulting in shrinkage, possible tears and distortion.

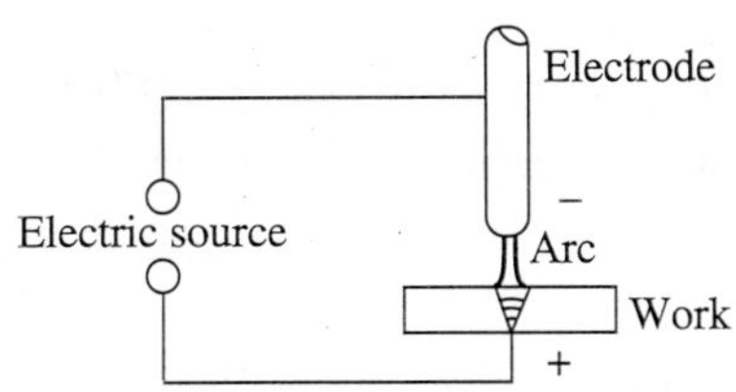

FIGURE 5.30 Arc welding scheme.

(v) **Corner radii.** There are two main factors that must be taken into account when selecting a small value for a corner radius. *First,* a small corner radius requires a sharp fillet in the die steel, which acts as a stress raiser. *Second,* the smaller the corner radius, the higher the forging pressure required to fill the die cavity.

In addition, some other factors affect the choice of the parting line and the forgeability of the metal being worked. The larger the distance from the parting line, the larger should be the corner radius. Also, whereas a corner radius of 0.0625 in. (1.5 mm) is generally considered adequate for aluminum forging, a corner radius of at least 0.125 in. (3 mm) is used for titanium forgings of similar shape and size. Besides, the product designer should try to keep the corner radii as consistent as possible, and avoid blending different values for a given shape in order to reduce the die cost (since there would not be any need for many tool changes during die sinking). Meanwhile, corner radii at the end of high, thin ribs are critical. A rule of thumb states that it is always advisable to have the rib thickness equal to twice the value of the corner radius. A thicker rib may have a flat edge with two corner radii, each equal to the recommended value.

(vi) **Fillet radii.** It is of great importance that the product designer allows sufficient radii for the fillets for abrupt diversion in the product. When the shape of the part to be forged is intricate, i.e., involving thin ribs and long thin webs, the metal may possibly flow into the gutter rather than into the die cavity. This results in a shear in the fibrous macrostructure and is referred to as flow-through. This defect can be avoided by using larger-than-normal fillets.

(vii) **Punchout holes.** Punchout holes are through-holes in a thin web, which are produced during, but not after, the forging process, punchouts reduce the net projected area of the forging, thus reducing the forging load required. If properly located and designed, they can be of great assistance in producing forgings with thin webs. The following are some guidelines regarding the design of punchouts:

1. Try to locate a punchout around the central area of thin web, where the frictional force that impedes the metal flow is maximum.
2. Whenever possible, use a gutter around the interior periphery of a punchout. This provides a successful means for the surplus metal to escape.
3. A single large punchout is generally more advantageous than many smaller ones that have the same area. Accordingly, try to reduce the number of punchouts, unless dictated to by functional requirements.
4. Although punchouts generally aid in eliminating the problems associated with the heat treatment of forgings, it may prove beneficial to take the limitations imposed by heat treatment processes into account when designing the contour of a punchout, i.e., try to avoid irregular contours with sharp corners.

In addition to the manufacturing advantages of punchouts, they serve functional design purposes such as reducing the mass of a forging and/or providing clearance.

(viii) **Pockets and recesses.** Recesses are used to save material, promote the desirable alignment of the fibrous macrostructure, and improve the mechanical properties by reducing the thickness, thus achieving a higher degree of deformation. The following guidelines will be of some assistance in die designs:

1. Recesses should never be perpendicular to the direction of metal flow.
2. Recesses are formed by punches or plugs in the dies. Therefore, the recess depth is restricted to the value of its diameter (or to the value of minimum transverse dimension for non-circular recesses).
3. Simple contours for the recesses, together with generous fillet, should be tried.

5.2.3 Joining Processes

Joining processes differ from production processes like casting or forging which produces a single component in a single act. Complex configurations can be built by joining different members to yield the desired results.

Welding, brazing, soldering and adhesive bonding are the most frequently used joining processes.

(i) **Pressure welding.** Solid state welding may be carried out at room temperature or at elevated temperature. The joint is formed owing to plastic flow (at the joint) due to applied pressure. In pressure welding at high temperature, heat is generated due to resistance at the joint as flow of current is high. Other methods of achieving high temperature include friction, induction heating, impact energy as in the case of explosive welding, seam welding, and projection welding. But welding is well known for resistance welding techniques.

(ii) **Fusion (liquid state) welding.** In fusion welding, the material around the joint is melted in both the parts to be joined. If necessary, a molten filler metal is added from a filler rod or from the electrode itself. The important zones in fusion welding are: (a) Fusion zone, (b) heat-affected unmelted zone around the fusion zone, and (c) the unaffected original part. Important factors affecting fusion welding processes are:

1. Characteristics of heat source
2. Nature of weld pool
3. Heat flow from the joint

4. Chemical reactions in the fusion zone
5. Contraction, residual stresses and metallurgical changes

(iii) **Arc welding.** Workpiece is positive and rod is negative; usually, 2/3 heat is at the anode due to impingement of high velocity electron. Temperature of arc is about 6000°C (see Figure 5.31(a)).

(iv) **Gas welding.** Chemical heat source such as Acetylene (C_2H_2) is used with Oxygen to liberate 1.275×10^6 kJ/kg mole of heat. C_2H_2 in the presence of excess oxygen produces CO_2. In limited oxygen supply, CO is formed, instead of CO_2, and heat = 0.448×10^6 kJ.

(v) **Thermit welding.** A mixture of aluminium powder and Fe_3O_4 is used:

$$8Al + 3Fe_3O_4 = 2Fe + 4Al_2O_3 + dH$$

where $dH = 0.24 \times 10^6$ kJ/k mol of atomic wt. of O_2. The temperature reached is 3000°C.

(vi) **Soldering.** The manual soldering method involves using a hard type soldering iron, made of copper. It is heated to a temperature of 300°C and its tip is dipped in flux and tinned with solder. Then the iron is used for heating the base metal as well as for melting and spreading the solder.

(vii) **Brazing.** Brazing uses silver, copper, etc. as the material. When the base metal is ferrous, copper enters grain boundaries (temperature 450°C), whereas in the case of gold, the (Ag–Cu) braze metal acts as a filler between sandwich.

Design considerations. As soon as a decision is made to fabricate a product by welding, the next step is to decide which welding process to use. This decision should be followed by selection of the types of joints, by determining the distribution and locations of the webs, and finally, by making the design of each joint. The following is a brief discussion of the factors to be considered in each design stage.

(i) **Selection of the joint type.** We have already discussed the various joint designs and realized that the type of joint depends on the thickness of the parts to be welded. In fact, there are other factors that should also affect the process of selecting a particular type of joint. For instance, the magnitude of the load to which the particular joint is going to be subjected during its service life is another important factor. The manner in which that load is applied (i.e., impact—steady or fluctuating) is another factor. While the square butt—simple-V, double-V and simple-U butt joint—is recommended for all loading conditions, the square-T joint is appropriate for carrying longitudinal shear under steady state conditions. When severe longitudinal or transverse loads are anticipated, other types of joints (e.g., the single-level T the double-level T and the double J) have to be considered. In all cases, it is obvious that cost is a decisive factor, whenever there is a choice between two types of joints that would function equally well.

(ii) **Location and distribution of welds.** It has been found that the direction of the linear dimensions of the weld with respect to the direction of the applied load does have an effect on the strength of the weld. In fact, it has been experimentally proved that a weld whose linear direction is normal to the direction of the applied load (such as that shown in Figure 5.31(b)) is 30 per cent stronger than a weld which is parallel to the direction of applied load. A product designer should, therefore, make use of this characteristic when planning the location and distribution of welds.

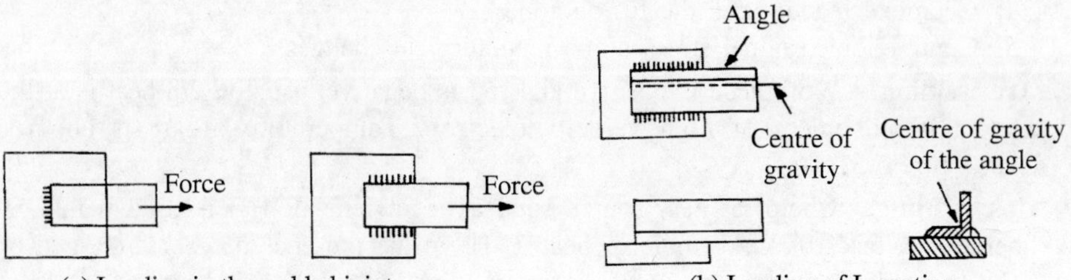

(a) Loading in the welded joint (b) Loading of L-section

FIGURE 5.31 Design of weld length for strength and stability.

Another important point that must always be considered is the prevention of any tendency of the welded elements to rotate when subjected to mechanical loads. A complete force analysis must be carried out in order to determine properly the length of each weld. Let us now consider a practical example to examine the cause and the remedy for that tendency to rotate. Figure 5.31(b) indicates an L-angle, which is welded to a plate. Any load applied at the angle would pass through its centre of gravity. Therefore, the resisting forces that act through the welds would not be equal; the force closer to the centre of gravity of the angle would always be larger. Consequently, if any tendency to rotation is to be prevented, the weld which is closer to the centre of gravity must be longer than the other one. It is also recommended that very long welds be avoided. For example, it has been found that two small welds are much more effective than a single long weld.

(iii) **Joint design.** In addition to the procedures and rules adopted in the common design practice, there are some guidelines that apply to point design:

1. Try to ensure accessibility to the locations where welds are to be applied.
2. Try to avoid overhead welding.
3. Consider the heating effect on the base metal during welding operation. Balance the welds to minimize distortion. Use short intermittent welds. Figure 5.32(a) indicates distortion caused by an unbalanced weld, whereas Figures 5.32(b) and (c) provide the methods for reducing that distortion.

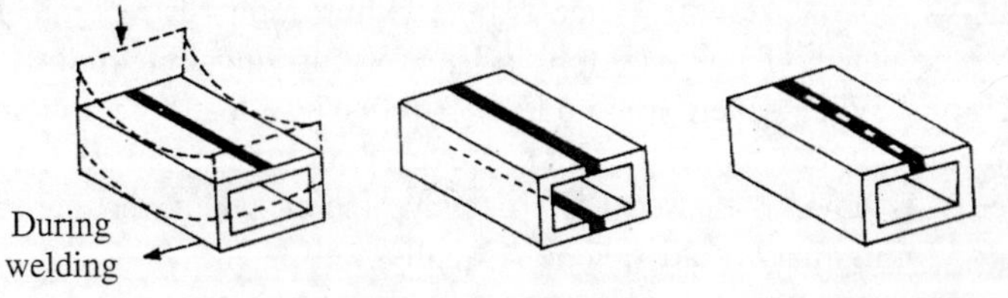

(a) Poor (b) Good (c) Acceptable

FIGURE 5.32 Avoiding distortion of welded component through balanced welding.

4. Avoid crevices around welds in tanks as well as grooves (and the like) that would allow dirt to accumulate. Failure to do so may result in corrosion in the welded joint.
5. Do not employ welding to joint steels with high hardenability.
6. Do not weld low-carbon steels and alloy steels by the conventional fusion-welding methods because they have different critical cooling rates and hence cannot be successfully welded.

7. When employing automatic welding (e.g., submerged arc), the conventional joint design of manual welding should be changed. Wider vees (for butt joints) are used, and single-pass welds replace multi-pass welds.

Design of brazed joints. For the proper design of brazed joints, two main factors have to be taken into consideration: The first factor involves the mechanics of the process, i.e., the fact that the brazing filler metal flows through the joint by capillary action. The second factor is that the strength of the filler metal is poorer than that of the base metals. The product designer should take the following steps:

1. The filler metal is placed on one side of the joint and allocating a space for locating the filler metal before (or during) the process.
2. The joint clearance is so adjusted that it ensures optimum conditions during brazing. The clearance is dependent on the filler metal used and normally takes a value less than 0.005 in (0.125 mm), except for aluminium, where it can go up to 0.025 in. (0.625 mm).
3. The distance to be travelled by the filler metal is shorter than the limit distance, as demanded/required by the physics of capillarity.
4. Enough filler metal is provided.
5. The arc of the joint is increased since the filler metal is weaker than the base metal.

There are actually three types of joint-area geometries—butt, skirt, and lap. The butt joint is the weakest, while the lap is the strongest. Nevertheless, when designing lap joints, one should make sure that the joint overlap is more than $3t$, where t is the thickness of the thinner parent metal. Examples of some good and poor practices in the design of brazed joint are shown in Figure 5.33, as guidelines in product design.

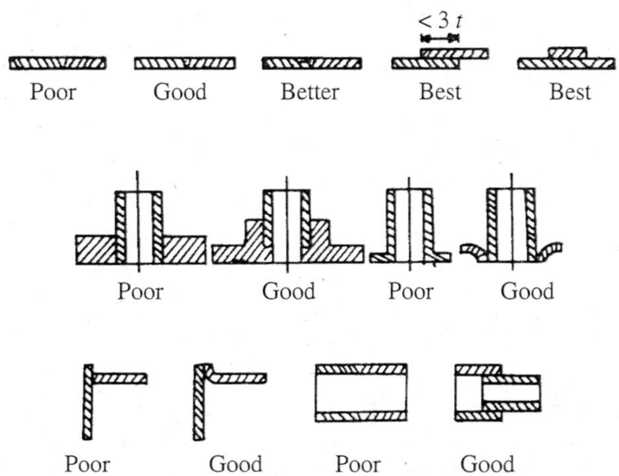

FIGURE 5.33 Design of brazed joints.

Adhesive bonding has gained popularity due to developments in polymer chemistry and is widely used now. Structural adhesives include one or more polymers. In the unhardened state, these adhesives can take the form of viscous liquids or solids with softening temperatures of about 212°F (100°C). The unhardened adhesive agents are often soluble in ketones, esters and higher alcohols as well as in aromatic and chlorine hydrocarbons. Nevertheless, the hardened adhesives resist nearly all solvents. The following is a brief description of the adhesives which are commonly used in industry.

Epoxies. These are thermosetting polymers (see Chapter 7), which require the additions of a hardener or the application of heat so that they can be cured. They are considered to be the best sticking agents because of their versatility, resistance to solvents, and ability to develop strong and reliable joints.

Phenolics. These are characterized by their low cost and heat resistance (up to about 930°F (500°C)). They can be cured by a hardener, by heating, or used in solvents that evaporate, thus enabling setting to occur. Like epoxies, phenolics are thermosetting polymers with good strength, but they generally suffer from brittleness.

Polymides. The polymide group of polymers is characterized by its oil and water resistance. Polymides are usually applied in the form of hot melts, but can also be used by evaporation of solvents in which they have been dissolved. Polymides are normally used as seam sealants and for other similar purposes. They are used as hot-melt for shoes.

Silicones. These adhesives can perform well at elevated temperatures. However, cost and strength are the major limitations. Therefore, silicones are normally used as high-temperature sealants.

Other adhesives that find industrial applications, in bonding two nonmetallic workpiece, include cyanoacrylates, acrylics and polyurethanes.

Joint preparation. The surfaces to be bonded must be clean and degreased, since most adhesives do not amalgamate with fats, oils or wax. Joint preparation involves grinding with sandpaper, grinding, filing, sand blasting and pickling and degreasing with tri-chlorethylene. Oxide films, electroplating coats and varnish films need not be removed (as long as they are fixed to the surface). Roughening of the surface is advantageous if it is not overdone.

Joint design for adhesive joining. There are basically three types of adhesive-bonded joints. These are shown in Figure 5.34 and include tension, shear and peel joints. Most of the adhesives are weaker in peel and tension than in shear. Therefore, when selecting an adhesive, one should always keep in mind the types of stresses to which the joint is going to be subjected. It is also recommended that one avoid using tension and peel joints and change the design to replace these by shear joints, whenever possible.

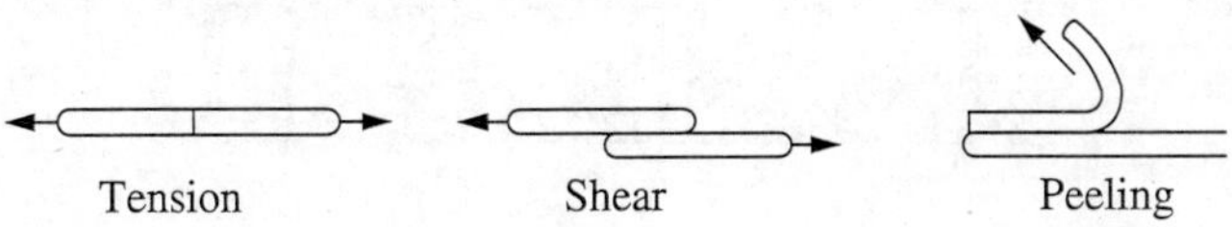

FIGURE 5.34 Design of adhesive joints and their loading.

5.3 WELDING PROCESSES

Welding processes are classified as shown in Figure 5.35.

5.3.1 Arc Welding

Arc welding also known as *shielded arc welding* is accomplished by producing an electric arc between the work to be welded and the tip of the electrode.

The arc column is generated between an anode, which is the positive pole of a DC power supply, and the cathode, the negative pole. Metal ions pass from the positive to the negative pole because they are positively charged and thus attracted to the negative pole.

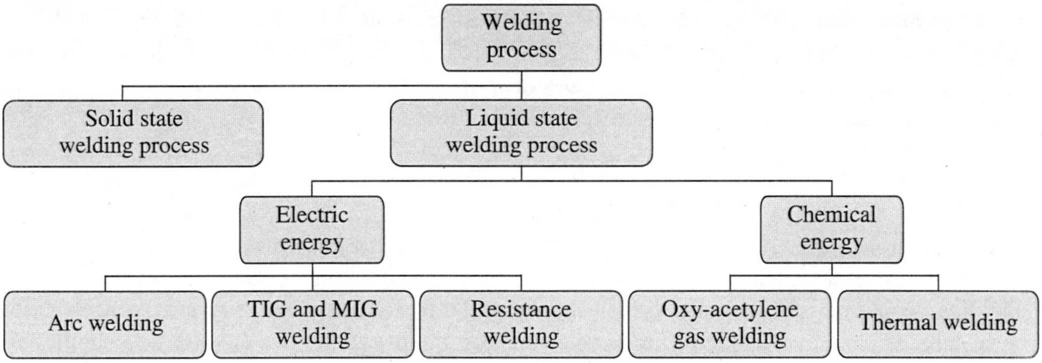

FIGURE 5.35 Types of welding processes.

The arc is one of the most efficient means for producing heat that is available to modern technology. Approximately, 50% of the electric energy put into the arc system comes out in the form of heat energy. Approximately two-third of the energy released in the arc column system is always at the anode (the positive pole). This is true in all DC systems. Another type of arc power source used in shielded-arc welding is alternating current (AC). When an AC power supply is used, the heat in the arc column generally is equalized between the anode and the cathode areas, so that the area of medium heat is then in the plasma area (Figure 5.36).

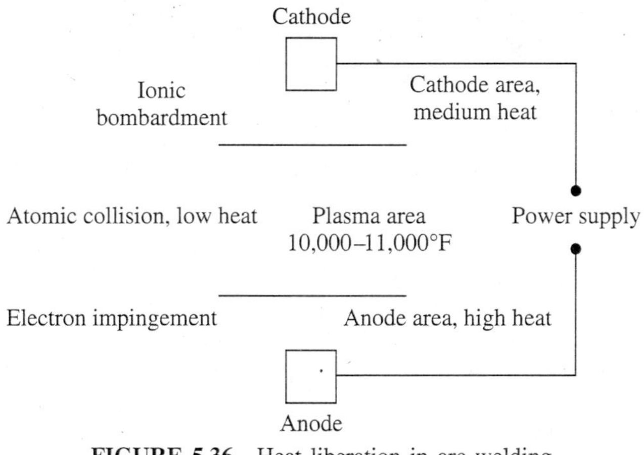

FIGURE 5.36 Heat liberation in arc welding.

The arc column and power sources. The welding circuit consists of a power source, the electrode cable, the ground cable and the electrode. The two basic types of power sources for arc welding are direct current and alternating current. Each of these two power supplies has distinct advantages. In DC welding, the electron flow is in one direction and in AC welding, the electron flow is in both directions. In DC welding, the direction can be changed by simply reversing the cables at the terminals located on the generator. The different settings on the terminals indicate that the electron flow will be either from the electrode to the work, which is the positive ground, or from the work to the electrode, which is the negative ground.

Two-third of the heat is developed near the positive pole while the remaining one-third is developed near the negative pole. As a result, an electrode that is connected to the positive pole will burn away approximately 50% faster than one that is connected to the negative pole. Knowing this information helps a welder to obtain the desired penetration of the base metal. If the positive ground is used, the penetration will be greater because of the amount of heat energy supplied to the work by the electrode force. At the same time, the electrode will burn away slowly. If the poles are reversed and there is a negative ground, two-third of the heat will remain in the tip of the electrode. For this reason, the penetration of the heat zone in the base metal will be shallow when compared to the penetration depth of the positive ground arc column. Alternating current yields a penetration depth that is approximately half that achieved by the DC positive ground. Since electron flow switches ground every time the AC cycle changes, the penetration of the heat zone in the base metal is approximately between the two DC types.

In straight polarity, the electrode is negative and the work is positive. The electron flow goes from the electrode into the work. When the electrode is positive and the work is negative, the electron flow is from the work to the anode, a characteristic called *reverse polarity* (Figure 5.37). When reverse polarity is used, the work remains cooler than when straight polarity is used.

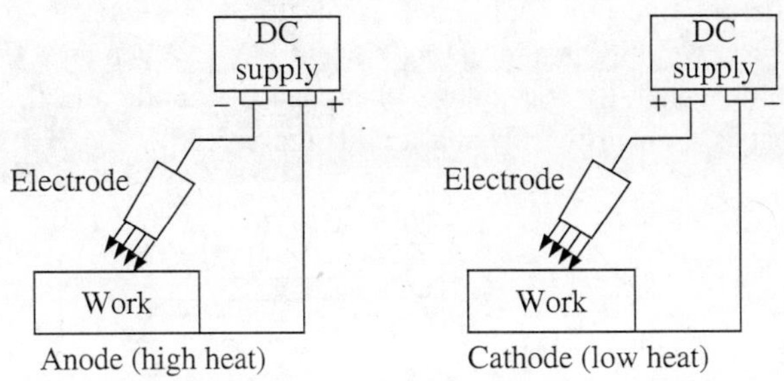

(a) Straight polarity (a) Reverse polarity

FIGURE 5.37 DC arc welding.

In both the AC and DC power sources, the arc serves the same purpose: producing heat to melt metal. If two pieces of metal that are to be joined are placed so that they touch or almost touch one another and the arc from the electrode is directed at this junction, the heat generated by the arc causes a small section of the edges of both pieces of metal to melt. These molten portions along with the molten portions of the electrode flow together. As the arc column is moved, the molten puddle solidifies, joining the two pieces of metal with a combination of electrode metal and base metal.

The coatings on the electrodes burn as the electrode wire is melted by the intense heat of the arc. As the electrode wire melts, the electrode covering, or the flux, provides a gaseous shield around the arc, preventing contamination. The force of the arc column striking the workpiece digs a crater in the base metal. This crater fills with molten metal. As the flux melts, part of it mixes with the impurities in the molten pool causing them to float to the top of the weld (Figure 5.38). This slag protects the bead from the atmosphere and causes the bead to cool more uniformly. The slag also helps to design the contour of the weld bead by acting as an insulator. By insulating the heat-affected zone, located in the parent metal or the base metal and completely surrounding the weld bead, the slag allows an even heat loss from this heat-affected zone, thus helping to control the crystal or grain size of the metal.

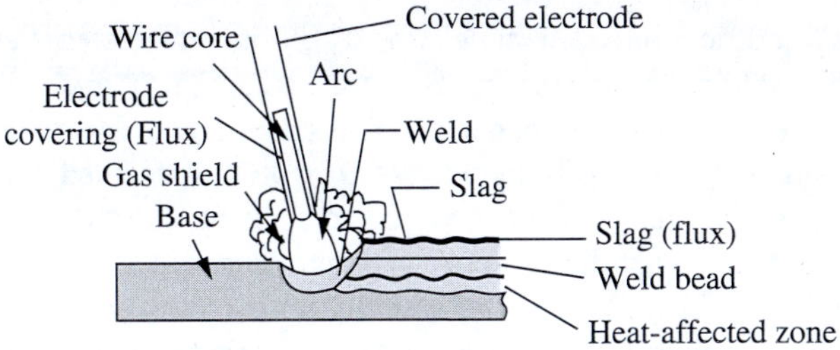

FIGURE 5.38 Scheme of arc welding.

The arc column reaches temperatures from 5000 to 7000°F. These temperatures have a harsh effect on the parent metal. The molten pool, which must maintain a temperature of approximately 2800°F, radiates heat outward and changes the crystals surrounding the weld bead. Many times after welding, a part must be heat treated to change the size of the grains in the weld bead and the surrounding area. The heating of the base metal by the arc stream and the resultant molten weld puddle or crater generally extend deep into the base metal. The extent of the heat-affected zone can be observed by studying the crystalline structure of the base metal in this zone. It generally is represented by a large grain. The grains in the unaffected areas of the metal are smaller. Because of the protection of the flux, the weld bead itself has medium-sized grains that extend to large grains at deeper penetration. It is not necessary to heat treat mild steel; but with many metals, the heat from welding will result in locked-in stresses that must be relieved either through peening or further heat treatment of the entire piece of metal.

Power supplies. Power is needed to supply the current that supports the arc column for fusion welding. There are three types of welding power supplies: DC motor generators, AC transformers, and AC transformers with DC rectifiers.

Voltage characteristics. There are three major current–voltage characteristics commonly used in today's arc welding machines to help control the fluctuating currents caused by the arc column.

They are: (1) the drooping-arc voltage (DAV), (2) the constant-arc voltage (CAV), and (3) the rising-arc voltage (RAV).

The machine that is designed with the DAV characteristics provides the highest potential voltage when the welding current circuit is open and no current is flowing. As the arc column is started, the voltage drops to a minimum and the amperage rises rapidly. With DAV, when the length of the arc column is increased, the voltage rises and the amperage decreases (Figure 5.39(a)). The DAV is the type of voltage–amperage relationship preferred for standard shielded-arc welding that is manually done.

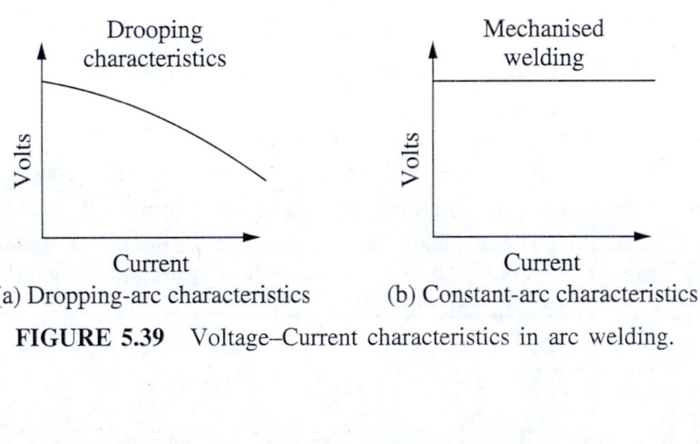

(a) Dropping-arc characteristics (b) Constant-arc characteristics

FIGURE 5.39 Voltage–Current characteristics in arc welding.

The CAV and a modification of it called the RAV are characteristics preferred for semi-automatic or automatic welding processes because they maintain a pre-set voltage regardless of the amount of current being drawn from the machine (Figure 5.39(b)). These voltage–amperage characteristics are sensitive to the short-circuiting effect of the shielded-arc mechanism of metal transfer. With these types, the spray arc method rather than the short-circuit arc method of metal transfer is used. The spray arc, much like a spray gun spraying paint, works on a principle different from that of the short-circuit pinch-off effect of welding with a stick electrode. An advantage of the RAV over the CAV characteristic is that as the amperage requirement is increased, the voltage is increased automatically, thus helping to maintain a constant-arc gap even if short-circuiting occurs. This RAV is adaptable to the fully automatic processes.

5.3.2 Tungsten Inert Gas (TIG)

In tungsten inert gas (TIG) welding, the weld zone is shielded from the atmosphere by an inert gas that is ducted directly to the weld zone where it surrounds the tungsten electrode. The two inert gases that are use most often are argon and helium.

The TIG process offers many advantages. TIG welds are stronger, more ductile, and more corrosion-resistant than welds made with ordinary shielded-metal-arc welding. In addition, because no granular flux is required, it is possible to see a wider variety of joint designs than in conventional shielded-arc welding or stick-electrode welding. The weld bead has no corrosion because flux entrapment cannot occur, and because of the fluxing, there is little or no post weld cleaning operation. There is also little weld metal splatter or weld sparks that damage the surface of the base metal as in traditional shielded-arc welding (Figure 5.40).

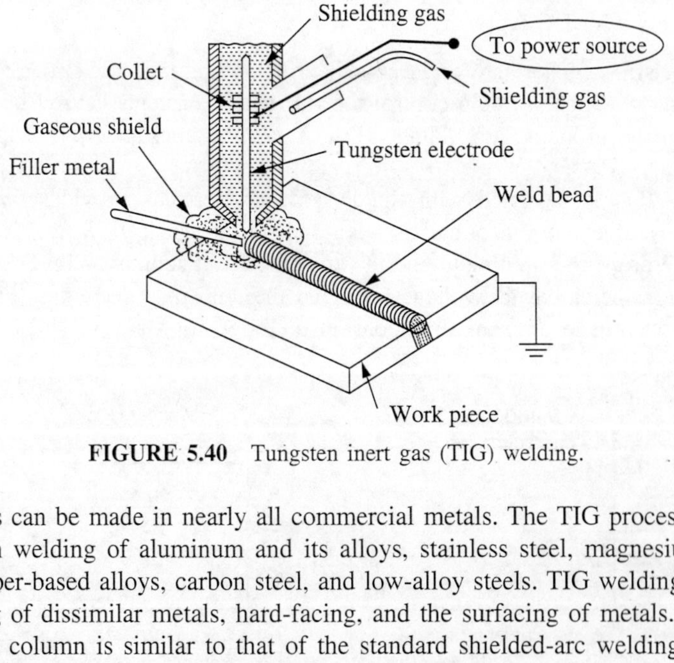

FIGURE 5.40 Tungsten inert gas (TIG) welding.

Fusion welds can be made in nearly all commercial metals. The TIG process lends itself very well to the fusion welding of aluminum and its alloys, stainless steel, magnesium alloys, nickel-based alloys, copper-based alloys, carbon steel, and low-alloy steels. TIG welding can also be used for the combining of dissimilar metals, hard-facing, and the surfacing of metals.

The TIG arc column is similar to that of the standard shielded-arc welding arc column. The electron travel is identical to that in shielded-arc welding.

5.3.3 MIG Arc Welding

Metal inert gas (MIG) welding uses consumable electrode and inert gas like CO_2 in case of mild steel to shield the welded joint (Figure 5.41). For other metals, the preferred inert gas shield is provided by argon and helium in proportions shown in Table 5.1.

TABLE 5.1 Proportion of gases

Metals	*Shielding gas*
Aluminium	Argon 25%, Helium 75%
Copper	Argon 25%, Helium 75%
Nickel	Argon 25%, Helium 75%
Steel low alloy	Argon 75%, Oxygen 25%
Mild Steel	Carbon dioxide

Carbon dioxide is used mostly to avoid surface oxides. Because CO_2 is cheap and mild steel is the material frequently welded, the above combination is most frequent.

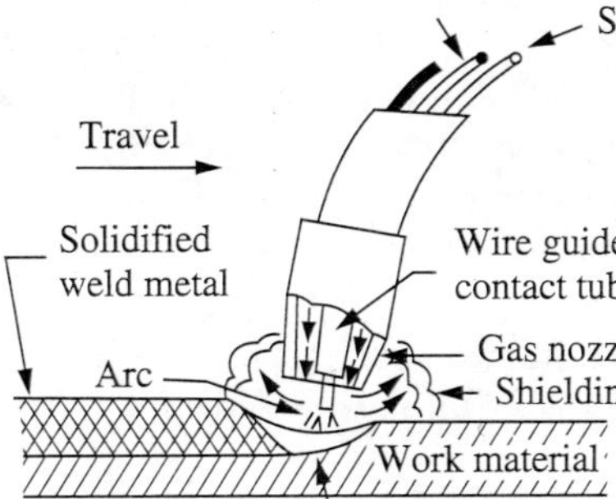

FIGURE 5.41 MIG welding scheme.

5.3.4 Resistance Welding

Resistance welding is based on the principle of heat being localized at a point where two metallic pieces are joined and heavy current flows through them. Electrodes of various designs (pointed, domed and flat) are used according to the weld desired. Pointed electrodes are the most widely used. They are used for ferrous materials. Domed electrodes are designed to withstand heavier current loads and more mechanical force, which make them applicable to non-ferrous metals. Flat electrodes are used when spot welding deformation is not wanted or when the spot-weld should be minimum. Usually, one flat electrode is used with one domed electrode.

Resistance welding process. The diameter of the electrode determines the diameter d of the fusion zone of the weld spot (Figure 5.42 (a and b)). The diameter of the fusion zone will be 0.01 in. plus twice the thickness of the thinnest member being spot-welded; however, this pre-set weld fusion size is chosen according to the application; that is, a sheet metal shop would determine the optimum sizes for their spot-welding needs, but an automotive body shop might require different electrode sizes. The amount of lap that is required for a good spot-weld depends on the size of the fusion weld.

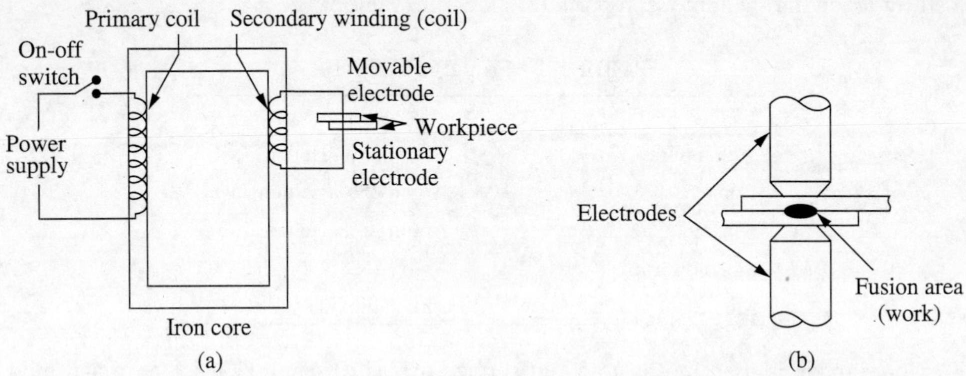

FIGURE 5.42 Resistance welding: (a) scheme of resistance welding and (b) weld bead.

High-frequency resistance welding. The phenomenon of high-frequency current which causes it to flow at or near the surface of a conductor and not through the entire thickness of a conductor makes it possible to resist welding of extremely thin pieces of *material*, as thin as 0.004 in. Another phenomenon of high-frequency current is the proximity effect (the current follows a path of low conductance rather than low resistance) which means that the effective resistance of the metal being welded is much higher with high-frequency current than standard 60-Hz current (Figure 5.43). Therefore, the amperage requirement for a given amount of calorie release or heat release is what a fraction of that needed for standard resistance welding.

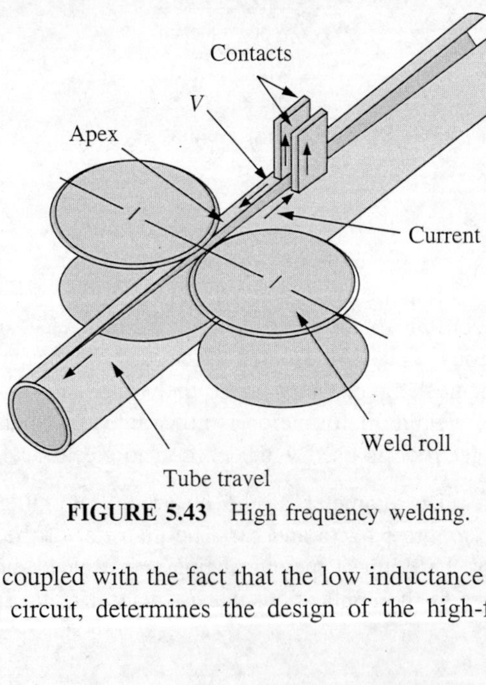

FIGURE 5.43 High frequency welding.

This characteristic, coupled with the fact that the low inductance path is the one that is closest to the conductor of the circuit, determines the design of the high-frequency resistance welding machine.

5.3.5 Oxy-Acetylene Welding

Oxy-acetylene welding is based on heat generation by gas burning. Heat is generated when acetylene (C_2H_2) burns with oxygen in atmosphere (Figure 5.44).

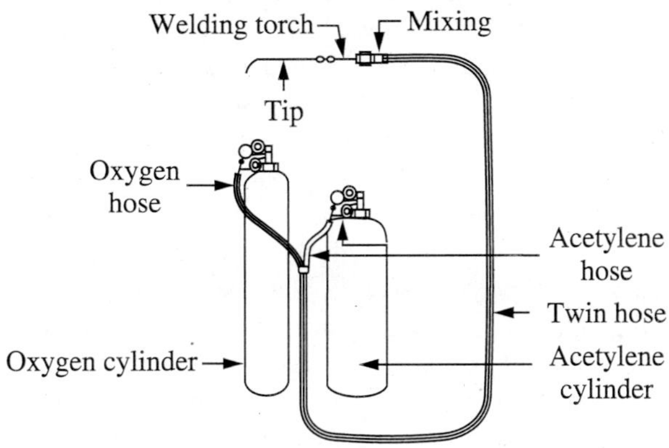

FIGURE 5.44 Oxy-acetylene gas welding scheme.

There are three types of flames: the carburizing, or reducing flame; the balanced or neutral flame; and the oxidizing flame. The carburizing, or reducing flame has an excess of acetylene and is characterized by three stages of combustion instead of two as in the other two types of flames. The extra combustion stage, called the *intermediate feather*, can be adjusted by the amount of acetylene imbalance induced by the torch body needle valve. The length of the intermediate feather usually is measured by eye in terms of the inner-cone length. A $2X$ carburizing flame, then, would be a feather approximately twice as long as the inner cone (Figure 5.45). The carburizing flame does not completely consume the available carbon; therefore, its burning temperature is lower and the leftover carbon is forced into the metal. This action is characterized by the molten weld puddle appearing to boil. After this carbon-rich weld bead solidifies, the weld will have a pitted surface; these pits can extend through the entire weld bead. The bead will also be hardened and extremely brittle because of the excessive amount of carbon that was injected into the molten base metal. This excess of carbon, however, is an ideal condition when welding high-carbon steel.

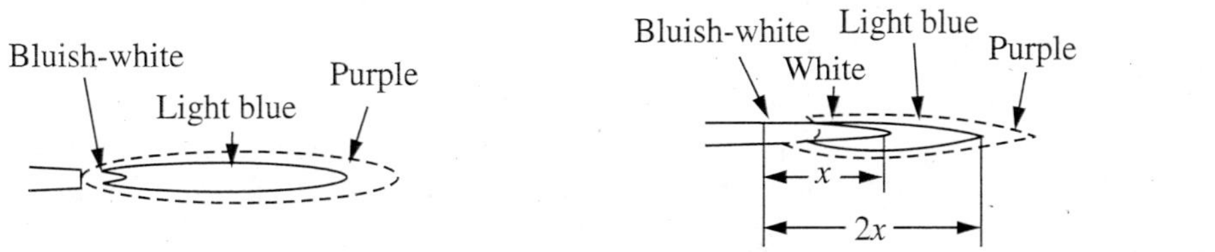

(i) Normal flame (5000–6300°F) (ii) Carburizing or reducing flame (up to 5700°F) (Suitable for high carbon steel)

FIGURE 5.45 Flame details.

Upon further adjustment of the torch needle valves, the intermediate feather can be drawn into the inner cone. The oxygen usually is increased in order to maintain the minimum amount of acetylene flow. Increase of the oxygen flow causes the intermediate feather to recede into the inner cone. The instant that the feather disappears into the cone, the oxygen–acetylene mixture produces a balanced or neutral flame. This two-stage neutral flame, which has a symmetrical inner cone and makes a hissing sound (Figure 5.45), is the most used flame in both the welding and the flame cutting of metals. It has little effect on the base metal or the weld bead and usually produces a clean-appearing, sound weld bead with properties equal to the base metal properties. The inner cone of the neutral flame is not hot enough to metals, and the secondary combustion envelope is an excellent cleanser and protector of ferrous metals.

Further opening of the oxygen needle valve on the torch body shortens the inner cone approximately two-tenth of its original length. The inner cone then loses its symmetrical shape, and the flame gives off a loud roar. These three actions characterize the oxidizing flame, the hottest flame that can be produced by any oxygen–fuel source. The oxidizing flame injects oxygen into the molten metal of the weld puddle, causing the metal to oxidize or burn quickly, as demonstrated by the bright sparks that are thrown of the weld puddle. Also, the excess of oxygen causes the weld bead and the surrounding area to have a scummy or dirty appearance. A slightly oxidizing flame is helpful when welding most copper-based metals, zinc-based metals, and a few types of ferrous metals, such as manganese steel and cast iron. The oxidizing atmosphere creates a base-metal oxide that protects the base metal. For example, in welding brass, the zinc alloyed in the copper has a tendency to separate and fume away. The formation of a covering copper oxide prevents the zinc from dissipating electrical resistance qualities, the current setting must be 20–30% higher than that use with argon or helium.

Other inert gases used for gas shielding include nitrogen oxygen, and hydrogen. When nitrogen is used as a mixing or carrier gas, a very small percentage is used. Oxygen can be used up to 10%. A higher percentage of oxygen will yield porosity in the weld bead.

5.4 MACHINING PROCESS

Machining is a secondary process in which a large quantity of material is removed from the workpiece to give the required shape and accuracy. The layer of excess material is removed in the form of 'chips'. The basic principle of generation is based on:

1. Cutting motion which is the main relative motion between the workpiece and the tool
2. Feeding motion which presents fresh surface for cutting to the tool

According to the principle of machinability developed by the Russian scientists, P. Rodin, N. Acherkan and the Indian Engineers, Bhattacharya [4] and Ghosh and Mallik [5], Directrix and Generatrix are essential basis for shape formation. Referring to Figure 5.46, feed motion is along Directrix and cutting motion is along Generatrix. Figure 5.46(a) indicates the generation of flat surface. Figure 5.46(b) shows the relationship between generation and direction.

Figure 5.46(c) shows the generation of cylindrical surface as in cylindrical turning on lathe. Figure 5.46(d) illustrates generation of flat surface, for example, a circular grinding wheel which generates a flat surface when the wheel spins and moves in a straight line. Table 5.2 shows the interaction of various feasible combinations of Generatrix and Directrix. In fact, the profile of the generated surface can be obtained by drawing a tangent envelop to successive positions of the cutter as it rolls on the workpiece, without slipping.

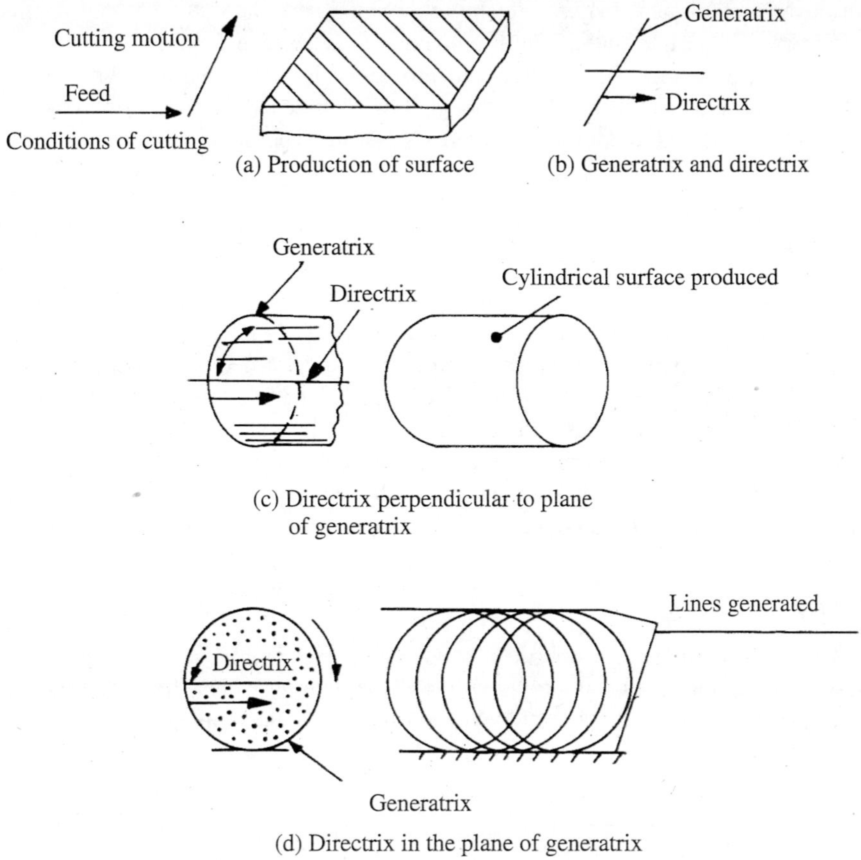

FIGURE 5.46 Principle of generation of surfaces.

TABLE 5.2 Generation of various surfaces

Generatrix	*Directrix*	*Process*	*Surface obtained*
Straight line	Straight line	Tracing	Plane
Circular	Straight line	Tracing	Cylindrical
Plane curve	Circular	Tracing	Surface of revolution
Circular	Straight line	Generation	Straight line (plain surface in practice)

We shall now give brief descriptions of the common machining processes.

5.4.1 Shaping and Planing

In shaping and planing, the surface obtained is plane as shown in column 4 of Table 5.1. In *shaping,* the cutting tool is given a reciprocating motion, and after every cutting stroke, the work is fed perpendicularly (during the return stroke the work is advanced by a small distance) in order to provide a layer of the uncut material to the tool. Since here the cutting is not continuous, the machining is known as an intermittent cutting operation, see Figure 5.47(a).

For a long job, it becomes inconvenient to provide long cutting strokes with the mechanism used in a shaping machine. In such a case, the work is provided with cutting motion, whereas the feed is given to the tool; this operation is known as *planing*. The basic geometry of the machining operation is the same as that of shaping.

5.4.2 Turning

This is a basic operation and produces a cylindrical surface. Of course, by facing, a flat surface can also be obtained. The machine tool used for this type of operation is known as lathe. Figure 5.47(b) shows a typical turning operation where a workpiece in the form of a cylindrical bar is rotated about the axis of symmetry. The tool is provided with a feed motion parallel to the work axis. With respect to the work, the tool has a helical motion and always encounters an uncut layer of the workpiece. Here, the machining operation is continuous. This operation results in a reduced work diameter and a new cylindrical surface. When the tool is fed in the radial direction along the face (Figure 5.47(b)), a flat surface is produced and the length of the workpiece gets reduced.

5.4.3 Drilling

This process is used for making a hole in a solid workpiece. Figure 5.47(c) shows the operation schematically. The cutting motion is provided to the two cutting edges (lips) by rotating the drill, and the feeding is done by giving a rectilinear feed motion to the drill in the axial direction. The final surface obtained is an internal cylindrical surface.

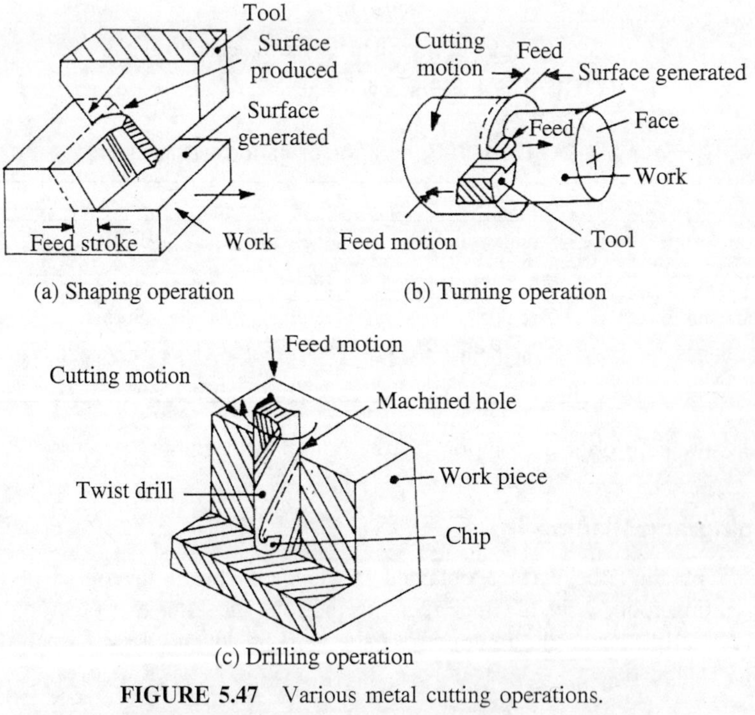

FIGURE 5.47 Various metal cutting operations.

5.4.4 Milling

Milling is a versatile machining operation; it can produce various types of surfaces. A plain slab operation is shown in Figure 5.48(a). The tool, known as a milling cutter, possesses a number of cutting edges. It is provided with a rotary motion and the work is gradually fed. Small chips are removed by each cutting edge during revolution, and finally a flat surface is produced.

5.4.5 Grinding

In grinding, the cutting tools are the sharp edges of the abrasive grains of the grinding wheel. These grains are very large in number and have a random orientation and distribution. However, if a particular grain is observed, its action would be as shown in Figure 5.48(b). Of course, the size of the chips removed by a grain is exceedingly small.

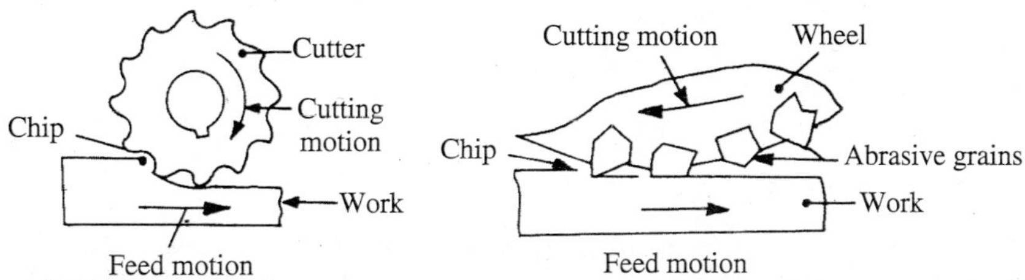

(a) Milling operation (b) Grinding operation

FIGURE 5.48 Machining with multipoint tools.

5.4.6 Chip Formation Mechanism

Machining or metal cutting occurs through the chip formation process shown in Figure 5.49. Research by Dr. M-Eugene Merchant in USA has shown that chip formation is a mechanism of localized shear deformation. The failure of the workpiece material immediately ahead of the cutting edge of the tool is through block-wise slip as shown in the Figure Thickness of each block can be assumed to be extremely small, almost 0.025 mm.

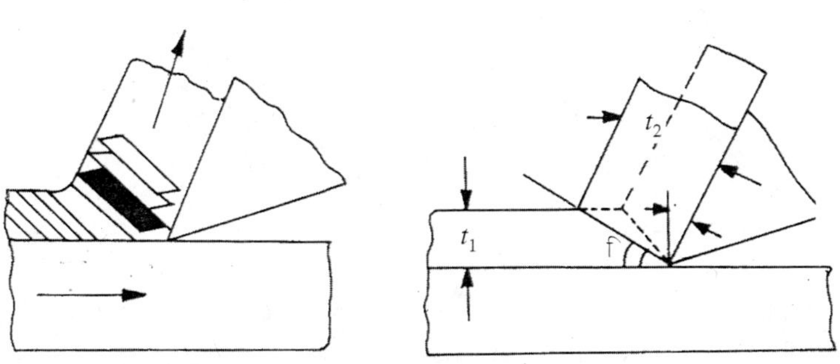

(a) Card analogy (b) Geometry of chip formation

FIGURE 5.49 Chip formation—idealized model.

The efficiency of metal cutting depends upon the sharpness of the tool edge. The rake angle of the wedge shape in the plane of chip of formation and friction at the chip tool interface. A rake angle up to 10° and use of cutting oil to reduce friction at the chip tool interface result in a value of shear plane angle of the order of 18–20°. Thin chips indicate reasonable values of shear plane angle, low shear plane areas, and reduced power needed for cutting. The opposite, i.e., thick chips, indicate poor machining conditions. The geometry of cutting process is shown in Figures 5.49(a) and (b). The notations are:

t_1 uncut thickness
t_2 chip thickness
α rake angle
ϕ shear plane angle

Whether it is turning, drilling, milling or any other metal removal process, the basic wedge shape in the plane of chip formation is present everywhere. It determines the case of cutting. To understand the action, of any cutting tool, it is essential to locate the basic wedge. The tool materials used for machining are high speed steel (18% tungsten, 4% chromium, 1% vanadium). Tips of inserts of tungsten carbide in a matrix of cobalt, produced by powder metallurgy and recently boron nitride have been introduced for metal cutting.

5.4.7 Analysis of Metal Cutting Process

Dr. Merchant was the first scientist who proposed a model for the cutting of metals. Merchant's model was based on the principle of minimum energy. Figure 5.50 shows a simple scheme of the metal cutting process in which a wedge-shaped tool removes material from the workpiece. The removed material appears in the form of chips. According to Merchant, following the natural law of minimum energy, the shear plane angle, ϕ, assumes a value, depending on the rake angle α of the tool, friction angle β at the chip-tool interface, and a constant C that expresses the machinability of the workpiece material. The relationship developed by Dr. Merchant is expressed as:

$$(2\phi + \beta - \alpha) = C$$

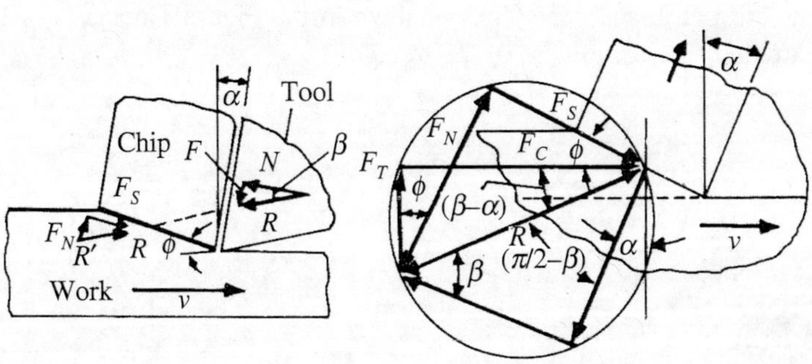

(a) Equilibrium of chip (b) Merchant's circle diargram

FIGURE 5.50 Merchants circle diagram.

Derivation of shear angle relation $(2\phi + \beta - \alpha) = C$: The chip is treated as a free body held in equilibrium due to equal and opposite forces acting on the chip (see Figure 5.50).

The first force is the force R exerted by the tool on the chip. This force is the resultant of the chip-tool interface friction, F and the normal force N at the chip-tool interface.

The second force is the force R' exerted by the workpiece on the chip, and the shear plane normal force, F_n. Merchant represented the vector diagram of forces on circle diagram as shown. Now, from the principle of minimum energy, the energy required in cutting depends only on the cutting force F_c (cutting force is not affected much by the cutting speed), for which the minimum is to be sought by setting $(\delta F_c/\delta\phi) = 0$.

From the geometry of the circle diagram.

$$F_c = R\cos(\beta - \alpha) \tag{5.9}$$

$$F_s = R\cos(\phi + \beta - \alpha) \tag{5.10}$$

Therefore,

$$F_c = \frac{F_s \cdot \cos(\beta - \alpha)}{\cos(\phi + \beta - \alpha)} = \frac{sA_s\cos(\beta - \alpha)}{\cos(\phi + \beta - \alpha)} \tag{5.11}$$

Now, the shear stress S on the shear plane depends on the normal stress σ, according to the relation

$$S = (S_0 + K\sigma)$$

Also, since $F_s = F_n\cot(\phi + \beta - \alpha)$ we have $S = \sigma\cot(\phi + \beta - \alpha)$ (from Merchant's circle). Therefore,

$$S_0 = S - K \cdot S\tan(\phi + \beta - \alpha) = S[1 - K\tan(\phi + \beta - \alpha)] \tag{5.12}$$

Substituting the value of S from Eq. (5.12) in Eq. (5.11), we have

$$F_c = \frac{S_0A_s\cos(\beta - \alpha)}{[1 - K\tan(\phi + \beta - \alpha)]\cos(\phi + \beta - \alpha)} \tag{5.13}$$

Further, substituting $A_s = (A/\sin\phi)$, we get

$$F_c = \frac{S_0A_s\cos(\beta - \alpha)}{[\sin\phi\cos(\phi + \beta - \alpha)][1 - \tan(\phi + \beta - \alpha)]}$$

$$F_c = \frac{\text{Numerator}}{[\sin\phi\cos(\phi + \beta - \alpha)][1 - \tan(\phi + \beta - \alpha)]}$$

Differentiating F_c w.r.t. ϕ, we have

$$\cot(2\phi + \beta - \alpha) = K$$

Setting $K = \cot C$,

$$2\phi + \beta - \alpha = C \tag{5.14}$$

The interpretation of C is the slope of S-σ curve. The value of C can be estimated by material testing. Its value usually lies between 70 and 80° for metals and 90° for plastics. Table gives the C values of some important metals.

(i) **Utility of Merchant's analysis.** The relationship

$$F_c = \frac{sA\cos(\beta - \alpha)}{\sin\phi\cos(\phi + \beta - \alpha)}$$

is of great importance. It can be used for estimating the cutting forces in metal cutting. Rearranging, we have

$$F_c = A\frac{s\cos(\beta - \alpha)}{\sin\phi\cos(\phi + \beta - \alpha)} = A[p] \tag{5.15}$$

where p is called specific cutting pressure. Its value depends on yield shear stress s of the workpiece material and thickness of cut. Practically, above a thickness of cut of 0.15 mm, p is constant. To be able to estimate the cutting force accurately, the Merchant's constant C should also be known (Table 5.3). Substituting $(\beta - \alpha)$ from Merchant's relation, we get

$$2\phi + \beta - \alpha = C$$

or

$$(\beta - \alpha) = (C - 2\phi)$$

Thus,

$$F_c = A_s\frac{\cos(C - 2\phi)}{\sin\phi\cos(C - 2\phi)} \tag{5.16}$$

where A denotes uncut area. The yield shear stress of the workpiece material can be estimated from indentation test and calculated as follows: Brinell Hardness Number (BHN) $\approx (6s)$ where s is the yield stress of the material in shear.

For good cutting conditions yielding continuous chips, polished tool surface and efficient cutting fluid, shear plane angle ϕ is of the order of magnitude $\approx 20°$.

TABLE 5.3 Values of Merchant's constant C.

Material	*C (degrees)*
AISI 1010	69.8
AISI 1020	69.6
AISI 1045	78.0
AISI 2340	76.2
AISI 3140	70.6
AISI 4340	74.5
Stainless 303	92.0
Stainless 304	82.0

For cylindrical turning, $A = (f \times d)$, where f is the feed rate in mm/revolution and d is the depth of cut. In drilling operation, $A = (f/2)\,(D - C)/2$, where D is the drill diameter and C the chisel edge length.

The thrust component F_t in metal cutting can be estimated from:

$$F_t = F_c \tan(\beta - \alpha)$$

$$F_t = F_c \tan(C - 2\phi)$$

Figure 5.40 indicates force system of drilling and turning showing F_i and F_t and other force components in the machine reference system.

(ii) **Drilling torque and thrust.** In drilling, the torque can be calculated from mechanics of cutting. As can be seen from Figure 5.51,

$$\text{Torque} = F_c \times (D + C)/2 = p \cdot f/2[(D - C)/2]\,[(D + C)/2 \tag{5.17}$$

$$= pf(D^2 - C^2)/8$$

$$\text{Thrust due to cutting} = 2F_t \sin p \tag{5.18}$$

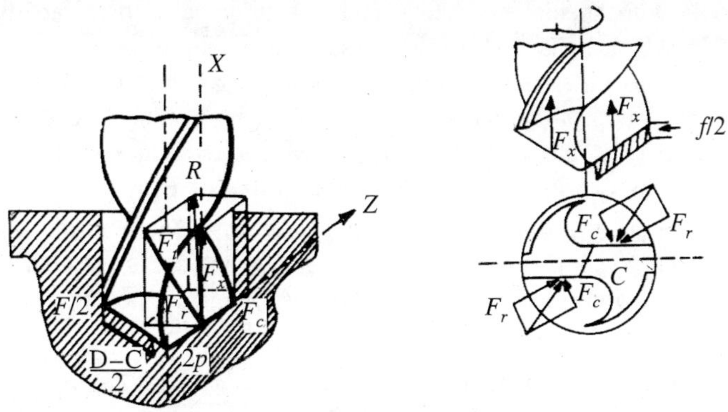

FIGURE 5.51 Mechanics of drilling process.

where p is the semi-point angle of the drill. In the drilling process, the chisel edge of a drill acts as an indentor rather than as a cutting tool. It functions as a wedge causing semi-hot extrusion. It has been shown by Bhattacharya [4] that the chisel edge contributes 50% to the total drill thrust. Hence, total drill thrust (due to cutting action of the drill tips + thrust due to indenting action of the chisel edge) is:

$$2[2F_t \sin p] = 4F_t \sin p \tag{5.19}$$

(iii) **Analysis of turning operation.** The various forces in turning are illustrated in Figure 5.52.

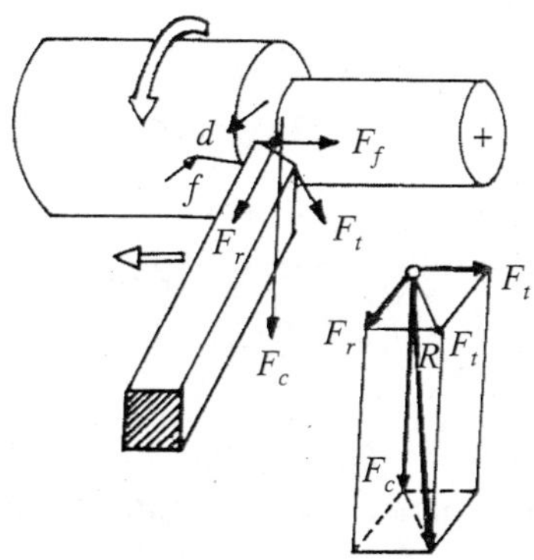

FIGURE 5.52 Mechanics of turning.

$$\text{Tangential cutting force} = F_c = p \cdot A = \text{p.f.d.} \tag{5.20}$$

$$\text{Thrust due to cutting} = F_t = (\text{p.f.d.}) \tan (\beta - \alpha) \tag{5.21}$$

The thrust force can be resolved parallel to the axis of workpiece, i.e., in the direction of feeding. The feed force, F_f, is given by the relation

$$F_f = F_t \sin (90 - C) = F_t \cos C \tag{5.22}$$

where C is the side cutting edge angle of the tool. The radial force F_r can be expressed as:

$$F_r = F_t \sin C \tag{5.23}$$

Cutting tools with special geometry having a high value of C are used for bar peeling operation, in which a hard skin on the surface of bar stock is to be removed at a high feed rate. On the other hand, slender workpieces are machined with cutting tools with low values of side cutting edge angle C, so that small radial forces are created. This helps maintain accuracy of the workpiece due to reduced deflection of the workpiece as a beam subjected to radial loading, owing to reduced value of F_r.

(iv) **System approach to metal removal processes.** Some authors like Alting, Leo [6] prefer to employ an approach different from shear plane analysis, to estimate power and forces in cutting. The following elementary relationships should be noted:

1. Energy/min consumed in cutting = $F_c\ V$ N m/min
2. Power consumed in watts = $F_cV/60$ Nm/s
3. Metal removal rate, $W = (fdV \times 10^3)/60$ mm^3/s

The power required to remove a unit volume of metal per minute is of high utility to machine tool engineers.

$$p = \text{specific cutting pressure} = F_c/d_f \text{ N/mm}^2$$

$$U_c = \text{power}/W = (F_cV/60)\ (60/fdV \times 10^3) = F_c/(d_f \times 10^3) = p/10^3$$

An illustrative example on system approach to metal cutting is now taken up to make the notion clearer.

Example. A lathe running idle consumes 325 W. When cutting an alloy steel at 24.5 m/min, the power input rises to 2580 W. Find the cutting force and torque at the spindle when running at 124 rpm. If the depth of cut is 3.8 mm and feed = 0.2 mm, find the power criterion.

Solution. The power consumed in cutting = 2580 – 325 = 2255 W

$$W = 0.2 \times 3.8 \times 24.5 \times 10^3/60 = 310 \text{ mm}^3/\text{s}$$

$$\text{Power criterion} = 2255/310 = 7.27 \text{ W/mm}^3/\text{s}$$

$$\text{Torque at spindle} = 2255 \times 60/(2\pi \times 124) = 174 \text{ Nm}$$

$$\text{Cutting force, } F_c = 2255 \times 60/24.5 = 5522 \text{ N}$$

The merit of the system approach is that it can be modified to multitooth operations of forming as well as generating, such as milling, gear generation, e.g., hobbing and shaping. The reader is referred to authentic works on the subject of metal cutting by, among others Alting, Leo [6], Bhattacharya [4], and Ghosh and Mallik [5] have expressed power criterion as dependent on undeformed chip thickness. That is,

$$U_c = \left[\frac{F_c}{1000 \times d \times f}\right] = U_0 f^{-0.4}$$

$$U_0 = \frac{F_c \times f^{0.4}}{1000 \times d \times f}$$

$$U_0 = \frac{F_c}{1000 \times d \times f^{0.6}}$$

Rearranging, we obtain:

$$F_c = (1000 \times d \times f^{0.6}\ U_0) \text{ Newton}$$

The values of U_0 are as given in Table 5.4.

TABLE 5.4 Values of U_0 (after Ghosh and Mallik [5])

Material			U_0 (J/mm^3)
Steel	BHN	85–200	1.4
	RC	35–40	1.6
		40–50	1.9
		50–55	2.4
		55–58	4.0
Stainless	BHN	135–275	1.4
CI		110–190	0.8
		190–320	1.6
Al alloy		30–150	0.35
Copper	RB	80	1.2
Copper alloys	RB	10–80	0.8

5.4.8 Analysis of Grinding Process

As already stated, grinding is a metal cutting operation which is analogous to milling and is termed *micromilling* (see Figure 5.53). Material is removed by abrasive grits of a very hard substance held together by bonding materials. Grinding wheels comprise grits, bonds and voids, the latter providing chip clearance and space for coolant supply. To continue material removal effectively, it is essential that blunt grits be released from the bond. This release of the grit at the end of active service is called self-sharpening action. Another requirement for a wheel to cut effectively is that the wheel should not get loaded, i.e., the space between grits should not be clogged with chips. Open structure wheels with grits spaced properly are suitable for grinding ductile materials producing continuous chips. A proper selection of grinding wheel and grinding conditions ensures that grits are released after they get blunt. This prevents rubbing through mechanical and metallurgical damage caused by high temperatures of the grinding process.

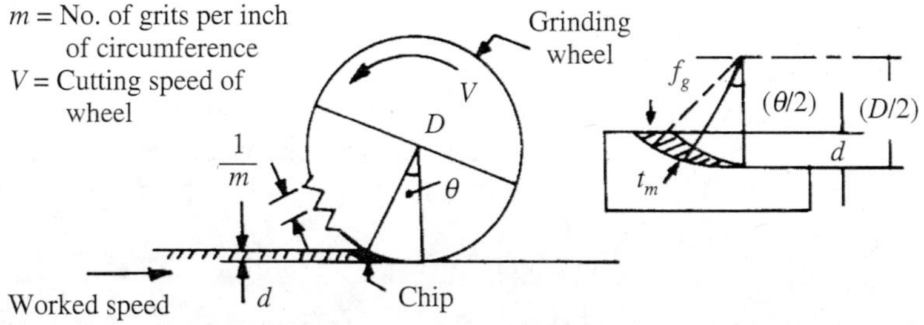

FIGURE 5.53 Grinding process and its geometry of chip formation.

Analysis of grinding as micromilling
NOTATION

t_m: Mean chip thickness,

m: No. of grits per unit length,

Wheel speed: mV grits/min

Equation for mean chip thickness:

$$t_m = f_g \sin \theta/2 = f_g[(1 - \cos \theta)/2]^{1/2}$$
$$= f_g[d/D]^{1/2}$$
$$= v/mV[d/D]^{1/2}$$ [In grinding, the value of $t_m \approx 0.002$ mm]

Analysis of equation for mean chip thickness. Equation for t_m indicates that by altering the work speed v, wheel speed V, depth of cut, d, and the grit chip thickness, the chip load can be controlled. Thus, if the chip load is less and the wheel behaves hard, i.e., the grit is not released, v and d can be increased and V decreased, to avoid damage to job. On the other hand, if wheel wear is excessive due to more chip load, the opposite steps can be taken.

Grinding wheel specification

Example. A typical grinding wheel specification is A-46-K-12-V. The letter A indicates material of Abrasive Al_2O_3; 9 Moh scale suitable for grinding steel. C stands for SiC, 9.5 Moh scale suitable for grinding, C.I. 46 refers to grit size (Mesh No.), i.e., the grit will just pass through mesh 46 holes/inch for good finish, larger mesh number and vice versa. Bond strength $E \rightarrow W$ in 19 grades: M is medium bond strength wheel.

The structure close–open is used depending on whether the material ground is ductile or brittle (1–12). For ductile work material, open structure such as 12 is preferred. V indicates vitrified or clay bond. Other bonds are Resinoid, Rubber, Shellac and Oxychloride.

The other factors for wheel selection are as follows:

1. For hard material, use ‘soft’ wheel, i.e., one of lower bond strength.
2. For surface grinding, the area of contact is more; so use soft wheel to ensure self dressing and for cylindrical grinding, use hard wheel as intensity of pressure is more due to small contact area.
3. In the case of unskilled workers or old machines, use hard wheels to ensure sufficient wheel life.

5.4.9 Machinability

Machinability of a work piece material is a property which enables easy chip formation, consistent with a good surface finish and reasonable tool life. This definition of machinability indicates the inherent paradox because soft materials which are easy to cut yield a poor surface finish and vice versa.

Some factors which influence machinability of work piece material are:

1. *Hardness.* Steels up to 300 HB are easy to machine if alloying elements raising the hardness during cutting (e.g., in case of stainless steels) are not present. Stainless steel is

austenitic at room temperature. During cutting, the stresses created result in the formation of martensite and cutting becomes a problem. Soft materials such as steels containing banded structures of ferrite do not yield a good finish due to tearing of ferrite rich areas.

2. *Microstructure.* In high carbon steels if cementite is in platelet form, it causes tool wear. In cast iron, graphite present in spheriodal form is desirable and gives good finish. Graphite present in cast iron as flakes acts as lubricant during cutting but such a cast iron is weak in tension and is good only due to its shock absorbing property.
3. *Free cutting properties.* The presence of sulphur as manganese sulphide inclusions in steel lends it free machining property. This is due to the formation of solid film of low shear strength at chip–tool interface in the form of (FES) which acts as a lubricant during metal cutting. Addition of lead to brass makes it easy to machine due to formation of lead film at chip tool interface assisting in lubrication.
4. *Ductility.* Ductile materials give rise to fast moving continuous chips which endanger the operator. Chip breaker grooves or steps are to be built in. The discontinuous or powdery chip shows high machinability, due to reduced risk to operator.

Machinability index or rating. It is defined as the ratio of cutting speeds when cutting the workpiece material to cutting of standard and high machinability steel for same tool life (usually 60 min). It is thus a speed ratio or metal removal rate ratio.

5.4.10 Economics of Metal Cutting

F.W. Taylor gave the tool life equation.

$$VM^n = C$$

where,

V – cutting speed
M – tool life mins
n – index depending upon tool material

It is as below:

n = 0.125 for high speed steel tool
n = 0.25 for carbide tip tool
n = 0.5 for oxide tools

C – constant depending upon cutting conditions.

During the machining of hard and brittle materials like cast iron, tool wear occurs along clearance surface. This is flank wear. Rake face wear or crater wear occurs during cutting of ductile materials.

Economic relationships in metal cutting

Let m: machine running cost, labor plus overheads (₹/min)
T: tooling cost (₹/tool change)
f: feed rate, d = depth of cut (mm)
V: cutting speed (mm/min)

Metal removal rate (mm³/min) = fdV

Time to remove unit volume of metal = $\dfrac{1}{fdV} = \dfrac{K}{V}$

Referring to Figure 5.54(a) on costs:

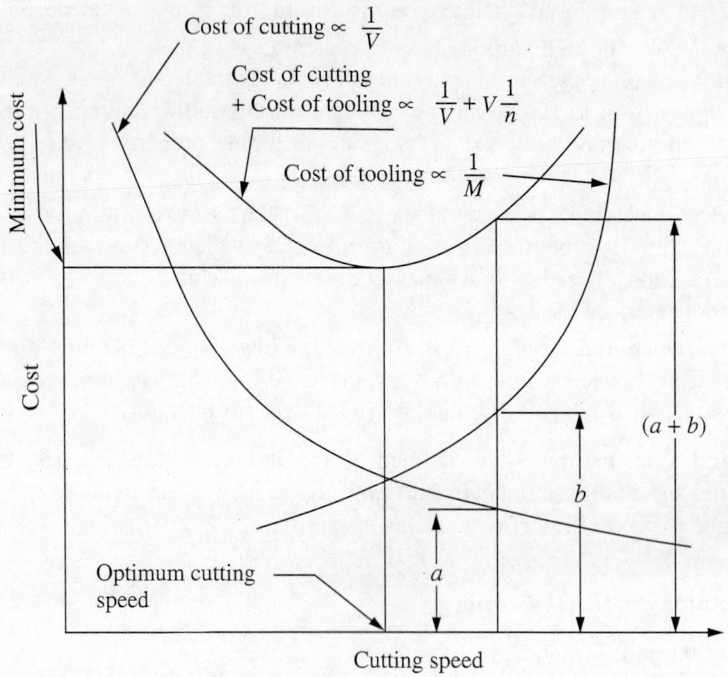

FIGURE 5.54(a) Economics of metal cutting–economic cutting speed.

Cost of metal cutting per unit volume of metal removal = $m\left(\dfrac{K}{V}\right)$

If M is the tool life or time per tool change,

The number of tool changes in time $\left(\dfrac{K}{V}\right) = \left(\dfrac{K}{MV}\right) = \left(\dfrac{K}{V} \cdot \dfrac{1}{M}\right)$

Cost of tool change per unit volume of metal $\left(\dfrac{K}{MV}\right)T$

Total cost of metal cutting and tooling $C_t = m\left(\dfrac{K}{V}\right) + \left(\dfrac{K}{MV}\right)T$

For economic conditions of optimization $\dfrac{dC_t}{dV} = 0$

Rewriting C_t by substituting $M = (C/V)^{1/n}$

We have,

$$C_t = \left[m\left(\frac{K}{V}\right) + \frac{TKV^{(1-n)/n}}{C^{1/n}} \right]$$

Writing

$$\frac{\partial C_t}{\partial V} = \frac{mK}{V^2} + \frac{1-n}{n}\frac{TK}{C^{1/n}}V^{(1-2n)/n} = 0$$

$$m = \left(\frac{1-n}{n}\right)T\left(\frac{V}{C}\right)^{1/n}$$

or

since

$$\left(\frac{V}{C}\right)^{1/n} = \frac{1}{M}$$

$\therefore$

$$m \cdot \frac{M}{T} = \frac{1-n}{n}$$

We get,

$$M = \left(\frac{1-n}{n}\right)\frac{T}{m}$$

Thus, the equation for most economic tool life M is obtained.

It is to be noted that the tooling cost consists of the following three cost components:

1. Original cost of tool (₹/edge) = T/(No. of edges + 1), where T is the original cost of insert.
2. Cost of tool change, i.e., tool change time $T_c \cdot m$
3. Cost of tool grinding, i.e., tool grind time $T_g \cdot m$

If we want to derive the tool life for maximum production rate or minimum time, only cost component due to tool changing time T_c is important and cost of tool edge and grinding the edge can be set equal to zero.

Thus,

$$(M)_{\text{mintime}} = \frac{T_c m}{m}\left(\frac{1-n}{n}\right) = T_c \frac{1-n}{n}$$

Figure 5.54(b) indicates the high efficiency range for machining which shows the cutting speed range between maximum production and minimum cost. The formulae for $(M)_{\text{mincost}}$ and $(M)_{\text{mintime}}$ are straightforward to apply.

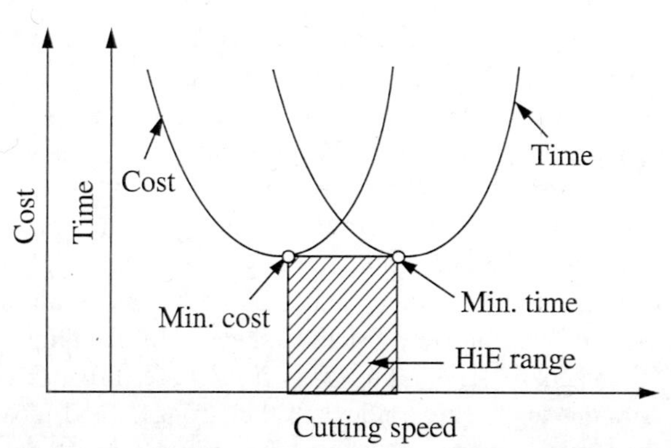

FIGURE 5.54(b) Economics of metal cutting—high efficiency (HiE) range.

For example, for a high speed steel tool ($n = 0.125$), if the tool changing time is, say, $T_c = 4$ min, the tool life for maximum production.

$$(M)_{\text{mintime}} = \left(\frac{1-0.125}{0.125}\right) \times 4 = 28 \text{ min}$$

The corresponding cutting speed can be found from Taylor's equation

$$VM^{0.125} = C$$

i.e.,

$$V = \frac{C}{(28)^{0.125}}, \text{ if } C \text{ is known.}$$

5.4.11 The Tool Material

One of the greatest steps forward in the machining of metals was made when Taylor discovered the heat treatment process used in producing high-speed, steel-cutting tools. Use of these cutting tools made higher metal removal rates possible owing to the improved tool wear behaviour. Since Taylor's heat-treatment discovery, development in metallurgical science and technology has led to other new tool materials, such as cast alloys, cemented carbides, and more recently, sintered oxides or ceramics.

Practical experience has shown which tool materials are most suited to particular operations; with single-point tools, where the manufacturing problems are not serious, the desirable property appears to be a high hardness value that is maintained at high temperatures. Unfortunately, an increase in hardness is usually accompanied by a decrease in the impact strength of the material; an increase in hardness also increases the tool manufacturing problems. Consequently, the materials found most suitable for continuous cutting with single-point cutting tools form only a small proportion of the total number of cutting tools used in practice; most metal cutting is still performed with tools manufactured from high-speed steel.

High-speed steels are alloy steels with the alloying elements consisting mainly of tungsten (about 18%) and chromium (about 4%); they may also contain cobalt, vanadium, or molybdenum.

Cast-alloy tools contain no iron and are cast into their final shape. They consist of cobalt, chromium, tungsten, and carbon. The carbide phase being about 25–30%, by volume of the matrix. These tools can usually be used at slightly higher speeds than high-speed steels and have less tendency to form a built-up edge during machining. They find the widest applications in the machining of cast iron, malleable iron, and the hard bronzes.

Cemented carbides are usually made by mixing tungsten powder and carbon at high temperatures in the ratio of 94 and 6%, respectively, by weight, this compound is then combined with cobalt, and the resulting mixture is compacted and sintered in a furnace at about 1400°C. This tungsten–carbon–cobalt material can maintain high hardness values at temperatures as high as 1200°C column and can therefore be used at much higher cutting speeds than high-speed steel or cast-alloy tool materials. However, as mentioned earlier, cemented carbides are not as tough and cannot be shaped after sintering. For this reason, they usually take the form of inserts, either brazed-on or clamped-on (Figures 5.55 and 5.56). The clamped-on inserts are thrown away after all the cutting edges have been worn. Straight tungsten carbides are the strongest and most wear resistant but are subjected to rapid cratering when machining steels. To improve resistance to cratering, tantalum carbide and titanium carbide are added to basic composition, resulting in tungsten–tantalum carbide or tungsten–titanium carbide.

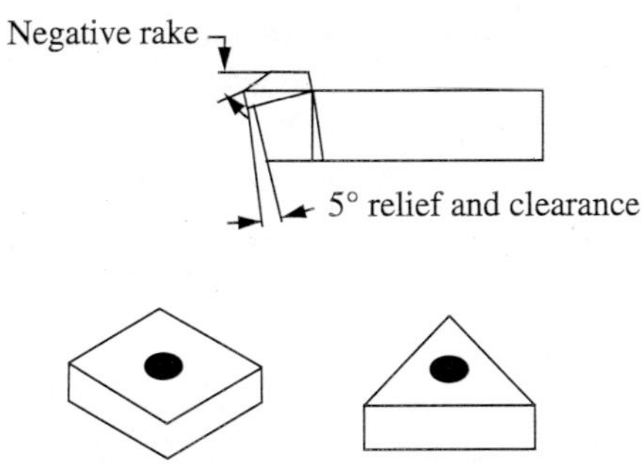

FIGURE 5.55 Single point brazed tool.

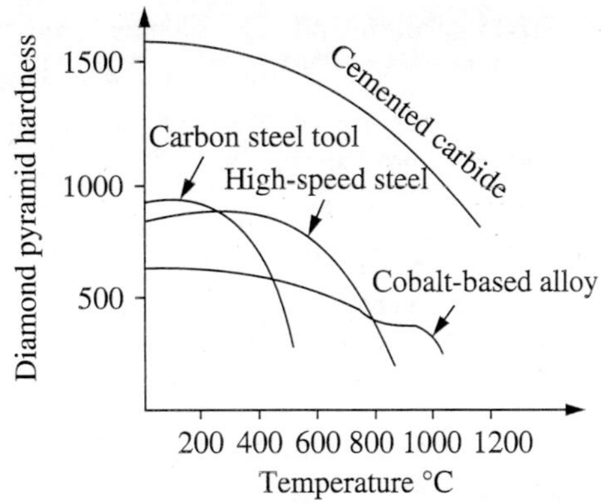

FIGURE 5.56 Hot hardness of cutting tool materials.

More recently, cemented titanium carbide has been available in the form of disposable inserts. This material is more wear-resistant than straight tungsten carbide but has the disadvantage of lower strength. However, development in the manufacture of this material has led to the production of superior grades that allow cutting speeds approaching those of ceramics; these superior grades can be used in the semi-rough cutting of steels and certain cast irons. Some believe that by the end of this decade, at least one half of all steel machining will be carried out using cemented titanium carbide.

The basic requirement for the efficient rough machining of steel is a tool material that exhibits the toughness of tungsten carbide while giving the superior wear resistance of titanium carbide. For this reason, much interest is being shown in the coating of cemented tungsten carbides with a thin layer of harder material. Successes have been reported with coatings of titanium carbide, titanium dioxide, and titanium nitride. These coatings are between 5 and 8 μm thick, and are found to practically eliminate inter diffusion between the chip and the tool. Eventually, when the coating has been worn away by abrasion, the wear rate becomes the same as that for the uncoated tool.

Sintered oxides, or ceramics, are made from sintered aluminium oxide and various boron-nitride powders; these powders are mixed together and sintered at about 1700°C. Sintered oxides can be used at cutting speeds of two or three times those employed with tungsten carbides, are very hard and have a high compressive strength and low thermal conductivity. They are, however, extremely brittle and can only be used where shock and vibrations do not occur. They are only available in the form of throwaway inserts, and their widest applications are in high-speed finish turning.

5.4.12 Cutting Fluids

Cutting fluids have the following two main functions:

1. To remove heat generated so as to limit rise of temperature of the tool's cutting edge.
2. To lubricate the area of contact between tool clearance face and work pieces and between the tool rake face and the chip, thus reducing friction, abrasive wear and built-up edge and so increasing tool life and surface finish.

Types of cutting fluid. Cutting fluids are required to carry away heat, e.g., in turning or carry away swart, e.g., in grinding. Cutting fluids which act as coolants are generally water based. Oils and emulsifying additives help in suppressing rusting. Oils also help in lubrication. Typical concentrations are: grinding (oil/water = 1/40 to 1/50); turning and milling (ratio of oil/water = 1/20).

- Straight cutting oils are blended from two types of oils (i) mineral oils, e.g. paraffin and other petroleum oils and (ii) fatty oils, generally organic oils of animal or vegetable origin.
- Cutting oils are sulphurized or chlorinated to develop extreme pressure oils. The sulphur and chlorine combine with steel to form FeS and FeC_3 at the chip–tool interface, which are solids of low shear strength. Thus, very efficient lubrication is possible.
- Chemicals such as carbon tetrachloride (CCl_4) are effective for reason given above.
- Gaseous cutting fluids such as CO_2 have also been tried. Oil in the form of a mist has been reported to be successful.

5.4.13 Friction at Chip-Tool Interface

The distribution of chip–tool interface normal pressure (σ) and shear stress (τ) are as indicated in Figure 5.57, value of coefficient of friction in the sticking zone at point 1, can be expressed as

$$\mu = \frac{K}{\sigma} = \frac{K}{6K} = \frac{1}{6} = 0.17$$

Because σ_{max} = Brinell Hardness Number (BHN) of workpiece material which is six times, yield shear stress K

Value of μ at point 2 is

$$\mu_2 = \frac{K}{\sigma_2} = \frac{K}{K} = 1$$

Value of μ at point 3 also tends to 1

$$\mu_3 = 1$$

Average value of kinetic coefficient of friction

$$= \frac{0.17 + 1 + 1}{3} = 0.7$$

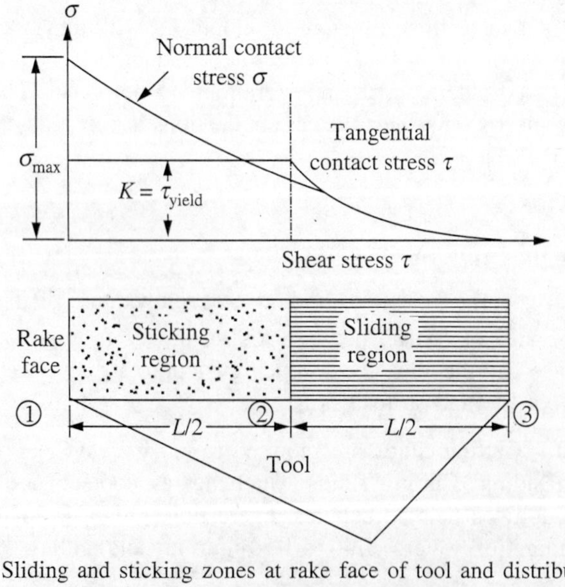

FIGURE 5.57 Sliding and sticking zones at rake face of tool and distribution of stresses.

Experiments indicate that the value of coefficient of friction in metal cutting tends to unity. Cutting fluids lower this value considerably.

5.5 MICROFINISHING OPERATIONS

The three microfinishing operations of importance in industrial practice are:

5.5.1 Lapping

This operation employs a lapping plate made of cast iron (the porosity helps to lodge the abrasive grains) or some softer material. During lapping, the fine abrasive which is mixed with grease and called lapping compound is smeared and rubbed under pressure against the hard workpiece surface. This causes erosion of the harder workpiece. The softer lap is now worn out during lapping because the abrasive grain gets embedded in the softer lap instead of cutting it. It is important that the lapping plate follows a non-repeating path such as a figures of eight to avoid formation of directional scratch pattern. Lapping gives high degree of flatness or roundness depending on the geometry of the lap. The tolerance grade achieved is below grade IT5 (Figure 5.58).

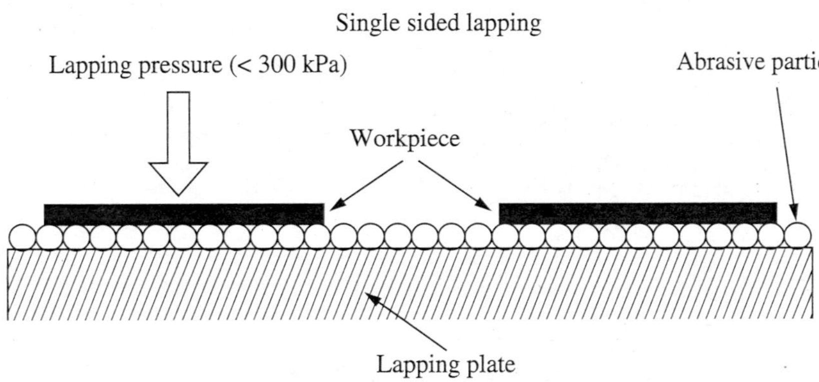

FIGURE 5.58 Lapping process.

5.5.2 Honing

Honing is usually applied to correct taper and out of roundness in holes such as engine cylinder bores. A honing tool carries 6–8 honing abrasive sticks along the circumference of a cylindrical tool body. The honing tool is driven by a rotating spindle through universal joints to achieve a floating condition for the tool inside the hole.

Honing of gears is done by a gear-shaped honing tool which is a soft grade bonded abrasive gear which rolls without slipping alongwith the workpiece gear to be honed. High accuracy and finish is obtained by gear honing but the tool is very costly (Figure 5.59).

5.5.3 Superfinishing

Superfinishing is a microfinishing process which employs a boned abrasive sector or flat disc which presses upon the surface to be microfinished. The surface and the abrasive piece are in very

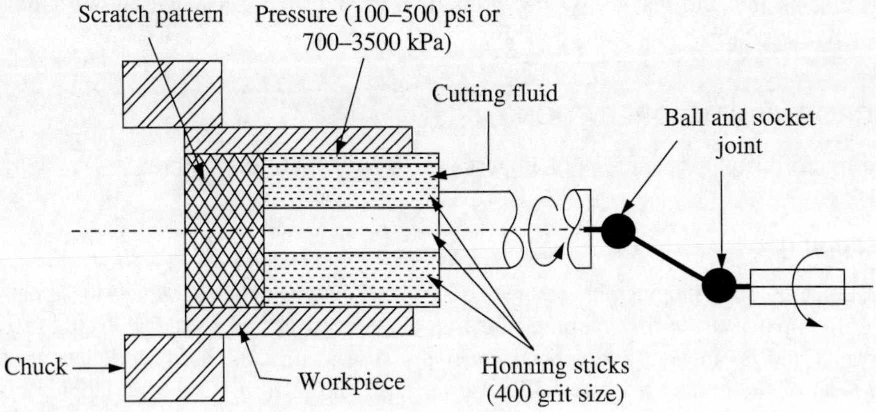

FIGURE 5.59 Honing process.

light contact under the influence of slight pressure. The two surface are separated by a thin film of viscous fluid. Contact between the abrasive disc and work surface at high spots results in the highest level of surface finish and to tolerance grade (even up to IT1).

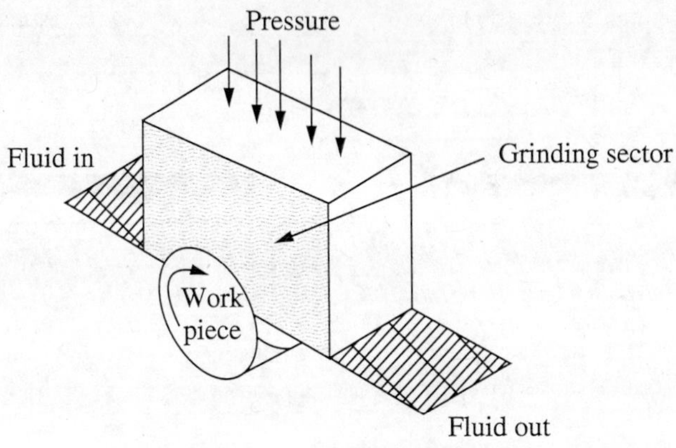

FIGURE 5.60 Superfinishing process.

5.6 NON-TRADITIONAL MACHINING PROCESSES

Many new materials have been developed recently, which possess very low machinability. Producing complicated shapes and geometries in such materials becomes extremely difficult with usual machining method. A number of new technological processes are discussed, outlining the basic principles involved.

5.6.1 Abrasive Jet Machining (AJM)

In AJM, material removal takes place due to impact of the fine abrasive particles. The particles move with a high speed aided by air discharge or gas stream. Figure 5.61 shows the process with some typical parameters of the process. The abrasive particles are typically of 0.025 mm diameter and the air discharges at a pressure of several atmosphere, see Figure 5.61.

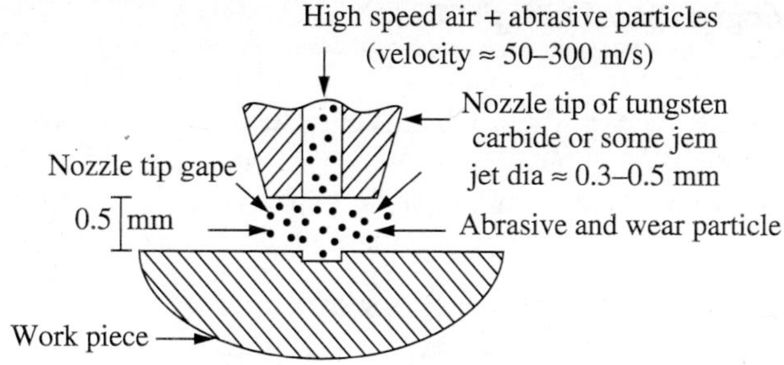

FIGURE 5.61 Abrasive jet machining.

5.6.2 Ultrasonic Machining (USM)

The basic USM process involves a tool made of tough and ductile material vibrating with a high frequency and continuous flow of an abrasive slurry in the small gap between the tool and work surface. The tool is gradually fed with a uniform force. The impact of the hard abrasive grains fractures the hard and brittle work surface, resulting in material removal. The tool material, being tough and ductile, wears out at a much slower rate, see Figure 5.62.

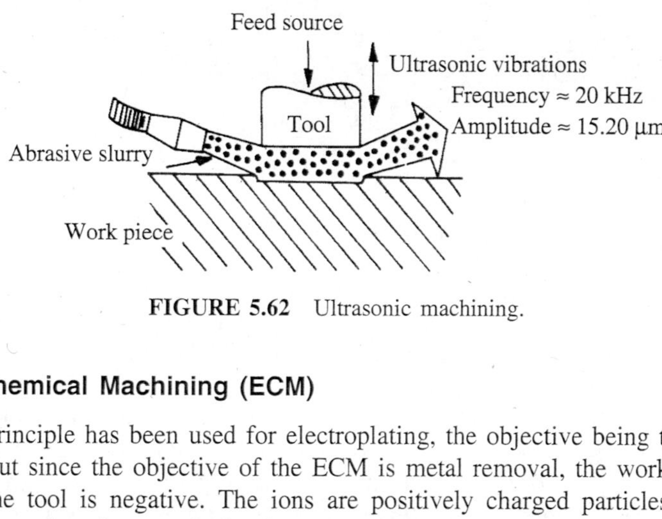

FIGURE 5.62 Ultrasonic machining.

5.6.3 Electrochemical Machining (ECM)

The electrolysis principle has been used for electroplating, the objective being to deposit metal on the work piece. But since the objective of the ECM is metal removal, the workpiece is connected to positive and the tool is negative. The ions are positively charged particles, eroded from the workpiece and attracted to the negatively charged tool. The work material is not allowed to deposit on the tool but is washed away by the electrolyte, see Figure 5.63.

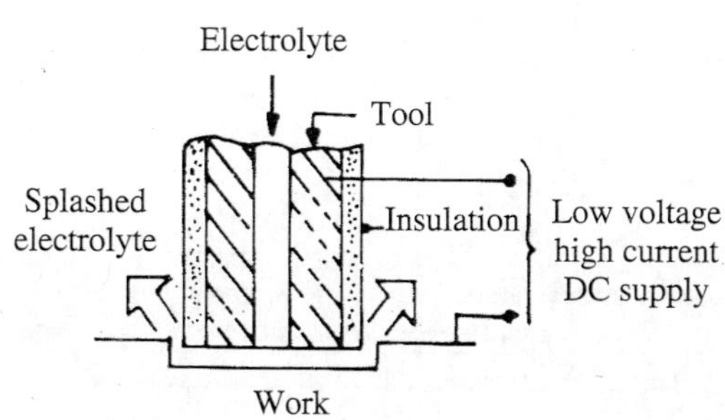

FIGURE 5.63 Electrochemical machining.

5.6.4 Electric Discharge Machining (EDM)

When discharge takes place between two points, anode (workpiece) and cathode (tool), the intense heat generated near the zone melts and evaporates the material in the sparking zone. The workpiece and the tool are immersed in direct fluid, e.g. kerosene (with toluene). There is a continuous charging and discharging resulting in intermittent sparking in the gap. The gap is sensed through suitable sensing circuit and a servomotor controlled feed given to the tool which maintains the gap, see Figure 5.64.

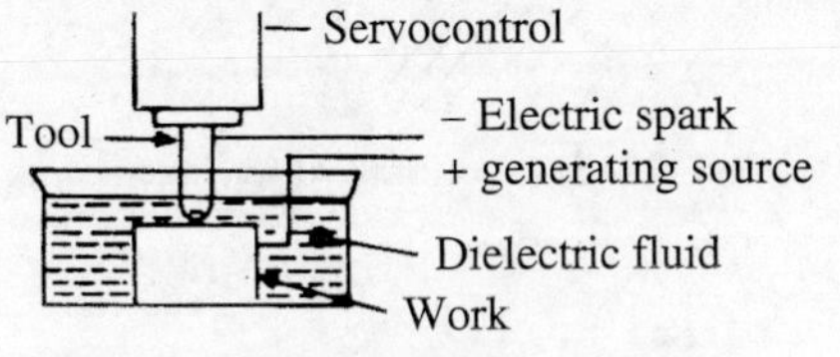

(a) Scheme of electric discharge machining

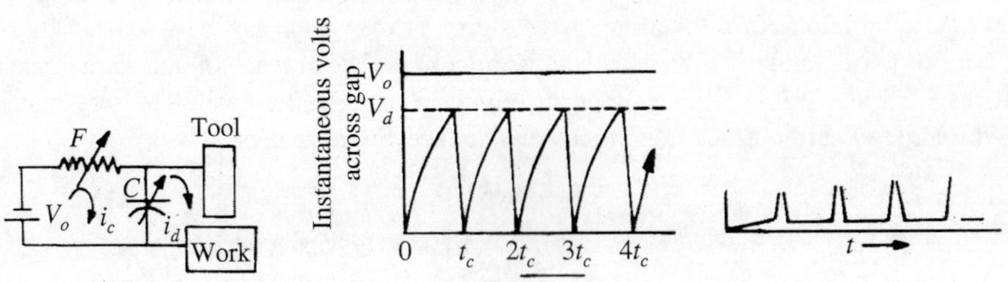

(b) Relaxation circuit (c) Variation of current and voltage

FIGURE 5.64 Electric discharge machining.

5.6.5 Electron Beam Machining (EBM)

Basically, electron beam machining is also a thermal process. Here, a stream of high speed electron impinges on the work surface whereby the kinetic energy transferred to the work material produces intense heating. Such heating melts and vaporizes the metal. The process has a high potential, and an accelerating voltage of 150,000 V can produce electron velocity of 228,478 km/s. For 10–200 microns area, the power density can go up to 6500 billion W/mm^2. Such a power density can vaporize any substance immediately. Processing capabilities of drilling holes 25–125 microns in 1.25 mm thick sheets are possible. A slot width up to 25 micrometer can be cut by EBM. The EBM can be manipulated with magnetic deflection coils. Figure 5.65 shows a schematic view of the EBM apparatus.

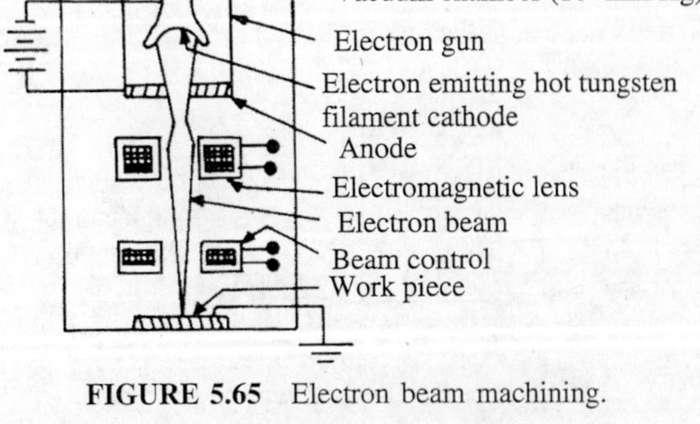

FIGURE 5.65 Electron beam machining.

5.6.6 Laser Beam Machining (LBM)

Like a beam of high energy electrons, laser (Light Emission by Stimulated Emission of Radiation) beam is also capable of producing high power density. Laser is a highly coherent beam of electromagnetic radiation of wavelength varying from 0.1 to 70 microns. The power requirement for machining needs wavelength, in the range of 0.4–0.6 microns. Power density is 10^{-7} W/mm^2. Generally, high power ruby is used. CO_2–N_2 laser has also been used for machining.

Xenon flashlight placed around ruby rod and internal walls of container are made reflecting. The capacitor is charged and a high voltage is applied. The atoms in the laser medium are excited to higher levels. When the electrons excited into outer orbits fall back into inner orbits, they emit photons as laser beam. The focussing beam confines the energy to a small area, causing ablution and melting of work surface, see Figure 5.66.

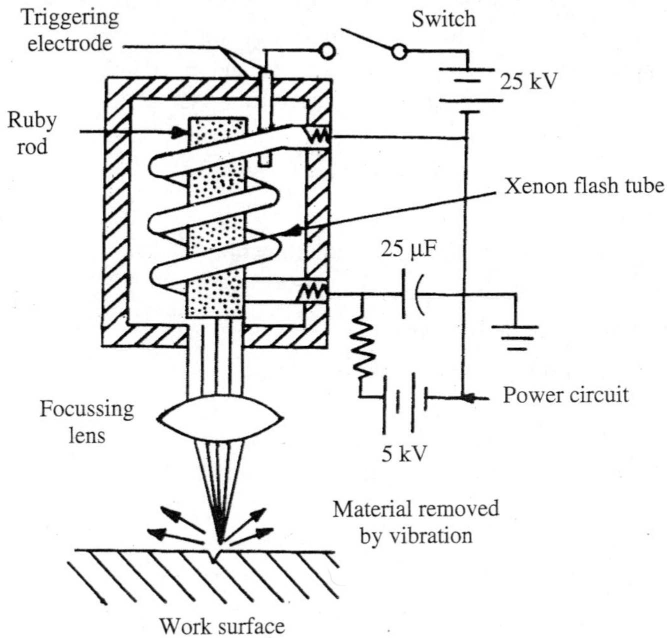

FIGURE 5.66 Laser beam machining.

Processing capabilities: holes up to 250 microns and slot with total area 0.25 mm can be cut. Work piece thickens about 0.25 mm and a taper of 0.05 mm/mm is noticed.

REVIEW QUESTIONS

1. Classify production processes into primary and secondary processes.
2. Describe the following casting processes and explain their differences. Sec. 5.2.1; P 101–106
   (a) Sand casting: greensand moulding, dry sand moulding, cement bonded sand moulds, CO_2 process;
   (b) Plaster moulding;
   (c) Loam moulding;

(d) Shell moulding;
(e) Ceramic moulding;
(f) Investment moulding and lost wax;
(g) Graphite moulding; and
(h) Permanent moulding

3. Develop expression for solidification time for casting.

[**Ans: Heat transfer**

The solidification time for various cases is:

(i) In case of a large casting in insulating mould (sand casting); solidification time $t = c(V/A)^2$

where V is total volume of casting and A is the area of mould–metal interface.

(ii) In case of permanent mould castings; film heat transfer coefficient h, latent heat L, temperatures on either side of film θ_1 and θ_2; density θ, volume V, area A, to determine the solidification time t, the formula is:

$$t = \frac{LV\rho}{hA(\theta_1 - \theta_2)}$$

Further, convex interface encourages solidification whereas concave interface increases solidification time.]

4. How Bernoulli's theorem is applied to casting process?

[**Ans: Role of fluid mechanics in casting process**

The fluid supply system as shown in Figure 5.67 should be so designed that the flow of liquid metal is laminar (smooth), though in practice, some turbulence is inevitable. The feeding system comprises (1) pouring basin and (2) sprue to transport fluid down the mould. Potential energy is converted to kinetic energy during the flow down the sprue and V_2 is greater than V_1. Bernoulli's equation can be applied as follows:

$$p_1 + \frac{\rho v_1^2}{2} + \rho g h_1 = p_2 + \frac{\rho v_2^2}{2} + \rho g h_2 + f$$

where p_1 and p_2 – pressures; v_1 and v_2 – velocities; f – friction loss and density ρ.

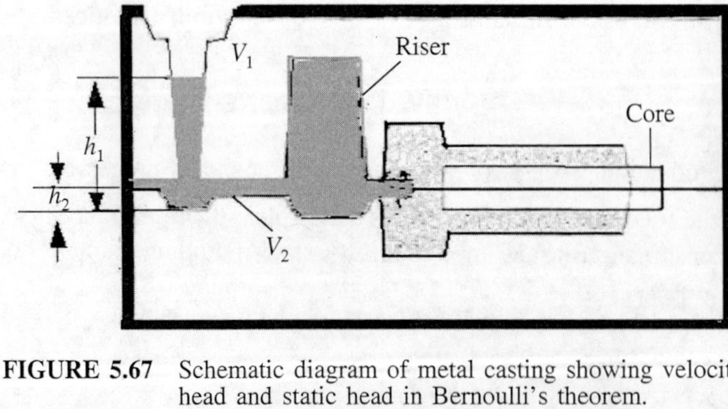

FIGURE 5.67 Schematic diagram of metal casting showing velocity head and static head in Bernoulli's theorem.

Excessive friction loss results in lower value of v_2 and consequent freezing at entrance to mould which is very undesirable. Gating ratio, i.e., ratio of areas of sprue/runner/gate is adopted 1.4/1.2/1 based upon continuity of metal flow.]

5. Illustrate plaster moulding and permanent moulding with sketches.

(i) Plaster and gypsum is added to water up to creamy consistency

(ii) Prepared plaster is poured over greased matchplated pattern in flask.

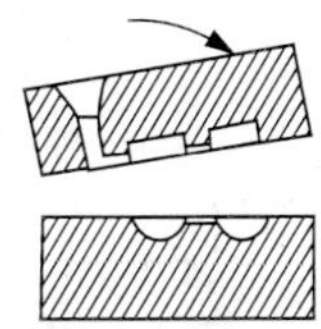

(iii) When plaster has set it is removed from the matchplate and the step are repeated for the other half of mould.

(a) Plaster moulding and its steps

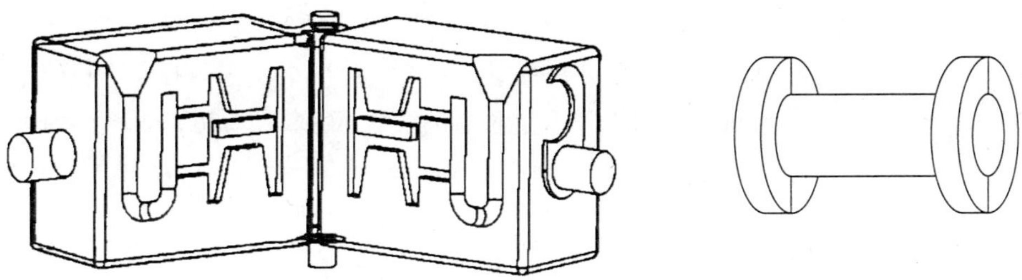

(b) Permanent mould part

FIGURE 5.68 Some typical moulding processes.

6. Explain the following types of cast iron: (i) grey cast iron, (ii) white cast iron, (iii) ductile cast iron, (iv) malleable cast iron and (v) alloyed cast iron. P 107–110
7. Describe the heat treatment cycle for producing malleable cast iron. P 108–109; Figure 5.4
8. What are the advantages of casting aluminium in combination with (a) copper, (b) zinc, (c) magnesium and (d) silicon? How are the ill effects of hydrogen in casting aluminium overcome? P 110
9. Write the special precautions in copper, zinc and magnesium alloy production. P 111
10. Describe the design considerations in casting of metals. P 111–113
11. Differentiate between hot chamber and cold chamber die casting processes. Sec. 5.8, 5.9, 5.10; P 113–114
12. Explain the application of centrifugal casting for producing engine cylinder liners. Figure 5.11
13. Explain the theory of metal forming with special reference to extrusion, wire drawing and tube drawing. Sec. 5.2.2; P 115–118

14. Explain the following metal working processes: P 118–120
rolling, forging, drawing, bending, extrusion, punching and blanking.

15. Discuss the design consideration for (a) impact extrusion, (b) conventional extrusion and (c) aluminium impact extrusion with reference to following aspects: (i) parting line, (ii) draft, (iii) ribs, (iv) webs, (v) corner radii, (vi) fillet radii, (vii) punchout holes, and (viii) pockets and recesses. P 120–128

16. What are the design considerations for welding from the following aspects:

(i) Selection of joint type (*hint:* butt joint is preferred to lap joint, single V joint or double V joint). P 129–130

(ii) Location and distribution of welds for stability.

(iii) Avoiding distortions after welding.

(iv) Materials to be welded.

17. How are brazed joints designed? Illustrate through sketches. P 131–132

18. How is joint preparation for adhesive joining designed? Figure 5.34

19. How are the forces in turning, drilling and milling estimated? P 147–149

20. Explain the utility of Merchant's circle diagram. P144–146

21. What is meant by the specification: A-46 K-12-V for a grinding wheel? P 150

22. Explain the working principle of the following non-traditional machining processes: Sec. 5.6; P 158–161

(1) Abrasive jet machining

(2) Ultrasonic machining

(3) Electrochemical machining

(4) Electric discharge machining

(5) Electron beam machining

(6) Laser beam machining

23. Classify machining processes into forming and generating processes, giving examples of each.

[**Ans: Generating principle of machining**

A surface may be generated by combining motions that not only accomplish the chip forming process (primary motion), but also move the point of engagement along the surface feed motion, the workpiece may rotate around its axis, as in turning; the tool is set to cut a certain depth and receives a continuous, longitudinal feed motion. When the workpiece axis and feed direction are parallel, a cylinder is generated (Figure 5.69(a)); when they are at an angle, a cone is generated (Figure 5.69(d)). If, in addition to the primary and feed motions, the distance of the cutting tool from the workpiece axis is varied in some programmed fashion—e.g., by means of cams, a copying device or numerical control—a large variety of shapes can be generated.

In turning, the generating point moves, diagonally from top to bottom across the workpiece, a hyperboloid is generated. A tapered cylinder is obtained when the generating point moves at an angle in plane view.

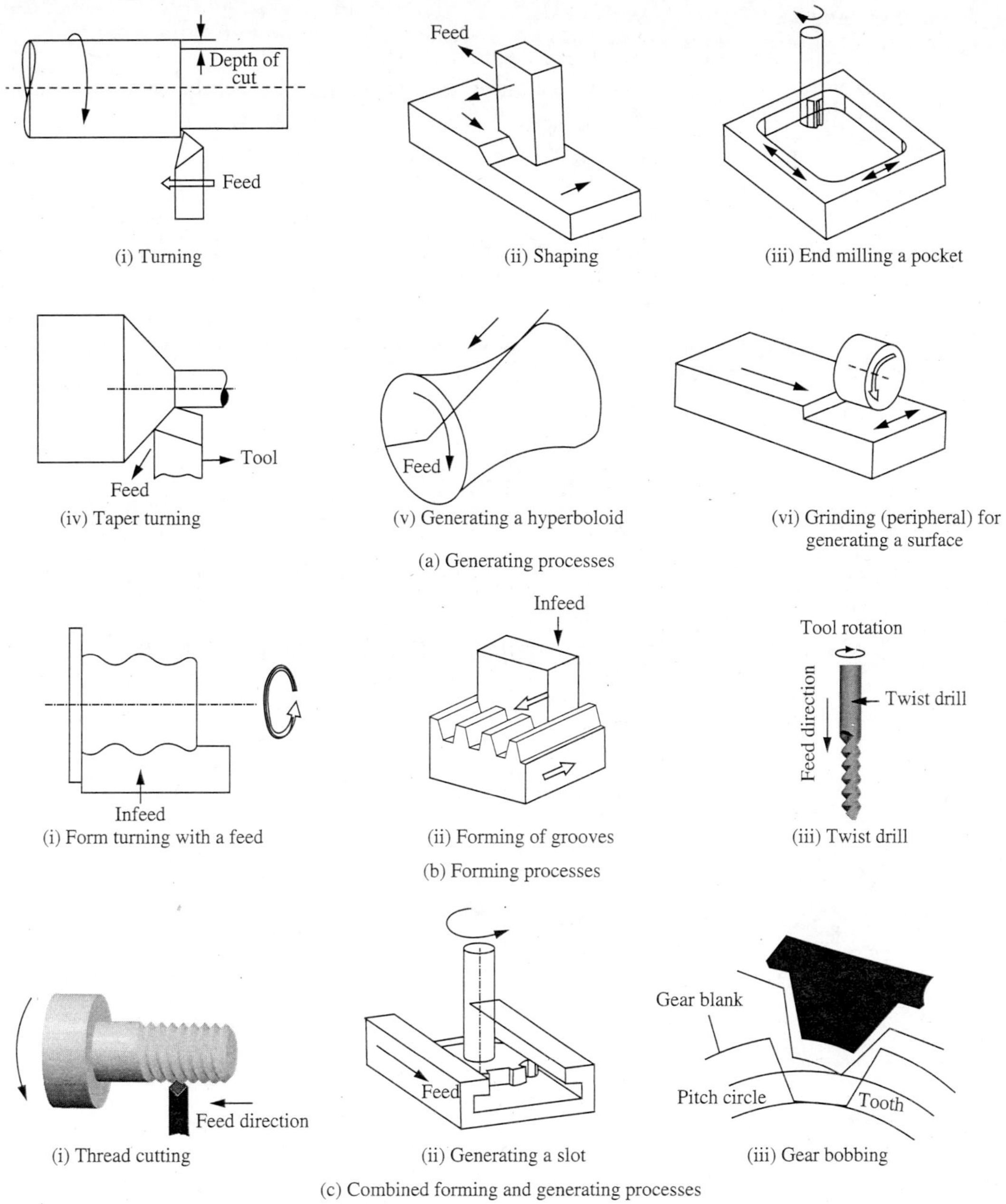

FIGURE 5.69 Generating, forming and combined forming and generating processes.

Programmed tool motion (feed) is necessary in generating a shape:

(a) turning a cylinder and (b) a cone; (c) shaping (planning) a flat and (d) a hyperboloid; (e) milling a pocket; and (f) grinding a flat. (Principal motions are marked with hollow arrows, feed motions with solid arrows).

Forming

A shape is said to be formed when the cutting tool possesses the finished contour of the workpiece in addition to the relative movement required to produce the chip (the primary motion), feed (plunge) the tool in depth to achieve the desired form.

How the primary motion is generated is immaterial. The workpiece can be rotated against a stationery tool (turning), or the workpiece and tool can be moved relative to each other in a linear motion (shaping or planning) or the tool can be rotated against a stationary workpiece (milling and drilling) or against a rotating workpiece (as in cylindrical grinding). The accuracy of the surface profile depends on the accuracy of the forming tool. Figure 5.69 indicates screw cutting and gear generation processes which are combinations of forming and generating processes. These are very important practical processes.]

24. Classify and give the outline of various liquid state welding processes. Sec. 5.3; P 132–140

REFERENCES

[1] Rao, P.N., *Manufacturing Technology*, Part I, Tata McGraw-Hill, New Delhi, 1987.

[2] Johnson, R.C., *Optimum Design of Mechanical Elements*, Wiley Interscience, New York, 1980.

[3] El Wakil, S.D., *Designing for Production*, Prentice-Hall, Englewood Cliffs, New Jersey, 1991.

[4] Bhattacharya, A., *Principles of Metal Cutting*, New Central Book Agency, New Delhi, 1988.

[5] Ghosh, A. and Mallik, A.K., *Manufacturing Science*, Affiliated East-West Press, New Delhi, 1986.

[6] Alting, Leo, *Engineering Manufacturing Processes*, Marcel Dekker, New York, 1988.

Chapter 6

Design for Production
Metal Parts

6.1 PRODUCIBILITY REQUIREMENTS IN THE DESIGN OF MACHINE COMPONENTS

It was pointed out in Chapter 2 that a design should be of such configuration geometrically that it should be easily producible by suitable manufacturing process. Designing and Production are two different specialities. However, a Process engineer who is an expert in both these areas should see to it that a design should be producible with ease. In this chapter, the following aspects are considered in the design of machine components that comply with production technique requirements. According to Kovan [1] the following are the requirements:

1. Requirements concerning the form of machine components and blanks manufactured from special purpose rolled stock, die-rolled stock, flat-die forgings, closed-die forgings obtained under hammers and in presses, upset forgings, headed parts, pressworked sheet metal parts and castings.
2. General producibility requirements concerning machine techniques. Requirements for elementary surfaces of machine parts; external surfaces of revolution and end faces, holes and bores, threads, flat surfaces, formed surfaces, slots and recesses.
3. The necessity of employing a certain manufacturing technique as determined by the design of components. Thus, design and process compatibility is a major factor.
4. Certain demands are imposed by the manufacturing techniques on the form of machine components. If these requirements are taken care of at the design stage, manufacturing difficulties are excluded or at least reduced. The production cycle time is reduced as well; labour productivity is increased and the cost of the machine components is minimized. Good production design considers production techniques both for primary processes such as blank production, and for secondary processes like machining.
5. Designing is a creative process and, therefore, it is impossible to recommend universal rules for the design of machine components that satisfy all production technique requirements. This is particularly so since each component is designed for a definite functional purpose. The general trends in solving this problem may be formulated as follows:

   The form of a component or part should consist of a number of simple geometric shapes that enable high-production techniques to be applied in their processing, and convenient, reliable, locating datum should be provided to set up the workpiece in production. When the surfaces of the components do not provide such a datum, special elements should be added (bosses, pads, bugs, holes, etc.) to locate and clamp the workpiece. These elements may be removed, if necessary, after machining.

6. The grade of accuracy and class of surface finish specified in the drawing must be based strictly on the function of the component in the machine. Unjustified, stringent requirements for accuracy or surface finish lead to additional operations in the manufacturing process and increase the production time, labour input and machining costs.
7. If machine components and parts as a whole and their elements are extensively standardized and unified, labour input as well as manufacturing cost is reduced. This reduction is due to their manufacture in larger batches and unification of machine tool set-ups.
8. As far as the producibility requirements of blank manufacture are concerned, the following factors should be taken into account:

The use of special-purpose rolled stock and die-rolled stock is justified in large batch and mass production. Blanks of such stock require considerably less machining time and cost and, in a number of cases, subsequent machining is almost completely eliminated. In some cases, the application of special shapes during design stage is useful. For example, in drop forging, such a shape analysis reduces the number of roughing die impressions and results in increased labour productivity.
Blank of shaped cross-section, requiring no further machining, may be obtained from bar stock by cold drawing in the engineering plant.

6.2 FORGING DESIGN

In forging techniques research is carried out for arriving at a shape called 'net shape' so that negligible machining is needed after forging. The following aspects are considered in the design of forging components that comply with production technique requirements:

1. If the blanks are to be produced by flat-die forging, intersections of two or more cylindrical elements should be avoided (Figure 6.1). Intersections of cylindrical and flat surfaces should also be avoided (Figure 6.2). Such combinations present difficulties when they are forged between flat dies; they should be designed as shown in Figure 6.3 and 6.4, respectively. Ribbed cross-sections should also be avoided, because ribs are unacceptable when flat-die forging is employed. Bosses, projections, pads, etc. should be avoided on the main surfaces of forgings (e.g. bosses "a" in Figure 6.5), as well as projections inside the prongs of fork-type parts (e.g. bosses "a" in Figure 6.6). In the first case (Figure 6.5), the holes may be spotfaced below the rough surface instead of providing bosses. In the second case (Figure 6.6), instead of making inner bosses, the height of the outer bosses can be increased.

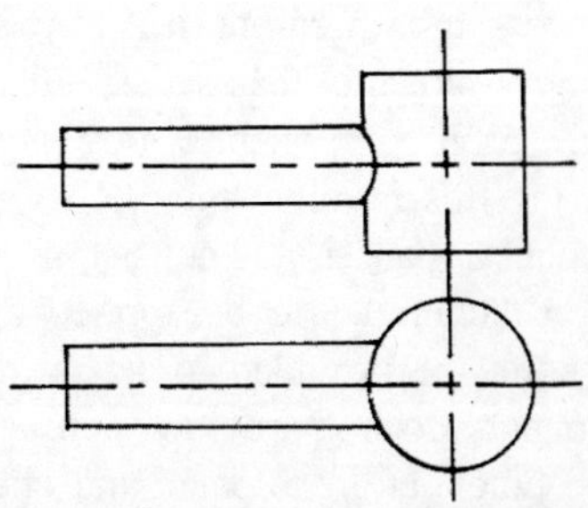

FIGURE 6.1 Undesirable shape for flat die forging.

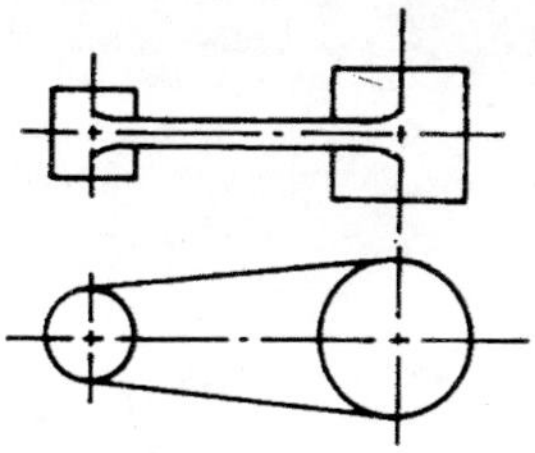

FIGURE 6.2 Undesirable shape for flat die forging.

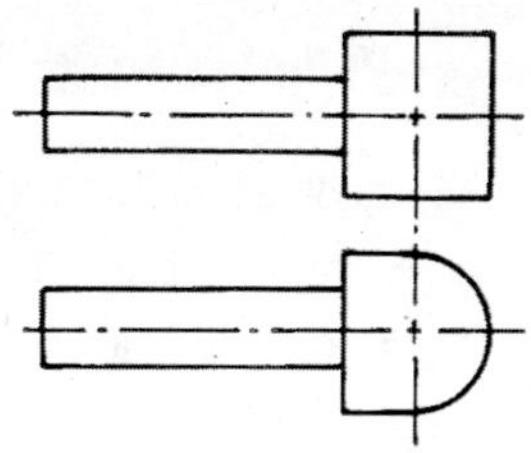

FIGURE 6.3 Desirable shape for flat die forging.

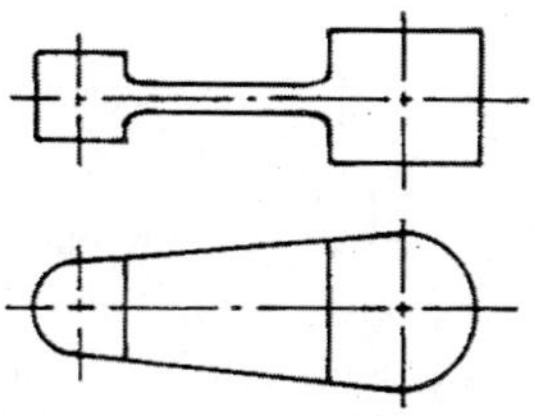

FIGURE 6.4 Desirable shape for flat die forging.

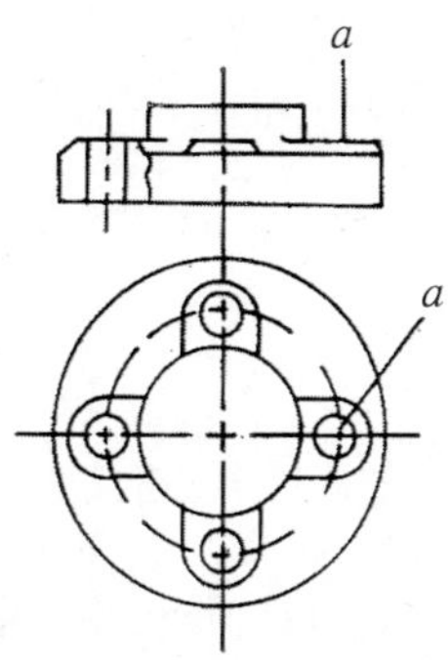

FIGURE 6.5 Component with four bosses.

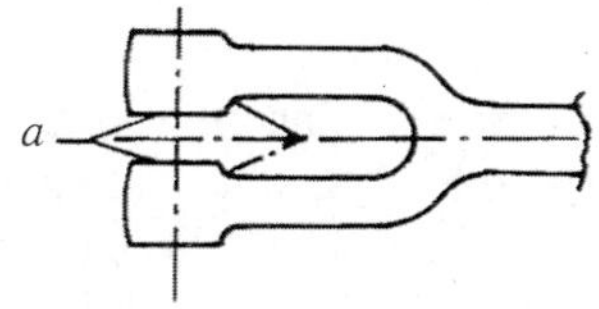

FIGURE 6.6 Component with bosses on inner and outer sides.

2. In a number of cases, it is advisable to replace components having such a complex shape by units consisting of simple welded or assembled elements.
3. The following discussion involves production design aspects of forgings produced in closed dies under hammers or in presses:

    The form of a drop forging should ensure easy removal from the die impression. The angle of draft on the side surface of forging should be designed from a plane square to the die parting surface. Draft and dowels should range from 5 to 15° for outer walls and from 7 to 15° for inner walls, when no ejectors are used. When ejectors are applied, it should be between 2 and 10° for outer walls and 3 and 12° for inner walls.
4. Transitions from one rough surface to another must be rounded fillets and corners. Sharp corners are inadmissible on closed-die forgings. To avoid forging rejects and to extend the die life, the fillets of inside corners should have larger radii than outside corners. Depending on the height and height-to-width ratio of the element, radii are taken from 1.5 mm to 12.5 mm for outer corners and 4 mm to 45 mm for inner corners. Adequate radii or chamfers should be provided for the junctions of machined surfaces on the component (Figure 6.7). In this case, the following condition is to be observed:

$$r_p \geq r_f - z_n$$

where,

r_p = corner radius of the machined part

r_f = corner radius of the rough-forging

z_n = nominal machining allowance

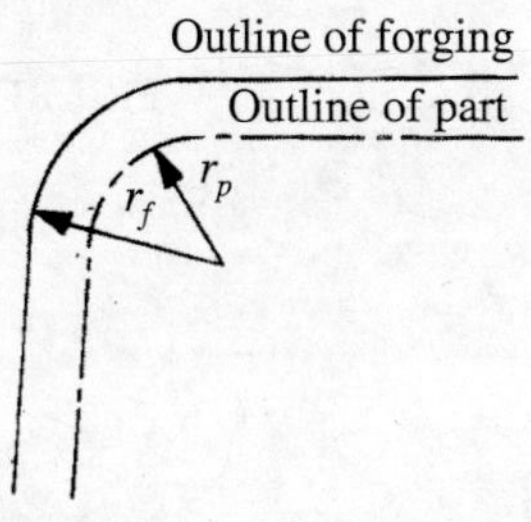

FIGURE 6.7 Profile of forging.

If the above condition is not observed, it will be necessary to increase the machining allowances for the adjoining surfaces to ensure that the specified radius is obtained on the finished part. When a chamfer is used instead of a rounded corner, it should be such as can be inscribed by the corner radius.

5. No sharp differences should be allowed in the cross-section areas along the forging because this complicates the forging process and may lead to an increase in rejects due to cramping and underfilling.
6. Thin walls in forgings reduce die life since the forging cools rapidly and its resistance to metal flow is increased. This also leads to underfilling and increase in the amount of rejects. If thin elements of forgings are adjacent to the parting plane of the dies, there will be a large metal waste and more rejects due to underfilling and breaking-off in the process of cold flash trimming.
7. Symmetrical shapes of forgings relative to die parting planes and symmetrical drafts of projectile walls simplify die-sinking procedures and forging operations, and reduce the number of rejects due to die mismatch. Asymmetrical shapes and non-uniform drafts result in forces tending to shift the upper and lower dies.
8. The sizes of bosses to be drilled and subsequently machined are determined on the basis of the required minimum wall thickness after machining the hole and the possible value of die mismatch. In many cases, oval bosses, with their major axis along the direction of probable shift, will enable minimum wall thickness to be maintained after machining the hole.
9. It is often better to substitute weld parts for one-piece components to have metal and simplify forging operations. For instance, the weldment shown in Figure 6.8 used in place of a drop forging provides for considerable amount of metal economy and simplifies, to a great extent, the forging process. However, the need for such changes should be checked in each definite case because, sometimes a one-piece drop forging may be more convenient in production and costs than a weldment (e.g., the lever shown in Figure 6.9).

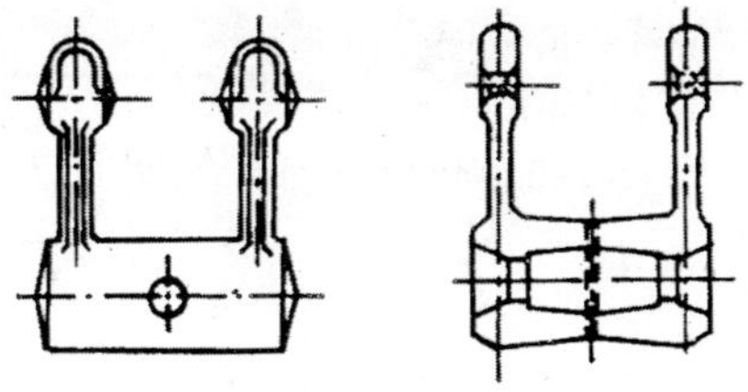

(a) Forged (b) Forged and welded

FIGURE 6.8 Forged and forged cum welded machine part.

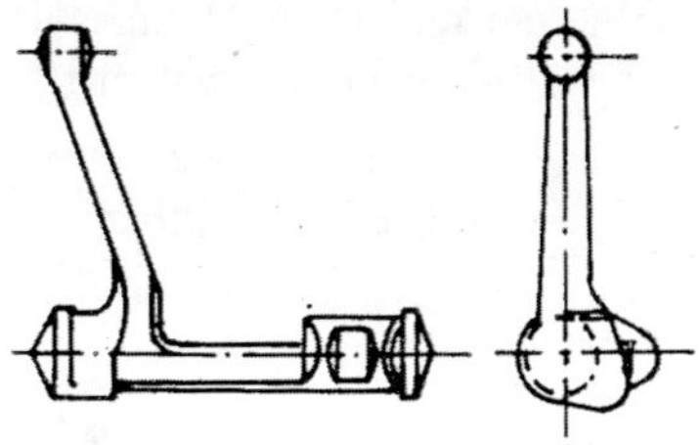

FIGURE 6.9 Lever design.

10. In designing forgings, which are to be produced in horizontal forging machines, the following considerations may be helpful:
    (a) Forgings of various forms may be obtained in horizontal forging machines, but the most suitable for this process are those having the form of solids or revolution of regular geometric shape with flanges, shoulder and through or blind holes. The wall thickness of forging with deep, through or blind holes should not be less than 0.15 of the outside diameter.
    (b) Reductions in cross-section along the length of forgings should be avoided because they impede metal flow during the forging process.
    (c) Shanks of taper form are also difficult to forge and they should be replaced by cylindrical shanks.
    (d) The volume of flanges located at the ends or in the middle of a forging must not exceed the volume of a bar having the given diameter d and a length of 10–12 d.
    (e) Draft for this type of forging may be very small. For instance, a draft of 0.5° is suitable for the cylindrical section of the forging up-set within the punch cavity and of a length more than one-half of the diameter. A draft of 0.5–1.5° is suitable for shoulders formed in the circular impressions of dies and 0.5–3° on the walls of blind holes with a length of five or more diameters.
    (f) Transition from one surface to another must have fillets with radii from 1.5 to 2 mm.
    (g) Carbon and alloy steel fasteners and similar parts having an annealed hardness, BHN = 120–207, are produced by cold heading.

    Cold drawn wire or rod is employed in cold heading. The headed elements or components should be, as far as possible, of simple form and with a minimum volume and diameter. Close tolerance should not be specified, unless required, for the headed parts, as die life will be reduced. Fillet radii of at least 0.2 mm should be provided at all corners.

6.3 PRESSED COMPONENTS DESIGN

The following factors should be taken into account while considering press worked sheet metal components (stamping):

1. Band, strip and sheet metal are mainly used in press working. Band material is used chiefly for the thin part (2.0–2.5 mm thick; strip material for thicker parts and sheet material for parts with overall dimensions that cannot be accommodated by the width of band or strip metal).

2. Stiffening ribs, flanges and similar structural elements designed for metal economy in press working often permit the thickness of the part to be reduced.
3. Welding may also substantially reduce metal consumption; Figure 6.10 and 6.11 show examples of welding used to save metal.

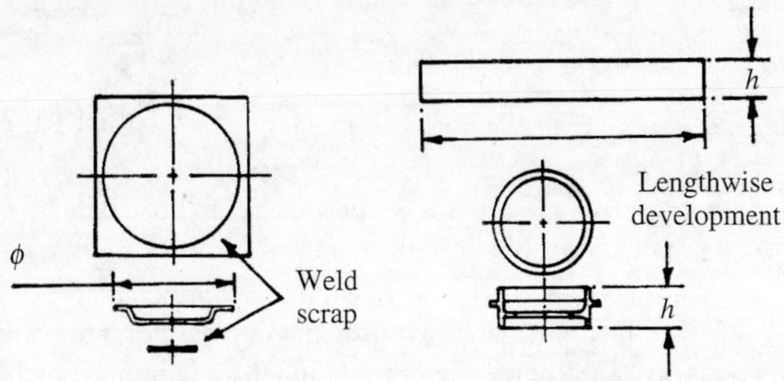

(a) Part produced by blank and drawing
(b) Part produced by welding and tube sinking

FIGURE 6.10 Combining sheet metal work with welding to save material.

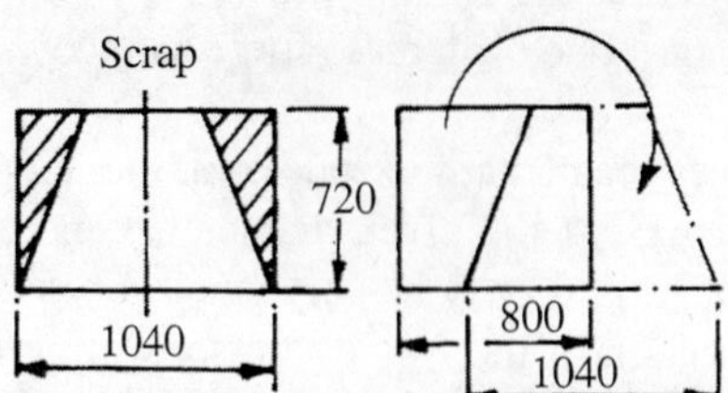

FIGURE 6.11 Saving effect of combining cutting and welding.

4. The form of a blank or part should be such that a minimum amount of material is converted into scrap in laying out the stock. Figure 6.12(a) shows a poor strip layout in which sheet metal is wasted as scrap. To this end, the outline of one side of the blanked part should be, as far as possible, complementary to the opposite side. This is illustrated by Figure 6.12(b) in which there is a perfect nesting providing for minimum scrap loss.

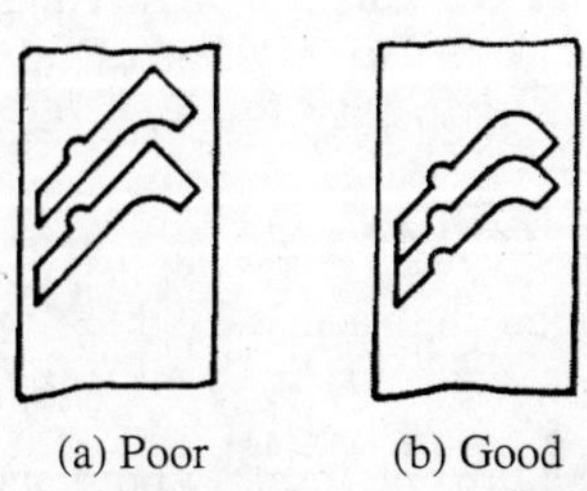

(a) Poor (b) Good

FIGURE 6.12 Nesting of parts in sheet metal blanking.

5. Economy of non-ferrous metals can be achieved by replacing one-piece components by units in which only certain elements are made of non-ferrous metals. These elements are secured to the basic component by press-fitting or other joining methods.

6. The minimum size of holes that can be punched by steel punches and dies is expressed as fractions of the material thickness and depends on the configuration of the holes (round, square or rectangular). These fractions are 1.0–0.7 for mild steel, 0.9–0.6 for brass and copper, 0.8–0.3 for aluminum and zinc, 0.7–0.4 for bakelite and fabric-based phenolic laminate, and 0.6–0.3 for cardboard and paper.
7. When contours are punched for blanks with steel punches and dies, minimum corner radii between sections of the contour are taken to the order of 0.9 of the material thickness. The minimum distance from a hole edge to the contour of the part or to the edge of an adjacent hole or blank is taken from 0.7 to 1.5 of the material thickness for mild steel. The minimum distance (x) from a hole edge to a wall in bent or drawn parts is determined by the following formula:

$$x = R + 0.5s$$

where R is the corner radius between the wall and the surface being punched and s the material thickness.

The minimum width of a blanked part of mild steel should be taken $1\frac{1}{2}$ times the material thickness.

8. In bending dies, the height of the straight portion of the bent walls should be more than twice the material thickness. If less height is required, it can be achieved by providing an indented groove at the base of the bend for the wall, or if a subsequent machining operation is carried out.

A reduction in wall thickness may occur in bends, as well as dents where the radius adjoins the vertical wall; these faults can be eliminated only by supplementary operations.

When angles and channels are bent in dies, the variation in flange thickness depends on the thicknesses of the material, and will be shown as follows:

s (mm)	up to 2	2–4	over 4
δ (mm)	± 0.15	± 0.3	± 0.4

9. In order to eliminate local bulges in drawn parts with very large flat surfaces, long intersecting stiffening ribs or beads should be formed in the surfaces.

If the design calls for a complex-shaped part, presenting difficulties in the drawing operation, then the part should be broken down into several simple components joined by press-working or welding.

6.4 CASTING DESIGN

The following principles of casting design must be observed to obtain sound castings.

1. The form of a casting should allow free withdrawal of the pattern from the mould. This may be accomplished by allowing a draft on the vertical surfaces of casting, the draft value being taken as a function of the surface height. For internal surfaces, draft values should be higher than those for external ones. Loose parts and complex parting lines should be avoided, if possible, on the patterns.
2. The position of the surfaces of the casting, when the metal is poured, is a major factor. It is necessary to avoid large horizontal surfaces at the top of the mould, since gas evolved

by the metal and in the mould may be trapped on these surfaces and cause cavities and pinholes in the casting.

3. The form of the casting should ensure unimpeded filling of the mould with molten metal, without abrupt changes, both in the direction and velocity of the flow.
4. Other important factors in casting design are shrinkage and its restriction by the friction of the mould and cores, as well as restriction by the difference in the rate of cooling of different parts of the casting. In order to eliminate internal stresses leading to warping and hot tears in castings, their design should, as far as possible, ensure an equal rate of cooling in all sections of the casting and allow unrestricted shrinkage.
5. The form of casting should be such that all feeding heads, risers, runners, sprues and gates can be easily cut off, all cores knocked out and core irons removed.
6. The drawings of cast parts should indicate, by special symbols, the datum surfaces to be employed in machining operations. Then, these surfaces can be used as measuring datum surfaces in checking patterns and castings. As far as possible, the datum surfaces should be obtained in the mould by the pattern and should be located in one flask, so that the effect of the flask and core shifts on the accuracy of the surfaces is eliminated. It is advisable to have only one datum surface along each of the three space coordinates.
7. The size and weight of the casting, the type of alloy employed, and the casting method should be taken into account while designing the wall thickness of a casting.

Designs, in which all changes in section are gradual and sharp corners have been avoided at adjoining sections, result in castings free from faults and stresses. It is a good practice to have all the fillets of a casting with the same radius or to limit the number of different radii to a minimum.

Abrupt changes in section are inadmissible; these changes should always be gradual (Figure 6.13–6.15). Corner radii (R and r) and transition lines (dimensions h and C) between

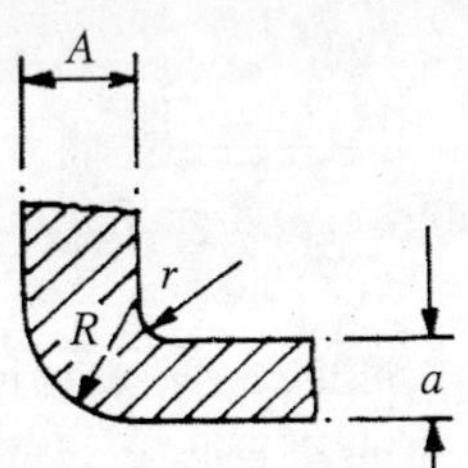

FIGURE 6.13 Providing radius on casting.

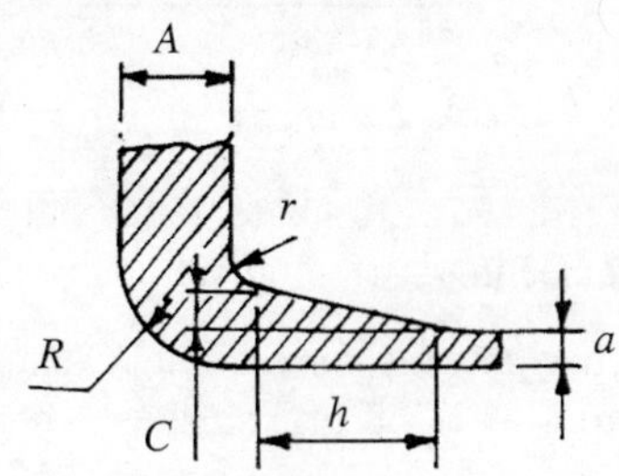

FIGURE 6.14 Providing flat surface for improved heat transfer.

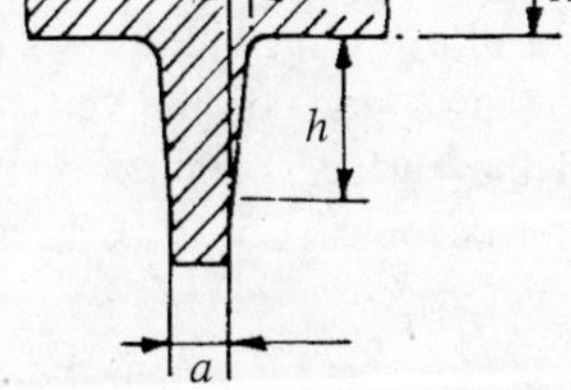

FIGURE 6.15 Providing a gradual transition in thickness.

adjoining sections of a single wall and angular junctions of two or three sections should have a definite magnitude, depending on the thickness of the adjoining sections (*A* and *a*).

8. Rib design depends on the overall dimensions of the casting; and their size is in definite relation to the wall thickness.
9. Corner radii at the junctions of surfaces may range from 2 mm to 120 mm, depending on the overall dimensions of the surfaces and the angle between them.
10. The rate of cooling for outside corners is always higher than that for inside corners. In this case, heat flow square to the surfaces of the casting intersects near inner corners, thus forming a "hot spot", which slows down the cooling process. At the apex of the corner, the wall thickness should be 20 to 25 per cent less than the thickness of the adjoining walls (Figure 6.16). It is advisable to design the form of the recess in casting so that no cores are required in the mould. The relation between the dimensions of recesses formed by parts of the mould without using cores depends on the location of these recesses in the mould. In machine moulding, recesses produced by parts of the mould in the drag (Figure 6.17) have a depth $H \leq D$, while those in the compress mould have a depth $h \leq 0.3d$. In hand moulding, these values are $H \leq 0.5D$ and $H \leq 0.15d$, respectively.

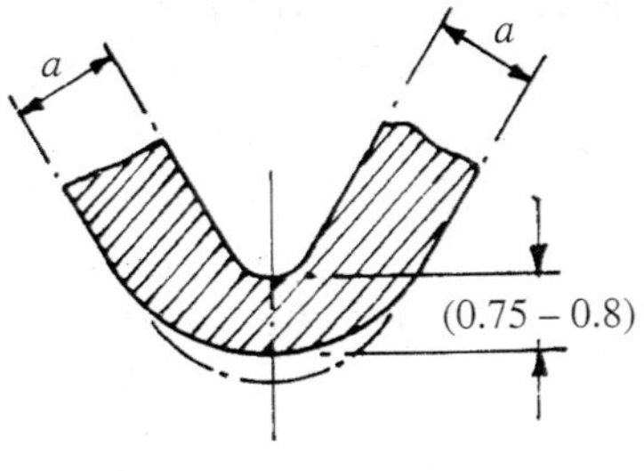

FIGURE 6.16 Design for external radius in casting.

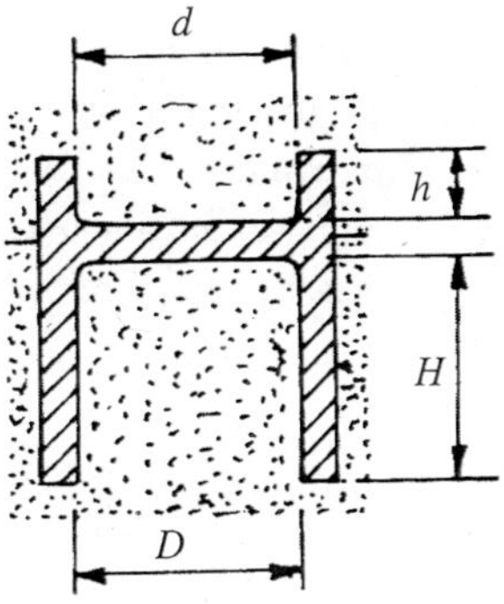

FIGURE 6.17 Recommended design for H-section.

It is a sound practice to unify cores when a large number of core cavities are present in the casting. For cores of length exceeding 2 diameters, the form of the cavities should provide for core prints to support the core on both ends. The sizes of cavities and diameters of holes produced by cores should permit the use of cast or wire core irons for reinforcing purposes.

The design of a casting should provide for the possibility of knocking out core sand and removing irons from the inner cavities, as well as through cleaning of the latter. Closed inner cavities must have special holes for the removal of burned core sand and core irons: after cleaning the cavities, the holes may be plugged.

11. Bosses are provided at places where holes are to be drilled to reinforce the walls of the casting. The minimum recommended height of bosses is 5 mm for castings with overall dimensions up to 500 mm; 10–15 mm for overall dimensions from 500 to 2,000 mm and 20–25 mm for overall dimensions over 2,000 mm.

6.5 DESIGN FOR MACHINING EASE

General producibility requirements meant for design of machine parts and machining techniques may be formulated as follows:

1. The amount of machining should be reduced, as far as possible, by assigning size tolerances only for fits between mating surfaces; all other elements should have free dimensions. Parts may be obtained without any machining if precise methods of blank manufacture are applied (see Figure 6.18).

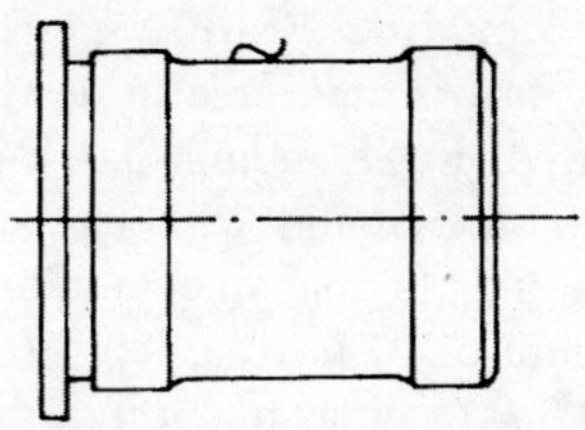

FIGURE 6.18 Reducing machining.

2. Convenient and reliable locating surfaces should be provided to set up workpiece for machining. Whenever possible, the measurement datum should be made to coincide with the set-up datum surface by proper dimensioning of the part drawing.
3. There should be sufficient rigidity of workpiece so as to eliminate significant deformation in the process of machining.
4. Provisions should be made for conveniently advancing rigid, high-production cutting tools to the surface being machined. Difference in height between adjacent, rough and machined surfaces should be sufficient, making adjustment for the machining allowances, to enable the cutting tools to clear the rough surface in its overtravel (when errors in rough blank size are within the permissible limits).
5. Clearance recesses: Dimension *A* should be provided to allow overtravel of the cutting tool whenever it is necessary, see Figure 6.19 and 6.20.

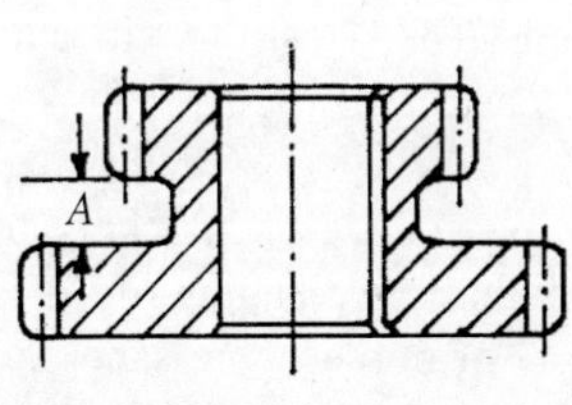

FIGURE 6.19 Provision of allowance for tool overtravel.

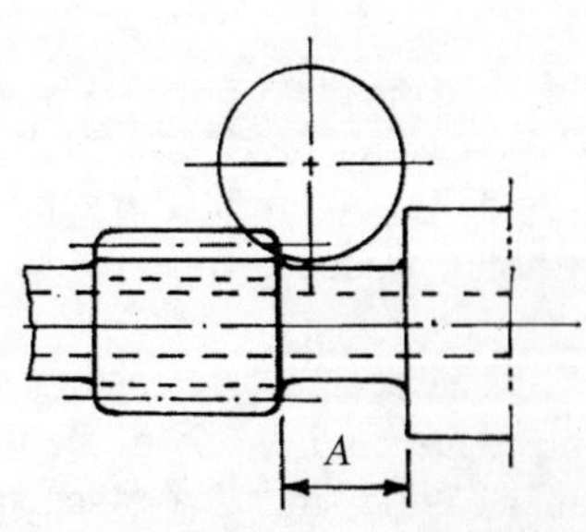

FIGURE 6.20 Provision of allowance for tool overtravel in milling a slot.

6. Parts should be designed so that several workpieces can be set up to be machined simultaneously, as shown in Figure 6.21. The following considerations are important for elementary surfaces of machine parts:

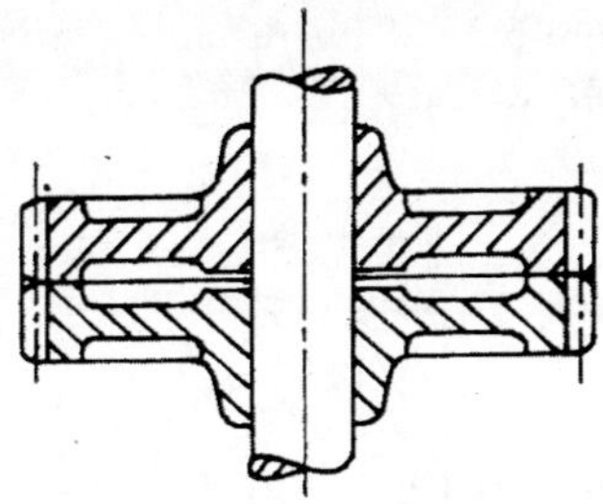

FIGURE 6.21 Increasing production through mounting two gears on one shaft during gear cutting.

7. External surfaces of revolution, upset heads, flanges and shoulders should be extensively applied to reduce machining and to save metal.
8. It is advisable to retain the centre holes on the finished components (shafts and similar parts) that were machined between centres.
9. The elements of shank design should be unified, whenever possible, so that the same multiple-tool set-up can be employed in machining them, as illustrated in Figure 6.22.

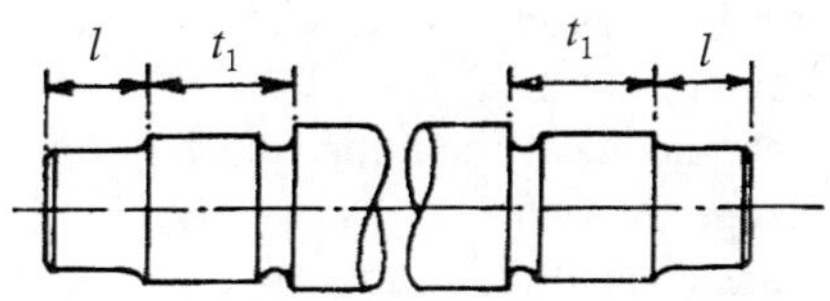

FIGURE 6.22 Unified shank design.

10. It is a good practice to provide a spherical convex surface with a flat end surfaced (see Figure 6.23).

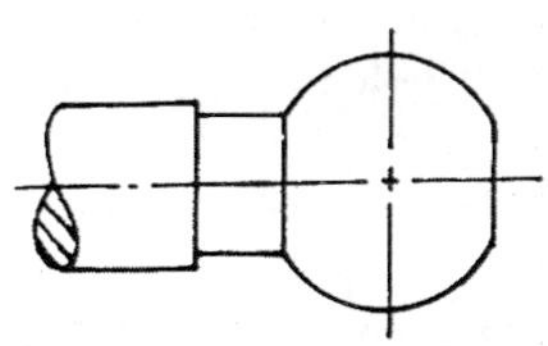

FIGURE 6.23 Provision of flat end surface on a sphere.

11. Holes:
    (a) Through holes are to be used, wherever possible, because such holes are much more simple to machine than blind holes. The form of blind holes should correspond to the design of the tool to be employed in machining for example, with the reamer (Figure 6.24(a)) or counterbore (Figure 6.24(b)).
    (b) Holes should not be located closer to a certain minimum distance from an adjacent wall of the

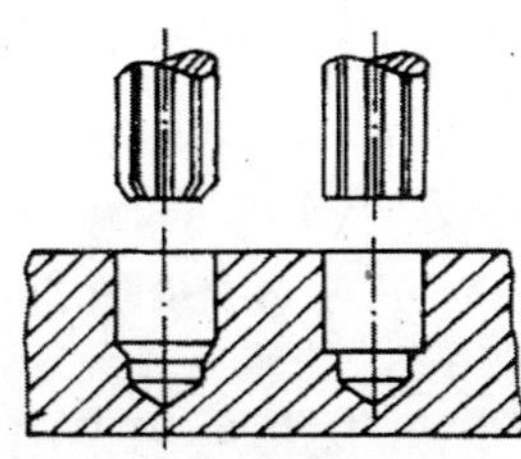

FIGURE 6.24 Design recommendation for reamed holes.

part: $A \geq D/2 + R$ (Figure 6.25). This distance for holes accommodating fastening bolts should be $A \geq D_n/2 + R$, where D_n is the diameter of a circle circumscribing the nut.

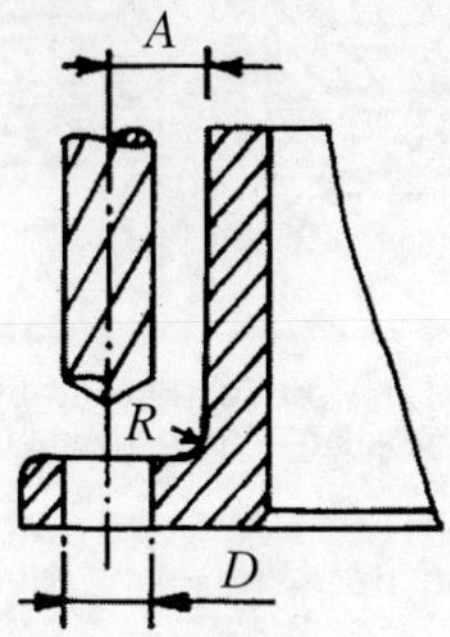

FIGURE 6.25 Allowance A for nut.

(c) Centre distances of holes should be specified, by considering the possibility of using multispindle drilling heads. For this purpose, the location and sizes of the holes in flanges have to be unified. The number of holes and their location in a flange should be designed so that the holes can be drilled by standard three or four spindle heads with subsequent indexing.
(d) Holes to be drilled should have their top and bottom surface square to the hole axis to prevent drill breakage.
(e) When several holes are located along the same axis, it is a good practice to reduce the diameter of each consequent hole by an amount exceeding the machining allowance for the preceding hole. This will enable a set-up to be used in which all the holes are bored simultaneously.
(f) In drilling holes at the bottom of a slot, their diameter should be less by 0.5–1 mm than the slot width.
(g) In stepped holes, maximum accuracy should be specified for the through step.
(h) Either a blind hole or a through hole should be provided on the axis in the design of concave spherical surfaces to avoid zero cutting speeds at the axis, as shown in (Figure 6.26), thus preventing damage to the tool point.

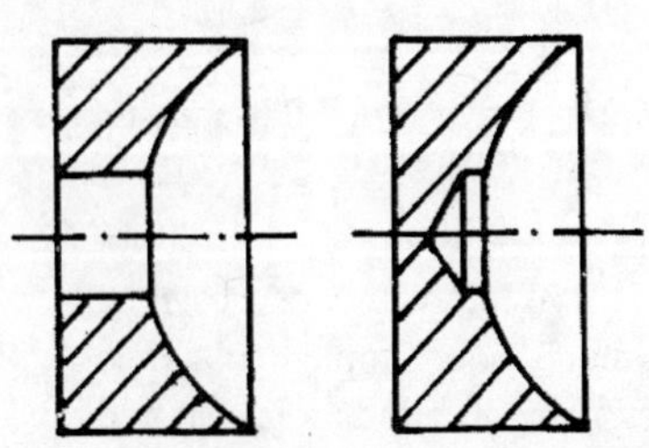

FIGURE 6.26 Design recommendation for concave spherical surfaces.

(i) It is advisable to avoid recesses in holes that are to be machined on single or multiple-spindle drilling machines since they complicate machining operations. Machined recesses should also be avoided by using cored recesses (see Figure 6.27).

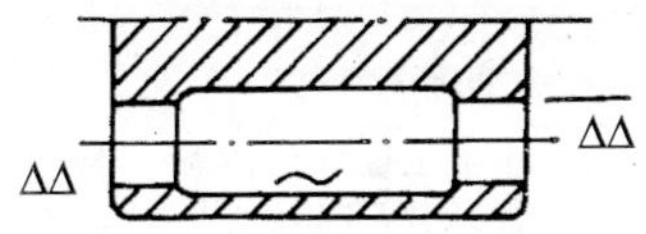

FIGURE 6.27 Provision of cored holes.

12. Threads:
    (a) It is advisable to use an entering chamfer on threaded holes.
    (b) The number of incomplete threads cut with a tap in a blind hole with no recess should be equal to three for grey iron casting and five for steel parts.
    (c) A neck at the end of a thread is not required for milled threads.
    (d) Preferred thread standards should pertain, not only to the machine under consideration, but to all the threads used in the plant or branch of industry. Small diameter threads (6 mm and less) should be avoided if they are cut.
13. Flat surfaces:
    (a) The outline of a machined flat surface should ensure, as far as possible, uniform and impactless chip removal.
    (b) The size of a machined flat surface should be in accordance with the sizes of standard milling cutters, i.e., the width of the surfaces should be unified to suit the standard services of face mill diameters or the widths of plain milling cutters.
    (c) If no elements are provided for cutting tool overtravel, the transition surfaces should correspond in size and form to the cutting tool (as illustrated in Figure 6.28 and 6.29).

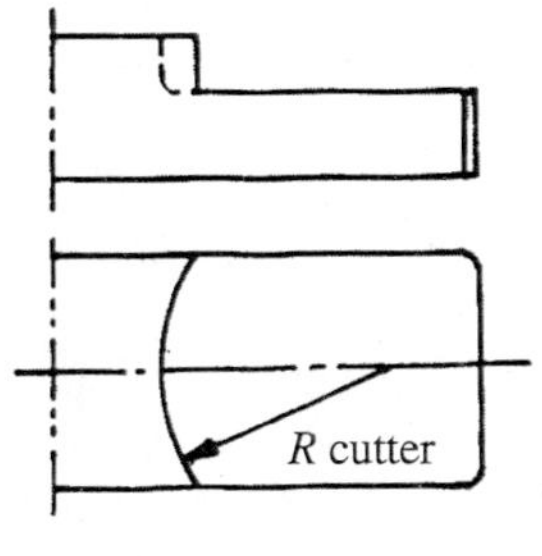

FIGURE 6.28 Assigning proper radius *R* on component.

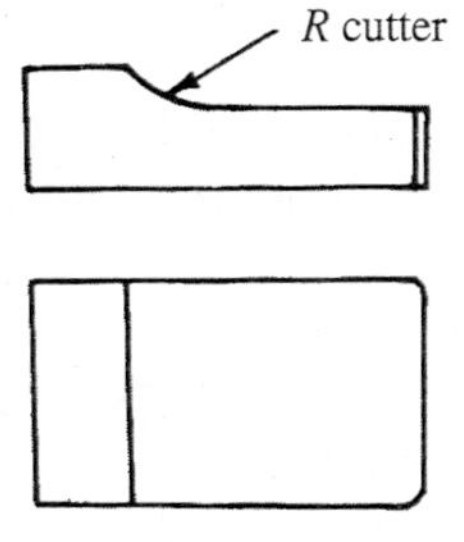

FIGURE 6.29 Assigning proper radius *R* on component.

14. Formed surfaces: The radii of concave and convex surfaces should correspond to those of standard convex and concave milling cutters.
15. Slots and recesses: Whenever possible, through slots should be employed. If through machining is possible, the end of the slot should correspond to the radius of the cutter, as shown in Figure 6.30.

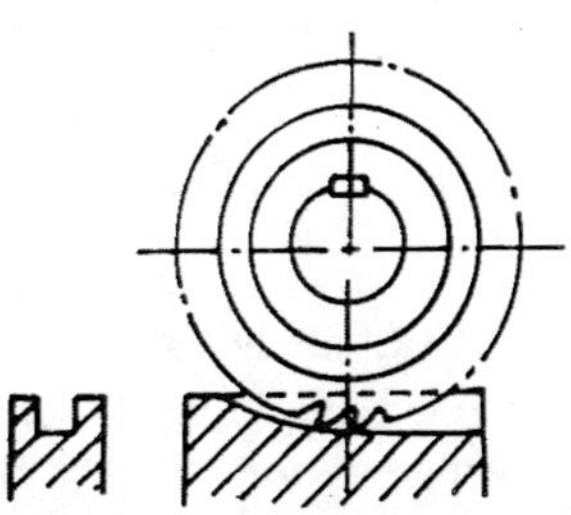

FIGURE 6.30 Assigning proper slot depth and radius.

The width and depth of slots should be specified according to the sizes of standard side milling, viz., end mills. The corner radii at the bottom of recess should be the constraint for all around recess (Figure 6.31), and should correspond to the size.

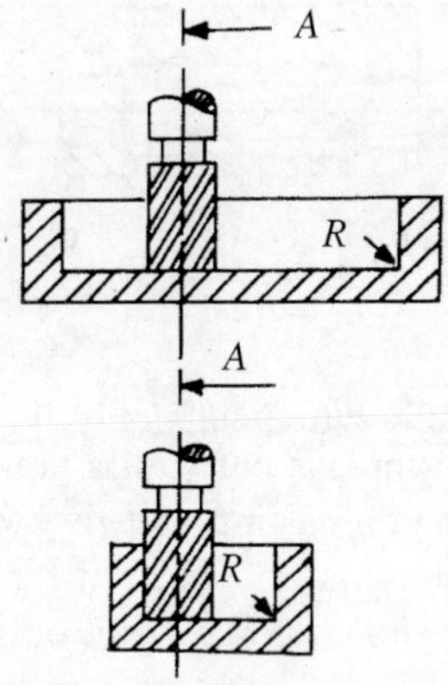

FIGURE 6.31 Assigning correct radii *R*.

6.6 THE ROLE OF PROCESS ENGINEER

The aforementioned producibility requirements made to the design of machine components cannot, of course, be considered as comprehensive in every detail. However, these requirements adequately illustrate the necessity of coordinating the design of machine components with the techniques for their production. The establishment of the general principles of producibility enables a complete analysis of a design from this standpoint. It is assumed that such an analysis may be carried out on the basis of the above-mentioned factors. It may prove more useful in this analysis to work back from the final stage of manufacture to the initial one, i.e., from producibility requirements for general assembly techniques to those for the process of blank manufacture. However, it is premature to leap to conclusions on the question of such a comprehensive analysis until the problem has been studied in more detail.

It should be noted that the design of a great variety of machine components, especially of the more complex type, in which all the principles of producibility are observed, may involve processing know-how possessed only by experts in various manufacturing fields (press-working, foundry, machining, etc.). There is no doubt, therefore, that it is indispensable and advisable to consult such experts in production techniques while machine parts are being designed. The experience of advanced enterprise in the development of new designs with the collaboration of processing engineers has given very good results. When such cooperation exists among designing and processing engineers, the lead time, i.e., the time that elapses between the release of the part drawings and the start of actual production, is substantially reduced and much less changes are required in the drawing to enable efficient production techniques to be applied.

6.7 EASE OF LOCATION AND CLAMPING

These two factors contribute to the time of machining and the accuracy of the machined part. A large flat surface is not good for positive positioning because any roughness of warpage causes the piece to rock. A three-point support is much better because it is less sensitive to casting defects. A piece with two feet or with a tilted bottom may be equipped with a temporary tab on the casting. After the piece is completely machined, the tab can be cut off. It is good to stay in one position or one alignment as much as possible. Figures 6.32–6.34 show three examples in which the effort

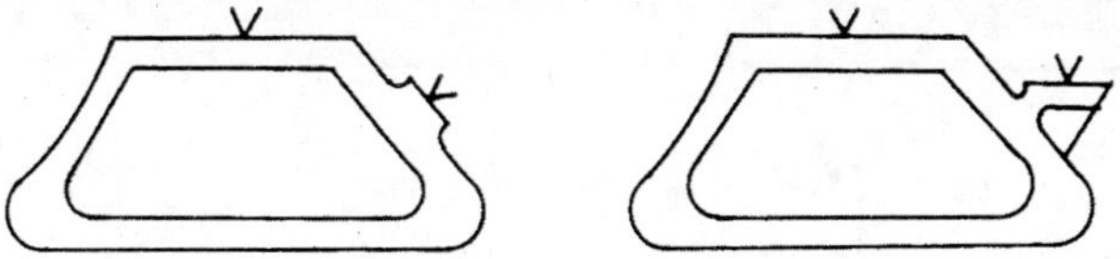

FIGURE 6.32 Simplifying drilling operation through good product design.

FIGURE 6.33 Advantage of uniform pad height.

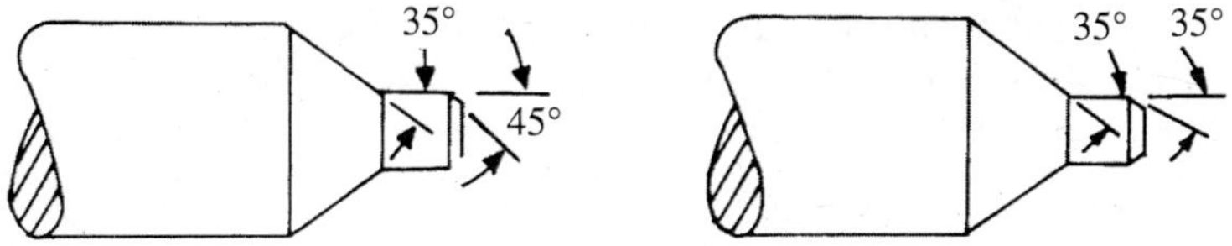

FIGURE 6.34 Minimizing tooling set-ups.

in positioning and aligning the workpiece is reduced by a careful design. The number of shoulders on shafts should be kept to a minimum. Curved surfaces should be excluded from machining.

Reducing tool changing and allowing for larger tools: Reducing the frequency of tool changing and allowing for larger tools shorten machining time. Larger tools are stronger and, therefore, they cut faster. They also wear longer because they have more cutting surfaces. To allow for larger tools means to leave enough clearance and overshoot space. It is also advisable to make the radius on the product the same as the radius of the tool so that no extra maneuvering is needed (Figure 6.35). If the holes have the same diameter, and radii on the workpiece are the same, the need to change tools would be reduced (see Figure 6.36).

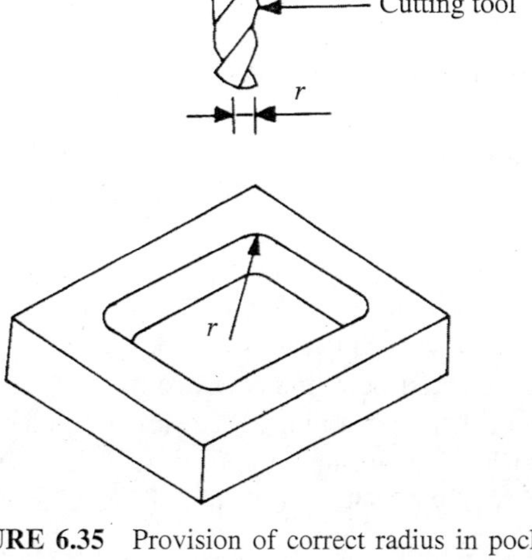

FIGURE 6.35 Provision of correct radius in pockets.

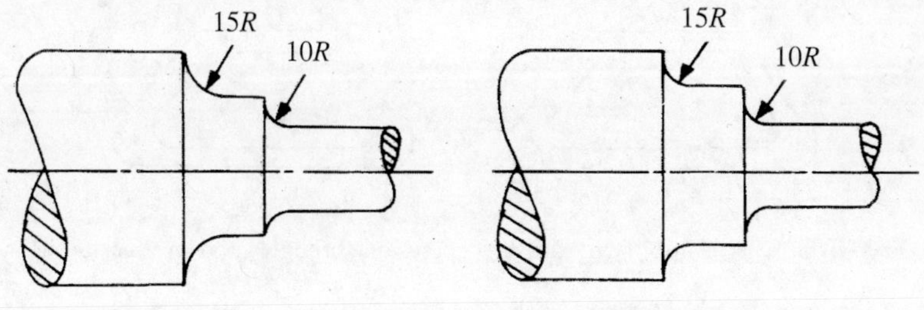

FIGURE 6.36 Equalizing radius R for minimizing tooling set-ups.

6.8 SOME ADDITIONAL ASPECTS OF PRODUCTION DESIGN

1. Sometimes, a slight modification in the features of a product can permit the use of a cheaper method of production. Figure 6.37 shows two similar products, one of which is produced by welding two stock pieces, whereas the other one is cast.

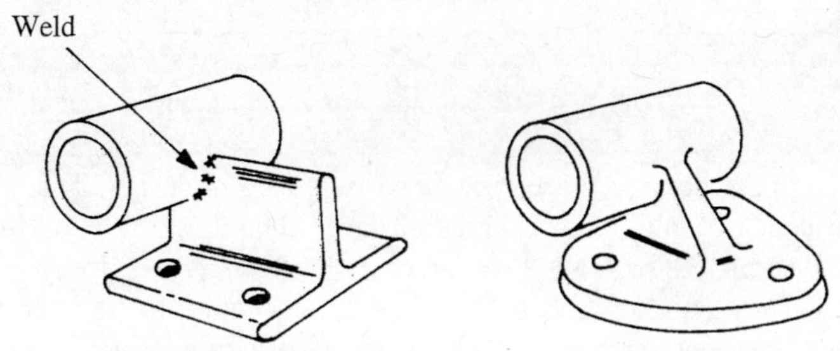

FIGURE 6.37 Welded bracket and cast iron bracket.

2. Normal good design of parts and moulds can decrease the number of rejects and lower the cost. There are also several methods to lower the material cost, labour cost and machining cost. The material cost can be lowered by using techniques of minimum weight designs. Compact design and wide tolerances can also lower material consumption.

6.9 DIE CASTING AND SPECIAL CASTINGS

The die casting companies are increasingly going into thin-wall castings, reducing 0.060 inch walls to 0.030 inch. The filling and flowing problem previously encountered with thin walls are compensated by improved design and better temperature control of moulds. If serious difficulty does occur, the wall can always be increased by grinding on the die. Labour is decreased by different ways of automation and by using multiple cavity moulds. Machining is a major area of cost reduction in casting design. If the dimensions can be closely controlled and the surface finish improved, much of the machining can be eliminated. Considering the cost of machining, the extra effort in mould-making can be very rewarding. Precision investment casting is already used on hard-to-machine metals, such as titanium and stainless steel, to eliminate machining completely. Casting offers design flexibility not available in welding or forging. Side cores can be used to save hole drilling. Many separate parts can be combined into an integral design to eliminate assembly and machining of the fittings.

Die casting is a high-speed, high-volume production process for small to medium components. The cycle time of the process is short because both the mould material and the casting material are good thermal conductors. The process is less expensive than other casting methods when the production volume is large enough. Because the molten metal is forced into the die under pressure, very fine details can be duplicated. The physical properties of a die-east piece are superior to a sand-cast piece of the same material. The precise dimensions and fine surface finish of a die-cast piece often eliminate machining. Die casting is used to produce engine components and housings for power tools and business machines. It is also used to produce small components such as gears, flywheels and decorative pieces.

6.10 DESIGN OF POWDER METALLURGICAL PARTS

Powder metallurgy has been developed as a production process after 1960. This process comprises mixing different metal powders with die lubricants and feeding the mixture into a press. The loose powders have a density which is 40% of the density of solid metals. The press cavity is about double the size of the piece obtained, after pressing and compaction. The 'green compact' derived after compaction is sintered in an oven in an inert atmosphere for about 20 minutes to obtain the desired component.

From the point of view of a product designer, the best design is purely prismatic in shape. The presence of flanges or protrusions results in uneven compaction and components of uneven density.

In certain cases, non-uniform densities are intentionally introduced in the P/M component. However, this is an exception rather than a rule.

The advantages of a P/M part are as follows:

1. Refractory metals such as Tungsten, Molybdenum and Tantalum can be fabricated only by this process. Tungsten carbide tips with cobalt binder are a typical example of P/M design application. Tungsten carbide tips have revolutionized the technology of metal cutting.
2. Very little scrap is produced in the P/M process and the form of the product obtained by P/M is final and requires little finishing.

Chow [2] has shown certain examples of P/M products which are introduced in Figure 6.38. Modifying a part with steps into two straight pieces can simplify the die and reduce the press capacity, as illustrated in Figure 6.38(a).

For a product manufactured by the P/M process design, the efforts should be made towards getting a proper fill, a uniform density, and a longer tool life. Wall thicknesses at a fin or a web, or between a core pin and the edge should be more than 1.5–2 mm to avoid filling problems (Figure 6.38(b)). Unevenly filled parts of a component have lower densities and lower strengths than the rest. Circular holes can be used at non-critical parts of gears or pulleys to reduce weight. Sharp contours or internal key holes will result in a weak die, since the dies have the same profile as the pressed piece (Figure 6.38(c)). Such a die is also expensive to make and needs more maintenance.

The female die is a hollow prism with the contour of the P/M component. The male die slides along this prism of constant area. Therefore, the P/M component should have a uniform thickness and straight sides. No draft is needed on the side walls and core holes. It is not possible to make a perfect sphere by P/M because the male die will have a feather edge. However, a sphere can be approximated by a shape, with a cylindrical section between two spherical domes.

The two pieces can be assembled before sintering and they will bond together during sintering. Sometimes, a small shoulder (0.010 in wide) is added to a piece with 45% chamfers so that the die will have a stronger edge. A shoulder is not needed for chamfers less than 30° (Figure 6.38(d)). Gear teeth should be at a larger diameter than the hub so that the die will not be weakened (Figure 6.38(e)).

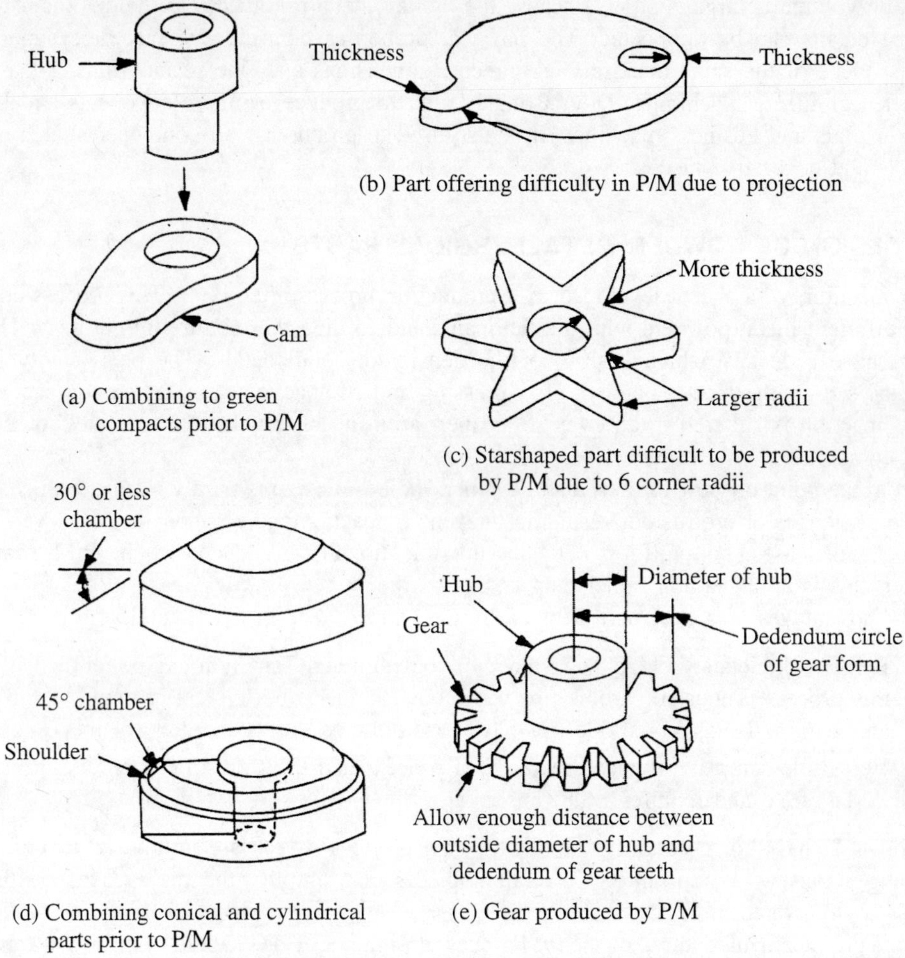

FIGURE 6.38 Product design practice for powder metallurgy parts.

P/M parts can also be made with controlled non-uniform densities. For many machine components, such as gears and engine connecting rods, it is advisable to have bearing properties at some locations and structural strength at others.

6.11 EXPANDED METALS AND WIRE FORMS

Expanded metals and wire forms are light-weight and high-strength structures which are economical to manufacture. They allow free passage of air, light, sound, and heat. With wire forms, the designer can control the distribution of material very closely. The following discussion will further clarify the advantages and design details of these structures.

6.11.1 Expanded Metals

Expanded metal processing is an effective strength-improving technique. Unlike punching and perforating, the expanding process does not create scrap. Regardless of whether expanding is achieved by stretching or back and forth bending, the production process operates at a high speed and a low cost.

Usual applications of expanded metals are: fences, catwalks, garden furniture, ventilators, and safety protective screens for fans, heaters, and so on. Figure 6.39 shows several kinds of expanded metals for different applications.

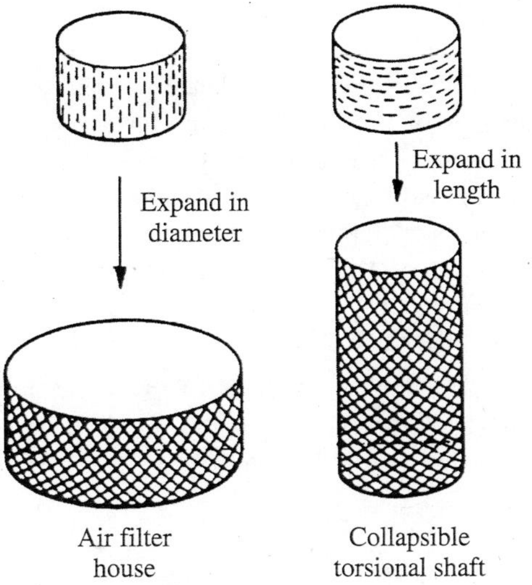

FIGURE 6.39 Expanded metal products.

Several inherent characteristics of the expanding process influence product properties and design. The standard expanded metals have diamond-shaped holes and three-dimensional textures make the materials more rigid in lateral bending. The diamond-shaped holes make the material extra strong in shear because forces are transmitted along 45° angled webs. In the expanded tube steering column for automobiles, the pattern gives high torsional rigidity and strength. The 3-D textures also provide good surface strength, which makes the materials prime candidates for catwalks. Figure 6.40

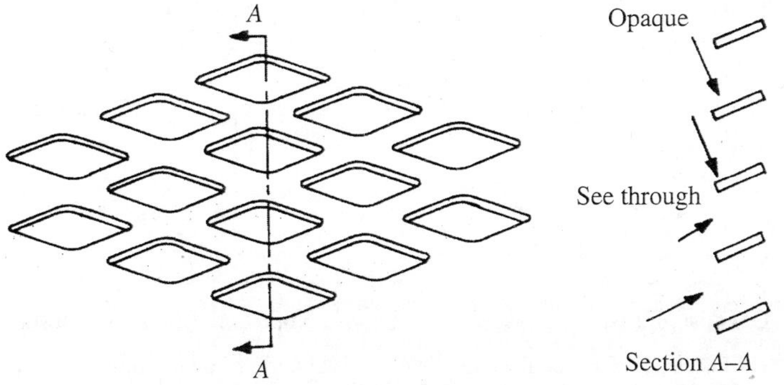

FIGURE 6.40 Louvre design.

shows a section of a three-dimensional texture. Such a texture resembles the Venetian blind, in that, in some angles, it is transparent and at other angles, it is opaque. Such a directional property can be used to shield light from an optical projector or provide decorative effects for a computer cabinet. It is not advisable to leave a blank margin at the trailing edge of the expanded sheet. The transition between an expanded area and an unexpanded blank area (with 5 to 1 material density difference) is a potential stress raiser. Perforation is one instead of expanding, if blank margins are needed from the point of view of design, to avoid stress concentration.

6.11.2 Wire Forms

Chow [2] has illustrated wire forms that are made by bending and forming wires of different diameters into different geometries which are "resistance-welded" into structures. The designer has a wide choice regarding the sizes or positions of wires for proper strength, rigidity and stability. Wires are stronger than cast materials of equal rigidity. In many applications, a wire-form structure has the least weight and is inexpensive to construct. It is also somewhat easy to incorporate spring components, clips, bearings, hinges and cranks, into a wire-form design. Due to this, integral design is applicable to wire forms with more effectiveness. Examples of wire-form structures are display racks, cages, trays, grills, fan guards, refrigerator racks, supermarket carts and baskets. Figure 6.41(a) shows several wire-form designs that can replace similar cast metal or sheet metal products. Repeated usage of wires of a standardized geometry within a product can reduce tooling and fixture costs.

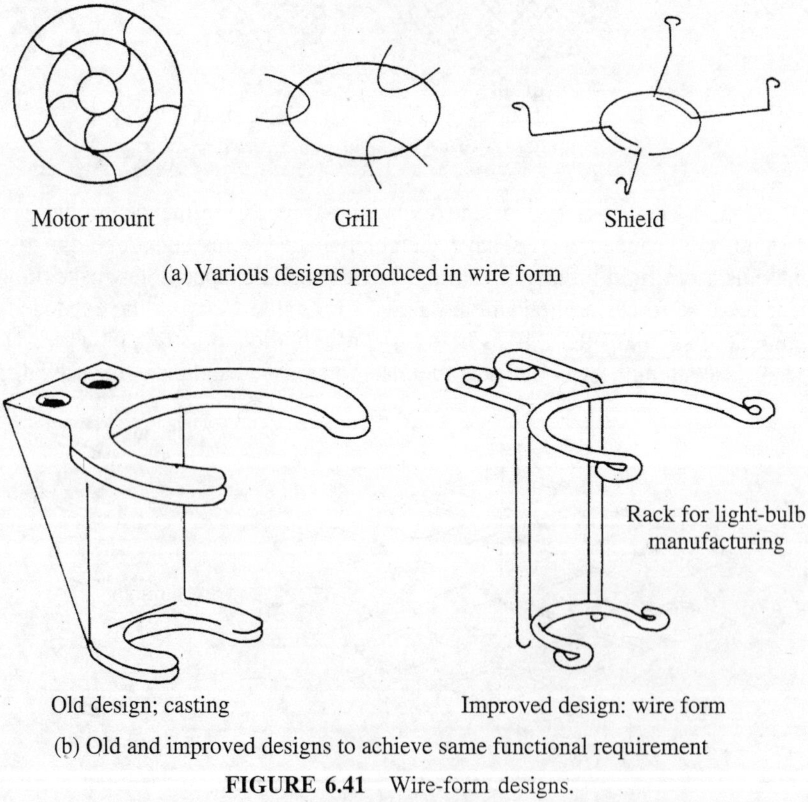

FIGURE 6.41 Wire-form designs.

Wire-form design variety is limited by the process capability of bending, forming and welding processes. Since different vendors may have different equipments, accepting design suggestions from the vendors can often reduce the piece cost. A wire-form design is quite accommodative to design changes without affecting functional efficiency. An example of a wire-form design replacing a casting is shown in Figure 6.41(b).

REVIEW QUESTIONS

1. Explain producibility requirement in the design of machine components. P 167–168
2. In a forging design, why intersection of cylinders at right angles and intersection of flat plate with cylinder are avoided? Sec. 6.2; Figure 6.2 to 6.6
3. Why bosses are avoided in flat die forging?
4. In which situation forging and welding are combined to generate final geometry of the component? Ref. Figure 6.8
5. Why some industries avoid casting and combine press-working and welding to produce certain components?

   [**Ans:** To avoid the pollution of air due to use of foundry processes, certain industries combine sheet metal working with welding to obtain similar geometry of the component. For a bowl of submersible pump suggests how press-working and welding can be combined (see Figure 6.42(b) to give a geometry similar to Figure 6.42(a))].

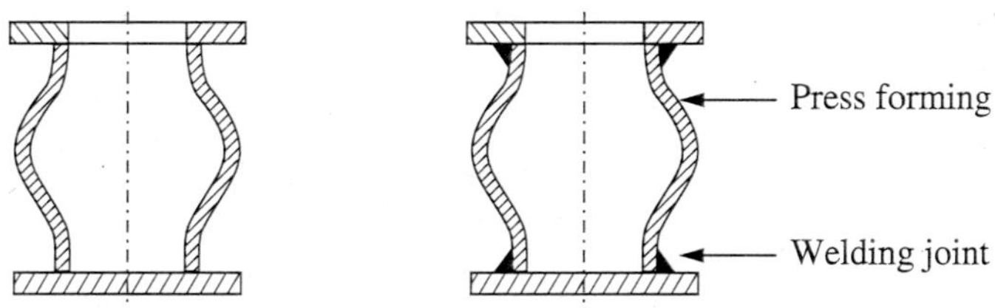

(a) Casting (b) Forming and welding

FIGURE 6.42 Bowl of multistage vertical submersible pump.

6. How efficient casting design shapes can be achieved? Sec. 6.4; P 173–175
7. Give examples of designing for machining: Sec. 6.5; P 176–180
   (i) Drill a vertical hole on an inclined surface.
   (ii) Drilling a hole in a flange adjacent to vertical casting wall.
   (iii) Provision of cored holes in casting.
   (iv) Minimizing machining surfaces.
   (v) Hobbing of two adjacent gears.
   (vi) Machining cluster gears.
   (vii) Provision for reamed blind holes.
   (viii) Provision of locating bosses for first operation fixtures.
   (ix) Provision of radii and slot width to suit standard cutting tools.

8. Compare a welded bracket for bearing with a bracket with a cast and machined bearing bracket. Sec. 6.8; P 182; Figure 6.37 (a) and (b)

9. Powder metallurgy can produce only prismatic shapes. How to achieve complex shapes by powder metallurgical process? Sec. 6.10; Figure 6.38

10. What are expanded metal products? What are their advantages? Sec. 6.11; P 184–186

11. How wire forms can replace casting or forging in certain situations? Explain through sketches. Sec. 6.11.2; Figure 6.41 (a) and (b)

REFERENCES

[1] Kovan, V., *Fundamentals of Process Engineering*, Mir Publishers, Moscow, 1969.

[2] Chow, W.W., *Cost Reduction in Product Design*, Van Nostrand Reinhold, New York, 1978.

Chapter **7**

Material Processing of Plastics, Rubber, Glass and Ceramics

7.1 PLASTICS

The history of rubber and plastics as commercially useful materials could not be contemplated about 150 years ago. Charles Goodyear discovered hard rubber in 1839 when he accidentally produced ebonite on his domestic stove. Chemists had not realized that by the combination of such basic materials as hydrogen, oxygen, nitrogen, chlorine, sulphur etc., a new material like commercial plastic could be created. In 1868, a shortage of ivory billiard balls was felt. An inventive young printer named James Wesley Hyatt mixed pyroxylin, made from cotton and nitric acid with solid camphor. The resulting material was called celluloid. This material found wide application in dentures, films, combs, etc. Forty years later in 1909, Les Henrik Bakeland developed phenol formaldehyde resin. Cellulose acetate was the next (1927) large volume plastic.

Plastics are a group of synthetic chemical compounds which are high polymers and which are at some stage plastic and could be shaped by heat, with or without pressure into useful products. They usually consist of one or more chemical compounds of organic origin which have indefinite melting points and have amorphous structures. (We are familiar with natural resins which are exudations from various plants and animals.)

Polymerization is an important reaction in plastics technology. A basic molecule is called a *monomer*, and any compound composed of basic molecules may also be termed a monomer. A polymer is composed of enlarged molecules or macromolecules which are formed by the recurring addition of monomers. This combining of many monomers to make macromolecules or polymers is known as *polymerization.* During polymerization, molecular weight is increased. As an example, the polymerization of ethylene C_2H_4 to produce polyethylene is shown by the following chemical reaction:

$$n \times \begin{bmatrix} H & & H \\ | & & | \\ C & = & C \\ | & & | \\ H & & H \end{bmatrix} \longrightarrow \begin{matrix} & H & & H & & H & & H & \\ & | & & | & & | & & | & \\ - & C & - & C & - & C & - & C & - \\ & | & & | & & | & & | & \\ & H & & H & & H & & H & \end{matrix} \text{(repeated many times)}$$

Monomeric ethylene   Polymeric ethylene

A polymer is often explained by the analogy of formation of spaghetti from small linear nodules joined together. When the number of repeating molecular units in a single molecule is below 500 (approx.), the compound is called a *low polymer.* Above 500 (approx.), repeating molecular units in a single molecule, the material becomes a high polymer reaching up to 4000 (approx.) in certain cases. In general, monomers are liquids, and as polymerization progresses, viscosity increases until the material becomes a solid. High pressure and chemical catalysts initiate or promote polymerization. Cooling below 0°C and inhibitors, which act as negative catalysts, prevent or retard polymerization. During polymerization, the units may grow in one of the following three different arrangements:

(i) linear polymer, (ii) branched-linear polymer, and (iii) cross-linked polymer (Figure 7.1(c)). In the cross-linked polymer, the ends of the branches are not free, as against those of branched-linear polymer. The molecules are fastened together to form a more rigid material. Cross-linked polymers are much more insoluble and infusible than linear polymers. Polymers are produced by either of the two types of processes. "Addition polymerization" (in which monomers combine together, as already described) or "condensation-polymerization" reactions such as that between an acid and an alcohol, forming an ester (polymer).

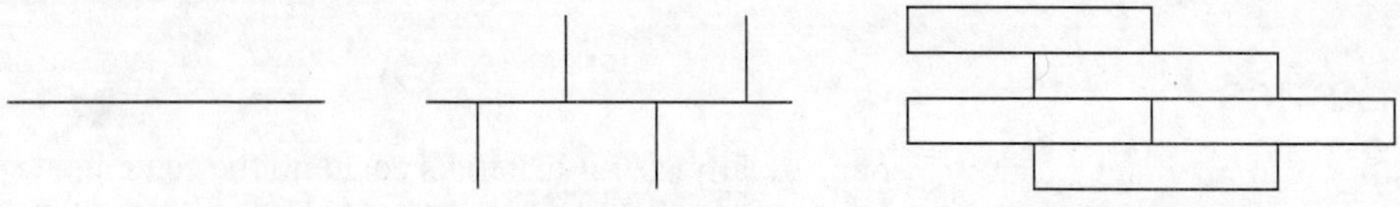

(a) Linear (b) Branched linear (c) Cross-linked

FIGURE 7.1 Molecular structures of polymers.

Co-polymerization is analogous to alloy formulation when two or more different repeating molecular units combine during polymerization. The new material produced is known as a "co-polymer". Low polymer and low co-polymers continue to have a tendency to polymerize until they become high polymers, reaching a stable condition. Polymerization is an irreversible process.

7.1.1 Some Definitions

Other terms used in connection with plastics include the following:

Accelerators or **hardeners** are catalysts used specifically for speeding up chemical reactions in which synthetic resins are polymerized.

Elastomers are materials which have the ability to deform considerably within elastic limits; synthetic rubbers and polyethylene are examples of elastomer.

Fillers are mixed into synthetic resins, primarily to dilute them so that less resin will be required. When using wood flour, which is the most common filler, 30 to 60 per cent wood flour by weight is mixed into the resin. Fillers may be wood flour, some type of fibres, mineral powder or any other material. It is essential that a filler gets wet by the resin. Fibrous fillers, such as fibreglass, cotton and linen fibres, are used to improve mechanical properties like tensile strength.

Modifiers are added chemicals used to change the properties of the base synthetic resin. Some modifiers are cross-linking agents, used to improve mechanical properties.

Plasticizers are chemical additions used either to soften resins at their forming temperatures or to make the final plastic products tougher or more flexible. A synthetic rubber may be mixed or blended, with a synthetic resin to produce a tough, shock-resistant moulding plastic. Stabilizers are added to prevent deterioration by the action of light and heat.

7.2 CONCEPTS IN CHEMISTRY OF PLASTICS

7.2.1 Types of Polymerization

Plastics are made by one of the two processing techniques:

(i) **Chain polymerization.** In this technique, aliphatic hydrocarbons form straight chains as shown in Figure 7.2(a). Alternative hydrocarbons can be represented as hexagonal rings (benzene) or aromatic hydrocarbons. Monovalent Cl, F, or Br may replace H in other polymers. In other instances, N, O, S, P, or Si may be present in backbone or side chains. Figure 7.2(b) shows formation of polyethylene, and Figure 7.2(c) the formation of polypropylene, polyvinyl chloride (single Cl atom) or polyvinylidene chloride (two Cl atoms). Figure 7.2(c) also depicts the formation of polystyrene and polyvinyl fluoride, respectively.

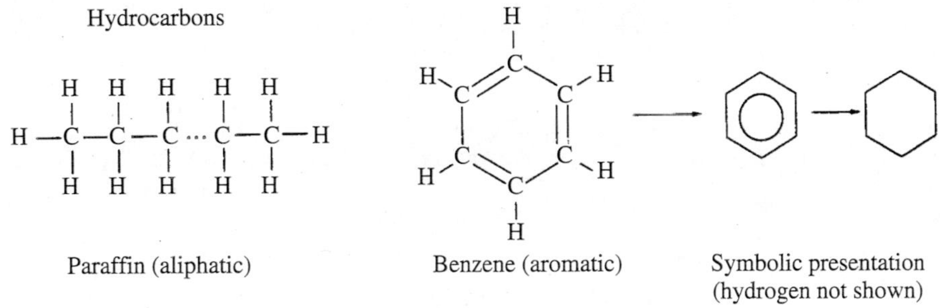

(a) Structure of some hydrocarbons

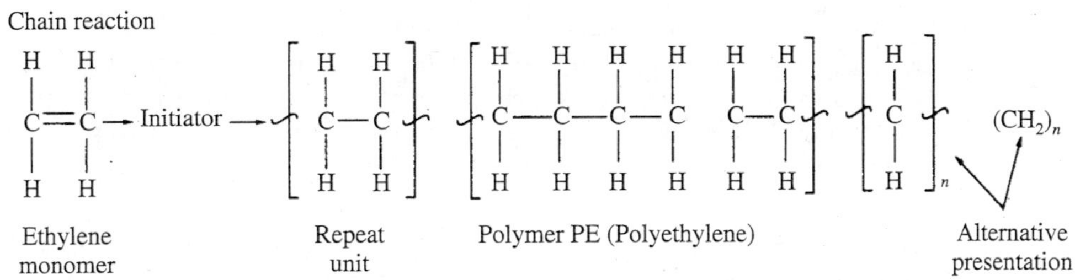

(b) Formation of polyethylene

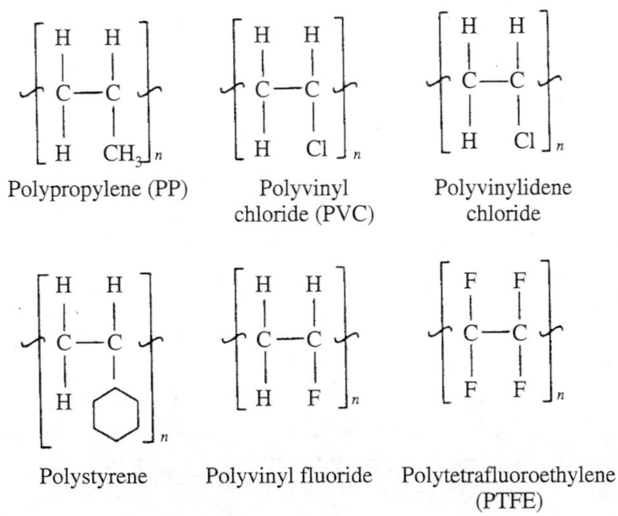

(c) Repeating units of some important polymers

FIGURE 7.2 *Contd.*

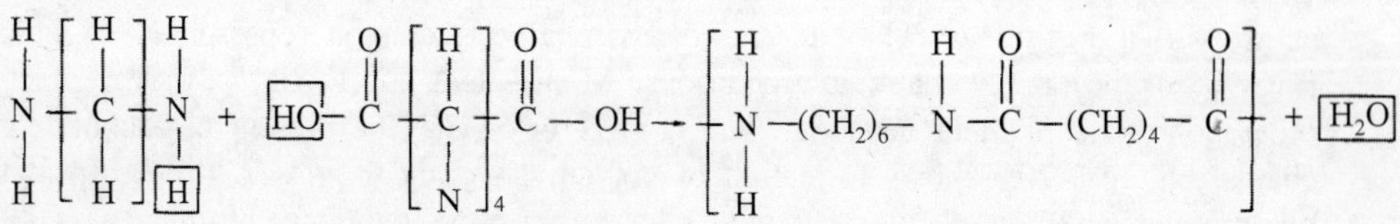

Hexamethylene diamine + Adipic acid Polyamide (nylon 66) + Water

(d) Step reaction in formation of Nylon 66

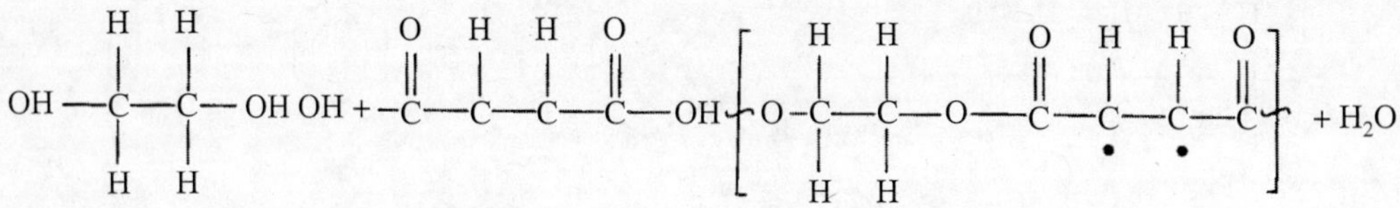

Ethylene glycol + Maleic acid Linear unsaturated polyester + Water

(e) Formation of polymer through condensation reaction

FIGURE 7.2 Chemical bond structure and some important chemical reactions in polymer chemistry.

Properties of these polymers depend on the atom which replaces H atom. For example, introduction of benzene ring gives polystyrene, which is in the form of a hard filament and is used in styrene butadiene rubber (Copolymer – alloy of two different polymers). Introduction of Si atom makes the polymer temperature resistant, N makes it inert and less susceptible to attack by chemicals, and Cl and F make it stable but capable of 'properties control' by heat treatment.

(ii) **Step polymerization or condensation polymerization.** As a result of reaction, usually between an alcohol and an acid, two different monomer groups are attached and water is formed. Figure 7.2(e) shows such a process during formation of polyester.

Example. This example is due to Schey [1]. An ultra-high molecular weight polyethylene has a molecular weight of 4 million. Calculate the degree of polymerization and length of straight chain.

Solution. The building unit is C_2H_4 with molecular weight $2 \times 12 + 4 \times 1 = 28$

$$\text{Degree of polymerization} = 4{,}000{,}000/28 = (143{,}000)$$

$$\text{Length of molecule} = 143{,}000 \times 1.26 = (180{,}000)\ \text{Å} = 18\ \mu\text{m}$$

7.2.2 Effect of Heating on Thermoplastic

A typical thermoplastic exists in three states: (i) elastic, (ii) viscoelastic, and (iii) viscous. The plastic undergoes change from elastic range to glassy range and then to viscous range. Viscoelastic range is called T_g range. Softening with rise in temperature is due to reduction of intramolecular forces. Figure 7.3 indicates change in specific volume of a thermoplastic with rise in temperature. From the point of view of plastic processing, the deformation should be carried out about 10 to 20°C above melting temperature, T_m which ranges from 100 to 300°C for various thermoplastics.

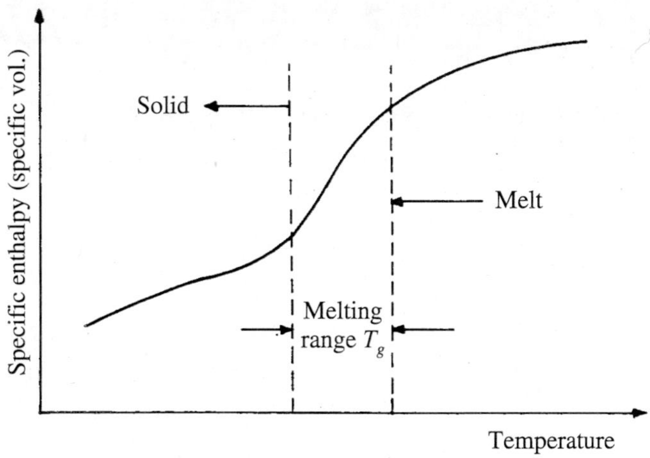

FIGURE 7.3 Thermal behaviour of a polymer.

7.2.3 Cross-Linked Polymers

In linear polymers, covalent bonds exist only within molecules as shown in Figure 7.4. However, when these bonds are present between molecules, no permanent deformation is possible.

Rubbers and elastomers. Elastomers are a special class of amorphous linear polymers containing a double bond of the micromolecule. In the case of elastomers, cross-links can be formed by addition of catalysts or additives, e.g., sulphur in isoprene rubber. When only a few cross-links are formed, the molecules can unwined to 200% of initial length because they are helical and spring like. Figure 7.4(a) indicates isoprene polyisoprene, and the formation of vulcanized rubber. Figure 7.4(b) indicates the cross-linking process. Figure 7.4(c) depicts polybutadiene–styrene copolymer and its molecular structure. The styrene segments segregate to form polystyrene such as glassy regions which act as cross-links in polybutadiene, e.g., rubbery regions. Figure 7.4(d) shows the molecular structure of polyurethane which forms an elastomeric spatial network.

Example. Calculate the amount of sulphur required to establish a cross-link between every 10 mers of polyisoprene. Assume that only one sulphur atom is required between each cross-link.

Solution. Each mer of isoprene (C_5H_8) has a molecular weight of $5 \times 12 + 8 = 68$ g. Sulphur has an atomic weight of 32 g. For 10 mers of 10×68 g of isoprene, sulphur needed = (32/680) or (4.7 g) of sulphur per 100 g of isoprene. The fraction of sulphur is $4.7/(4.7 + 100) = 0.045$ or 4.5% by weight of vulcanized rubber. Since sulphur forms chains by itself, a somewhat higher percentage of sulphur is required.

7.2.4 Thermosetting Polymers

These are a different class of materials in which once the polymerization is completed, no further deformation is possible. These polymers get permanently hardened by heat. In certain cases, there is a stage-wise transformation from Stage A → Stage B → Stage C. Stage B is that in which the material is in the form of a viscous liquid and can be processed into solid, and stage C is by application of temperature. Figure 7.5 shows the reaction of phenol formaldehyde.

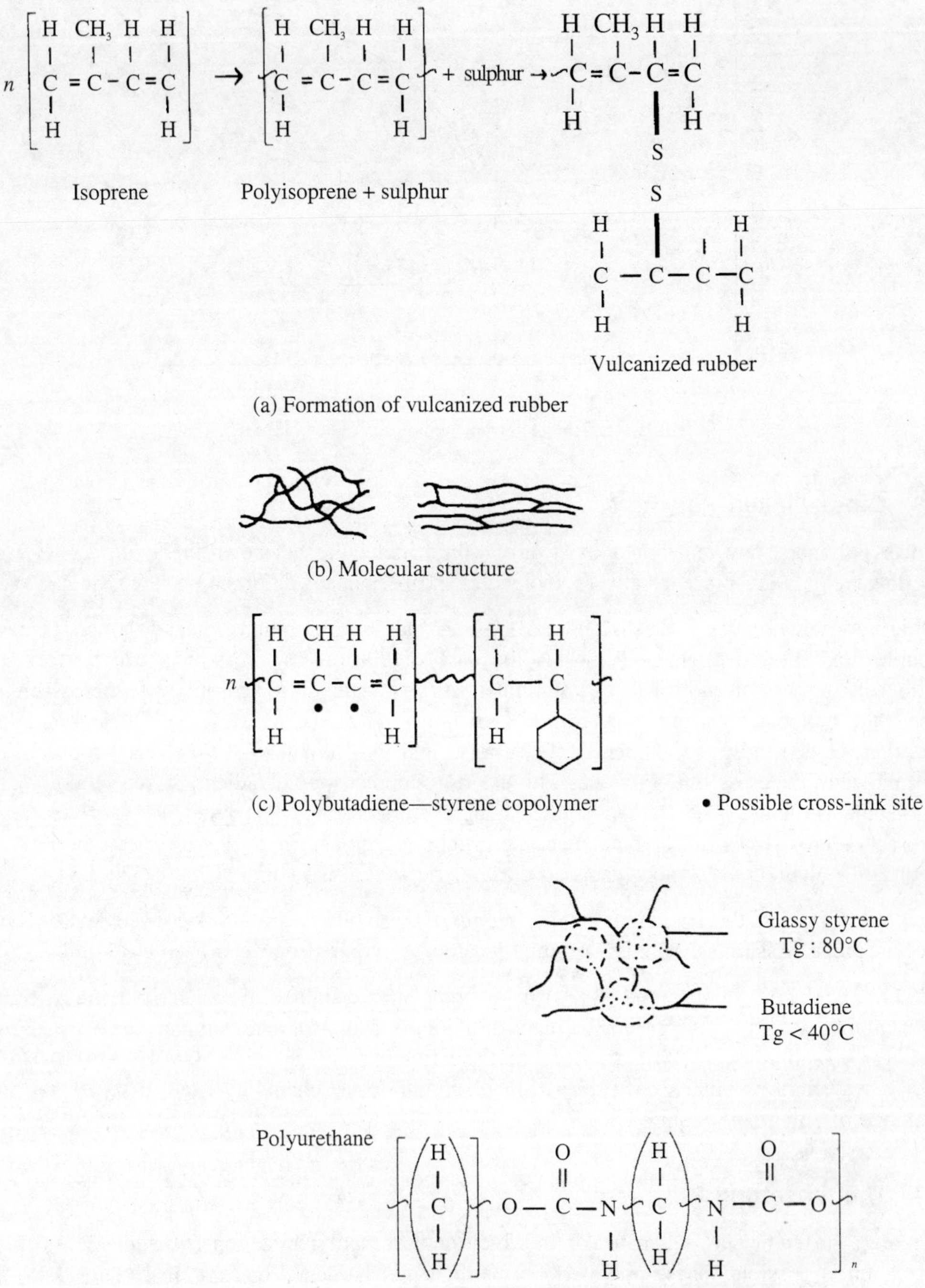

FIGURE 7.4 Chemical reactions in the formation of rubbers and elastomers.

Thermosetting polymers

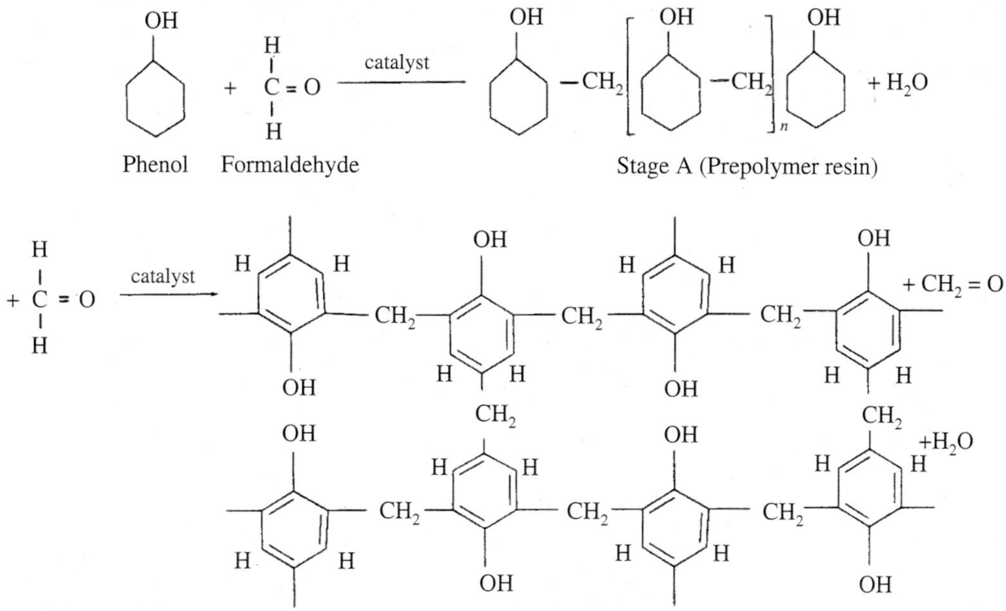

Stage C (Phenol formaldehyde resin)

FIGURE 7.5 Formation of stages A and C in thermosetting process.

7.3 PROPERTIES OF PLASTICS

Because of their unusual combination of properties, plastics occupy an important position among engineering materials. In general, plastics are light in weight, resistant to most chemicals (also corrosion-resistant), excellent electrical insulators, easy to shape into finished parts, adequately strong for many applications, sufficiently hard and, in some cases, flexible. Disadvantages of plastics include: costs of materials are comparatively higher and most plastics cannot withstand even moderately high temperatures. Ultimate tensile strength of plastics ranges from about 2,000 to 15,000 psi. When reinforced with fibreglass or certain other fibres, tensile strengths of up to about 50,000 psi are obtainable. The shapes of stress-strain curves for thermoplastic materials are similar to those for metals. At light loads, stress is proportional to strain, up to the proportional limit. Thermosetting materials, which are high polymers, will have practically no elastic or plastic deformation before rupturing, and thus are somewhat brittle. Important electrical properties of plastics include dielectric strength and power factor. Dielectric strength is obtained by placing the material as an insulator between two plates which are to be charged as a capacitor. The dielectric strength is the maximum voltage which the material can withstand before breakdown occurs, and it is expressed as so many volts per mil of thickness. Dielectric strengths may be measured at various AC frequencies, depending on their use for the plastic material. Power factor is a measure of the energy absorbed by an insulating material in the presence of an alternating electrical field. With perfect insulators, no power is absorbed or lost. Since it is important in electronics, power factor is measured at various frequencies, such as 60, 1,000 or 1 million cycles per second.

7.4 CLASSIFICATION OF PLASTICS

Numerous plastics have been discovered since the discovery of phenol formaldehyde, and the discovery of new plastics continues. Research in the field of plastics is one of the most active fields in organic chemistry today. A synthetic resin, such as phenol formaldehyde, may exist in a number of different forms. In addition to existing in one or more different forms, a plastic can often be blended with another plastic or modified to obtain a variety of properties. When two or more plastics are blended, the principal resin is known as the *base resin.* Resins may be classified as natural, synthetic, cellulose derivative, or protein. Natural resins are those produced by nature, and by definition, they are not included under plastics. The term 'plastics', however, does include three other classifications.

(i) **Synthetic resins.** According to this classification, plastics are complex organic materials made by the chemical reaction of relatively simple substances. A *cellulose derivative* is made from cellulose, which has a large complex molecule already built by nature. It is already a polymer, and is only modified by chemical methods to produce various cellulose derivatives. A *protein resin* is made using a protein, such as casein, as its base.

(ii) **Thermosetting resin.** All resins are either thermoplastics or thermosetting. Thermosetting resin is one that is hardened by heat, causing a chemical change which is irreversible. Thermosetting materials are sometimes called heat-setting materials; a common example is a waffle, which is hardened by heat.

(iii) **Thermoplastic resins.** These are softened by heat, and are sometimes called cold-setting resins. An example is paraffin, which may be softened by heat and hardened by cooling. This process may be repeated as many times as is required. The line of separation between thermoplastic and thermosetting materials is well defined. There cannot be a material which is both heat-setting and cold-setting at the same time. Cross-linked polymers are normally thermosetting and linear and branched-linear polymers tend to be thermoplastics. Thus, a cross-linking agent may be used to change a resin from thermoplastic to thermosetting. The method of moulding or forming to final shape is determined largely by whether a plastic is thermosetting or thermoplastic.

7.5 PHENOL FORMALDEHYDE AND UREA FORMALDEHYDE RESIN PRODUCTS

The chart developed by Campbell [2] in Figure 7.6 briefly shows, how some of the phenol formaldehyde and urea formaldehyde products are produced. It can be seen that the structure of phenol formaldehyde is quite complex. Phenol formaldehyde has the peculiar ability of being produced by either the one-step or the two-step process. The principal difference in these two processes is that the one-step process uses a basic catalyst and an excess of formaldehyde, whereas the two-step process requires an acid catalyst and a deficiency of formaldehyde. The A-stage resins are liquids and low polymers. When completely hardened (a high polymer), the resin is in what is known as the *C stage*. Between the A and C stages, there may be a B stage. This is a partially cured gelatinous condition, which may exhibit different properties. Liquid resin products, such as liquid core binders, casting resins and adhesives will ordinarily polymerize slowly at room temperature. In doing so, they become progressively thicker until they are worthless. The maximum storage life is usually considered to be about 9 months, unless such a material is kept in a cool place like refrigerator.

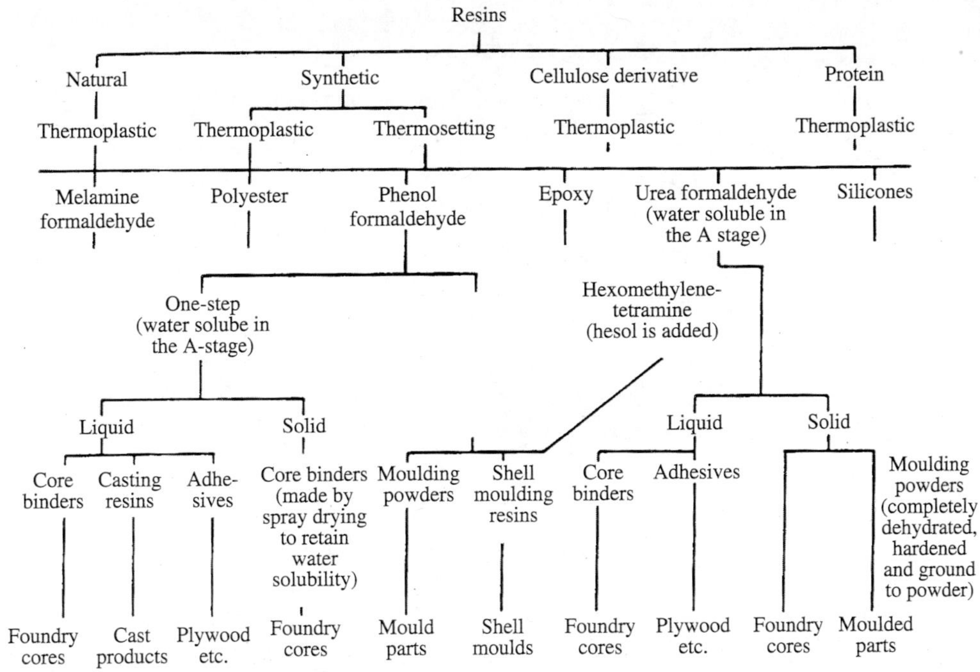

FIGURE 7.6 Classification of resins and their industrial applications.

7.6 COMPRESSION MOULDING

In compression moulding, the steel mould cavities have horizontal parting surfaces. The moulding powder is heated and compressed as the mould halves are forced together by the press. Since it is subjected to a high pressure (around 2,000 psi) and heat (at about 350°F), the material first becomes sufficiently fluid to fill the mould cavity completely. In the next step, additional heat then causes the fluid thermosetting moulding material to harden. From 20 s to 10 min are required for the curing, depending on the part thickness and the moulding material. If thermoplastic moulding materials were used, hardening would have to be accomplished by turning off the heat and cooling the mould because alternate heating and cooling of a mould would be a waste of time, thermoplastic materials are not suitable for compression moulding. When producing sufficiently large quantities, moulding powder is first automatically pressed into preforms in order to eliminate weighing out the correct amount of powder for each charge. The weights of preforms are quite uniformly held, and the operator can easily place the proper number of preforms into a mould cavity (see Figure 7.7). Preforms are usually shaped like tablets, but some have special shapes, which may simplify moulding material nearer to its final shape. Preforms should be preheated before loading into mould cavities to eliminate moisture, improve flow characteristics and decrease curing time. After the first compressing, a mould may be momentarily separated slightly, to allow any gases produced to escape. This is known as "breathing" a mould. After sufficient time (for curing), the mould is finally opened and the moulded part is ejected, as illustrated in Figure 7.7.

It should be noted that since the moulding material is placed directly into the mould cavities, no gazing is necessary for compression moulds. Fibre-reinforced parts, such as panels, ducts and armrests, are made using a thermosetting moulding material which is first placed into the mould

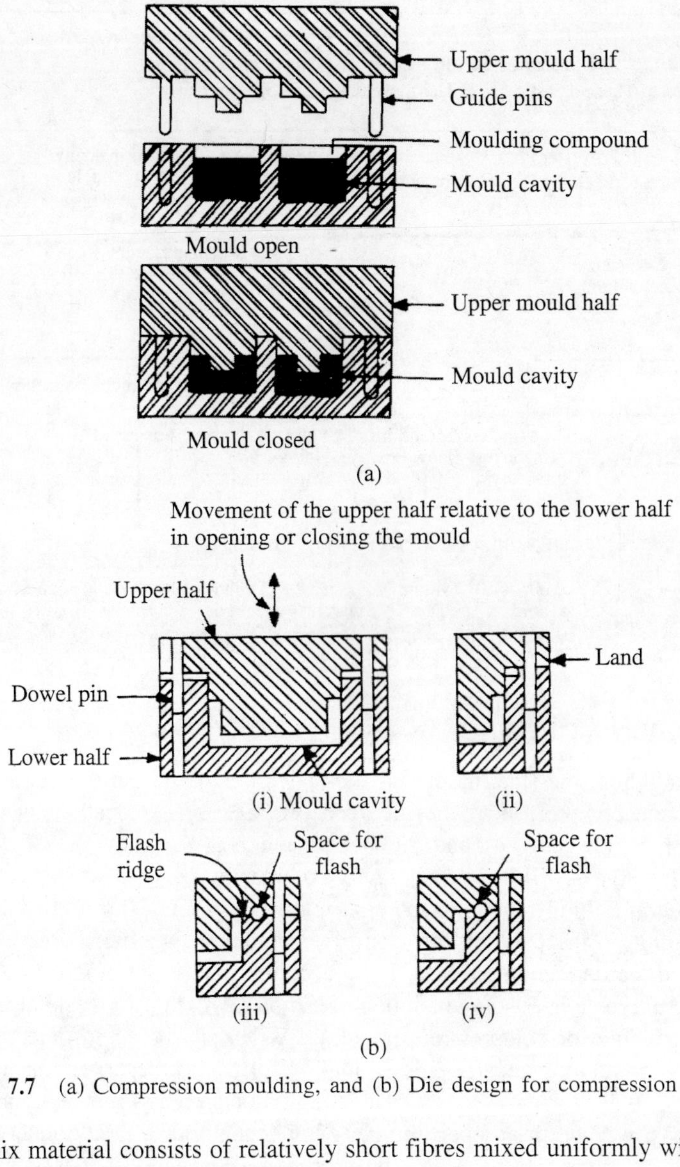

FIGURE 7.7 (a) Compression moulding, and (b) Die design for compression moulding.

cavity. This premix material consists of relatively short fibres mixed uniformly with a viscous resin. After mixing, it is extruded to obtain a uniform cross-section. It is then cut to proper lengths to obtain charges of correct weight.

7.7 TRANSFER MOULDING

This process is similar to compression moulding, with the exception that in transfer moulding, the moulding material is loaded into a separate loading chamber. Under heat and pressure, the material becomes fluid and flows through a sprue from the loading chamber to all parts of the mould cavity or cavities. Additional heat then causes the thermosetting moulding material to harden. Transfer moulding is especially suitable for parts with slender cores or metal inserts. In comparison with compression moulding, parts made by transfer moulding ordinarily have better mechanical properties, more accuracy, less flash at the parting line to clean off. In a sprue-type transfer mould, as shown in Figure 7.8, the sprue will break near the moulded part when the plunger returns upwards at the end of the curing period. The sprue, together with a small amount of excess material, called a "cull", may be removed by pushing it from a tapered dovetail impression at the end of the plunger. Since it is thermosetting, this material cannot be reclaimed and used again. A plunger-type transfer mould, as shown in Figure 7.9, must be used with a double-action press. One action is used for opening and closing the mould, and the other action operates the plunger.

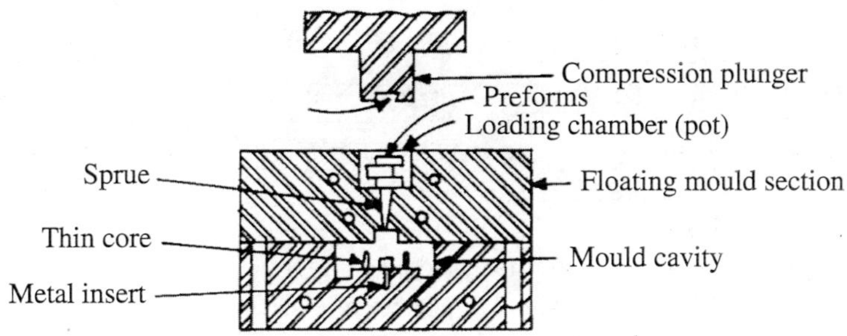

FIGURE 7.8 Transfer moulding.

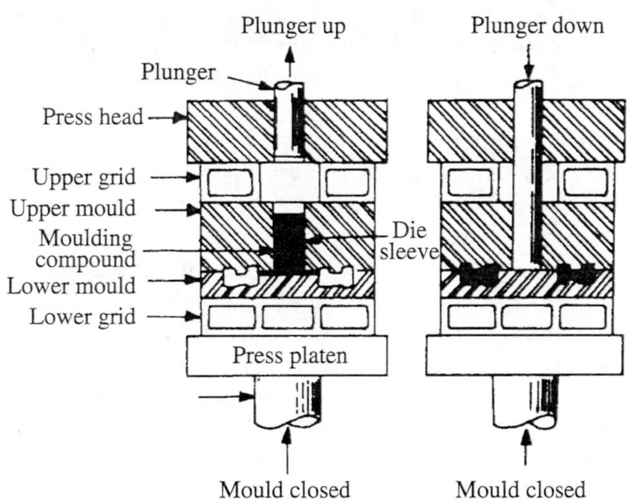

FIGURE 7.9 Transfer moulding with opposed dies.

7.8 INJECTION MOULDING

As can be seen from Figure 7.10, moulding powder, which has been heated to drive off moisture, is loaded into the feed hopper, and when the plunger moves backward, some of the moulding powder drops down in front of the plunger. Then the mould is closed tightly, and the plunger moves forward, applying pressure behind the powder. This forces some plastic, which has softened sufficiently, through the nozzle into the water-cooled mould. After some period of time (for hardening), the plunger returns backwards, and the mould opens to eject the plastic parts. A spreader, called a

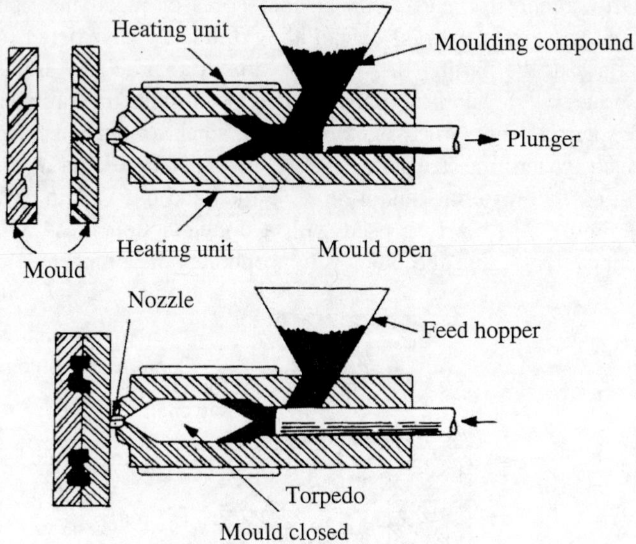

FIGURE 7.10 Injection moulding.

'torpedo', causes the moulding material to be inserted completely into the material which reaches the nozzle. It should be sufficiently fluid.

Injection moulding is primarily used for the moulding of thermoplastic parts. The gating and sprue which are formed in the mould are ejected with the parts and, since they are of thermoplastic material, they can be reclaimed and used again. The temperature range for the material, as it enters the mould, is between the minimum processing and the decomposition temperatures of the thermoplastic material. Heating unit temperatures normally range from 350 to 575°F, and injection pressures vary from 10,000 to 25,000 psi. The operation of an injection moulding machine is normally arranged to be semi-automatic so that the operator has only to start the machine at the beginning of each cycle and take out the parts at the end of the cycle. The operation is fast, up to six shots per minute on some machines. It is evident that injection moulding will be much more economical for production in large quantities than compression or transfer moulding.

A variation of injection moulding, especially adapted for thermosetting plastics, is known as *jet moulding*. Here, a suitably high mould temperature is maintained for hardening the thermosetting plastic. The heating chamber is kept at a moderate temperature, which will not harden the material. The nozzle, however, is heated to a high temperature during injection, and at all other times, it is kept at a moderate temperature to prevent hardening of the material.

Moulds for the compression, transfer and injection-moulding processes are similar in many respects to the dies used in die casting. They are precisely made of alloy steel and heat-treated. The slipperiness of the chromium plating serves as a lubricant. In some cases, a lubricant such as oil, wax or soap may be mixed with the moulding powder to assist in the lubrication.

Extruding of plastics. This is similar to the forward-extrusion process for metals. All thermoplastic resins can be extruded. Thermosetting resins are generally not suitable for extrusion. Moulding powder is loaded into the feed hopper as shown in Figure 7.11. Below it, a continuously rotating feed screw forces the moulding powder slowly through a heating chamber, where it is properly softened.

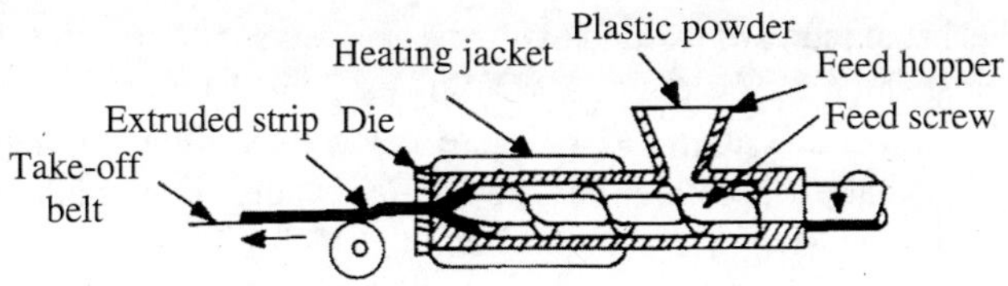

FIGURE 7.11 Extrusion of plastics.

Under pressure, the softened resin flows through a die opening to form a continuous section. The speed of the take-off belt is important in controlling the final dimensions of the cross-section, since the material is soft and easily deformed as it emerges from the die. Extruding is useful for producing fibres, rods, tubes, film, decorative strips and electrical insulation which is extruded around the wire. Hollow sections such as tubing require a mandrel supported in the die opening. The mandrel should have ports on its periphery to assist material flow. A mandrel may be supported by three or more thin streamlined connections, for enough backup from the die opening, so that the material will reunite again after passing them. Air may be introduced through one of these connections to the inside of a tubular plastic product. This is done to help maintain its shape until it is properly cooled. Relatively thin film may be produced by extrusion, either through a narrow straight opening or through a narrow circular opening, producing a thin-walled tube. This thin-walled tube may be extruded vertically. Air is admitted into the interior of the tubular product which causes it to resemble a large cylindrical balloon, since the end is closed. These tubes are later slit longitudinally to make sheets up to 8 feet or more in width.

Casting of plastics. This is similar to the casting of metals. A liquid resin, after it has been poured into a suitable mould, is hardened. Suitable materials for moulds are rubber, gypsum plaster, wood or metal.

7.9 HIGH-PRESSURE LAMINATES

Laminates are plastic products that consist of layers of reinforcing fibrous cloth-like material impregnated and bonded together with a suitable resin. High-pressure laminates are those which are cured under higher pressures in the range of 1,200–2,000 psi. They are made using the following steps:

1. The reinforcing material, such as paper, cotton cloth or woven fibreglass, is impregnated with a suitable resin. Usually the material is passed through a resin bath and allowed to dry.
2. The resin-impregnated sheets, depending on the resin, may be advanced to the B stage.
3. The impregnated sheets are cut to the desired size and stacked to obtain the desired thickness.
4. Heat and pressure are applied to soften the resin, bond the layers together and cure the resin.

Because of the high pressures used, parts made by high-pressure lamination in matched metal moulds are limited in size, due to the size of presses which are available. High-pressure lamination is useful for the production of laminated plastic sheets, plates, rods and tubes. In the manufacture of a laminated sheet, a number of impregnated reinforcing sheets are placed between two smooth polished stainless-steel plates. This is then placed into a large heated platen press for curing. Laminated tubing is made, by first winding the impregnated sheet under pressure, on a steel mandrel with the desired diameter. The mandrel is wound with the impregnated sheet, as it is rotated between three large steel rollers, which apply pressure. Curing is done later in a suitable oven, and after curing, the mandrel is removed. Laminated rods are made by rolling impregnated paper or cloth on a mandrel having the smallest possible diameter. This mandrel is withdrawn before the heating, and the rolled material is placed into a suitable mould, which closes the central hole as heat and pressure are applied for curing. High pressure laminated sheets, tubes and rods are usually further processed by machining to the desired shapes.

7.10 REINFORCED PLASTIC MOULDING OR LOW-PRESSURE LAMINATING

This process includes several methods for producing relatively large plastic parts, such as boats, automobile bodies, luggage and radomes. Reinforcing materials like fibreglass cloth or fibreglass mats help provide excellent strength-weight ratios. Some of the plastics used cure at atmospheric temperatures and pressures.

Contact lay-up method. Here, the moulds used may be of wood, plaster or reinforced plastic. Mould surfaces, if porous, should be well sealed. A parting agent should be applied to facilitate release of the moulded part from the mould surface. After a sufficient number of layers have been built up, the resin is allowed to cure, and the part is removed from the mould. Generally, a "postcuring" at a suitable temperature is given to the part. Advantages of the contact lay-up method include:

1. Low cost of the mould
2. Ease of reinforcing sections subjected to high stresses
3. Unlimited range of sizes in which parts can be made

Disadvantages include:

1. Non-uniformity of wall thickness
2. Finish on one side only
3. Relatively long period of time required for curing

Rubber bag method. This method is illustrated in Figure 7.12. Like the mould for the contact-lay-up method, only mould-half is needed, and it is ordinarily made of metal to withstand pressures up to about 50 psi. A rubber bag, or diaphragm, serves as the other mould half. Layers of impregnated reinforcing fibrous material are placed on the mould, and then covered with the rubber diaphragm.

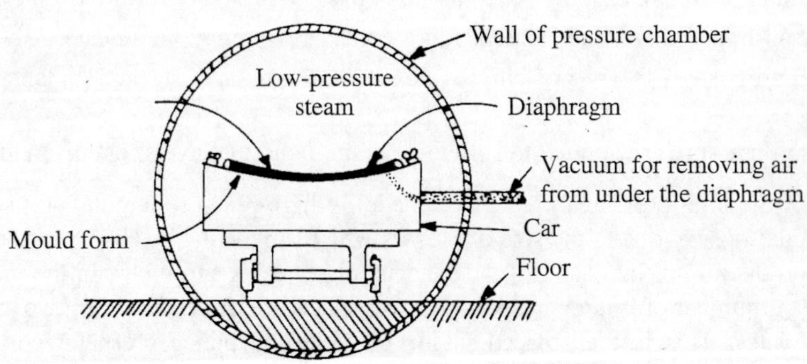

FIGURE 7.12 Vacuum moulding of sheets (Rubber bag process).

Thereafter, the mould goes into a steam chamber where the plastic is softened and subjected to a pressure of about 50 psi for the curing. This method is faster than the contact-lay-up method. The product is more uniform, and the wall thickness too is more uniform. It still provides an accurately finished surface on one side only.

Matched-metal moulding method. This method can be used in order to obtain accurately finished surfaces on all sides. Since a complete metal mould is required, mould costs are much higher. Higher pressures ranging from 50 to 1,500 psi are used and parts with better mechanical properties are produced. This method approaches, or may become, high-pressure laminating.

To make the ideas on fibre reinforced composites clearer, a numerical example cited by Schey (1987) is now taken up.

Example. A container is to be made of epoxy resin reinforced with glass fibre. An elastic modulus of 20 GPa is desired in the structure. Calculate (a) the proportion of glass fibre required, by volume; (b) the density of the composite; and (c) how much of the imposed load is taken up by the fibres. Assume that E_{glass} = 70 GPa and E_{epoxy} = 350 kpsi = 2.4 GPa.

Solution.

(a) From the equation of the "rule of mixtures",

$$E_c = fE_f + (1-f)E_m$$

where,

E_c = elastic modulus of composite
E_f = elastic modulus of the filler
E_m = elastic modulus of matrix
f = fraction of filler by volume

Thus,

$$20 = 70f + (1-f)2.4$$

$$f = 0.26 \quad \text{or} \quad 26\% \text{ by volume}$$

(b) The density of epoxy is 1.2 g/cm^3 and that of glass is 2.49/cm^3. In 100 cm^3 composite, there is 26 (2.4) = 62.4 g. Glass and (100 – 26) (1.2) = 88.8 g epoxy

$$\text{Total weight} = 62.4 + 88.8 = 151.2 \text{ g of mixture}$$

Out of this,

$$\frac{62.4}{151.2} = 0.413$$

Or, 41.3 wt% is of glass and 88.8/151.2 = 0.587, or 58.7 wt% is of epoxy.

(c) To determine the load carried by glass fibres, if e is the engineering strain and σ the stress, then

$$e = \sigma/E = P/AE$$

If P_f is the load carried by glass fibre and P_m the load carried by matrix of epoxy, then

$$P_f/P_m = A_fE_f/A_mE_m = 0.26(70)/0.74(2.4) = 10.24$$

In other words, about 10.24 times, i.e., 90% of the load, is carried by fibres which constitute 26% of the volume of the composite.

7.11 FORMING AND DRAWING OF PLASTIC SHEETS

Most forming and drawing operations require that first the plastic material be heated to a suitable temperature. The press operations used for sheet metals can also be applied in many cases to plastic sheets. These include blanking, stretch forming, forming and drawing with suitable dies. Thermoplastic sheets can be readily formed and drawn. Certain thermosetting laminated sheets can be formed by a process known as *postforming*. This is believed to be possible because a small percentage of the thermosetting resin, between the laminations, is still uncured (in the B stage).

There are two other processes which can be used, viz., vacuum forming (Figure 7.13) and pressure drawing (Figure 7.14). Blowing is also used to produce bottles and other hollow articles. Two plastic sheets can be clamped together by the two halves of a die, and air can be blown into the space between them, causing them to expand and take the form of the die cavity. At the edges of the die cavity, the plastic sheets are fused to gather, and the excess material is pinched off. Another method of blowing uses suitable lengths of extruded plastic tubing with one end closed. These may be placed into a split die, blown to a desired shape and ejected when properly cooled.

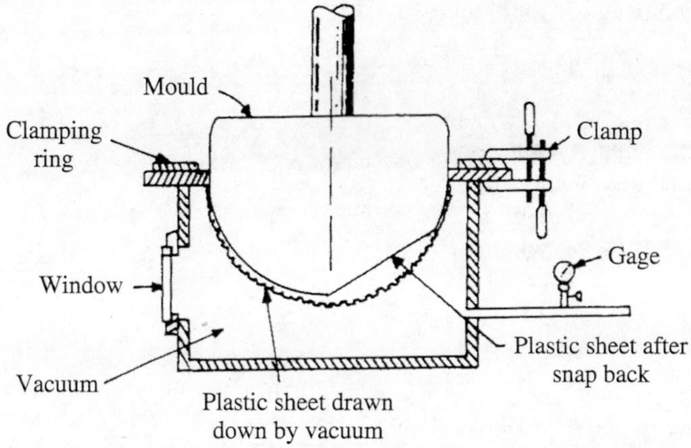

FIGURE 7.13 Vacuum moulding with male die.

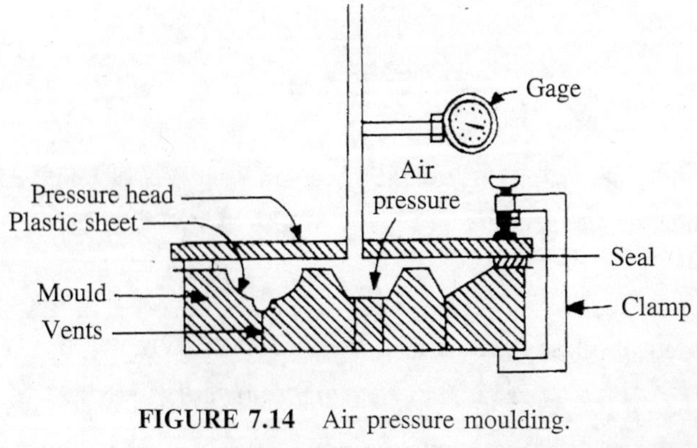

FIGURE 7.14 Air pressure moulding.

Expanded plastic may be manufactured by (a) whipping gas into a resin by mechanical agitation, (b) incorporating a gas or liquid which expands on reducing pressure or raising temperature, and

(c) releasing a gas throughout a resin by the breakdown of a chemical material. The resulting plastic is cellular or foam-like containing many small bubbles of gas. The material is impermeable and extremely light with high strength to weight ratio. Application for these plastics includes: use in an interior material for sandwich structures in building panels, aeroplanes, boats and building panels, insulation for refrigerators, buoyancy materials for boats sound proofing and decorative items.

7.12 DESIGN OF PLASTIC PARTS

Many of the design rules for moulded plastic parts are similar to those which apply for die castings, permanent mould castings and sand castings. Some of the design rules for plastic-moulded parts may be given as follows:

1. Allow for shrinkage after moulding.
2. Specify only dimensional tolerances as close as actually necessary. Tolerances closer than 0.005 inch, the usual commercial limit, generally increase costs.
3. Allow at least the minimum draft of 1/2° to 1° to facilitate removal of parts from the mould.
4. Avoid undercuts which require cores or split-cavity moulds.
5. Locate the mould parting in one plane, if possible.
6. Locate holes at right angles to part surfaces. Oblique holes add to mould costs.
7. Avoid long cored holes, this is particularly necessary if the holes are not in the direction of mould closing. It is necessary to provide support for sufficiently long core pins not in the direction of mould closing. Avoid design that necessitates weak cores.
8. Design projections in order to have circular sections. Irregularly shaped holes are generally more expensive to obtain in the mould.
9. Locate all holes and projections in the direction of mould closing, if possible. Otherwise, holes must be formed by the use of retractable core pins.
10. Locate lettering to be embossed or debossed on surfaces perpendicular to the direction of mould closing.
11. Arrange ejector pin locations so that marks will occur on concealed surfaces.
12. Design grille elements parallel to the flow of the plastic in a mould.
13. Continue grille lines as a false grille.
14. All ends to be held within the plastic should be knurled for adequate gripping. Some rules for the design of plain inserts and threaded inserts are now enumerated:
    (a) Use brass inserts rather than steel, as their coefficient of thermal expansion nearly equals that of plastics.
    (b) Use inserts that are sturdy and not too small. Small fragile inserts are difficult to handle and slow down the moulding cycle.
    (c) Avoid long slender inserts, since moulding pressure may deflect them out of position.
    (d) Make the plastic section around an insert heavy enough, to hold the insert securely and prevent cracking after moulding.
    (e) Make the projecting portions of inserts cylindrical for minimum mould cost.
    (f) Design projecting threaded inserts with a slightly projecting unthreaded shoulder to help prevent plastic from filling the threads during moulding.
    (g) Always specify metal inserts for small threaded holes (no. 6 or smaller), when the thread will be subjected to mechanical stress or wear.

15. Specify as shallow a draw as feasible. Deep draws require higher moulding pressures, thus restricting the types of presses that can be used.
16. Design toward uniform section thickness and uniform distribution of mass for optimum flow of the plastic in moulding.
17. Design corners with ample radii or fillets. This makes possible a more durable mould and improves the flow of the plastic in moulding.
18. Use ribs to add strength and rigidity, to minimize distortion from warping and to improve the flow of the plastic during moulding.
19. Avoid sharp discontinuities that might become locations of stress concentrations, particularly where internal ribbing is used for support.
20. Restrict rib height to not more than twice the thickness of the rib section. Otherwise, "sink" marks may occur on the flat surfaces opposite the ribs.
21. Break up large flat surfaces with beads, steps or other geometric designs to increase rigidity. Improved appearance too can be obtained.

7.13 NATURAL RUBBER

Natural rubber is a high molecular weight hydrocarbon polymer represented by the formula $(C_5H_8)_x$. It is obtained from a milky emulsion, called latex, by tapping the bark of the tree *Hevea brasiliensis.* This tree was originally found along the Amazon river in South America, and its seedlings were planted in Ceylon.

Rubber plantations flourish best in the equatorial climate. In India about 95% of the plantations are in Kerala, the remaining are in the states of Tamil Nadu, Karnataka, Goa, Assam and Maharashtra; the total production in 1977 was 151,000 tonnes.

When the trees are 6 years old, spiral grooves are cut in the bark; the sap flows slowly and is collected in cups. It has about 35% rubber. The latex is diluted with water and filtered to remove coagulated rubber, bark etc. and acetic or formic acid is stirred in it, which causes the rubber to coagulate. Rubber is separated from the liquid by squeezing between rolls and is then washed with water. The sheets so obtained are dried either in air when 'crepe' rubber is obtained, or in hot smoke when 'smoked' sheet rubber is obtained.

The product so obtained is a high polymer of isoprene.

$$
\begin{array}{c}
\quad\quad CH_3 \\
\quad\quad | \\
-CH_2-C{=}CH-CH-
\end{array}
$$

In a normal position, the molecule is like a coiled helix and uncoils in tension. When tension is removed, the molecule recoils and returns to the original coiled state. This accounts for the elasticity of rubber. If rubber is stretched too much, one molecular chain slips over another and a permanent deformation takes place. In this process of uncoiling and recoiling, some energy is lost. This gives rubber the property of absorbing shock and reducing vibrations in machines. Raw rubber has some serious defects, e.g., it becomes soft and sticky with heat, and stiff and brittle in cold. It is not very tough and deteriorates through slow atmospheric oxidation, giving a bad odour. These defects are removed by vulcanization.

7.13.1 Vulcanization of Rubber

When raw rubber is passed between hot rolls, both physical and chemical changes take place and the mass becomes plastic. Before vulcanization, proper substances are added in order to control properties like strength, toughness and hardness and to make it resistant to abrasion, chemicals, solvents, oxygen, light and oil. Some fillers like barytes ore, cotton etc. are also added. Zinc oxide and zinc soaps are added to decrease the vulcanization time and are called accelerators. The vulcanized rubber deteriorates with age; hence some age-resistors, mostly organic nitrogen compounds, are also added. Antioxidants are used to give resistance to oxygen. Carbon black increases abrasion resistance and is an important reinforcing agent. Raw rubber, when in a plastic slate during hot rolling, is mixed with these ingredients and sulphur, which is the most important vulcanizing agent. Soft rubber is obtained when 0.5–5% sulphur is used. Addition of over 30% sulphur produces hard rubber or ebonite. For uniformity of composition, the material is passed many times between the rolls. This operation, called milling, requires considerable power, and the temperature rises. Rubber is then cut into pieces of suitable size, placed in moulds, and formed into the desired shape and vulcanized in a single operation by the simultaneous application of heat and pressure. The rubber flows and fills the cavities and sets by vulcanization, giving the desired shape. The moulds are opened and the finished products are obtained.

Vulcanization involves complex and not too well understood chemical reactions. The helix-like molecules of unvulcanized rubber deform readily, i.e., it does not regain the original shape. In vulcanization, cross links are formed between the long unsaturated hydrocarbon chains of the original molecule. The cross links provide anchoring and prevent inter-molecular movements, with the result that, when the vulcanized rubber is subjected to stress, elastic strain is produced. On removing the stress, it regains its original shape. The cross links may be directly from carbon to carbon or through a sulphur atom or through an oxygen atom or through all the three. Thus, the vulcanized rubber is of higher molecular weight than the raw rubber and it less unsaturated.

On vulcanization, the properties of rubber change considerably. For instance, the unvulcanized rubber very readily deforms, becomes plastic and soft on working between hot rolls, and becomes viscous in hydrocarbons like benzene. Vulcanized rubber, on the other hand, is elastic, crumbles between hot rolls and retains its form in solvents. Besides bringing about these changes in properties, vulcanization enables the manufacturer to manipulate the material to produce the desired shapes.

7.14 ARTIFICIAL RUBBER

Strictly speaking, synthetic rubber is not produced in the sense that the synthetic product differs in chemical composition and properties from those of the natural rubber. 'Synthetic' rubbers are only rubber-like products. Therefore, the term 'artificial' rubber is more appropriate than 'synthetic' rubber. The development of the automobile industry brought a revolution, not only in the petroleum industry, but also in the rubber industry. Rubber from the plantations could not meet the demand, and attempts were made to synthesise natural rubber. As this did not succeed, rubber-like materials were synthesized. Further, due to several specific and specialized applications, a need was felt to retain elastomeric properties over a wider range of conditions than natural rubber processes. As natural rubber is produced in tropical regions, the industrialized countries felt the urgency for having their own resources of rubber. With the development of the petrochemical industry, an attempt was made to increase artificial rubber production. In India, its production was 28,000 tonnes in 1976. In 1980, world production of synthetic rubber was 8 million tonnes and Indian production in India was 50,000 tonnes.

At present, the following major types of artificial rubber are in large scale use. These are now described.

(i) **Buna S.** It is a co-polymer of butadiene, $CH_2=CH-CH=CH_2$ (75% by weight) and styrene, $C_6H_5-CH=CH_2$ (24% by weight). In the early days of its synthesis, sodium was used as a catalyst; hence the name, bu (for butadiene), na (symbol Na, for sodium) and S (for styrene). It is also called GR–S (Government Rubber Styrene) or SBR. Buna S rubber can be mixed with natural rubber, thus combining the useful properties of both, and is used for the manufacture of tyres. This rubber has lower strength and flexibility than natural rubber.

An emulsion of butadiene and styrene is made in water with the help of soap-like emulsifying agents. A catalyst is added and the mass is heated under pressure when a latex-like liquid is obtained. It is then steam distilled to remove the uncombined hydrocarbons. Rubber is coagulated and processed in a manner similar to natural rubber using sulphur as the vulcanizing agent. Buna S rubber is synthesized more than other types of rubber.

In 1985, Synthetics and Chemicals Ltd. located at Bareilly (UP) had an artificial rubber plant of 20,000 tonnes a year capacity. Today, it has a planned capacity of about 1 lakh tonnes. The plant annually uses about 70 million litres of ethyl alcohol, which is supplied by the various distilleries, and 9 million litres of benzene obtained from the coke oven plants of the steel industry. Alcohol is dehydrogenated in the presence of a catalyst, to give acetaldehyde. Acetaldehyde mixed with more alcohol is passed over another catalyst when butadiene is obtained:

$$CH_3CH_2OH \longrightarrow CH_3CHO + H_2$$

$$CH_3CHO + CH_3CH_2OH \longrightarrow CH_2=CH-CH=CH_2 + 2H_2O$$

Dehydration of ethyl alcohol gives ethylene which, along with benzene, in the presence of catalysts, gives styrene:

$$C_6H_6 + CH_2=CH_2 \longrightarrow C_6H_5CH_2CH_3 \longrightarrow C_6H_5CH=CH_2 + H_2$$

$$C_6H_5CH_2CH_3 \longrightarrow C_6H_5CH=CH_2 + H_2$$

Copolymerization of butadiene and styrene gives Buna S rubber which has a structural unit of:

$$-[CH_2-CH=CH-CH_2-CH_2-\underset{\displaystyle CH_3}{\underset{|}{CH}}]$$

(ii) **Buna N (GR–A and GR–N).** It is a copolymer of butadiene and acrylonitrile, $CH_2=CHCN$, and its structure is similar to that of Buna S rubber, styrene being replaced by acrylonitrile. The stable nitrogen component makes Buna N rubber highly resistant to solvents, oils and chemicals. It has also good resistance to abrasion, aging and low temperatures. The rubber is vulcanized with sulphur and is used for hose, conveyor belts, tank linings and for high altitude aircraft. In India, a plant with installed capacity of 2000 tonnes of nitrile rubber was started in 1976, which produced 360 tonnes of rubber in 1977.

(iii) **Butyl rubber (GR–1).** 98% of this rubber consists of isobutylene which polymerizes to give a saturated polymer:

Since butyl rubber is saturated, no cross links can be formed; hence it cannot be vulcanized. To overcome this difficulty, about 2% of butadiene is copolymerized with

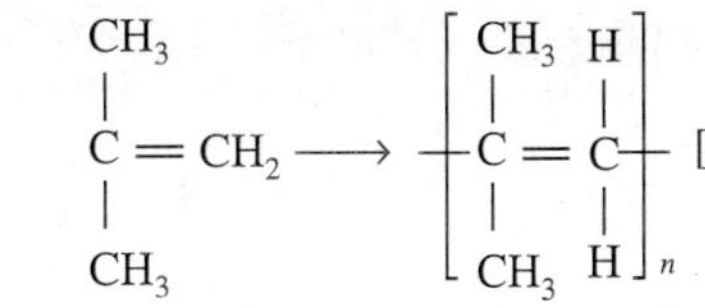

Isobutylene Polymer unit

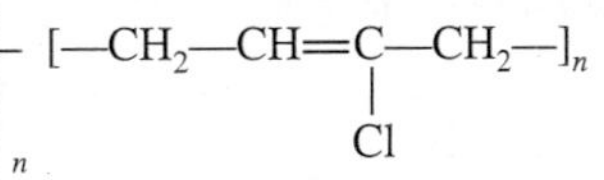

isobutylene. Butadiene provides centres for cross links and, thus, the rubber can be vulcanized. A plant for 20,000 tonnes per annum capacity of polybutadiene was commissioned in India in 1973.

Butyl rubber is cheaper than other varieties of artificial rubber. Another advantage of this rubber is that it is impermeable to gases, and is thus satisfactory for making cycle and automobile tubes. It is also resistant to aging, ozone, acids or alkalis. Its other uses are for hose tank linings and electrical insulation. A limiting factor of butyl rubber is that, because of very low unsaturation, it cannot be hardened much.

(iv) **Neoprene (GR–M).** It is a polymer of chloroprene:

Starting materials for neoprene are acetylene and hydrogen chloride. Neoprene is vulcanized by zinc oxide or magnesium oxide. It has very useful properties and resembles natural rubber, but is more expensive than other rubbers. It has very good resistance to aging and to oil and is used for hose, wire insulation and belts.

(v) **Thiokol (GR–P).** Several types of rubbers of this group are made by copolymerization of organic dichlorides, like ethylene dichloride, with inorganic polysulphides, e.g. Na_2S_x. Such kind of rubber resembles natural rubber neither in structure nor in properties. They have very good resistance to solvents and can withstand cold but not heat. They are cheap and can be easily shaped, but have an unpleasant smell. Since they are practically unaffected by petrol, fuel oils and lubricating oils, these are mostly used for making hose pipe and, tank linings for handling these materials.

7.15 ENGINEERING PROPERTIES OF RUBBER

Rubber has several properties which make it useful as an engineering material. It has large deformability. Most structural materials, if deformed more than 10%, exceed their elastic limit, but some types of rubber can be stretched 10 times without rupture and regain almost the original shape after the removal of the stress. This constitutes both an advantage and a disadvantage, depending on the service requirement. Rubber has low modulus, i.e., low stresses produce deformation or change in shape. This property enables rubber to absorb shocks and to be used for cushioning and sealing. Since it regains its original shape after large deformation, rubber can store energy more than most other materials. When rubber is subjected to cyclic (i.e. alternating) loading, as in automobile tyres which are cyclically stressed when the automobile is moving, not all the energy is recovered. This results in some hysteresis loss of energy which appears as heat energy and the rubber gets heated. It shortens the life of rubber. This loss of energy enables rubber to reduce vibrations. Rubber continues to deform under steady load with passage of time, i.e., it has high creep. This behaviour limits the use of rubber as a structural material.

Rubber is a bad conductor of electricity. Soft rubber is used as an insulator and hard rubber or ebonite is used as a high grade dielectric. Rubber is impermeable to water and, to a large extent, to gases.

Natural rubber is superior to synthetic rubber in mechanical properties but is inferior in resistance to solvents and oils.

7.16 GLASS

Glass may be defined as an "Inorganic product of fusion which has been cooled to a rigid condition without crystallization". It is an undercooled liquid of very high viscosity. The glassy state is a condition which is continuous with, and analogous to, the liquid state of that substance.

7.16.1 Glassy State

In the glassy state, the atoms form a random three-dimensional network. The glasses are non-crystalline or amorphous.

X-ray diffraction techniques have thrown light on the structure of glass. Glass produces only a few diffused bands, showing that little order is present, whereas the X-ray spectrum of a crystal has many sharp lines. The crystals fracture along definite cleavage planes related to the structure of the crystal. On the other hand, when glasses break, the fracture cannot be predicted. Mostly, the cleavage follows curves, except in flat glasses in which fracture lines are practically straight for considerable length. Thus, the glassy state is a vitreous state. Appearance of tiny crystals in glass is called *devitrification.*

The most important behaviour of glasses, from practical as well as theoretical point of view, is exhibited when they are heated or cooled. When they are cooled from the liquid state, viscosity steadily increases and the rigid, elastic condition of ordinary glass is reached without any sudden change. On heating from the solid condition, the glasses eventually soften and gradually become more and more fluid. They do not have melting points (see Figure 7.15). Some arbitrary methods have been designed to fix some degree of mobility or ductility and to designate the corresponding temperature as softening temperature, e.g., for the common soda-lime glasses it is about 700°. In this respect also, the glasses differ from crystalline materials, winch, at a certain fixed temperature (the melting points), suddenly absorb heat without rise in temperature.

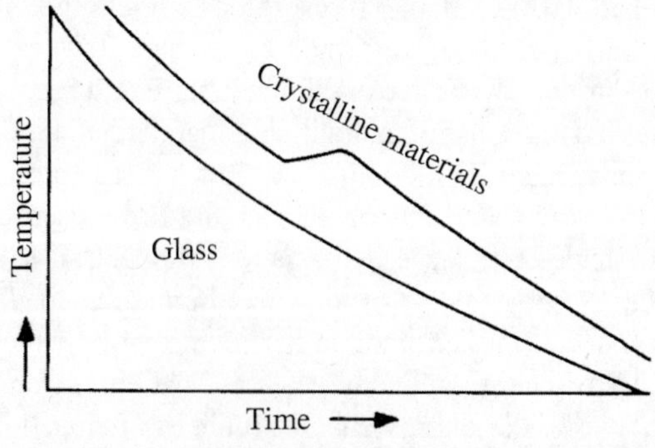

FIGURE 7.15 Cooling curves for crystalline and glass type materials.

The glassy state, not being quite a stable state, tends to attain the crystalline state. If glasses are kept for a long period at a temperature slightly above the softening temperature, crystals begin to appear or they devitrify. At the ambient temperature also, this process takes place, but the rate is imperceptibly slow. The effect is seen only in glassware made centuries ago.

7.16.2 The Glass Making Oxides

The glass-making oxides (Figure 7.16) can be grouped into the following three classes:

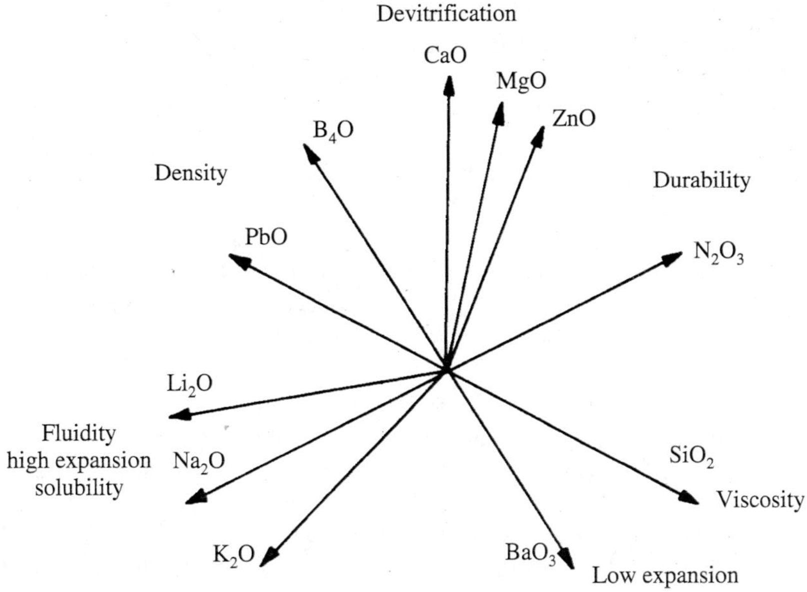

FIGURE 7.16 Effect of glass making oxides.

(i) **Network formers.** These can produce glass by themselves. These are oxides of elements whose atomic diameters are such that they can be surrounded by four oxygen atoms each, in the form of a tetrahedron. They form chains and networks that may exist in a completely random manner. The rules stated by Dr. Zacharisen lay down four conditions:

1. Each oxygen atom must not be linked to more than two cations.
2. The number of oxygen atoms around any one cation must be small, i.e. not more than four.
3. The oxygen polyhedra must share the corner positions, not the edges, to form a three-dimensional network.
4. At least three corners of each tetrahedron must be shared.

The most important network forming oxide is SiO_2. Other important ones are B_2O_3, GeO_2, P_2O_5 and As_2O_5. Other less important oxides are Sb_2O_3, As_2O_3, Bi_2O_3 and BeF_2. On melting, all these can give glass without the addition of any other oxide. Some others of this category are of purely theoretical interest. In general, these are acidic oxides. Silica may be considered to be the most important raw material for glass making, not only because it can produce glass by itself but also because of its availability at low cost. It is an important constituent of most of the glass manufactured. Deposits of glass sand are available in different parts of India, in addition to other crystalline forms being available. Its melting point is high (1723°C), and molten silica is so viscous that the gas bubbles formed in melting are not easily removed. It is difficult to form many articles from molten silica because it becomes rigid so quickly that it is not easy to give it shape. Its high melting point makes it suitable for making glass, for use at high temperatures. Its coefficient of thermal expansion is low, has good electrical properties and high transmission for ultraviolet light. Silica glass is expensive.

The most harmful and common impurity in glass sand is iron oxide. For glass of good colour, Fe_2O_3 should be less than 0.04%, and for optical glass, it should be less than 0.015%. Lime and alumina, once considered as impurities, are now not considered so, because they are incorporated in glass compositions. It needs to be seen that they are uniformly distributed.

Boric oxide is another network former and about 20% of it is present in borosilicate glass, with a small per cent of alkali, the remaining being silica. The glasses have a low coefficient of thermal expansion, are resistant to corrosive action of acid, can be used to higher temperatures and are resistant to thermal shocks. These properties make the borosilicate glasses suitable for shock resistance, and for many industrial and laboratory applications. Boric oxide is used in small amounts in other glasses, mainly for giving lower coefficient of expansion.

(ii) **Network modifiers.** To this class belong a large number of elements whose atoms have larger diameters and, therefore, can have more than four oxygen atoms as their nearest neighbours. In other words, their coordination numbers are higher. These, when melted alone, cannot form glass, but on melting with network formers, can enter into the holes of the network. They loosen the bounds of the network formers, with the result that the softening point as well as chemical resistance is lowered, but the coefficient of thermal expansion is increased.

Important network modifiers are the oxides of the alkali metals and alkaline earths. Lead, zinc and some other oxides are of lesser importance. In general, these are basic oxides.

Soda ash is the most widely used alkali metal oxide, although for special purposes, potash is also used. In tonnage, its amount is next to silica. The requirements of the glass industry have led to improvement in its manufacturing process. Its chief impurity is sodium chloride. In soda of good quality, sodium chloride is less than 0.5% and iron oxide is negligible. For glass making, granular soda ash is preferred since it is not blown off easily by the furnace gases. The most important effect of soda is the fluxing action, i.e., lowering the melting temperature. When it is used in larger amounts, it increases thermal expansion, and lowers tensile strength, elasticity, and resistance to weathering.

Lime and limestone come next to soda in glass-making on the basis of weight. Limestone of good quality is widely available in India. There are points in favour of both of them. Limestone is cheaper and is easier to store. Carbon dioxide evolved from it during glass-making helps stir the material, whereas the use of lime saves heat of the furnace—which is a distinct advantage—and the transportation cost is less but the storage is more expensive. Good limestone should contain less than 0.1% Fe_2O_3. Dolomite, which contains carbonates of calcium and magnesium, is also used.

When added in correct amounts, lime contributes to glass stability or permanency, hardness, and facilitates melting and refusing.

(iii) **Intermediate glass formers.** These too cannot form glass by themselves, but on fusion with the network formers, may act like network formers, taking up their coordination numbers. Under suitable conditions, they may even form glass with other non-glass-forming oxides. For example, Al^{3+} may partially substitute Si^{4+} in the network. The intermediates are amphoteric oxides.

Oxides of lead are prepared by heating lead in a current of air. Red lead, Pb_3O_4, is preferred to ligharge, PbO, because it helps to ensure oxidizing conditions and is free from metallic lead, which is highly undesirable in glass. In most cases, PbO content is less than 15%, but can be as high as 80%. It increases brilliance and improves working quality. Lead glasses are used in electric lamps, neon signs, lubes, optical glasses, and for absorbing X-rays.

Barium is introduced in the form of $BaCO_3$ which gives BaO in the glass melt. It is prepared by reducing $BaSO_4$ to BaS by heating with coke, which is then dissolved in hydrochloric acid, and then $BaCO_3$ is precipitated by adding Na_2CO_3. It is used only in small amounts, but is an important constituent of heat resistant glasses and optical glasses.

Alumina is more widely used than any other intermediate oxide. Its deposits in the form of bauxite are abundant in India. It is purified by Bayer process (described in the section on aluminium). The alumina so obtained, though expensive, is free from iron oxide. The use of feldspar, $K_2O \cdot Al_2O_3 \cdot 6SiO_2$, and other clay minerals has increased in recent times not only because of lower costs but also because alkali, which is expensive, is supplied at a lower cost when a material such as clay is used.

Up to 3% alumina can be advantageously used in the ordinary soda glasses as it contributes to resistance to weathering, decreases tendency to devitrification, and lowers thermal expansion. Alumina along with boric oxide is an important constituent of all types of low expansion glasses.

7.17 THE FUNCTIONS OF THE GLASS-MAKING OXIDES

In brief, it may be stated that silica is the best glass-former, but its melting point (1723°C), as also its viscosity on melting, is very high. Alkalis act as flux and facilitate the melting of silica and reduce the viscosity, but resistance to chemicals, weathering and even water is greatly decreased. For example, addition of 25% Na_2O to silica reduces its melting point to 850°C but makes it water-soluble. The alkaline earths, like lime, make glass resistant to water, weathering and chemicals. Thus, silica, soda and lime are the most widely used raw materials and are known as soda-lime-silica glass.

Other oxides are added to improve the properties or to incorporate certain desirable properties such as devitrification (i.e. prevention of crystallization or maintenance of the glassy state), reduction in coefficient of thermal expansion, modification of optical properties, high temperature properties, fluidity, durability, and resistance to weathering and chemicals. Colourants may be added for coloured glasses. Special glasses, of course, need special consideration. In Figure 7.15, the effect of common oxides used in glass-making is represented in an oversimplified manner. The effects are, however, not as distinct and sharply defined as the simple diagram may suggest, but one can get from it a fairly good idea of the role played by the common raw materials as also some idea about the guiding principle in choosing the raw materials. The difference in the cooling curve of crystalline state and glassy state is highlighted in Figure 7.16.

7.18 MANUFACTURE OF GLASS

The raw materials are analyzed, especially with a view to judging the purity and to take care of the objectionable impurities. They are then taken in the correct proportions. It may be noted that, even in the case of simple common glass whose raw materials are sand, soda and lime, small amounts of several other oxides have to be added. For example, ferrous oxide, which is a common impurity, gives a greenish tinge. An oxidizing agent like sodium nitrate needs to be added to oxidize it to ferric which gives a yellowish tinge and is less noticeable to the eye. Alternatively, manganese oxide is introduced which gives a pink colour, complementary to the green colour of ferrous iron. Molten glass will have a large number of bubbles, due to the air entrapped between the grains of the raw material and due to the CO_2 liberated. Reduction in the viscosity helps to eliminate them, but refining agents like arsenic oxide have to be added to help the bubbles to rise to the surface. Small amount of feldspar may be introduced in the batch with a view to give certain desirable properties which have already been discussed.

Besides purity of the raw materials, the particle size is of importance. Large grains may not react fully and remain behind as "stones". ("Stones" is the name given to any non-glassy material embedded in glass.) Too finely divided material causes dusting. Materials should be fine and of uniform grain size. Waste or broken glass is always available in the factory. It is called "cullet" and forms, say, one-third to three-fourths of the total charge. Cullet has to be carefully sorted out before adding.

The furnaces used for glass-making are of two types. In the first type, separate pots, may be from 1 to 20 pots, are kept in the furnace. The pots may be open, in which case the glass is heated from the surface also. The covered pots protect the glass from the furnace atmosphere. The pots of capacity up to two tonnes are in use, but for special glasses, pots of smaller capacities are used.

The second type of furnace is the tank-furnace which has an open hearth over which flames pass from one end to the other. In the continuous tank furnace, the raw materials are fed at a rate equal to that at which molten glass is withdrawn. This type of furnace is used where mechanical or continuous working on a large scale is required.

The common fuel used is either oil or producer gas. The furnace is worked on a regenerative system of heat economy, which has been explained in detail in the section on open-hearth furnace for steel-making.

The refractory materials used in the construction of the pots and the furnaces are carefully chosen. The batch, along with the cullet, fining agents and colourants, is introduced in the furnace either by shoveling by hand or mechanically. During the melting, a series of reactions take place as the temperature rises. Around 800°C, the alkali silicates are formed and limestone begins to decompose. Lime and other basic oxides gradually begin to enter the solution, forming double silicates with the alkali silicates. As the temperature increases and viscosity decreases, the excess of silica begins to dissolve. The gases, mostly CO_2, liberated due to the reactions with the carbonates violently agitate the molten mass. The reactions continue for some time, after the maximum temperature is reached. In fact, molten glass is heated to 1400–1500°C, which is higher than is needed for the completion of the reactions. This is done so as to reduce the viscosity of the melt and thereby facilitate the escape of the entrapped gas bubbles. Once the fusion process starts, it should proceed rapidly. Therefore, the design and working of the furnace should be such that heat in transferred properly to the charge.

The molten glass is cooled to several hundred degrees below the maximum temperature so that the glass has satisfactory viscosity for working. It is then given the final shape by various methods of glass working. The principal methods are: pressing in mould, blowing for making bottles and jars, and so on; drawing into sheets, tubes, rods etc.; and spinning for making fibres.

After giving the shape, the sharp edges are made smooth by fire polishing, i.e., local application of heat. Some glasswares require grinding and polishing on a wheel.

Glass is a bad conductor of heat; therefore, great care has to be exercised in cooling the finished product. Rapid cooling will cause the surface to become hard and rigid, whereas the interior still remains soft. Severe thermal stresses will result and the glassware will be weak and break easily. It is therefore kept for annealing, i.e., for slow cooling at a controlled rate, either in an oven or placed on a belt moving slowly in a furnace, one end of which is hot. As the glassware moves, the temperature gradually drops.

7.19 CERAMICS

A very broad definition of ceramic is anything which is not a metal or of organic origin. However, the present discussion will be confined to clay-based ceramics—majority of ceramics are designed on and manufactured from clay. Particulate processing is the method of manufacture of clay-based ceramics. Figure 7.17 indicates, on a ternary diagram, various ceramic products of common use.

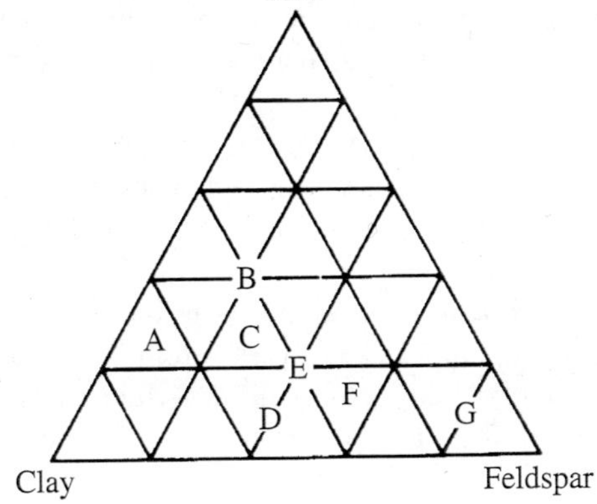

FIGURE 7.17 Ternary diagram for ceramics.

Ceramics, pottery and porcelain are taken together as their basic raw material is clay. Also, their method of manufacture involves similar processes. Pottery, also known as earthenware, refers to all ceramic bodies that are not vitrified. Consequently, they are slightly porous and coarser. The vitrified clay product is known as stoneware or porcelain. The distinction between these two is very vague and, in this section, the term *porcelain* will be used. All these products may either be glazed or unglazed.

The igneous rocks contain feldspar. The common feldspar is the potash feldspar which may be approximately represented as $K_2O \cdot Al_2O_3 \cdot 6SiO_2$. In place of K_2O, soda. Na_2O, or lime-CaO may be used to give soda or lime feldspar. Over the years, its slow chemical decomposition by the action of carbon dioxide and water, and mechanical disintegration gave Kaolinite, $Al_2O_3 \cdot 2SiO_2 \cdot 2H_2O$. It occurs mixed with particles of feldspar, sand and other impurities and is washed to give white clay, kaolin or china clay, which is the basic raw material for the pottery and porcelain industry.

Clay has two important properties. First, when ground and mixed with water, it is plastic, i.e., it can be moulded into the desired shape which it retains. Secondly, on firing, it forms a brittle product which is highly resistant to corrosive agents that attack most metals and organic materials. The clay pots, when dried in the sun, become soft and collapse in contact with water, but on heating to about 600°C, are unaffected by water. China clay is a refractory material and does not deform at high temperature. Therefore, it forms the framework of the porcelain or chinaware body. On heating to very high temperature, the clay vitrifies or fuses to give a glassy, non-porous body. The temperature can be reduced by mixing with more readily fusible materials which seal the pores of the unfused materials.

The earthenwares are made of cheaper raw materials and are fired to lower temperatures (1000–1550°C). These are not vitrified.

Of all types of clays, it is only kaolin which yields a white translucent, vitreous ceramic, when fired. For making porcelain, 40–50% of it is mixed with fusible materials like feldspar and silicon of various types. To give an example, a composition containing equal parts of clay and feldspar vitrifies (i.e., fuses to form a glassy substance) at 1200°C, becomes translucent at 1250°C and melts at 1400°C. About 10–15% of ball clays are mixed with the raw materials. These clays have a high degree of plasticity and make the body more workable and help in fusing or vitrification. Flint or pure silica has to be added to lower the shrinkage, cracking and warping of the body during firing. Feldspar acts as a flux and is the first to melt and dissolve the other materials and fuse them into a vitreous mass. On cooling the ware, feldspar hardens and acts as a binding agent that increases hardness and translucency of the fired ware.

The raw materials, in proper proportions, are mixed with the correction amount of water and ground in a ball mill. The muddy mass is passed through a screen to remove particles of larger size and then between electromagnets, so as to remove iron impurities which cause discolouration. It is passed through a filter press to remove extra water. This gives a soft, plastic mass of clay from which bubbles are removed, which could cause defects in the finished product.

After giving the desired shape, the wares are very carefully packed in the kiln for firing. Firing transforms the soft, dull-coloured clay body into a brilliant white, translucent porcelain or chinaware. The temperature of firing required for maturing the body, glaze and decorations varies widely. For ordinary pottery, it may be as low as 900°C and for good porcelain, 1500°C. The ware moves on kiln cars or movable trays through a kiln. It passes through zones of different temperatures, gradually increasing to the maximum and then cooling as the ware approaches the exit. Industrial Uses: Commonly, one thinks of the potteries and porcelain mainly in terms of its use as domestic crockery. The production figures in 1987 in India, in tonnes, are given after each item: crockery 15,700; sanitary wares 20,000; stoneware jars 4,200; stoneware pipes 47,200; glazed tiles 40,000; high tension insulators 18,000, and low tension insulators 1,300. Power generation and transmission require special ceramic products, and there is a rapid increase in the demand for insulators for these uses.

REVIEW QUESTIONS

1. What are plastics? How does polymerization take place? What are low polymers and high polymers? Sec. 7.1; P 189
2. What are linear, branched and cross-linked molecular structures of polymers? Figure 7.1
3. What is the difference between 'addition polymerization' and 'condensation polymerization'? What is co-polymerization? Give examples. Figure 7.2; P 190–192
4. What are fillers, accelerators or hardeners, modifiers, plasticizers and elastomers? Sec. 7.1.1
5. What is the effect of heating on thermoplastic? Plot a graph between temperature and specific volume. Sec. 7.2.2; Figure 7.3
6. How is rubber formed from latex? What is the reaction called? Figure 7.4
7. Phenol formaldehyde is a thermosetting plastic. How does it react to heating? Figure 7.5; P 195

8. Describe: (with reference to plastics)
   (i) Compression moulding Sec. 7.6; P 197–198
   (ii) Transfer moulding and Sec. 7.7; P 198–199
   (iii) Injection moulding. Sec. 7.8; P199–200

9. Sketch and explain extrusion of plastics. P 200–201; Figure 7.11

10. What is reaction injection moulding (RIM) of plastics?
[**Ans:** Reaction injection moulding is a plastic and rubber manufacturing process in which the reacting liquid chemicals are mixed at high presses and quickly pushed in a closed mould. Nitrogen or some inert gas is mixed with the plasticizing materials. The gas–resin mixture is shot in the mould cavity. The gas expands producing internal less dense structure with a tough external coating (skin) on the mould face. This special structure is called *integral skin*. It has properties superior to homogeneous plastic or rubber products.]

11. Sketch the following FRP processes:
   (a) Hand lay up process
   (b) Filament winding process
   (c) Matched SMC moulding
[**Ans:** Refer Figure 7.18(a), 7.18(b) and 7.18(c) which indicate the processes.

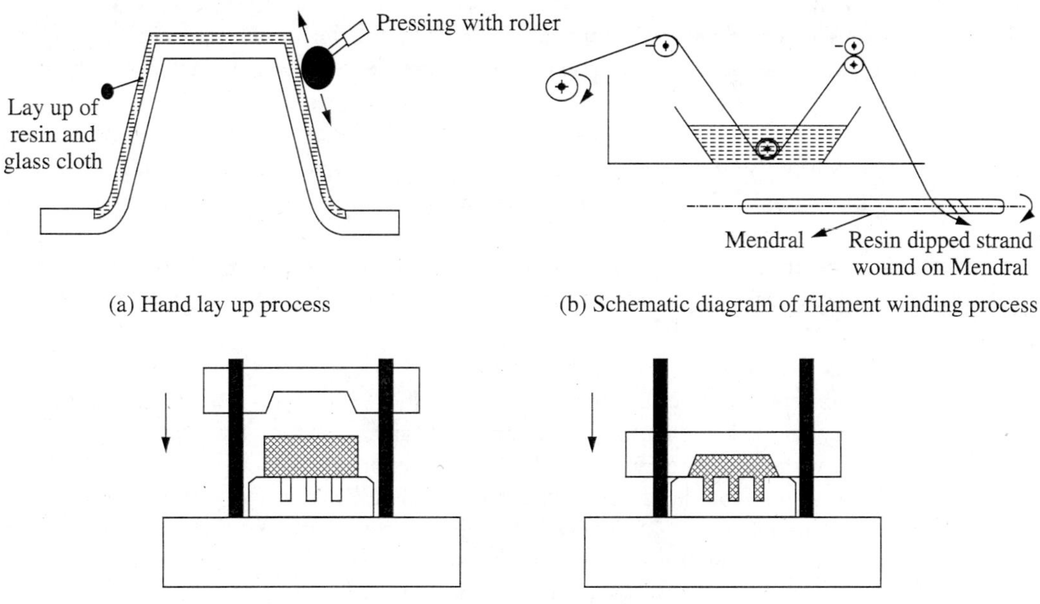

(a) Hand lay up process

(b) Schematic diagram of filament winding process

(c) Matched SMC moulding

FIGURE 7.18 Some fiber glass moulding processes.

12. List various design considerations for fiber reinforced plastic parts.
[**Ans:** Design rules for FRP

It is difficult to generalize about part design for the entire gamut of FRP engineering resins because of their different inherent properties and processing requirements. However, part design rules of any specific unmodified resin become the starting point for design in glass (or other) reinforced version of that resin.

The most significant factor to note is that glass FRP parts are stronger than their non-reinforced counterparts, and consequently, a part can be designed using less material to achieve the same function. The basic percept for planning, therefore, is not to over-design. It is always easier to add ribs and stiffeners, from the mould than it is to add material to mould to part size or dimensions. Over designing results in moulding problems and loss of speed. Working with reliable resin and glass suppliers, mould designers and toolmakers provide an excellent starting point, even if they are partially inexperienced in FRC.

The different mould and part design parameters are discussed below, together with the well-known practices.

1. **Moulded part wall thickness.** In designing walls, the general rule to follow is that part walls should be as uniform in thickness as possible in order to prevent distortion and promote rapid and uniform thermal solidification of material. Depending upon the resin, the wall thickness can be 10–50% less than that would be necessary when using unreinforced material. To avoid heavy wall sections, use ribbing and other strengthening devices which help achieve faster moulding cycles and better part strength.

   The optimum wall thickness for nylon material is approximately 1/8 in. Polycarbonate and styrene-based materials are about the same thickness. Polyolefins, however, require walls about 50% heavier. The minimum wall thickness with nylon materials can range from 0.018 to 0.020 in. For polycarbonate and styrene-based materials, minimum thickness of 0.025 in. is possible.

2. **Dimensional tolerances.** The tolerances that can be achieved with glass FRP approach are same as those possible with metal parts. The mould shrinkage of reinforced material is 1/10 to 1/2 that of the unreinforced resin. Various small threads and gears have been designed and moulded to tolerances of 0.00025 to 0.0005 in. (Commercial Class III gears).

3. **Fillets and radii.** As with non-reinforced materials and metals, sharp corners should be avoided in all the parts made of FRP. Elimination of sharp corners helps to promote resin flow during moulding and also to reduce the possibility of notch-sensitive failure of the finished part. Reinforced materials possess greater rigidity and are more susceptible to notch-type impact failures than are the non-reinforced types.

   A radius that is 25–75% of the adjacent wall thickness should be added on all inside corners, with a minimum radius set at 0.005 in. In general, the designer will find that he will be successful in designing parts for glass FRP (Figure 7.19(a)).

4. **Ribs.** For unreinforced plastic, it is always recommended that ribs be located at the junction of two walls or that decorative beads or surface effect be added opposite a rib to hide the effects of shrinkage. Because the reinforcement tends to reduce shrinkage on cooling. It is less of a problem with reinforced thermoplastics than with non-reinforced. It is recommended that the part be designed without ribs at the start,

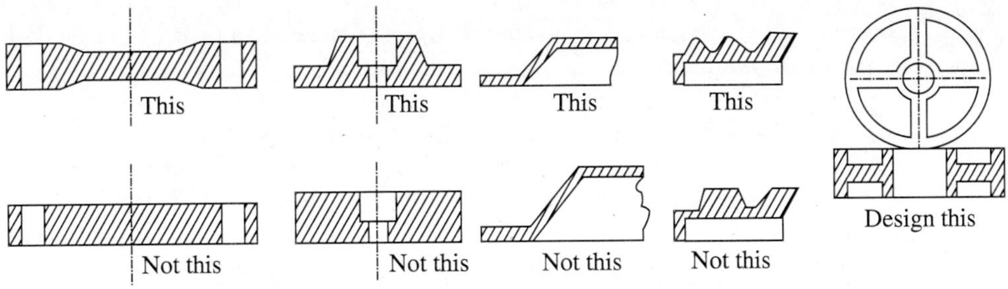

FIGURE 7.19(a) Good and bad FRP design practices.

because in many cases the greater inherent strength in the reinforced material will make ribs unnecessary.

The standard recommendation for unreinforced material is that ribs should be no higher than three times the wall thickness and less than one-half the thickness of the adjacent wall. These guidelines are considered safe for reinforced material too. With reinforced materials, a rib design should be originated with a height only to 1 to 1½ times the wall thickness (see Fig 7.19(b)).

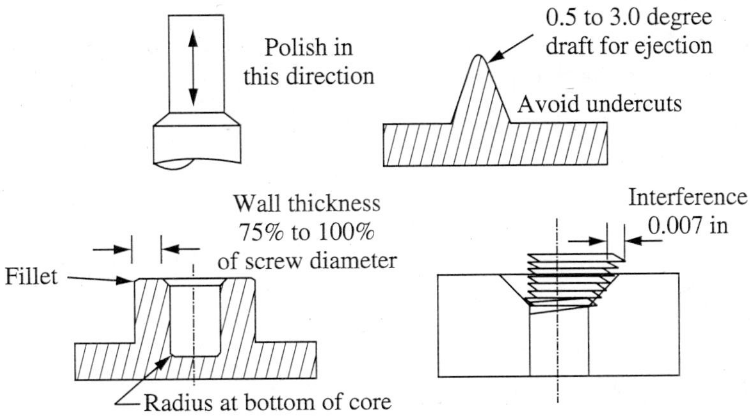

FIGURE 7.19(b) Ribs, bosses and studs.

5. **Bosses and studs.** Generally, it is recommended that bosses be no higher than a dimension twice their diameter. With unreinforced materials, studs should always be placed at the convergence of an angle in order to minimize the effects of sinking. This problem assumes less significance with glass FRP, because with 50% less shrinkage, the problem sink marks is ameliorated.

   Long studs should usually be designed with an adequate taper in order to facilitate removal from mould. Deep holes and core pins should be polished to remove all undercuts caused by lathe turning. Adequate venting of the mould on studs, bosses, or any extended section is also important for reinforced material.

   Screw holes in studs or bosses should be designed with less interference because of the greater hardness of the FRP material. It is recommended that the original part design be made with 0.007 in. interference as opposed to 0.030 in. for unreinforced material. The interference should be built up in increments of 0.004 or 0.005 in. at a time until the correct interference is achieved.

Holes should be designed with a chamfer at the opening to lead the screw in and with a radius at the bottom of the core. The wall thickness around the hole should be 75–100% of the diameter of the screw to be used. The usable depth of the core is 1–1½ times the diameter of the screw (see Figure 7.19 (a) and (b)).

6. **Surface Finish.** Grain or texture etched or embossed into the mould surface for transfer to the moulded parts should not exceed 0.002–0.0025 in. in depth. This parameter is related to the ejection of the part from the mould. The greater the amount of texture designed into the part, the larger should be the amount of draft provided for ejection of the part from the mould. A reliable factor to follow is to allow one degree of draft per inch for each 0.002 in. of texture depth.]

13. What are composite materials? Describe particulates and fibre-reinforced plastics. Explain the rule of mixtures.

[**Ans:** Composites refer to structures which are made of two distinct starting materials, the identities of which are maintained even after the component is fully formed. The starting materials may be metals, ceramics, or plastics, Two-phase materials are also composites.

Types of composites. Depending on the relative distribution of the two materials, the following groups are identified:

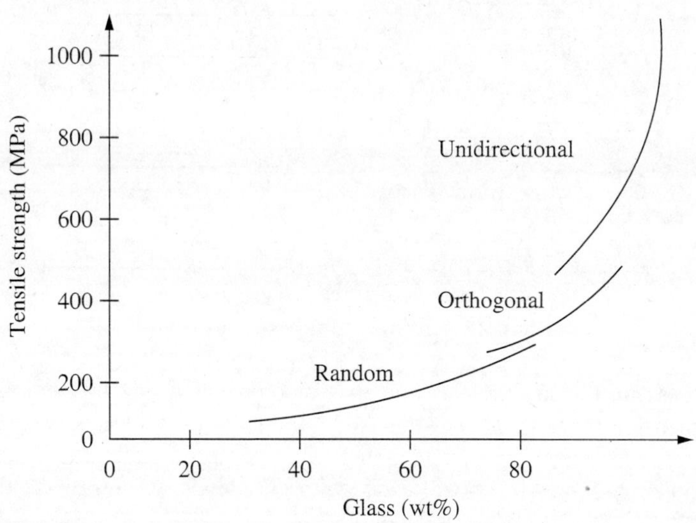

FIGURE 7.20 Effect of orientation and percentage of glass fibres on tensile strength of polyester glass fibre composites.

Coatings and laminations. Tin-plate, galvanized sheet and terneplate with a mild-steel base are fairly well known. Tools coated with TiC, TiN, or Al_2O_3 are examples of ceramics on steel. Polymers are applied in large quantities to paper (milk cartons), textiles (seat covers, carpets), metals (wire insulation, beverage cans), and to polymers (multilayer films and bottles), combining the impermeability of one polymer with the mechanical and processing advantages of another, usually lower-cost plastic.

Particulate composites. There are several examples including metal–metal (Cu-infiltrated iron), ceramic reinforced metal (dispersion-hardened metals), metal-bonded ceramics (cermets including cemented carbides), and metal polymer structure (metal bearings infiltrated with PTFE or nylon).

The mechanical properties of composites are calculated from the rule of mixture: each component contributes to the properties of the composite in proportion to its volume fraction. Thus, the yield strength of the composite r_c is:

$$r_c = fr_c + (1 - f)r_m \tag{1}$$

where f is the volume fraction of the filler, r_f and r_m are the yield strengths of the filler and matrix, respectively. Similarly, the composite elastic modulus E_c is:

$$E_c = fE_t + (1 - f)E_m \tag{2}$$

Thus, the elastic modulus (and flexural modulus) can be increased by incorporating into polymer a material of higher modulus, typically a metal or ceramic.

Fibre reinforced composites. When a stronger or higher modulus filler is in the form of thin fibres, strongly bonded to the matrix, the properties depend on the strength of fibres (Table 7.1), on the proportion of the fibres, and on their orientation to load application (Figure 7.21).

TABLE 7.1 Properties of some reinforcing fibres

	Young's modulus (GPa)	*Tensile strength* (GPa)	*Density* (kg/m^2)
High-strength steel	210	2.1	7830
Tungsten	350	4.2	19300
Beryllium	300	1.3	1840
E Glass	73	3.5	2480
S Glass	85	4.6	2540
Alumina	175	2.1	3150
Graphite			
– High modulus	390	2.1	1900
– High strength	240	2.5	1900
Boron	420	4.0	2600
Nylon	5	1.0	1140
Dacron	14	1.1	1380
Kevlar 29	62	2.8	1440
Kevlar 49	117	2.8	1440

Critical fibre length $l = dr_f/2k_m$ = where, d is diameter of fibre, r_f is tensile strength of fibre, K_m is shear strength.

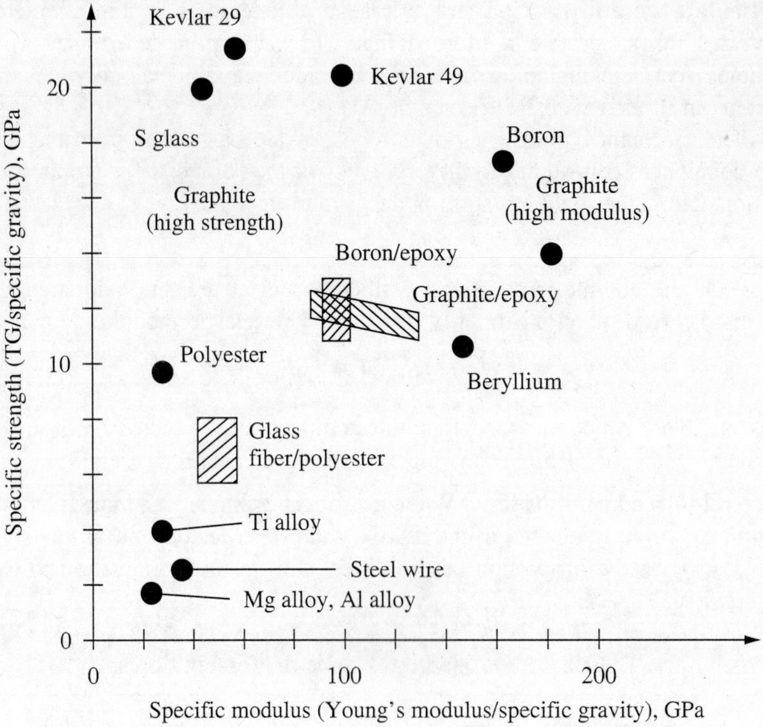

FIGURE 7.21 Improvement of specific strength of composite materials.

For a given weight, composite materials with fibres oriented in the direction of loading offer tremendous gains in strength and stiffness, as shown by their specific strength and modulus (shaded areas). For comparison, typical values are shown for bare fibres and for the highest, strength members of alloy groups.]

14. How is foam plastic produced?

15. Explain the role of silicon, nitrogen, chlorine and fluorine in modifying the properties of plastics.

16. Classify various types of rubber. Sec. 7.14; P 208, 209

17. What are the various glass-making oxides? What is the composition of glass? What is the percentage of SiO_4, Na_2O and CaO in glass?

[*Hint:* SiO_4 (72%) Na_2O (14%) CaO (11%)]

18. What are the applications of glass? What is usual melting point of glass?
[**Ans:** 60% of glass is used in containers, 15–20% in flat glass for windows, automobiles, etc., 15% in fibre glass and textiles (borosilicate glass), 10% application is in glazing and decoration of composites and ceramics, usual melting point is about 1200°C–1500°C. Recently, the purity of glass has been increased tremendously due to applications in fibre optics and stereolithography.]

19. Explain the proportion of flint, clay and feldspar in various ceramics through a ternary diagram.

20. Draw a ternary diagram for a grinding wheel and explain how it helps in identifying the useful zone of proportioning of bond, grit and abrasive. What proportion of bonding agent is used?

[**Ans:** A grinding wheel consists of vitrified clay bond, abrasive grain and porosity.

A grinding wheel is a three phase system as shown in Figure 7.22 with grit = 40%, bond = 25%, porosity = 35%. In this figure, the feasible zone is enclosed by lowest packing density (LPD) line, maximum packing density (MPD) line, maximum bond equivalent (MBE) line, lowest bond equivalent or LBE line.

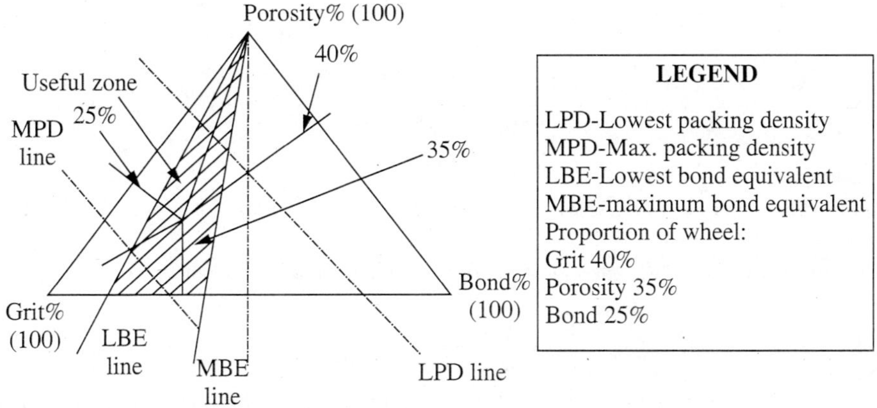

FIGURE 7.22 Ternary diagram for vitrified bond in grinding wheel.

The raw materials for the bonding agent are, flint China clay and feldspar as shown on another ternary diagram (Figure 7.23). China clay 50%, feldspar 36%, flint 14%, sawdust or any carbonaceous material is added so that during firing in the kiln length CO_2 is formed which escapes and forms porosity in the grinding wheel. Typical dimension of the kiln length is 100 m (Figure 7.24). The trolley takes 144 h for covering 100 m so that proper sequence of the following essential operations takes place:

(1) predrying, (2) preheating, (3) firing, (4) quenching, (5) annealing, and (6) drying.

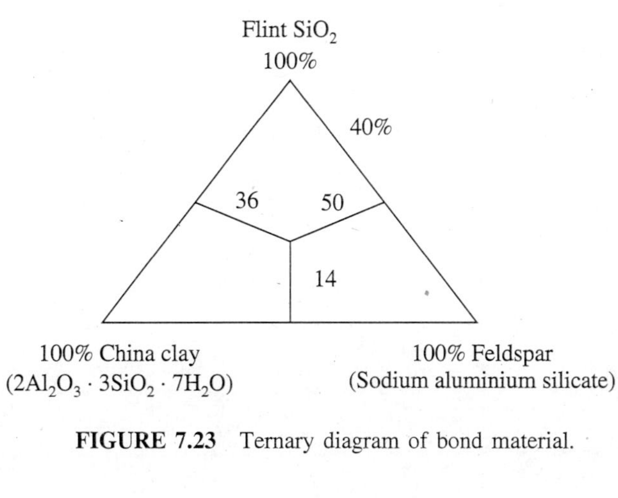

FIGURE 7.23 Ternary diagram of bond material.

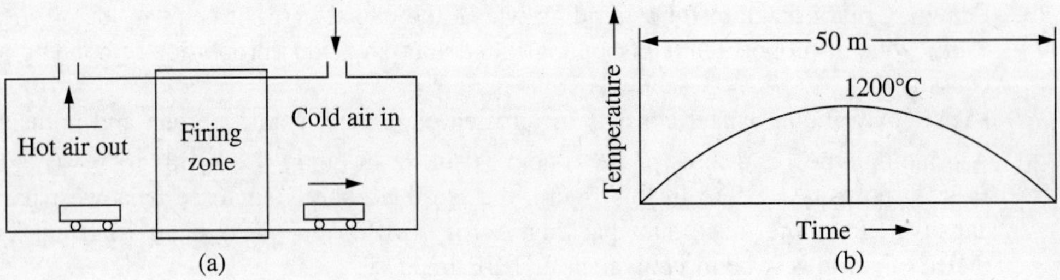

FIGURE 7.24 (a) Schematic diagram of kiln for producing abrasive wheels (vitrified) and (b) temperature (Time chart in vitrification in ceramic grinding wheels).

REFERENCES

[1] Schey, John, *Manufacturing Processes*, McGraw-Hill, New York, 1987.

[2] Campbell, J.A., *Principles of Manufacturing Materials and Processes*, Tata McGraw-Hill, New Delhi, 1985.

[3] Ogorkiewicz R.M., *Engineering Properties of Plastics,* The Design Council, London, 1977

Chapter 8

Designing with Plastics, Rubber, Ceramics and Wood

In this chapter, we discuss how designing with plastics, rubber, ceramics and wood is done. Novel ideas on designing with plastics, some of which were highlighted by Chow [1], are covered in the beginning of the chapter. This is followed by design recommendations on product design for low cost, with rubber and ceramics, according to Bralla [2]. At the end of the chapter, the application of wood and design of its various joints in furniture and construction work is illustrated.

8.1 APPROACH TO DESIGN WITH PLASTICS

Every elastic material deforms under external forces. This property is expressed by the stiffness of the material (the ratio of force to deflection of the material). Metals, especially steels, are good spring materials, because they have very high strength and resilience $R_f(R = 1/2S_y e_y) = (1/2S_y^2/E)$, where S_y is stress and e_y, strain. Plastics are unsuitable as spring materials, because they reach the yield point at low values of stress and behave viscoelastically. If they are used in springs, a low stress can prevent plastic deformation. A short duration of the load is a common design criterion for plastic springs, due to 'creep' tendency of plastics. Creep occurs in materials when, under a constant load, the material starts yielding and 'flowing' before failure.

Viscoelastic behaviour manifested by plastics is characterized by the following aspects:

1. The modulus of elasticity is not constant and depends on the rate of loading.
2. At a constant stress, the strain will increase with time. This flow effect is called *creep*.
3. A plastic material with history of locked-up stresses tends to unlock and reaches a lower level of stress.

Viscoelastic effects are serious obstacles to choose plastics as engineering materials for certain heavy duty applications. If a plastic gear is transmitting load without rotating, the load may cause the gear teeth to creep. This flow will result in pitch variation and noise in the gear train. Newly developed high-strength engineering plastics are favoured for plastic springs because the magnitude of stress can be kept tower as compared to the yield stress.

Figures 8.1 and 8.2 show two designs of plastic springs. Figure 8.1(b) depicts a leaf spring for a door latch, whereas Figure 8.2 depicts a plastic bevel spring. The leaf spring is the most widely used, because of its simple geometry. The width of a leaf spring can be tapered in-some designs so that the stress is more uniform and the material utilization is better.

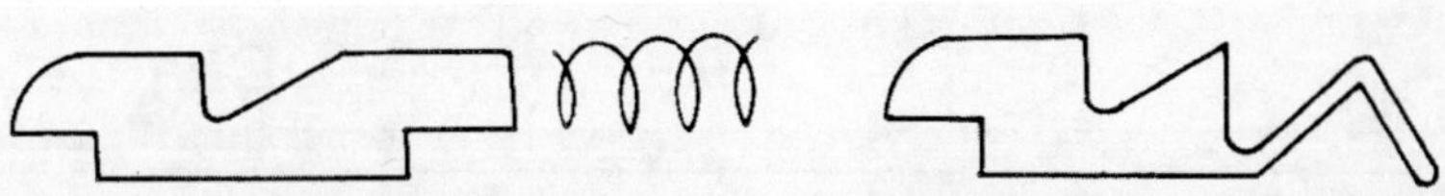

(a) Conventional design (b) Integral design with plastic

FIGURE 8.1 Design of door latch in plastics.

(a) Single conical spring with plastics (b) Stack of conical springs in plastics

FIGURE 8.2 Design of conical springs in plastics.

8.2 PLASTIC BUSH BEARINGS

Plastics make cheap bearings that can easily replace wood, steel and zinc bearings. Plastic as bearings material is favoured in chemically aggressive environments, without the use of any lubricant and needs no maintenance. Plastics suitable for bearing applications are phenolic, nylon, fluorocarbon, polycarbonate, acetal, and ultra-high molecular weight polyethylene. The above materials are used with steel shafts of fine finish. When plastic rubs against plastic, the wearing is higher. Figure 8.3 illustrates two applications of plastic as bearing material for bush for pinjoint and pedestal bearing, respectively.

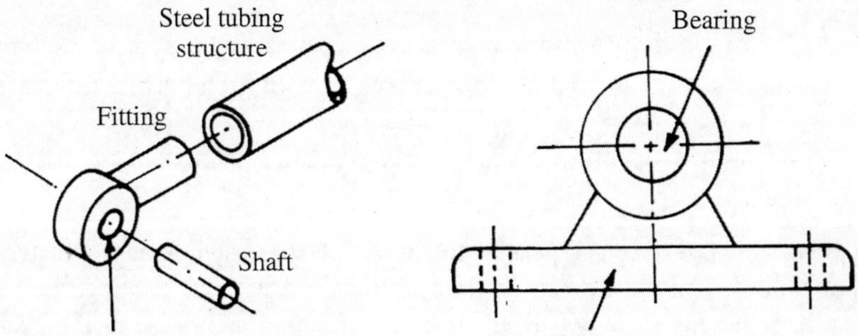

(a) Pin joint with plastic bush bearing (b) Bracket bearing with plastic bush

FIGURE 8.3 Bearing design with plastics.

Table 8.1 shows the wear and friction data for acetal, nylon, and polysulphone. Wear factors of 240 or less are considered very good for most design purposes. The pressure at the bearing is the load divided by the projected area of the bearing (length × diameter). Nylon and fluorocarbon

TABLE 8.1 Friction coefficients and wear factors of plastics (after Theberge et al. [3])

Bearing material	*Shaft material*	*Wear factor* $= \dfrac{\text{Radial wear}}{P \times V} = \dfrac{(\text{cm/h} \times 10^{-8})}{\text{kg/cm}^2 \times \text{mpm}}$	*Coefficient of friction*	
			Static	*Dynamic*
Acetal	Acetal	10,200	0.19	0.15
Acetal	Steel	78	0.14	0.21
Acetal (20% TEF)*	Steel	21	0.07	0.15
Nylon 6/6	Nylon 6/6	1380	0.12	0.21
Nylon 6/6	Steel	240	0.20	0.26
Nylon (20% TEF)	Steel	144	0.10	0.18
Nylon (30% glass) (15% TEF)	Steel	192	0.19	0.26
Polysulphone (30% glass) (15% TEF)	Steel	66	0.12	0.10
Polycarbonate	Steel	3000		
Polycarbonate (30% glass) (25% TEF)	Steel	36		

*Theberge, J.E., B. Arkles, and P.J. Cloud, How plastics wear against plastics, *Jour. Machine Design,* Oct. 31, 1974, pp. 60–61.

Operating conditions and formulae for Table 8.1 are tabulated as follows:

$$\text{Radial wear (cm/h)} = \text{wear factor} \times P \times V$$

The wear factors in the above table were measured at

$$P = 2.8 \text{ kg/cm}^2,\ V = 150 \text{ mpm},\ \text{TEF} = \text{fluorocarbon}$$

All fillers are percentage by weight.

bearings have a tendency to creep under moderate pressures. The contact pressure can be decreased by increasing the length of the bearing. The product of pressure and velocity, *PV*, is the power rating of the bearing per unit area. The product of *PV* and the coefficient of friction gives the energy dissipation (or the rate of heat generation). The wear rate is the product of the wear factor and *PV*. Increasing the material hardness by glass filler or metal backing can reduce wear. Glass reinforcement is an important feature of most of the bearings because the hardness of the resin alone is insufficient to protect a bush from wear.

Friction and wear. Plastic bearings are sensitive to temperature. When the temperature rises above a certain point, wear becomes extremely fast. Because of the slow heat conduction through plastics, one of the methods used in removing heat is by a fluid such as oil or water.

8.3 GEARS IN PLASTIC

Theberge, Cloud and Arkles [4] have given specific guidelines on production of accurate plastic gears. Making an accurate plastic gear is more difficult than making a similar machined gear because a plastic gear is made by moulding process. The engineer has to consider errors in the machining of the mould in the moulding of the product, and the shrinkage of the particular material after moulding.

8.3.1 Moulded Plastic Gear: Manufacturing Technique

Production of moulded plastic gear involves the following steps:

1. Cut a gear in a brass blank by hobbing.
2. With the brass gear as the tool, use EDM to create mould cavity in the die.
3. Inject molten plastic into the mould to obtain plastic gear.

The final moulded plastic part will shrink and become smaller than the mould cavity.

Design calculations to combat shrinkage of plastic in the mould. The diameter of the mould cavity should be the final diameter of the piece multiplied by $(1 + s)$, where s is the fractional shrinkage. In order to have the same number of teeth on a larger diameter, the pitch on the mould has to be nonstandard. The module of female gear in the mould has to be increased by the factor $(1 + s)$. The ratio of the cosines of the pressure angles of the female mould gear and the final piece is also $(1 + s)$. The pressure angle in the mould should be smaller than the standard angle, in order to get a moulded piece with the standard pressure angle. As an illustration, the shrinkage (S) in acetal is 0.023. In order to get a 50 mm diameter gear of module m = 1.04 and 20° pressure angle, the mould should be made with 51.15 mm diameter, with a module of 1.065 and a pressure angle of 15.99°.

8.4 FASTENERS IN PLASTIC

Designing for assembly is a new strategy in which a product designer starts thinking at the design concept stage itself, in terms of ease of assembly of the final product from its component and subassembly levels. Research and development with plastics has resulted in several new designs of fasteners. These plastic fasteners are specially made for non-plastic components. These fasteners reduce the assembly time to a minimum. There are five general kinds of plastic fasteners:

1. Screw assemblies
2. Snap and press-fits
3. Inserts
4. Ties and twists
5. Shrink wraps

8.4.1 Design Creativity with Hinges

Hinges can be used effectively to reduce the number of parts in an assembly. A small tool box can be moulded with a hinge connecting the lid and the box. One often comes across lunch boxes with novel designs of hinges and snap fitting lids. Figure 8.4 indicates design with plastic hinges. A hinge can improve alignment and provide a free joint. Since the hinge is practically free, the cost of these products is just the cost of the material and the moulding. The ease of assembly of such boxes is remarkable. Although very inexpensive to manufacture, propylene is technically unsuitable

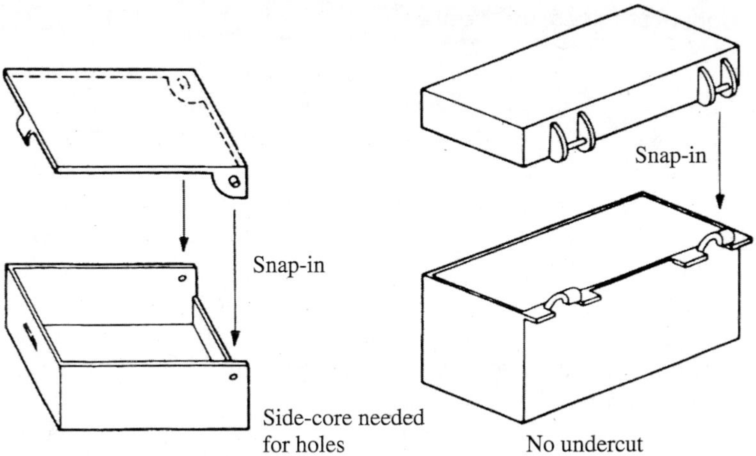

FIGURE 8.4 Box design with plastics.

material for plastic springs owing to its viscoelastic behaviour. The main reason for its wide use at present is its low cost.

8.5 RUBBER PARTS

Rubber can be classified into hard rubber and thermoplastic rubber. Rubber parts are formed to the desired shape, mainly by moulding and extruding. Figure 8.5 shows some typical sections of extruded rubber. Most rubber products are vulcanized with sulphur at high temperatures during moulding or after extruding. Thermoplastic rubber has useful rubber properties, only after sufficient cooling, below moulding or extruding temperatures.

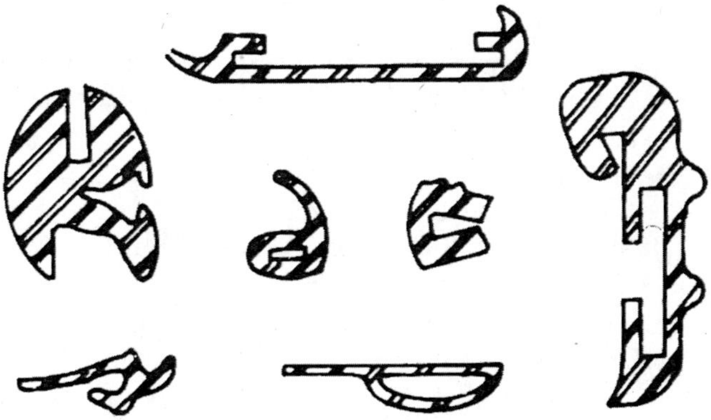

FIGURE 8.5 Extruded sections in rubber.

Most rubber (available mostly from Kerala or imported), when they arrive at the shop, is a very high viscosity or dough-like material in bale form (malleable rubber). Eight or more different additives, including fillers, plasticizers, vulcanizing agents, etc. are added, depending the desired end-use properties. These additives are generally incorporated into the rubber by using an internal mixer, followed by forming the compound into sheets on a two-roll mill.

8.5.1 Production Processes for Rubber

(i) **Injection moulding.** While long strips or pellets cut from the sheet are used to feed extruders and injection-moulding machines, injection moulding is done at high temperatures, typically 180°C (360°F) using high injection pressures (14 kg/cm^2) and in shorter cycles (typically 3 min) as compared with compression and transfer moulding. In compression moulding, a rubber blank is placed directly in an open mould cavity. In transfer and injection moulding, rubber is forced through transfer ports or channels into a closed mould providing greater control of closure dimensions.

(ii) **Dipping and other processes.** Rubber parts are also prepared by techniques such as dipping of patterns or 'forms' in rubber latex or liquid. After dipping the 'pattern' or 'form' a number of times, the desired thickness of rubber latex is deposited on the form. Then the form is removed from the latex part. Other techniques include die cutting of vulcanized sheets formed by moulding, calendering or extruding. The production of circular parts such as washers is done by cutting rubber tubes on a lathe. Products manufactured from thermoplastic rubber are typically extruded or injection-moulded from granules as received, but other materials may be added before extruding or moulding.

8.5.2 Popular Rubber Products

1. Rubber is combined with cord or fabric to form composites which possess both flexibility and high strength. Typical examples are reinforced V belts, hose and tyres. The wall thickness of rubber parts varies considerably. For example, the wall thickness of an injection moulded automotive brake diaphragm is about 1.3 mm, whereas the thickness of rubber bridge bearings may be 180 mm. As thickness increases, longer time is generally needed to cross-link rubber or to cool thermoplastic rubber before it is removed from the mould.
2. *Rubber products prepared by latex dipping* are hollow and have extremely thin walls (about 0.25 mm). Latex-dipped products are in the shape of bellows and similar designs.
3. *Gaskets* are frequently prepared by die-cutting rubber sheets, while rubber tubes may be cut on a mandrel in a lathe to form washers. Rubber washers lend shock absorbing property to fasteners.
4. *O rings* and *metal insert seals* with lip contact are moulded from a variety of rubber compounds to provide resistance to leakage of fluids. Since they are used in critical sealing applications, tolerances are much closer for O rings and metal insert seals, than for most other rubber products.
5. *Polyurethane parts manufactured by RIM (reaction injection moulding)* have a dense skin and a porous core and are usually much stiffer than conventional rubber parts. Rubber is a popular material with product designers. It has a high compressive strength (approx. 700 kg/cm^2) as maximum value and high resilience or shock absorbing ability because of its low average elastic modulus E (resilience $\propto f^2/2E$).

Some of the important applications of rubber in mechanical design are now described.

1. *Water lubricated rubber bush bearings.* These bush bearings in rubber are pressfitted in metallic housing. They have grooves parallel to their axis for retaining water which acts as lubricant. These bearings can tolerate and lubricate shafts when water contains sand particles and other materials.

2. Flexible mechanical couplings for transmission of power from one shaft to another with a slight permissible angle of twist utilize a rubber cross for connecting driving jaw with a driven jaw. A spider or cross made or rubber is the connecting element between the jaws of driving and driven shafts.
3. Rubber pads for absorbing high frequency vibrations are widely used in foundations. Due to its high stiffness in compression but lower stiffness in shear, rubber is favoured in vibration reduction during torque transmission. It should be noted that natural frequency of vibration is proportional to $\sqrt{K/m}$, where K is stiffness and m is mass density. Rubber, which has a high value of K, can be used when the forcing frequency is high.

8.6 DESIGN RECOMMENDATIONS FOR RUBBER PARTS

Rubber moulding is similar to moulding of plastics, and design principles are somewhat similar. Rubber parts can be designed with complex shapes. However, it is always better to make the design simple, avoid projections, overhangs, undercuts, etc. Designs should be reviewed with the rubber manufacturer who has good acquaintance with processing properties. In the following subsections, various design features and production design aspects are considered as outlined by Sommer (see Bralla [2]).

8.6.1 Gating

Consideration must be given to the location, size and shape of the gate. The rubber in the gate region should permit both easy removal of parts from cavities and easy trimming. The gate should be extra large in the case of RIM (reaction injection moulding).

8.6.2 Holes

1. Holes in rubber are the easiest to form and most economical to produce during moulding by providing core pins in the die. Drilling holes in cured rubber by conventional means is difficult because of its flexibility.
2. Holes should be as shallow and as wide as possible, consistent with functional requirements (see Figure 8.6).

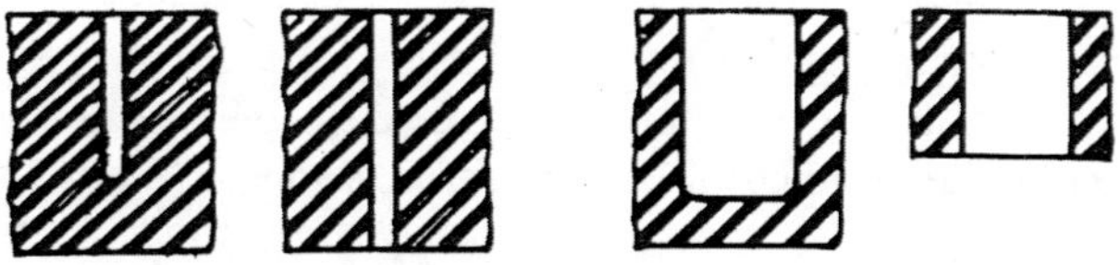

Not these These

FIGURE 8.6 Shallow, wide holes are preferred.

3. Through holes are preferable to blind holes, because the core pins forming them are well supported in the die.
4. Through holes can be moulded as small as 0.8 mm in diameter to a depth of 16 mm.
5. Deep blind holes having a small diameter should be avoided because the core pin forming them buckles during moulding. Instead, blind holes from tapered or stepped core pins are preferred (see Figure 8.7).

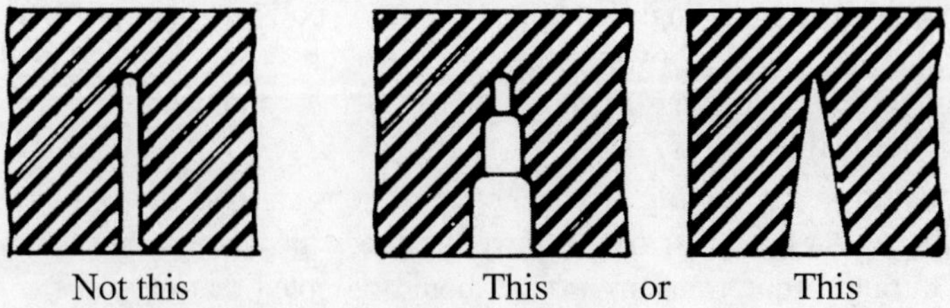

FIGURE 8.7 Design recommendation for holes in rubber.

6. Sufficient wall thickness should be incorporated around holes to minimize the danger of tearing of rubber from the hole, as illustrated in Figure 8.8.

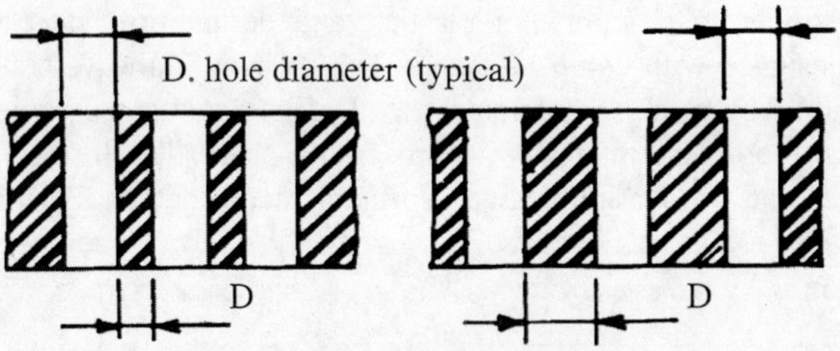

FIGURE 8.8 Design recommendation of distance between holes.

8.6.3 Wall Thickness

The wall thickness of parts should be kept constant, because it helps in cross-linking and more uniform properties throughout the product. It also minimizes distortion.

8.6.4 Undercuts

Undercuts should be avoided, if possible. However, they can be incorporated in low and medium hardness rubber, owing to the flexible nature of rubber.

1. If undercuts are required in hard rubber, they can be produced by machining, but not by moulding.
2. An internal undercut like the one shown in Figure 8.9 should be avoided, if possible, because it causes difficulty during removal of part from the mould.

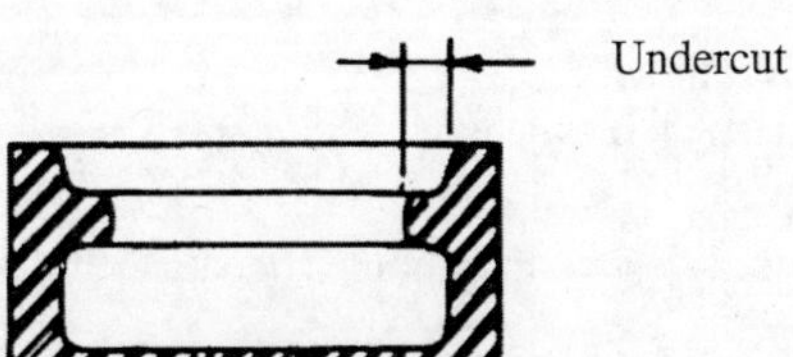

FIGURE 8.9 Illustration of the need to avoid undercut that makes moulding more difficult.

3. External undercuts are satisfactory if they are not so deep that they cause demoulding problems (see Figure 8.10). An undercut with a radius aids both demoulding and removal of trapped air. Softer rubbers can tolerate larger undercuts.

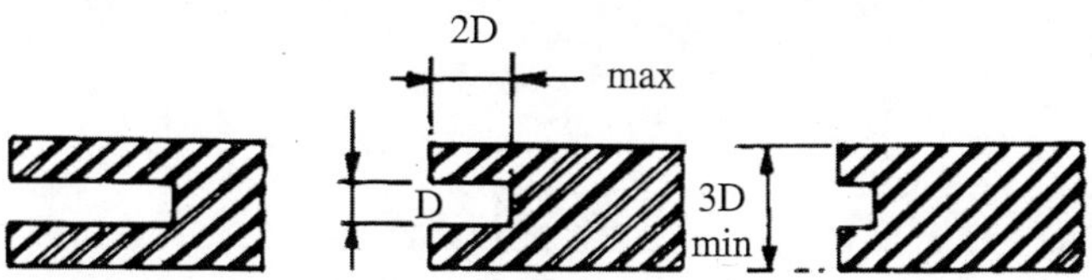

FIGURE 8.10 Undercut with round corners and limited depth are desirable.

8.6.5 Screw Threads

Screw threads are moulded only on hard rubber, which has greater strength. For softer rubber, threaded-metal inserts are often used for attachment purposes.

8.6.6 Inserts

1. The location of nonflush threaded inserts is staggered to keep more uniform rubber thickness which prevents stress concentration (Figure 8.11). Inserts with flush heads are used to reduce stress concentration further.

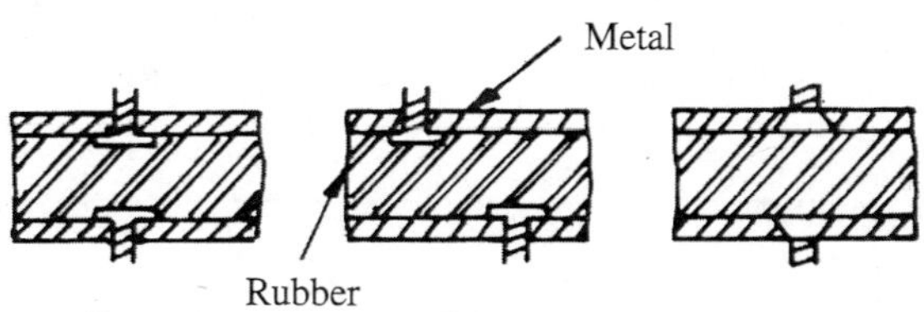

FIGURE 8.11 Design recommendations for inserts in rubber parts.

2. Inserts with sharp edges should be avoided, as shown in Figure 8.12, to prevent cutting the rubber.

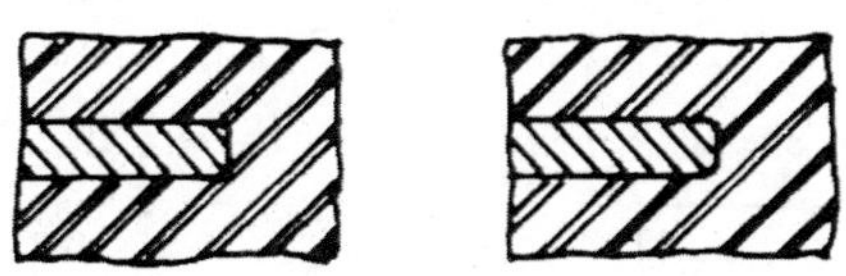

FIGURE 8.12 Inserts in rubber parts.

8.6.7 Draft

The provision of draft in moulded rubber parts varies with both the part design and the nature of rubber. For many soft rubber parts having hardness below 90 Shore A hardness, draft is not needed.

For soft thermoplastic rubber, a draft angle of 1/4 –1° is recommended (see Figure 8.13). For hard rubber, at least 1° draft is provided.

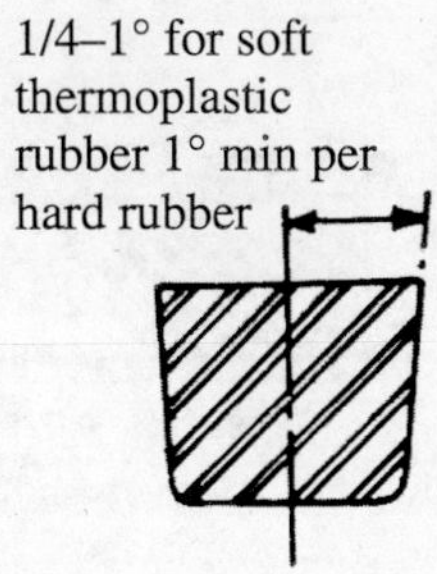

FIGURE 8.13 Draft on rubber parts.

8.6.8 Corners

Radii and fillets. Radii and fillets are generally desired on the corner of rubber parts, to facilitate a streamlined flow of rubber during moulding and to minimize stress concentration at the corners in the part and the mould.

1. Lower-cost parts are made by parting off from an extruded sleeve to length instead of moulding the parts. The square corner caused by parting off is satisfactory for some applications (see Figure 8.14).

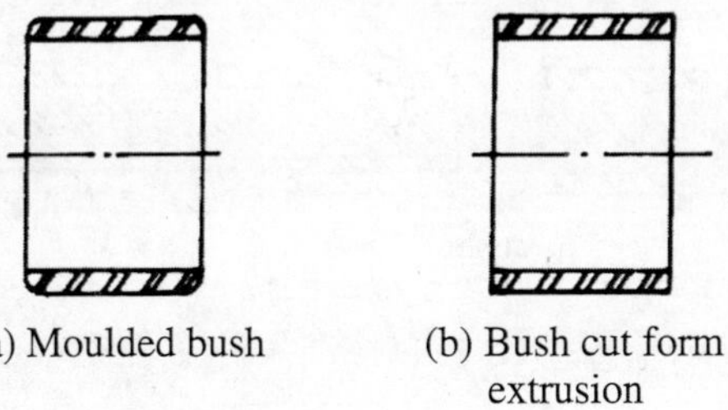

FIGURE 8.14 Moulded and extruded bushes in rubber.

2. Avoid sharp edges as they are difficult to obtain (see Figure 8.15(a)). A minimum thickness of 0.8 mm is recommended as illustrated in Figure 8.15(b).

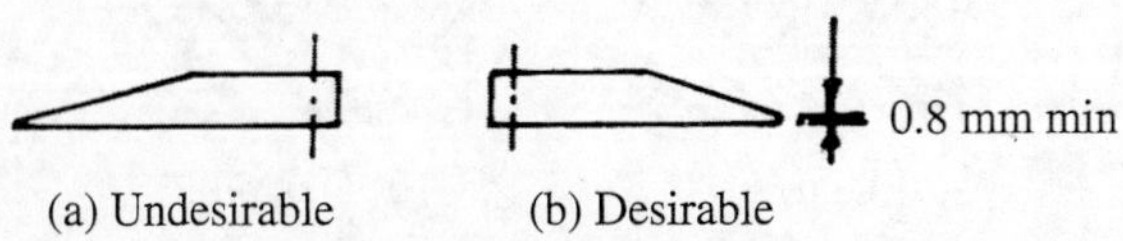

FIGURE 8.15 Recommended thickness of lips in rubber.

3. Only one mould half is needed to be machined if sharp corners rather than chamfers or radii are used at the parting line. The part shown in Figure 8.16(b) is preferred over Figure 8.16(a) because mould design is simpler for the former.

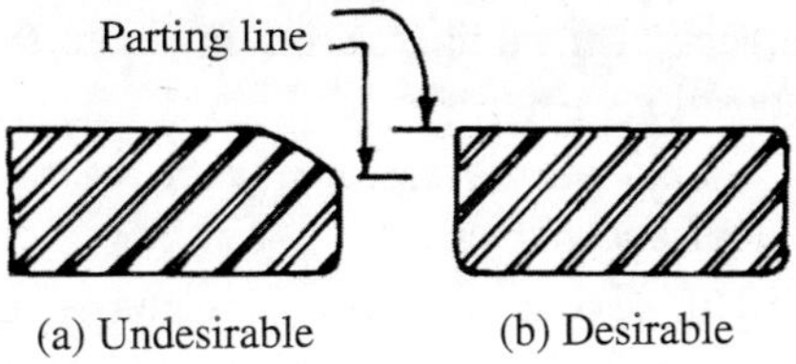

FIGURE 8.16 Illustration of how moulding can be facilitated.

4. The minimum radius for forming a tubing on a mandrel depends on the wall thickness and outside diameter. The minimum radius should be at least 1.5 times the outside diameter as shown in Figure 8.17 to prevent cracking or warping.

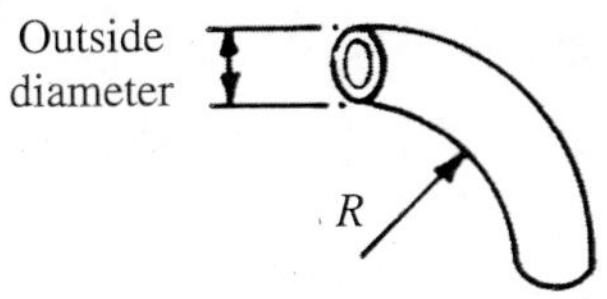

min $R = 1.5 \times$ outside diameter

FIGURE 8.17 Rubber hose dimensions.

5. Generous radii should be provided in the walls of rubber bellows to minimize stress concentration and to make removal from mould easier. Bellows find wide application in mechanical design.
6. In forming dipped latex products such as balloons, avoid sharp corners, as these cause weak points.
7. Polyurethane tends to build up dead material zones in sharp corners of moulds used for RIM and adversely affects part aesthetics. To minimize this tendency, radii of about 1.3 to 2.5 mm are provided at corners.

8.6.9 Flash

Flash tends to form at the mould parting line. In compression moulding, excess rubber flows into the flash gutter. The amount of flash permissible depends on the function of the rubber part. Flash extension is the extension beyond the part edge and should be shown on the part drawing. For material saving and economy, a mould is designed to produce a thin flash or, for some precision moulds, no flash at all. However, some moulds with multiple die cavities for mass production are designed to produce a thick flash and the parts are later cut off with a die in large batch quantities.

8.6.10 Parting Line

A parting line is formed at the junction of the two halves of a curing mould. As far as possible, the mould-parting line should be in a plane.

8.6.11 Venting

Venting in the die is effective at the final closure to avoid defects by releasing trapped air, during injection moulding, in which the air has only a short time to escape. There are a large number of shots per minute. Other design rules for vents are as follows:

1. Parting-line vents for injection moulding should be about 0.1 mm deep by 3.15 mm wide for high-viscosity compositions.
2. The depth of the vent should be decreased and the width increased, for lower-viscosity compositions and thermoplastic rubbers.
3. Provide vents in moulds for very low-viscosity, castable compositions to avoid trapped air at the top of the cavity.

8.6.12 Surface Texture

Although smooth, glossy surfaces on moulded rubber parts are aesthetically desirable, they are more costly than commercial grade finishes. Recommended commercial finish and other standard finishes of the RMA are influenced by the following factors:

1. Mould-release agents may cause an oily surface on the moulded part.
2. Lettering, identification letters, numbers and surface decoration on moulded-rubber parts are generally raised, because it is preferable to form them from depressions in the mould. Generally, identification has to be raised 0.5 mm maximum for legibility.

8.6.13 Shrinkage

For typical cross-linked rubber containing normal filler content, the shrinkage is about 1.5 per cent, but it may be as low as about 0.6 per cent for some highly filled compounds. Shrinkage is as high as 4 per cent for fluorocarbon rubber which is post-cured in an oven at high temperature. Shrinkage for RIM polyurethane is 1–2 per cent, but it can vary outside this range, depending on composition and process parameters.

For rubber compounds containing reinforcing fibre, such as glass, shrinkage is lower along the fibre axis. Higher amounts of filler or fibre increase hardness of a rubber compound and reduce the shrinkage. Shrinkage may also be non-uniform for rubber in rubber metal composites. This effect is seen in products like a bridge bearing, in which shrinkage is considerably lower in the plane of the metal plates than at right angles to the plates.

8.7 DISTORTION IN RUBBER

As a result of shrinkage and other factors, exposed rubber surfaces are seldom truly flat, particularly if metal reinforcing members are used. Metals have a lower coefficient of thermal expansion than rubber, and this causes distortion in the composite part during cooling after moulding. Figures 8.18 and 8.19 illustrate two examples of distortion.

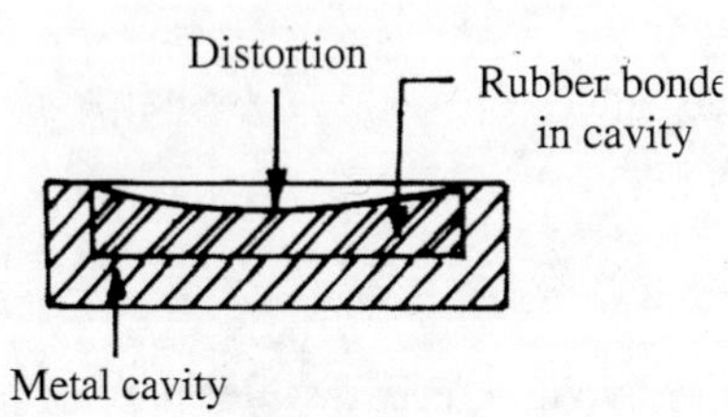

FIGURE 8.18 Suitable metal cavities for rubber.

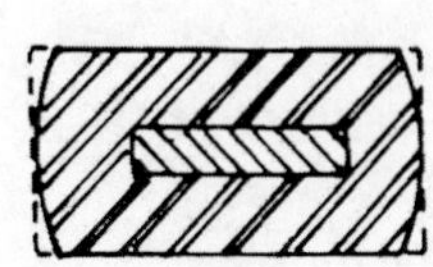

FIGURE 8.19 Inserts in rubber.

8.8 DIMENSIONAL EFFECTS

Rubber parts with very close tolerances can be produced, but their costs will be significantly higher, because of higher tooling costs, more strict process controls, and more number of defectives. Increasing the number of cavities per mould to achieve mass production reduced both the cost per part and promotes interchangeability of the parts. Support for some rubber products may be necessary during manufacture and subsequent packaging. The dimensions of rubber parts may change after moulding due to relaxation effects. Some moisture absorbing rubbers like polyurethane undergo dimensional change with time.

8.9 TOLERANCES

The tolerances of parts designated as "A-high precision" are so critical that errors in measurement may be large, in relation to tolerances. Products requiring post-curing should not be included in this designation.

In die-cutting, closed-cell parts thicker than 12 mm, a dished effect occurs on the edges which may affect tolerances.

Other dimensional factors of specific importance to certain rubber products are lack of concentricity, parallelism and squareness. Figure 8.20 shows correct and incorrect ways to use external metal reinforcement. The correct reinforcement provides more and better adhesion as compared with the square reinforcement in Figure 8.20(b).

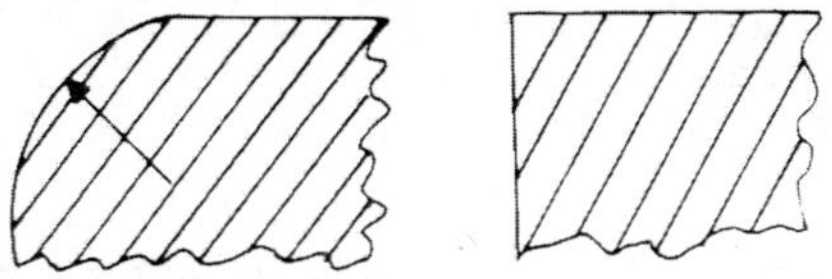

(a) Desirable (b) Undesirable

FIGURE 8.20 Provision of radius.

Wobble and eccentricity. To explain the concept of wobble and lack of concentricity, an example of a 75 mm diameter wheel is taken up. The wobble and eccentricity should be within 0.75 mm (see Figure 8.21). Squareness for a bonded-rubber product can typically be held to a tolerance of 1°, as illustrated in Figure 8.22.

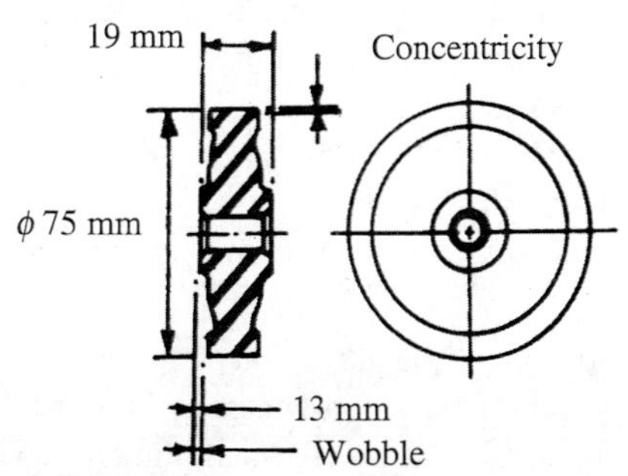

FIGURE 8.21 Desirable wheel dimensions.

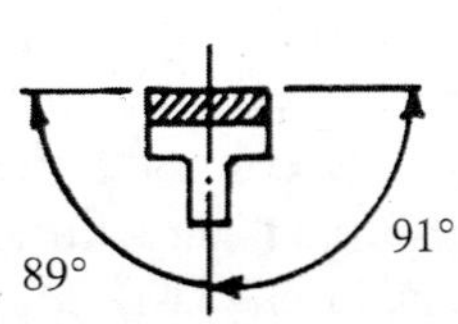

FIGURE 8.22 Sandwiching of rubber with metal.

8.10 CERAMICS AND GLASS PARTS

Ceramics are inorganic, non-metallic materials and are classified into the following groups:

(i) **Whitewares.** These include, in addition to mechanical and electrical components, earthenware, china, tiles and porcelain.

(ii) **Glass.** Glass is a mutual solution of fused, inorganic oxides cooled to a rigid condition without crystallization. A variety of hard, transparent objects are produced from glass. It is yet to be replaced totally by polymers.

(iii) **Refractories.** These include heat-resistant and insulating blocks, bricks, mortar and fireclay. They are used for furnace linings and briquettes.

(iv) **Structural clay products.** These consist of bricks, tiles and piping made from natural clays.

(v) **Porcelain enamels.** These are ceramic coatings on cast-iron, steel and other metal products. They find application in kitchenware and household utensils.

8.10.1 Properties of Ceramics and Glass

(i) **Ceramic parts.** Ceramic parts meant for industrial applications are hard and extremely strong in compression; they are also highly chemical, corrosion resistant and non-flammable, and are suitable for use at extremely high operating temperatures. Ceramic whitewares have good thermal shock resistance and low thermal expansion. High modulus of elasticity and high radiation resistance are two additional properties of importance in some applications. Most ceramics are dielectrics and, except for ferrites, they lack magnetic properties. Ferrite rods are used in induction welding in steel tube manufacture.

Excellent abrasion-resistant surfaces are possible. These surfaces also offer a pleasing gloss or patina and can be vitreous and non-porous. In addition to their resistance to chemical substances and corrosive materials, ceramics are relatively immune to fire, heat and weathering.

Generally, all ceramic materials are brittle. Tensile strengths are somewhat limited. There are also some limitations in freedom of design because of processing complexities and certain undesirable mechanical properties. Because of high firing temperatures, metal inserts cannot be moulded into ceramics.

The size of commercial ceramic components ranges from the very small electronic components to large nose cones and radomes. Typical ceramic parts for mechanical application are bearings, turbine blades, cams, cutting tools, extrusion dies, thread and wire guides, nozzles for abrasive materials, wear plates, seals, valve seats, filters, pump parts, crucibles and trays. Typical parts for electrical and electronic applications include coil forms, tubes, insulators, lamp housings, printed-circuit boards, radomes, resistor bases, vacuum tube-element supports and terminals. The Japanese have produced an automobile engine with ceramics.

(ii) **Glass.** Glass is solid at room temperature and becomes plastic on heating to 1200°C. Though the atomic structure of glass resembles ceramics, its processing is done like thermoplastics. Glassy phase is characterized by molecular array like a liquid. In special glasses (ceramic type), while heating, crystals are formed. Transparency is the most important property of glass and is responsible for most of its applications. Other properties are similar to those of whiteware but with less favourable strength and high-temperature characteristics. The poor resistance of glass to thermal shock can be improved by tempering, which also provides increased mechanical strength. (The concepts and practice of toughening of glass has already been discussed in Chapter 3.)

Glass products range in size from microspheres of fractional-millimeter diameter used as fillers for plastics, to large plate-glass windows. Normally, pressed parts are about 9 kg or less in weight, while blownware ranges up to 16 kg.

Typical pressed-glass components are electrical insulators, baking dishes, stoppers and stopcocks for laboratory vessels, eye glasses and ornamental pieces. Typical blown-glass components are bottles and other containers, incandescent lamps, electron tubes, laboratory glassware, and television picture tubes.

Tubes and pipes of glass made by drawing are used for laboratory, chemical industry, high-temperature applications and thermometers. Flat glass for mirrors, tabletops and other purposes is made, either by drawing or by rolling, which, in the case of plate glass, is followed by grinding and polishing, or by the newer process of floating onto molten tin and drawing horizontally. Glass powders are sintered to make filters and other porous objects. Glass fibres are a major reinforcing medium for many products and for insulation.

Cellular glass is black or dark coloured. Its pore size can be varied, depending on the method of introducing porosity. Thermal expansion of cellular glass is the same as that of the base glass.

Colour can be incorporated into most glass, white-ware porcelain and other ceramic materials by introducing proper pigmentation medium to the material before firing.

8.11 PRODUCTION DESIGN FACTORS FOR CERAMIC PARTS

Although technical ceramics can be fabricated into complex shapes, it is always desirable to keep shapes as simple as possible for economic reasons. Tolerance also should be as liberal as possible. It is important for a designer to impart geometry that avoids problems which result from the low tensile strength and lack of ductility of ceramics.

8.11.1 Problems of Manufacture of Ceramic Parts

These problems are common to all particulate processing techniques and equally applicable to ceramics:

1. It is not possible to keep height-to-diameter ratio of more than 2, with 'one plunger' set-up. This is because of higher density of the particulate near the plunger surface and lower density away from the plunger-compact interface (refer Figure 8.23).
2. Sliding-type (spring loaded movable) dies at the lower end are a partial solution to the above problem of non-uniform compaction of the 'green' ceramic part.
3. Having plungers from both ends to apply pressure on the ceramic powder green compact is the best, though, costly solution.
4. Thin-walled parts cannot be made without the danger of breakage of the ceramic. Thus, the punch and die design should be proper, leaving enough wall thickness. Ample draft should be given on punch/die when possible. Perfectly spherical parts are not possible as they give rise to the need for sharp-edged punches (feather edge) with short lives. Figure 8.23

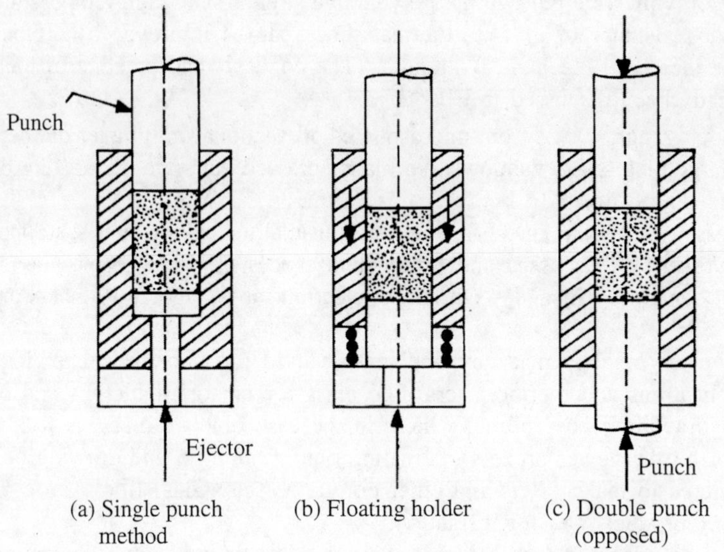

FIGURE 8.23 Ceramic moulding practice with composite and split dies.

shows constraints imposed by processing limitations on compaction process for production of 'green' compacts.

J.G. Mohr (see Bralla [2]) gives specific design recommendations for technical ceramics as follows:

1. Edges and corners should have chamfers or generous radii to minimize chipping and stress concentration and help in forming. When parts are machined, the outside radii should be 1.5 mm or more, and the inside radii at least 2.4 mm. For dry-pressed parts, outside edges should be beveled in a manner similar to that employed for powder-metal parts; 0.8 mm by 45° is a desirable minimum. The inside radii should be as large as possible: 6 mm is adequate.
2. Since parts in green state may sag or be distorted, if not properly supported during firing, it is preferable to avoid large overhanging or unsupported sections.
3. Pressed parts should be designed with as uniform a wall thickness as possible. Unequal shrinkage of sections of non-uniform thickness, during drying and firing, induces stress, distortion, and cracking. Sections should not exceed 25 mm in thickness.
4. Other factors being equal, simple symmetrical shapes without deep recesses, holes and projections are recommended. Gently curved surfaces are normally preferred with most ceramic-forming processes.
5. When hollow pieces are cast in a mould (e.g. cup-shaped parts), a draft angle of at least 5° must be provided to facilitate removal of the green body. Refer Figure 8.24 for recommendation on draft. If the part is left in the mould too long, drying shrinkage will cause adhesion of the material against the mould, resulting in cracking. Dry-pressed parts do not require draft on either outside surfaces or in walls of through holes. Wet-pressed parts should have at least 1° draft on exterior surfaces and 2° draft on interior surfaces (see Figure 8.24).

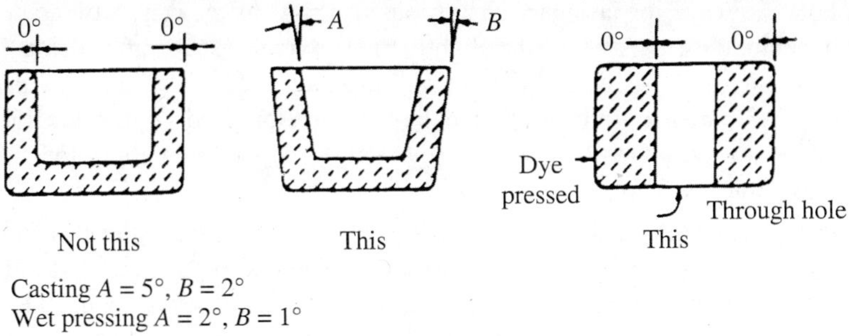

FIGURE 8.24 Design recommendation for draft in ceramics.

6. Undercuts should be avoided in ceramic components, if possible. Although, some undercuts can be incorporated through the use of mould cores, machining is the normal method for producing them.
7. Cavities, grooves and blind holes in pressed parts should not be deeper than one-half of the part thickness and, preferably, only one-third of the thickness (see Figure 8.25).

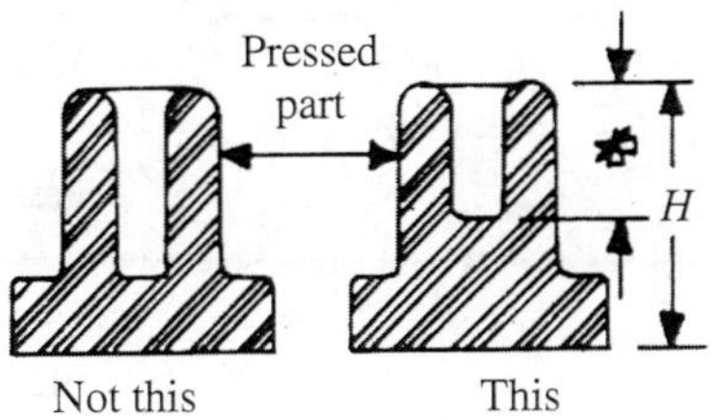

FIGURE 8.25 Design recommendation on grooves etc.

8. Extruded parts should be symmetrical, with uniform wall thickness. The minimum wall thickness for extrusions should be 0.4 mm or, for circular sections, 10 per cent of the extrusion diameter. For long extrusions, 150 mm in length or more, the wall should be thicker, at least 20 per cent of the outside size of extrusion (see Figure 8.26).

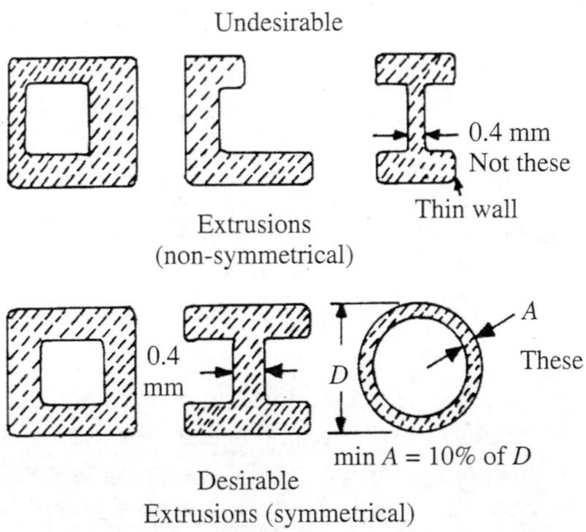

FIGURE 8.26 Design recommendations for extended parts.

9. When holes are used for fasteners, distortions from shrinkage can cause assembly problems. Holes in ceramic parts may become slightly out of circular shape after firing. To compensate for variations in hole spacing, multiple holes, which are to be aligned with corresponding holes in other parts, must be further enlarged (or elongated in the direction of the other holes). The amount of enlargement or elongation depends on the allowable hole-to-hole tolerance of the two parts.
10. Moulding of screw threads in ceramic parts is not feasible. Screw threads can be machined in 'green' ceramic workpiece, but they constitute a potential problem, and it is better to design parts without screw threads, if possible. If incorporated, threads should be coarse and not smaller than 5 mm. Holes should not be tapped to a depth more than six threads, because dimensional variations in the thread pitch from firing shrinkage may cause assembly problems, if too long a thread is used. All tapped holes should be countersunk (see Figure 8.27).

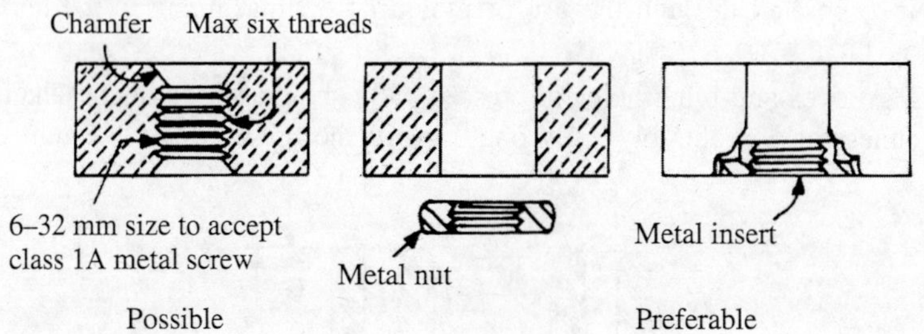

FIGURE 8.27 Design recommendations for screw threads in ceramic parts.

External threads should also be as coarse as possible and have a well-rounded thread form to reduce edge chipping and stress cracking. Coarse-pitch threads with a truncated form or knuckle thread can also be used to increase the strength of the threaded ceramic part. As with internal threads, it is recommended that the number of threads in engagement be limited to six. Glass bottles are provided with knuckle thread of semi-circular thread profile.

11. Ribs and fins should be well rounded, wide and well spaced, and should have normal draft. Figure 8.28 illustrates design rules for ribs.

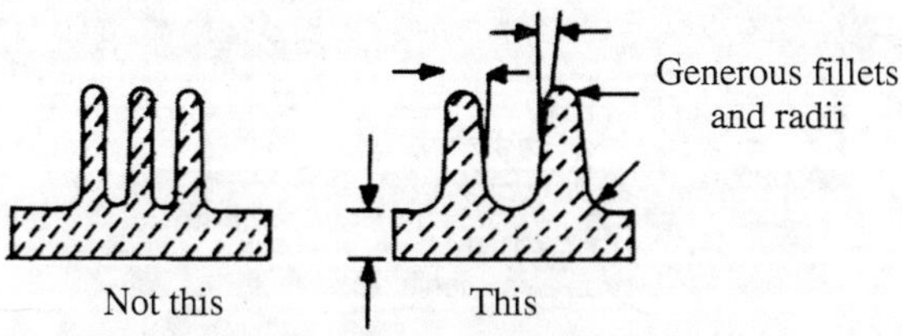

FIGURE 8.28 Desirable dimensions for ribs.

12. Grinding after firing can produce ceramic parts of high accuracy, but stock-removal rates are slow and the operation is expensive. When the operation is necessary, it is advisable to reduce the area of the surface to be ground, as much as possible, and provide clearance for the grinding wheel, at the ends of the surface (see Figure 8.29). Special diamond grit surface grinding wheels are needed for grinding of ceramics.

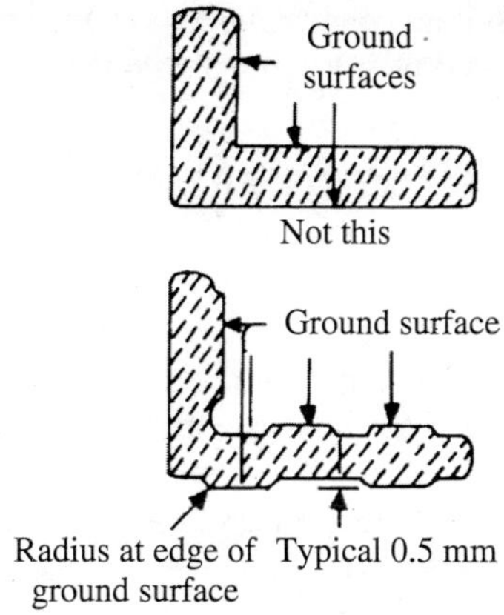

FIGURE 8.29 Minimizing grinding on ceramics.

8.12 SPECIAL CONSIDERATIONS FOR DESIGN OF GLASS PARTS

1. Holes, cavities and deep slots can cause moulding problems and should be included in a part, only if absolutely necessary. Holes are normally not punched through in the pressing operation but are machined from the thin web or hollow boss, as shown in Figure 8.30. Holes are made in glass with special 'mounted points' type grinding wheels fitted at the end of shafts. These conical diamond grit grinding wheels are suited for drilling of holes in glass.

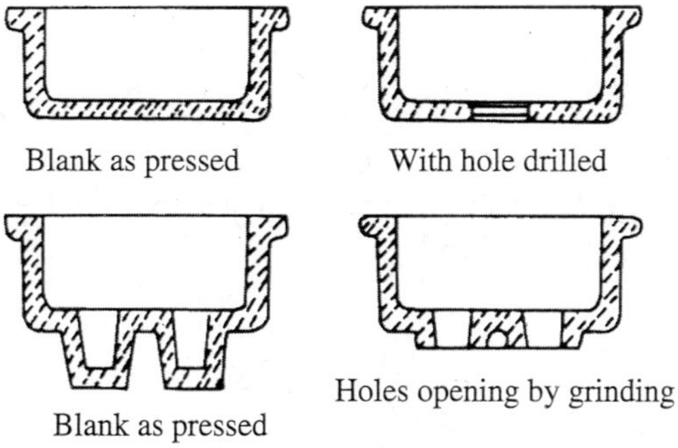

FIGURE 8.30 Holes in glass parts (drilling or grinding with point grinding).

2. As in the case of whiteware parts, best results are obtained when walls are uniform in thickness, as the part is designed for compressive, rather than tensile strength and, when gently curved, rather than sharp-angled shapes are employed.
3. Lettering or other irregular surface features may be incorporated as long as they are aligned in the direction of, and not perpendicular to, the mould opening.
4. Ribs and flanges can be incorporated in pressed-glass components, but they are not practicable in blown parts.
5. While bosses may be incorporated in some items like electrical insulators, they are normally not practicable for general-purpose design and manufacture.

6. Threads for bottle caps or similar connecting devices may be incorporated in blown-glass parts as they are with blow-moulded plastics, and the same screw thread designs are recommended.

8.13 DIMENSIONAL FACTORS AND TOLERANCES

8.13.1 Ceramic Parts

Ceramic parts are affected dimensionally, primarily by drying shrinkage and firing shrinkage, which can total as much as 25 per cent for high-clay ceramics and about 14 per cent for porcelains. Other factors affecting the accuracy of ceramic parts are mould accuracy and mould wear. Processing variables such as the amount of material pressed, pressing time and pressure affect the dimensions of pressed parts. Machining variations affect green-state machined and finish-ground parts.

8.13.2 Glass Parts

Glass parts are dimensionally affected by job weight, temperature of the melt and mould, mould tolerance, and wear and shrinkage of the glass on cooling. Shrinkage rates vary from the equivalent of that of steel (92×10^{-7} cm/cm°C) down to that for pure silica glass (7×10^{-7} cm/cm°C).

8.14 WOOD

Wood is a unique natural material that is used in structural products and fibre products. It is a very useful material as a source of certain oils, chemicals and source of energy. The discussion here is confined to wood as a structural material.

8.14.1 Some Engineering Properties of Wood

Wood has highly directional properties and represents a material with marked anisotropy. It behaves like a bunch of straws bonded together (see Figure 8.31). Typical values of strength for pine wood are: Axial tensile strength 140 kg/cm^2; axial compressive strength 120 kg/cm^2; transverse compressive

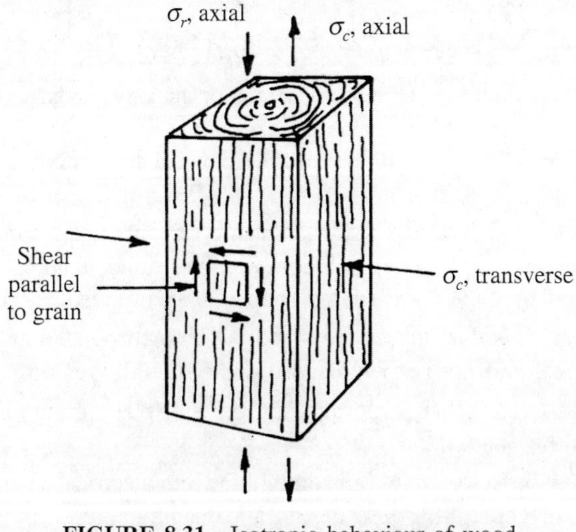

FIGURE 8.31 Isotropic behaviour of wood.

strength 32 kg/cm^2; transverse tensile strength of wood is very low (i.e., it is about 3% of axial tensile strength): 4.2 kg/cm^2; shear strength parallel to grain 8.4 kg/cm^2. The elastic modulus E = 120 kg/cm^2, which is about l/20th of steel. However, being a lightweight material, the specific strength of wood is comparable to steel. The density of wood is in the range of 0.2 to 0.9 g/cc. The heavier wood with more fibres is stronger than lighter wood. Since the shear strength of wood across the fibre is much more, a designer can select the depth of the beam without bothering about transverse shear. However, a wooden beam subjected to bending has to be protected from longitudinal tensile failure.

8.14.2 Wood-based Composite Materials

Plywood, particle board, hard board, etc. are resin bonded wood composites. The advances made in the processing of composite wood products have resulted in the elimination of directional properties and increased the confidence level of the designer. Even rice husk and cottonseed husk, which used to be waste materials in the past, are now being utilized for making particle boards.

8.14.3 Joinery in Woodwork

Joints occupy an important place in woodwork. One of the problems with wood is the dimensional change which it undergoes as a result of moisture absorption. Figure 8.32 gives a comparison of the conventional and improved ways to install a flush door. The door in Figure 8.32(b) will fit well even if a dimensional variation up to 2 cm takes place. Various methods of joining wood in a straight line and at right angles are illustrated in Figures 8.33(a) and 8.33(b), respectively.

(a) Conventional (flush) door (b) Improved installation

FIGURE 8.32 Door hinge designs.

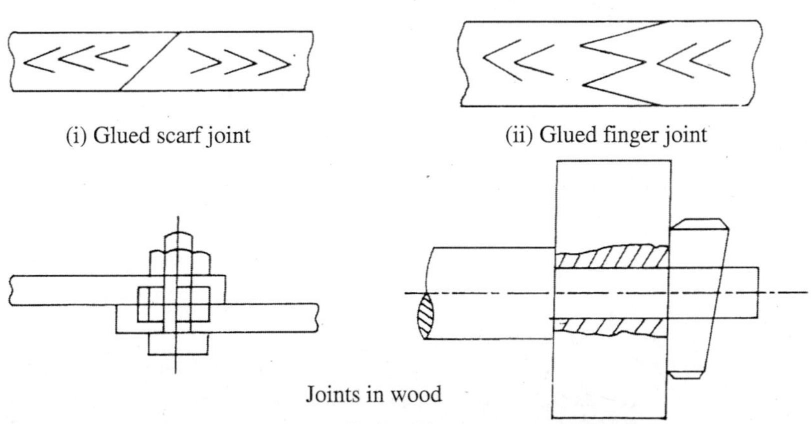

(i) Glued scarf joint (ii) Glued finger joint

(iii) Bolted lap joint (iv) Wedge type joint

(a) In a straight line

FIGURE 8.33 *Contd.*

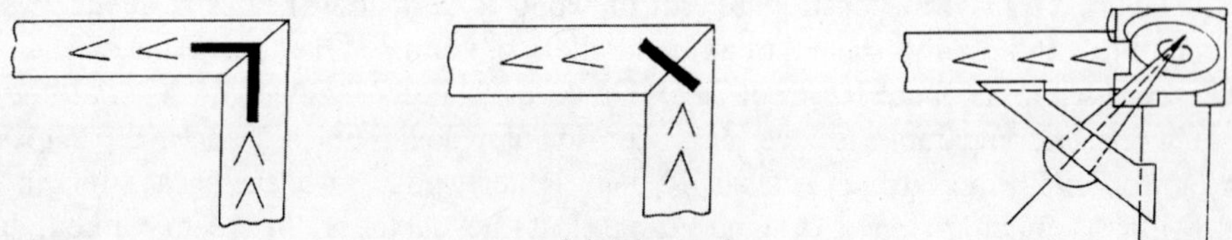

Joints in wood

(i) Joint with *L*-type insert (ii) Joint with straight insert (iii) Joint with wood screw

(b) At right angles

FIGURE 8.33 Design ideas with wood joints.

REVIEW QUESTIONS

1. Which property of plastics poses a difficulty to designers? [*Hint:* Creep?] Sec. 8.1; P 225
2. How are springs designed with plastics? Figure 8.1, 8.2
3. Write a note of plastic bush bearings. Which design criteria for plastic bearings are important? (wear and friction μ). Sec. 8.2; P 226–227
4. How accurate gears in plastics are manufactured keeping in view standard modules and pressure angles? Sec. 3.1; P 228
5. Give two examples of creative design of a lunch box made with plastic. Sec. 8.4.1; Figure 8.4
6. Describe injection moulding and dipping method of production of rubber products. What is reaction injection moulding (RIM)? Sec. 8.5, 8.5.1
7. List a few prominent rubber products. What are the desirable elastic properties of rubber? Sec. 8.5
8. Discuss rubber moulding with reaction injection moulding with following details: gating, holes, wall thickness between holes, undercut, screw threads and metal inserts, draft, avoidance of sharp edges, flash parting line, venting. Sec. 8.5.1
9. Classify ceramics according to their application. Sec. 8.10
10. What are the problems of production of ceramic parts? How draft, grooves, symmetry of section, screw threads, ribs, minimizing of grinding are optimized in engineering ceramics? Sec. 8.11, 8.11.1
11. How tolerances are maintained in ceramic and glass products?
12. How wood-based composites have superseded natural wood? Sec. 8.14

    What precautions are to be taken in using wood as material for beams?
13. Show a few design concepts with wood joints and wooden doors. Figure 8.32, 8.33
14. Explain the design and production aspects of automobile tyre with neat sketches.

    [**Hint: Design:** Figure 8.34 shows a local section of a segment of automobile tyre. The main features of a tyre are tread, the body with sidewalls and beads. Tread is the raised pattern in contact with the road; body along with sidewalls supports the tread and gives it the shape. The body is made up of strips of cloth like fabric covered with rubber called the ply. The ply can be diagonal are radial depending upon design. Belts are additional covers above ply to provide strength to be tyre. There can be steel belted covers to provide extra strength to the tyre. The beads are rubber covered metal wires bundle that hold the tyre and help fitting the tyre on the rim of the wheel.

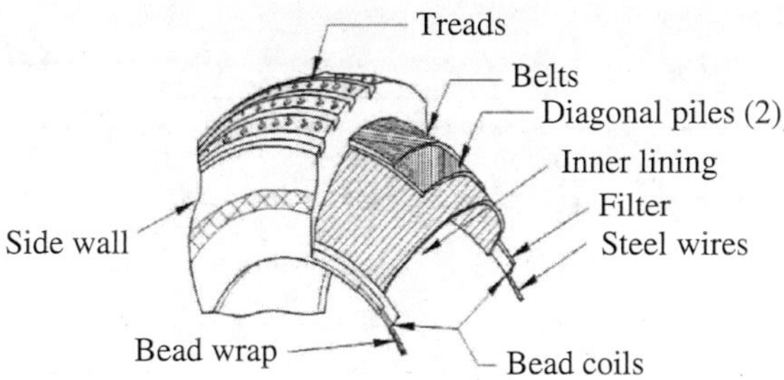

FIGURE 8.34 Local section of an automobile tyre.

Production steps:

1. **Pre forming of components:** The bead coil (rubberized steel wire), the plies (fabric), belts (continuous fabric or steel), tread (extrusions as a continuous strip) and sidewall (extruded as a continuous strip).
2. **Assembling of components in a carcass on a building drum:** Skilled assembler wraps specially cut pieces of rubber around the collapsible metal drum. The pieces are assembled to prepare the green tyre. Then the drum is collapsed and the green tyre shown in Figure 8.35 is ready for moulding and curing.
3. **Moulding and curing:** The uncured tyre is placed over expandable diaphragm, the mould is closed and the diaphragm is expanded to force uncured (green) tyre against mould cavity, pressing tread pattern on rubber. Mould and diaphragm are heated to cure rubber. Small and thin tyre can be cured in a few minutes while large tyre takes several hours to cure.

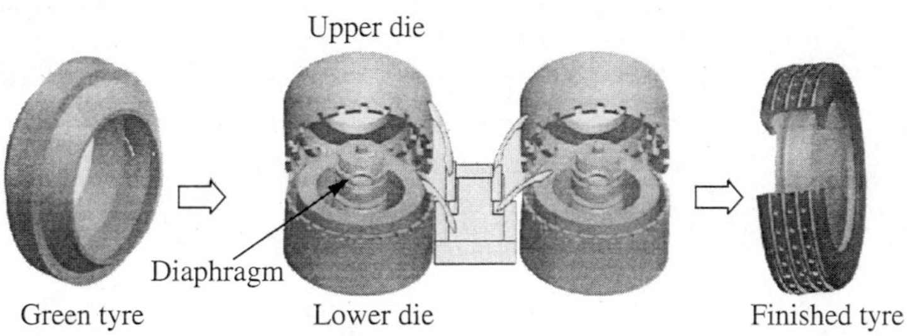

FIGURE 8.35 Process for moulding to obtain finished tyre from green tyre.

REFERENCES

[1] Chow, W.W., *Cost Reduction in Product Design*, Van Nostrand Reinhold, New York, 1978.

[2] Bralla, James (Ed.), *Handbook of Product Design for Manufacturing*, McGraw-Hill, New York, 1986.

[3] Theberge, et al., How plastics wear against plastics, *Jour. Machine Design,* Oct. 31, 1974, pp. 60–61.

[4] Theberge. J.E., Cloud, P.J., and Arkles, B., How to get high accuracy plastic gears, *Jour. Machine Design,* Sept. 6, 1973, pp. 140–45.

Chapter 9

Optimization in Design

9.1 INTRODUCTION

It has already been emphasized in Chapter 1 that design is an iterative process. We start with a primitive problem, refine it, develop a model and arrive at a solution. Usually, there is more than one solution, and the first one is not always the best. Thus, in engineering design, we have a situation in which there is a search for the best solution. Therefore, optimization is inherent in the design process.

As stated in Chapter 1, **optimization** forms phase II of *morphology of design.* Several mathematical techniques of optimization have been developed since 1950, and they have been gradually applied to a variety of engineering design situations. The concurrent development of the digital computers, with their inherent ability for rapid numerical calculations and search, has made the utilization of optimization procedures practical, in many design situations.

Optimal design means the best of all feasible designs proposed in phase one, i.e., the conceptual design. Optimization is the process of maximizing a desired quantity or minimizing an undesired one. Optimization theory is the body of mathematics that deals with the properties of maxima and minima, and how to find maxima and minima numerically. In the typical design optimization situation, the designer has already created a general configuration for which the numerical values of the independent variables have not been fixed. An objective function that defines the value of the design in terms of the independent variables is established.

$$U = U(x_1, x_2, ..., x_n) \tag{9.1}$$

Typical objective functions could be cost, weight, reliability and so forth. Essentially, the objective function is subject to certain constraints arising from physical situations and limitations, or from compatibility conditions on the individual variables. The functional constraints F specify relations that must exist between the variables:

$$\begin{aligned} F_1 &= f_1(x_1, x_2, \ldots, x_n) \\ F_2 &= f_2(x_1, x_2, \ldots, x_n) \\ \vdots \quad & \quad \vdots \\ F_m &= f_m(x_1, x_2, \ldots, x_n) \end{aligned} \tag{9.2}$$

For example, if we were optimizing the volume of a rectangular storage tank, where $x_1 = l_1$, $x_2 = l$, and $x_3 = l_3$, then the functional constraints would be $v = l_1 l_2 l_3$. The regional constraints Z are imposed by specific details of the problem:

$$
\begin{aligned}
Z_1 &= Z_1(x_1, x_2, \ldots, x_n) \le L_1 \\
Z_2 &= Z_2(x_1, x_2, \ldots, x_n) \le L_2 \\
\vdots & \qquad \vdots \\
Z_p &= Z_p(x_1, x_2, \ldots, x_n) \le L_p
\end{aligned}
\tag{9.3}
$$

A type of regional constraint that arises naturally in design situations is based on specifications which are points of interaction with other parts of the system. Often, a specification results from an arbitrary decision to carry out a suboptimization of the system.

A common problem in design optimization is that there is more than one design characteristic which is of value to the user. In formulating the optimization problem, one predominant characteristic is chosen as the objective function, and the other characteristics are reduced to the status of constraints. Frequently, they show up as strictly defined specifications. Such specifications are usually subject to negotiation (soft specification), and should be considered as target values, until the design progresses to such a point that it is possible to determine the penalty that is being paid in trade-offs to achieve the specifications. Siddal [1] has shown how this may be accomplished in design optimization through the use of interaction curve.

The following example should help to clarify the above definitions. It is desired to insulate a building to save fuel. A decision must be made about the thickness of the insulation. We wish to find the optimum thickness of insulation, x, that balances the increased capital cost of insulation against the savings in fuel. Fuel cost is a per year cost; insulation is a one-time (capital) cost, but it can be converted to an annual cost by applying a capital recovery factor. The objective function can be written as:

$$C = \frac{K_1}{x} + K_2 x \tag{9.4}$$

where C is in dollars per year and K_1 and K_2 are the fuel and insulation costs, respectively. Now, we must consider the constraints on x. There are no functional constraints in this simple example, but there are several regional constraints:

1. The insulation cannot exceed the thickness of the wall space ($x \le 100$ mm),
2. Insulation does not come in thickness less than 25 mm ($x \ge 25$ mm),
3. There may be a constraint on the total money available for the project ($K_3 x \le M$).

9.2 SIDDAL'S CLASSIFICATION OF DESIGN APPROACHES

Siddal [1], who has reviewed the development of optimal design methods, gives the following graphic description of optimization methods.

(i) **Optimization by evolution.** There is a close parallel between technological evolution and biological evolution. Most designs in the past have been optimized by an attempt to improve on an existing similar design. Survival of the resulting variations depends on the natural selection of user acceptance.

(ii) **Optimization by intuition.** The art of engineering is the ability to make good decisions, without being able to provide a justification. Intuition is knowing what to do, without knowing why one does it. The gift of intuition seems to be closely related to the unconscious mind. The history of technology is full of examples of engineers who made use of intuition to make major advances. Although the knowledge and tools available today are so much more powerful, ultimately intuition continues to play an important role in technological development.

(iii) **Optimization by trial-and-error modelling.** This refers to the usual situation in modern engineering design, where it is recognized that the first feasible design is not always the best. Therefore, the design model is exercised for a few iterations, in the hope of finding an improved design. However, this mode of operation is not true optimization. Some refer to satisfying, as opposed to optimizing, to mean a technically acceptable job done rapidly and economically. Such a design should not be called an optimal design.

(iv) **Optimization by numerical algorithm.** This is the area of current active development in which mathematically based strategies are used to search for an optimum. Computer is widely used for such an approach.

There is no unique technique for optimization in engineering design. How well a technique works depends on the nature of the functions represented in the problem. All optimization methods cannot be covered in a brief chapter; an attempt is made here to discuss a number of such methods, as they are applied in engineering design.

9.3 OPTIMIZATION BY DIFFERENTIAL CALCULUS

The use of the calculus to determine the maximum or minimum values of a function has become the modern trend. Figure 9.1 illustrates various types of extrema that can occur. A characteristic property of an extremum is that U is momentarily stationary at each point. For example, as E is approached, U increases; but it does not increase and soon decreases to the right of E. The familiar condition for a stationary point is:

$$\frac{d^2U}{dx_1^2} \tag{9.5}$$

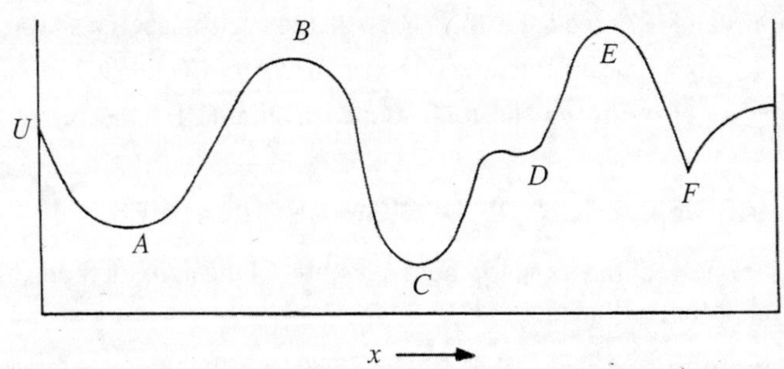

FIGURE 9.1 Graph between U and x indicating maxima, minima, saddle, point and inflexion.

If the curvature is negative, then the stationary point is maximum. The point is a minimum if the curvature is positive.

$$\frac{d^2U}{dx_1^2} < 0 \text{ indicates maximum} \tag{9.6}$$

$$\frac{d^2U}{dx_1^2} > 0 \text{ indicates minimum} \tag{9.7}$$

Both points B and E are mathematical maxima. Point B, which is similar to the two maxima, is called a local maximum. Point D is a point of inflexion. The slope is zero and the curve is horizontal, but the second derivative is zero. When $d^2U/dx^2 = 0$, higher order derivatives must be used to determine maxima or minima. Point F is not a minimum point, because the objective function is not continuous at it. Point F is only a cusp in the objective function.

We can apply this simple optimization technique to the insulation problem in Section 9.1. The objective function is given by Eq. (9.4). The optimum is given by:

$$\frac{dC}{dx} = 0 = -K_1(1/x^2) + K_2 \tag{9.8}$$

$$x = \sqrt{(K_1/K_2)} \tag{9.9}$$

The values of insulation thickness established by Eq. (9.9) results in minimum cost, because the second derivative of Eq. (9.8) is positive. In using Eq. (9.9), we apply the regional constraints that $25 \le x \le 100$.

9.4 LAGRANGE MULTIPLIERS

The Lagrange multipliers provide a powerful method for finding optima in multivariable problems involving functional constraints. We have the objective function $U = U_1(x, y, z)$ subject to the functional constraints, $F_1 = F_1(x, y, z)$ and $F_2 = F_2(x, y, z)$. We establish a new function, the Lagrange expression LE.

$$LE = U_1(x, y, z) + Q_1F_1(x, y, z) + Q_2(x, y, z) \tag{9.10}$$

where Q_1 and Q_2 are the Lagrange multipliers. The following conditions must be satisfied at the optimum point:

$$\frac{dLE}{dx} = 0, \quad \frac{dLE}{dy} = 0, \quad \frac{dLE}{dz} = 0, \quad \frac{dLE}{dQ_1} = 0, \quad \frac{dLE}{dQ_2} = 0$$

We will illustrate the application of the Lagrange multipliers and the optimization method with the help of an example taken from Stoker [2].

Example. A total of 300 m length of tubes must be installed in a heat exchanger, in order to provide the necessary heat-transfer surface area. The total dollar cost of the installation includes:

1. The cost of the tubes, \$ 700
2. The cost of the shell = $25D^{2.5}\,L$
3. The cost of the floor space occupied by the heat exchanger = $20DL$,

The spacing of the tubes is such that 20 tubes will fit in a cross-sectional area of 1 m^2 inside the shell. The optimization should determine the diameter D and the length L of the heat exchanger to minimize the purchase cost.

The objective function is made up of three costs, due to shell, tube and floor space:

$$C = 700 + 25D^{2.5}L + 20DL \tag{9.11}$$

Subject to the functional constraint:

$$\frac{\pi D^2 L}{4}\,(20\ \text{tubes/m}^2) = 300\ \text{m} \tag{9.12}$$

$$5\pi D^2 L = 300$$

$$F_1 = L - \frac{300}{5\pi D^2}$$

The Lagrange expression is:

$$LE = 700 + 25D^{2.5}L + 20DL + Q\left(L - \frac{300}{5\pi D^2}\right) \tag{9.13}$$

$$\frac{dLE}{dD} = 62.5D^{1.5}L + 20L + 2Q\frac{60}{\pi D^3} = 0 \tag{9.14}$$

$$\frac{dLE}{dD} = 25D^{2.5} + 20D + Q = 0 \tag{9.15}$$

$$\frac{dLE}{dQ} = L - \frac{300}{5\pi D^2} = 0 \tag{9.16}$$

From Eq. (9.16), $L = 60/\pi D^2$, and from Eq. (9.15), $Q = -25D^{2.5} - 20D$. Substituting the value of Q into Eq. (9.14), we get:

$$62.5D^{1.5}\frac{60}{\pi D^2} + 20\frac{60}{\pi D^2} + 2(-25D^{2.5} - 20D)\frac{60}{\pi D^3} = 0$$

$$62.5D^{1.5} + 20 - 50D^{1.5} - 40 = 0$$

$$D^{1.5} = 1.6,\ D = 1.37\ \text{m}$$

Substituting the optimum value of diameter into the functional constraint, we obtain $L = 10.2$ m. The cost for the optimum heat exchanger is \$ 1540.

This example is simple and could be solved by direct substitution and finding the derivative, but the method of Lagrange multipliers is quite general and could be used for a problem with many variables.

9.5 LINEAR PROGRAMMING (SIMPLEX METHOD)

Before solving any linear programming problem, we reduce the problem in the standard form. The major characteristic points of standard form are:

1. Objective function is of the maximization or minimization type.
2. All constraints are expressed as equations.
3. All decision variables are restricted to be non-negative.
4. The right-hand side constant of each constraint is non-negative.

In general, we find that the linear programming problems are not in the standard form.

9.5.1 Inequality Constraints

As mentioned above, the standard form of LP requires all the constraints in equation form, but in real life, these are generally in inequality form. These inequality constraints have to be converted into equations. This can be done by introduction of new variables to represent the slack between the left-hand side and the right-hand side of each inequality. These new variables are called as *slack* or *surplus variables.* For example, consider a constraint:

$$x_1 \leq 8$$

This can be converted into an equation by introducing a slack variable, say x_2, as follows:

$$x_1 + x_2 = 8 \tag{9.17}$$

Here x_2 is non-negative.

To illustrate the use of surplus variables, consider a constraint

$$2x_1 + 3x_2 \geq 10 \tag{9.18}$$

By introducing a surplus variable, say x_3, the above inequality can be expressed as an equation in the following manner:

$$2x_1 + 3x_2 - x_3 = 10 \tag{9.19}$$

The slack and surplus variables are as much a part of the original problem of the linear program.

Example. Convert the given L.P. problem into standard form:

$$\text{Maximize } z = x_1 + 2x_2 \tag{9.20}$$

subject to

$$x_1 + 2x_2 \leq 10$$

$$x_1 + x_2 \geq 1$$

$$x_2 \leq 4$$

$$x_1, x_2 \geq 0$$

Solution

$$z = x_1 + 2x_2 \tag{9.21}$$

subject to

$$x_1 + 2x_2 + x_3 = 10 \tag{9.22}$$

$$x_1 + x_2 - x_4 = 1 \tag{9.23}$$

$$x_2 + x_5 = 4 \tag{9.24}$$

Here, x_3 and x_5 are slack variables and x_4 is a surplus variable.

9.5.2 Simplex Method: Maximization

Data for the problem: Two products x_1 and x_2 are to be produced, each yielding a profit of ₹ 5 per piece and ₹ 3 per piece. The two products are processed in two machines having time as a scarce resource.

Time per piece

	x_1	x_2	*Time (h)*
Machine 1	1	2	8
Machine 2	3	1	7

Determine the optimum values of x_1 and x_2. Formulate this problem as a linear programming problem, assuming that the imaginary products x_3 and x_4 yield profit (loss) of ₹ –1 per piece and ₹ 1 per piece, respectively. Product x_3 requires to be processed exclusively on machine M_1, whereas product x_4 requires to be processed exclusively on machine M_2. Each of the imaginary products x_3 and x_4 takes 1 hour on machine 1 and machine 2, respectively.

Solution. Problem formulation:

Objective function: maximize profit:

$$z = 5x_1 + 3x_2 - 1x_3 + x_4 \tag{9.25}$$

Subject to the time constraints:

$$x_1 + 2x_2 \leq 8 \tag{9.26}$$

$$3x_1 + 1x_2 \leq 7 \tag{9.27}$$

$$x_1, x_2 \geq 0$$

or

$$x_1 + 0.2x_2 + 1x_3 + 0x_4 = 8 \tag{9.28}$$

and

$$3x_1 + 1x_2 + 0x_3 + 1x_4 = 7 \tag{9.29}$$

In the above formulation, x_1 and x_2 are termed *decision variables* and x_3 and x_4, *slack variables.* Objective function: maximize:

$$z = 5x_1 + 3x_2 - x_3 + x_4$$

Subject to:

$$x_1 + 2x_2 + 1x_3 + 0x_4 = 8$$

$$3x_1 + 1x_2 + 0x_3 + 1x_4 = 7$$

***Step* 1.** Put the above equation in a tabular form. We start with slack variables x_3, x_4 in the initial program. With an iterative process, we shall bring decision variables x_1, x_2, in the final program.

TABLE 1

C_B	*Basis*	5	3	–1	1	*Quantity*
		x_1	x_2	x_3	x_4	
–1	x_3	1	2	1	0	8
1	x_4	3	1	0	1	7
		Body matrix		Identity matrix		

In the final table, we want to identity matrix under columns x_1, x_2 when the "Quantity" column will give us optimal values of x_1 and x_2.

***Step* 2.** Add one additional row to Table I to include Net Evaluation Value (NEV) or opportunity cost not to have each column variable in this initial program. For example, NEV for x_1 = profit due to introduction of 1 unit of x_1 = loss due to not making equivalent units of x_3 and x_4.

$$\text{One unit of } x_1 = 1 \text{ unit of } x_3$$
$$= 3 \text{ units of } x_4$$
$$\text{NEV} = 5 - [(-1)(1) + 1\ (3)] = 3$$

The term in the square brackets is characterized by the so-called inner product rule:

TABLEAU 2

C_B	*Basis*	5	3	–1	1	*Quantity*
		x_1	x_2	x_3	x_4	
–1	x_3	1	2	1	0	8
1	x_4	3	1	0	1	7
	NEV *C*	3	4	0	0	

***Step* 3.** Refer Tableau 3. To determine the entering variable in the new program, select the variable with the maximum NEV and to determine the outgoing variable, apply the minimum ratio rule. Ratio 4 in row 1 indicates that 4 units of x_2 can be produced in row 1, whereas a ratio 7 in row 2 indicates that 7 units of x_2 can be produced in row 2. However, a decision to make 7 units of x_2 is not feasible, as it will violate the time capacity of row 1. Thus we select lower ratio 4.

TABLEAU 3

C_B	*Basis*	5	3	–1	1	*Quantity*
		x_1	x_2	x_3	x_4	
–1	x_3	1	2	1	0	8 8/2 = 4
1	x_4	3	1	0	1	7
	NEV	3	4	0	0	

The entering variable is x_2, because its NEV (4) is maximum and the quantity of x_2 which is feasible is 4 as given by the ratio in row 1. This makes row 1 as the key row and variable x_3 of row 1 as the outgoing variable.

***Step* 4.**

TABLEAU 4

C_B	*Basis*	5	3	–1	1	*Quantity*	
		x_1	x_2	x_3	x_4		
3	x_2	1/2	1	1/2	0	4	8
1	x_4	5/2	0	– 1/2	1	3	6/5
	NEV *C*	3	–4	–2	0		

The entered variable x_2 is written in the new Tableau 4. Next we achieve $\begin{bmatrix} 1 \\ 0 \end{bmatrix}$ matrix under x_2 in Tableau 4. For this purpose, row 1 of Tableau 3 is divided by key number 2 and the corresponding values are entered as shown above. To achieve 0 in row 2, in column x_2, each element of key row of Tableau 3 is multiplied by (–1/2) and added to each element of row 2 of Tableau 3 columnwise. The row operation is very similar to the elimination procedure used in simultaneous equations.

To make the calculation for row 2 of Tableau 4 clearer, we refer to Tableau 3 and obtain the result:

–1/2 (1,	2,	1,	0,	8)	
+ (3,	1,	0,	1,	7)	
= (5/2,	0,	–1/2,	1,	3)	row 2 of Tableau 4

The result is displayed in Tableau 4.

***Step* 5.** Referring to Tableau 4, the incoming variable for this step is x_1 and the outgoing variable is x_4.

TABLEAU 5

C_B	*Basis*	x_1	x_2	x_3	x_4	*Quantity*
3	x_2	0	1	3/5	–1/5	17/8
5	x_1	1	0	–1/5	2/5	6/5
	NEV	0	0	–9/5	–2/5	

Identity Matrix

As in step 4, the value 1 has to be achieved in x_1 column, by dividing each element of row 2 of Tableau 5 by 5/2. Zero is achieved by multiplying row 2 by (–1/5) and adding each corresponding element columnwise to row 1 of Tableau 5.

Result: An identity matrix is achieved for decision variables and the final answer is x_2 = 17/5, x_1 = 6/5.

9.6 GEOMETRIC PROGRAMMING [3]

Geometric programming is a nonlinear optimization method gaining wide acceptance in engineering design. It is particularly useful when the objective function is the sum of a number of polynomial terms. An example would be an expression such as:

$$U = x_1x_2 + 5x_2 + 12/\sqrt{x_2} + 3.4x_1^3 \tag{9.30}$$

A polynomial expression in which all the terms are positive is called a *polynomial.*

The geometric programming method is best understood through an example. Consider the insulation example in Section 9.2, where the objective function is given by:

$$U = 120x + \frac{150,000}{x^4} \tag{9.31}$$

Total cost = insulation cost + fuel cost

This is an objective function with two terms, T and a variable N. By definition, the degree of difficulty is $T = (N + 1) = 2 - 2 = 0$. We can rewrite the objective function in the standard form:

$$U = u_1 + u_2 = C_1x_1^a + C_2x_2^a \tag{9.32}$$

$$u_1 = 120x, \qquad u_2 = \frac{150,000}{x^4}$$

where,

$$C_1 = 120,\ C_2 = 150,000$$

$$a_1 = 1,\ a_2 = -4$$

The approach in geometric programming is as follows:

1. Write down the function to be minimized in the form of arithmetic mean (AM) by inspection.
2. Write down the geometric mean (GM) corresponding to the above arithmetic mean.
3. Write down the conditions which result in a maxima of the geometric mean. These conditions automatically define the conditions for the minima of the original function AM:

$$U = 120x + 150,000x^{-4}$$

$$\text{AM form of } U = w_1(120x/w_1) + w_2(150,000x^{-4}/w_2)$$

The corresponding geometric mean is:

$$(120x/w_1)^{w1} + (150,000x^{-4}/w_2)^{w2}$$

$$GM = \left(\frac{120}{w_1}\right)^{w_1}\left(\frac{50,000}{w_2}\right)^{w_2}\left(\frac{x}{w_1}\right)^{w_1}\left(\frac{x^{-4}}{w_2}\right)^{w_2} \tag{9.33}$$

The maxima of GM will occur when the middle term becomes 1, i.e., when the exponent of x becomes zero. Thus

$$\text{in } x^{w_1-4w_2},\ \text{the exponent, } w_1 - 4w_2 = 0.$$

Also, $w_1 + w_2 = 1$ (sum of weightage factors which should be 1).
On solving, we get $w_1 = 4/5$ and $w_2 = 1/5$.

$$(\text{GM})_{\text{max}} = (\text{AM})_{\text{min}} = x^{4/5}\left(\frac{120}{4/5}\right)^{4/5}\left(\frac{150,000}{1/5}\right)^{1/5}\left(\frac{1}{x^4}\right)^{1/5}$$

$$= 150^{4/5}\ (750,000^{1/5})\ (x^{4/5})\ (x^{-4/5})$$

$$= 55.06(14.96)\ (1) = 824 \tag{9.34}$$

Also,

$$(120x/w_1) = (150,000x^{-4}/w_2)$$

or

$$\frac{120x}{4/5} = \frac{150,000x^{-4}}{1/5}$$

$$x^5 = 5000$$

Therefore,

$$x = 5.49$$

We note that w_1 is the weighting function that expresses what fraction $u * 1$ is of the total U*.

The objective function is the sum of the insulation cost, u_1, and the fuel cost, u_2. The insulation cost is four-fifths of the minimum total cost; the fuel cost is one-fifth. If the cost of insulation is increased from $120x$ to $200x$, the total cost at the optimum would be higher and the optimum thickness of insulation would be less but the fraction of the total cost contributed by the insulation would be the same. This is so because the relative fraction of the cost is determined by the exponents of x. Thus, when costs are constantly changing (rising!), the distribution of costs among various cost drivers remains constant, so long as the functional cost relation remains unchanged.

Example. Consider now an example with three variables, taken from Wilde [3]. We wish to design a rectangular box to haul V ft³ of material each load. The objective function is:

$$V = \frac{40}{LWH} + 10LW + 20LH + 40HW \tag{9.35}$$

$$U = U_1 + U_2 + U_3 + U_4$$

where the first term is the cost of transporting a load and the other three terms are the costs of material and labour in building the bottom sides and ends of the box. This is a problem with zero degrees of difficulty because $T - (N + 1) - 4 - (3 + 1) = 0$.

By inspection,

$$AM = w_1\left(\frac{40}{(w_1)LWH}\right) + w_2\left(\frac{10LW}{w_2}\right) + w_3\left(\frac{20LH}{w_3}\right) + w_4\left(\frac{40HW}{w_4}\right)$$

$$(GM) = \left(\frac{40}{w_1}\right)^{w_1}\left(\frac{10}{w_2}\right)^{w_2}\left(\frac{20}{w_3}\right)^{w_3}\left(\frac{40}{w_4}\right)^{w_4}(L^{-w_1+w_2+w_3}W^{-w_1+w_3-w_4}H^{-w_1+w_3+w_4})$$

and

$$w_1 + w_2 + w_3 + w_4 = 1$$

$$L: -w_1 + w_2 + w_3 = 0$$

$$H: -w_1 + w_3 + w_4 = 0$$

$$W: -w_1 + w_2 + w_4 = 0$$

which results in $w_1 = 2/5$; $w_2 = w_3 = w_4 = 1/5$.

$$(\text{GM})_{\max} = \left(\frac{40}{2/5}\right)^{2/5}\left(\frac{10}{1/5}\right)^{1/5}\left(\frac{20}{1/5}\right)^{1/5}\left(\frac{40}{1/5}\right)^{1/5}$$

$$= 5(20^2 \times 10 \times 20 \times 40)^{1/5}$$

$$= 5(3{,}200{,}000)^{1/5} = 5(20) = 100$$

$$w_2 = \frac{u_2^*}{U^*} = \frac{10LW}{100} = \frac{1}{5}, \qquad LW = 2$$

$$w_3 = \frac{u_3^*}{U^*} = \frac{20LH}{100} = \frac{1}{5}, \qquad LH = 1$$

$$w_4 = \frac{u_4^*}{U^*} = \frac{40HW}{100} = \frac{1}{5}, \qquad HW = \frac{1}{2}$$

Therefore, to achieve a minimum cost of $ 100 per load, the optimum dimensions of the box should be $L = 2$, $W = 1$ and $H = 1/2$.

An important aspect of geometric programming is that, when the problem has zero degrees of difficulty, the solution is obtained with a set of linear equations in W_1. If the problem had been solved with calculus, it would have required the solution of simultaneous nonlinear equations. Thus, when the degree of difficulty is zero, geometric programming is an efficient optimization tool.

Many realistic design problems have at least one degree of difficulty. One approach to a solution is the technique called condensation. We can convert the gravel box problem to a problem with one degree of difficulty, if we add runners to the box to make it a gravel sled. The cost of runners is 10 per unit length, and hence the objective function becomes:

$$U' = U + 10L = \frac{40}{LWH} + 10LW + 20LH + 40HW + 10L \tag{9.36}$$

We see that

$$T - (N + 1) = 5 - (3 + 1) = 1$$

The cost of this new design is 100 + 10(2) = 120. We wish to find a new minimum by changing the values of L, W and H. The technique of condensation combines two of the terms, so as to reduce the problem to one or zero degree of difficulty. In selecting the terms to combine, we pick terms with exponents that are not very different. In this case, the second and fifth terms are:

$$t_2 + t_5 \geq \left(\frac{10LW}{1/2}\right)^{1/2}\left(\frac{10L}{1/2}\right)^{1/2} = 20LW^{1/2} \tag{9.37}$$

where we have used equal weighting factors for each term.

The resulting objective function is:

$$U' = \frac{40}{LWH} + 20LW^{1/2} + 20LH + 40HW \tag{9.38}$$

which is a posynomial with zero degree of difficulty.

$$U^* = \left(\frac{40}{w_1}\right)^{w_1}\left(\frac{20}{w_2}\right)^{w_2}\left(\frac{20}{w_3}\right)^{w_3}\left(\frac{40}{w_4}\right)^{w_4}$$

and

$$w_1 + w_2 + w_3 + w_4 = 1$$

$$L: -w_1 + w_2 + w_3 = 0$$

$$W: -w_1 + 1/2w_2 + w_4 = 0$$

$$H: -w_1 + w_3 + w_4 = 0$$

which result in

$$w_1 = 3/8, \quad w_2 = 2/8, \quad w_3 = 1/8, \quad w_4 = 2/8$$

Therefore,

$$U'^* = \left(\frac{40}{3/8}\right)^{3/8}\left(\frac{20}{2/8}\right)^{2/8}\left(\frac{20}{1/8}\right)^{1/8}\left(\frac{40}{2/8}\right)^{2/8}$$

$$= \left[\left(\frac{320}{3}\right)^3 (80^2)(160)(160^2)\right]^{1/8} = 115$$

Other techniques that can be used, when the degree of difficulty is not zero, are partial invariance and dual geometric programming. These can be referred to from any textbook on Operations Research.

9.7 JOHNSON'S METHOD OF OPTIMUM DESIGN

A method of optimum design was developed by Johnson [4] in the early seventies. This method is unique in the following respects:

1. A number of possible solutions can be generated.
2. Realistic solutions are obtained because constraints are imposed on the objective function.
3. The objective function could be either minimum weight or minimum cost. Constraints such as maximum permissible stress, available space for the part, etc. can be imposed.

The method of optimum design (MOD) is illustrated with an example.

Example. A tensile rod of circular cross-section is to be designed with minimum weight as objective function.

Data:

$$\text{Load to be transmitted} = 10{,}000 \text{ kg}$$

$$\text{Length of rod: } L_{min} = 250 \text{ cm}$$

$$L_{max} = 300 \text{ cm}$$

Due to space limitation, the maximum diameter of the rod is

$$d_{max} = 1.2 \text{ cm}$$

$$\text{Factor of safety SF} = 1.2$$

The data on (density/yield stress), i.e., ρ/σ_y are tabulated as follows:

Material	ρ/σ_y	$\rho(\text{kg/cm}^3)$
Titanium alloy	0.5×10^{-6}	1.608
Aluminium alloy	0.56×16^{-6}	1.045
Steel	0.57×16^{-6}	2.76
Magnesium alloy	0.80×10^{-6}	0.742
Cast phenolic	2.0×10^{-6}	0.67

Solution

(a)

$$\text{Weight } W_{win} = (\pi/4)d^2 \rho l_{min} \tag{9.39}$$

$$\sigma_y = \frac{P(\text{SF})}{A} = \frac{P(\text{SF})}{\left(\frac{\pi}{4}\right)d^2} \tag{9.40}$$

(b) Eliminating $(\pi/4)d^2$ from Eq. (9.39),

$$W_{min} = P(\text{SF})\ L_{min}\ (\rho/\sigma_y) \tag{9.41}$$

The minimum values of W_2, W_3, W_1, W_4, W_5 are, 1.5, 1.68, 1.71, 2.4, 6 kg, respectively.

(c) From Eq. (9.39), taking the logarithm of both the sides, we get:

$$\log W = \log(\pi/4)\ L_{\min} + 2 \log d + \log \rho \tag{9.42}$$

The linear graphs between log W and log d are as shown in Figure 9.2. The points corresponding to $(W_1)_{\min}$, $(W_2)_{\min}$ ..., $(W_5)_{\min}$ are located on the straight lines. The constraint of d = 1.2 is superimposed on the graph as a vertical line parallel to the Y-axis. Among the various designs, steel rod with weight W_1 qualifies the constraint.

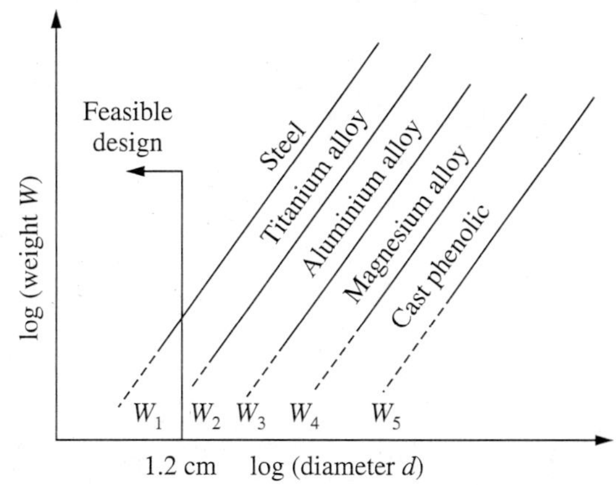

FIGURE 9.2 Log-log plot between diameter (d) and weight W of tensile bar.

If the constraint on space is removed, the lightest design is offered by titanium alloy, with weight W_2 = 1.5 kg.

REVIEW QUESTIONS

1. What is meant by optimal design? Is it feasible design? Or does it have an objective function subject to constraints? Give an example. Sec. 9.1; P 248
2. Give Siddal's classification of design approaches. Sec. 9.2; P 249, 250
3. Explain classical optimization by calculus approach.

Problem. A strut is subject to a tensile force of P 20 kN. The value of σ_t = 100 N/mm^2. If the material cost is ₹ 30/kg and the metal cutting cost per surface is ₹ 10/mm^2, calculate the section dimensions for cost minimization. The strut length is 800 mm. Assume density of the material ρ = 8000 kg/m^3.

Solution Cost of production C_{total} = Material cost + Machining cost

$$= C_m \times whl\rho + 2\ell(b + h)C_c \tag{i}$$

Now
$$\sigma_t = P/wh \tag{ii}$$

Eliminating h from Eq. (i)

$$C = C_m \cdot l\rho w \times \frac{P}{\sigma_t w} + 2\ell C_c\left(w + \frac{P}{w\sigma_t}\right)$$

$$\text{Putting } \frac{C_m \ell \rho P}{\sigma_t} = \text{Constant} = S$$

Differentiating C with respect to w:

$$\frac{\partial C}{\partial w} = 0 + 2\ell C_c\left(w + \frac{P}{w\sigma_t}\right) \quad \text{(iii)}$$

$$\therefore \quad w = \sqrt{\frac{P}{\sigma_t}} = \sqrt{\frac{20,000}{100}} = 14.14 \text{ mm} \quad \text{(iv)}$$

$$\text{Now} \quad h = \frac{P}{w \times \sigma_t} \quad \text{(v)}$$

Substituting $w = \sqrt{P/\sigma_t}$ from Eq. (iv) in (v), we have

$$h = \sqrt{\frac{P}{\frac{P}{\sigma_t} \times \sigma_t}}$$

$$\therefore \quad h = \sqrt{\frac{P}{\sigma_t}}$$

$$= \sqrt{\frac{20,000}{100}} = 14.14 \text{ mm}$$

Thus, the optimum section of the strut is square and $h = w \approx 14.14$.

4. How geometric programming is utilized to arrive at the dimension of a rectangular box? P 258
5. What is Johnson's method of optimal design? Illustrate with an example. Sec. 9.7; P 260–261
6. What is meant by reliability based design? A cable has standard deviation of mean strength (μ_s) as 5%. In a crane, the dynamic load has 20% standard deviation from the mean load μ. Calculate factor of safety for 99.9% reliability. Also calculate mean strength of the cable for lifting a load of 1000 kg, of the cable (Figure 9.3).

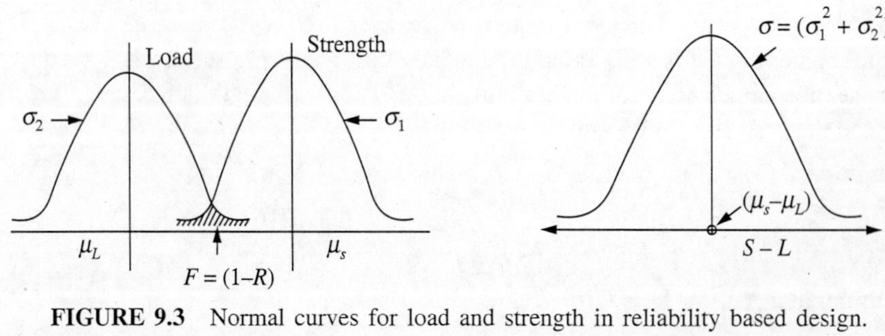

FIGURE 9.3 Normal curves for load and strength in reliability based design.

Solution As shown in Figure 9.3, μ_s is mean strength of material with standard deviation σ_1 and μ_2 is mean load with S.D. σ_2.

$\therefore$ $(S - L)$ is a normal variate with mean $(\mu_s - \mu_L)$ and S.D. $(\sigma_1^2 + \sigma_2^2)^{1/2}$

Thus
$$Z = \frac{(S - L) - (\mu_S - \mu_L)}{(\sigma_1^2 + \sigma_2^2)^{1/2}}$$

In the limiting case, for no failure $S = L$, i.e. $(S - L) = 0$

$\therefore$
$$Z = \frac{(\mu_S - \mu_L)}{(\sigma_1^2 + \sigma_2^2)^{1/2}}$$

$$\text{Factor of safety (FS)} = \left(\frac{\mu_S}{\mu_L}\right)$$

Dividing numerator and denominator by μ_L, we have

$$Z = \frac{\text{FS} - 1}{\left[(\text{FS})^2\left(\frac{\sigma_1}{\mu_S}\right)^2 + \left(\frac{\sigma_2}{\mu_L}\right)^2\right]^{1/2}}$$

It is given that

$$\frac{\sigma_1}{\mu_S} = 0.5 \text{ and } \frac{\sigma_1}{\mu_S} = 0.2,\ R = 99.9\%$$

From standard normal tables, $Z = 3.08$

Substituting the above values : $3.08 = \dfrac{\text{FS} - 1}{\left[(\text{FS})^2(0.05)^2 + (0.2)^2\right]^{1/2}}$

The value of FS = 1.67

Conclusion. The cable should have mean strength of 1670 kg to lift a load of 1000 kg with factor of safety 1.67 and 99.9% reliability.

REFERENCES

[1] Siddal, J.L., Optimization Criteria in Design, Transactions of ASME; *Journal of Machine Design*, 101, 674–81, 1979.

[2] Stoker, W.F., *Optimal Design of Thermal Systems*, McGraw-Hill, New York, 1980.

[3] Wilde, D.J., *Globally Optimum Designs*, Wiley Interscience, New York, 1978.

[4] Johnson, R.C., *Optimum Design of Mechanical Elements*, Wiley Interscience, New York, 1980.

Chapter 10

Economic Factors Influencing Design

In this chapter, we shall discuss a number of topics not directly related to the function of a product but, nevertheless, are important to the success of the product. The cost of the product is one such factor, in comparing alternative designs.

First, we shall introduce some basic notions of value engineering, which deal with the relationship between performance and cost. A product may have undesirable effects, such as accidents, failures and environmental damage, the absence of which increases the value of the product indirectly. We shall study the safety and reliability requirements of a product and their relationship. In the end, break-even analysis, which is an important tool of economics, is discussed along with break-even chart and profit-volume chart.

The main objective of this chapter is to show how product design is influenced by various economic factors. Technology and engineering represent alternatives only, which can be used, if required. What is actually done is governed by economic factors.

10.1 PRODUCT VALUE

Value Engineering (VE) is a very important subject and is dealt with, in detail, in Chapter 12. In this section, we introduce the notion of value. For instance, if small pastries sell for ₹ 70, per dozen and large pastries sell for ₹ 85, per dozen, which kind of pastry has a better value? We must reduce the pastries to a common base, in order to compare them rationally. Suppose that each large pastry weighs 2 oz and each small pastry weighs 1.7 oz, then the value of small party is 0.291 oz/₹. Thus, the small pastry has a better value!

In the design of a typing machine, for example, the following options are available: electric type, manual, and tabulator. Let the speed be chosen to quantify performance. Hypothetical costs and values are shown in Table 10.1. The basic manual typewriter has a value of 1.5 word/min per rupee. Those options with a value greater than 1 are more desirable than the basic version. Those options

TABLE 10.1 Analyzing values of typewriter options

	Speed (word/min)	Cost, ₹ (× 00)	Value (word/min/₹)
Electric	50	50	1
Manual additional	30	20	1.5
Tabulator additional	5	2	2.5

with a value less than 1 cannot be justified, on the basis of typing speed only. As the table shows, the tabulator has the best value. Of course, a broader view of performance includes low noise, tidiness of type and appearance, convenience of the typewriter, and other intangible aspects of value.

Functional requirements. It is true that, in order to do exactly what is needed without wasting effort, one must be able to state one's objective clearly and precisely. The definition of a function in value engineering and product design is rather unusual. Value and performance are sought from an abstract and conceptual approach, without implying any particular mathematical model or physical quantity. As an example, let us examine the bicycle tail light. Its function may be described in a primitive need statement as: improve safety, draw attention, or illuminate bicycle. The three descriptions tend towards increasing the safety of a bicycle, but they involve different degrees of attraction. "Illuminate bicycle" is the most exact description, but it implies the use of light bulbs and limits the scope of the solution. "Drawing attention" may allow the use of sound, motion, glare, flags, reflectors, bright paint, etc. "Improve safety" may suggest the construction of special bicycle paths or the use of helmets or bumpers. If an engineer is brought into the design of a tail light, he might reduce cost, by using cheaper materials and easier manufacturing methods. Optimization may lead to a better lens angle and, hence visibility. The abstract analysis of a function can bring out totally different ideas. For this reason, function definition in value engineering can be considered as a technique to identify the problem. Most other engineering methods are problem-solving methods, in which the problems are intuitively assumed. In value engineering, emphasis is laid on analyzing the function, and not on the hardware that performs the function.

Many products have a variety of functions. There is usually a principal function and a host of secondary functions. To define a function means to find out what the consumer wants the product to do. In this sense, value analysis is related to marketing research. Consumer testing and ratings have been used regarding the taste of different drinks and riding comfort of automobiles.

After a function is defined or measured, the value is obtained by dividing the function by the cost. At this time, the engineer should seriously consider all the alternatives that could perform the function. There are several questions that may help:

1. How does the product meet the function?
2. Which features of the product do not contribute to the function?
3. What else can do the job?
4. Can an additional component or a change in material improve the performance?

10.2 DESIGN FOR SAFETY, RELIABILITY AND ENVIRONMENTAL CONSIDERATIONS

Safety, reliability and ecology are important considerations in design. These factors add extra cost to the product, or the production process, and they put an additional burden on the designer. Safe, reliable and ecologically sound products will enrich society and win acceptance in the long run.

Safety is a very important consideration in product design. Whether the people paying for the accidents are the consumers, the distributors, the manufacturers or the insurance companies, it is the consumer who suffers. An unreliable machine may result in the termination of service or it may result in an accident. A machine that has a short useful life is uneconomical. Therefore, reliability is also good economics.

Product design, from the point of view of environment, is vital. Pollution of air, water and soil is a means of saving money by abusing and exploiting the environment. A polluted environment is a source of discomfort and is harmful to human beings and animals. Yet, zero pollution is too heavy a burden for most industries. If the cost of a product has to include the cost of all the pollution control, probably the price would be beyond the reach of the common man. So, we have to tolerate some damage to the environment, for our short-term well being. Consider automobiles as an example. With pollution control devices, they have a higher initial cost and lower fuel mileage. Some cars even suffer in performance and reliability.

10.2.1 Design for Safety

Besides the explicit warranty which a manufacturer supplies to the consumer, the former is also committed to an implied guarantee of safety to the user. If the user suffers from an accident during the normal usage of a product, he would expect compensation from the manufacturer. There are many conditional safety standards for products:

1. As safe as they can possibly be
2. Safe, according to industry-wide standards
3. Safe, if used in the manner and situations specified in the instructions
4. Safe for a child who may behave impulsively

Engineers and designers are concerned about the legal aspects of safety. Often, decisions in court involve judgments, not obvious to the designer. Moreover, the enforcement of laws and the interpretation of constitutional rights vary from one country to another, and may change with public awareness. The information given here presents a general outline for designers. In most countries, specific details are available from government agencies, for instance, in USA from agencies such as the National Highway Traffic Safety Administration (NHTSA), Food and Drug Administration (FDA), Consumer Product Safety Commission (CPSC), and the Occupational Safety and Health Administration (OSHA), under the Department of Labour.

Reducing the responsibility of the manufacturer, by specifying narrow situations and particular procedures, does not always work. In court, the user is often not responsible, for not following the minute details included in the instructions. It all depends on how reasonable and obvious the instructions are. Products are required to function in real-life situations, allowing for human error as permitted by ergonomic factors. Real-life conditions may include power failure, poor maintenance, accidental overheating, and a corrosive environment. Human errors include slight ignorance, negligence and abuse. Though instructions do not exclude responsibility on the part of the manufacturer, clear and explicit warnings are often the best defence. Whenever possible, safety warnings should be placed on the product. Crucial warnings are sometimes included as part of advertising.

Quality assurance is aimed at removing faulty designs, miscalculations and inherent defects. The decision by quality assurance often necessitates design and drawing changes. Quality control curbs manufacturing defects and variations in quality such as assembly defect. The methods of quality control include visual inspection, non-destructive testing, and random sampling. Date coding, batch coding and serial numbering are widely used in high-volume consumer products. In case a defect is noticed after the product leaves the company, the date and batch codes will enable traceability.

10.2.2 Mistake Proofing

A defect-free or fail-safe design is one that will not lead to accidents, in the case of functional failures. Since a functional repair is much cheaper than a damage from an accident, fail-safe designs are recognized as superior and necessary in many products. Take power steering as an example. Most power steering systems are designed so that the wheels can still be controlled without the power booster. If the fluid pump fails or the engine stalls, the car can still be steered.

Large soft drink bottles have foam plastic coatings for increased safety. Uncoated bottles are known to explode upon impact, under the pressure of carbon dioxide. Photographic flash bulbs also have plastic coatings, to prevent shattering due to sudden heating. Automobile windshields are engineered to prevent shattering.

The clothing or hair of an employee may be caught between rollers and dragged into a machine. Slip clutches, shear pins, fuses, circuit breakers and pressure-relief valves are used to prevent overloads. If a bicycle is jammed under an electric garage door (or an elevator door), a slip clutch can prevent uncontrolled large forces that might damage both the bicycle and the garage door.

Interlocks are used to prevent human errors. For instance, the keys for a car with an automatic transmission cannot be removed unless the shift is in 'park' position. In some cars with manual transmissions, the engine cannot be started unless the clutch is depressed. Safety switches are installed at the bottom of some portable heating appliances. If an appliance, such as an electric room heater, is accidentally tipped over, it would automatically shut off. All of these are introduced because humans do not function perfectly, and the design parameters invariably take into account the human errors.

Emergency equipment in buildings has greatly improved, during the last decade, due to fire hazards. Many buildings are equipped with emergency exits, emergency lights, which have self-contained battery packs, fire doors, smoke detectors and automatic sprinkling systems. Emergency elevators are also installed in some tall buildings.

10.2.3 Factor of Safety and Reliability

Factor of safety is the ratio of strength to load. Strength is a characteristic of the machine component: the maximum force it can bear. The load is the actual force imparted to the component, when the machine operates. The strength of a component may vary, because of uncertainties in material properties and finishing processes. The load may exceed the estimated load, when the machine is missed. A factor of safety larger than 1 leaves a margin for an overload, and for the discrepancy between what is calculated and what actually happens. Sometimes, a factor of safety as large as 10 is used, because the estimation of strength and load is extremely inaccurate. Since excess strength results in material wastage, a better engineering practice is to obtain an accurate evaluation of the strength and the load, and to use a small factor of safety.

Reliability is a statistical estimate of the probability of success. Such an evaluation includes the statistical distribution of strength and load. The concept of product reliability is largely associated with warranty and liability. A good practice is to make the product 99.9% reliable, and to replace the one out of 1000, which is defective. The probability of failure is the complement of reliability: $(F = 1 - R)$.

Reliability is a statistical evaluation to the real situation. The factor of safety is a simple ratio to aid design. A product with a safety factor of 1, 5, 2 or 4 presumably will not fail.

For components in series, the one with the smallest factor of safety determines the overall safety factor. As the load increases, the weakest component always fails first; thus, the weakest component acts like a fuse to protect the stronger components. Therefore, the safety factor of the system equals the smallest safety factor of the components. Reliability is a random occurrence, where the cause of failure may not be the load. The reliability R of components in series is the product of all component reliabilities:

$$R = R_1 \cdot R_2 \cdot R_3 \cdot R_4 \cdot R_5 \cdots R_n \tag{10.1}$$

where R_1, R_2, R_3, ... are the reliabilities of the components and n is the total number of components in series. Occasionally, a more dependable component will fail, before a less dependable component. The addition of more components in series will decrease the overall reliability. Figure 10.1 illustrates the safety and reliability factor of a series system.

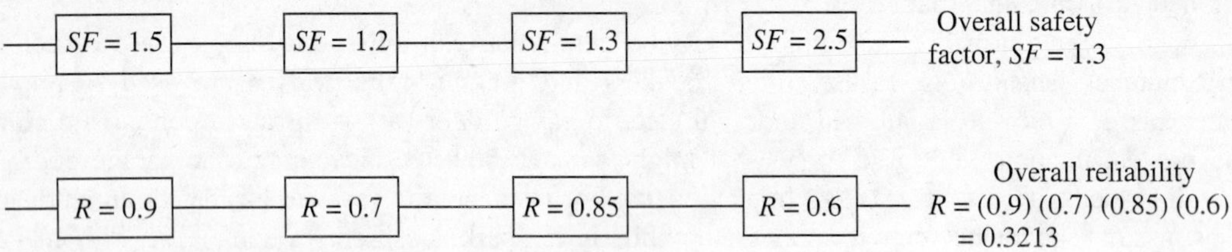

FIGURE 10.1 Safety factor and reliability.

The evaluation of the reliability of components in parallel is rather different. A parallel system will fail only if all the redundant components fail. The probability of system failure F is the product of the individual component's probability of failure. Reliability is the complement of the chance of failure. A system with 10% probability of failure has a reliability of 90%. Suppose we have a system of n components in parallel. Let F_i and R_i be the probability of failure and the reliability of the component, respectively. Also, let F and R be the probability of failure and reliability of the system. Then

$$F_i = 1 - R_i$$

$$R = (1 - F) = (1 - F_1 \times F_2 \times F_3 \times \cdots \times F_n)$$

$$R = 1 - [(1 - R_1)\,(1 - R_2)\,(1 - R_3)(1 - R_4) \cdots (1 - R_n)] \tag{10.2}$$

To illustrate the dramatic difference in the overall reliabilities of a series system and a parallel system (see Figure 10.2), let us connect four components of $R_1 = 0.8$ in two different ways:

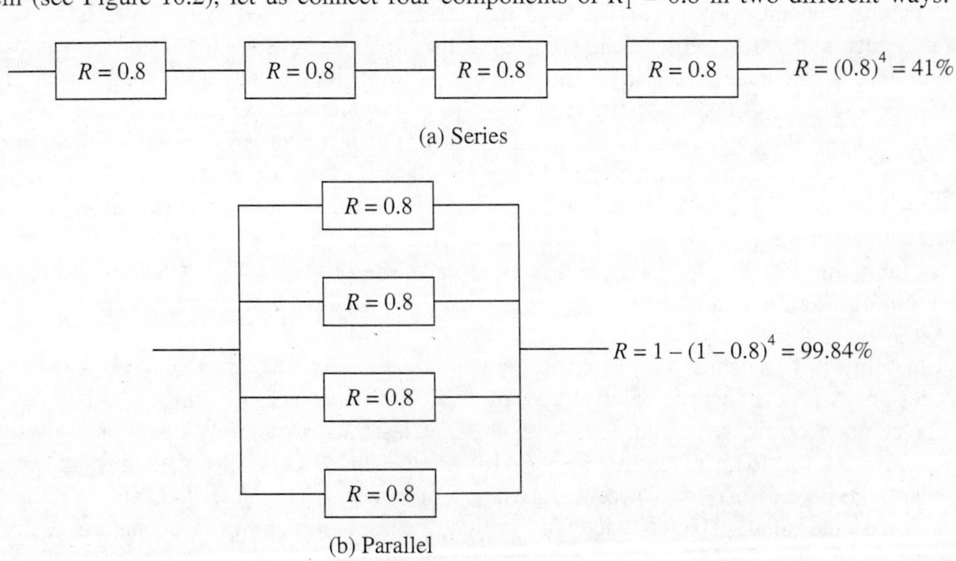

FIGURE 10.2 Series and parallel configurations in reliability.

1. If connected in series, the overall reliability is

$$R = (R_1)^4 = (0.8)^4 = 0.41$$

2. If connected in parallel, the overall reliability is

$$R = 1 - (1 - R_1)^4 = 1 - (0.2)^4 = 0.998.$$

10.2.4 Design for Reliability

The safety factor and reliability can be converted from one to another, if statistical data are available about the load and the strength.

A tensile bar with a mean strength μ_s would have a frequency distribution as shown in Figure 10.3. If the load is very precise, the probability of failure is represented by the area to the left of the load line. The difference between the strength and the load, which is the safety margin $(\mu_s - \mu_L)$ can be expressed as x times the standard deviation of the strength, σ_s, as illustrated in Figure 10.4(a). If $x = 0$, the load line coincides with the mean strength, μ_s, and there would be 50% failure. If x is very large, the load line would be at the extreme left of the strength distribution. Thus, the failure rate would be very small. Table 10.2 shows x vs. reliability. This relationship being a characteristic of the assumed normal distribution, the safely factor can be related to x and σ_s/μ_s (the ratio of standard deviation of strength to mean strength) by the following equation:

$$\text{Safety factor SF} = \frac{\text{strength}}{\text{load}} = (\mu_s/\mu_L) = \frac{1}{1 - x(\sigma_s/\mu_s)} \tag{10.3}$$

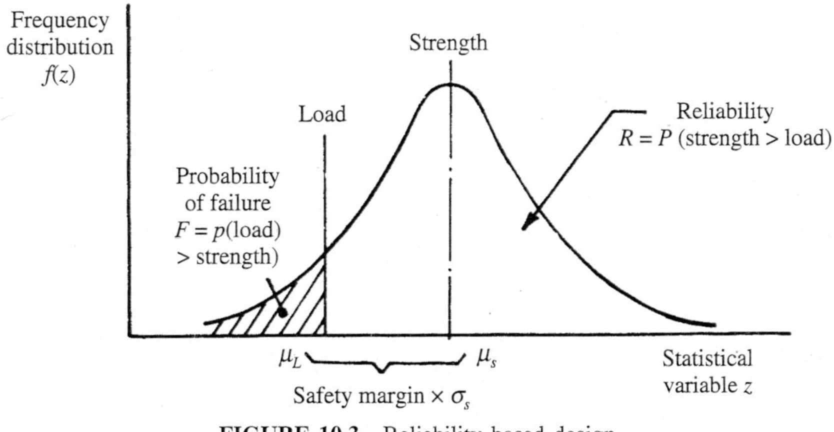

FIGURE 10.3 Reliability based design.

Using the value of 0.08 for (σ_s/μ_s), in Eq. (10.3), the values of reliability and corresponding SF values are tabulated. In actual machines the load may vary, and there should be a wider safety margin. The combined effect of load and strength distributions is shown in Figure 10.4(b).

The conversion from reliability to safety factor depends on the following factors:

z = interference variable
σ_s = standard deviation of strength
σ_1 = standard deviation of load
μ_s = mean strength
μ_L = mean load

TABLE 10.2 Tabulation of reliabilities and safety factors for static loading (deterministic)

$R = P(z > \mu_L)$ (per cent)	(*based on* $\sigma_s/\mu_s = 0.08$)	*SF*
50	0	1
80	0.84	1.07
90	1.28	1.114
95	1.645	1.15
99	2.33	1.23
99.9	3.08	1.327
99.99	3.7	1.42

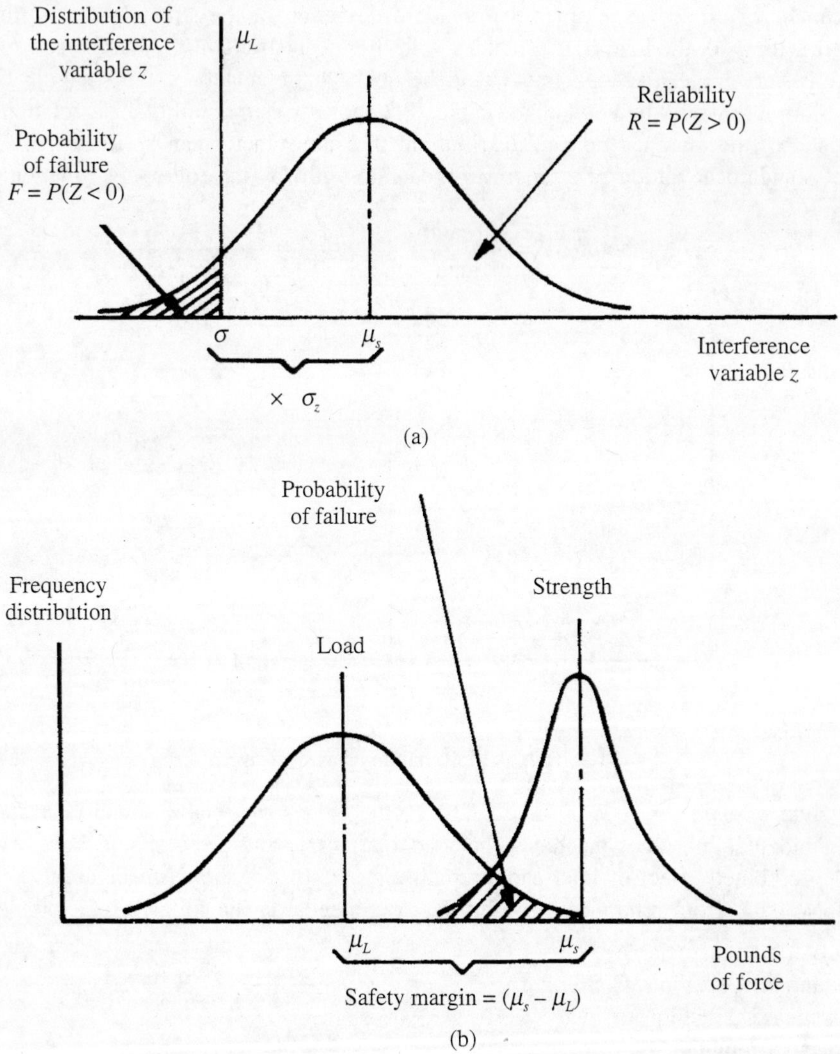

FIGURE 10.4 Interference (shaded area) between strength and load in reliability based design.

Given (σ_s/μ_s) and (σ_L/μ_s), the following formula (given the safety factor) can be derived:

$$\text{SF} = \frac{1}{1 - x\sqrt{(\sigma_s/\mu_s)^2 + (\sigma_L/\mu_L)^2}} \tag{10.4}$$

Since, in practice, variation in material property is most frequent and loading is static, Eq. (10.4) reduces to Eq. (10.3), and hence the calculation in Table 10.2 is based on Eq. (10.3).

10.3 MANUFACTURING OPERATIONS IN RELATION TO DESIGN

Figure 10.5 shows the price structure of a modern manufacturing company. The selling price can be decided on the basis of indirect cost, direct cost, tax, and profit. The direct cost includes the costs of material, labour and equipment. As a means to simplify cost estimation, normal ratios are established between the material cost, the direct cost and the selling price. A typical ratio is:

Material cost : Direct cost : Selling price = 1 : 3 : 9

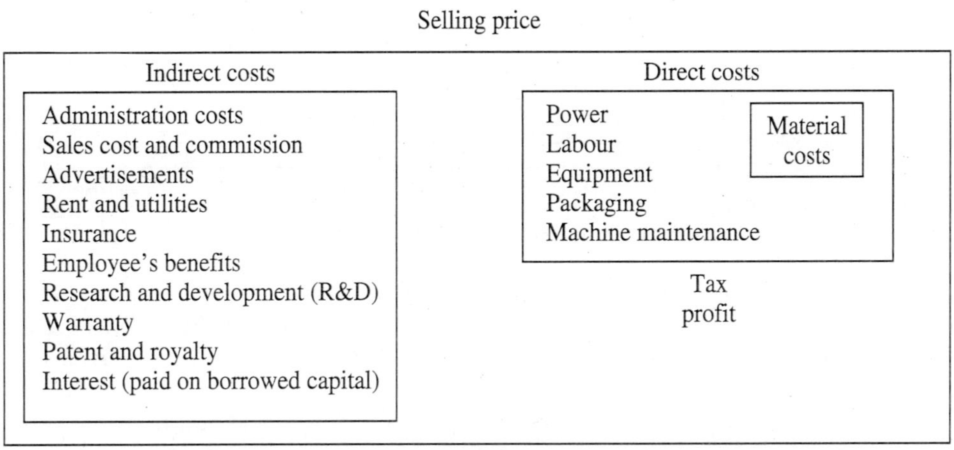

FIGURE 10.5 The price structure of a modern manufacturing company.

In this case a product, whose raw material costs are ₹ 10 and manufacturing costs ₹ 30, should have a selling price of ₹ 90 in order to make a reasonable profit.

This nominal cost formula works well, as long as we have a narrow group of similar products. Using the above ratios, plastic products that cost about ₹ 60/kg in terms of raw material would have a selling price of ₹ 540, Because of this cascading effect, a 10 per cent saving in the material cost could lead to 90% reduction in the selling price. The nominal ratio may be quite different for a completely different industry. The food packaging industry may have a ratio of 1 : 2 : 5. The ratio between the selling price and the direct cost is sometimes called the operational overhead ratio. This ratio describes the efficiency and the risks involved during the operation. Typically, for companies specialized in advanced technology or speculative products, the operational overhead ratios are high.

Since we are mostly interested in the design of a product, we will concentrate on the direct cost of a product.

$$\text{Direct cost} = \text{material} + \text{power} + \text{labour} + \text{equipment} \tag{10.5}$$

Usually, the costs of material, power and labour are directly proportional to the production volume. The equipment cost is independent of the production volume. The cost component which is proportional to the production volume is a variable cost.

$$\text{Total cost} = \text{variable cost} \times \text{quantity} + \text{fixed cost} \tag{10.6}$$

$$\text{Unit cost} = \text{variable cost} + \frac{\text{fixed cost}}{\text{quantity}} \tag{10.7}$$

Equations (10.6) and (10.7) are illustrated in Figure 10.6. A mathematical model for break-even analysis is discussed in detail in Section 10.6.

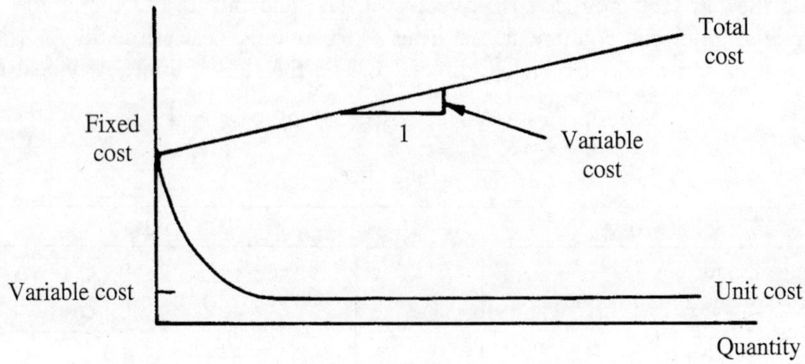

FIGURE 10.6 Graph showing cost of production vs. quantity.

The distinction between the fixed and the variable costs is critical in the profit-volume relationship. Sometimes it is difficult to distinguish between variable and fixed costs. Take labour, for example. If workers can be hired and laid off from day-to-day to match the production need, the labour cost would be a variable cost. If recruiting efforts or labour unions prevent the change of personnel, with the fluctuation of production need, the labour cost would be a fixed cost. Some cost accountants prefer to use accounting data from the history of the company, to determine whether the cost of one constituent varies with the company's sales.

A question that frequently arises is, whether a company should purchase components or make them in-house. Figure 10.7 shows a simplified model, which assumes that the unit purchase price is constant (independent of quantity). There is a break-even quantity, at which a manufactured item is comparable in cost to purchased item. For quantities larger than the break-even quantity, it is more economical to manufacture the parts and vice versa. If the unit purchase price decreases with quantity, the break-even point will be at a larger quantity, causing the break-even point in Figure 10.7 to be shifted to the right. The question of make or buy should consider some other factors too. There is more control over the quality of a component, if it is manufactured in-house. There is less shipping, receiving and inspecting. The company would also be building up its strength, instead of possibly helping a potential competitor. On the other hand, a company cannot just get into a new business and expect to make money. It might be better to stay in one's speciality and leave unrelated jobs to others. Purchased items are cheaper for small quantities, because there is no capital tied up. Purchasing parts from outside also has the advantage of flexibility. Assume that a component of a car is purchased. The drop in sales of one motor company and an increase in the sales of another would not influence this component supplier, as long as the total automobile

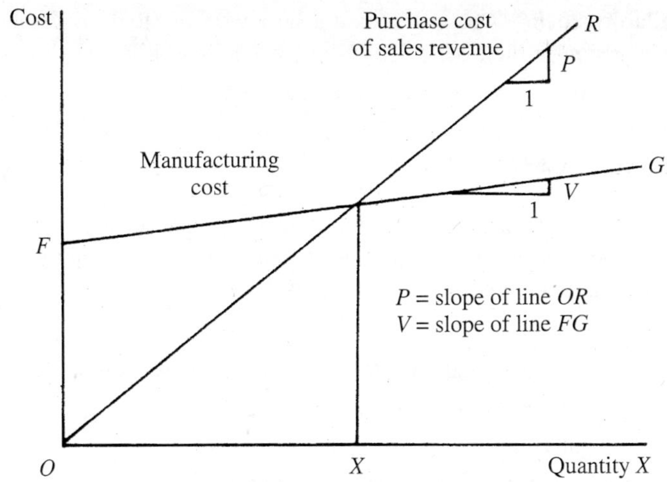

FIGURE 10.7 Break-even chart.

market is constant. The component supplier can make the part cheaper than an individual motor company because of a larger volume. The motor company is hurt less by the fluctuation in sales because of less capital investment.

The following list includes 10 aspects of manufacturing operations that will lower the cost of products if they are considered in the design stage.

(i) **Standardization.** A product should be so designed that it should comprise standard parts, components and subassemblies. This will ensure interchangeability and competitiveness in world market place. Several industries today are trying to get ISO 9000 certification to be able to enter world market.

(ii) **Modular design.** As distinguished from integral design, modular design offers advantages of product assortment through various combinations of modules by assembly operation. Examples of modularity are filing cabinets, meroform furniture, and using 18 threaded holes in a ball for erecting structures of various designs.

(iii) **Group technology.** In manufacturing, grouping products according to similar processes in cellular GT cells is a great advantage in reduced material handling.

(iv) **Automation.** Low-cost automation can speed up production and is cost effective too.

(v) **Assembly line.** Flow shop type lines with dedicated machines arranged in U-type offer the best utilization of machines.

(vi) **Specifications and tolerances.** Tolerance T is the permissible variation in a dimension specified by the designer. Suitable machines with process capability P should be chosen so that the C_p or relative precision index of 2 (approx.) is achieved.

(vii) **Compact design.** Compact design conserves material, reduces storage and transportation costs, and is user friendly.

(viii) **Foldable, stackable design.** It reduces storage space and transportation cost. Sometimes, customer-assembled design can be offered.

(ix) **Complementary product planning.** Firms dealing in seasonal products should widen their scope through multiple product strategies.

(x) **Use of available stock.** Designers should be aware of stock available even in the junk market, for inclusion in their designs. Value engineering philosophy aims at *function* rather than part drawing.

10.4 ECONOMIC ANALYSIS

Economic analysis is the key to management decision, in product design policy. Having obtained sufficient information about customer's requirement and market potentialities, and detailed study about the functional, operational and quality aspects of the proposed product, the economic analysis can be evaluated by seeking an answer to the following questions:

1. What capital expenditure is required for manufacturing the new product?
2. What total production costs per piece are envisaged?
3. What is the reasonable margin of profit that can be expected?
4. Do the price (= total costs + profit) and the features of the product render it competitive in the market?
5. In what numbers is the product expected to be sold?

Here, the interdependence of variables should be clearly emphasized. Not one single question in this list can be isolated and solved independently of the others. The economic analysis is, in fact, a cyclic and repetitive procedure. Each question is weighed in the light of the answer and the data provided by the preceding question, and all the answers are checked when their turn comes again to be re-evaluated in the following cycles, until a state of equilibrium is reached and no further modifications to these answers are required.

10.5 PROFIT AND COMPETITIVENESS

The measure of competitiveness of the product corresponds to the portion of the market it succeeds in capturing. This is largely dependent on the value the customer is prepared to put on the product and on the ratio of this value to the price. As customer assessment of value is not uniform everywhere, but subject to preference of features and performance or taste, the ratio of value to price varies with customers. A state of equilibrium is formed, in which the market is divided between different preferences. This equilibrium may change if the ratio of value of price of the product becomes more favourable, when compared with other products. Thus, the product increases its share of the market and becomes more competitive. Such an equilibrium is shown in Figure 10.8, where the total costs include set-up, materials, overheads, storage and distribution. The total profit is determined by the margin of profit per unit and by the sales volume. If the organization seeks to increase its profit, it can try one of the following methods.

(i) **Pure pricing strategy.** Increase the sales price, but leave the total production to costs unchanged. If such a course does not affect the sales volume, the total profit will be proportional to the increase in the margin of profit per unit. Such an increase, however, can upset the market equilibrium unfavourably, in that the ratio of customers' value of the product to its price will deteriorate and the products of competitors will become more attractive. The market may shrink, and the total profit may, in extreme cases, fall below its original level.

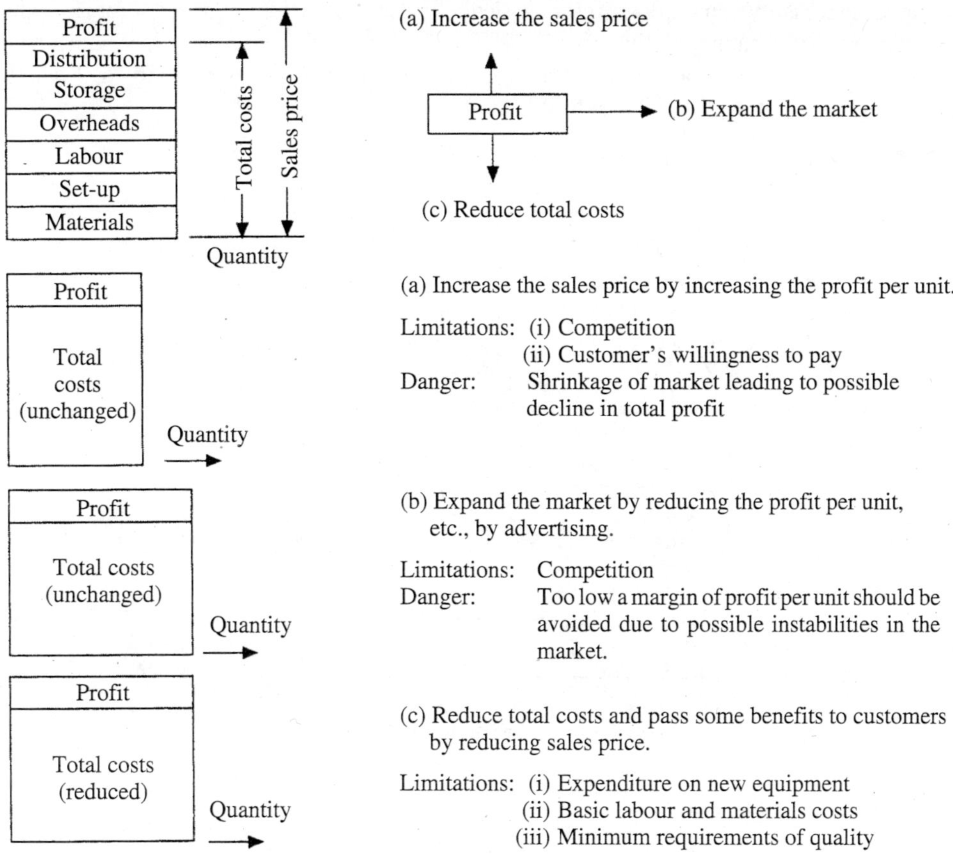

FIGURE 10.8 Methods of increasing total profit.

(ii) **Marketing strategy (through design, advertising and pricing).** Leave the total costs unchanged, but try to improve the ratio of value to price, and thus widen the market. This can be done: (i) by producing a better or more attractive product at the same cost, (ii) by launching an intense advertising campaign in order to boost the customer's assessment of the product value, or (iii) by reducing the sales price, at the expense of the margin of profit per unit, in the hope that the market will expand enough to increase total profit. A very marginal profit per unit is, however, undesirable, as it allows little protection from possible fluctuations in the market, and even slight instabilities may turn a small profit into a sizable loss.

(iii) **Reduction of in-house production cost.** Reduce the total production costs and pass some of the benefits to customers in the form of reduced sales price. If both the profit per piece and the size of the market increase, a substantial improvement in total profits will be achieved. This necessitates a continuous search for better methods, better processes, better materials and their utilization, and better management to reduce overheads. There are, however, some limitations to the rate of improvement one can attain, such as basic labour and material costs and limited resources or expenditure on new equipment and machines. However, reducing production costs and thereby expanding the market, while sustaining accepted quality standards, offer a challenge to the production engineer. Probably, the most characteristic feature of this process is that it is both dynamic and continuous that each success is a further advance along the spiral of increasing productivity and standard of living, as illustrated in Figure 10.9.

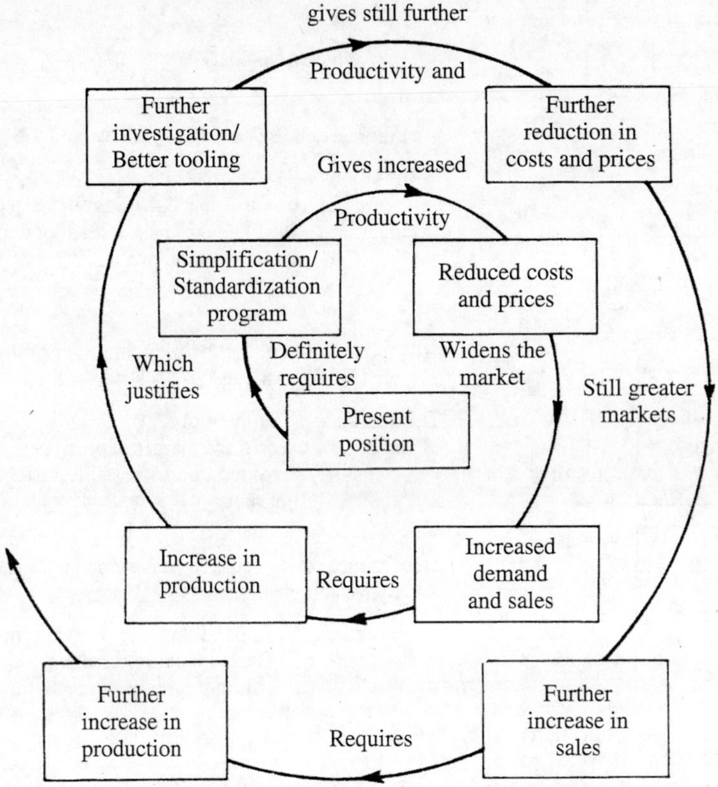

FIGURE 10.9 Spiral of increasing productivity.

10.6 BREAK-EVEN ANALYSIS

Two approaches to break-even analysis are widely used:

1. Conventional break-even chart
2. Profit-volume chart.

10.6.1 Conventional Break-Even Chart Approach

The effect of volume of production on profit is illustrated in Figure 10.10. The line of sales revenue is shown by the straight line bQ, where b is the slope and Q, the sales volume; b is also the sales revenue per piece sold. In the linear model shown in Figure 10.10, the production costs involve the following:

1. Fixed costs F which are independent of the number of pieces produced and include salaries, depreciation of plant and machinery.

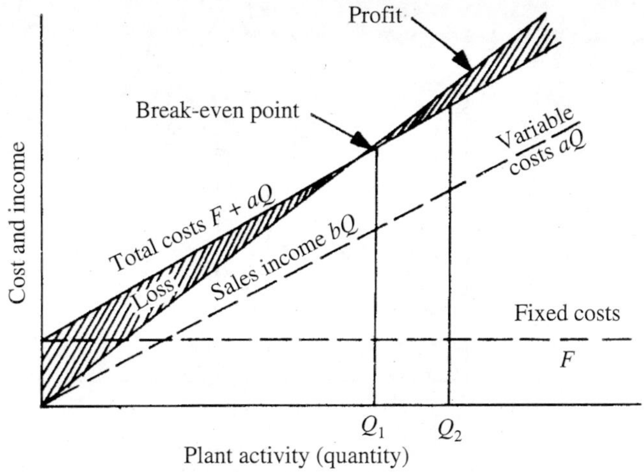

FIGURE 10.10 Break-even chart showing loss and profit zones.

2. Variable costs aQ which consist of direct material costs, labour costs, etc. These vary directly with production volume.

The point of intersection of line representing ($F + aQ$) with line bQ is termed the *break-even* point. The profit to the firm at this point is zero. A firm must produce more pieces than break-even volume Q_1 to make a profit.

Mathematical model for break-even volume. Equating cost ($F + aQ$) with sales revenue bQ results in the following equation:

$$F + aQ_1 = bQ_1$$

Rearranging, we get:

$$Q_1 = \frac{F}{b - a} \tag{10.8}$$

Margin of safety. A plant is operating with a margin of safety (s) if the production volume Q_2 is more than the break-even point (BEP) denoted by Q_1:

$$\text{Margin of safety } (s) = \frac{Q_2 - Q_1}{Q_1} \tag{10.9}$$

A very interesting simplification for margin of safety is as below: As can be seen from Figure 10.11,

$$b(Q_2 - Q_1) = P$$

where P denotes profit. It can be shown that

$$s = \frac{P}{F} \tag{10.10}$$

Thus,

$$Q_2 = Q_1\ (1 + s) = Q_1(1 + P/F) \tag{10.11}$$

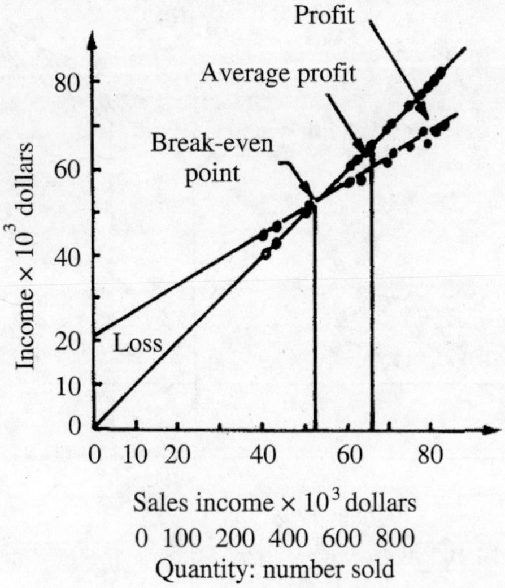

FIGURE 10.11 A monthly break-even chart.

Illustrative example (on break-even chart). Data on sales, total cost, and quantity sold for a firm for 12 months is gathered. Figure 10.12 gives a graphical plot of sales vs. quantity sold.

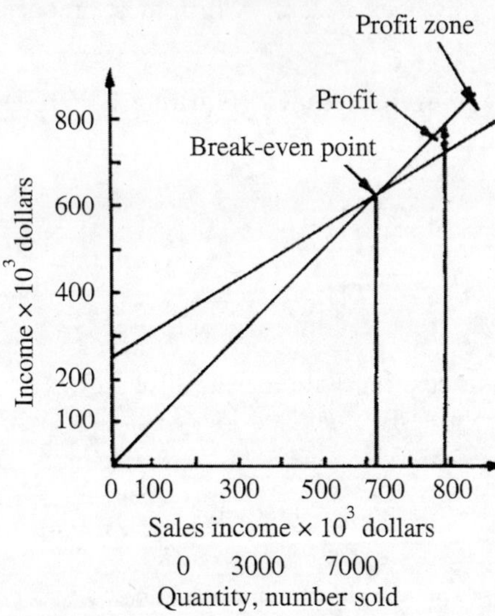

FIGURE 10.12 An annual break-even chart.

Other data are as tabulated below:

	Annual data × 10^3	*Derived monthly data* × 10^3
Quantity sold	7931 pieces	661 pieces
Sales income	793.1 monetary units	66.1 monetary units
Total cost	723.2 monetary units	60.3 monetary units

The fixed cost F on monthly basis is 21×10^3 monetary units. Calculate the BEP and safety margin (s).

Solution

$$a = \frac{C - F}{Q}$$

where,

C = average total costs
F = average fixed costs
Q = average quantity

Then
$$a = \left[\frac{60.3 - 21.0}{661}\right] \times 10^{-3}$$
$$= 59.5 \text{ monetary units/piece}$$
$$b = \frac{S}{Q}$$

where,

S = average sales income

$$Q = \text{average quantity sold} = \frac{66.1 \times 10^3}{661}$$
$$= 100 \text{ monetary units/piece}$$

The BEP is given by

$$Q_1 = \frac{F}{b - a} = \left[\frac{21}{100 - 59.5}\right] \times 10^3 = 520 \text{ pieces}$$

A BEP on annual basis is shown in Figure 10.12, in which break-even occurs at 12 × 520 = 6240 pieces.

$$\text{Margin of safety } s = \frac{P}{F} = \frac{5.83}{21} \times 10^3 = 27.1\%$$

For graphical solutions, Eilon [1] has suggested a simplified technique in which along the x-axis, the sales volume is expressed in monetary units. Thus,

$$a = \frac{C - F}{S} = \frac{(60.3 - 21.0)10^3}{(66.1)10^3} = 0.6$$

$$\text{Slope } b = \frac{S}{S} = 1 \text{ (slope 45°)}$$

10.6.2 Profit-Volume Chart Approach

The profit-volume chart is shown in Figure 10.13, where the firm starts with a negative profit F, being the initial fixed investment. The slope of profit-volume chart is given by ϕ:

$$\phi = \frac{F}{Q_1} \tag{10.12}$$

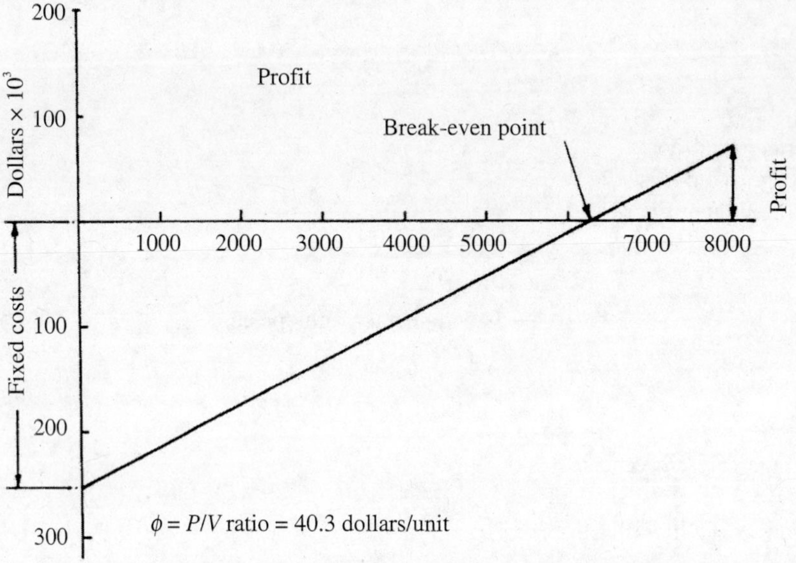

FIGURE 10.13 An annual profit-volume chart.

where Q_1 is the volume of production at the break-even point. Now, since

$$Q_1 = \frac{F}{b - a}$$

we have

$$\phi = \frac{F}{F/(b-a)} = (b - a)$$

For the example considered in Section 10.6.1,

$$\phi = \frac{F}{Q_1} = \frac{252 \times 10^3}{6250} = 40.3 \text{ monetary units/piece}$$

10.6.3 Multiproduct Profit-Volume Chart

For a firm making products *A*, *B* and *C*, a multiproduct profit-volume chart can be plotted as shown in Figure 10.14. Such a chart has the utility of showing whether the product-mix followed by a firm is desirable or not. The BEP and profit for each of the products *A*, *B* and *C* can be displayed on a single chart. A careful study of the profit-volume chart in Figure 10.14 shows that making product *A* alone results in a loss to the firm whereas making products *A* and *B* results in some profit. It is further noted that substantial profits are made by making products *A*, *B* and *C*, as shown in Figure 10.14. Making an equivalent quantity of about 80 units results in sales income of \$32500 and a total profit of \$8000.

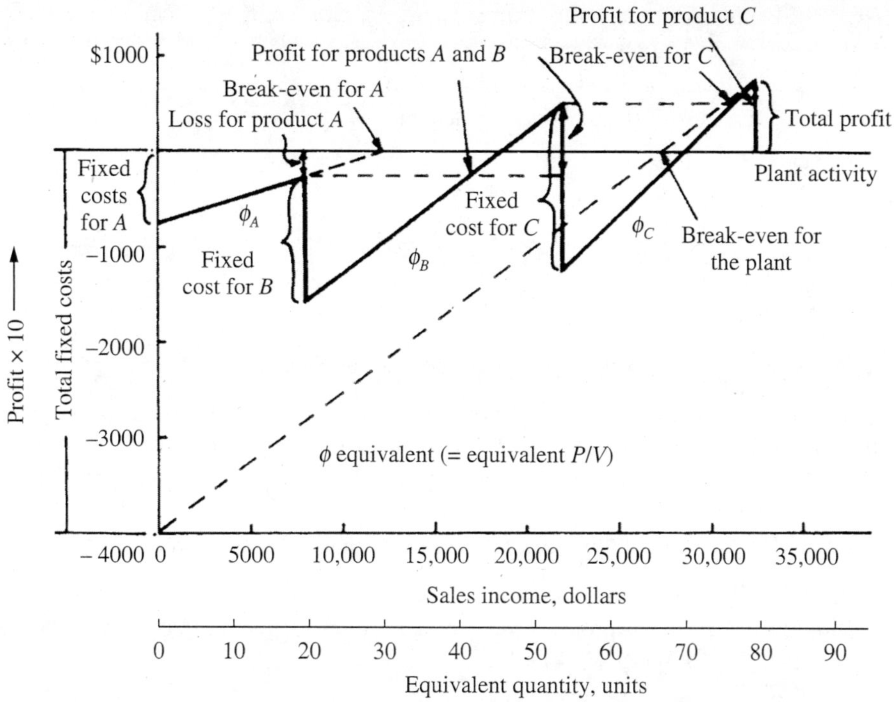

FIGURE 10.14 Multiproduct profit-volume chart.

10.7 ECONOMICS OF A NEW PRODUCT DESIGN (SAMUEL EILON MODEL)

In order to survive in the competitive atmosphere of industrial world, new products or modification of existing products is essential. The mathematical model of profit-volume analysis is a useful tool to determine whether the additional investment of (s) monetary units (due to process change, design change and material change) is desirable or not. If the profit accrued after investing (s) is P_2 and profit before investing this amount is P_1, a comparison between P_2 and P_1 can be done and a decision made.

$$\phi_1 = \frac{P_1 + F}{Q_1}$$

or

$$P_1 = (\phi_1 Q_1 - F) \tag{10.13}$$

where Q_1 is the quantity sold. After investment (s),

$$\phi_2 = \frac{P_2 + F + s}{Q_2}$$

where Q_2 is the quantity sold, or

$$P_2 = \phi_2 Q_2 - F - s \tag{10.14}$$

for the new model. Then

$$\text{Profit difference} = (P_2 - P_1) \geq (\phi_2 Q_2 - \phi_1 Q_1 - s) \leq 0$$

Setting $P_2 - P_1 \geq 0$, we have, after substituting, the relation

$$D = \frac{\phi_1}{\phi_2} = \frac{P/V \text{ ratio for old design}}{P/V \text{ ratio for new design}}, \text{ in equation for } (P_2 - P_1),$$

We finally have

$$\frac{Q_2}{Q_1} \geq \left[1 + \frac{s}{P_1 + F}\right] D \tag{10.15}$$

Equation (10.15) indicates that $D = 1$, Q_2 must be greater than Q_1 to justify investment (s) on design change.

A numerical example is taken up to make the notions clear.

Illustrative example. For a product, the annual fixed cost (F) is 20,000 monetary units. While the annual profit is 4000 and average monthly sales are 82 pieces. A new design is being planned with investment (s) of 8000 to be returned in 2 years. With the new design, the P/V ratio shall increase by 5%.

Calculate the annual sales figure for the new design under two different conditions, as follows:

1. Net profit remains constant
2. In addition to the above profit, a yield of 10% of investment 8000 is to be accrued. (The value s per year is 8000/2 = 4000)

(a) $$\frac{Q_2}{Q_1} \geq \left[1 + \frac{s}{P_1 + F}\right] = \left[1 + \frac{4000}{4000 + 20,000}\right] 0.95 = 1.11$$

Then

$$Q_2 \geq 1.11 Q_1 = 1.11 \times 12 \times 82 = 1092 \text{ pieces}$$

(b) In the first year, 10% of total (s) value of 8000 = 800 is to be added to profit value in the equation, i.e. $P_2 = 4800$.

$$\frac{Q_2}{Q_1} = \frac{P_2 + F + s}{P_1 + F} = \left[\frac{4800 + 20,000 + 4000}{4000 + 20,000}\right] 0.95 = 1.14$$

then $Q_2 = 1.14 \times 12 \times 82 = 1122$ pieces. Thus, the firm should be able to sell at least 1122 pieces to obtain a profit of 4800 monetary units.

REVIEW QUESTIONS

1. What are the courses of action open to management in improving profits? What are the likely hazards linked with each course of action? Sec. 10.5; P 274, 275; Figure 10.8
2. What is a break-even chart? How does it help in arriving at profit or loss corresponding to a certain quantity of production? P 272, 273; Figure 10.7, 10.10; P 276, 277
3. What is a profit–volume chart? Sketch a profit volume chart showing profit (P), break-even quantity Q, fixed cost (F), slope ($b - a$) of the (P/v) line. Sec. 10.6.2
4. How does profit? Volume break-even chart help in determining product-mix of three products A, B, C. Why some firms continue making products giving some loss along with their premier products? Sec. 10.6.3; Figure 10.14

5. Develop a model to determine whether a firm making a profit P_1 should launch a new product yielding a profit P_2 when the additional investment is s. Sec. 10.7; P 281

6. What are the merits of following strategies in affecting production costs? Discuss.

   (a) modular design, (b) group technology, (c) automation, (d) assembly line, (e) compact design, (f) specification and tolerances, (g) foldable and stackable design, and (h) use of available stock. P 273

7. What is meant by spiral of increasing productivity? Figure 10.9; P 273

8. What is the approach to reliability based design? What is the relationship between reliability and factor of safety? Derive a formula linking reliability and factor of safety.
   Sec. 10.2.4; Figure 10.3, 10.4; P 269–271

9. Write in brief about design for safety and mistake proofing. Sec. 10.2, 10.2.1, 10.2.2, 10.2.3

REFERENCE

[1] Eilon, S., *Elements of Production, Planning and Control*, Macmillan, London, 1962; 3rd ed. reprinted by Universal Publishing Corp., Bombay, 1991.

Chapter 11

Human Engineering Considerations in Product Design

11.1 INTRODUCTION

In this chapter we discuss Ergonomics as applied to design. Intensive work in this field has been done by Singleton [1] for WHO, and by McCormic and Sanders [2].

Ergonomics or *human factors engineering* is the science of fitting tasks to man. The word "Ergonomics" is derived from the Greek words *ergon* and *nomos,* meaning "work" and "natural laws", respectively. Ergonomics and human factors engineering are synonymous and cover a very wide field, including the human operator and his working environment. The areas of study covered under human factors engineering are one group comprising Anatomy, Physiology and Psychology, and the other group consisting of engineering sciences such as Physics, Mathematics, Materials Science and Design. Human factors engineering brings together two groups of specialists: those who know about machines and processes, and those who know about human capabilities. Thus, human factors engineering is the link between engineering sciences and social sciences. The role of human factors in product and equipment design assumes importance in three respects:

1. Man, as occupant of space, i.e. to operate a machine, the human operator should have adequate space, as dictated by human body dimensions or anthropometry.
2. Man, as reader of display from the machine. That is, based on the display data, man processes the data and takes action.
3. Man, as one who takes action through operating controls which form a part of the machine.

Thus, man acts as applicator of force and controls the machine. It will be obvious that human engineering in design should consider application of forces and study of displays and controls. These aspects are covered in the subsequent sections.

11.2 HUMAN BEING AS APPLICATOR OF FORCES

Refer to Figures 11.1 and 11.2. Energy is converted into useful work by the human motor system. The body can be regarded as a set of rigid members: the part of the limbs between joints, the main parts of the trunk and head. All these parts are quite heavy in relation to the available forces. Thus, available forces may be wasted in moving the parts of the body. Two consequences follow from this. *First,* action will not be efficient if the direction of force is such that the limb or any other part of the body is moving against the force of gravity. *Second,* the most effective way of generating

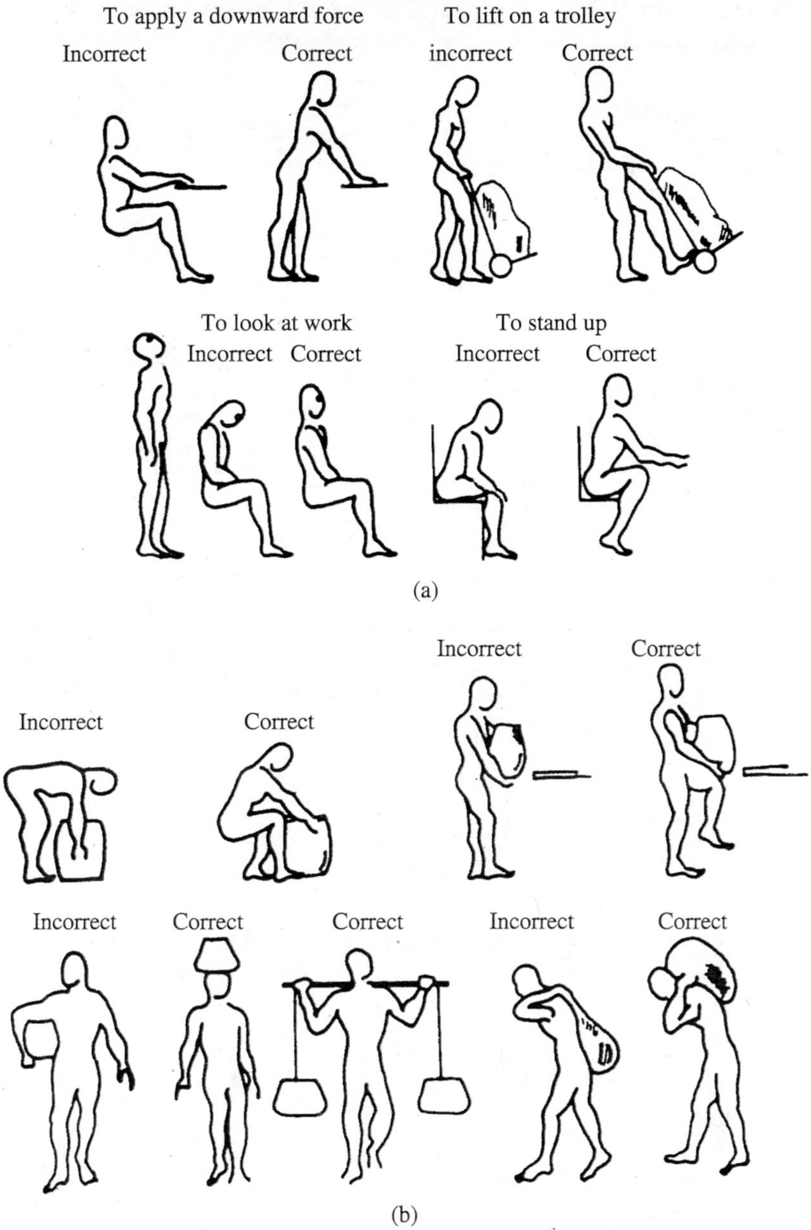

FIGURE 11.1 (a) Aspects of weight distributions, (b) Lifting and carrying.

forces is to use the muscles and joints to get the body in a position such that use of body weight is made to overcome forces. For example, in lifting a weight off the ground, if the body and head are moving upwards against gravity as the weight is lifted, then most of the available force will be wasted within the body. Correspondingly, if a worker is required to exert a downward force, for instance, to fit an object into its surrounding part, then this task might well be accomplished more easily, from a standing rather than a sitting position.

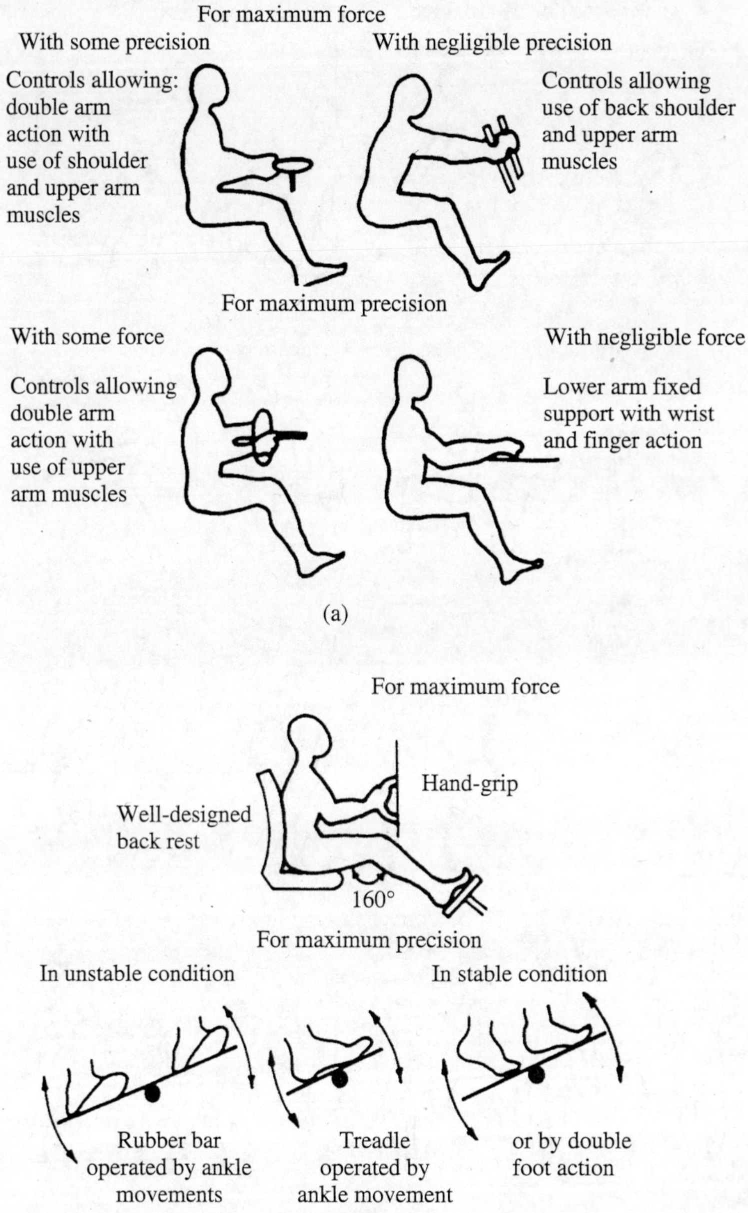

FIGURE 11.2 (a) Use of hand controls and (b) Use of pedals (stable foot rest required).

(i) **Momentum.** One other way in which body masses can be utilized is by the provision of forces from momentum. The force exerted is proportional to the mass of the moving part, as also to the relative velocity of the limb and the object on which the force is to be exerted. Machine operators are trained to use momentum to operate handwheels, etc.

To achieve precision in limb movement, a worker uses two sets of muscles about each joint—those involved in causing the required movement (the agonists) and a complementary group opposing the movement (the antagonists). This is the best way to achieve high precision. Assuming that these two sets of muscles are required, the greatest precision will be achieved when the limbs are in the middle part of their total path of movement.

(ii) **Muscle contraction and energy release.** Economy and spread of effort occur within a muscle. All muscles consist of a large number of fibres and bundles of fibres that can be regarded as motor units. The greater the force, or the faster the movement, the greater will be the number of motor units involved. A slight change in the movement of a particular joint may result in a drastic change in the order, number and identity of motor units involved.

(iii) **Isometric application of forces and isotonic action.** In mechanics, the principle that no work is done unless a force moves its point of application is used. The human operator is certainly capable of work, either by isometric (static) muscle action or by isotonic action, in which there is limb movement. Isometric activity probably is superior in reaction sensitiveness as it is called *kinesthetic feedback.* In kinesthetic feedback, the operator receives more information feedback from the feel of what he is doing than from observing the results of the activity. Isotonic action, in which muscle fibres are moving in relation to each other, facilitates the blood flow and thereby the supply of oxygen and the removal of waste products. Thus, for maximum precision, isometric action is often best, but for maximum power output and for postponing fatigue, isotonic action is superior.

11.3 ANTHROPOMETRY: MAN AS OCCUPANT OF SPACE

Refer to Figures 11.3 and 11.4. The starting point of the design of work spaces must be the dimensions of the people who are going to operate within given spaces. Thus, one of the primary responsibilities of ergonomics is to provide data about body size. Such a study, which is part of the domain of the anatomist, is called *anthropometry.*

The variations between individuals are usually large enough to be important and so the statement of averages is not enough. Ranges are required, but since human dimensions are distributed normally in a statistical manner, there are very few individuals at either extreme. The question, therefore, arises as to what proportion of actual ranges of size should be taken into account in design. For example, most adults are between 1.50 m and 1.85 m tall, but some men exist whose height is as much as 2.05 m. It would clearly be absured to make all doorways at least 2.50 m high, to cater to a few individuals in the total world population.

Anthropometric data are often expressed in the form of 5th, 50th and 95th percentiles. A dimension quoted at 5th-percentile level means that 5% of the population considered are estimated to be smaller than this. Correspondingly, only 5% of the population is larger than the 95th percentile. The range from 5th to 95th percentile covers 90% of the population.

Even when anthropometric data has been gathered, there are problems of data presentation and application. The compilers of the data usually have background in Biology, but the users have a practical industrial or engineering background. It is of little use to the work-place designer to know that the popliteal height is 40 cm, unless this information is presented in such a way that he can appreciate its relevance to the height of seats. This problem of specific terminology can be overcome by the proper use of diagram or manikins. A manikin is a scale model of a human operator, usually in two dimensions only, with swivel points, corresponding to the sites, at which joints permit movement. These can be made for different percentile levels, so that the question of ranges is properly dealt with. Table 11.1 indicates anthropometric data as reported by McCormick [2].

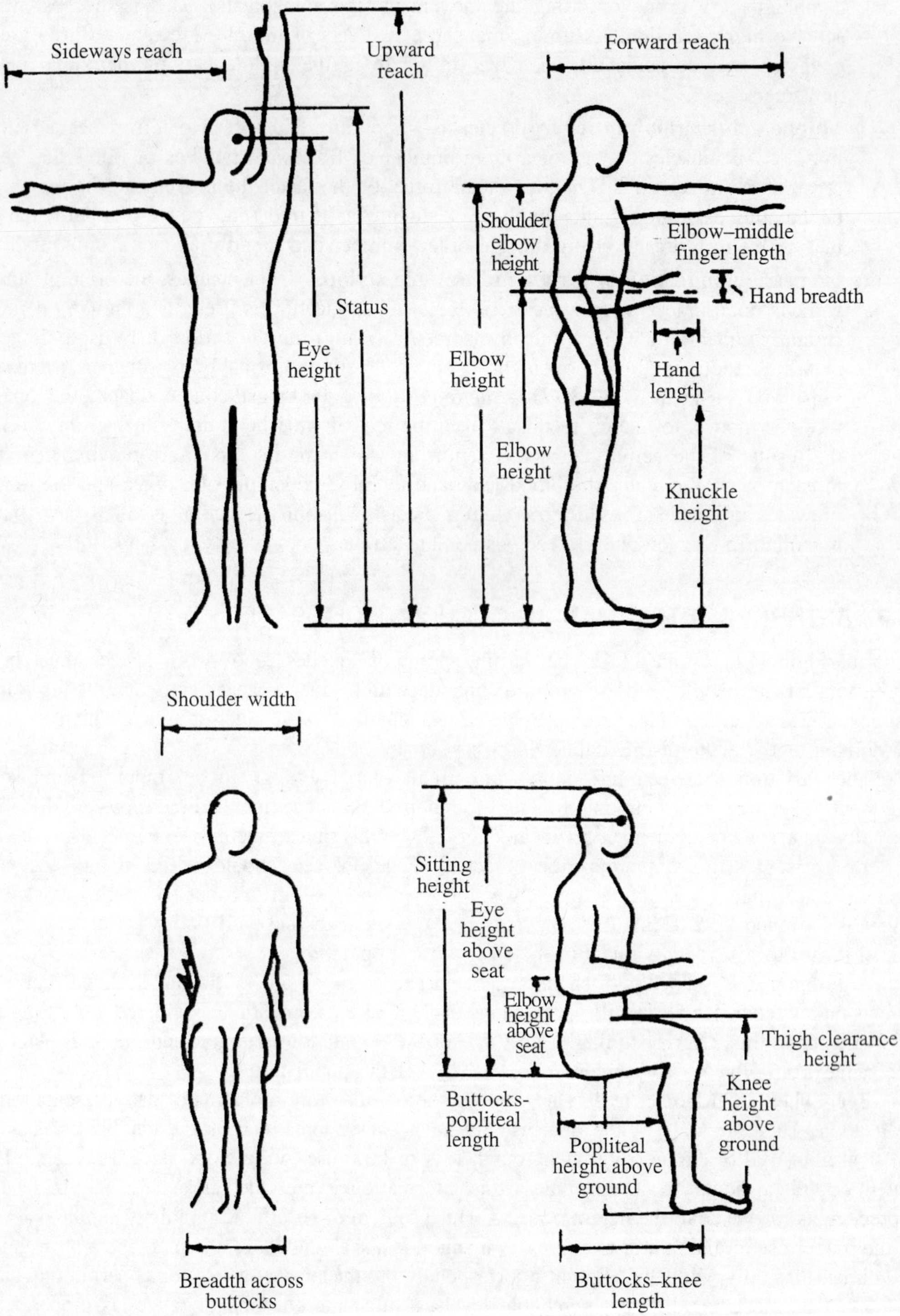

FIGURE 11.3 Body size and posture.

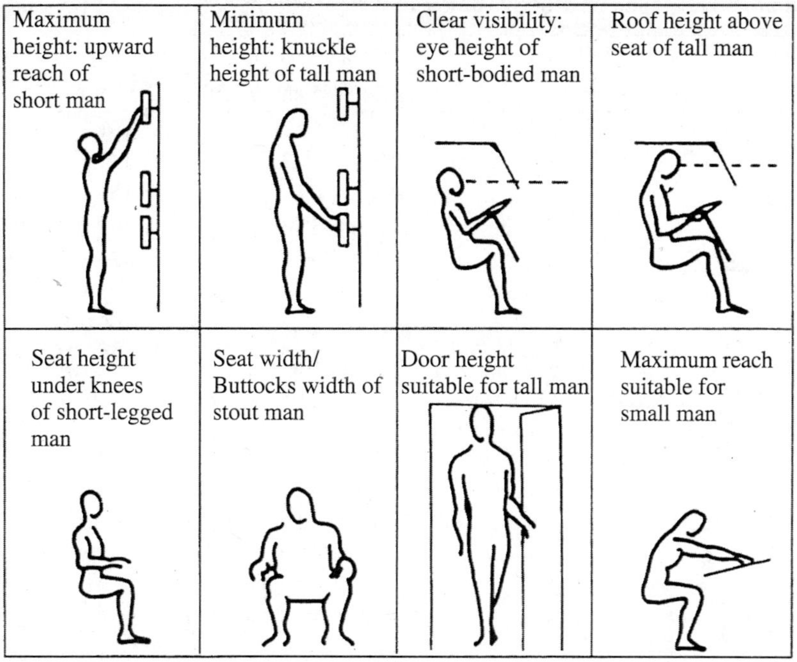

(a)

Body part	Desirable posture	Design implications
All	Small variations of all postures should be possible including movement of inactive parts.	All aspects of work space should allow for these minor changes.
Head and neck	Head should be more or less balanced on shoulders with horizontal line of sight. Extensive, frequent or rapid head movements should be avoided.	Main display element should be at eye height or below. Angular separation of display elements should be limited.
Trunk	More or less vertical with normal spinal curvature to minimize effort of stabilizing musculature. Facilitates breathing and maintaining maximum stability.	Provision of back rest and appropriate location of display and controls.
Upper limb	Upper arm roughly vertical; forearm roughly horizontal wrist such that the palm faces downwards and inwards.	Provision of arm rest and placement of hand controls.
Lower limb	Thigh roughly horizontal; lower leg at obtuse angle to thigh; foot at right angles to lower leg.	Size, height and slope of seat; provision for adjustments and perhaps foot rest; placement of foot controls.

(b)

FIGURE 11.4 (a) Importance of range of body size in design, and (b) Postural aspects of seating.

Table 11.1 Selected body dimensions and weights of US adult civilians

Body dimension	*Sex*	*Dimension (in.)*			*Dimension (cm)*		
		5th	50th	95th	5th	50th	95th
1. Stature (height)	Male	63.7	68.3	72.6	161.8	173.6	184.4
	Female	58.9	63.2	67.4	149.5	160.5	171.3
2. Eye height	Male	59.5	63.9	68.0	151.1	162.4	172.7
	Female	54.4	58.6	62.7	138.3	148.9	159.3
3. Shoulder height	Male	52.1	56.2	60.0	132.3	142.8	152.4
	Female	47.7	51.6	55.9	121.1	131.1	141.9
4. Elbow height	Male	39.4	43.3	46.9	100.0	109.9	119.0
	Female	36.9	39.8	42.8	93.6	101.2	108.8
5. Knuckle height	Male	27.5	29.7	31.7	69.8	75.4	80.4
	Female	25.3	27.6	29.9	64.3	70.2	75.9
6. Height, sitting	Male	33.1	35.7	38.1	84.2	90.6	96.7
	Female	30.9	33.5	35.7	78.6	85.0	90.7
7. Eye height, sitting	Male	28.6	30.9	33.2	72.6	78.6	84.4
	Female	26.6	28.9	30.9	67.5	73.3	78.5
8. Elbow rest height, sitting	Male	7.5	9.6	11.6	19.0	24.3	29.4
	Female	7.1	9.2	11.1	18.1	23.3	28.1
9. Thigh clearance height	Male	4.5	5.7	7.0	11.4	14.4	17.7
	Female	4.2	5.4	6.9	10.6	13.7	17.5
10. Knee height, sitting	Male	19.4	21.4	23.3	49.3	54.3	59.3
	Female	17.8	19.6	21.5	45.2	49.8	54.5
11. Buttock-knee distance, sitting	Male	21.3	23.4	25.3	54.0	59.4	64.2
	Female	20.4	22.4	24.6	51.8	56.9	62.5
12. Popliteal height, sitting	Male	15.4	17.4	19.2	39.2	44.2	48.8
	Female	14.0	15.7	17.4	35.5	39.8	44.3
13. Chest depth	Male	8.4	9.5	10.9	21.4	24.2	27.6
	Female	8.4	9.5	11.7	21.4	24.2	29.7
14. Elbow-elbow breadth	Male	13.8	16.4	19.9	35.0	41.7	50.6
	Female	12.4	15.1	19.3	31.5	38.4	49.1
15. Hip breadth, sitting	Male	12.1	13.9	16.0	30.8	35.4	40.6
	Female	12.3	14.3	17.2	31.2	36.4	43.7
16. Weight (lb and kg)	Male	123.6	162.8	213.6	56.2	74.0	97.1
	Female	101.6	134.4	197.8	46.2	61.1	89.9

Source: Kroemer, et al., Ergonomics: How to design for ease and efficiency, Prentice-Hall, Englewood Cliffs, New Jersey, 1994.

Two techniques for utilizing anthropometry have been developed. The first is to design and present data for a special problem. For example, a chart is available that indicates the area of acceptable centre-line heights for lathes as a function of certain design variables. The task of translating the raw data provided by anthropometrists into a form directly usable by lathe designers has been carried out by an ergonomist who took into account such factors as variations in size of likely user populations and the need to manipulate controls and materials. In this case, the range of application of the data has been reduced, in order to make the data more readily communicable.

The second and a more general technique is to use 'fitting trials'. This is effectively the use of live subjects instead of manikins. In its simplest form, a full-scale model of the workspace is built and various people from the user population try it, and their opinion is taken.

Figure 11.5 illustrates the relationship between human body dimensions and a chair and a table with it.

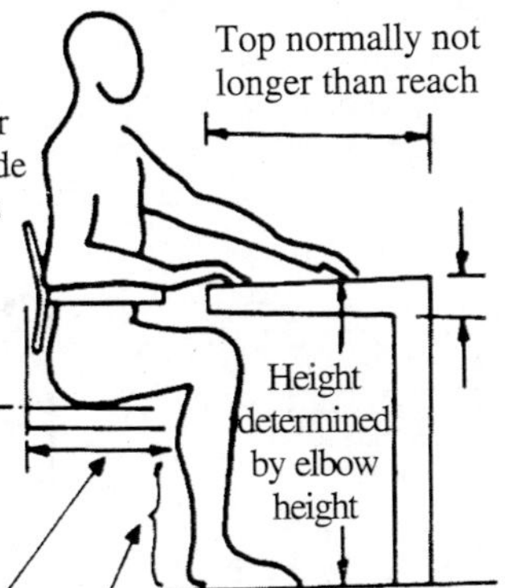

FIGURE 11.5 Seating at the workspace.

11.4 THE DESIGN OF CONTROLS

Refer to Figures 11.6–11.8 for the study of various types of controls. A control is a device that enables an operator to change the state of a mechanism. It converts the output of an operator into the input of a machine. Since controls are pieces of hardware, they are often regarded as parts of a machine, out for design purposes, they can be more effectively considered as connecting links between the machine and the operator.

The following is a list of some controls:

1. Handwheel
2. Crank
3. Thumbwheel
4. Knob
5. Slider
6. Toggle switch
7. Joystick
8. Roller ball
9. Lever
10. Foot pedal
11. Treadle
12. Detent switch
13. Handle

	Use	Special design requirements
	In arrays for rapid selection between alternatives.	To avoid slipping finger and accidental activation.
	For definite, rarely used action involving only choice of two (normally on/off).	To avoid excessive finger pressure or nail damage.
	For more than two and less than ten choices.	To avoid excessive wrist action make total movement less than 180°. Do not use simple circular shape.
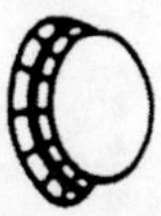	For continuous variables.	Size depends mainly on resistance to motion. Use circular shape with serrated edge.
	When rotated through more than 360° is needed.	Grip handle should turn freely on shaft.
	For higher forces or very definite activity.	Identification of neutral or zero.
	For precise activity involving large angles or rotation.	Identification of particular positions avoid slipping.

(a)

Anatomical			
Which limb?	Which joint?	When used	
		Force	Precision
Hand	Shoulder	High	Low
	Elbow	Medium	Medium
	Wrist/Figner	Low	High
Foot	Ankle	High	Low
	Thigh/Knee	Maximum	Minimum

Psychological	
Identification	Position Size Shape Colour Legend
Selectivity	Position in sequence relative importance Frequency of use

(b)

FIGURE 11.6 (a) Types of control, and (b) Criteria for control positions.

Method		When used
Position	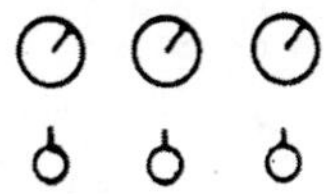	Best placed near to controlled function (mechanical device or dial) provided access is reasonable and high speed is not essential.
Size		Important in relation to high frequency of use (e.g. space bar on typewriter) or in relation to operating force. Size should be increased with required force.
Shape		Useful when controls must be operated without visual attention.
Colour		Useful only as secondary cue or as warning unless there are many controls together. Even so number of colours used should not be more than five.
Legend	Main stand-by	Useful secondary cue. Should not be obscured when control is operated.

(a)

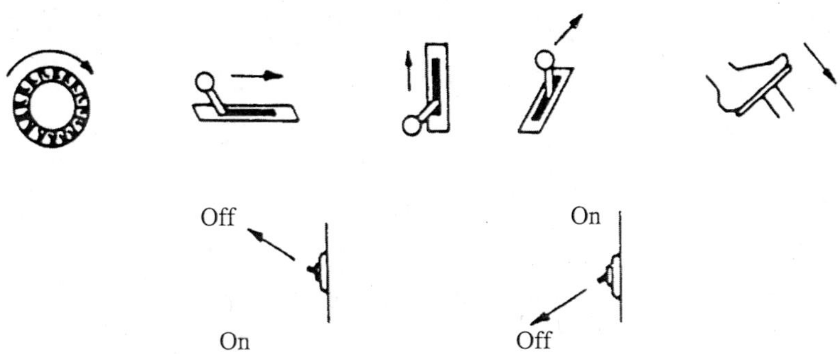

(Arrows indicate direction of movement; standard position of switch indicating "on" or "off" differs from one country to another.

(b)

FIGURE 11.7 (a) Identification of controls, (b) Control stereotypes.

An important problem involves deciding as to which limb is to be used for which purpose. Broadly speaking, foot controls are best for the provision of powerful continuous forces and hand controls are best for speed and precision.

The variety of hand controls is commensurate with the versatility of the hands. The steering wheel is the hand equivalent of the rudder-bar, and has the corresponding advantage of achieving precision by balancing forces between the two hands. It makes possible a wide variety of positions and types of hand-grip and operations by either hand or by both hands, besides providing a large torque. As in the case of the bicycle, had it not been invented as a result of long experience, it would by now have been designed by the ergonomist. The handlebar is a specialized form of steering wheel with a reduced range of possible hand-grips. Cranks are the hand equivalent of rotating pedals,

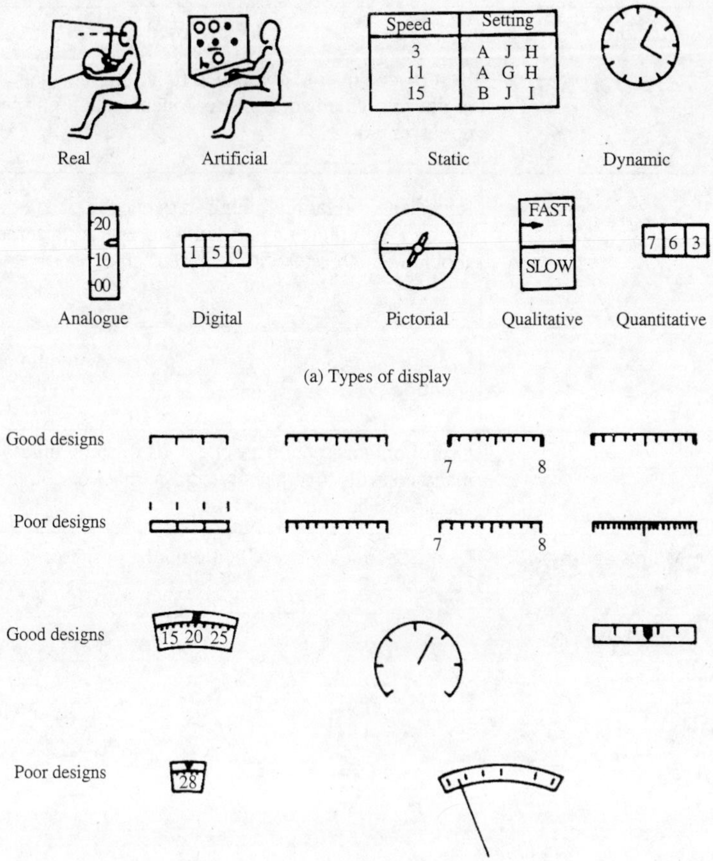

(b) Space patterns

FIGURE 11.8 Design of displays.

and since they are used to generate power, rather than information, it is usually pertinent to ask whether a pedal system might not be superior. The more precise hand controls such as selectors, toggles and buttons pose problems of identification and grouping, rather than of individual design.

Population stereotypes and interaction between man and machine. The simple aspect of this relationship is in the direction of motion of controls. Particular populations have certain habitual expectations about how a control or a display or a control/display relationship should behave. These are called *population stereotypes*. The main control stereotypes are that an increase (e.g. in volume, speed, voltage, and height) should be effected by a clockwise rotation, a movement downwards for a pedal and upwards or to the right or away from the body for a hand level. These seem to be common to most populations.

11.5 THE DESIGN OF DISPLAYS

Refer to Figures 11.8 and 11.9. A display is a part of the environment of the operator that provides him with information relevant to the task he is performing. Common examples of display are: (a) display on a TV screen, (b) dial type display with pointer, and (c) simple mechanical display, e.g., an advertisement card on a visiting card.

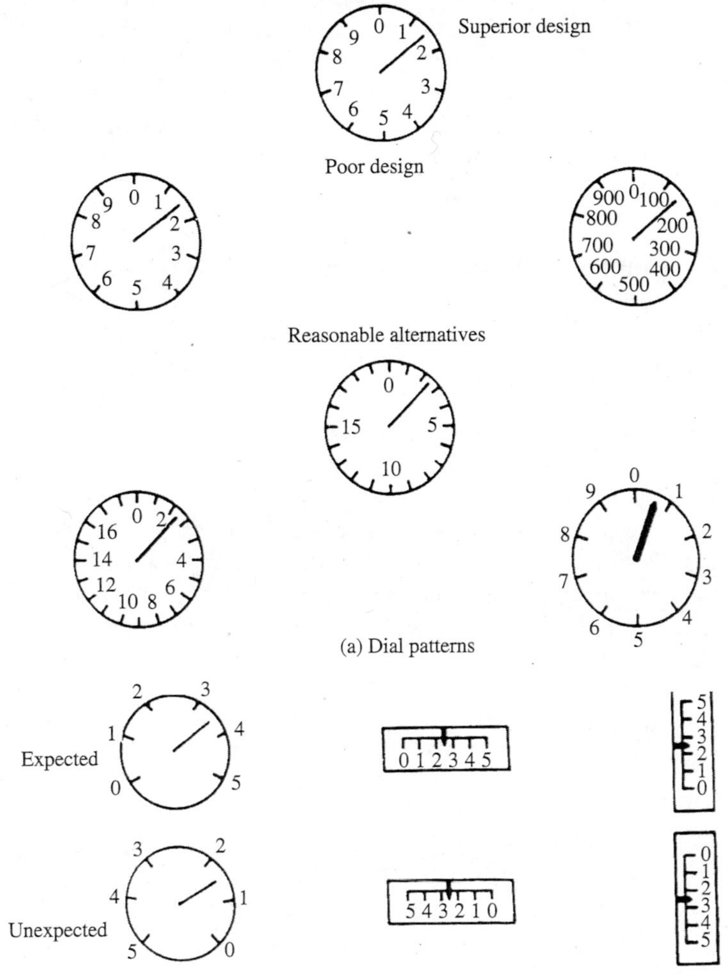

(b) Display stereotypes

FIGURE 11.9 Design of display.

Various types of display

(i) **Pictorial display.** This consists of some level of direct representation of the real situation, for example, a spot moving across a map representing position, or a tiny model aircraft and an associated line, with the model and line moving in synchronization with the real aircraft and the horizon.

(ii) **Qualitative display.** This indicates a general situation, rather than a numerical description of it. This is often quite adequate for the needs of the operator. For example, a light showing when the oil pressure is too low is satisfactory for most car drivers, rather than a gauge that indicates the pressure in units.

(iii) **Quantitative display.** This presents a number denoting the value of some variable in the situation. There are two main types—the moving-pointer fixed scale display and the digital display. The fixed-pointer moving scale display—a hybrid of the two—is not commonly used, because of the confusing nature of the relationship between the scale direction, the scale movement and the pointer. Design guidelines of markers, distance between markers, graphics and visual communication are important areas of product design, recommended by Woodson and Conover. The height of the letter, h (mm) and the width of the letter, w (mm) can be expressed as a function of viewing distance s in metres.

$$W_{\text{mm}} = 0.15 \text{ mm}$$

TABLE 11.2 Letter size as function of viewing distance

Class	h	w
Major index	$8s$	$1.5s$
Intermediate index	$6s$	$1.2s$
Minimum index	$4s$	$1s$

This last point is one aspect of the more general problem of population stereotypes, already mentioned in relation to controls. For displays, the expected patterns in Europe and USA are that scales should increase from down to up, from left to right and clockwise.

There are only three important channels through which the operator receives information—the eyes, the ears, and the sense of force and motion, or, to use more scientific terminology, the visual, the auditory and the kinesthetic sensory channels. The task of the ergonomist is to allocate the required information between these channels, according to their relative advantages and disadvantages and to ensure that, for each channel, the signals are above the threshold value.

11.6 MAN/MACHINE INFORMATION EXCHANGE

Refer to Figures 11.10 and 11.11. The man/machine interface is an imaginary plane across which information is exchanged between the operator and machine. Information is conveyed from the machine to the man by the display elements of the interface, and from the man to machine by the control elements of the interface. The separate problems of displays and control have already been discussed, but there are also the more general aspects of man/machine information exchange.

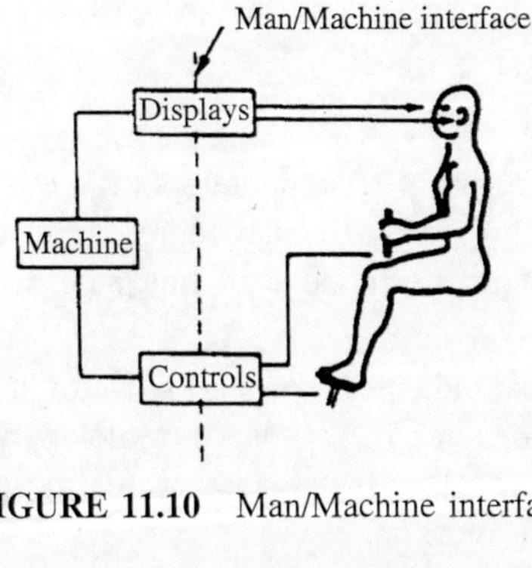

FIGURE 11.10 Man/Machine interface.

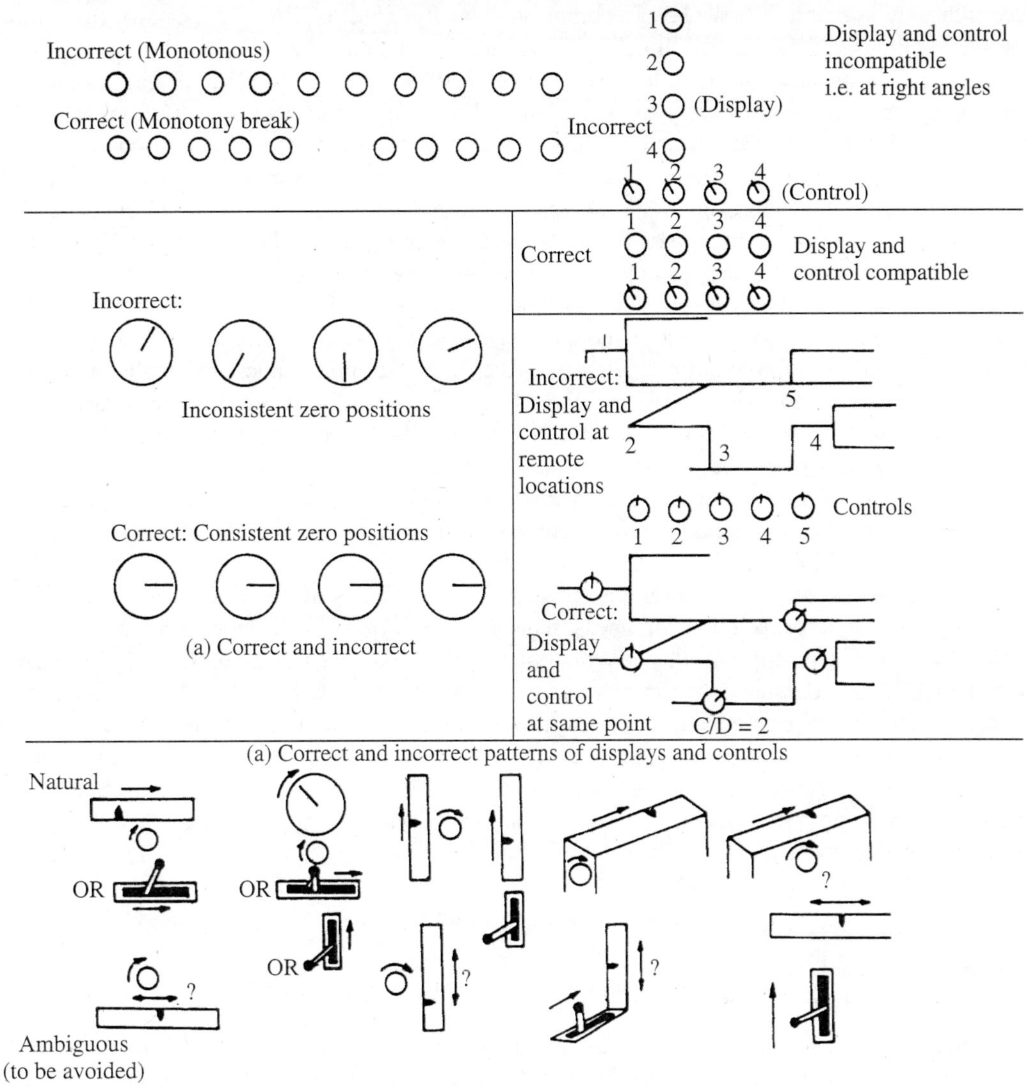

(b) Control/display relationships: Natural and ambiguous (?) cases

FIGURE 11.11 Design of controls.

This is inherently a difficult design problem that cannot be left to chance, to common sense or to tradition. The machine is fast, accurate, powerful, and inflexible; the man is slow, subject to error, relatively weak, and yet highly versatile. The nature of these properties explains why the man/machine combination is so useful but only if these two fundamentally different units can be efficiently linked together.

The higher the speed of the equipment, the more crucial it is to conform to the basic principles of interface design. Population stereotypes have already been mentioned for both displays and controls, but there are also stereotype aspects of control/display relationship. Optimal values of control/display of ratio of 2 have been recommended by ergonomists. Broadly speaking, these follow from the relationships established in natural situations. Movement should follow the line of force: if a control moves upwards, left or away from the body, then the corresponding display should move respectively upwards, left or away from the body. The relationship between rotary movements of controls and linear movements usually follow the logic of the simplest mechanical connection. For example, right-hand threads are such that a clockwise rotation causes an away movement, and this is the expected relationship even when there is no mechanical connection between the control and the display. Stereotypes for rotary controls adjacent to linear display follow simple ratchet or pulley/belt type movements. Relationships between display movements at right angle to control movements are usually ambiguous because there are a variety of equally valid ways in which a mechanical connection could be envisaged. These should be avoided. Unexpected display/control relationships may result in longer response times, greater errors, longer training times and high fatigue rates. Even when a new relationship has been learnt for a new situation, there may be a regression to earlier habits when an emergency arises. For example, if the brake and accelerator pedals of a car were interchanged, it would be perfectly possible, with extra care, to drive such a car. However, if the car had to be stopped suddenly, there will be a tendency to press the accelerator pedal which would, of course, have the contrary effect. There have been many serious accidents resulting from situations similar to this.

Given that almost all the power transmission occurs within the hardware, interface problems are almost entirely informational. The measurement of work or effort in functioning at an interface is, therefore, extremely difficult. Physiological measures of load are not appropriate, and even when used indirectly as measures of strain (e.g., muscle tension of sinus arrhythmia), it is not possible to make comparisons between systems. Psychological measures of information processing, and level of skill (e.g., required channel capacity or precision of timing) are obviously more relevant, but at present, they are unreliable and tedious. Even if it is possible to quantify the amount of information crossing the interface, this does not incorporate the critical encoding and dynamics variables. Informational measures of difficulty have been proposed and used for simple laboratory situations, but they have not been extended to cover even simple practical interfaces. Obviously, there is considerable scope for interface design research.

11.7 WORKPLACE LAYOUT FROM ERGONOMIC CONSIDERATIONS

A general-purpose machine should be designed for the average person. However, if one considers an operator who may be of either sex, seated or standing at a workplace, there are very few persons with average dimensions for all limbs. Therefore, a workplace should be so proportioned that it suits a chosen group of people. Adjustment may be provided (on seat height for example) to help the situation. If one considers the workplace (driving control area) in a modern motor car which will be required to suit one or two people from a large population, the benefits of adjustment will be appreciated. Ideally, the seat should be adjustable for height, rake and position, the steering wheel for height and the control levers and pedals for length.

Detailed anthropometric information is available for the different sexes, but simpler information could be obtained once the group of persons liable to use workplace is known.

Figure 11.12 shows the maximum working area and the normal working area. These are defined as:

1. *Normal working area:* The space within which a seated or standing worker can reach and use tools, materials and equipment when his elbows fall naturally by the side of the body.

2. *Maximum working area:* The space over which a seated or standing worker has to make full-length arm movements (i.e., from the shoulder) in order to reach and use tools, materials and equipment.

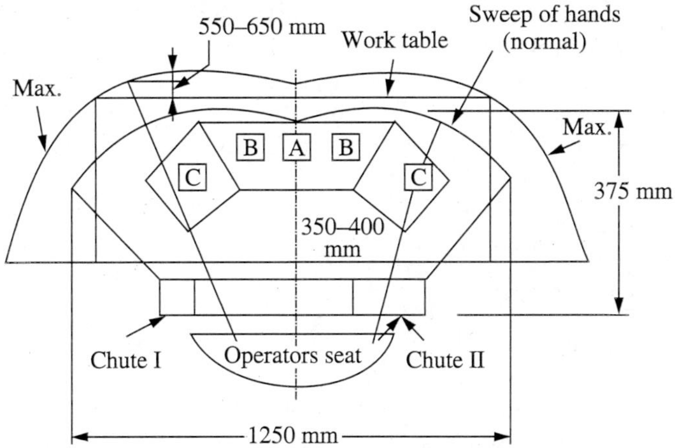

FIGURE 11.12 Assembler's (operator's) work place layout.

Assume the work is some operation, requiring equipment, tools, bins, etc., should be placed within the area shaded so that they can be seen and reached quickly and easily. The body dimensions given in the simple example shown in Figure 11.12 must be the smallest in the group, not the average, in order that all can reach the equipment.

The seat should be adjustable for height and rake. It is not usually convenient to have adjustable benches or work tops (and the value of range 712–762 mm is probably the best compromise dimension). With fixed bench height, varying thickness footboards are a help for varying sized operators, particularly where the operator is standing. The design of seats is a specialist activity, and much data is available for dimensions and shapes. A seat should give good support for back, buttock and thighs as it is a springboard for seated muscular activity. The criterion of support can be seen to conflict with that of comfort if a seat is required to meet both. Yet again, a good compromise usually gives best overall results. Ideally, with a seated workplace, the feet should be firmly on the floor or footboard, body well supported and comfortable, and work top on or below elbow height when seated.

If an instrument display forms part of the workplace, then the size of the display should be such as to be easily readable by all. Also the display panel should be at right angles to the line of sight of the operator.

In the case of total boxes, bins, loose or portable tools, etc., there should be a definite place for their location within the working area. Hence, the operator can develop habitual, confident movements when reaching for equipment often without any need for the eyes to direct the hands. The mental effort and strain are less. For the same reason, material and tools used at the workplace should always be located within the normal working area to permit the best sequence of operation. This is shown in Figure 11.12.

The operations shown consists of assembling stacks of three parts *A*, *B* and *C* (two assemblies at a time) using both hands. As finished assemblies are placed in chutes, parts assembled are in the next bins as they are required first for the next assembly.

11.8 NOISE

Many engineering factories are noisy, and given the choice most people would prefer rather less noise than more. Noise can be very annoying, and where concentration is required of an operator in the industrial task he is undertaking, it can be distracting, therefore, he may work with less efficiency and in some instances, the risk of accident increases. Much research is being carried out now on the question of aircraft noises at and near airports, as it generally believed that they cause a decrease in the health of people who live near the airports. Another factor is that some noises can damage the hearing and cause deafness, and worse. Still these noises may not necessarily be the loudest or the most annoying. On the grounds of reduced efficiency and damaged hearing then, it is obviously worthwhile to consider how the situation of industrial noise can be improved.

11.8.1 Measurement of Noise

Consider a horizontal milling process where the nature of the operation often causes undue vibration and noise. The vibration causes a rapid rise and fall in the pressure of the surrounding air. These pressure changes travel through the air in the form of waves and hence may eventually strike the ear of a person. Whether the person hears the sound or not depends upon the amplitude of the sound wave, and how rapidly the source is vibrating, i.e., the frequency.

Two units are used in the measurement of sound. The first is the unit of hertz (Hz) which is a measure of the frequency of sound. (*Note:* Hz is an SI unit which is in common use in noise technology (5 Hz = 5 cycles per second). When this number is small in value, the sound will have a low note, and when large in value, the sound will be high pitched. A human being can hear sounds between values of 20 and 15,000 Hz. Ultrasonic flaw testing equipment, for example, operates at a frequency to the order of a value of 3 MHz. A sound produced at this frequency is not audible to the human ear.

The second unit of sound is the decibel (dB) which is a measure of the intensity of sound. The higher the number of decibels, the louder the sound. It can be seen than that frequency measures the pitch of noise and decibel measures the intensity of noise. A very low whisper some few feet away to the order of 20 dB at 1000 Hz say would just be detectable to a person with acute hearing. The ears of a capstan lathe operator might be receiving noises to the order of 90 dB at many varying frequencies. One would have to shout to be heard above a noise of this intensity. Decibels are measured on a logarithmic scale such that a 10-fold increase in the intensity of noise, whether from 10 to 100, or 100 to 1000, is measured by 10 dB. Therefore, the lathe noise of 90 dB is 10^9 (i.e., 1,000,000,000) times as intense as a whisper of zero dB. Some industrial noises will be of the order of 140 dB (electricity generator room) depending upon how close to the offending process one stands.

Expert opinions that industrial noise first causes hearing loss to occur in the 4000 Hz region and this damage can spread over a wider range with more prolonged exposure to the noise. To measure industrial noise, meters are available which give a direct reading in decibels, and the frequencies of individual sounds can be isolated and measured using more sophisticated equipment.

11.8.2 Precautions against Noise

All noise problems are best tackled at source, and can most economically be taken into account at the design stage. Many machines can be made quieter by improved maintenance procedures, and machines that give rise to vibration should be mounted on properly designed vibration mountings to prevent vibration transmission through the base. Compressed air operated mechanisms are particularly noisy and some parts should be connected to silencers. When this type of attack has been carried out on noise, often at some considerable expense and if it will be found that the level of noise is still intolerable, then the protection of the operator from the noise must be considered. It may be desirable to enclose all or part of a machine in a soundproof booth. In such cases, the cost must be balanced against the cost of operative's health, and also against the increased efficiency of the working staff which will almost certainly result. Sound proofing materials are available which can be applied to walls and roof. These materials are basically of two types which are different in physical character and design. The first type is acoustic material which is in general dense and non-porous, whilst the other type is light and porous, and is classified as an absorbent. These are required in the design of most acoustic enclosures.

11.9 HEATING AND VENTILATING

The bodily comfort of the worker depends upon the room temperature in which he works as being neither high nor low, and ventilation being adequate. As with noise, if these factors are not controlled to a desirable level, then loss of efficiency will occur, health may suffer and rate of accidents may increase. Therefore, heating and also ventilating must be considered part of the field of study, which the ergonomists must consider and apply. However, the ergonomists appear to have a range of values fairly well established for our climate, and the Factory Acts have something to say on the subject. It must still be remembered that in the hotter processes, an environment exits which the operator trained to the work gets used to, and can work in, without apparent detriment to his health. In the pottery industry for example, men work around and near to kilns, which operate at very high temperatures.

11.9.1 Standard for Industrial Thermal Comfort

There are four factors, which the ergonomist will consider when tacking the problem of thermal comfort. These are:

1. Air temperature
2. Radiant temperature
3. Air humidity
4. Rate of air movement

Of these four, the first is usually classed as the most important. Consider each factor in turn.

1. *Air temperature.* The Factory Acts state that a reasonable temperature must be maintained in each workroom by non-injurious methods. In rooms in which a substantial proportion of the work is done sitting and does not involve serious physical effort, the temperature must not be less than 60°F after the first hour of working. It is generally conceded that 18.3°C (65°F) is a satisfactory standard to aim for although the following values give a more detailed standard:

   Workers engaged upon heavy task: 12.8°–15.6°C (55°–60°F); workers engaged upon light task: 15.6°–20°C (60°–68°F), workers engaged upon sedentary occupation 19.4°–22.8°C (67°–73°F).

The effect of a process in the workroom such as a furnace, giving off radiant heat, must be taken into account.

2. *Radiant temperature:* This is measured using a globe thermometer which records the mean radiant temperature. The desirable standards are as for air temperature. Where radiant heat is being given off from a high temperature process, it is important that workers are shielded from the heat.
3. *Air humidity:* This is measured by means of a hygrometer. Absolute humidity is a measure of the actual moisture content in given weight of air and is not affected by changes in temperature. Relative humidity is the commonly used measurement and is the ratio of the actual moisture content of the air to that which would exist if the air was saturated at the same temperature. It is expressed as a percentage. Sixty-five per cent relative humidity may be considered as the maximum value, which should be allowed if personal comfort is to be maintained. As the temperature falls so humidity may cause discomfort through dryness of the nose and throat, and high humidity may cause discomfort through a feeling of stuffiness and closeness. On a very cold day; for example, the relative humidity may fall as low as 20% which can be uncomfortable for some people.
4. *Rate of air movement:* The speed at which air moves through a workroom can affect the comfort of the staff. At 0.5 m/s, people will complain of draught, and at 0.1 m/s, the atmosphere will be classed as airless. It has been found that 0.15 m/s is ideal provided that the air temperature and radiant temperature are correct. On the other hand, if the temperatures are well above those recommended then an increase in rate of air movement will be welcomed.

In process industries where dust or fumes are a hazard, these are best extracted at source and exhausted outside.

Figure 11.13 is a plot of moisture content in g/kg (humidity) vs. temperature to define a zone of comfort on a psychrometric chart. Outside the shaded zone feeling of hot, cold, dry and damp will be felt.

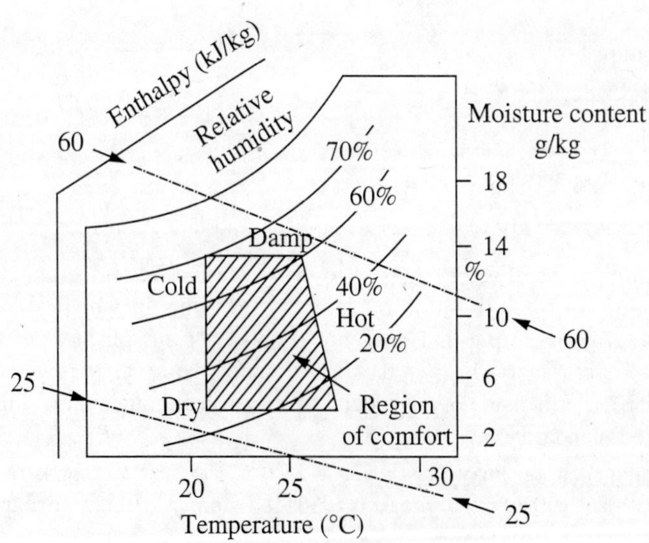

FIGURE 11.13 Region of comfort.

11.9.2 Air Conditioning

It is generally taken to mean the processing of air to control the factors of temperature, humidity and cleanliness at the required levels. An air conditioning system usually consists of an air circulating system which extracts air from the required rooms, treats it under automatic control and delivers it back to the rooms. In most cases, a proportion of outside air will be added to the returned air, humidifying (or de-humidifying) the air, and cleaning the air. Heating is usually done by means of steam or hot water filled coils, or electric elements. Humidifying is usually done by means of water sprays, or steam generating arrangement. Many types of air filtration equipment are available depending upon efficiency of air cleaning required, space available and type of dust in the atmosphere, if any, etc. Apart from personnel comfort, many processes require air conditioning in order to function correctly. Fine measurement was mentioned earlier as an example. Computers for another, will only function correctly in a controlled atmosphere.

Individual heat sources may be used to improve working conditions even if a full air conditioning system is not installed.

11.9.3 Heating Methods

These will be designed to give off heat by radiation, convection or a mixture of the two.

Radiators or convectors. Hot water filled radiators transmit both radiant heat and convected heat, and should not be obstructed by equipment. Modern electric convector heaters are very efficient and have the advantage of being portable. Radiant heaters, like electric fires or infrared wall heaters are useful means of applying a local source of heat directed at a particular working area. They are particularly used outside on loading bays, open sheds, etc., where it is difficult for workers to keep warm.

Floor and ceiling heaters. Floor heating systems are popular as they keep feet warm; cold feet being universally unpopular. They are often impracticable for industrial buildings, but are ideal for offices. It is recommended that the floor temperature is not allowed to rise above 25°C (77°F).

Overhead unit heaters are very popular and have adjustable louvers to enable warm air to be directed where required. They can, however, if badly sited become uncomfortable, giving the people closest to them hot heads. They can also give an uneven distribution of heat throughout a work room. The fan type has the advantage of being dual purpose; they can be used as fans in hot weather, blowing cold air instead of heated air. Radiant ceiling heating is a more efficient but more expensive form of overhead heating. It consists of mounting a battery of radiant heating panels at a suitable overhead height.

Where a heating system only is provided, as against a full system of air conditioning, problems can arise with open windows. They will in some cases be the only means of circulating air in the room if it becomes stuffy. Draughts can arise due to windows being open and can be both unpleasant and injurious to health. Air conditioning, of course, is the complete answer to thermal comfort.

These, and many other questions, are being investigated by many researcher in ergonomics.

11.10 LIGHTING

If light is controlled at a desirable level, satisfactory and comfortable to the working staff, efficiency will be high. Hence, productivity will be higher as a result, health will be improved and less accidents should occur.

11.10.1 Measurement and Amount of Light

The unit of light (luminous flux) is the lumen, which can be defined as the amount of light emitted by a point source having a uniform intensity of 1 cd. The minimum amount of light required for reading, writing, etc., is 10 lm/m^2, i.e., the light give off by 10 (international) candles at a distance of 1 m from the work. Note here that the SI unit of illumination is called the *lux* which means an illumination of one lumen per square metre. The Factories Act states that there must be sufficient and suitable lighting in every part of the factory in which persons are working or passing, and requires a minimum of 65 lux. The Illuminating Engineering Society of Great Britain publishes a Code of Good Interior Lighting Practice (1961) in which it is proposed that a lighting level of 160 lux should be regarded as minimum in all work places as a general amenity. The code also gives specific recommendations, a few of which are given in Table 11.3.

TABLE 11.3 Specific recommendations of lighting level

Visual task	*Recommended illumination (lux)*
Rough assembly work	300
Very fine assembly and inspection work	1000
Weaving light cloth	400
Weaving dark cloth	800
Sheet metal work	400
Plaining wood at machine or bench	600

11.10.2 Types of Electric Lamps

Three main types of lamps are available for industrial use. These are: (1) tungsten filament, (2) tubular fluorescent, and (3) colour corrected mercury discharge. In modern installations, the choice usually lies between (b) and (c), but they both have the disadvantage of flicker. This flicker has a frequency of twice that of the 50 Hz supply and can be serious where moving machinery is in use because of the *stroboscopic* effect it produces. This can give the operator the impression that the machine has stopped when in fact it has not. Various devices, such as a lead-lag circuit, can help to reduce flicker from discharge lamps.

1. *Tungsten filament lamps:* These produce light when the tungsten wire inside the glass bulb is heated by the passage of electric current to incandescence. They are cheap with a colour rendering which is acceptable for many purposes. They are not suitable for supplementing daylight.
2. *Fluorescent tubes:* The tube is, in which the discharge takes place, is coated on the inside with a fluorescent material. They are far more efficient than tungsten filament lamps but their great limitation is low loading. The most common industrial fitting take two tubes of 1.5 m length giving a lamp wattage of only 160. The tubes are available in a wide range of colours.
3. *Mercury discharge lamps:* These, when not colour corrected, give off the similar blue–green colour which are seen from street lighting; unsuitable for use in working areas. The colour corrected lamp incorporates a large outer bulb coated on the inside with a

fluorescent material causing more orange and red light to be discharged. Unlike fluorescent tubes, a single lamp can have a loading of 1000 W or more contained in a fitting of 0.6 m diameter. Therefore, installation and running costs are less. The efficiency is about the same as fluorescent tubes.

Lamps of typical ratings can be compared in Table 11.4.

TABLE 11.4 Lamps of typical rating

Type of lamp	*Wattage*	*Light output (lm)*	*Efficiency (lm/m2)*	*Rated life (h–W)*
Tungsten	300	4300	14	1000
filament	1000	17300	17	1000
Fluorescent	80	4640	49	5000/White
tube	80	4680	47	5000/Daylight
Mercury	400	18800	44	5000
lamp	1000	48000	46	5000
CFL	50	2600	60	10000
	100	4500	72	10000
LCD	20	3000	80	30000
	50	4500	85	30000

11.10.3 Glare

There may be ample light for comfortable working in a work area, but the operation may suffer visual discomfort because of glare. Take the example of an engineering inspector working at a marking off table which has a good reflective surface. Glare from a badly positioned light source can be reflected from the table top reducing its visibility to such an extent that operator cannot clearly see the graduation upon his measuring instrument. The amount of glare can now be expressed precisely by means of a glare index in terms of the brightness and position of the light sources causing the glare. Some examples of limiting glare index are given in Table 11.5 as per I.E.S. Code.

TABLE 11.5 Limiting glare index

Visual task	*Lighting glare index*
Rough assembly and inspection work	28
Very fine assembly and inspection work	19
Weaving light cloth	19
Weaving dark cloth	19
Sheet metal work	25
Plaining wood at machine or bench	22

11.11 CONCLUDING REMARKS

Ergonomics or human factors engineering is a blend of Human Sciences: Anatomy, Physiology and Psychology on one hand and Engineering Sciences like Mechanics, Electronics and allied physical sciences on the other. Applied Ergonomics is a highly useful branch concerned with design of equipment and products for efficient use by human beings. Industrial design is concerned with two major aspects: aesthetics and ergonomics. Improvement in human productivity should focus on safety, health and environment. The present chapter has summed up concepts of ergonomics including anthropometry, design of displays and controls and man–machine information exchange. In the end, issues of workplace design and environmental factors such as noise, air-conditioning, lighting and illumination are discussed in view of their importance to product design and manufacturing.

REVIEW QUESTIONS

1. Explain how ergonomics is a combination of human sciences and engineering sciences.

   [*Hint:* Figure 11.14 shows how ergonomics is an integration of engineering sciences and human sciences.

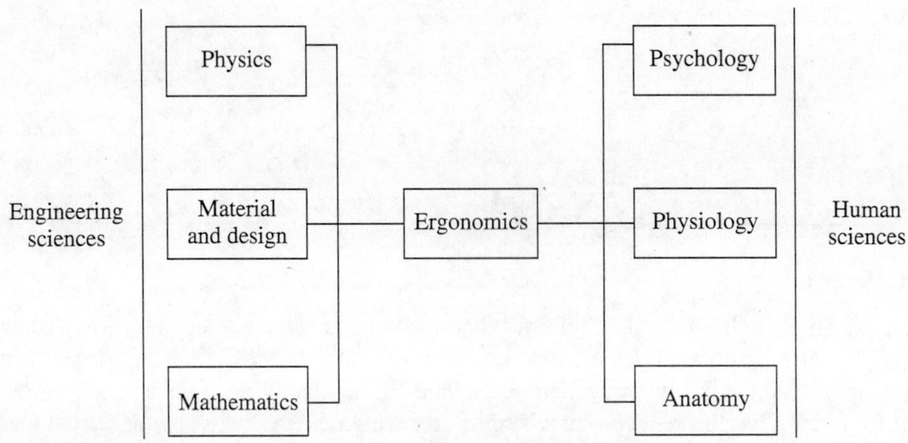

FIGURE 11.14 Ergonomics as integration of engineering sciences and human sciences.

   The group of specialists who know about machines and processes are engineers. Those who know about human capacities and psychology are experts in human sciences.

   An ergonomic study covers the following aspects:

   (i) Man as occupants of space should have comfortable posture and space at workplace according to anthropometry.

   (ii) Man as applicator of force should able to apply the force at the controls with a mechanical advantage.

   (iii) Man should be able to read the display with ease.

   (iv) There should be proper relationships between controls and displays called *stereotypes*.

2. What are the advantages of a proper 'fit' between man and machine?

   [*Hint:* The benefits of a proper fit are: (i) reduced fatigue, (ii) reduced errors, (iii) reduced chance of accidents, (iv) reduced training periods, (v) reduced response time or reaction time, and (vi) increased outputs.]

3. How is ergonomics applied to displays and controls? Give a list of controls and displays used in ergonomics. Sec. 11.4; Figure 11.6–11.8

4. Discuss the role of human being as applicator of forces. Explain the aspects of weight distribution, in lifting and carrying of weights. Sec. 11.2; Figure 11.1 (a), (b); P 285

5. What is meant by use of momentum? What is muscle contraction and energy release? Compare between isometric action and isotonic action. P 286–287

6. Which dimensions of work/workplace are designed for 95 percentile and 5 percentile, respectively? Explain with sketches. What is the percentile applied for door clearance height? What is the percentile applicable for switch positioning on a wall?

   [**Ans:** Refer to Fig 11.4(a) two top left figures for switch positioning on wall. For door clearance, use Figure 11.4(a) Number 7. For switch positioning, the percentile should be between 5 percentile for tall man's lowest reach and 95 percentile of short man's highest reach. This gives a percentile of 90. For door height, it should permit 95 percent of tallest men to pass through.]

7. How a suitable workplace layout can be designed from ergonomic considerations?
   Sec. 11.7; P 298–299

8. How environmental factors such as noise can be taken care of to ensure worker efficiency?
   Sec. 11.8, 11.8.1, 11.8.2; P 300

9. What are thermal factor considerations in ergonomics? How comfort zone considering humidity and temperature can be determined and displayed on a psychometric chart?
   Sec. 11.9.1, 11.9.2; P 301

10. How effective lighting can be planned for efficient working condition? Sec. 11.10, 11.10.2; P 303–305

11. Define glare. Discuss how to reduce glare at workplace. Sec. 11.10.3; Table 11.5

REFERENCES

[1] Singleton, W.T., *An Introduction to Ergonomics*, WHO, Geneva, 1978.

[2] McCormick, E.J. and Sanders, W., *Human Factors Engineering*, McGraw-Hill, New York, 1993.

Chapter 12

Value Engineering and Product Design

12.1 INTRODUCTION

In 1961, Miles [1], the founding father of Value Engineering (VE), defined *value analysis* (VA) as: "An organized creative approach, which has for its purpose the efficient identification of unnecessary cost, i.e., cost which provides neither quality nor use, life, appearance or customer features." Numerous other definitions of value engineering, including the one given by the Society of American Value Engineers (SAVE), have been used. We perceive VE as the systematic application of recognized techniques to identify the functions of a product or service, and to provide those functions at the lowest total cost. The philosophy of VE is implemented through a systematic rational process consisting of a series of techniques, including (a) *function analysis*, to define the reason for the existence of a product or its components, (b) *creative and speculative techniques*, for generating new alternatives, and (c) *measurement techniques*, for evaluating the value of present and future concepts. The techniques used in the VE process are not unique to VE. They are a collection of various techniques from many fields. As Bouey [2], President of SAVE, says: " 'VE'... holds no respect for proprietary concepts that are merely ways of thinking. VE will adopt any technique or method (or price thereof) for use, in any of its procedural phases".

Value engineering should not be confused with modern or traditional cost reduction analyses; it is more comprehensive. Based on function analysis, the process concentrates on a detailed examination of utility, rather than on a simplistic examination of components and component cost. The improvement of value is attained without any sacrifice in quality, reliability or maintainability. Collateral gains are often realized in performance, productivity, parts availability, lead time and quality. Historically, VE has returned between \$15 and \$20 for every \$1 expended on effort. It was originally developed and traditionally applied in the hardware area. However, recent years have witnessed an increase in its use in numerous new and nontraditional areas. It should be viewed as applicable to almost any subject. Its use is limited only by the user's imagination. The literature offers examples of applications in construction, administration, training, nonhardware, management, systems and procedures, vendor analysis, forecasting, resource allocation and marketing.

12.2 HISTORICAL PERSPECTIVE

Value engineering has its origin in studies of product changes, resulting from material shortages during World War II. The substitution of materials in designs without sacrifice in quality and performance caught the attention of Miles [1] and the purchasing people at the General Electric Company (GEC). Miles, who is considered to be the inventor of value analysis and value engineering introduced a formal methodology in which several teams examined the function of products (function analysis) manufactured by GEC. Through team-oriented creative techniques, they made changes in products that lower their cost without affecting their utility. This new methodology was VA. Although most of the original techniques used were not new, the philosophy of a functional approach was unique.

The term 'value analysis' is used interchangeably, here with the term 'value engineering' (VE). Traditionally, VE has been used to refer to the design stage, whereas VA has been used to refer to an existing product.

The definition of *product* used in this chapter is the one developed by Mudge [3]: "Anything which is the result of someone's effort". Therefore, product is not limited to hardware.

What emerged from the early experience of GEC and other organizations was the discovery and development of some fundamental concepts that provided the function for the development of VA methodology. These basic concepts were:

1. The use of interdisciplinary teams to effect change
2. The development of change through the study of function
3. A basic questioning logic
4. A job plan

Over the years, the techniques of VA were expanded, as were the areas of its application. Today VA or VE is a widely recognized discipline for improving the value of products or services.

12.3 WHAT IS VALUE?

A product or service is generally considered to have good value if that product or service has appropriate performance and cost, or, by reverse definition, a product is considered not to have good value, if it lacks either appropriate performance or cost. It can almost be said without any hesitation that, by this definition, value can be increased by either increasing the performance or decreasing the cost. More precisely:

1. Value is always increased by decreasing costs (while, of course, maintaining performance).
2. Value is increased by increasing performance, if the customer has needs and wants, and is willing to pay for more performance.

12.4 NATURE AND MEASUREMENT OF VALUE

Quantitative measurement of value has been provided by Salvendy [4]. It would be inappropriate to discuss VE and some of its techniques without a brief explanation of the nature and measurement of value. Value can be perceived as the ratio of the sum of the positive and negative aspects of an object. The following equation represents this simplistic interpretation:

$$\text{Value} = \frac{\Sigma(+)}{\Sigma(-)} \tag{12.1}$$

In reality, this equation is more complex, since we are dealing with many variables of different magnitudes. A more descriptive equation is:

$$\text{Value} = \frac{(mb_1 + mb_2 + \cdots + mb_n)}{(mc_1 + mc_2 + \cdots + mc_n)} \tag{12.2}$$

where,

m = the magnitude of a given factor or criterion
b = a specific benefit
c = a specific cost

Equations (12.1) and (12.2) are both general and can be used to measure the value of items and alternatives. The field of psychophysics has provided us the means with which to measure the parameters of Eqs. (12.1) and (12.2). Thurstone, Stevens, and others have discovered and proved the validity and utility of quantitative and subjective estimation applied to both physical and nonphysical stimuli. The principles of these psychophysical experiments have been used by others, to develop several value measurement techniques. They can be used to quantify the importance of beneficial functions and characteristics present in objects and services. They can also be used to measure cost, difficulty, risk and other negative factors present in new or old designs. They are very effective in evaluating alternatives. The quantification of these parameters allows value, as expressed in Eqs. (12.1) and (12.2), to be measured. This psychophysical principle of subjectively quantifying parameters forms the basis for deriving value, by means of the value measurement techniques discussed in Section 12.9.4.

12.5 MAXIMUM VALUE

Maximum value is probably never achieved. The degree of value of any product depends on the effectiveness with which every usable idea, process material and approach to the problem have been identified, studied and utilized. The purpose of the special techniques and knowledge of value analysis is to bring with less expenditure of time and money, more of the better value combination into focus.

12.6 NORMAL DEGREE OF VALUE

In normal usage, value is considered good, if the product contains somewhat better combination of ideas, processes, materials and functions, costwise, than competition. It is considered bad because, if the opposite is true, it would lead to loss in sales volume. This method of determining the degree of value often comes too late and has serious limitations.

Selected typical products have been given considerable amount of attention in order to determine more closely the amount of unnecessary cost they involve, when compared, not with competition, but with the optimum combination of available ideas, processes, materials and design concepts. Such studies have shown that unnecessary cost which can be so identified varies between 25 and 75 per cent of the product cost.

We all recognize that these unnecessary costs are not hanging like pears from a tree, for those who wish to pluck. Identification and removal are the reward for a well-organized effort, using effective value-oriented tools and involve appropriate use of money and competence.

12.7 IMPORTANCE OF VALUE

In a free enterprise system, with competition at full play, success in business over the long-term hinges on continually offering the customer the best value for the price. Competition, in other words, determines in what direction one must go, in setting the value content in order for a product or a service to be competitive. This best value is determined by two considerations: performance and cost.

Over the years, it has been generally recognized that an acceptable product must serve the customer's needs and wishes to the degree that he expects. That is to say, the product must have performance capability. In recent years, it has been clearly noticed that the cost of product must be such that the customer can buy the product at competitive prices, while leaving adequate difference between customer's cost (selling price) and production cost, to assure a continuing healthy business. Keeping appropriate performance, while securing appropriate cost, introduces the value concept.

12.8 THE VALUE ANALYSIS JOB PLAN

In the job plan, the problems are recognized and faced, with the functions to be accomplished clearly in mind. It is a five-step process. First, information surrounding the problem area is intensively and extensively procured. Then, it is thoroughly analyzed for meaning and sense of direction. Next, the essential creative work is done. Afterwards (in a separate process), evaluation of alternative solution is done, followed by suitable development work. Each of the first four steps is a different type of mental activity. Each is exclusively followed and thoroughly completed, before any of the other steps are begun.

(i) **Information step.** The foundation for effectiveness is built in the information step. What are the facts? What are the truths? What have been thought to be truths? Only when thorough and complete knowledge of the situation is obtained, can valuable new thinking be done. Often, when complete information is available, good solutions grow rapidly. Carefully separate out the assumptions. Review each. Determine if facts can be substituted for part of the assumptions.

What is to be accomplished? What is it that the customer really needs or wants? What are the desirable characteristics with respect to size, weight, appearance, durability, etc.? Get all pertinent information on costs, quantities, vendors, drawings, specifications, planning cards and manufacturing methods data, as well as actual samples of parts and assemblies, where practicable. In the case of new products, secure all available information: all design concepts, preliminary sketches and drawings, preliminary cost estimates, etc.

Examine the basic engineering. When the engineer asks questions, listen and develop through him a thorough understanding of the experience with the product to date. Examine the basic manufacturing with the manufacturing experts; ask questions, listen and study manufacturing methods that have been adopted for the operation in question. Make three lists: (i) facts, (ii) assumptions (beliefs), and (iii) information needed, but not known. Allow no interpretation, analysis, or idea generation.

What is known? What is believed? What is done? Where? By whom? When? At what cost? What are the service factors? What are the maintenance factors? What are other customer factors? Why was it done this way? When? What changes? Why were changes done? Why not other changes? What are marketing, engineering, manufacturing, purchasing, inventory and all other factors?

Record all the relevant hard or soft information pertaining to the problem. This work may be done by individuals or by groups of any number of persons, provided each person present has some information or knowledge or assumptions used, and further that the leader manages the meeting, so that there is deep "dredging" for pertinent information, with positively no wandering, half thoughts of analysis or possible solutions.

(ii) **Analysis step.** In the analysis step, extensive essential "function" thinking is developed. Functions are "evaluated" and problem setting is made precise; functions are separated for single study and then they are grouped as needed for best solutions. Moreover, it is readily discerned that, in effect, the preceding information step is an essential prerequisite to precise and final problem setting.

What are the meanings? What is the total problem? What are the individual problems? What are the reasonable goals and plans? What are the key problems to be solved first? What solutions seem reasonable? What end result is reasonable? What steps—first, second, third, etc. are indicated? What additional information is required? What unlisted assumptions are being made? Are the assumptions now valid? What solutions does it make sense to search for? Approximately what savings or benefits might each of the best approaches bring? Exactly what parts of the problem or overall problems should we seek, for better solutions, at first? What specific needs, when well met by better solutions, would "unlock" beneficial solutions for the project?

(iii) **Creativity step.** Einstein said that, when there is a problem to be solved: "Creativity is more important than knowledge." Having acquired understanding and information, we have laid the foundation for the application of various techniques, to generate every possible solution to the overall problem involved, to the part of problem, and to the individual problems. To derive the fullest benefit from our creative power, we must now encourage free use of imagination. It is useful to consider the human mind, as containing certain knowledge in bits or pieces, and having an ability to bring these diverse knowledge bits, which have never before appeared in the "same mental picture", together into one focus, long enough to consider. "What benefits to my present project might result, if I combined them in the solution?" By this concept, creativity is maximized if the individual is in possession, of (a) the knowledge bits required to deal with the task at hand, and (b) the mental ability to readily join diverse, unrelated bits of knowledge into one temporary picture.

To meet real-life situations, the strategy of value engineering must be to:

1. provide logic,
2. communicate emotionally in credible terms,
3. identify new types of knowledge needs,
4. provide research techniques that will find that knowledge efficiently, and
5. cause creativity that will usefully combine the knowledge from diverse sources.

Neither a chemical, not yet compounded, nor a metal, not yet developed, does exist, not because they are not possible, but because the required combination of creativity and knowledge is not to be found.

To accomplish the functions that the customer wants, for half or a third of the historical or expected cost and at less than the competitor's cost, a situation must be created in which the necessary creative idea and essential knowledge are blended extensively and intensively. The important roles to be followed during creativity step are:

- Three to ten people are optimum.
- Defer all judging. This will be much more difficult than expected.

Use the various methods to accelerate creative activities from the mind. (These were originated by the late Alex Osborn and are extended and taught by the Creative Problem Solving Institute, University of Buffalo, USA and elsewhere.) Since creativity is joining bits of knowledge in new combinations, it may be desirable to include, in this step, people who have some knowledge of the subject. However, they must accept the discipline of deferred judgement, or they must not be there.

Penetrate each of the problems in classes 1 to 3 thoroughly, listing all suggested approaches.

Encourage free association of ideas.

(iv) **Use preliminary judgement.** Select the approaches that show so much promise than it is believed. They should be thoroughly studied, extended and judged.

(v) **Evaluation.** This phase is a feasibility and cost analysis phase. It is explained in Section 12.13.4 through an example.

Value analysis job plans recommended by several experts in the field/organization are given in Table 12.1.

TABLE 12.1 Various value analysis job plans

	Miles	*Mudge*	*Fallon*	*Dell'Isola*	*GSA (General Services Admn.)*
1.	Information	Selection	Information	Information	Orientation
2.	Analysis	Information	Analytic	Speculative	Information
3.	Creativity	Function	Creative	Analytical	Function
4.	Judgement	Creation	Evolution	Proposal	Creative
5.	Development	Evaluation	Presentation		Judicial
6		Investigation	Implementation		Development
7.		Recommendation			Presentation
8.					Implementation
9.					Follow-up

12.9 CREATIVITY

The creativity phase in a value analysis program is most important. Creativity is the development of ideas, new to an individual, not necessarily new to someone else. It is creativity that leads to the discovery of alternative designs, methods, systems or processes that will accomplish the basic function at minimum cost.

Analysis of function through the use of creativity is the root of VE. Normally, an individual's creative ability is much more than he assumes. Training and practice can increase the growth of innate creativity.

There are two general approaches to problem solving: the analytical approach and the creative approach. The aim of analytical approach is to arrive at the final solution through a standard step-by-step procedure; the creative approach banks on the idea-generating ability of the problem solver and his ability to embark on the best out of a number of possible solutions.

12.9.1 The Creative Process

In the creative process, the past experience is combined and recombined to form a new combination, which will satisfy the need.

Steps in the creative process:

1. Orientation: Problem definition and decision on the path to be taken.
2. Preparation: Information gathering and fact-finding.
3. Ideation: Production of alternative solutions to the problem.
4. Incubation: Sorting and combining the information and slowing the pace to invite illumination.
5. Synthesis: Bringing the ideas to gather into a complete whole.
6. Verification: Evaluation of the proposed solution or resulting ideas.

12.9.2 Blocks to Creativity

(i) **Habitual blocks**
  (a) Continuing to use "tried and true" procedures even though new and better ones are available.
  (b) Rejection of alternative solutions which are incompatible with habitual solutions.
  (c) Lack of a positive outlook, lack of determined effort, conformity to custom and reliance on authority.

(ii) **Perceptual blocks**
  (a) Failure to use all the senses of observation.
  (b) Failure to investigate the obvious.
  (c) Inability to define terms.
  (d) Difficulty in visualizing remote relationships.
  (e) Failure to distinguish between cause and effect.

(iii) **Cultural blocks**
  (a) Desire to conform to "proper" patterns, customs or methods.
  (b) Overemphasis on competition or on cooperation.
  (c) The drive to be practical above all things and being too quick to make immediate judgements.
  (d) The belief that all indulgence in fantasy is a waste of time.
  (e) Having confidence and faith, only in reason and logic.

(iv) **Emotional blocks**
  (a) Fear of making a mistake or of appearing foolish.
  (b) Fear of supervisors or colleagues and subordinate's distrust.
  (c) Overmotivation to succeed quickly.
  (d) Refusal to take any detour, in reaching a goal.
  (e) Inability to reject decisions which are adequate, but which are obviously sub-optimum.

12.9.3 Factors Conducive to Creativity

Problem sensitivity: Being aware that a problem exists.

Idea fluency: Being able to produce plenty of ideas.

Flexibility: Open-minded and adaptive in the approach to a problem.

Originality: The ability to produce a great number of new and unique ideas.

Constructive discontent: A dissatisfaction with existing conditions, with an attitude of mind which seeks to improve the conditions. This type of person usually asks why and how.

Observation: Alertness to the environment.

Facility at combination: The ability to combine and recombine information in a variety of ways.

Orientation: Development of the proper frame of mind towards creativity.

Motivation: The mustering of the necessary energy to work towards a goal and achieving it.

Permissive atmosphere: An environment in which new ideas are encouraged. A free atmosphere is characterized by freedom of expression, job satisfaction, effective communication, mutual respect and encouragement from co-workers.

12.9.4 Creative Techniques

The ground rules for creative techniques are:

1. Do not attempt generating new ideas and judge them at the same time. Let them be separated by time, space and people, if possible.
2. Generate a large quantity of possible solutions. Multiply the ideas produced first, by inspiration, by 5 or even 10.
3. Seek a broad-spectrum attack approach.
4. Watch for opportunities to combine or improve ideas as they are generated.
5. Consider all possible ideas, even apparently impractical. Do not ridicule them. Never eliminate any idea summarily.

(i) **Brainstorming technique.** It is a problem-solving conference method based on stimulation of one person's mind by the mind of another. An average group consists of 4 to 6 people sitting around a table, and spontaneously producing ideas designed to solve a specific problem. The following rules should be followed:
   (a) Criticism is ruled out.
   (b) Free-wheeling is welcome.
   (c) Any number of ideas is welcome and desirable.
   (d) Combination and improvement are sought.

(ii) **Gordon technique.** This technique is closely related to brainstorming, with the difference that the group leader opens the session with a statement of the broad area to be discussed, not pinpointing to the actual problem. For example, the problem is to review procedures for cleaning windows. So the topic selected is "removing, dirt".

(iii) **Checklisting technique.** Here, checklists are aimed at solving a specific problem. They aid our faulty memory. The most famous checklists for VE are: What is it? What does it cost? What does it do? What else will do the job? What does that cost?

(iv) **Synectics technique.** This is an analogy method, utilizing personal analogy which makes you feel yourself to be an integral part of a thing you are designing. For instance, imagine yourself as a guard and think of redesigning it for a lower cost. Symbolic analogy to think of mental images to symbolically represent something you have seen, heard etc., e.g. "Strong as a horse", "Small as a peanut".

(v) **Morphological analysis.** It is structured in a comprehensive way to list and examine many possible combinations that may be useful in solving a problem.

An example of this technique, using a window as product under consideration was cited by Parker [5] is shown in Figure 12.1. There are many possible combinations of windows for a new building. The three variables considered are size (shape), type and glazing material. One axis of the cube lists all the different sizes to be considered. The second axis displays the different types of windows, and the third axis lists the various choices of glazing materials. The resulting three dimensional matrix displays up to 125 possible combinations. Each of these combinations could be evaluated on a systematic basis, creating many more ideas.

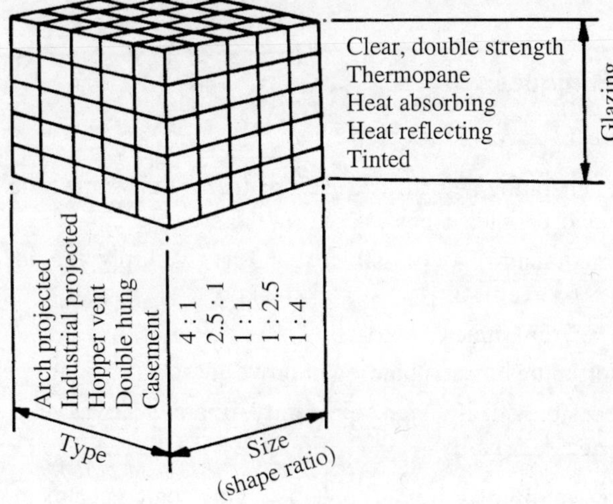

FIGURE 12.1 Morphological approach for generation of ideas in design of window pane.

(vi) **Attribute listing technique.** There are two steps in the attribute listing technique. The first is to list all the various characteristics of the study object. The second is to deliberately change or modify these characteristics. By means of this technique, it is possible to bring together new combinations of characteristics or attributes that will fulfill some existing needs in a better way.

Example 1. Consider a type of cast-iron radiator which was common, a few years ago. Its characteristics are multiple iron tubes, four legs to allow freestanding, high inlet and low outlet, valve to control 50 cm to 60 cm high by 10 cm to 20 cm deep and installed 3 cm to 30 cm from walls. Next, each attribute could be changed as follows:

(a) Multiple tubes changed to single tube with fins to increase heat transfer area.
(b) Leg eliminated to allow attachment to wall brackets, inlet and outlet placed at same low level.
(c) Dampers and attractive cover added for control and beauty.
(d) Height decreased to 25 cm and width to 6 cm.
(e) Installed flush with wall.

Example 2. Consider a standard Venetian blind, developed years ago. Its characteristics are: multiple slots, horizontally pivoted for opening and closing, opened and closed by vertical pull on a cord and stored in use by vertical raising. Each attribute could be changed as follows

- Horizontal slots changed to vertical slots.
- Horizontal pivoting changed to vertical pivoting.

- Pulling on a cord changed to twisting on a fibreglass rod.
- Overhead storage through vertical raising, changed to side storage by horizontal sliding.

(vi) **Evaluation comparison technique.** This is a forced creativity technique for developing unique verbal solutions, by forming measurable comparisons between the elements of dimensions, physical properties, mechanical properties, electrical and magnetic properties, cost consideration and other properties. Table 12.2 shows a checklist used to force these comparisons.

TABLE 12.2 Creative evaluation—the comparison checklist

Dimension	*Physical properties*	*Mechanical properties*
Size	Weight	Compressibility
Shape	Density	Elongation
Geometry	Thermal conductivity	Tensile strength
Configuration	Boiling point	Elasticity
Height	Freezing point	Compressive strength
Length	Melting point	Shear strength
Depth	Shrinkage	Creep strength
Width	Corrosion resistance	Ductility
Breadth	Alkalinity	Hardness
Volume	Acidity	Fatigue strength
Perpendicular	Inertness	Damping
Parallelism	Colour	Wear resistance
Circumference	Smell	Formability
Complexity	Texture	Mouldability
Simplicity	Feel	Machinability
Angularity	Taste	Flexibility
Area	Appearance	Impact strength
Proportion	Radiation effect	Stiffness
Amplitude	Porosity	Resilience
	Bonding	Toughness
	Cementability	
	Chemical stability	
	Reflectivity	
	Absorptivity	
	Water absorption	
	Impurities	
	Viscosity	
	Temperature	
	Hardness	

(Contd.)

TABLE 12.2 Creative evaluation—the comparison checklist (Contd.)

Electric and magnetic properties	*Cost considerations*	*Others*
Resistance	Time	Sound
Capacity	Location	Light
Power factor	Place	Heat
Conductivity	Material	Power
Permeability	Quality	Energy
Inductance	Reliability	Force
Coercive force	Flexibility	Action
Residual flux	Safety	Position
Field strength	Lead time	Velocity
Core loss	Surface finish	Acceleration
Arc resistance	Tooling	Jerk
Dielectric constant	Work-in-process	Process
Dielectric strength	Mechanization	Specification
	Direct labour	Environment
	Set-up time	Customer
	Training	
	Tolerance	

(vii) **Phillips 66 Buzz session technique.** This technique is useful in developing creative ideas from large audience situations. First, the audience is divided into a large number of groups of six people each. Within each group, a leader and recorder are appointed; they should be selected and briefed before the meeting, if possible.

The problem to be tackled should be announced before the meeting gets started. Using the group brainstorming method, each group develops creative alternatives. After a period of time and a signal from the leader, each group stops producing ideas and begins evaluating the ideas and selecting the best solution.

The leader of each group is called upon to present the ideas produced, to the rest of the audience. The multiplicity of good, diversified ideas makes an excellent, large group convincing, creative demonstration.

(viii) **Crawford slip writing technique.** This is another technique specially suited to large audience. The technique is a form of individual brainstorming. This technique provides many ideas for a wide range of different problems in one session in a short period of time.

Each person in a large audience is given a coloured slip of paper on which he is asked to make a statement relating to the problem. A different coloured paper is used for each problem. The slips are collected to be evaluated later.

(ix) **Using Idea stimulators.** When the flow and development of ideas seem to be slowing down, during use of the creative problem-solving techniques, the use of idea stimulators can be introduced. In Section 12.10, we present some questions that can be used to stimulate and trigger more ideas.

12.10 STEPS TO PROBLEM-SOLVING AND VALUE ANALYSIS

Creative problem-solving techniques are the tools an individual can use to expand his creative ability. Creative techniques are forcing techniques. These are the techniques that relieve the individual from mental fixity.

Up to a point, the human mind is superior to the most elaborate computer. It can store almost infinite number of data, but regrettably, it can only process and integrate up to about seven bits of these data simultaneously. Because of our mind's limitations, we find the following idea generation checklist helpful, in applying, either the analytical or the creative approach to problem solving, and developing greater personal creative ability:

Establish a specific time and place for creative thinking.
Set a deadline or quotes for creative ability.
Write down ideas as they occur.
Go through the elements of the problem several times.
Take notes of observations.
Suspend judgement—don't jump or be led into false conclusions.
Rearrange the elements of the problem—get a new viewpoint.
Take a break, when you are stuck.
Discuss your problem with others; let it incubate.

TABLE 12.3 Additional checklist for value analysis of products—(after Parker [5])

Eliminate/Combine
Can it be eliminated entirely?
Can part of it be eliminated?
Can two parts be combined into one?
Is there duplication?
Can the number of different length, colours, and types be reduced?
Standardize/Simplify
Could a standard part be used?
Would a modified, standard part work?
Does the standard contribute in cost?
Does anything prevent it from being standardized?
Is it too complex?
Can connections be simplified?
Is it over-detailed or over-specified?
Challenge/Identify
Does it do more than is required?
Does it cost, more than it is worth?
Is someone else buying it at a lower cost?
What is special about it?
Is it justified?
Can tolerances be relaxed?
Have drawings and specifications been coordinated?

(Contd.)

TABLE 12.3 Additional checklist for value analysis of products—(after Parker [5]) (Contd.)

Maintain/Operate
Is it accessible?
Are service calls excessive?
Would you like to own it and pay for its maintenance?
Is labour inordinate to the cost of materials?
How often is it actually used?
Does it cause problems?
Have users established procedures to get around it?
Requirements/Cost
Are any requirements excessive?
Can less expensive materials be used?
Is it proprietary?
Are factors of safety too high?
Are calculations always rounded off on the high side?
Would higher gauge materials work?
Could a different finish be used?

12.11 VALUE ANALYSIS TESTS

Figure 12.2 illustrates 10 tests for value analysis, as suggested by the Anglo-American Council on Productivity in 1953. Each product or component is subjected to the following tests:

1. Does its use contribute value?
2. Is its cost, proportionate to its usefulness?
3. Does it need all its features?
4. Is there anything better for the intended use?
5. Can a usable part be made by a lower cost method?
6. Can a standard product be found, which will be usable?
7. Is it made on proper tooling, considering the quantities used?
8. Will another dependable supplier sell it for less?
9. Is anyone buying it for less?

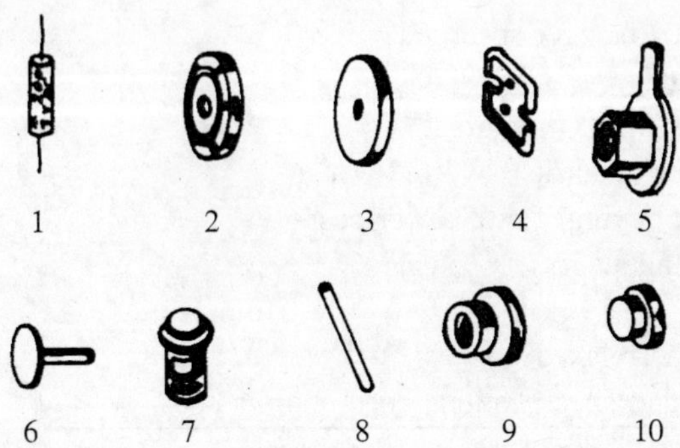

FIGURE 12.2 Value analysis checklist with typical products.

12.11.1 Details of Value Analysis Tests

(a) Does its use contribute value?

Part: Condenser used across contacts of a relay to provide arc suppression as contact opens.

Cost: 5,000,000 per year, at 10 cents each.

When cobalt again became available after the war, an alnico magnet was used to provide snap action. Analysis was done to re-evaluate the necessity of the condenser, with this magnet. It was found that the condenser did not add value, and it was eliminated.

Saving: $ 50,000 per year, 100%

(b) Is its cost proportionate to its usefulness?

Part: Spacer hub for mounting light aluminium disks.

Cost: $ 0.90 per unit.

Considering its simple function in the assembly, this cost was not proportionate to its usefulness. Cost was high, due to undercutting to reduce weight, which was an important-consideration. Value analysis study showed that, by making the part of aluminium, the undercutting could be eliminated and a resulting 20 per cent part provided identical performance, with still further reduced weight.

Saving: 70% per unit.

(c) Does it need all of its features?

Part: Stainless steel disk in dispensing machine.

(d) Is there anything better for the intended use?

Mica stack used for insulation COST: $ 40 per machine.

By changing to Micalex, cost of $ 34 per machine was available and, due to the moulded contour of the Micalex, the parts of the assembly were more rigidly mounted.

Saving: 15% and a better assembly.

(e) Can a usable part be made by a lower cost method?

Part: Hub assembly.

Cost: $ 30 per machine.

Earlier, designed and made as a two-part riveted or staked assembly. Study showed that part could be made as casting, eliminating assembly operation and simplifying production.

Saving: $ 20 per machine: 67%

(f) Can standard product be found, which will be usable?

Part: Stud contact.

Cost: $ 27 per machine.

This part was made to special design. Search revealed that a standard stud contact was available at about half the cost, equally suitable and providing identical performance. Another case of a well-directed, intensive, purchasing.

Saving: $ 13 per machine: 48%

(g) Is it made on proper tooling, considering the quantities used?

Part: Stainless weld nipple.

Cost: 20 cents each.

Because of the relatively small quantities required, procedure had been established, to purchase a standard stainless fitting and machine, a part of which was meant to provide the desired weld embossing. Re-evaluation disclosed that production requirements had stepped up sufficiently, that it was now economical to make it on an automatic screw machine. Cost by the latter method was reduced to 8 cents each.

Saving: 15 cents per unit: 75%

(h) Do material, reasonable labour, overhead and profit total its cost?

Part: Stainless dowel pin.

Cost: $ 3 per machine (50,000,000 a year).

This dowel pin is purchased according to special design and specifications. Value analysis indicated that the cost was out of proportion with reasonable standards. Every detail of the specification, manufacturing process and inspection was studied with the vendor's manufacturing people. As a result, some wastage of material and labour eliminated. It is now purchased at $ 2 per machine.

Saving: $ 1 per machine: $ 50,000 per year: 33%

(i) Will another dependable supplier provide it for less?

Part: Bushing.

Cost: $ 18 per machine.

Numerous examples similar to this are being developed of the buyers, in virtually every product classification. In this case, an exploration of the market resulted in finding an equally reliable source of supply that would furnish the identical part at $ 13.50 per machine.

Saving: $ 4.50 per machine: 25%

(j) Is anyone buying it for less?

Part: Button

Cost: $ 2.50 per machine (used in large quantities).

This phase of cost measurement draws no line of comparison, whether within, or outside the company itself. The extensive purchasing activities of the GE organization provided a ready means of comparison and are a logical starting point, in considering this question. In this case, a similar button was being purchased in another GE high production factory, at $ 1 per machine, which would give identical performance in the application under study.

Saving: $ 1.50 per machine: 60%

12.12 VALUE ENGINEERING IDEA GENERATION CHECK LIST

Figure 12.3 shows a three-dimensional matrix which involves all possible combinations of five materials, seven designs and five manufacturing methods. The designer should select the best combination from these 175 alternatives. Similar matrices can be constructed for various features of a product. Obviously, some combinations in the matrix are completely useless. We only need the best idea among the long list of alternatives.

In each product category, there are usually special areas where cost reduction is particularly fruitful. The design engineer should consult the records of cost reduction and product improvement. Value engineering case study can be used for the same purpose. The following list is representative of the questions the designer may have in mind while finalizing a design:

1. Can a material change improve the product performance?
2. Can lubricants and catalysts improve the performance of the product?
3. Should the appearance of the product be associated with major sports or cartoon figure?

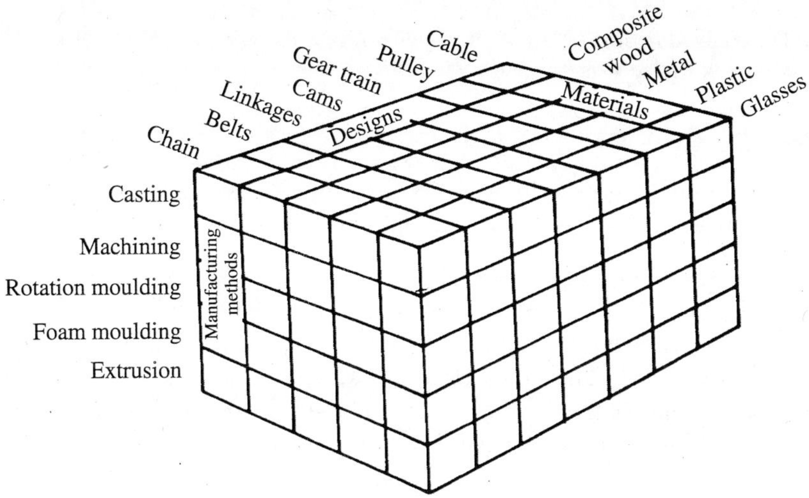

FIGURE 12.3 Morphological approach for machine element, material and process.

4. Can a colour change make the product more attractive (e.g., day-glow colour, chrome plating, glow-in-the-dark paints, ultraviolet colour, and reflective paints)?
5. Should fragrants be added to the product?
6. Would a change in surface texture improve the appeal of the product?
7. Can the product be made with a special click sound to demonstrate positive engagement?
8. Where two components join or interact? Can the male and female components be interchanged?
9. Can the handles and buttons be repositioned to improve man–machine interaction?
10. Can the order of operation, direction of cut, or direction of movement be improved?
11. Should the product be made foldable?
12. Can miniaturization lead to low cost production?
13. Can the number of components be reduced to improve strength and decrease assembly?
14. Are the packaging and labelling of the product appropriate in terms of cost and function?
15. Are all the components and manufacturing processes standard?

12.13 COST REDUCTION THROUGH VALUE ENGINEERING CASE STUDY ON TAP SWITCH CONTROL ASSEMBLY

This section summarizes the VE study carried out on Tap Switch Control Assembly used on distribution transformers, as illustrated in Figure 12.4. The objectives of study were to bring down cost, simplify design and find an alternative to high cost material, without detriment to quality and reliability.

12.13.1 The Problem

Transformer is one of the major products manufactured in a wide range, in national and international markets. In order to improve market and continue to have profit in the high inflation world, VE study was carried out on "TAP SWITCH CONTROL ASSEMBLY", used on distribution and power transformers. The main function of this unit is to facilitate the adjustment of turn ratio of primary to secondary windings of the transformer.

12.13.2 The Objective

The objectives of this study were to bring down cost, simplify design, and to find alternatives to high cost material, without detriment to quality and reliability.

12.13.3 The Team

As value engineering is inherently a team task, a group was formed consisting of personnel from all disciplines, such as Design, Manufacturing, Quality Assurance, Marketing and Value Engineering to achieve the set goal. Team members were given training to enable them to use value engineering techniques more effectively and meticulously during the study.

12.13.4 The Methodology

The value engineering study was carried out in a systematic and organized way, as per VE job plan, consisting of information phase, functional analysis phase, function-cost-worth analysis, creative phase, evaluation phase, recommendations, and implementation. These are now discussed.

(i) **Information phase.** In this phase, team members collected all the relevant information about the items under study. The study of drawings, material specification, design, processes cost, procurement and quality problems, as also in-house and field complaints was made in detail.

The tap switch control assembly is a subassembly used in all distribution and power transformers. It is often required to change the turn ratio of primary to secondary windings of transformers, to adjust for the voltage drop in a feeder or main supply as also to match the varying requirements of load. The simplest arrangement for ratio adjustment was to bring taps from one or both windings to terminals of selector switch (tap switch). This can be operated by an insulated shaft brought out through an "oil tight gland" mounted on the side of the transformer tank. This case study mainly concentrates on oil tight gland assembly (tap switch control assembly) consisting of 13 items, as shown in Figure 12.4.

The cost details of each item and its material specification are given in Annexure A.

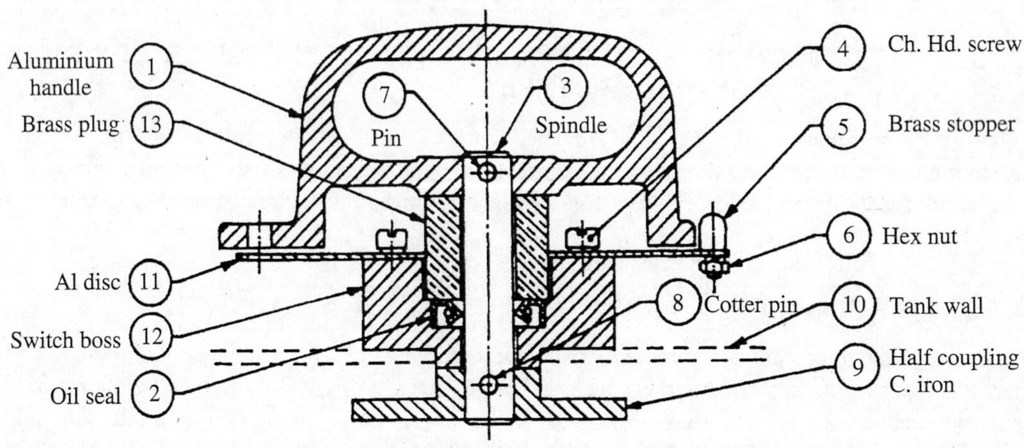

FIGURE 12.4 Transformer tap control switch before value analysis.

(ii) **Functional analysis phase.** The results of a value engineering exercise, generating good alternatives for achieving the desired functions at optimum cost, mostly depend on how well the functional analysis is done. The functional requirement of the tap switch assembly as a whole is analyzed and recorded as below:

Verb	*Noun*	*Basic/Secondary*
Facilitates	Tap change	Basic
Transmits	Rotation	Basic
Prevents	Leakage	Basic
Indicates	Position	Secondary
Facilitates	Locking	Secondary
Prevents	Rusting	Secondary

Further, the details of the functions of each component in the Assembly were analyzed and listed (Annexure B).

(iii) **Function-cost-worth analysis.** In this phase, the team found the worth of each item of the subassembly. After identifying the desired functions of each item, the team established the worth of each item, depending on its essential function. While establishing the worth, the definition of value, i.e., the lowest price one has to pay to reliably accomplish a given function, was used as the basis. The estimated worth was also based on other factors such as: (a) state of art, (b) the accuracy of the available information, (c) thoroughness of the functional analysis of the item, (d) an uncommon amount of commonsense, and (e) the experience and subject knowledge of team members.

Critically examining the present design, the following points can be made:

1. The basic function of oil-tight gland (switch boss assembly) is to prevent oil leakage and provide support to the spindle (shaft).
2. Item 12, "Switch boss", is welded to the transformer tank. It is bigger in size, because it has to accommodate brass plug which has lesser worth (see Figure 12.4).
3. Item No. 13, "Plug" is made out of brass. Its function is to position the oil seal. The cost of the brass plug is about 40% of the total cost of the subassembly. When compared to its basic function, the worth of the plug is much less.
4. The stopper provided on anodized aluminium plate is made out of brass material to resist corrosion.
5. Spindle is machined in order to get smooth surface where the oil seal comes into contact with it.

With the above information, the team members analyzed function cost worth of each item of the subassembly and arrived at the value gap in each item, as given in Annexure C.

(iv) **Creative phase.** The poor value (hidden cost) areas, identified earlier, were subjected to brainstorming, to find out alternative ways of accomplishing the functions. Criticisms and evaluation are avoided in the brainstorming session, to prevent the premature death of potentially good ideas. Even wild ideas were noted down in line with basic VE principles.

During the brainstorming session, a large number of ideas were generated for each item to perform the same function. Help was taken from experts who were involved in similar design and process. Vendors were contacted to contribute alternative ideas. In all, 35 ideas were generated for items of the subassembly, these are listed in Annexure D.

(v) **Evaluation phase.** The alternative ideas suggested during the creative phase were refined and analyzed with a view to ascertain, whether they could achieve the desired functions. This was carried out in two stages: In the first stage, all suggestions were studied and those which could not be adopted because of quality, reliability or other basic reasons were eliminated, and the others were shortlisted.

In the second stage, the ideas shortlisted after first evaluation were critically studied and discussed with the concerned personnel, for feasibility and practicability of production. Thus, the ideas were further shortlisted and assigned for feasibility ranking matrix. For judging the ideas, the following designs were considered:

A Function
B Cost
C Maintainability
D Quality and reliability
E Space

Each of these design criteria was given a weightage factor. This was carried out as follows: Each of the above criteria was compared with others, and depending on their relative importance, three categories were formed, viz. major, medium, and minor. A score of 3, 2 and 1 respectively was assigned to each of the levels. The details are as follows:

Weightage analysis	**Points**
Major difference	3
Medium difference	2
Minor difference	1

Paired comparison

	B	*C*	*D*	*E*	Score
A	*B*2	*A*2	*A*1	*A*3	6
	B	*B*2	*B*1	*B*3	8
		C	*D*2	*C*2	2
			D	*D*3	5
				E	1

Example. Note that the function *A* and quality *D* are closely connected with the weightage factor 3.

Weightage for Each Criterion	
A: Function	6
B: Cost	8
C: Maintainability	2
D: Quality and reliability	5
E: Space	1

The following shortlisted ideas for the brass plug were taken for evaluation:

(a) M.S. cover plate instead of plug to hold oil seal
(b) Nylon plug
(c) Internal circlip to hold oil seal
(d) Handle itself as cover plate for oil seal.

Feasibility Ranking

	A	*B*	*C*	*D*	*E*	*Score*	*Rank*
Design ideas	6	8	2	5	1		
a	1/6	2/16	1/2	1/5	3/3	32	IV
b	3/18	2/16	2/4	2/10	1/1	49	II
c	1/6	2/16	2/4	1/5	2/2	33	III
d	2/12	3/24	3/6	2/10	3/3	55	I

Note. 2/16 means score of 16 is achieved as 2 × 8 in row of a column of *B*. Similarly, the shortlisted ideas for other components were also evaluated.

(vi) **Recommendations.** Based on the feasibility ranking of ideas, team members made the following recommendations:

(a) Eliminate brass plug, and its function has to be obtained by redesigning the handle suitably.
(b) Standard bright bars of shorter length to be used without machining O.D. for spindle.
(c) Switch boss has to be redesigned to lesser width.
(d) Stopper to be redesigned with internal thread and to be made out of aluminium rod.

Figures 12.4 and 12.5 show the present and proposed designs of the tap switch control assembly.

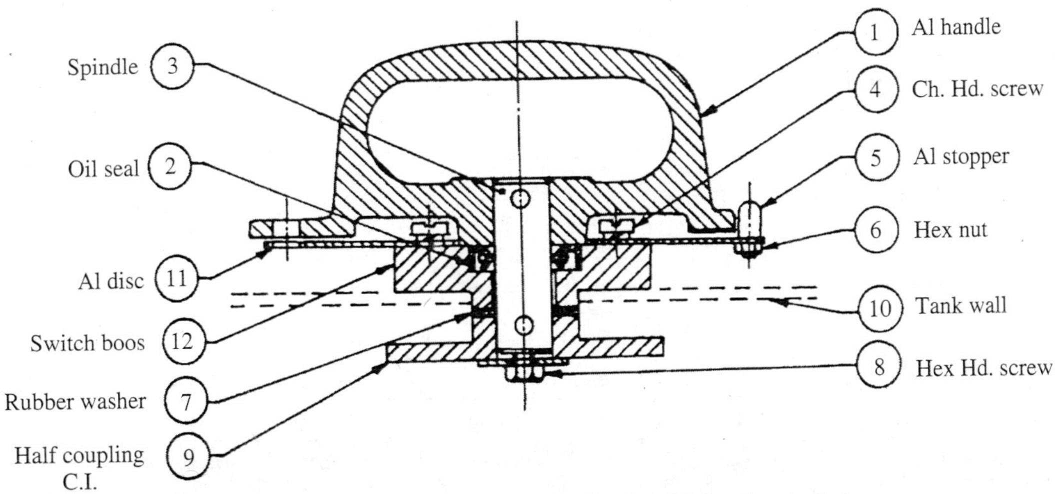

FIGURE 12.5 Transformer tap control switch after value analysis.

(vii) **Implementation.** One prototype was built, as per VE team recommendation and tested for its performance and reliability. Based on the test results, thorough discussions were held with the concerned department, i.e., Production shop, Design office, Quality Assurance and Sales and Servicing, and their comments were obtained. Five more assemblies were made as per the proposed design and sent for field trials. After successful field trials and ensuring that quality and reliability were unaffected, the proposed designs were introduced in regular production.

12.13.5 Benefits of Value Engineering

1. *Cost benefits:*
   (a) Cost of subassembly before value engineering — ₹ 165.00
   (b) Cost of subassembly after value engineering — ₹ 85.00
   (ref. Annexure E for cost benefit on each item)
   (c) Savings per subassembly — ₹ 80.00
   (d) Expected annual savings — ₹ 96,000.00
2. *Other benefits:*
   (a) Simplified design
   (b) Reduction in assembly time
   (c) Reduction of components
   (d) Less inventory

Annexure A Bill of material

Component	*No. per assembly*	*Bought or made*	*Material*	*Cost per piece*	*Cost per assembly*
Handle	1	B.O.	Aluminium casting	20.00	20.00
Spindle	1	B.O.	Steel bright bar	12.00	12.00
Brass plug	1	B.O.	Brass (Hex)	67.00	67.00
Switch boss	1	B.O.	Mild steel	26.00	26.00
Dial plate	1	B.O.	Aluminium plate	16.25	16.25
Switch stopper	2	B.O.	Brass	4.00	8.00
Oil seal	1	B.O.	Rubber	12.00	12.00
Hardware	–	B.O.	Steel		3.75
Total					165.00

Annexure B Function analysis

Component	*Basic function*		*Secondary function*	
	Verb	*Noun*	*Verb*	*Noun*
Handle	Changes	Position	Provides	Locking
	Provides	Grip	Locates	Position
	Transmits	Rotation	Withstands	Operative force

(*Contd.*)

Component	Basic function		Secondary function	
	Verb	Noun	Verb	Noun
Spindle	Transmits	Rotation	Prevents	Rust
	Connects	Mechanical	Locates	Handle
Plug	Positions	Oil seal	Provides	Support
			Prevents	Rust
			Guides	Spindle
Switch boss	Guides	Spindle	Connects	Mechanical
	Holes	Oilseal	Prevents	Leakage
			Holds	Dial plate
Dial plate	Indicates	Position	Facilitate	Locking
			Holds	Stopper
			Prevents	Rust
Switch stopper	Restricts	Overtravel	Prevents	Rust
Oil seal	Prevents	Leakage	Reduces	Friction
Hardware	Connects	Parts	Prevents	Rust
	Withstands	Operative force		

Annexure C Function-cost-worth analysis

Component	Present cost (₹)	Functions			Worth (₹)	Value gap	Remark
		Verb	Noun	BS			
Handle	20.00	Transmits	Rotation	B	15.00	5	
		Changes	Position	B			
		Provides	Grip	B			
Spindle	12.00	Transmits	Rotation	B	8.00	4	
		Locates	Handle	S			
Brass plug	67.00	Holds	Oil seal	B	6.00	61	
		Prevents	Rust	S			
Switch boss	26.00	Holds	Spindle	B	16.00	10	
		Seats	Oil seal	B			
Dial plate	16.25	Indicates	Position	B	15.00	1.25	
		Holds	Stopper	S			
		Facilitates	Locking	B			
Switch stopper	8.00	Restricts	Overtravel	B	2.00	6	
Oil seal	12.00	Prevents	Leakage	B	12.00	0	
Hardware	3.75	Connects	Parts	B	3.75	0	
		Prevents	Rust	S			

Annexure D Through brainstorming

Item	*Ideas generated*
Handle	1. Cast iron handle 2. Extended boss in handle for positioning the oil seal 3. M.S. fabricated handle, with plating 4. Spindle and handle one piece made of aluminium or cast iron 5. Spindle and handle one piece made of DMC or polymer
Spindle	1. Standard bright bar for spindle 2. Short length spindle 3. Made out of DMC 4. Aluminium rod 5. Polymer rod 6. Bakelite rod
Brass plug	1. M.S. cover plate instead of plug to hold oil seal 2. M.S. plug with plating 3. Plastic plug 4. Nylon plug 5. Internal circlip to hold oil seal 6. Die cast aluminium 7. Hard rubber plug 8. Spring loaded pressure plate 9. Handle itself as cover plate for oil seal 10. Threaded wooden plug 11. Eliminate brass plug from the assembly 12. Dial plate itself as cover plate
Switch boss	1. Lesser boss width 2. Cast iron switch boss 3. Put switch outside the oil
Dial plate	1. Fibre reinforced plastic or plastic painted plate 2. Sticker on tank wall instead of dialplate 3. Bakelite plate with engraving
Switch stopper	1. Mould steel plated stopper 2. Internal threaded stopper 3. Internal threaded aluminium stopper 4. Small dia. stopper 5. Steel screws instead of special stopper 6. DMC with metal inserts.

Annexure E Benefits of value engineering

Tap switch control assembly

Items	*Before VE*	*After VE*
	₹	₹
Handle	20.00	22.00
Spindle	12.00	8.00
Brass plug	67.00	—

(*Contd.*)

Annexure E Benefits of value engineering

Tap switch control assembly

Items	*Before VE*	*After VE*
Switch boss	26.00	16.00
Dial plate	16.25	16.25
Switch stopper	8.00	2.00
Oil seal	12.00	12.00
Hardware	3.75	3.75
Total	165.00	80.00

12.14 MATERIAL AND PROCESS SELECTION IN VALUE ENGINEERING*

An engineer must not only understand the problems of engineering economy associated with production runs, but also how design and production interact. In the past, because of the limited number of materials and processes, a product engineer could prepare the majority of designs. Geometric designs were evaluated initially with the materials and processes which were available. This approach is no longer acceptable and the design methods of the past must necessarily be updated. Any product design today, particularly through value engineering, must undertake a rigorous study of the materials and process possibilities.

12.14.1 The Problem

Many companies in India have been oriented to a particular manufacturing process, such as a foundry. With the greater emergency of product-oriented companies, they have the know-how to effectively utilize many different materials and processes to produce a particular product. This is one factor that has contributed to the need for a much more rigorous consideration of materials and processes. We are in the midst of a technological revolution. New processes and materials are being developed at an accelerating rate, and these have opened up whole new possibilities for product design and manufacturing.

Further, manufacturing companies are facing increased competition today, and the importance of materials and process considerations in terms of this competition are quite clear. A product may have excellent functional utility and sales appeal to the customer, but it is useless if it cannot be manufactured at a competitive cost. Since material and process are major contributors to the product cost, it is desirable that these are given considerable attentions before the product is put on the market. Once a product is released for production, there is a natural resistance to major changes in product design in the minds of persons who have been working with the existing design. It must be realized that "Process Selection saves rupees while Process Optimization saves paise". The potential effect of materials and processes on the competitive effect of a product is a very important factor contributing to the need for a rigorous consideration of materials and process in product design.

*The authors are thankful to Professor M. Vasantrao, NITIE, Bombay, for permitting the inclusion of his research on Value Engineering.

12.14.2 Design, Material, Process and Supplier Decisions

The manufacturing cost of a product is dependent on the decisions related to the following:

1. Design
2. Materials
3. Process
4. Supplier

There is a close connection between the selection of design, materials and process (DMP). The major efforts in selecting materials and processes will have to be accomplished during "Concept Formulation". This is where a considerable amount of creativity is required with the main emphasis on generation of good ideas. The ultimate in good ideas is a solution to the design problem which will satisfy all the functional,and aesthetic requirements, and costs almost nothing. This will, however, never be achieved, but it is surprising how much difference can be seen in the results of two designers working independently on the same problem.

In many cases, a geometric design will inherently dictate a particular material and process. However, DMP are important integrated aspects of the total product design. They are all mutually dependent. It is, therefore, important that the product alternatives considered be total in terms of their geometric design aspects, material aspects, and processing aspects. These product alternatives may be called DMP alternatives. This, however, does not mean that these three items cannot be considered independently in some phase of the design process. In fact, of 3 designs, 3 materials and 3 processes to be considered independently can lead to 27 possible combinations. If one more material were to be added, the number of alternatives could be increased by 9 rather than 1. Many of the combinations will not be feasible, such as steel combined with pressure die casting. But with the very large number of metals and alloys available, the number of alternatives will still be unmanageable.

One is therefore faced with the problem of reducing the DMP alternatives to a realistic number, depending on the situation. However, the consideration of materials and process must be as rigorous as possible. The degree to which the various DMP alternatives are considered is limited primarily by the cost of decision making which includes salaries, testing etc. along with the opportunity cost associated with the time delay due to the rigorousness of decision making. What is also of interest is that the actual cost of a product is a function of its design, material and process.

As shown in Figure 12.6, the product cost will decrease with the increased design effort. There is therefore, an optimum design effort at which the total cost of decision-making cost and product cost will be minimum.

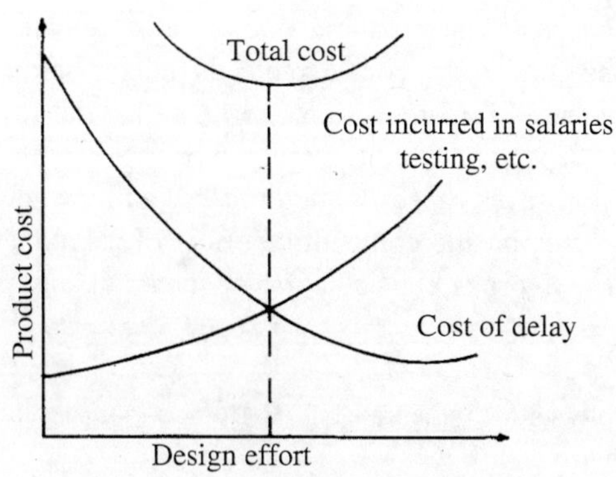

FIGURE 12.6 Optimal design effort.

12.14.3 Product Parameters

The consideration of materials and processes during product design requires setting up of product parameters in order to establish boundary conditions. This provides a basis for the evaluation of materials and processes. The product parameters spell out the design requirements in terms of those factors which affect the choice of materials and process. These factors generally can be classified as

1. Process Selection Factors:
   (a) Shape requirements
   (b) Size requirements
   (c) Tolerance requirements
   (d) Surface finish requirements
   (e) Annual volume requirements
   (f) Material characteristics (if material is determined)
2. Material Selection Factors:
   (a) Material requirements
   (b) Process characteristics (if process is determined)

The product parameters, properly defined, will establish the problem definition at a given design level based on the above factors. No attempt is made to cover cost consideration in the definition of the product parameters as an awareness of potential costs will permeate the entire design effort. A detailed cost analysis will be accomplished only after the DMP alternatives have been generated.

12.14.4 Process Selection

Process selection requires a broad and extensive knowledge of various manufacturing processes. In many instances, value engineers well versed in a few processes have a tendency to use these more often to the exclusion of others.

The need for consideration of alternative processes can well be seen by the changes occurring in manufacturing, forgings are replaced by heavy stampings and castings. Stampings are being replaced by die-casting and plastic moulding. These changes are only representative of what is occurring continuously in today's manufacturing technology.

Process selection is the initial selection of a manufacturing process, which in combination with a geometric design and material, fulfils the design requirements. This, however, has various problems associated with it. A process may require various additional subprocesses to achieve the design requirements, which complicate the problem of process selection. Besides, there is a lack of adequate information on the capabilities and limitations of the various processes available with different Indian manufacturers and vendors, and the costs associated with them. This means that in many situations due to a lack of readily available information, adequate screening and evaluation of processes can be achieved. Since the capabilities of various manufacturing organizations vary according to their know-how and equipment, the evaluation of processes in terms of capabilities and limitation is normally done in relation to a specific manufacturing organization rather than using general information.

There is, therefore, a need for communication between the production engineers of various manufacturing firms, and between the designers and production engineers of a particular firm. It must be emphasized again that the selection of a process is done and evaluated in the form of design-material-process alternatives.

12.14.5 Process Selection Parameters

The following factors have a primary influence on the selection of a manufacturing process.

(i) **Geometry.** The consideration of processes is done in terms of a specific geometric design of a component or product in terms of its shape, size, general tolerance, surface finish, etc. The determination of geometric parameters must take into consideration any secondary processes that may be required.

The geometric shape has a significant effect on the selection of process. B.W. Niebel and Baldwin have suggested the following shape classifications:

(a) Solid concentric
(b) Hollow concentric
(c) Cup or cone concentric
(d) Solid or hollow nonconcentric
(e) Cup or cone nonconcentric
(f) Flat and flanged parts
(g) Spiral, repetitive, irregular concentric
(h) Miscellaneous complex

Howard G. Lestle has classified various processes in the following four shape classifications:

(a) Solid concentric
(b) Hollow concentric
(c) Spiral, repetitive, irregular concentric
(d) Non-concentric

(ii) **Material requirements.** Unless material requirements severely limit the number of acceptable materials, it is generally recommended that the process alternatives be developed before material alternatives, as it is normally easier to fit a material to a process than to fit a process to a material. However, in some cases where material requirements are stringent, it may be more practical to establish specific material alternatives prior to the consideration of processes. The fact that normally material requirements are not generated prior to process selection does not mean that material parameters do not influence process selection.

(iii) **Production volume.** The production volume requirements greatly affect the economic feasibility of a process. In many cases, the need for a re-evaluation of an existing process arises due to a sudden change in volume. Though the actual volume requirements for some future period cannot be determined exactly, a decision under risk of uncertainty may have to be taken considering the different levels of production. In addition, the anticipated volume significantly influences the amount of process selection effort. The greater the volume, the greater would be the process selection rewards, but this does not mean that the small volume product should be overlooked.

12.14.6 Material Selection

The selection of a sound, economic material for product design is in itself a difficult problem. The additional consideration of design material and process-material interactions complicates the problem further. In many situations, development work on the creation of new material leads to a solution of a design problem. Therefore, the continuous development of new and better materials must always be anticipated and exploited.

The general problem of material selection is choosing one material from the many available. In the design process, this proceeds from the initial consideration of broad classes of materials to the testing and evaluation of very specific materials. It is essential that the material requirements be specified in terms of product function and end use.

The generation of material alternatives is a major problem as there are thousands of metallic alloys. In addition to these are the large number of nonmetals, which further enlarge the scope of the problem. In the initial stages of design, the broad material groups can be considered, such as ferrous, nonferrous, plastics, and other nonmetals. Only in the later stages of design, can the specific materials be considered. The determination of what alternatives are to be considered is done largely intuitively. With proper computer programs, the material selection process can be speeded up to a point where the consideration of large number of materials becomes practical.

In the initial evaluation of material alternatives, many can be rejected on the basis of absolute product parameters, such as strength, conductivity, magnetic permeability, etc. This is fairly straightforward in that either the alternative meets some absolute requirement or it does not. Once the materials which do not meet the requirements have been eliminated, the problem is far more difficult. Though all the remaining 'alternatives are acceptable, the question is how good they are compared to one another. The decision matrix is used in the final evaluation of specific alternatives. In addition, the materials finally selected are with respect to a particular geometric design and process, taking into account the DMP interactions.

12.14.7 Material Selection Parameters

The primary conditions affecting the choice of a material in terms of various requirements are:

(i) **Function.** Many of the parameters developed for material selection are related to the functions the product must perform in terms of mechanical, physical, electrical, and thermal properties of materials. This has to be based on a thorough understanding of the product application.

(ii) **Appearance.** The material makes a major contribution to the aesthetics of product. Though it is difficult to establish any quantitative parameters for this, this must necessarily be included for material selection.

(iii) **Reliability.** This is related to the probability that the material will meet all the requirements during the product life, and is closely tied to the other types of material. Reliability is gaining greater importance as a criterion for material selection due to increasing consumer demands for trouble-free products.

(iv) **Service life.** The length of service life over which the material maintains its desirable characteristics is a very important consideration in material selection.

(v) **Environment.** The environment to which the material is exposed during the product life is a very important consideration, depending on whether the environment is beneficial or harmful.

(vi) **Compatibility.** This is an important factor influencing material selection, whenever more than one type of material is used in a product or assembly, consideration of the possibility of galvanic action is essential.

(vii) **Producibility.** The selection of material in relation to the ease of producibility of an item is an important consideration, in the context of DMP interactions.

(viii) **Cost.** The material cost is a significant factor contributing to the overall cost. However, it must be remembered that the total product cost is of primary importance. It is conceivable that a DMP alternative having a high material cost could have a very low overall product cost.

12.14.8 Multivariable Chart

Computer programs can be developed for the evaluation of process alternatives in terms of various parameters related to the geometric design and materials. The major problem, however, would be the usefulness of the output data which is limited by the accuracy and applicability of the process capabilities data fed in. Programs could more easily be developed on the basis of published data. However, data developed and used in a manufacturing company would result in a more useful program.

A device often used by Industrial Engineers for combining two-dimensional matrices in one decision chart is known as a *multivariable chart*, first developed by Phill Carroll in his book, *How to Chart Data*.

A multivariable chart for process selection has been developed, for some ferrous materials based on published data in various reference books and surveys carried out in some manufacturing companies in Mumbai (Bombay).

The chart includes the following parameters for selection:

1. Geometric form
2. Surface finish
3. General tolerance
4. Production volume
5. Material

Use of multivariable chart grid. Starting from the column associated with the geometric shape classification based on the component shape, one goes vertically to reach the row associated with the required surface finish. One then goes along the row till the column associated with the required general tolerance is reached. Go down along this column until the row for the required production volume is reached. One then goes along this row until the column for the desired material is reached. The acceptable processes are listed in this column which meet the process selection parameters. From an initial consideration of the many processes, all but a few would have been eliminated because of shape surface finish, general tolerance, production volume, and material requirements. If the material requirements are not constraint, the process in the final row is acceptable.

There are many advantages in the use of multivariable chart in process selection. These are:

1. They are very fast, and many process alternatives can be considered in a very short time.
2. They can be used by a value engineer anywhere, and do not require the use of a computer.
3. The input parameter can be easily varied, and many combinations of these can be evaluated in a short time.
4. If a particular process is to be added or deleted, the chart can be immediately corrected.

5. It is easy to identify the parameters which significantly affect the results.
6. The chart can be useful to any value Engineer who has only a basic engineering knowledge of processes.

12.14.9 Organizing for Material and Process Selection

One question that could logically be asked regarding materials and process selection is who should do this work. Basically, this work is a part of design or product engineering activity. Because of the accelerating advances being made presently on materials and processes, there is a need for close interaction between design and engineering. A process engineer who could act as a link between design and production should be an effective interface between the two functions.

REVIEW QUESTIONS

1. Define value. What is the background of evolution of value engineering as a subject? Sec. 12.1 Introduction, 12.2 Historical Perspective; P 308, 309

2. What are the various steps of value analysis (VA) job plan? Describe the following steps of a VA job plan: Sec. 12.8; P 311–313

(i) Information step, (ii) analysis step, (iii) creativity step, (iv) use of preliminary judgement, and (v) evaluation.

3. What are the value analysis (VA) job plans proposed by: Miles, Mudge, Fallon, Dell'Isolla, General Services Administration? Table 12.1; P 313

4. What is creativity? How does design by creative routes differ from Engineering design?

[**Ans:** The essential differences are as under:

Creative design	Engineering design
1. Creative approach with the steps: (a) Preparation (b) Soaking in the problem (c) Relaxation (d) Illumination or Eureka (e) Recording and documenting	1. Analytical approach based on engineering, cut-dried principles, does not need heuristic and instinctive approach. Use of handbooks is done for selection-based design, e.g., ball bearings, shafts, seals, gaskets, etc.
2. Individualistic approach	2. Team based approach
3. Heavy dependence on synectics, i.e., analogies like personal analogy, symbolic analogy, direct analogy, fantasy, etc.	3. Emulation and experience with similar earlier designs.

Personal analogy: The designer imagines that he is himself the machine.

Symbolic analogy: Strong as an ox, small as a pea.

Direct analogy: Tough as the turtles back to simulate isotropic material, cob web of a spider to represent lightweight structure.]

5. What is cost-worth approach to value analysis?

6. What are the roadblocks to creativity? Sec. 12.9.2; P 314

7. Discuss the role of materials, design, process and supplier in enhancement of value.

[*Hint:* Value = Function/Cost, Any improvement in function and decrease in cost should increase value. Cost can be brought down by proper design, low cost process for in-house produced components; proper supplier can supply at a low price. In present times, companies buy 90–95% of parts from vendors and limit in-house production of components to their core competency.]

8. (a) How is a multivariable chart used? How does it help in material-process selection?

(b) If a component is solid concentric, surface finish 3 μm and tolerance = 0.4 mm, lot size = 500. Find suitable material and primary process for producing the component.

Solution (b) Surface finish of 3 μm = Code (3)

Tolerance of 0.4 mm = Code (2)

Solid concentric = Code (1)

Lot size 500 is between 101 and 999 = Code (2)

Outputs: For stainless steel, high alloy steel, high carbon steel, the process code is (5) – Investment casting.

For low carbon steel the process code is (5, 11), i.e. 5–, … 11– Impact extrusion

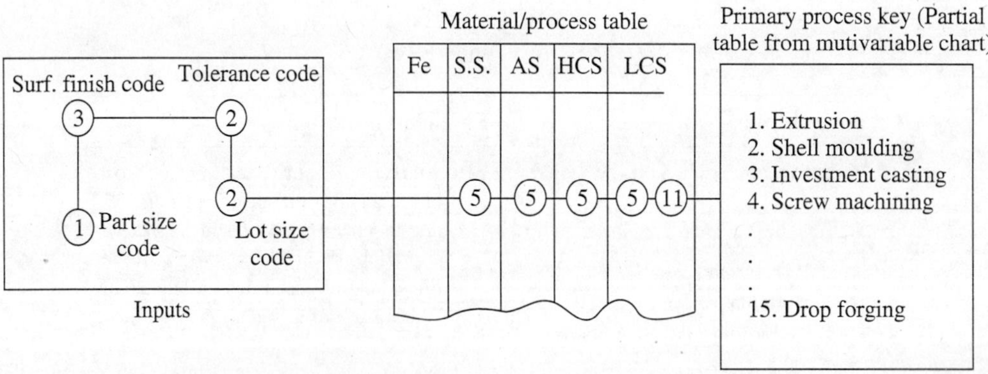

FIGURE 12.7 Use of multivariable chart.

9. What is check-listing approach to creativity? Explain. What are the questions asked about existing design? Sec. 12.9.4; P 315(iii); Sec. 12.12; P 322–323; Figure 12.3

10. Explain Functional Analysis System Technique (FAST) diagrams. Illustrate with an example.

[*Hint:* Example of overhead projector is taken (Figure 12.8).]

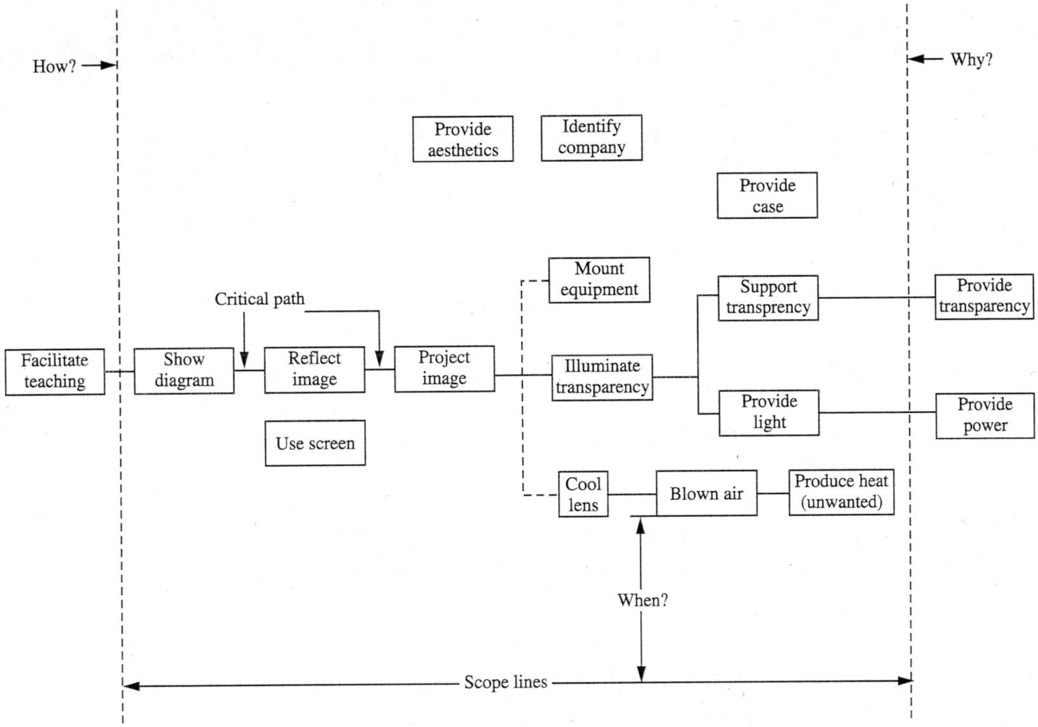

FIGURE 12.8 FAST diagram for overhead projector.

11. Why does the value of a part reduce with increasing weight? Why small parts have a higher cost per kilogram than larger parts? What is 'comparative analysis' technique? Explain.

[**Ans:** This technique compares similar parts, e.g., die castings, through the use of graph with X-axis as weight of part and Y-axis as price of part per kg. Small parts have higher cost per kg since mould costs are same for both.]

REFERENCES

[1] Miles, L.D., *Techniques of Value Analysis and Engineering*, McGraw-Hill, New York, 1961.

[2] Bouey, E., 'Value Engineering is Unique, *Interaction*', December 1979.

[3] Mudge, A.E., *Value Engineering—A systematic approach*, McGraw-Hill, New York, 1971.

[4] Salvcndy, G.J. (Ed.), *Handbook of Industrial Engineering*, Wiley, New York, 1984.

[5] Parker, D.E., *Value Engineering Theory*, Lawrence Miles Value Foundation, Washington, DC, 1977.

Chapter 13

Role of Computer in Product Design, Manufacturing and Management

The computer has brought about a revolution in the entire manufacturing system which comprises product design, manufacturing and management. In fact, computer, to a great extent, has been responsible for linking together the above areas of manufacturing into a single market and product driven system which is called Computer-Integrated Manufacturing (CIM). We shall discuss CIM later in Section 13.6, but first we focus our attention on CAD (Computer-Aided Design) and CAM (Computer-Aided Manufacturing).

13.1 CAD/CAM: SOME DEFINITIONS

Computer aided design can be defined as the use of computer system to assist in the creation, modification, analysis or optimization of a design.

Computer aided manufacturing can be defined as the use of computer system to plan, manage and control the operations of the manufacturing plant. These include the following:

NC part programming. Here, control programs are prepared for automated machine tools.

Computer-Aided Process Planning (CAPP) involves listing of operation sequence required for processing a particular part.

Production scheduling and material requirements planning. This is a planning tool for taking decisions like when to order and how much to order for raw materials and other purchased parts. This helps in achieving proper schedule.

13.2 PRODUCT CYCLE AND CAD/CAM

Product cycle starts from customers and markets and involves three steps:

1. Product identification
2. Design and optimization engineering
3. Drafting.

The three phases are well known primary phases of design. Computer-Aided Design provides support in step 1, i.e., product concept development is aided in CAD modelling in which a large number of alternative designs can be generated on the computer screen. The best option can be selected from these designs. The types of models used in CAD are:

- Wireframe models
- Surface models
- Solid models

Step 2, design engineering and optimization, can be done on a CAD terminal through sophisticated methods such as finite element analysis in which the proposed product is divided into triangular shaped (usually) elements. The effect of loading the structure with expected loading is seen, and the deflections and stresses at various nodal points defined by vertices of finite element triangle are determined. Stress concentrations in object can be displayed through colour graphics.

Step 3 of design, namely, drafting, can be effectively executed on a CAD terminal using input devices such as digitizing tablet in which any line drawing can be done and stored/displayed by the computer on the CRT screen. The digitizing tablet helps in converting x and y movements of the tablet into digital signals which are stored in the computer for possible retrieval. CADD (Computer- Aided Design and Drafting) replaces the conventional tee board with CRT screen. Other input hardware includes the track ball, the mouse, and the joystick.

13.3 ROLE OF COMPUTER IN MANUFACTURING

CAM accomplishes process planning which determines that the sequence of operations is done through CAPP. Currently, there are two methods in use:

1. *Variant type*, in which standard process plans are available for standard components.
2. *Generative type*, which is based on the part coding decided by products geometry, and a processing sequence is generated by the computer accordingly.

(i) **Scheduling.** Material requirements planning determines what materials are required on the shop floor at what time and in what quantity so that a master schedule is implemented. This can be processed by the computer.

(ii) **Production.** Computer numerical control machines (CNC), material handling devices, inspection devices such as coordinate measuring machines operated by a master computer produce the desired product in batches as required, Just In Time (JIT).

Figures 13.1 and 13.2 show product cycle with and without the aid of computer, respectively.

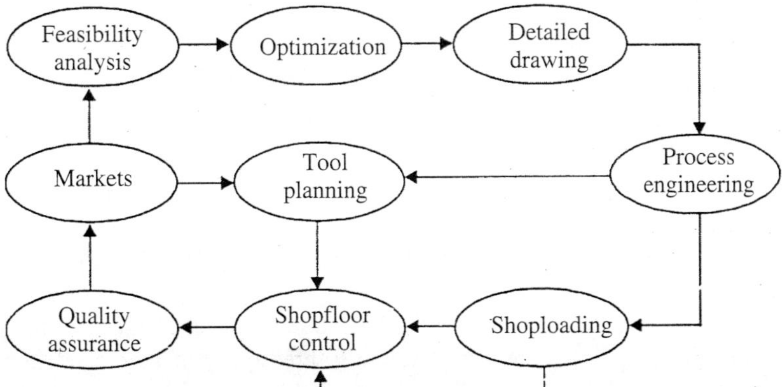

FIGURE 13.1 Product cycle without computer.

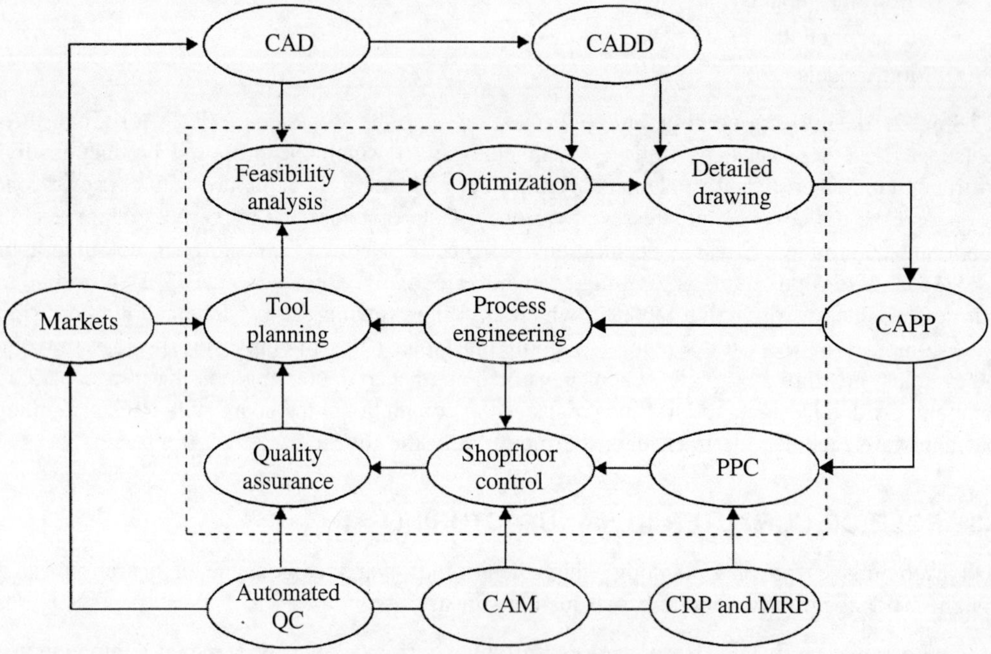

FIGURE 13.2 Product cycle with computer.

13.4 ROLE OF COMPUTER IN DESIGN PROCESS

The design-related tasks which are performed by a modern CAD system can be grouped into four functional areas:

1. Geometric modelling
2. Engineering analysis
3. Design review and evaluation
4. Automated drafting.

Figure 13.3(a) shows design morphology as stated by Shigley [1]. Figure 13.3(b) illustrates the role of computer in the design process.

13.4.1 Geometric Modelling

In CAD, geometric modelling involves computer compatible mathematical description of the geometry of an object. Trie mathematical description allows the image of the object to be displayed and manipulated on a graphics terminal through signals from the Central Processing Unit (CPU) of the CAD system.

In geometric modelling, the designer constructs the image of the object on the CRT screen of the interactive computer graphics system, by inputting three types of command to the computer:

1. The first type of command generates basic geometric elements such as points, lines and circle.

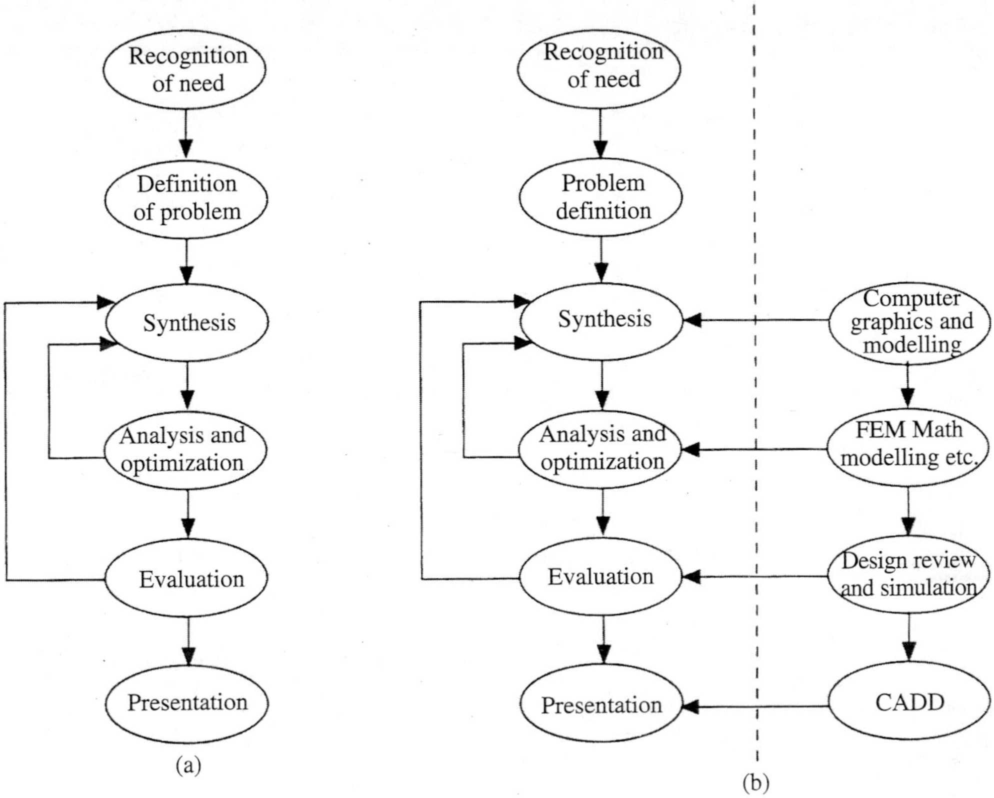

FIGURE 13.3 (a) Design morphology according to Shigley and (b) Role of computer in design process.

2. The second type of command is meant to accomplish translation scaling (size change), rotation or other transformations of the elements.
3. The third type of command joins the various elements to give the desired object.

During the above process, the computer converts the commands into a mathematical model, stores it in the computer data files and displays it as an image on the CRT screen.

Example. An example cited by Bedworth et al. [2] to design a component is given in Figure 13.4. The user has chosen to build the part by describing the outer turned profile cross-section, generating a solid from the cross-section and adding a rectangular block at the end.

The cross-section of the solid of revolution can be input by specifying the coordinates of the vertices in the cross-section, similar to the procedure used by a draftsman to draw a 2-D orthographic projection. The actual coordinate specification depends on the user interface. One method is to indicate points on a graphics terminal. The vertices are connected in order from point to point using a LINE command. Only half of the cross-section must be defined, since the part is symmetrical. When all points have been connected, a SPIN command generates a solid of revolution. The box on the end may be generated by using a CREATE BLOCK command. With parameters which specify the length, width, height, location and orientation of the box, by executing a UNITE command, the box and round solids are jointed and become one solid. For verifying solidity of the objective, Euler relationships can be used.

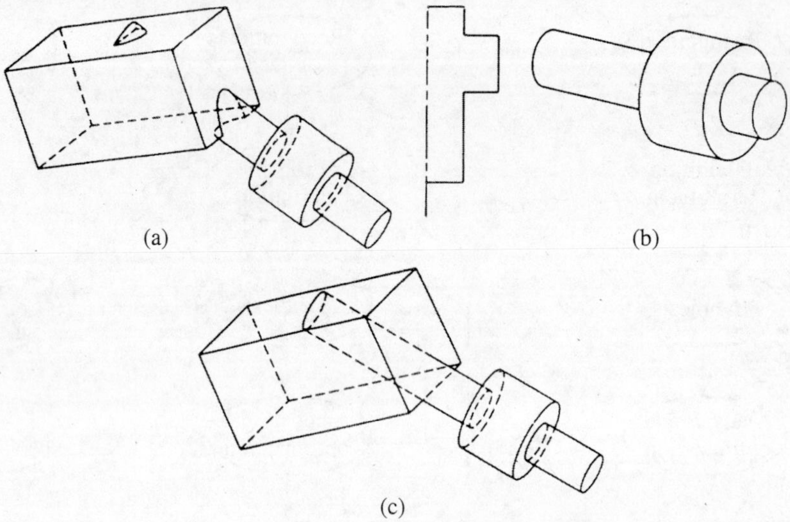

FIGURE 13.4 (a) Box and Cylindrical solid become one object after command HIDDEN LINE REMOVAL, (b) Profile and corresponding solid of revolution created by SPIN command, (c) Rectangular box penetrated by Cylindrical solid by UNITE command.

There are essentially three methods of representing objects in geometric modelling.

1. The first method uses wire frames to represent the object. Figure 13.5 shows the development of a wireframe model. Wireframe models are often confusing because of extra lines. Some CAD systems have "Hidden line removal" feature.

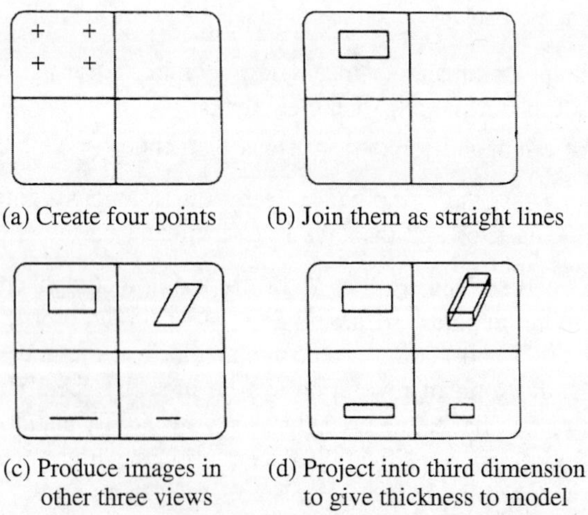

FIGURE 13.5 Development of a wireframe model on computer.

2. Surface modelling is an improved version which defines the outside part geometry precisely but is unable to highlight inner details.
3. Solid modelling is the most advanced method of modelling. It allows computation of such properties as mass and moment of inertia. It is very useful for rendering, which shows the inner details of an object after it is cut away (Figure 13.6).

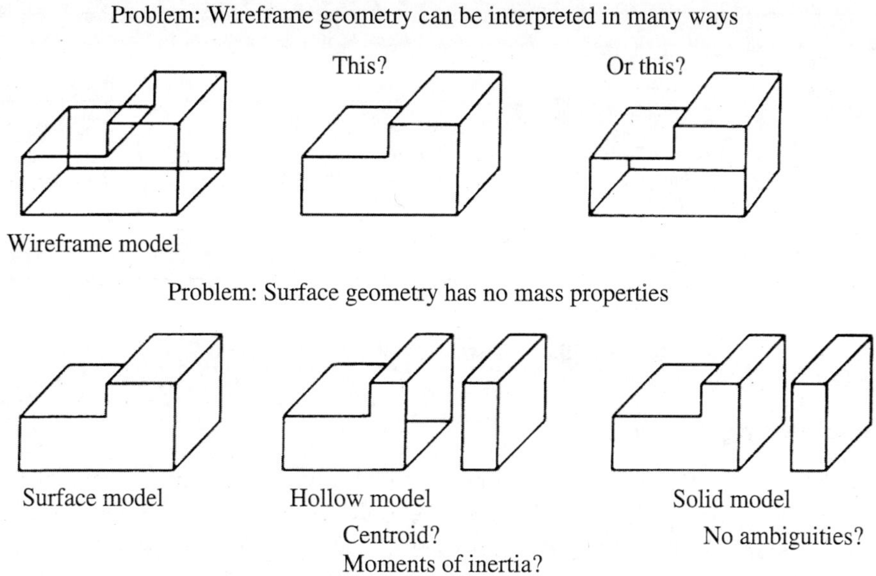

FIGURE 13.6 Various methods of modelling a solid.

Dimension of models. Models can be two dimensional, $2\frac{1}{2}$-dimensional or three-dimensional as shown in Figure 13.7. Two-and-a half dimensional models define axis-symmetric objects without side wall details. In boundary modelling, the shapes defined have to follow a set of Euler relationships which state in polyhedra:

$$(\text{Vertices} + \text{Faces} - \text{Edges}) = 2 \tag{13.1}$$

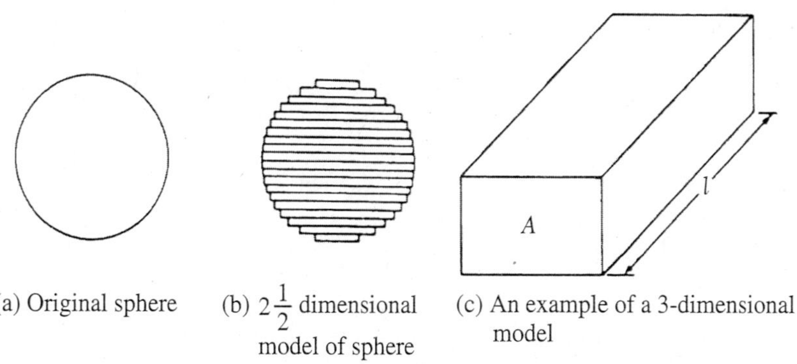

(a) Original sphere (b) $2\frac{1}{2}$ dimensional model of sphere (c) An example of a 3-dimensional model

FIGURE 13.7 Dimensions of solids modelling.

When the bodies contain holes and passages:

$$\text{Vertices} - \text{edges} + \text{faces} - \text{holes in faces} + 2 \times \text{passages} - 2 \times \text{shells} = 0 \tag{13.2}$$

$$(V - E + F - H + 2P - 2S) = 0$$

Figure 13.8 illustrates Euler's equation as applied to a solid object, with holes and passages.

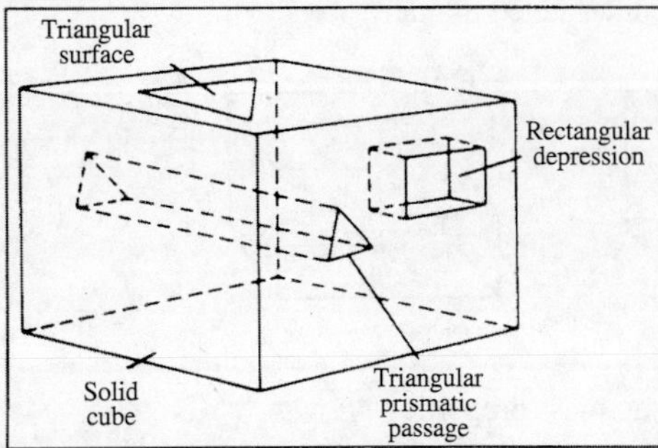

	F	E	V	H	S	R
1. Cube	6	12	8	0	1	0
2. Triangular passage	3	9	6	2	0	1
3. Rectangular depression	5	12	8	1	0	0
4. Surface	1	3	3	1	0	0
	15	36	25	4	1	1

FIGURE 13.8 Illustrations of Euler's equations.

13.4.2 Engineering Analysis

In the formulation of any design project, some sort of analysis is required. The analysis may be stress-strain calculations, heat transfer computations or the use of differential equations to describe the dynamic behaviour of the system being designed. The computer can be used to assist in this work. Turnkey CAD/CAM systems can be interfaced to engineering analysis software to test a given product design.

Probably the most powerful analysis feature of a CAD system is the Finite Element Method (FEM).

As an example of the FEM, we consider a cantilever loaded at one end (see Figure 13.9). The FEM approach is as follows:

1. The object to be analyzed is divided into small elements, usually triangular elements.
2. An equation is assumed between displacement u, v and the coordinates x and y in the X and Y directions. The strain ε_x in the X-direction, the strain ε_y in the Y-direction and shear ε_{xy}, are expressed from the theory of elasticity as:

$$\varepsilon_x = \frac{du}{dx} \qquad \varepsilon_y = \frac{dv}{dy}$$

$$\tau_{xy} = \frac{du}{dy} + \frac{dv}{dx}$$

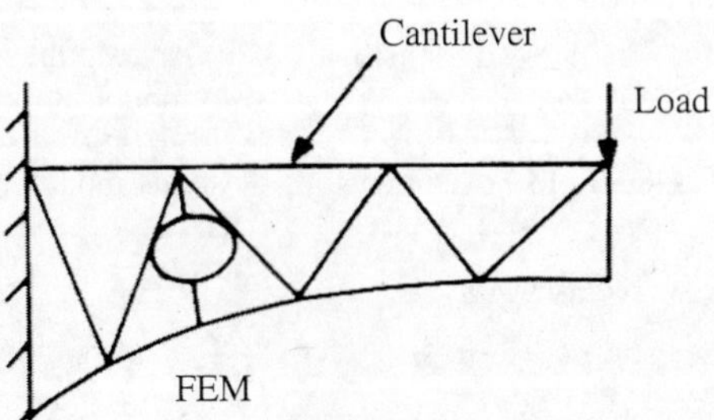

FIGURE 13.9 Finite element approach for stress analysis in a cantilever with end loading.

The matrix connecting ε and δ, i.e. u or v is B:

$$[\varepsilon] = [B]\ [\delta] \tag{13.3}$$

3. From the theory of stress and strain, we can derive the relation between stress σ and strain ε as

$$[\sigma] = [D]\ [\varepsilon] \tag{13.4}$$

where D is a function of Elastic modulus and Poisson's ratio.

4. From force analysis for the element under consideration, we obtain a relation

$$[f] = [\mathrm{A}]\ [\sigma] \tag{13.5}$$

5. Combining Eqs. (13.3–13.5), we get

$$[f] = [A]\ [D]\ [B]\ [\delta] = [k]\ [\delta]$$

where (k) is the element stiffness matrix.

Now, as a result of the relation between external forces (F) which are known from loading and reaction for the structure, the deflection (δ), and (K) obtained for the calculation of the stiffness matrix, we have the equation.

$$F = [K]\ [\delta] \tag{13.6}$$

Thus, the deflection δ can be calculated at various nodal points. Hence ε can be calculated from Eq. (13.3) and σ from Eq. (13.4). In FEM, a graphics display to indicate the final output data through stress contours, colour graphics, etc. is very useful.

13.4.3 Design Review and Evaluation

Checking the accuracy of design can be accomplished conveniently on the graphics terminal. Semi-automatic dimensioning and tolerancing routines, which assign size specifications to surfaces indicated by the user, help in reducing the possibility of dimensioning errors. The designer can zoom in on any details and closely scrutinize the magnified image. Animation helps in checking kinematic performance of like mechanisms without resorting to pinboard experiments. Gear simulation can be carried out and tooth contact analysis can be done. Interference checking of shaft-hole assemblies and the link can be done.

13.4.4 Automated Drafting

This procedure results in saving a lot of time and labour. Computer-aided drafting is known as the *design workstation*. The CAD workstation is the system interface with the outside world. A good CAD workstation must accomplish five functions: It must—

1. interface with the central processing unit of the computer;
2. generate a steady graphic image for the user;
3. provide digital description of the graphic image;
4. translate computer commands into operating function; and
5. be user friendly.

Figure 13.10 shows the block diagram of a CAD workstation.

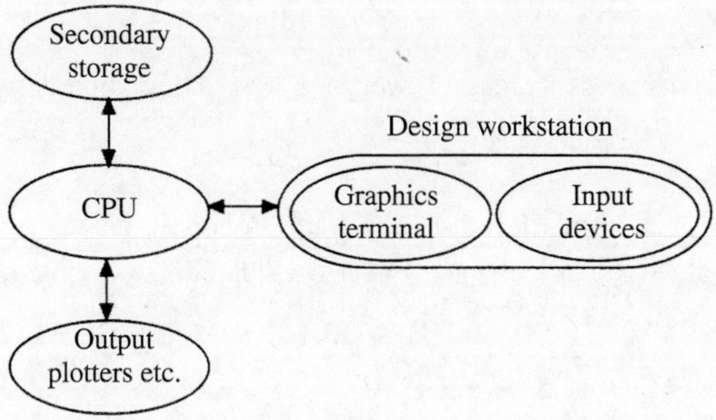

FIGURE 13.10 Block diagram of a CAD workstation.

13.5 CREATION OF A MANUFACTURING DATABASE

Apart from increasing the productivity of the design department of a company, an important reason for adopting CAD is that it offers an opportunity to create the database for manufacturing the product. In the conventional manufacturing cycle, engineering drawings are prepared by draftsmen and used by manufacturing engineers to develop the process plan ("Route Sheets"). Thus, design and processing are separated from one another. In an integrated CAD/CAM system, the aim is not only to automate designing through part code as input but also to utilize the very same part code for automated process planning. Figure 13.11 depicts the CAD/CAM integration.

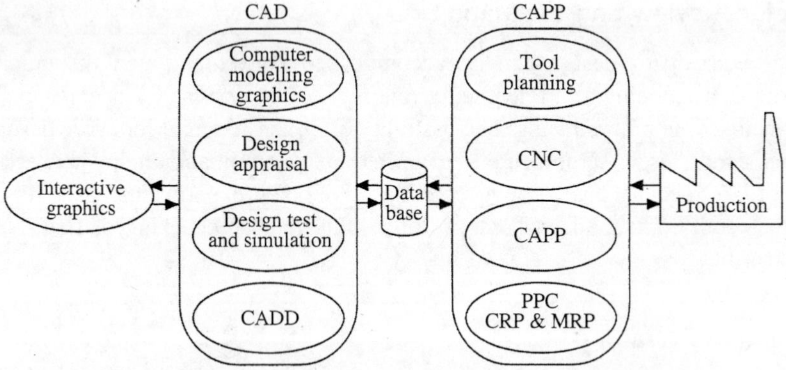

FIGURE 13.11 Block diagram of CAD/CAM integration.

Benefits of CAD/CAM

- Improved productivity
- etter costing
- Shorter lead times
- Fewer errors in NC part programming

- Reduced engineering personnel requirement
- Reduced tooling costs
- Possibility of easy modifications
- Better design for manufacture
- Reduced subcontracting
- Operation at optimal conditions
- Improved design accuracy
- In analysis, easier recognition of component interaction
- Assistance in inspection of complex parts
- Reduced prototype testing
- Better teamwork and system integration
- Increased standardization

13.6 COMPUTER-INTEGRATED MANUFACTURING

Figure 13.12 shows a flow chart of computer-integrated manufacturing. The industry has been undergoing continuous progress since the industrial revolution. Introduction of machines resulted in increased productivity of workers. With the beginning of the twentieth century, concepts such as "assembly lines" resulted in mass production. With further developments, factory organization was planned on functional divisions such as finance, design, production planning and manufacturing. Introduction of the computer led to improved efficiency of each functional area. However, this resulted in the creation of 'islands of automation' without a common link. This is shown in Figure 13.13(a). The ideal situation is the one that integrates Computer-Aided Design (CAD) with Computer-Aided Manufacturing (CAM). When this concept of CAD/CAM integration is extended to company wide operations through the use of a mainframe computer, the system is termed Computer-Integrated Manufacturing (CIM), as shown in Figure 13.13(b).

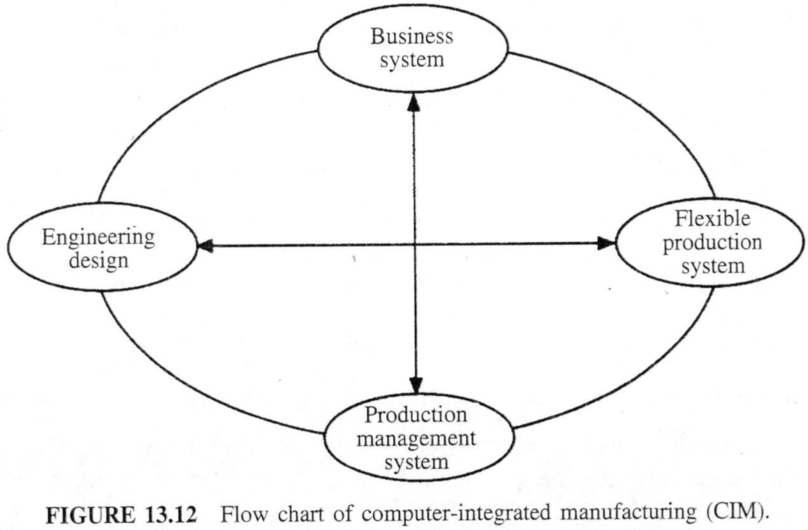

FIGURE 13.12 Flow chart of computer-integrated manufacturing (CIM).

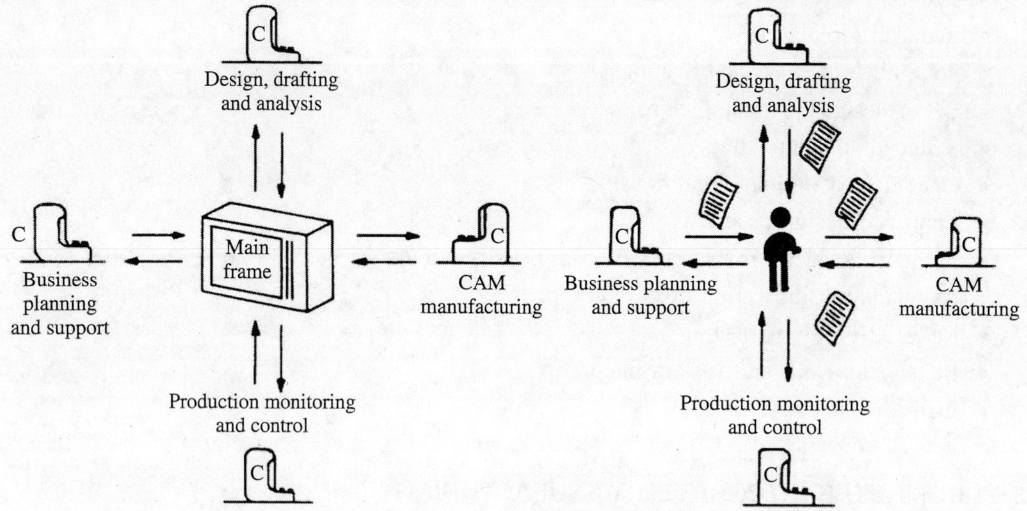

(a) Computer-Integrated Manufacturing (CIM) through mainframe computer

(b) Computer-Aided Manufacturing (CAM) without mainframe computer and resulting islands of automation

FIGURE 13.13 Information flow in CIM.

13.6.1 CIM: Definition

An interesting definition of CIM was given by Dr. M. Eugene Merchant (the Father of metal cutting theory) as:

A closed loop feedback system whose prime inputs are product requirements and product concepts and whose prime outputs are finished products. It comprises a combination of software and hardware product design, production planning, production control, production equipment and production processes.

Another definition given by Richard G. Abraham, which was adopted and published by CASA (The Computer and Automated Systems Association of the Society of Manufacturing Engineers) is as follows:

A truly integrated CAD/CAM or CIM system provides computer assistance to all business functions from marketing to product shipment. It embraces what historically have been classified as "business systems" applications, including order entry, bill of material processing, and inventory including drafting, design and simulation: manufacturing planning, e.g., process planning, routing and rating, tool design; and parts programming; and shop floor applications such as numerical control, assembly automation, testing and process automation.

It is of importance to note that both definitions are very general and applicable to any business, they are not confined to engineering activities alone.

13.6.2 Integrating Product Design, Manufacturing and Production Control

Based on the foregoing discussion, it is obvious that in future the roles of engineers involved in design, manufacturing, and production planning will change. As a result of integration, product design will not be dominated only by the function but will also be affected by production considerations. It is, therefore, certain that the boundaries now existing between the design and the production phases will disappear in the very near future. Thus, the engineers who carry out product design must have a good knowledge of production techniques as well. Similarly, an upgradation in the skill of other personnel, including everyone from blue-collared workers to top management, will become essential in a CIM environment. The field of Management Information Systems with computer application will also assume more importance in times to come. Major enablers for CIM are Group Technology, Material requirements planning (MRP) and flexible manufacturing systems (FMS).

13.6.3 Benefits of CIM

(i) **Improved product design.** Improved product design is a result of the CIM concept of developing the product within the computer, thus basing the product-development process on rational and profound analysis instead of today's common philosophy of "produce and test". Desktop prototyping is the recent technique of developing prototypes on a computer.

(ii) **Quality improvement.** Other factors that contribute to improve the product quality and consistency include elimination of human error and ensured uniformity of product quality because of on-line computer-aided inspection and quality control.

(iii) **Better labour utilization.** Automating the information flow would result in a decrease in workforce and increase the efficiency of information transfer. Any decrease in workforce would lead to decrease in unit cost of production. Also, increasing the efficiency of information transfer would lead to more effective management. The concept of paperless offices is the ultimate in computerization.

(iv) **Improved machine utilization.** Factors like programming of equipment and computerized monitoring and control of the whole manufacturing facility would largely improve the efficiency of machine utilization.

(v) **Expansion in market through product variety.** CIM increases the flexibility of the manufacturing facility, thus enabling it to react quickly to fast-changing market tests. There is much less delivery lead time taken to develop a product in a corporation where CIM is implemented.

13.6.4 Installing CIM

As already seen, the development of a totally computer-integrated manufacturing system is a very hard task that requires long-term commitment.

CIM development in an existing organization has to be carried out gradually. Each computerized subsystem has to be developed slowly and carefully. CIM is a philosophy that will stand by a company on a long-term basis. It is a programme with short-term goals.

Two steps involved in the development of CIM are:

1. Study and review of the activities to be performed in each subsystem. This involves the study of information flow into and out of the system.
2. Verification of the economic and financial feasibility of a CIM project.

13.6.5 Database Development in CIM

The heart of integration is a well-structured database, which enables designers, production engineers, production managers, marketing and purchasing personnel, as well as vendors to have access to the same set of factual data about products, production, and inventory. The typical architecture of a CIM system should be based on a group of computer systems (CAD, CAM and others), a neutral data format, a number of processors, each linked to a computer system to convert local data into neutral data (free format) and vice versa and, finally, a database management system (DBMS). The major aim of a DBMS is to ensure that all users or elements automatically receive the updated version of data. As a practical example if, for some reason, the manufacturing engineers in the CAM department modify the design to facilitate the manufacturing phase, all modifications made would be transmitted directly to the database and to the CAD department. Such adaptive ability is a must for a good database.

Classes of CIM database. For easier and logical management of the CIM database, it is appropriate to classify the data in that database into four categories:

1. Product data
2. Manufacturing data
3. Production control and operational data
4. Business data

Product data involve geometries of the products to be manufactured. Manufacturing data deal with process plans, whereas production planning (business) data involve lot sizes, schedules, routes, etc. These three classes are mostly technical as compared with business data, which deal with resources, people and money.

13.7 COMMUNICATION NETWORKS

A CIM system is a complex system involving a large number of separate, but interconnected computers that must communicate with each other through many computer networks as shown in Figure 13.14. These computers must be able to communicate with each other on real time basis and must also be able to process each other's data and execute each other's programs. Computer-integrated manufacturing utilizes local area network (LAN) in which the system consists of computers, machine controllers, etc. located close together. The individual LANs are connected together through internetworking to form the CIM system. The network configuration takes different forms. All networks and LANs consist of two components: (i) switching elements (specialized computers or interface message processors and (ii) transmission lines (circuits).

Network structure. The structure of networks can be either point-to-point channels or broadcast channels. In the first type, the network contains several channels, each one connecting a pair or nodes or Interface Message Processors (IMPs), which are the switching elements. Figure 13.14 shows some topologies. The star configuration shown in Figure 13.14(a) is an obsolete configuration. Since star-type LANs have the disadvantage of being decentralized, ring topology (Figure 13.14(b)) became more common because of its decentralized structure and decentralized access techniques. Nevertheless, since this topology requires passing messages from one node to another until they reach their destinations, any failure at single node can bring the network down. This reduces its reliability. The second kind of communication structure, viz., broadcasting channels, involves a single communication channel shared by all interface message processors (nodes), as illustrated in Figure 13.14(c). In this type, messages sent by any interface message processor are simultaneously received by all other IMPs (nodes). This type is usually referred to as bus topology when it is used in LANs.

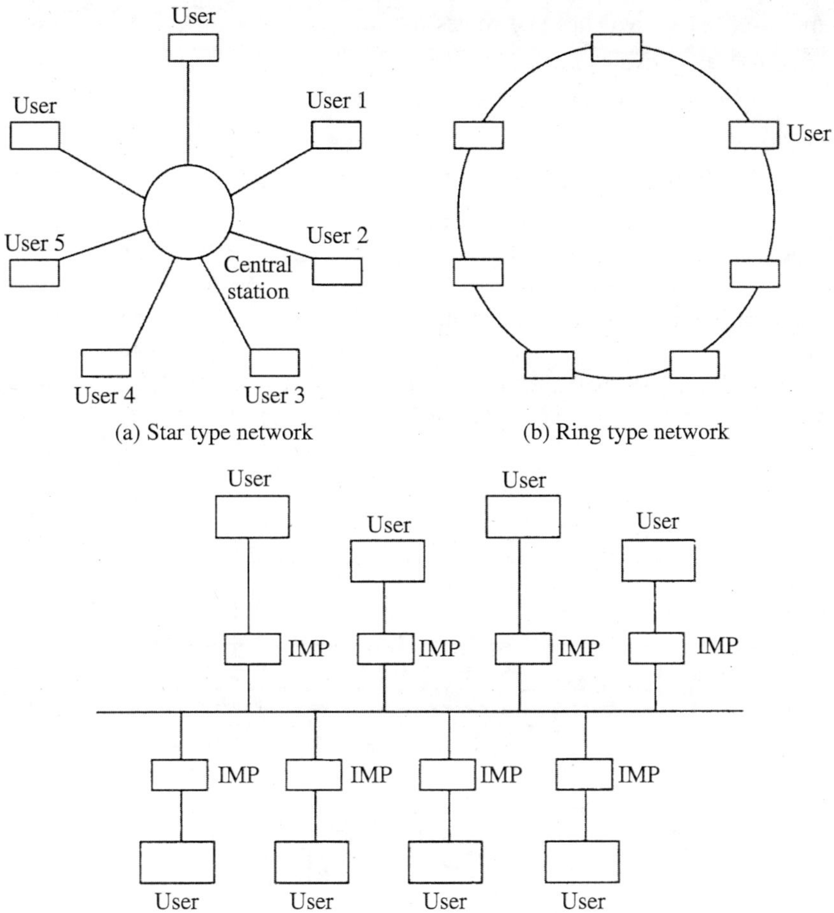

(a) Star type network (b) Ring type network

(c) Bus bar type topology with interface message processors.

FIGURE 13.14 Communications networks.

Network architectures. Layers in communication CIM networks are organized as a series of layers or levels. Each layer is designed to provide certain services to the higher-level layers without involving them in the details of how those services are provided. According to this architecture, a layer with a certain level on one machine communicates only with a layer having the same order on another machine. The set of rules and conventions stating how these two layers should interact during a dialogue are known as the *protocol*. Actual physical communication between two machines takes place only at the lowest layer, whereas communication between higher layers is only virtual. Each layer passes data to the layer directly below it until it reaches the lowest layer, where physical communication is possible. This idea is illustrated in Figure 13.15, which also shows the need for an interface between each two successive layers to define the basic operations and services that are offered by the lower layer to the upper one. In manufacturing automation protocol (MAP), the network architecture comprises seven layers:

1. Physical layer: provides actual physical link through cable
2. Datalink layer: transfers units of data

3. Internetwork layer: switches and routes data
4. Transport layer: provides quality of service
5. Session layer: does coordination between the two ends
6. Presentation layer: provides code convention and data refining
7. Application layer: selects appropriate service.

Taking an analogy from telephone connection, the physical layer is the actual cable connection. Data link layer (2) is analogous to picking up the receiver and informing the central office that a call is on the way. If something is wrong, layer (2) informs layer (4) about it. The network layer (3) may be regarded as the agency responsible for selecting the best telephone route when more routes are available. Transport layer (4) has the responsibility to see that the data passed is error free. Session layer (5) decides when to turn a communication 'On' or 'Off. Presentation layer (6) is responsible for transporting the data into the language acceptable to the Application layer (7). This is illustrated in Figure 13.15 which also shows the main function of each layer.

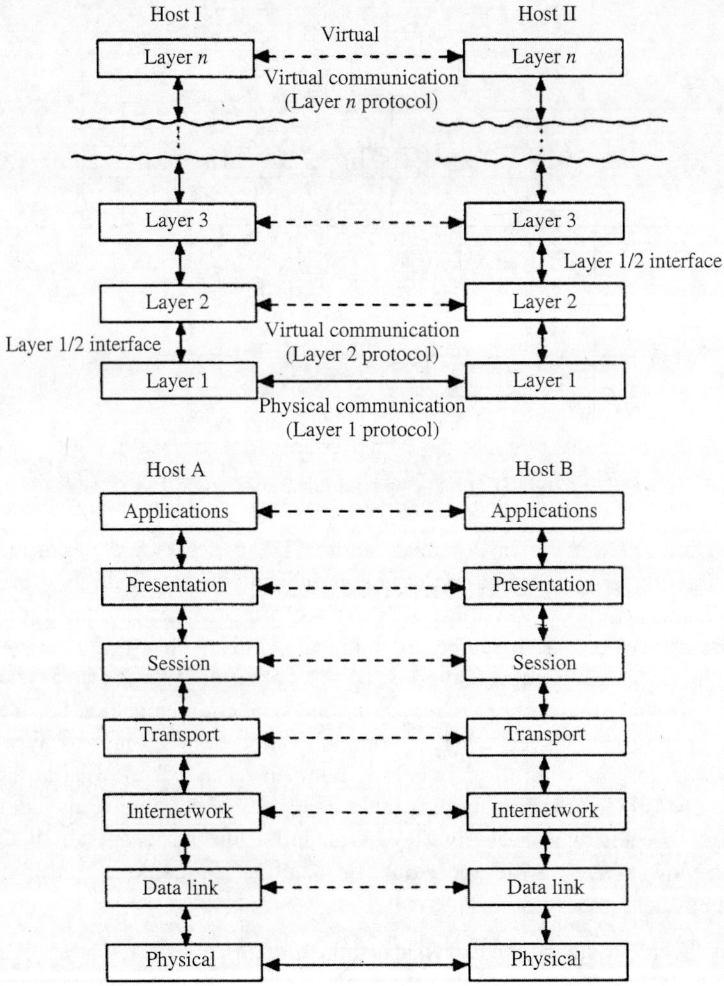

FIGURE 13.15 Network architecture showing various layers when MAP is used.

13.8 GROUP TECHNOLOGY

Group technology involves grouping components having similar attributes in order to take advantage of their similarities in the design or manufacturing phases of the production cycle. It is implemented through the application of well-structured classification and coding systems and supporting software to take advantage of the similarities of components, in terms of design attributes and processing sequence.

13.8.1 Reasons for Adopting Group Technology

Growing international competition and fast-changing market demands have put considerable amount of pressure on industries to streamline their production. Such marketing challenges, which are shown in the following list, can be successfully met by group technology:

1. Today, there is a trend in the industry towards low-volume production of a wider variety of products in order to meet the rising demand for specially ordered products for the affluent societies. The concept of mass markets of early 20th century has vanished. The share of the batch-type production in industry is growing each day, and it is expected that 75 per cent of all manufactured parts will be in small batch quantities.
2. As a result of the first factor, the conventional shop layout, i.e., process type or functional layout is becoming very inefficient and obsolete because of messy routing paths of the products between the various machine tool departments. Figure 13.16 explains this concept. Modern management concepts like business process and reengineering highlight the need for breaking of barriers between departments of an industry. Group technology and cellular manufacturing streamline material flow and reduce nonvalue adding activities.
3. There is a need to cut short the lead time, thus winning a competitive situation in the international market.

13.8.2 Benefits of Group Technology

(i) **Benefits in product design.** As far as design of products is concerned, the principal benefit of group technology is that it enables product designers to design a product that was previously designed since a variety of engineering designs are already available for storing in the computer, and it facilitates easy retrieval of these designs. When an order of part is released, the part is first coded, and then the existing designs that match that code are retrieved from the company's library of designs software stored in the computer. This saves considerable amount of time in design work.

(ii) **Standardization of tooling.** Since parts are grouped into families, a flexible design for jigs or fixtures can be made for each family in such a manner that it can accommodate every member of that family, thus bringing down the cost of fixturing by reducing the number of that family. A machine set-up can be made once for the whole family instead of a machine set-up for each of the individual parts.

(iii) **More efficient material handling.** When the plant layout is based on the group technology principles, i.e., dividing the plant into cells, which is termed cellular manufacturing, results in easier material handling. This is in contrast with the "messy" flow lines in the case of the conventional layout. That comparison is clearly illustrated in Figure 13.16.

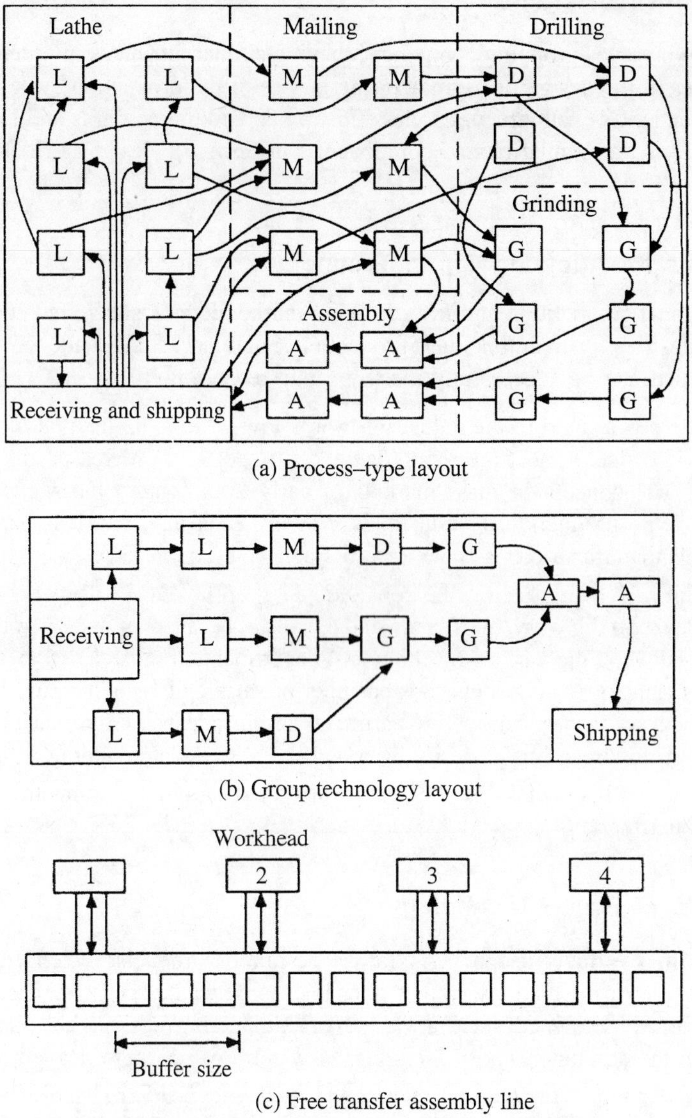

FIGURE 13.16 Various types of layouts in production systems.

(iv) **Improving economies of batch-type production.** Usually, batch-type production involves a wide variety of nonstandard parts, seemingly with nothing in common. Therefore, grouping parts (and processes) in families enable achieving of economies that are comparable to mass production.

(v) **Easier planning and control.** Grouping the parts into families facilitates the task of scheduling, since this work will be done for each family instead of for each part.

(vi) **Reduced work-in-process and lead time.** Reduced Work-In-Process (WIP) and lead time result directly from reduced set-up and material handling time.

(vii) **Faster process planning.** Group technology paves the way for automated process planning. This can be achieved through proper parts classification and coding system where a detailed process plan for each part is stored under its code and thus can be easily retrieved.

13.8.3 Obstacles to the Application of Group Technology

1. **Problems associated with rearrangement of physical equipment.**
2. **The large amount of development work needed.** In order to implement group technology, it would seem that every single part in the inventory of the industrial corporation must be coded so that part families can be established. This appears to be a huge task, which creates a barrier in implementing group technology.
3. **Resistance to change.** Most people have a resistance to change. They do not dare to experiment or innovate. Thus, we find that many managers and administrators avoid adopting new concepts and philosophies such as group technology.

13.8.4 Classification and Coding of Parts

In order to implement a classification and coding system based on group technology principles successfully, parts must be classified according to suitable features. Then a meaningful code is assigned to reflect the particular features of the classification and coding scheme. The PIN code indicates a geographic location by progressively classifying it into subdivisions. Codes that are numerically close indicate locations that are, in reality, geographically close as well.

Development of a coding system. A coding system may be based only on number or only on alphabets, or it can also be alphanumeric. When using alphabetical codes, each position (or digital location) can have 26 different alternatives, but the values of alternatives are only limited to 10 per position when numerical codes are used. Consequently, alphabets are employed to widen the scope of a coding scheme and make it more flexible.

There are basically two types of coding systems: monocodes and polycodes. These are now discussed.

Monocode. Monocodes, which are also referred to as hierarchical, or tree-structure codes, are based on the approach that each digit amplifies the information given in the preceding digit. It is, therefore, essential that these codes be short and shape-oriented. However, the monocodes do not directly indicate the attributes of components because of their hierarchical structure. Consequently, they are normally used for design storage and retrieval and are not very useful for manufacturing applications.

Polycode. Unlike in the monocode, the meaning of each digit in a polycode is completely independent of any other digits and provides information that can be directly recognized from its code. An illustration of a polycode is given in Figure 13.17(a). A polycode is generally manufacturing-oriented, because its easily identifiable attributes help the manufacturing engineer to determine the processing requirements of parts. Moreover, it has a string of features, a structure that makes it particularly suitable for computer analysis. Nevertheless, polycodes tend to be long, and a digit location must be reserved whether that particular feature applies to a part or to a family of codes. It is, therefore, a common industrial practice to use a hybrid construction, combining the advantages of each of the two basic codes while eliminating their disadvantages. In a combination type, the first digit divides the whole group of parts into subgroups, where or not shorter polycodes are employed.

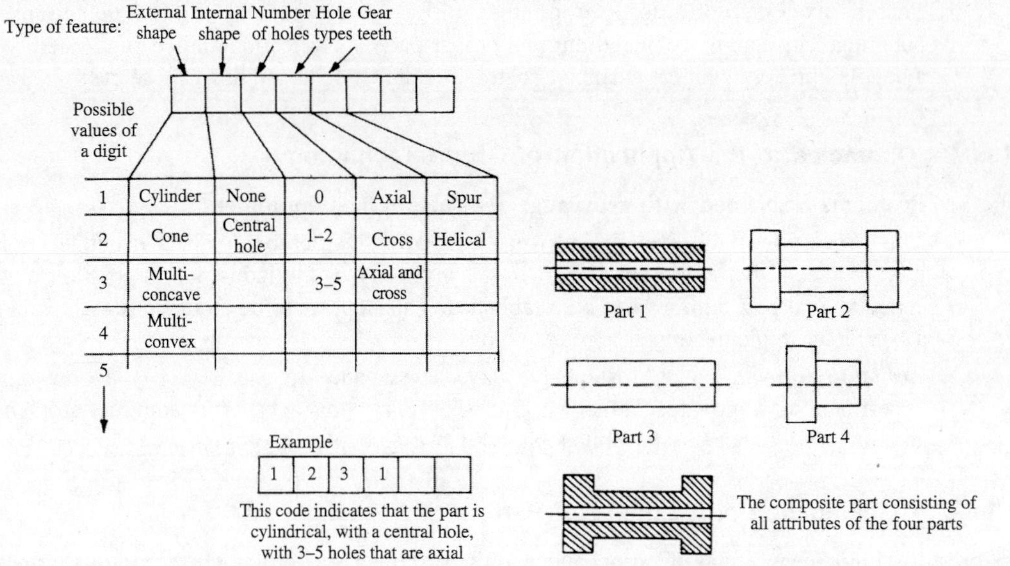

(a) Polycode as applied to a component (b) Concept of composite part

FIGURE 13.17 Polycode classification and concepts of composite part in group technology and cellular manufacturing.

13.8.5 Concept of a Composite Part

It is essential to know the concept of a composite part. A composite part is a hypothetical part that has all the attributes possessed by every individual part of a family. Consequently, the processes required to manufacture the parts of a family would be employed to produce the composite part representing that family. Any part belonging to a member of that family can then be obtained by deleting, wherever necessary, some of the operations required for producing the composite part. Figure 13.17(b) illustrates the concept of the composite part consisting of the processing attributes of all the parts of the family.

The next step is to design the machining cell to provide all machining capabilities based on the processing attributes of the composite part for the family of parts that is to be manufactured in that machining cell. The number of each kind of machine tool depends how frequently that machining operation is needed. In other words, the number of each kind of machine tool in a machining cell is necessarily the same for all the different machine tools in the cell. After determining the kinds and numbers of machine tools in the cell, the layout of machines within that cell is planned so as to achieve efficient flow of workpieces through the cell. This also ensures easy flow of material into the system.

13.9 PRODUCTION FLOW ANALYSIS (PFA)

Production Flow Analysis (PFA) is a method in which part families are identified and machine tools are grouped based on the analysis of the sequence of operations for the various products manufactured in the plant. Parts which may not be similar in shape but require similar sequence of operations are grouped together to form a family. The resulting families can then be used to design or establish machine cells. Production flow analysis employs clustering algorithms to obtain manufacturing cells.

After gathering the needed data, i.e., the part number and machine routing for every product, the computer is employed to sort out the products into groups, each of which contains parts that require identical process routings and is called a *pack*. Each pack is then given an identification number, and packs having similar routing are grouped together. Next, zoning is used to identify the machine tools that form 'rational' machine cells, as shown in Figure 13.18.

Pack identification letter

Code number of machine tools	A	B	C	D	E	F	G	H	I	J	K
1	X	X	X	X	X				X		X
2	X	X	X		X				X	X	
3			X							X	X
4	X				X						
5											
6	X			X		X		X	X		X
7	X	X	X		X	X	X	X		X	
8											
9				X		X			X		X
10	X	X	X		X				X		
11											X
12		X				X	X			X	
13						X	X			X	
14		X					X				

(a) Initial PFA chart codes of machine tools for each pack

Pack identification letter

Code number of machine tools	E	B	C	A	I	D	K	F	G	H	J
1	X	X	X	X	X	X	X				
2	X	X	X	X	X						X
3			X				X				X
4	X			X							
5											
6				X	X	X	X	X		X	
7	X	X	X	X				X	X	X	X
8											
9					X	X	X	X			
10	X	X	X	X	X						
11							X				
12		X						X	X	X	X
13								X	X	X	X
14		X								X	

(b) The PFA chart after arrangement with possible cells of machine tools

FIGURE 13.18 Establishing machine cells using PFA.

13.10 COMPUTER-AIDED PROCESS PLANNING (CAPP)

According to the American Society of Tool and Manufacturing Engineers, process planning is "the systematic determination of the methods by which a product is to be manufactured, economically and competitively". In fact, it is the manufacturing engineer's task to set up a process plan for each new product design released from the design office. This process plan is an important stage linking design and manufacturing in an industrial organization. Any process plan involves the sequence as well as the details of the operations required to manufacture a part whose design is given. That sequence of detailed operations is documented on a route sheet. The routing must be optimal to make the product economically competitive.

In order to design a process plan intelligently for manufacturing a product economically and competitively, a process planner has to study all possible alternatives, i.e., different combinations or sequences of operations, machine tools available, process parameters, and the like. Obviously, such a task requires thousands of lengthy calculations. Consequently, a computer must be used if that task is to be accomplished within a reasonable period of time. In fact, time is a decisive factor, since optimal process plans do not usually remain static but change with changing conditions, such as lot sizes available, equipment, and any emerging new technology. In other words, a process plan which is developed today for a part may be different from the plan that would be developed for the same part after a year in the same manufacturing facility. It is, therefore, a major advantage of CAPP that it accounts for any variation in the manufacturing parameters.

13.10.1 Benefits of CAPP

(i) **Productivity improvement.** Improved productivity is due to the more efficient utilization of resources such as machines, tooling, stock material and labour. This is a result of rationalization, which is based on accurate, lengthy computations, as against conventional process planning, where personal experience, preference, and sometimes even prejudice are decisive factors.

(ii) **Product cost reduction.** It is obvious that improved productivity leads to cost savings in direct labour, tooling and material and, finally, results in lower product cost.

(iii) **Elimination of human error.** Since the plans are based on the same analytical logic, with every planner having access to some updated database, we can see that two planners would come up with the same plans for the same part. This also occurs because of the elimination of human error during the lengthy computations performed on a computer.

(iv) **Reduction in time.** This is required to develop a process plan. As a result of computerizing the work, a job that used to take several days, is now done in a few minutes.

(v) **Factor response to meet design changes.** The fact that the logic is stored in the memory of the computer makes CAPP more responsive to any changes in the production parameters than the manual method of process planning. In the case when CAPP is used, it takes the process planner a few minutes to input updated data, such as lot size, machines available, and cost of raw material and obtain a modified optimal version of the process plan.

(vi) **Reduced paperwork.** We can see that paper work would be far less than in manual process planning, since routing of the planning paper work through the system is largely reduced or even eliminated.

13.10.2 Types of CAPP

There are basically two types of CAPP: variant and generative, which are now described. They are based on two completely different approaches.

(i) **The variant type.** The variant approach involves preparing beforehand a group of standard process plans, each for one of the part families produced by the plant. Those part families should be identified based on the principles of group technology, through an appropriate parts classification and coding scheme. These standard process plans are filed and stored in the memory of a computer, and each one can be retrieved and edited by inputting its associated group technology code. When a new part is given to the process planner, he can relate it to an appropriate family. Next, the standard plan for that part family is edited and modified by deletion or addition of some operations to suit the given part (recall the earlier discussion about the concept of composite part).

(ii) **The generative type.** In the generative approach, the computer is used to synthesize each individual plan automatically and without reference to any prior plan. In other words, what is stored in the memory of the computer are the rationale and algorithms that enable the appropriate technological decision to be made. The human role in running the system is minimal and includes inputting the group technology code of the given part design and monitoring the function; it is the computer that determines the sequences of operations and the manufacturing parameters. It is, therefore, the role of the computer to select the processes and the machines, to determine the sequence of operation and, finally, to sum these up into an optimum process plan.

13.11 MATERIAL REQUIREMENT PLANNING (MRP)

Let us now look at what material requirement planning (MRP) is, and why it is important. Consider a plant which is well operated by an active, qualified manufacturing staff and which is suddenly faced with a shortage of stock material. Production will stop, although machine tools and manufacturing personnel are available, because there is simply nothing that can be manufactured. It is, therefore, of paramount importance to manage inventories to ensure a continuous supply of stock material if production is to run uninterrupted. In fact, MRP software has to update continually all information about inventory, has to check whether the necessary raw materials and purchased parts will be available when required, and has to issue purchase orders whenever the situation demands.

MRP software packages can be obtained from various vendors, but they have to be tailored to the specific needs of the client. Also, major computer producers provide MRP packages as part of the software developed for their machines. In addition, software houses and consulting bureaus offer MRP packages that can be run on different types and makes of computers. It is even possible, in some cases, to obtain MRP on a time-share basis.

A recent trend in MRP development calls for linking inventory planning with the financial and capacity planning of the company in order to achieve a total business plan. In that case, MRP is referred to as *manufacturing resource planning*, or MRP II. Whenever MRP or MRP II was employed, the gains have been impressive, i.e., they have led to elimination of late orders and delays, increased productivity, and reduced WIP inventories. A further benefit is that it promotes the integration of various departments of a firm.

Example. Table 13.1 shows a typical MRP worksheet highlighting the time phasing and lot sizing concept. It will be seen how the master schedule of projected requirements drives the system and generates a planned order release of materials in lot sizes of 500 with a lead time (LT) = 2 weeks.

TABLE 13.1 Time phasing in MRP

	Weeks							
Order quantity = 500 Lead time = 2 weeks	1	2	3	4	5	6	7	8
Projected requirements	150	150	150	150	200	200	180	320
Scheduled receipts			500		500		500	
On-hand at end of 300 period	150	0	350	200	500	300	620	300
Planned order release	500		500		500		500	

|← LT 2 wks →|

13.12 MOVING TOWARDS TOTAL AUTOMATION: ROLE OF ARTIFICIAL INTELLIGENCE

The Latin root of the word "intelligence" is *intellegere*, which literally means to gather, assemble, or to form an impression. The word "intelligence" thus has meaning that involves understanding and perceiving, followed by the skilled use of logic. Assuming that we have a device which gathers knowledge, chooses among facts based on sound reasoning, understands, perceives, and knows, then it is said to have *artificial intelligence* (AI). That desired device or 'reasoning' machine must have a special capability, i.e., the ability to process knowledge information at very high speeds. In fact, this is the goal of the Japanese who established, in 1982, an institute to guide a 10-year research program aimed at developing hardware and software for the fifth generation of computers, or the KIPS (knowledge information processing systems).

The fifth generation of computers involves new computer architecture, new memory organization, and new programming languages. There are special AI programming languages, the most commonly used being LISP and PROLOG.

13.12.1 Expert Systems

An expert system is an intelligent computer program that comprises both knowledge and capability which are adequate to allow it to operate at the expert's level, i.e., it can solve extremely difficult problems which can be solved only by employing the expertise of the best practitioners in the field. AI program usually consists of a large number of if-then rules, and a person called knowledge engineer has the expertise to develop AI programs.

Applications in manufacturing. It is expected that expert systems will have widespread application in CIM systems. They can be employed in maintaining the system and quickly detecting any fault or disturbance that may occur. Another emerging application involves intelligent control of machine tools; tool path has to be established beforehand through a program. The person who prepares the programs utilizes his experience in order to bring the processing time to minimum, and not to cause any damage or distortion to the workpiece. Obviously, this is exactly where an adaptive control or expert system is needed.

13.12.2 Artificial Vision

Artificial vision is currently an emerging area in AI technology. Considerable amount of research is being carried out on more advanced aspects of technology of artificial vision. Artificial vision is aimed at locating, identifying, and guiding the manipulation of industrial components. As research continues in computer science to develop a superior pattern-recognition technique, we could expect to see more and more commercial and industrial applications of artificial vision.

13.12.3 Robots with AI

The robot with AI has always been the ultimate goal of manufacturing engineers, in order to make the fully automated factory of the future attainable. It is artificial intelligence that will make that dream come true. By definition, an intelligent robot is one that is able to think, sense, and effect, so that it can tackle a changing environment and learn from experience. Since thinking is a brain function, it is obvious that it would fall within the domain of artificial intelligence, if it is to be performed by a computer. An integration between sensing, reasoning, and effecting would unify artificial intelligence and robotics, the final outcome being a robot with AI.

13.13 FLEXIBLE MANUFACTURING SYSTEMS

Refer to Figures 13.19 to 13.24. Flexible manufacturing is one of the emerging automation concepts. In order to understand this concept, we must discuss automation in general. As we already know, mechanization started with Industrial Revolution, when machines performed some of the functions of labour. Automation included mechanization and went beyond it. With the beginning of twentieth century came a new concept, *mass production*. The automation at that time, i.e., the assembly

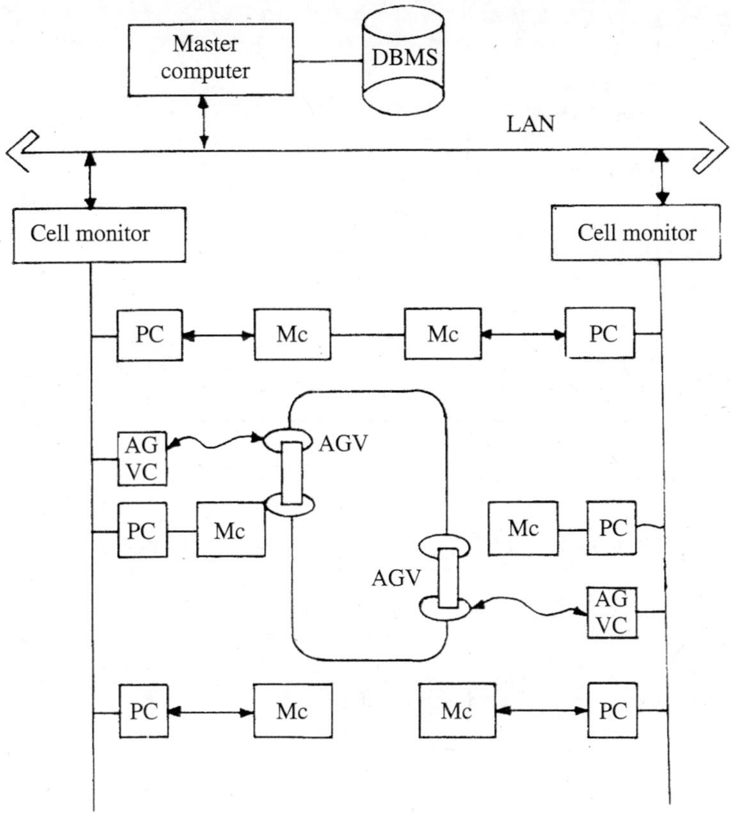

FIGURE 13.19 Schematic layout of a flexible manufacturing system.

line, markedly increased the productivity of workers, and the United States grew to lead all other nations, both in productivity and prosperity. In fact, both the assembly line and transfer line belong to the field of fixed automation, in which the sequence of processing operations remains unchanged throughout the production run. It can, therefore, be seen that the fixed automation has three characteristic features:

1. It requires very high initial capital cost.
2. It is suitable only for high production volume.
3. It is inflexible, and cannot handle product changeover or even minor changes in the product design.

As compared with fixed automation, programmable automation is flexible and can handle a large variety of parts. A good example of that kind of automation is a single CNC machine tool, where new part designs are accommodated simply by preparing new part programs without the need for changing the machine. Programmable automation is characterized by its low production volume, its flexibility, and ability to tolerate product changeovers, and the fact that its initial capital cost is not as high as that of fixed automation.

The domains in Figure 13.20 show that there exists a gap between the high production-volume transfer lines (fixed automation) and the low production, though flexible, individual NC machines.

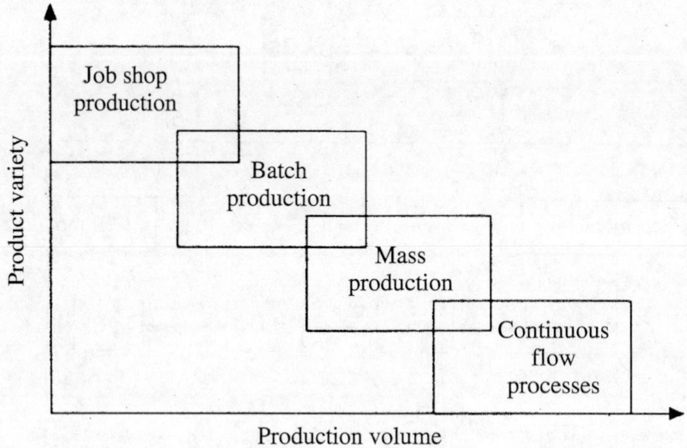

FIGURE 13.20 Production system as decided by production volume.

This gap involves medium-volume production accompanied by a limited variety of part designs. In fact, it is this "limited variety" production that is most required nowadays because of the customers desire to own something tailored to their needs. This calls for flexibility and the tailored products demanded by customers are required in quantities not suitable for mass production.

A practical solution to this problem is to develop a hybrid of fixed and programmable automations, which combines the best features of both.

13.13.1 Elements of Flexible Manufacturing System (FMS)

Figure 13.20 shows a typical architecture of an FMS. Figures 13.21 to 13.24 give details of flexible manufacturing centre and flexible manufacturing cell.

Although flexible manufacturing systems may slightly differ in features, depending on the manufacturers of the systems, they are all based on the same principle of incorporating several individual automation technologies into a unified, highly responsive production system. Figure 13.19 provides a simplified diagrammatic representation of the architecture of an FMS. It can be seen that FMS—the new method of automation—is actually based on three main elements: (i) machine tools, (ii) an automatic material handling system, and (iii) a computer control system that coordinates the functions of the other two elements. Figure 13.23 shows a chart of the elements of an FMS.

(i) **Machine tools.** An FMS always consists of a mixed range of CNC machine tools. The kind and characteristic features of those machine tools depend on the flexibility of the system. Therefore, some manufacturing experts tend to divide flexible manufacturing systems into two categories: dedicated FMS and random FMS. The former possess a lower degree of flexibility and are built to meet long-term, well-defined manufacturing requirements. Such a system can, therefore, tolerate only a limited variety of processing needs. Special machine tools form the backbone of this type of system. On the contrary, a random FMS is designed to machine (or process) a wide range of different parts in random sequence. Newer part designs can always be handled by a random FMS. Therefore, the machine tools used must be highly flexible. Four and five-axis CNC machine tools are commonly used with this type of FMS.

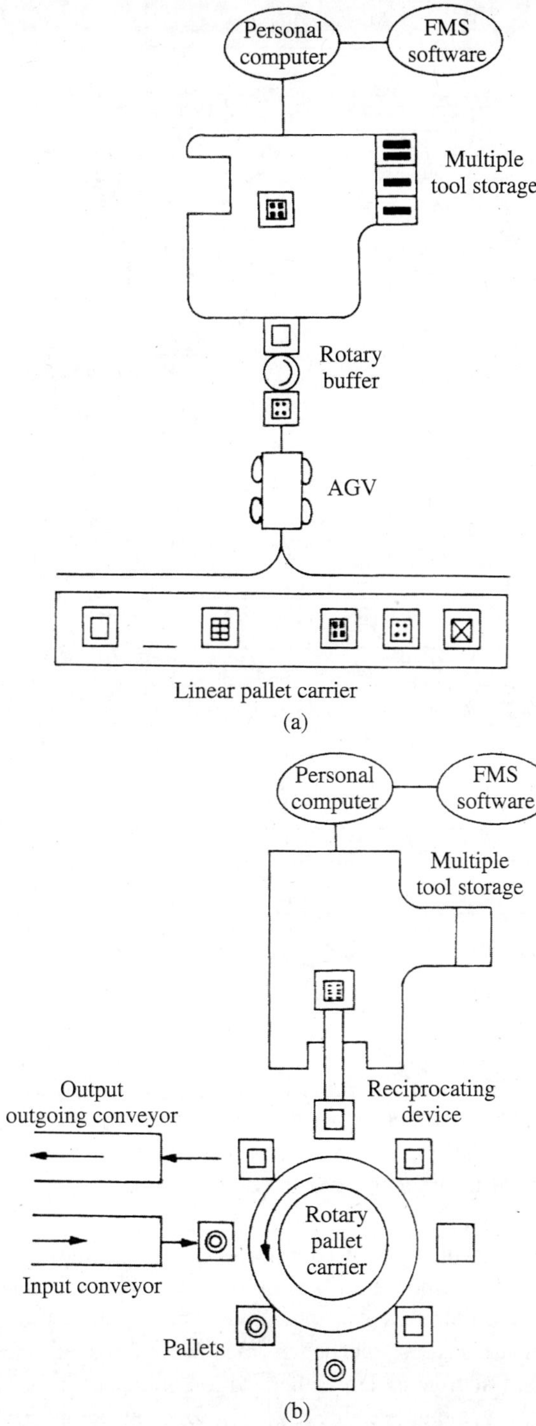

FIGURE 13.21 (a) Machine centre with pallet pool and rotary buffer, and (b) Machine centre with a rotary indexing table.

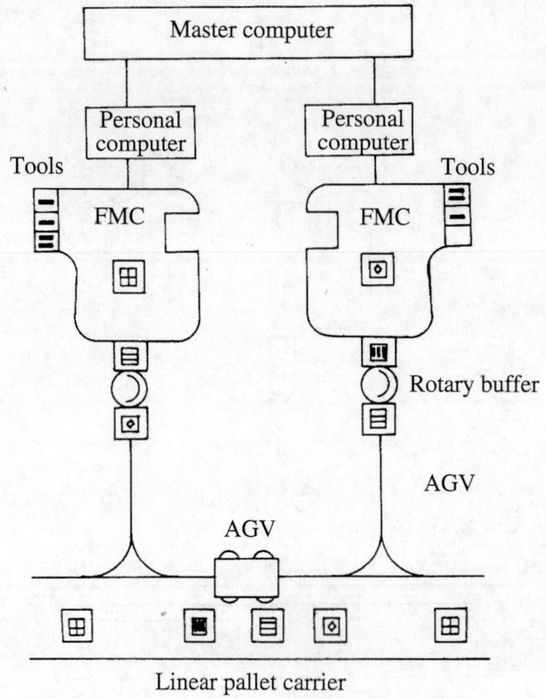

FIGURE 13.22 A flexible manufacturing cell with two machine centres.

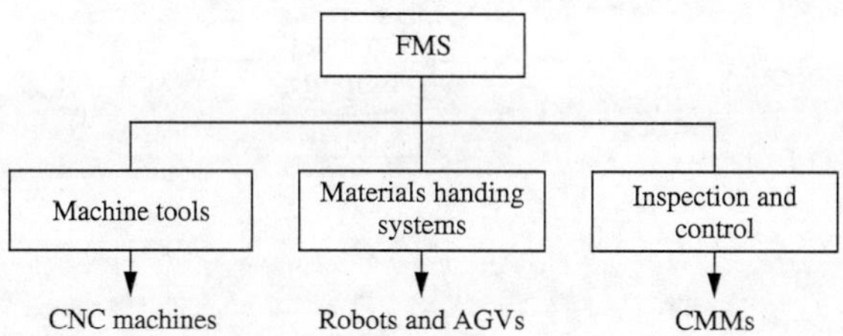

FIGURE 13.23 Elements of a flexible manufacturing system.

Although the machining processes involved differ from one FMS to another, they often include operations like turning, milling, drilling, tapping, cylindrical grinding, spline hobbing, and broaching. Batches usually fall within the range of 25–100 and can be completed, in most cases, in two days or 50 days. The system and the machine tools are designed and planned in order to operate without human supervision.

(ii) **Material-handling system.** The material-handling system involves two main elements. These include robots, which are used for automatic loading and unloading of machine tools, and a means of transportation that links the various machine tools together. Such a means for moving parts around can be a conveyor or automatic guided vehicles (AGV) on fixed tracks. In the system, the pallets must be randomly independent, i.e., parts can move from any one station to any other station independently without interference by each other. Those movements are directly controlled by the master computer of the FMS. This is achieved by coding each pallet uniquely so that it can be tracked by the computer.

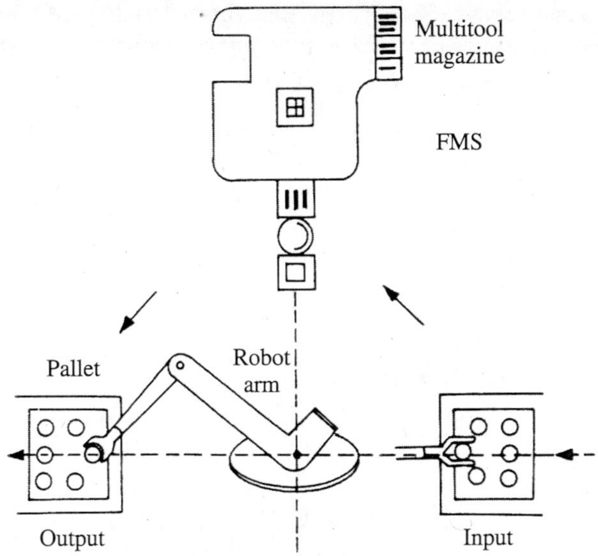

FIGURE 13.24 Machine centre with a robot.

Codes (which are usually binary) are affixed to a coding tag, which in turn, is mounted onto the pallet identification strip. This enables the computer to use sensors to identify and accurately locate pallets. Industrial robots are then used to unload pallets and/or parts placing them in the machine, and return pallets loaded with machined parts to the transport system. A temporary storage is provided at each machining station so that a workpiece can be promptly loaded in the machine as soon as a machined part is removed from it, thus eliminating waste of time. Another function of the robots is to select components for inspection under computer control on coordinate measuring machines (CMM).

(iii) **Computer control.** A flexible manufacturing system cannot be operated without a digital computer, because of the complexity of the system and the need for real-time planning and control of the different subsystems. The function of the computer is not limited to the storage and distribution of the NC part programs, the operation of load-unload robots, and the control of AGV's traffic between stations. In fact, it goes beyond that to cover tool monitoring (following each tool throughout the whole system and monitoring its life) and production control. For this reason, a data entry unit is employed in the load-unload station in order to act as an interface between the operator and the computer.

13.13.2 Flexible Manufacturing Cells

A flexible manufacturing cell (FMC), as shown in Figure 13.23, usually consists of two CNC machining centres which are linked together with each other as well as with their tool store through an industrial robot. Figure 13.24 indicates an example of those automated cells. Because of the flexibility inherent in the design of an FMC, its productivity is higher than that of the separate stand-alone machines, and it can also handle a larger variety of parts configurations. FMCs are, therefore, used when the production volume cannot justify the purchase of an FMS and cannot be met well by stand-alone machines. In other words, FMCs are a kind of automation which fill the gap between flexible manufacturing systems and individual stand-alone CNC machine tools. The domain of successful application of FMCs, therefore, involves a production volume between 20 and 500 pieces and variation in configuration, ranging from 30 to 500 different shapes.

Economics of FMC. The economic advantage of using FMC can be noted when comparing each with individual machine tools with regard to the production cost per component. Figure 13.25, which shows the cost per piece versus the volume of production for each of the different kinds of automation also indicates break-even points between various automated production systems.

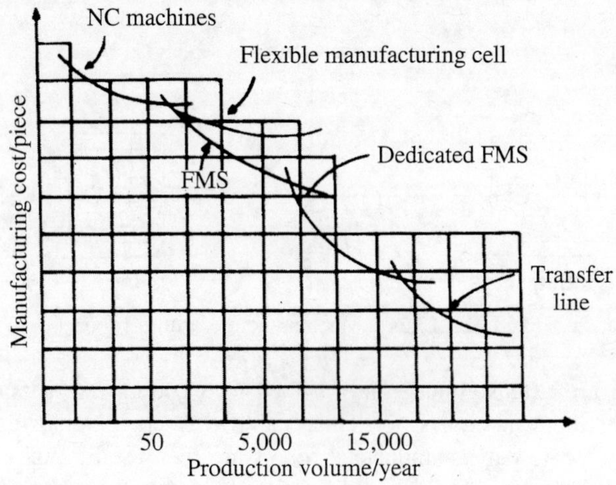

FIGURE 13.25 Economics of various production systems.

13.14 JUST-IN-TIME (JIT) MANUFACTURING

13.14.1 Introduction to JIT

The Toyota Motor Company of Japan developed the Just-in-time manufacturing system under the inspired leadership of Taichi Ohno [3], the Company's Vice President. The Just-in-time system evolved out of Henry Ford's assembly line concept. Ford, in the early twentieth century, introduced the assembly line which comprised a number of work centres or work stations arranged in a series. Each station performed some value addition to the product so that at the inlet end or upstream of the assembly line, there were raw materials and at the outlet or downstream side, there was a Ford T model car. This was a revolution in production system and made the United States the leading industrial power in the world.

Taichi Ohno, working for Toyota Motor Company, developed the assembly line concept with certain modifications which resulted in a highly flexible, fast and effective production line, termed the *JIT line*.

The key features of the Just-in-time system are as follows:

1. Single vendor to supply raw materials and parts to the assembly line with minimum lead time.
2. Use of mistake-proofing devices at every operation so that defectives are prevented in production. If a component is wrongly located in the jig or fixture, there is a provision in

the machine that will prevent it from doing the processing of the part. Thus quality is built into product right at the source.

3. Taichi Ohno regarded mass production as a continuous flow of very small batches of components from upstream to downstream. According to Ohno, this enabled one to discover defects quickly, which was not possible in large batch production systems that characterized the US approach to manufacturing. By reducing the set-up time of machines drastically from several hours to a few minutes, Ohno justified the use of small batch quantities flowing between machines.
4. Use of 'pull system' along the line instead of conventional 'push system', substantially reduced work-in-process in case of Just-in-time systems.

Figure 13.26 shows, through dashed lines and solid lines, the flow of information and material respectively in a typical JIT system. It is to be noted that the direction of arrows of information (which indicates requisition or pull) results in supply of material on demand indicated by arrows in the opposite direction on a just-in-time basis.

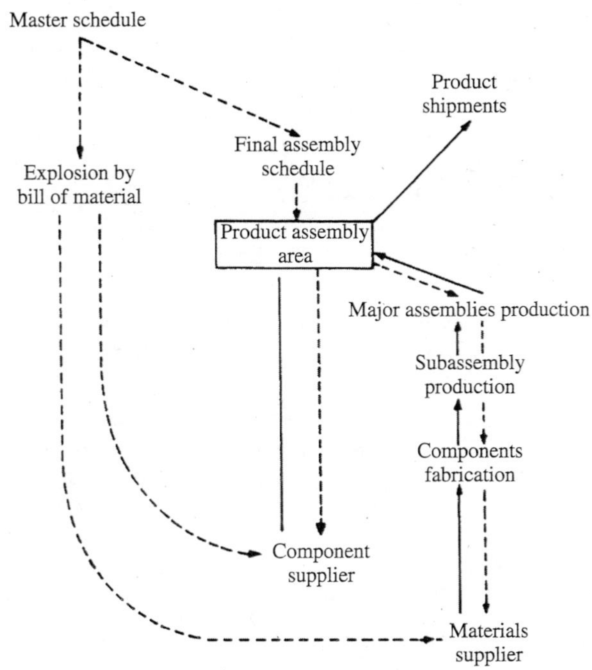

FIGURE 13.26 An overview of JIT system.

Figure 13.26 illustrates the network comprising the material supplier-component fabrication-subassembly—major assembly-product assembly-product shipment, typical of a JIT system. Such requisition based Just-in-time material flow results in negligible bottle-necks and drastically reduces work-in-progress inventory.

Figure 13.27 shows how a Kanban or Visible card system operates on the shop floor to supply materials to the downstream work centre when it uses a withdrawal card M giving a requisition to the upstream work centre. The withdrawal card M is a license for a downstream work centre to pull material when it is starved of material.

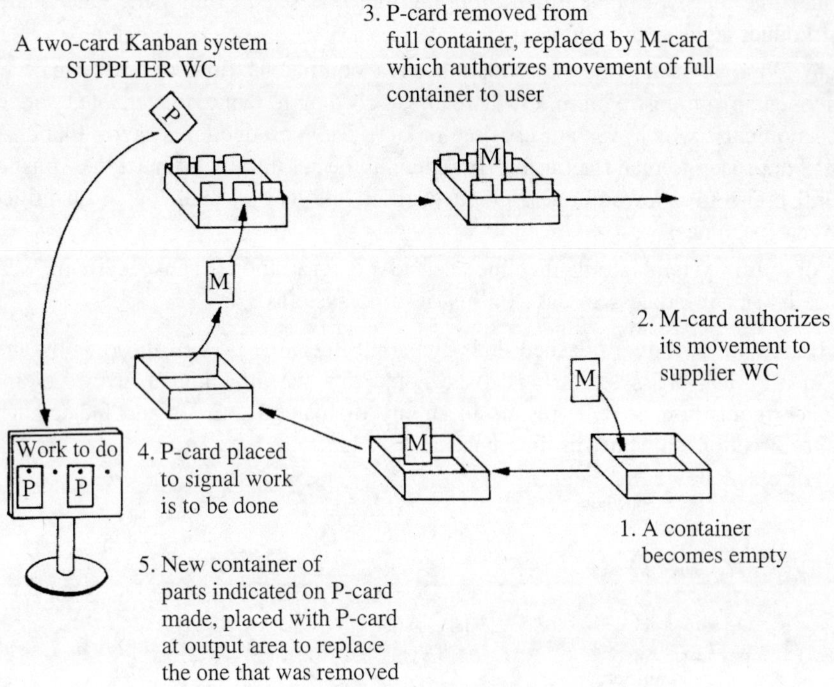

FIGURE 13.27 The Kanban system.

When material is taken from upstream work centre, a production Kanban P is posted on the billboard which authorizes the operator at the upstream work centre to produce an extra batch. This is depicted in Figure 13.27.

Thus, a pull effect is exerted by the downstream centre on the upstream centre.

The beauty of the Kanban System is that no work centre needlessly performs operations until it is informed by a downstream work centre. Thus, unnecessary collection of materials at work centres is prevented.

13.14.2 Just-in-Time and Product Design

The Just-in-time system has revolutionized the concept of manufacturing management. It has also triggered corresponding evolution in product design. This is because, for a JIT System to be successful, certain golden rules of product design are to be adhered to. Following is a list of product design rules which are an outcome of the JIT System. Several authors, including Schonberger [4], have outlined similar design rules.

1. Design improvements: A product designer should improve existing designs based on past experience and difficulties with earlier component designs, resulting in design modifications.
2. Quality should be assigned top priority instead of price or cost. To start with, Japanese industries often assign close tolerances. Later on, if necessary, the tolerances are relaxed.
3. JIT being a supplier-based system, it is essential that product designers assist the company in deciding on the best quality supplier.

4. Products should be designed based on the principles of ease of assembly. Proper chamfers, radii, undercuts, etc. should be indicated which promote assembly. If possible, use jigless assembly based designs.
5. Reducing the number of parts in an assembly is desirable for quickening assembly and increasing production rate.
6. Design for testability: A product should be so designed that diagnostic points of future failure can be easily traced. Repairability is another essential quality for a product, which should be conceived at the design stage.
7. Spare parts requirement: A product designer should identify at the design stage as to which parts would need replacement by making spare parts available. Field service department should be appraised of such eventuality.
8. Every product should be designed on the basis of certain reliability goals. The individual components should be assigned proper reliability allocation to achieve a system reliability goal. Simple algebraic methods to complex *dynamic programming* techniques are utilized for reliability allocation.
9. Product design simplification should be done because repetitive production and Kanban System require easy-to-manufacture products that need less floor-to-floor time.
10. Very often, it is assumed that, in order to install Just-in-time, a totally new and costly capital equipment and tooling is essential. This is far from the truth. With the same tooling, but with introduction of novel location and clamping system, it is possible to introduce mistake proofing of the product so that quality is built into the product right at the source.
11. Rationalize and simplify specifications so that they are easily understandable to the supplier. Try to understand suppliers process capabilities before writing specifications.
12. Before deciding to purchase components for customer-specified assemblies, it is essential for the product designer to visit suppliers, factory before finalizing the purchase order.
13. Make a study of output from a plant. Japanese JIT or Kaizen, i.e., continuous improvement, always results in an increase in output. However, low production is often an indicator of poor product design. The product designer should look for design modifications in the event of reduced production.
14. If the quality of the final product does not satisfy the customer, the product designer should also try to diagnose design fault.

The above design rules are the results of JIT environment, but they are general and can be helpful to designers in building quality into the product in non-JIT environments as well.

APPENDIX

Classification of Parts and Coding

Three methods of classification of various engineering components are well known, which are now discussed.

(i) **Physical observation.** Parts looking similar can be grouped together based on their physical form and shape. This is the most direct but crude method.

(ii) **Codification of parts.** By assigning a code number to each digit corresponding to a certain specific geometrical feature, e.g., external shape and internal shape, additional features, etc. The Opitz code is quite popular and is described in detail in this section.

(iii) **Production flow analysis.** Similar parts are subject to similar machining sequence. Thus, the rotating of similar parts from one machine to another should be identical. This can form the basis for grouping parts together. The detailed procedure comprises developing an initial matrix between jobs and machine on which they are processed. The machines or jobs are shifted from their respective positions in the matrix to form cohesive groups or clusters. These clusters represent the way in which machines can be grouped together in a 'Group Technology' cell.

Opitz Product Classification through Grouping

In 1961, Opitz developed the broad field of application of parts classification system as a methodical procedure. The basic theme was to show that technological processes are related with shapes and sizes of products. Tables A13.1–A13.4 show a part classification system with a decimal base.

Component shapes can be classified as *Rotational* and *Non-rotational*. The former are machined on lathe, boring machines, and cylindrical grinders. The latter are machined on shaper, planer, milling machine, etc.

The basic geometric code (see Tables A13.1–A13.4) number consists of five digits:

The first digit describes component class, i.e., whether disc, cylinder or rodlike, depending on L/D ratio; similarly, whether flat plate, long component or cubic component, depending on the A/B ratio and the A/C ratio, i.e. length ratio and thinness ratio.

Explanation: $L/D \leq 0.5$ is a disc, $0.5 \leq L/D \leq$ is cylinder, $L/D \geq 3$ is rodlike; a similar logic applies to non-rotational parts.

The second digit describes external shape elements, e.g., whether the cylinder has a step on one side or on both sides, or it has a screw thread or a groove.

The third digit describes internal shape elements such as a bore or internal thread or a groove.

The fourth digit describes plan face machining or facing, circular graduations of face, etc. For prismatic parts, it represents machining on top/bottom flat surface.

The fifth digit describes auxiliary holes and gear teeth, if any. The absence of any of the above five features results in entry 0 in that position during coding.

The supplementary code indicates code numbers depending on dimension, materials, initial form of raw material, and accuracy.

Tables A13.1–A13.4 can be utilized to determine the coding for any part. The coding system is illustrated through two examples which are due to Boothroyd [5].

Examples

1. From Figure 13.28 and Table A13.1, let us decide the Opitz code (form code only). The L/D ratio = 2, the first digit of code is 1 since it lies between 5 and 3. The second digit is 2 since there is a step to one end with a screw thread. The third digit is 0 since there is no internal feature. The fourth digit is 0 since there is no facing operation. The fifth digit is also 0 since there are no auxiliary holes/gear teeth. Thus, the Form Code is 12000.
2. From Tables A13.2 and A13.3, it can be seen that the nonrotational part of the first digit is 6 because A/B is 1.2 and A/C is 4.5, the former being less than 3 and the latter being greater than 4. The second digit is 1 since the external shape indicates a deviation, being a cut in the plate type part. The third digit is 1 to account for one principal bore. The fourth digit is 0 since there is no machining on top or bottom forces of the plate. The fifth digit is 3 to represent auxiliary holes, drilled in one direction with a pattern only. Thus, the Opitz code is 61103.

TABLE A13.1 Geometric code for rotational components*

1st digit

Code		Component class
0	Rotational components	$\frac{L}{D} \le 0.5$
1		$0.5 < \frac{L}{D} < 3$
2		$\frac{L}{D} \ge 3$

2nd digit

Code			External shape, external shape elements
0			Smooth, no shape elements
1	Stepped to one end		No shape elements
2		or smooth	With screwthread
3			With functional groove
4	Stepped to both ends (multiple increases)		No shape elemente
5			With screwthread
6			With functional groove
7			Functional taper
8			Operating thread
9			Others (> 10 functional diameters)

3rd digit

Code		Internal shape, internal shape elements
0		Without through bore blind hole
1		No shape elements
2	Smooth or stepped to one end	With screwthread
3		With functional groove
4	Stepped to both ends (multiple increases)	No shape elemente
5		With screwthread
6		With functional groove
7		Functional taper
8		Operating thread
9		Others (> 10 functional diameters)

4th digit

Code	Plane surface machining
0	No surface machining
1	External plane surface and/or surface curved in one direction
2	External plane surfaces related to one another by graduation around a circle
3	External groove and/or slot
4	External spline and/or polygon
5	External plane surface and/or slot and/or groove spline
6	Internal plane surface and/or groove
7	Internal spline and/or polygon
8	External and internal splines and/or slot and/or groove
9	Others

5th digit

Code		Auxiliary hole(s) and gear teeth
0		No auxiliary hole(s)
1	No gear teeth	Axial hole(s) not related by a drilling pattern
2		Axial holes related by a drilling pattern
3		Radial hole(s) not related by a drilling pattern
4		Holes axial and/or radial and/or in other directions not related
5		Holes axial and/or radial and/or in other directions related by drilling pattern
6	With gear teeth	Spur gear teeth
7		Bevel gear teeth
8		Other gear teeth
9		Others

*After Opitz.[2] © Verlag Wu. Giradet 1970.

TABLE A13.2 Second digit* of geometric code for flat and long non-rotational components†

1st digit: Component class	2nd digit		Overall shape
	0	Plane	Rectangular
	1	Plane	Rectangular with one deviation (right angle or triangular)
	2	Plane	Rectangular with angular deviations
	3	Plane	Rectangular with circular deviation
	4	Plane	Any flat shape other than 0 to 3
	5	Plane	Flat components, rectangular or right angled with small deviations due to casting, welding, forming
6 Flat components $\frac{A}{B} \leq 3, \frac{A}{B} \geq 4$	6		Flat components, round or any shape other than position 5
	7		Flat components regularly arched or dished
	8		Flat components irregularly arched or dished
	9		Others

1st digit: Component class	2nd digit			Overall shape
	0	Shape axis (straight)	Uniform cross section	Rectangular
	1	Shape axis (straight)	Uniform cross section	Rectangular with one deviation (right angle or triangular)
	2	Shape axis (straight)	Uniform cross section	Any cross section other than 0 and 1
	3	Shape axis (straight)	Varying cross section	Rectangular
	4	Shape axis (straight)	Varying cross section	Rectangular with one deviation (right angle or triangular)
	5	Shape axis (straight)	Varying cross section	Any cross section other than 3 and 4
7 Nonrotational components	6	Shape axis curved (bent)		Rectangular, angular, and other cross sections
7 Nonrotational components: Long components $\frac{A}{B} > 3$	7	Shape axis curved (bent)		Formed component
	8	Shape axis curved (bent)		Formed component with deviations in the main axis
	9	Shape axis curved (bent)		Others

† After Opitz.[2] © Verlag Wu. Giradet 1970.

TABLE A13.3 Geometrical code

Code	*1st digit* Component class	*2nd digit* Overall shape	*3nd digit* Principal bore rotational surface machining	*4th digit* Plane surface machining	*5th digit* Auxiliary hole(s) forming, gear teeth
0		Rectangular prism	No rotational machining or bore(s)	No surface machining	No auxiliary holes gear teeth and forming
1		(Block and block-like components) Rectangular with deviations (Right angle or triangular)	One principal bore smooth	Functional chamfers (e.g. welding prep.)	(No gear teeth, no forming) Holes drilled in one direction only
2		(Block and block-like components) Compounded of rectangular prisms	One principal bore stepped to one or both ends	One plane surface	(No gear teeth, no forming) Holes drilled in more than one direction
3		(Block and block-like components) Components with a mounting or locating surface and principal bore	One principal bore with shape elements	Stepped plane surface	(No gear teeth, no forming; Related by a drilling pattern) Holes drilled in one direction only
4		(Block and block-like components) Components with a mounting or locating surface principal bore with dividing surface	Two principal bores parallel	Stepped plane surfaces of right angles inclined and/or opposite	(No gear teeth, no forming; Related by a drilling pattern) Holes drilled in more than one direction
5		(Block and block-like components) Components other than 0 to 4	Several principal bores, parallel	Groove and/or slot	(Forming no gear teeth) Formed no auxiliary holes
6		(Box and box-like components; Not split) Approximate or compounded of rectangular prisms	Several principal bores other than parallel	Groove and/or slot and 4	(Forming no gear teeth) Formed with auxiliary holes
7	(Nonrotational components)	(Box and box-like components; Not split) Components other than 6	Machined annular surfaces annular grooves	Curved surface	Gear teeth, no auxiliary hole(s)
8	(Nonrotational components) Cubic components $\frac{A}{B} \leq 3, \frac{A}{C} < 4$	(Box and box-like components; Split) Approximate or compounded of rectangular prisms	7-principal bore(s)	Guide surface	Gear teeth with auxiliary hole(s)
9		(Box and box-like components; Split) Components other than 8	Others	Others	Others

TABLE A13.4 Geometrical code

1st digit

		Component class
3	Rotational components	$\frac{L}{D} \le 2$ with deviation
4	Rotational components	$\frac{L}{D} > 2$ with deviation

2nd digit

		Overall shape
0	Around one axis no segments	Hexagonal bar
1	Around one axis no segments	Square or other regular polygonal section
2	Around one axis no segments	Symmetrical cross section producing no unbalance
3	Around one axis no segments	Cross sections other than 0 to 2
4		Segments after rotational machining
5		Segments before rotational machining
6	Around more than one axis	Rotational components with curved axis
7	Around more than one axis	Rotational components with two or more parallel axis
8	Around more than one axis	Rotational components with intersecting axis
9		Others

3rd digit

		Rotational machining
0		No rotational machining
1	External shape	Machined
2	External shape	With screwthread(s)
3	Internal shape	Smooth
4	Internal shape	Stepped towards one or both ends (Multiple increases)
5	Internal shape	With screwthread
6	External and internal shape	Machined
7	External and internal shape	Screwthread(s)
8		External shape element
9		Other shape elements

4th digit

	Plane surface machining
0	No surface machining
1	External plane surface and/or surface curved in one direction
2	External plane surface related to one another by graduation around 0 circle
3	External groove and/or slot
4	External spline and/or polygon
5	External plane surface and/or slot and/or groove spline
6	Internal plane surface and/or groove
7	Internal spline and/or polygon
8	External and internal spline and/or slot and/or groove
9	Others

5th digit

			Auxiliary hole(s) gear, gear, teeth
0			No auxiliary holes gear teeth and forming
1	No forming no gear teeth		Axial holes(s) not related by drilling pattern
2	No forming no gear teeth		Holes axial and/or radial and/or in other directions not related
3	No forming no gear teeth	Related by a drilling pattern	Axial holes
4	No forming no gear teeth	Related by a drilling pattern	Holes axial and/or radial and/or in other direction
5	Forming no gear teeth		Formed no auxiliary holes
6	Forming no gear teeth		Formed with auxiliary holes
7			Gear teeth no auxiliary holes
8			Gear teeth with auxiliary hole(s)
9			Others

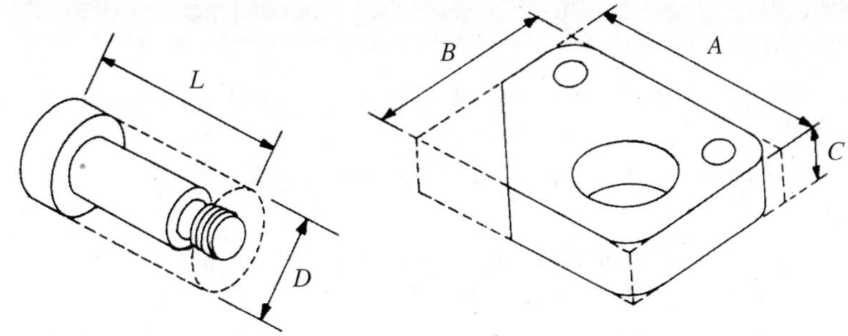

(a) Rotational (b) Nonrotational

FIGURE 13.28 Basic component shapes.

More examples are illustrated to make the ideas clear. Refer to Figure 13.29. The coding has been derived by taking cognizance of form elements.

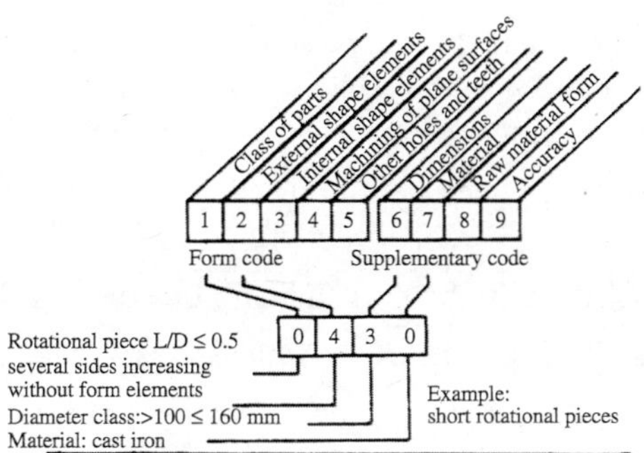

Work piece		Form code	Suppl. code
		04100	3072
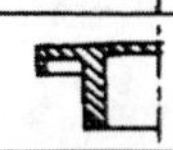		04100	3075
		04703	3072

Suppl. = Supplementary

FIGURE 13.29 Component families using the characteristic data.

REVIEW QUESTIONS

1. What is meant by CAD and CAM? Sec. 13.1, 13.2; P 340–341
2. How the computer has played a role in automating product cycle. Make flowcharts of product cycle without the intervention of computer and with the intervention of computer. Sec. 13.3; Figure 13.1, 13.2
3. How is feasibility analysis facilitated using computer?
[*Hint:* use of CAD]. Figure 13.3
4. How detailed drawing and design is achieved using a computer?
[*Hint:* CADD]. Figure 13.2

5. How process engineering is facilitated by the use of computer?
[*Hint:* CAPP].
6. How production planning and control is simplified by the use of a computer? (*Hint:* CRP and MRP).
7. How shop floor control is achieved by using a computer?
[*Hint:* CAM].
8. How quality control is achieved by using a computer?
[*Hint:* In process QC with sensors and CMM].
9. What are the four functional areas related to design are achieved by a modern CAD system?
10. What is the morphology of design defined by Shigley and how does a computer help in achieving it? Figure 13.3
11. Explain geometric modelling? How does a graphics terminal achieve a geometric model?
12. What are the different methods of representing objects in geometric modelling? Give the merits and demerits of each method. Figure 13.5, 13.6, 13.7
[*Hint:* Wireframe model, surface model and solid model].
13. What are the commands which help in developing a composite component? P 343–344; Figure 13.4
14. What is Euler's rule for verifying the solidity or otherwise of a model? P 342; Figure 13.2
15. How engineering analysis is done using 'finite element method' (FEM)?

Take a simple example highlighting the fundamentals of FEM?

[***Example.*** Calculate the stresses induced in a stepped bar with areas A_1, A_2 and subjected to an axial load 1000 kg. The bar is fixed at one end (Figure 13.30).

$$A_1 = 1 \text{ cm}^2;\ A_2 = 2 \text{ cm}^2$$

Solution Treating system in Figure 13.30 as one dimension spring sytem

$$\begin{bmatrix} S_1 & -S_1 \\ -S_1 & S_1 + S_2 \end{bmatrix} = \begin{Bmatrix} F_1 \\ F_2 \end{Bmatrix}. \text{ But } S = \frac{AE}{l} \quad \therefore \quad \frac{AE}{l}\begin{bmatrix} 1 & -1 \\ -1 & 1+2 \end{bmatrix} = \begin{bmatrix} F_1 \\ F_2 \end{bmatrix}$$

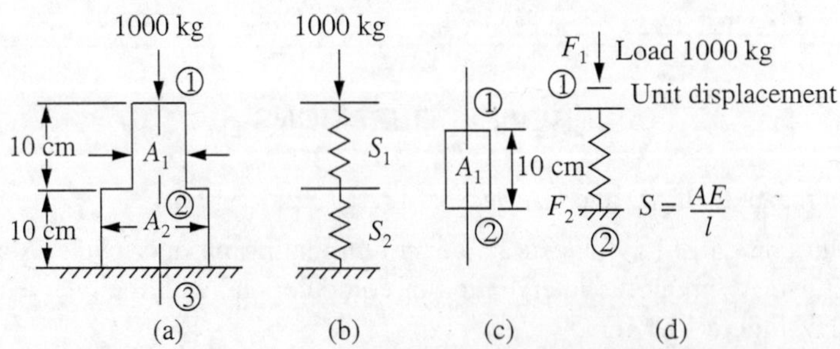

FIGURE 13.30 Axially loaded bar with its analogy with spring.

Substituting $\frac{AE}{l} = \left[\frac{E}{10}\right] \quad \therefore \quad \frac{E}{10}\begin{bmatrix} 1 & -1 \\ -1 & 3 \end{bmatrix}\begin{Bmatrix} u_1 \\ u_2 \end{Bmatrix} = \begin{Bmatrix} 1000 \\ 0 \end{Bmatrix}$ Eq. (1)

To determine $\{\delta\} = \begin{Bmatrix} u_1 \\ u_2 \end{Bmatrix}$, Eq. (1) will have to be multiplied on LHS by the inverse of

$\frac{E}{10}\begin{bmatrix} 1 & -1 \\ -1 & 3 \end{bmatrix}$ which is called *Gauss Jordan elimination procedure.*

Calculation of inverse I: Usually the inverse of 3 × 3 and larger matrices is determined by computer.

Being 2 × 2 matrix, a manual calculation is done.

$\frac{E}{10}\begin{bmatrix} 1 & -1 \\ -1 & 3 \end{bmatrix}$ the determinant D will be first calculated.

(i) $|D| = \frac{E}{10}(3-1) = \frac{2E}{10} = \frac{E}{5}$

(ii) Now $[K]^{-1} = \frac{1}{|D|}\begin{bmatrix} 3 & +1 \\ +1 & 1 \end{bmatrix} = \frac{5}{E}\begin{bmatrix} 3 & 1 \\ 1 & 1 \end{bmatrix}$

$$\delta = \begin{Bmatrix} u_1 \\ u_2 \end{Bmatrix} = \frac{5}{E}\begin{bmatrix} 3 & 1 \\ 1 & 1 \end{bmatrix}\begin{bmatrix} 1000 \\ 0 \end{bmatrix}$$

$$\begin{Bmatrix} u_1 \\ u_2 \end{Bmatrix} = \frac{5}{E}\begin{Bmatrix} 3000 & + & 0 \\ 1000 & + & 0 \end{Bmatrix} = \begin{Bmatrix} 15000/E \\ 5000/E \end{Bmatrix}$$

$\therefore$ $$u_1 = 15000/E \text{ and } u_2 = 5000/E$$

$$\text{Strain } \varepsilon_1 = \frac{\Delta\ell}{\ell} = \frac{u_2 - u_1}{\ell} = \left[\frac{5000}{E} - \frac{15000}{E}\right]\frac{1}{10} = -\frac{1000}{E}$$

$$\varepsilon_2 = \frac{u_3 - u_2}{\ell} = \left[0 - \frac{5000}{E}\right]\frac{1}{10} = -\frac{500}{E}$$

$\therefore$ Stresses: $\sigma_1 = E\varepsilon_1 = 1000$ kg/cm^2

$\sigma_2 = E\varepsilon_2 = 500$ kg/cm^2

Note: In FEM problems, the important matrices are matrix **B** linking displacement with strain, called *B* matrix. The matrix which links stress with strain is termed *D* matrix or material properties matrix, which generally speaking is a function of Young's modulus *E* and poisson's ratio v. It is usual to divide plate like structures into triangular elements for which the *B* matrix is evaluated as a first step. The reader should refer to any standard text on FEM for deriving a '*B*' matrix for triangular element.]

16. What is the essential difference between CAD/CAM and computer integrated manufacturing?

[*Hint:* CIM uses a main frame computer accessible to islands of automation created by CAD/CAM]. Sec. 13.6 P 349, Sec. 13.6.1 to 13.6.5 P 349 to 352

17. What are the benefits of CIM? How is CIM installed in a factory? Sec. 13.6.4

18. What is DBMS in computer-integrated manufacturing? What is adaptive ability for a good database? Sec. 13.6.5

19. What categories of CIM database are essential? Sec. 13.6.5

20. What is the role of communication networks in CIM? What different topologies are available in CIM? Sec. 13.7

21. What are the different layers when communication networks are used? Discuss what is manufacturing automation protocol. P 353, 354; Figure 13.14

22. What is meant by 'Group Technology'? What are the methods of coding classification of parts? Sec. 13.8

23. Which method of coding is superior from the point of view of improved shop layout:
    (i) Coding based on geometrical features
    (ii) Production flow analysis?

24. (a) In coding and classification of parts, what is meant by: Sec. 13.8.4
    (i) monocode and (ii) polycode.
    (b) What is hybrid coding?

    [**Ans. (b):** Hybrid code adds supplementary code in digits 6789 as dimensions material, raw material shape and accuracy, respectively, in addition to, the 5 digits of geometrical code. Show the supplementary code.]

25. What is concept of a composite part? How the composite part helps in identifying a group of parts belonging to the same family? How does it help in variant type of computer-aided process planning? Figure 13.17

26. How does variant type CAPP differ from generative type CAPP? What are the factors which should be considered in designing a computer-aided process planning system?

    Show on a diagram, the area of application of variant type CAPP and generative as well as manual process planning.

    [**Ans:** There are several factors that must be considered when one attempts to implement a process planning system. These include:

    1. Manufacturing system components
    2. Production volume/batch size
    3. Number of different production families

    1. **Manufacturing system components.** The planning function is affected directly by the capability of the manufacturing system that will be used to produce the component. A manufacturing system has several methods. It is essential, however, that the user interact with the system so that he or she can easily change the process knowledge base. This must be considered when purchasing or creating a generative process planning system.
    2. **Production volume/batch size.** Production volume is a major consideration in the selection of production equipment. As a basic rule of thumb, special purpose machines and tooling are used for mass production, and general-purpose equipment is used for

small-batch production. The economics of production determines this decision. These same "economies of scale" must also be applied to process planning.

Different process plans should be used for the same component design when the production volume is significantly different. For example, it is appropriate to turn a thread on an engine lathe if we only need one screw. However, when 10,000 screws are required, a threading die should be considered. Similarly, machining a casting is also more desirable than complete part fabrication for large production volume.

In a variant process planning system, the production volume can be included as a code digit. However, standard plans must be prepared for different levels of production. Preparing standard plans for each production level may not be feasible, since components in the same family may need quite different processes when the production volume increases. When the batch size is not included in the family formation, manual modification of the standard plan for different production volumes is necessary.

In a generative process planning system, the production volume can be considered a variable in the decision model. Ideally, the knowledge base of a system includes this variable. Processes, as well as machines and tool selection, are based not only on shape, tolerance, and surface finish but also on the production volume.

3. **Number of production families.** The number of different production families used is a function of the number and difference in the components being planned. A variant process planning system is of little value if there are many families and few similar components (family members), because the majority of effort will be spent adding new families and standard plans. A generative process planning system is more desirable for this type of manufacturing environment.

Certain manufacturing systems specialize in making similar or identical components for different assemblies. These components can usually be designated by their features (we typically call them composite components). Since each feature can be machined by one or a series of processes, a model can be developed for each family. In the model, processes corresponding to each feature are stored. A process plan can be generated by retrieving processes that correspond to the features on a new component. This type of generative process planning system utilizes the major benefit of group technology. It is easier to build this type of system than a general generative precision machining centre can produce most of its products on a single machining centre. However, in other systems, several machines may be required to achieve the same precision. This is true for both process and machine selection, and even more true for machine parameter selection or optimization. The process knowledge database depends on the manufacturing system.

A variant process planning system contains no process knowledge per se. Process plans are retrieved from a database. The standard process plans in the database are prepared manually by human process planners. The capability of the manufacturing system was embedded in the process plans by the process planners when they prepared the system. Consequently, the standard plans must be changed when major factory renovation takes place. Variant process planning structures have been adopted by different manufacturing systems; however, the database must be rebuilt for each system. The lengthy preparation stage is unavoidable. Implementation of a variant planning system requires that a unique database of component families and standard plans be constructed.

On the other hand, a generative process planning system has its own knowledge base, which stores manufacturing data. The user modifies the knowledge base in order to suit the particular system. A generative process planning system provides the user with a method to describe the capabilities of the manufacturing system. The process knowledge representation can be created and stored using process planning system; yet, it can provide very detailed plans (depending upon the part families being produced).

For a moderate number of component families and many similar components in each family, a variant process planning system is usually the most economic automated planning alternative. Although a long variant preparation stage is still necessary, a variant process planning system is much easier to develop. Such a system can be used very effectively when there are many similar components. On the other hand, significant product variation usually dictates generative process planning as the most economic alternative. Figure 13.31 illustrates the economic regions for the different planning alternatives.]

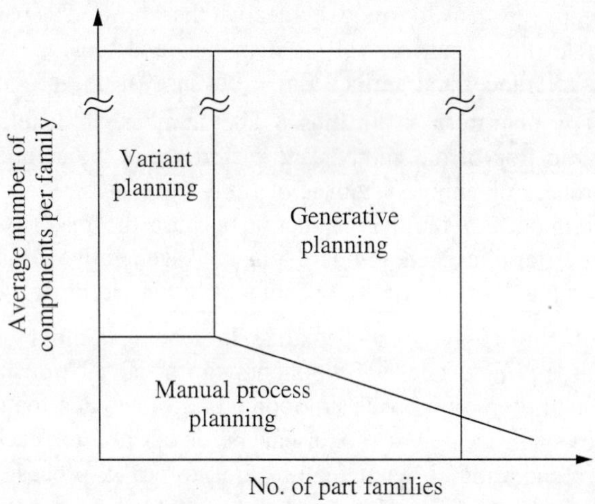

FIGURE 13.31 Economic regions for different process planning systems.

27. Show with a sketch on FMS suitable for internal broaching and hobbing of gear teeth.

[**Ans:** Cell control in manufacturing is shown in Figure 13.32 which gives layout for gear broaching and hobbing. On a shift basis, the remote host computer loads the cell controller with numerical data for parts to be processed for that time period. The cell controller downloads the appropriate NC information to the machine tools memory unit. Semi-finished gear blanks are subjected to metal cutting in the cell which has conveyer for material handling, stores, machine tools, programmable logic controllers (PLC) for driving machine tools, cathode ray tube for having information on processing, tool positioning and tool wear. Figure 13.32 also shows robot and robot controller (RC). A local area network links the various 'islands of automation' which is essential in CIM. In 1982, General Motors mandated that any computerized device installed in its factories would communicate via Manufacturing Automation Protocol (MAP). The objective was to establish a local area network to have CAD/CAM/Business Process Integration.

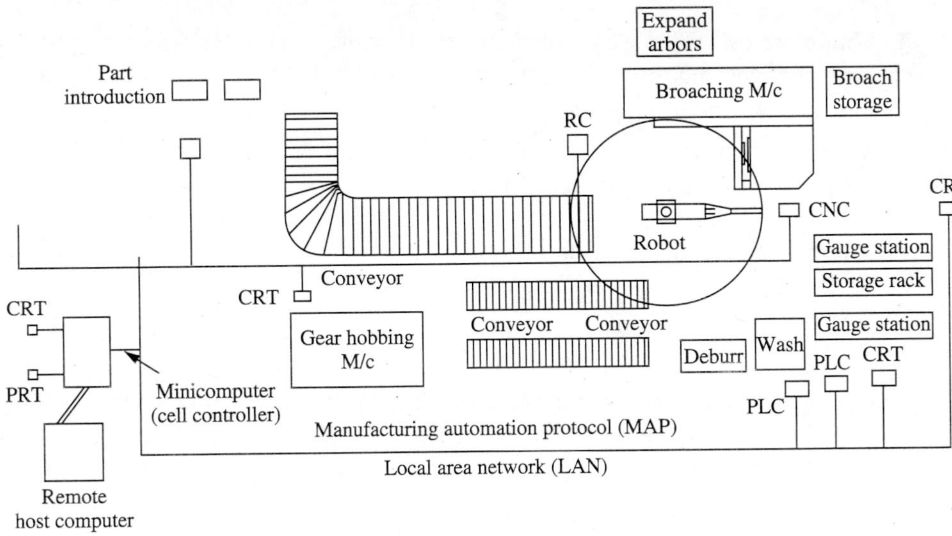

FIGURE 13.32 Spur gear cell for broaching and hobbing.

28. What are automated vehicles? Explain their types and principle of working.

[**Ans:** Refer to Figure 13.33. Automated guide vehicle (AGV) is operated with on-board batteries and moves on a fixed path without driver. The guidance control is a method by which AGVS pathway is defined and controlled. Various technologies are available for guidance control, following three are important from the subject point-of-view. The actual use of a particular guidance technology mainly depends upon application, environment and need.

1. Guide wires
2. Paint strips
3. Self-guided vehicles

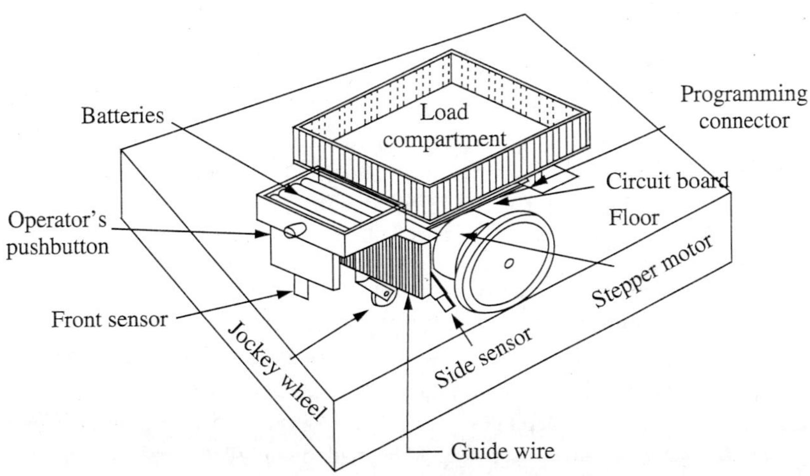

FIGURE 13.33 Automatic guided vehicle based on electromagnetic sensors: operation of the on-board sensor system that uses two coils to track the magnetic field in the guide wire.

1. **Guide wires.** The wire guidance is the most commonly used method in the manufacturing industries. The principle of wire guidance is shown in Figure 13.33. The different elements shown are:
   - Electric wires
   - Small cut channel into floor surface
   - Frequency generator
   - On-board sensors for each vehicle
   - Steering motor

   Electric wire. Electric wires are placed in a small channel cut into the surface of floor, along which the vehicle is to be guided.

   Small cut channel into floor surface. Small channel is cut into the surface of the floor. The channel is typically 3–12 mm wide and 13–26 mm deep. After guide wires are embedded (installed), the channel is filled with cement to eliminate the disorder in the floor.

   Frequency generator. A frequency generator is connected to guide wire, which emits a low-voltage, low current signal with a frequency in the range of 1–15 kHz. This induces a magnetic field along the pathway that can be followed by sensors on board each vehicle.

   On-board sensors for each vehicle. Two sensors are mounted on the vehicle on either side of the guide wire. They sense the induced magnetic field and guide the vehicle along guide wire. They feedback the information to the controller.

   Steering motor. A steering motor is attached with the vehicle which, after getting signals, is able to steer the vehicle in required direction.

2. **Paint strips.** In this guiding technology, an optical sensor is used to track the paint strips. The major elements used are:

   Paint strips. 1 in. wide paint strips can be taped, sprayed or painted on the floor. The paint strips contains fluorescent particles that reflect an UV (ultraviolet) light coming from the vehicle.

   On-board sensor. An on-board sensor detects the reflected light from the strip and controls the steering motor.

   Paint strip guidance technology is used where: (i) the installation of guide wires in the floor surface is not practical and (ii) electrical noise renders the guide wire system unreliable. Paint strips must be kept clean and periodically repaired, as they deteriorate with time.

3. **Self-guided vehicles.** These are computer controlled latest technology. These vehicles have the capability to follow a given route without any guide way in the floor. The movement of the vehicle is controlled by computing the wheel rotations and specified steering angles. This computation is performed by the vehicle's on-board computer. One of the major advantages of self-guided vehicles over other conventional guided vehicle is the flexibility of path. The path network can be changed by entering the required data into the navigation computer. This method allows quick changes and modification in the pathway without altering the plant facilities.]

29. What are automated storage and retrieval systems (AS/RS).

[**Ans: Automated Storage and Retrieval Systems**

Automated storage and retrieval systems (AS/RS) play a central role in the automated factory. An AS/RS can be defined as "a storage system that performs storage and retrieval operations under a defined degree of automation, with better speeds and more accuracy". The AS/RS not only controls inventories, but also keeps track (record) of parts and materials in process. In another way, "A combination of equipments and control, which handles, stores and retrieves materials with precision, accuracy, and speed under a defined degree of automation".

An AS/RS consists of racks and shelf system and pathways called aisles for material storage. It also consists of an automated mechanized crane used for automated storage and retrieval of material to and from aisles. Each AS/RS aisles has one or more input/output station where materials are delivered into the storage system or moved out of the system. The input/output stations are known as *pickup-and-deposit (P&D) stations*. This P and D stations can be manually operated or interfaced with automatic conveyor system. A typical unit load AS/RS is shown in Figure 13.34. The physical arrangement of the aisles in AS/RS is also shown in Figure 13.34.

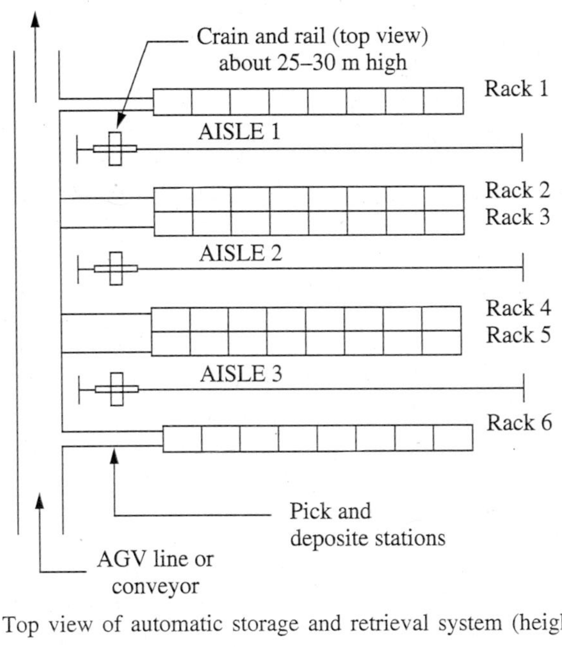

FIGURE 13.34 Top view of automatic storage and retrieval system (height about 22–25 m).

Objectives of AS/RS

The main objective of AS/RS is to store materials for a period of time and permit easy access to those materials and when required. Other possible objectives are:

1. Increase storage capacity
2. Increase storage density
3. Increase throughput

4. Improve control over inventories
5. Improve safety and security of storage
6. Improve stock rotation
7. Improve customer service
8. Improve floor space utilization
9. Improve real-time access
10. Improve productivity and overall performance of system
11. Reduce labour cost
12. Reduce wastage and pilferage

Types of AS/RS

There are various designs available for AS/RS, some of them are horizontal while other are vertical framed. Table 13.2 gives five basic designs of AS/RS along their properties.

TABLE 13.2 Five basic type of AS/RS

S.No.	*Type*	*Properties*
1.	Unit load AS/RS	A large automated system designed to handle unit load stored on pallets or containers. System is computer controlled. Storage/retrieval cranes are automated.
2.	Deep-lane AS/RS	A high density unit load storage system. Uses two automatic S/R cranes, one for load input another for load pickup.
3.	Miniload AS/RS	Smaller than a unit load AS/RS. Used to handle small loads that are contained in bins or drawers in the storage system. P and D station is usually operated by a human worker. Generally, enclosed for security of the items stored.
4.	Man-on-board AS/RS	A human operator rides on the carriage of the S/R crane. The man pickup the individual items directly at their storage locations.
5.	Vertical lift AS/RS	It is vertical type of AS/RS. Aisle is vertical. Capable of holding large inventories. Saving valuable floor space in the factory.

30. What are the programmable logic controllers? What is the role of PLC in flexible manufacturing systems?

[**Ans: Functions performed by PLC**

The programmable logic controllers (PLCs) were originally designed to perform logic control and sequencing functions. However, PLCs are evolved to include several capabilities in addition to the above. Some of these additional capabilities or basic functions performed by many commercially available PLCs include:

(i) *Analog control functions.* This function involves the capability of PLC to regulate the analog devices directly. Analog control devices are used to accomplish proportional, integral, and derivative control functions. Proportional-integral-derivative (PID) control is available on some more powerful PLCs which using digital computers.

(ii) *Arithmetic functions.* This function includes addition, subtraction, multiplication and division. Hence, it is possible to use the PLCs for more sophisticated processes where complex calculations are involved.

(iii) *Matrix functions.* This function equipped the capability to perform matrix operations on stored values in memory. This capability can be utilized to compare the actual values of a set of inputs/outputs with the values stored in the PLC memory, to error detection, if any.

(iv) *Data processing and reporting functions.* This function includes the business applications of PCs, PLC manufactures included these PC capabilities in their PLC products, to clear the gap between PCs and PLCs.

(v) *Logic control function.* This function involves the generation of an output signal according to the logic stored in the PLC memory. This is the basic function of PLC, for which PLC is designed.

(vi) *Timing functions.* This function allows the programming in which an output signal is generated with time delay, after an input signal has been received. This function also comes in the category of basic function of PLCs.

(vii) *Counting function.* This function involves the counting of inputs/outputs. For example, how many components passed the conveyor, so that after a pre-set value, the process starts or stops, depending upon the programming logic stored in PLC memory. This function is also basic function of PLC.

As we have seen above, the first four features or functions are additional and available only in more powerful PLCs while last three are basic functions for which PLCs were designed.

Basic structure or components of PLC

The programming logic controller (PLC) consists of number of component housed in a suitable cabinet designed for the factory environment. The basic components of the PLC are shown in Figure 13.35, it shows an internal structure or architecture of a PLC. It consists essentially of following components:

(i) The central processing unit (CPU)
(ii) Memory unit
(iii) Power supply
(iv) Input/output unit
(v) Programming device

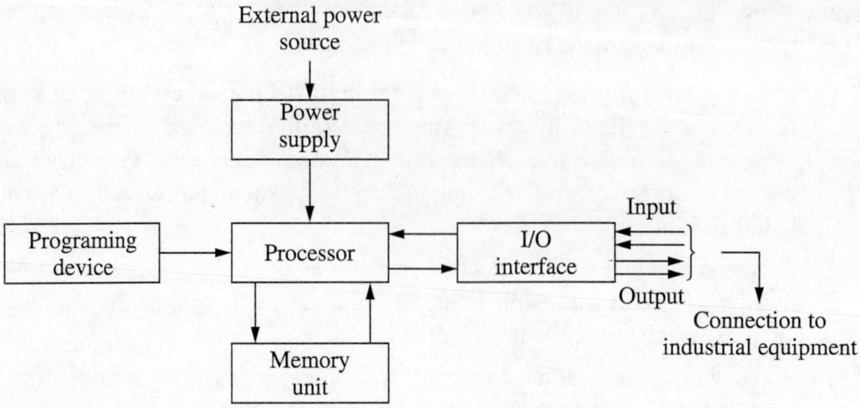

FIGURE 13.35 Components of PLC.

31. Explain the principle motions of a polar robot. How a robot sensor works?

[**Ans: Robots**

Robot Institute of America defines a robot as under:

"A reprogrammable multifunctional manipulator designed to move materials parts, tools or specialized devices, through variable programmed motions, for the performance of a variety of tasks"

Reasons for employing robots (Figure 13.36):

(1) Working in hostile environments.
(2) Performing dull or monotonous jobs.
(3) Lifting and moving heavy objects.
(4) Working during unfavouring hours.
(5) Providing repeatability and consistency.

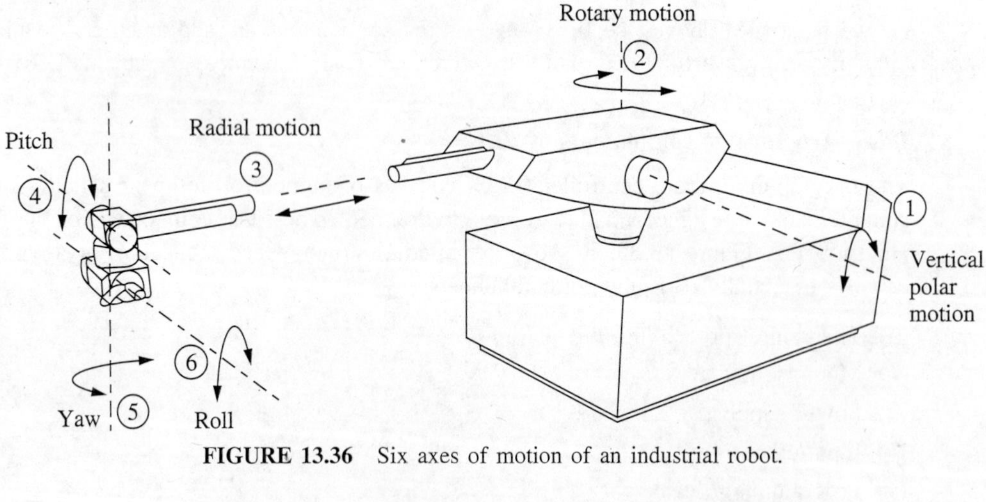

FIGURE 13.36 Six axes of motion of an industrial robot.

Classification of robots:

(1) According to control system, i.e., whether servo controlled or not.

(2) Geometry of coordinate system:

Whether it works in accordance with cartesian, cylindrical, polar coordinates. Another variety is articulated arm type robot which provides human arm type versatility. The workspace envelope in each case is different.

(3) Degrees of freedom

(4) Classification according to method of programming:

(i) Walk through programming wherein a robot is 'taught' a sequence which it will playback.

(ii) Lead through programming is for real time movements given to robot as in painting operation.

(iii) *Offline programming.* In places unsafe for humans, the first two methods are unsuitable. A separate computer drives the robot in such application.

Components of a robot

(1) Base, (2) Manipulator with gripper, (3) Control unit, (4) Feedback device, and (5) Powerpack for gripping; mechanical, magnetic or vacuum type grippers are used.

Sensor. In case of robots with artificial intelligence, these are built in devices to sense any overload or any obstacle to the path. Sensors are of the following types.

Tactile sensors. Material handling robots needs to know weight, surface roughness, etc. of the part. Special elastomer (rubber) undergoes excess deflection if there is overload on gripper. This is sensed by tactile sensor.

Distance sensors. They are ultrasonic transducers to get an idea between object and gripper. Other methods such as capacitance type transducer are also used.

Arc welding sensors. Utilize flaw in the welded seam by sensing the welding current.

Visual sensors. Camera vision system is used to match the edges of the object (as in perspective geometry) and a computer creates a picture of the object.

Thus, visual sensors are eminently suited for measurement of position and location of objects.]

32. Numerical control is the basis of various advances in manufacturing. Explain the basic working principle of working of a NC machine tool?

[**Ans. Numerical control of machine tools**

Numerical control of machine tools such as milling machine or lathe is possible by controlling the machine table movements in case of the former and the front slide and cross slide in case of the latter. Figure 13.37 shows the situation for a vertical spindle milling machine. A tape reader allows light from a light source to pass through perforations made in a tape to excite electrical impulses generated by a photoelectric cell. These impulses are amplified in the motor control unit (MCU). The MCU then drives the servomotors S_1 or S_2 to achieve table movements in X and Y directions with respect to a vertical end mill which is set to desired depth. Thus, any rectangular slot can be cut. The values of X and Y depend upon the holes made in the tape. The tape control was developed by Electronic Industries Associates.

Open loop and closed loop systems

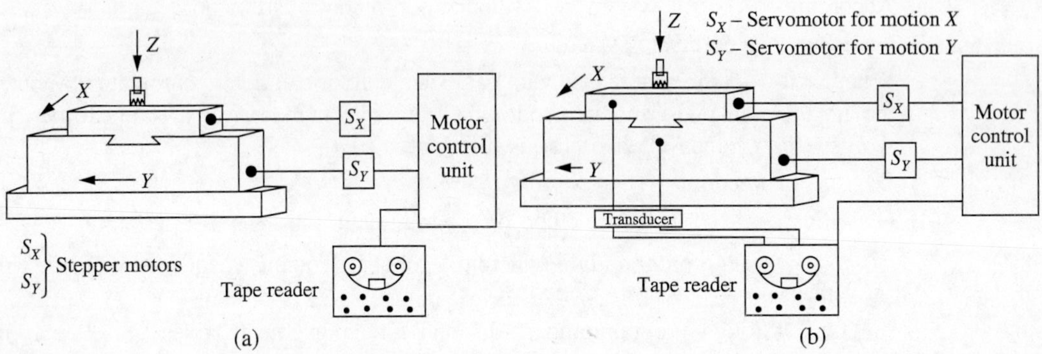

FIGURE 13.37 (a) Shows on open loop system in which there is no feedback to the MCU, through tape control, once the distance *X* or *Y* is covered. A stepper motor is preferred in case of the low cost open loop system. (b) Shows how a transducer gives a feedback once the distance *X* or *Y* is covered by the table as per the initial command given by the tape to the MCU.

Binary coded decimal system

The binary coded decimal system combines the binary and the decimal system on the tape, eight channels are available. By assigning values to each of the eight channels, different numbers can be achieved. For example, channel 1 is assigned (2°), channel 2 is assigned (2^1), channel 3 is assigned (2^2), channel 4 is assigned (2^3), channel 5 is for parity check or error correction, channel 6: values of 0, channel 7–*X* or *Y* and channel 8: end of block.

If we want a number 6 across the width of tape, it can be done by punching hole in channel 3 to yield number $2^2 = 4$ and one hole in channel 2 to yield $2^1 = 2$. Thus adding across, we get 4 + 2 = 6. Parity check establishes that an EVEN number of holes to assign desired number is done. If this is not achieved in that case, a parity check hole is added to achieve even number of holes. This is a convention of EIA.

1. **Tape format.** Figure 13.38 shows how a tape is punched to achieve: $x = 03.715$, $y = 04.612$, speed = 00–325 rpm, feed = 0000.3 in./rev.
2. **Computer formats.** Some of the shortcomings of the tape format such as inability to handle the programming of more complex programs resulted in the evolution of computer-assisted programming. One such program is the Automatic Programmed Tools (APT). The APT program uses geometric forms and English terminology to program the machine tool.

An example of APT program is taken up to clarify the point.

Example of APT language (Refer to Figure 13.39)

Define coordinates of P_0 P_1 P_2

P_0 = Point 0.0, 3.0, 0.1

P_1 = Point 1.0, 1.0, 0.1

P_2 = Point 2.0, 1.0, 0.1

```
Program FROM/PO
                GO TO/P1
                GO DLTA/0, 0, – 0.7
                DO DLTA/0, 0, + 0.7
```

GO TO/P2
GO DLTA/0, 0, – 0.7
GO DLTA/0, 0, + 0.7
GO TO/PO

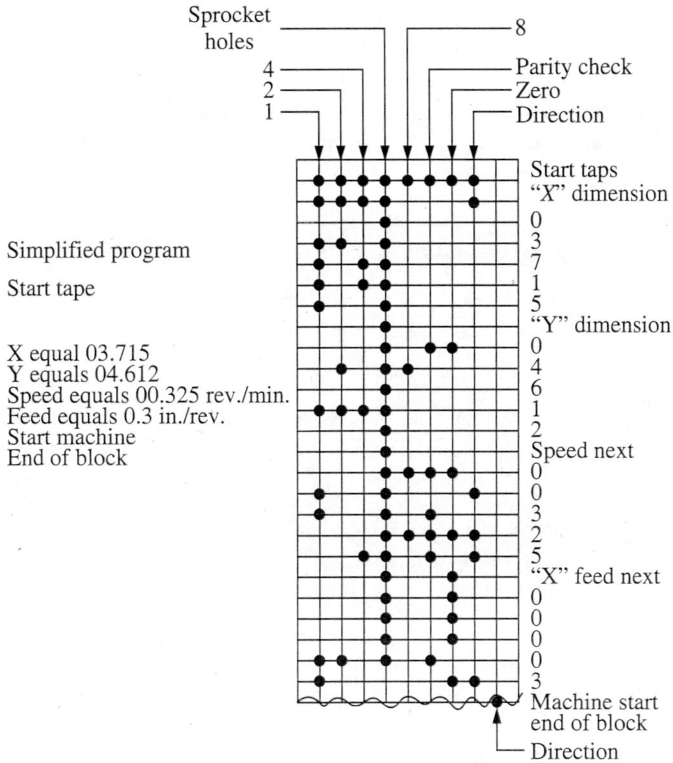

FIGURE 13.38 Tape sample in EIA system.

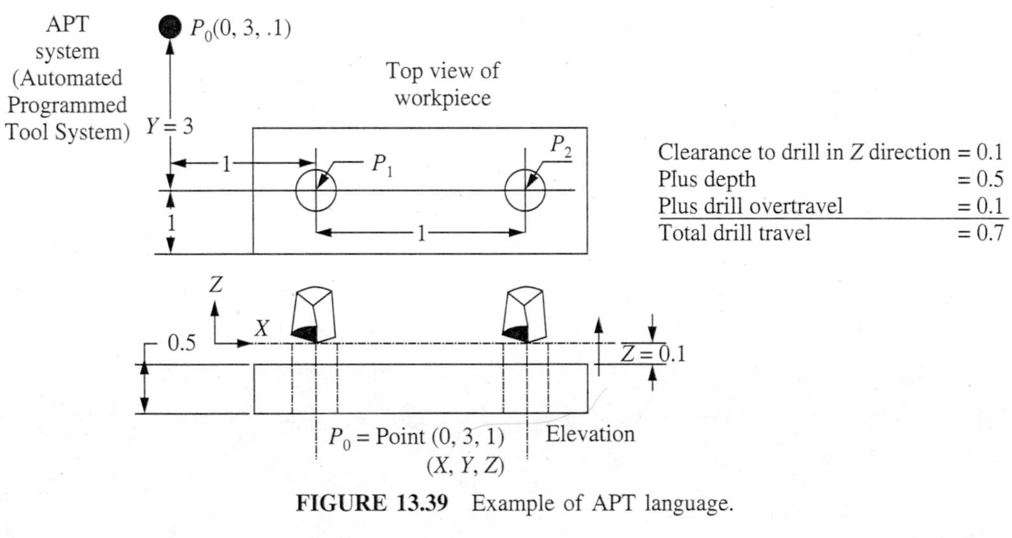

FIGURE 13.39 Example of APT language.

Drill penetration. Goto point P_1 (–0.05 –0.1–0.1 = –0.7)

Drill penetration 0.7, drill withdrawal 0.7, return to point P_0.

For other advanced programming involving G code and M code, the reader must refer to some specialized text on CAD/CAM.]

33. What is meant by just in time manufacturing? How does a pull system differ from a push system? Sec. 13.14

34. What is a 'Kanban' card? What is the difference between withdrawal Kanban and production Kanban? Illustrate through a diagram the Kanban system. How does a Kanban system work, explain through a flow chart.

[*Hint:* The flow chart in Figure 13.40 illustrates how a withdrawal Kanban (WK) pulls raw material (RM) across casting line to m/c line to assembly to final assembly.]

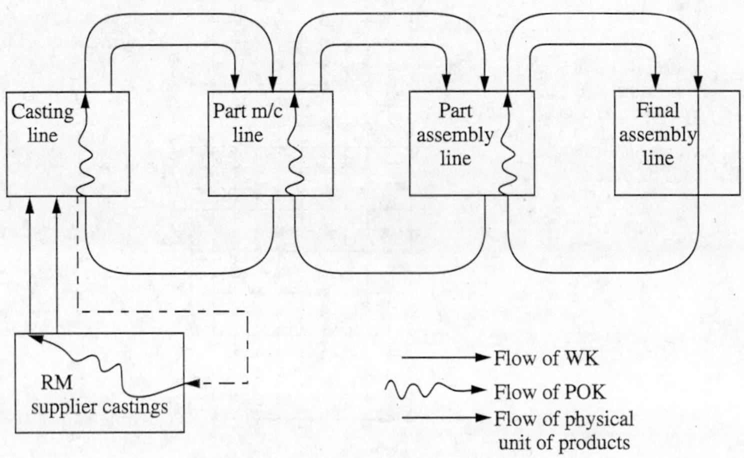

FIGURE 13.40 Kanban system.

35. What are design considerations for components used in a JIT environment? Sec. 13.14.2

36. What is meant by 'Poka-yoke' or mistake proofing?
[**Ans:** In Poka-yoke, there is provision that component cannot be located on fixture incorrectly.]

REFERENCES

[1] Shigley, J.E., *Design of Machine Elements*, McGraw-Hill, New York, 1985.

[2] Bedworth, David, Hendersen, M. and Wolfe, P.M., *Computer Integrated Design and Manufacturing*, McGraw-Hill, New York, 1992.

[3] Taichi Ohno, Kanban, *Productivity Inc.*, Stamford (Conn.), 1989.

[4] Schonberger, R.J., *Japanese Manufacturing*, Free Press, New York, 1992.

[5] Boothroyd, R.J., *Principles of Metal Machining and Machine Tools,* McGraw-Hill, New York, 1980.

Chapter 14

Modern Approaches to Product Design

In recent years, the competition between American and Asian (mainly Japanese) corporate world has given rise to two important and novel approaches to Product Design. The first approach is *concurrent design* while the second approach is *quality function deployment.* In this concluding chapter we shall highlight these two important approaches to design.

14.1 CONCURRENT DESIGN

Development from concept to product requires the consideration of four basic elements. Central to this concept is the function of the product. Related to the function are the shape, material, and production techniques used to manufacture and assemble the product.

Concurrent design is the simultaneous planning of the product and the process for producing it. Prior to the 1980s, team formation was not a preferred idea, and many designers worked in isolation. The role of manufacturing was to build what the designer conceived, improve the manufacture and assembly of the product. A certain industry survey showed that 60 per cent of all manufactured parts were not made exactly as represented in the drawings. The reasons varied: (a) The drawings were incomplete. (b) The parts could not be made as specified. (c) The drawings were ambiguous. (d) The parts could not be assembled if manufactured as drawn.

Many of these problems have since been overcome by evolution of the design team and of the philosophy of concurrent design. The process of translating from concept to a manufacturable product is rarely accomplished now by the designer alone. Generally, a team comprising a design engineer, a manufacturing engineer and a materials engineer plays a major role in supporting the chief designer. There are too many materials and manufacturing processes available for the designer to be able to make good decisions without the help of specialists.

14.1.1 The Design Team

Design is both a private, individual experience and a social, group experience. The ability to recall previous designs from memory and to synthesize partial concepts together to form new ideas is unique to an individual designer. However, since most design projects are large and require knowledge in many areas, they are generally accomplished by teams of engineers with varying views and backgrounds.

We now provide a list of individuals who may fill a role on a product design team. Their inclusion on the design team will vary from product to product, and their titles will vary from company to company. Each position on the team will be described as if filled by one person, but for large design projects, there may be many persons filling that role.

(i) **Product design engineer.** The major design responsibility is carried by the product design engineer. He must be certain about the needs for the product are clearly understood and that engineering requirements are developed and met by the product. This usually requires both creative and analytical skills. The design engineer should bring knowledge about the design process and about specific technologies to the project. The person who fills this position usually has a four-year engineering degree. However, especially in smaller companies, he may be a designer who has extensive experience in the product area.

(ii) **Marketing manager or product marketing manager.** In many companies, the marketing manager has the ultimate responsibility for the development of the product and represents the major link between the product and the customer. Because the product manager is accountable for the success of the product in the market, he is also often referred to as the *marketing manager* or the *product marketing manager.* The product manager also represents the interests of sales and service.

(iii) **Production engineer.** It is not possible for the design engineer to have the necessary know-how about production processes. This knowledge is provided by the person who must have a grasp not only of in-house manufacturing capabilities, but also of what the industry as a whole has to offer.

(iv) **Design detailer.** In many companies, the design engineer is responsible for specification development, planning, conceptual design, and the early stages of product design. The project is then turned over to detailers (often called designers), who finish detailing the product and developing the manufacturing and assembly documentation. Detailers usually are those who have passed two-year technology courses.

(v) **Testing engineer.** The testing engineer aids the design engineer in developing test apparatus, performing experiments, and gathering data in the development of the product. The insights gained from the technician's hands-on experience are usually invaluable.

(vi) **Materials engineer.** In some products, the choice of materials is forced by availability. In others, materials may be designed to fit the needs of the product. The more a product moves away from the use of known, available materials, the more a materials specialist is needed as a member of the design team. Many suppliers actually provide design assistance as part of their services.

(vii) **Quality control specialist.** A quality control (QC) specialist has training in techniques for measuring a statistically significant sample to determine how well it meets specifications. This inspection is done on incoming raw material, incoming products from vendors, and products manufactured in-house.

(viii) **Industrial designer.** Industrial designers are responsible for how a product looks and how well it interacts with human users; they are the stylists who have a background in fine arts and in human factors analysis. They often design the scope within which the engineer has to work.

(ix) **Assembly engineer.** While the production engineer involved in making the components from raw materials, the assembly manager is responsible for putting the product together. Concern for the assembly process is an important aspect of product design in modern times.

(x) **Supplier's representative.** Very few products are made entirely inside one factory. Usually there will be many suppliers of both raw material and finished goods. Often it is important to have critical suppliers on the design team because the success of the product may be highly dependent on them.

14.1.2 Benefits from Concurrent Design Approach

The application of a concurrent design approach results in reducing product design and development time and speeds the product to market. A recent example is that of the Reliance Industries where involvement of design team reduced the premarket time from 120 days to 14 days. Today this approach is also termed the *Business Process Reengineering (BPR)* approach. Michael Hammer and Champy, in their pioneering work*, have cited design process carried out as a concurrent engineering by Eastman Kodak Ltd., Rochester, USA to meet the high quality and smaller lead times of their competitor Fuji Corporation of Japan. They have met with some success.

14.2 QUALITY FUNCTION DEPLOYMENT (QFD)

QFD is the latest approach to product design. It essentially consists of converting customer's need statement (which is usually qualitative) into technical specifications. For example, a user of automobile insists upon "easy closure" of the door. This voice of the customer enables the design task force to derive the specifications of door closing mechanism in terms of kilograms of force required for the mechanism. QFD enables organizations to be proactive rather than reactive in QC. QFD involves (a) the customer, (b) what the customer wants, and (c) how to fulfill the customer's wants.

The first step of a QFD exercise is to objectively determine what group or groups constitute the customer base. For the design engineer, this implies answering the question: Who will benefit from the successful production or implementation of this product or program?

Once the customers have been identified, the wants of each customer or customer group must be determined. In QFD terminology, these are commonly referred to as the WHATs (i.e., What does the customer want?).

These WHATs can be ascertained by either interviewing representatives of the customer group, through survey, or mailing questionnaire based on the knowledge and judgement of the QFD team participants.

As stated by Robert Hall in his book, *Attaining Manufacturing Excellence,* design engineers are greatly maligned for concentrating so much on the technical aspects of design, yet giving so little thought to how everything fits together. Through the structured QFD process, these engineers are forced to first consider what the customer wants, then the means of achieving that end.

When defining the WHATs in a QFD exercise, it is important to use the same terms and phrase as would the customer. The best way to do this is through an interview/questionnaire process. As is often the case, time and budgetary constraints may prevent this approach. However, the QFD team must be able to empathize with the customer so as to correctly identify what the customer demands of the product.

Next, the QFD team must determine a means by which to satisfy these WHATs. In QFD terminology, these will be the 'HOWs', and will consist of the items or attributes of the product or

*Michael Hammer and Champy, *Reengineering the Corporation*, Harper & Row, New York, 1995.

program under development. When formulating a program strategy, the HOWs will constitute many of the action agendas in the strategic plan. The WHATs and HOWs are now ready for entry into the QFD matrix. This matrix table, often referred to as an A-l quality table, is a simple table of rows in which the WHATs are recorded and columns used to record the HOWs (see Table 14.1).

After meeting the three objectives, QFD transitions from a qualitative to a quantitative methodology. The QFD team assigns numeric values of 1.5, 1.2 and 1.0 to each of the WHATs, with 1.5 going to the most important WHAT, 1.2 to the second most important, and 1.0 to all others. These values are referred to as the *sales points* and reflect the relative importance of these customer demands.

The next step is to determine the correlation between each HOW and WHAT in the matrix. The following correlation and values are used:

Possible correlation 1
Some correlation 3
Strong correlation 9

Example. Gearbox top cover—GBS 40 Tata Truck.

TABLE 14.1 Simple QFD matrix—quality characteristics

Customer demands (WHATs)	*Technical requirement* / *Customer requirement*	*Integral casting*	*Reduce finger length*	*Reduce bush length*	*Redesign interlock pin*	*Increase interlock cable hole*	*Reshape checkplate and lug*	*Provide thick gasket*
	Ease of assembly	9	3					
	Easy of manufacturing	9			3		3	
	Ease of gear shifting	1	9	3	3	3	3	
	Ease of maintenance	9						1
	Economy	9		1			3	
	Low weight	9	1	1				
	No leakage	3						9

Many cells within the matrix will receive no value, indicating no correlation.

Each WHAT must also be analyzed and assigned a B value from 1 (for relatively low importance) to 5 for most important. These values should be recorded within the QFD matrix in the "Ratio of importance" column (see Table 14.2).

Next, an objective evaluation of the current performance of the organization in meeting each WHAT should be done, and a realistic projection as to where the organization will be in a given period of time has to be carried out. The ratings range from 1 (very poor) to 5 (very good). These values are recorded in the QFD matrix under the headings of "company now" and "Plan", respectively.

The final steps are the basic task of number crunching. The "Ratio of improvement" should be calculated by dividing each WHATs "Company now" score into its "Plan" score. The absolute weight of each WHAT is then calculated as follows:

$$AW = A \times B \times C$$

TABLE 14.2 Quality table

Cell value = Relationship weightage × DW
e.g. 243 = 9 × 27

Quality characteristic (HOWs)

Customer Demands (WHATs)

Technical requirement / *Customer requirement*	*Integral casting*	*Reduce finger length*	*Reduce bush length*	*Redesign interlock pin*	*Increase dia cable hole*	*Reshape checkplate and lug*	*Provide thick gasket*	*T*	*B*	*N*	*P*	*A*	*C*	*AW*	*DW*
Ease of assembly	9/243	3/81						324	4	3	4	0.75	1.5	4.5	27
Ease of manu-facturing	9/81			3/27		3/27		135	2	3	4	0.75	1	1.5	9
Ease of gear shifting	1/27	9/243	3/81	3/81	3/81	0.3/81		(594)	5	3	5	0.6	1.5	4.5	27
Ease of maintenance	9/108						1/12	120	2	4	4	1	1	2.0	12
Economy	9/99		1/11			3/33		143	3	2	4	0.5	1.2	1.8	11
Low weight	9/81	1/9	1/9					99	3	2	4	0.5	1	1.5	9
No leakage	3/15						9/45	60	1	3	4	0.75	1	0.75	5
Column weight	(654)	333	101	108	81	141	57			Totals					100
Function weight	44	22	7	7	5	9	1	100							

Relationship: Strong 9
Medium 3
Weak 1
Sales points = 1.5, 1.2, or 1.0
AW = A × B × C
A = P/N

Note:
T = total
B = rate of importance
N = company now
P = plan
A = ratio of improvement
C = sales point
AW = absolute weight
DW = absolute weight

where,

AW = absolute weight
A = ratio of improvement
B = ratio of importance
C = sales point

Once all WHATs have been similarly calculated, the demanded weight is computed by normalizing the column of absolute weights. The WHATs with the largest demanded weights represent the most critical customer demands.

A similar exercise yields the corresponding critical HOWs. In order to quantify the HOWs, the demanded weights of each corresponding WHAT are multiplied by the correlation factor previously recorded in the cells of the matrix. By summing the column, and again normalizing the sums of all columns, the most significant HOWs are derived.

As can be seen from Table 14.2, integral casting is the most important design change, and ease of gear shifting is the most important "WHAT". Necessary implementation at the shopfloor should be done as a part of continual quality improvement of products.

Though the mechanics of QFD are reasonably simple, its application enforces a rigour of planning and detail from its users. Participants in a QFD exercise must be capable of viewing the product from the vantage point of the customer. In order to do this, it is often advantageous to personalize the exercise by imagining yourself as a particular person within the customer group, then answering the question, "What do I want?" as you feel that the customer would.

Implementation of QFD in production. A four-fold strategy for production engineering division can be emphasized as follows:

1. *Establish* a single centre for the integration and dissemination of tools to support the concurrent engineering process needed for QFD implementation on the shopfloor.
2. *Develop* and validate analytical tools which increase the quality and quantity of information available to support the development of systems needed for incorporating the change in product or process.
3. *Reduce* the time and effort required to develop and transform systems into production by eliminating nonvalue adding activities.
4. *Broaden* the technology base by providing the ability to rapidly produce critical items for test, evaluation, and field trials.

The aim is to either locate or develop knowledge base or other tools related to the production function, evaluate its effectiveness and utility to other groups, then promote the transfer of this technology throughout the departments. The desired result is a more efficient and cost effective means for all organizations involved in the production process to share their collective knowledge and resources between various industries.

14.3 RAPID PROTOTYPING

During product design, physical models called *prototypes* are prepared and evaluated as a part of design evaluation. Conventional prototype manufacture is a very time-consuming process involving all stages of manufacture such as process planning, machining, and assembly, in addition to production planning. Due to the delay caused by the conventional prototyping procedure, R&D people in industry and academics started looking for some strategy which could enable the conversion of a 3D computer model to a 3D prototype form. Thus, the need of industry to reduce time to market resulted in the unique concept of rapid prototyping.

14.3.1 Principle of Rapid Prototyping

In the rapid prototyping process, the 3D object is sliced into several 2D sections on a computer. This simplifies 3D part producing process to 2D layer manufacture. By 'gluing' the produced layers, the desired part can be produced directly from its geometric model. Thus, rapid prototyping consists of two steps: Data preparation and Model production.

14.3.2 Rapid Prototyping Technologies

(i) **Stereolithography.** In this technology, the part is produced in a vat containing a liquid which is a photo-curable resin acrylate (see Figure 14.1(a)). Under the influence of light of a specific wavelength, small molecules are polymerized into larger solid molecules. The SLA machine creates the prototypes by tracing the layer cross-sections on the surface of liquid polymer pool with a laser beam. In the initial position, the elevator table in the vat is in the topmost position. The laser beam is driven in x and y-directions by programme driven mirrors to sweep across the liquid surface so as to solidify it to a designed depth (say, 1 mm). In the next cycle, the elevator table is lowered further. This is repeated until the 3D model is created. Figure 14.1(b) shows a modified design in which a contact window allows the desired area to be exposed to light, masking the area which remains liquid.

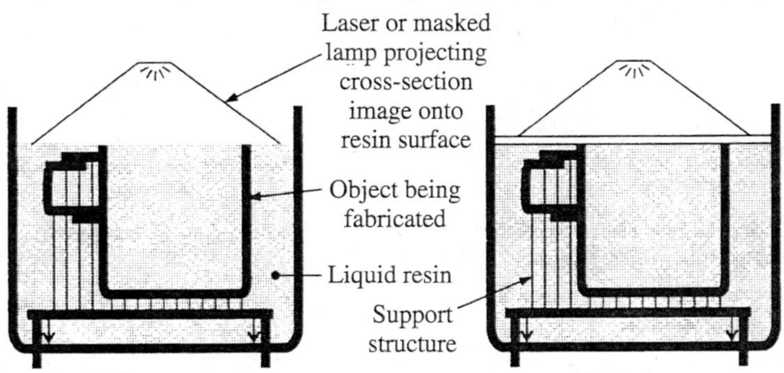

FIGURE 14.1 SLA technology.

(ii) **Photomasking technique or solid ground curing.** This method has certain unique features:

1. A mask is generated by electrostatically charging a glass plate with a negative image of cross-section of the part.
2. In the meantime, a thin layer of liquid polymer is spread across the surface of the workplane.
3. The mask plate with negative image of the cross-section slice is positioned over the thin polymer layer and exposed under the ultraviolet laser lamp for two seconds. All the parts of the exposed photopolymer layer are solidified with one exposure. However, the

area shaded by the mask is left in a liquid form and is wiped off with vacuum suction head and replaced by hot wax which acts as a support to the solidified polymer layer.

4. A face mill makes the surface of wax and polymer flat and to desired thickness.
5. The above four steps are repeated until the final model which is embedded in wax is obtained. The wax can be removed.

(iii) **Selective laser Sintering (SLS).** In the SLS process, a thin layer of powder is applied at the workplace with a roller. Carbon dioxide laser is often used to sinter successive layers of powder (instead of liquid resin).

(iv) **Fused deposition modelling.** In the FDM process, a spool of thermoplastic filament feeds into a heated FDM extrusion head. The *x* and *y*-movements of the FDM head are controlled by a computer so that the exact outline of each cross-section of the prototype is obtained. Each layer is bonded to the earlier layer by heating. This method is ideal for producing hollow objects.

(v) **Laminated object manufacturing (LOM).** The LOM process is especially suited for producing parts from bonded paper, plastic, metal, etc. A laser beam cuts the contour of part cross-section. Several such sections, when glued or welded, yield the prototype.

(vi) **Ballistic particle manufacturing (BPM).** The BPM system uses piezo-driven inkjet mechanism to shoot droplets of molten materials, which cold weld together on a previously deposited layer. A layer is created by moving the droplet nozzle in *x* and *y*-directions. After a layer is formed, the baseplate lowers a specified distance and a new layer is created on top of the previous one. Finally, the model is created.

(vii) **Three-dimensional (3D) printing.** Three-dimensional printing was developed at the MIT (USA). This technique also uses an inkjet printing head with a binder material to bind ceramic and other powders which are spread by a roller prior to application of the binder gun.

The aforementioned methods of rapid prototyping are still in a stage of development, even in developed countries. In India, intensive research is in progress at the Indian Institute of Technology Bombay and the Indian Institute of Science, Bangalore. Interested readers are advised to refer to the works of Burns [1], Ghosh [2], Knrunakaran [3], and Gurumoorthy [4]. skim

REVIEW QUESTIONS

1. What is meant by concurrent design? How does concurrent design reduce time to market?

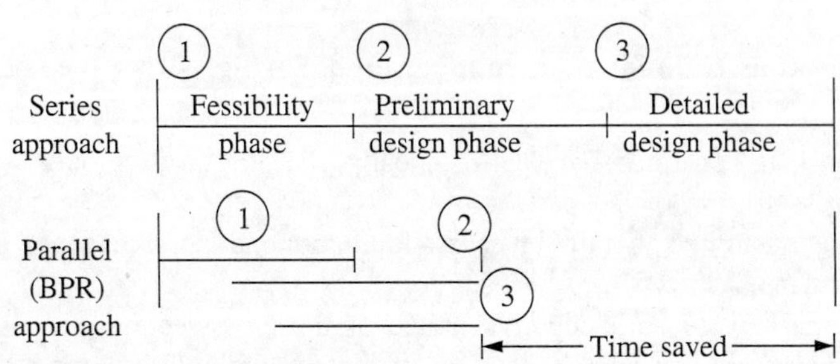

FIGURE 14.2 Reduction in customer waiting time through BPR.

[*Hint:* Conventional design contains design processes in series; concurrent design involves various interested members in a round table meeting. The design processes are overlapped as parallel concurrent processes.]

2. Who are the members of the concurrent design team ? What are their roles? Sec. 14.1.1; P 393–395

3. Who is the founder of business process re-engineering (BPR)? What are the benefits of re-engineering? Is there any flaw in BPR philosophy?
[**Ans:** Founders of BPR were Michael Hammer and James Champy].

[*Hint:* Knowledge showing with non-members of the team is not possible. BPR is a narrow concept.]

4. What is quality function deployment (QFD)? What is step-by-step QFD for customer-driven product design? What are the different steps of QFD? How does Japanese QFD differ from US approach? Explain.

[*Hint:* Quality function deployment (QFD) is design approach which gives maximum importance to 'voice of customer'. Various phases of QFD are (Figure 14.3):

(1) Developing customers' demands into engineering specifications.

(2) Converting product design specifications into component level specifications. It is called *parts deployment.*

(3) Converting part specifications into process specifications.

(4) Converting process specifications into production specifications which tell which machines will be used, how quality and maintenance charts will be developed to fulfill the process requirements.

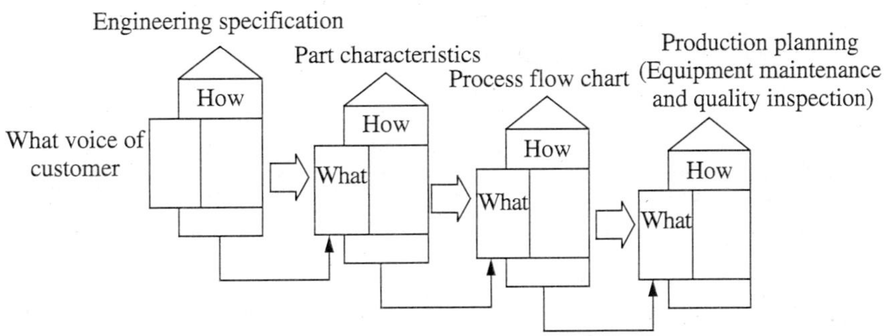

FIGURE 14.3 Stages of quality function deployment.]

US and Japanese approaches to product development

In Japanese approach, product development is done with intensive planning, forecasting difficulties caused by prototype failures. The Western engineers are overanxious to quick develop prototypes and test them with urgency. The design changes prior to production are too many. This is a costly affair. The Japanese do very detailed planning using QFD approach which reduces product development time to half. Dr. Yoji Akao is the father of QFD. It is only in the early 21st Century that US experts like Dr. Glen Mazur learnt the Japanese language and embraced Japanese QFD (Figure 14.4).

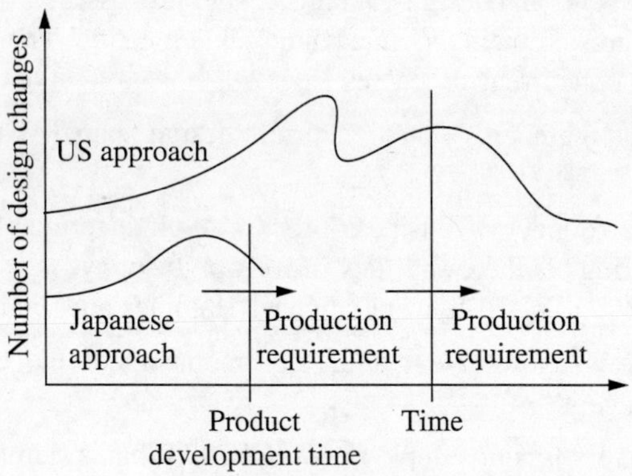

FIGURE 14.4 US and Japanese approaches for product development.

5. What is meant by rapid prototyping? What are different methods of rapid prototyping?
6. Explain through sketches the following techniques of rapid prototyping.
   (i) Stereolithography method
   (ii) Selective laser sintering
   (iii) Fused deposition modelling
   (iv) Laminated object manufacturing
   (v) Solid ground curing
   (vi) Three-dimensional printing

[**Ans: Rapid prototyping methods**

Principle. A three-dimensional geometric model of the object to be made is developed on a CAD workstation (Figure 14.5).

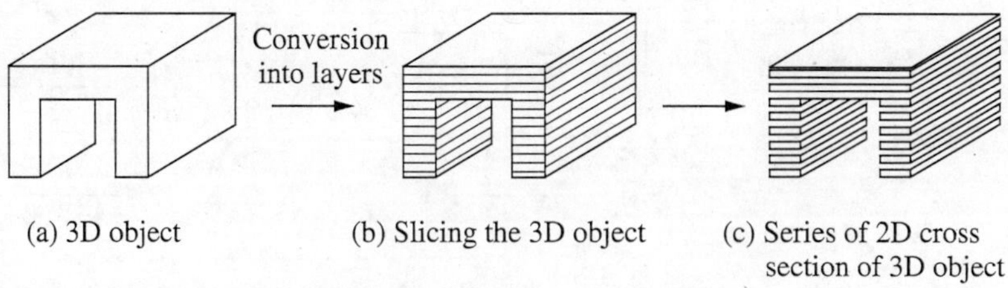

FIGURE 14.5 Basics of rapid prototyping.

Rapid prototyping is based on additive manufacturing technology. The machine needs data from CAD drawing and puts in successive layers of liquid, powder or sheet material and builds up a model from a series of cross sections. These layers, shown in Figure 14.5(c) are joined together or fuse automatically to create the final shape. Advantage of additive fabrication is taken in rapid prototyping. Sometimes, apart from the basic material, one more material to support basic material is needed. After the model is complete, the supporting material is removed.

The various processes and corresponding material are tabulated and shown in Table 14.3.

TABLE 14.3 Various processes and materials

S.No.	*Process*	*Material*
1.	Stereolithography	Photosensitive polymer
2.	Selective laser sintering	Thermoplastic powders
3.	Fused deposition modelling	Eutectic materials, polymers
4.	Laminated object modelling	Paper
5.	Solid ground curing	Various materials
6.	Inkjet printing	Various materials

1. **Stereolithography.** In stereolithography, the principle of working is based on the solidification of a photosensitive liquid polymer. When a laser beam falls on it, there is a creation of solid layer of thickness say 0.1 mm or the vertical movement of the elevator table in each cycle. Thus, the solid model is created as a result of a number of vertical movements of the elevator table. Figure 14.6 (a) shows beginning of model creation, (b) shows model is being partly created, and (c) shows model is completed.

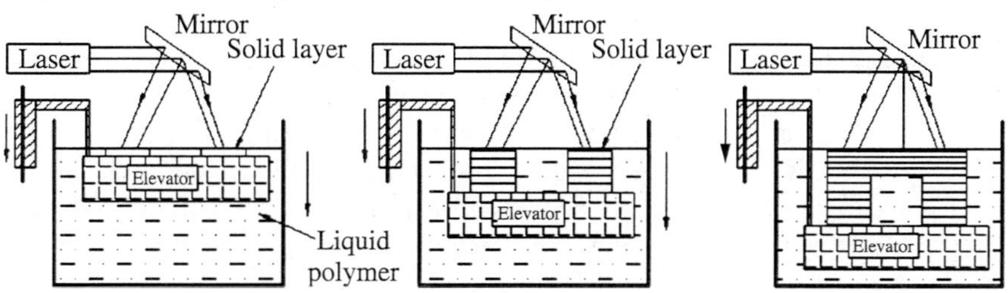

(a) Stage I – Elevator initial high position (b) Stage II – Elevator intermediate high position (c) Stage III – Elevator lowest position

FIGURE 14.6 Three stages of stereolithographic process.

2. **Selective laser sintering (SLS).** Particles of 50 μm diameter are molten by laser beam. Solidified layer is lowered in powder bed by piston and new layer is spread over the surface (Figure 14.7).

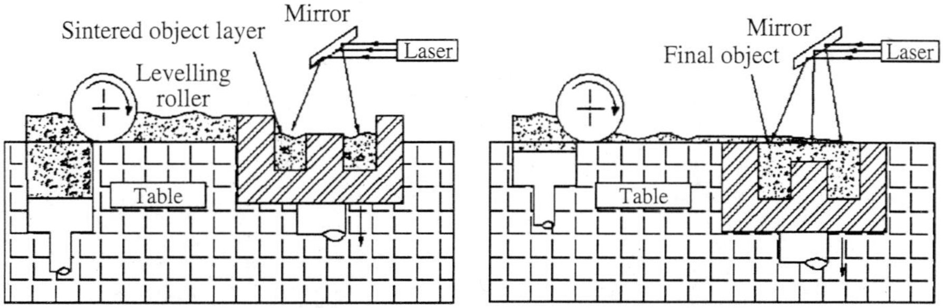

(a) Initial position of piston (b) Final position of piston

FIGURE 14.7 Two stages of selective laser sintering.

3. **Fused deposition modelling (FDM).** The process has been compared with a baker covering the cake with decorations. The heated thermoplastic material filament coming

out of the conical hopper is deposited in *X* and *Y* direction under the instruction from computer. The table is lowered in *Z*-direction of each cycle of deposition.

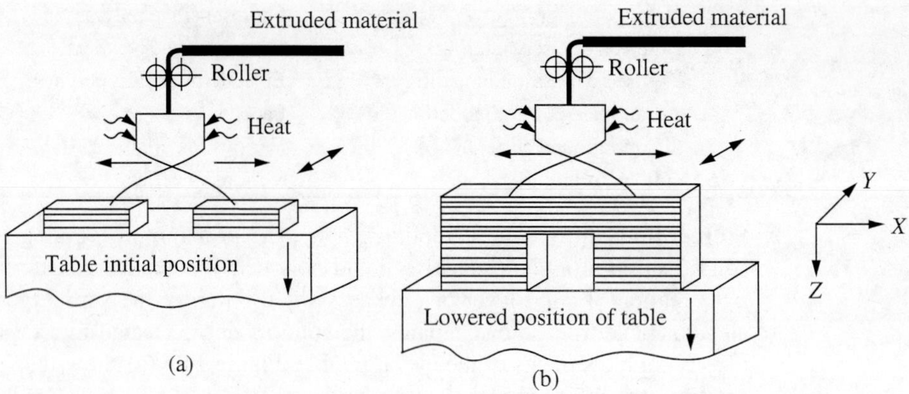

FIGURE 14.8 Two stages of fused deposition modelling.

4. **Laminated object modelling (LOM).** In this process, laser beam cuts contour of each layer and glue activated by hot roller presses the layers together. The cross hatch material remaining in the final object is removed later on. For example, if the object is an octagonal prism with a circular hole in the middle, the cross hatched material remaining attached to the object is removed after the process is complete. This is shown in Figures 14.9 and 14.10.

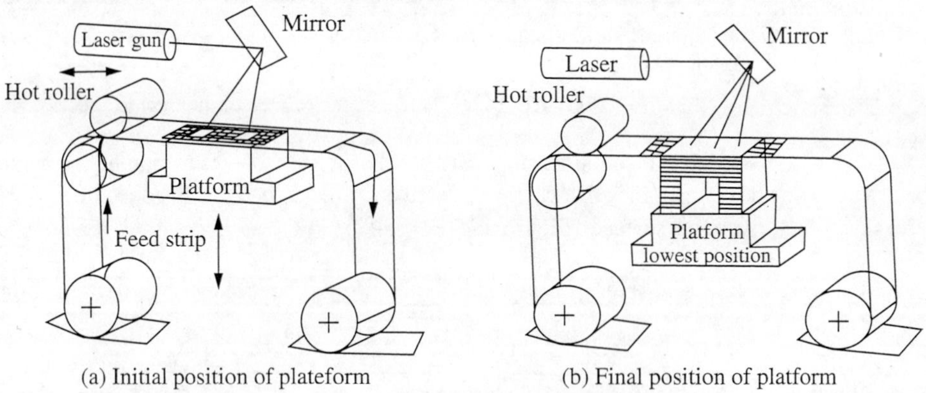

FIGURE 14.9 Two stages of laminated object modelling.

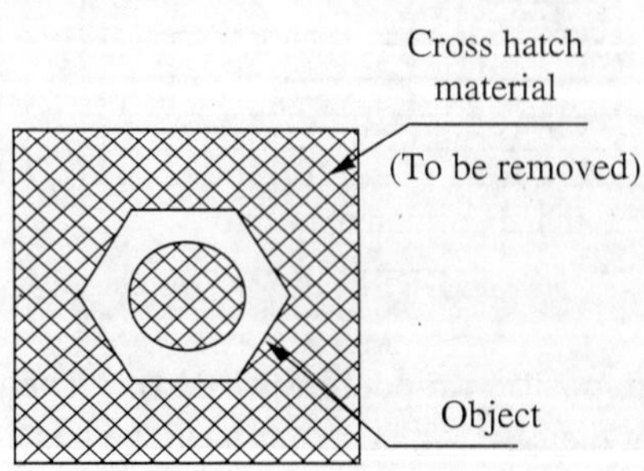

FIGURE 14.10 Job piece obtained by LOM.

5. **Solid ground curing.** This process is similar to stereolithographic process in principle. Ultraviolet rays solidify resin material which is exposed to them and a layer is formed in each exposure. The uncured resin which remains liquid because its exposure to UV rays is blocked by the mask. The uncured resin is removed by vacuum technique. Next, wax is sprayed in the gap left due to removal of uncured resin (Figure 14.11).

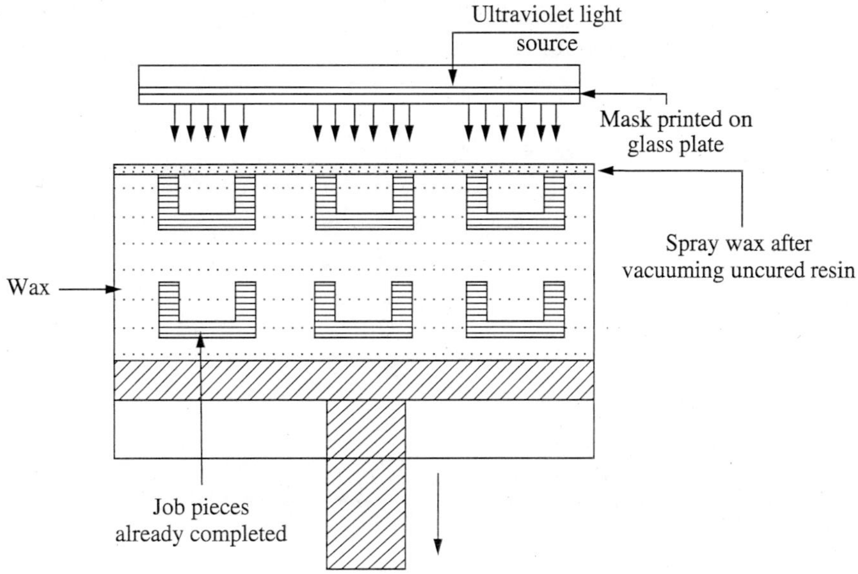

FIGURE 14.11 Scheme of solid ground curing.

6. **Three-dimensional printing.** Referring to Figure 14.12, the parts are built upon a platform situated in a bin full of powder material. An inkjet printing head selectively 'prints' binder to fuse the powder in the desired areas. Unfused powder does the function of supporting the part. The platform is lowered, more powder and binder are added and leveled, and the process is repeated. When finished, the green part is sintered and then removed from the unbound powder.

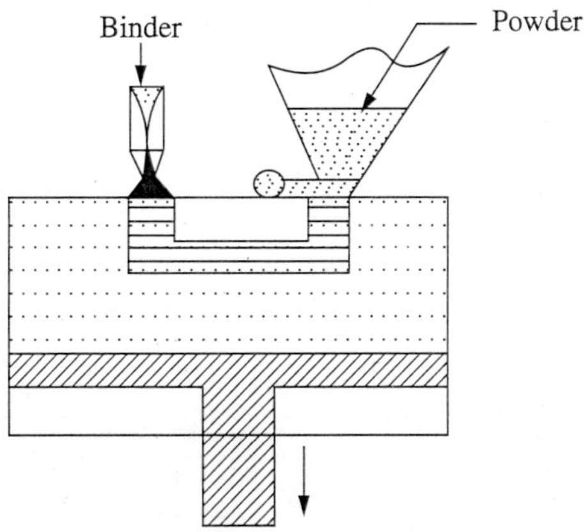

FIGURE 14.12 Three-dimensional printing process.

REFERENCES

[1] Burns, M., *Automated Fabrication*, PTR Prentice Hall, Englewood Cliffs, New Jersey, 1998.

[2] Ghosh, Amitabha, *Rapid Prototyping—An introduction*, Affiliated East-West Press, New Delhi, 1998.

[3] Karunakaran K.P., *Rapid Prototying—Technologies and challenges.* Second SERC School on Advanced Manufacturing Technology, Indian Institute of Technology Bombay, December 1996.

[4] Gurumoorthy, B., *Rapid Prototyping, CAD/CAM/Rapid Prototyping*, QIP Programme, Indian Institute of Science, Bangalore, August 1998.

Chapter 15

Quality Assurance in Product Design and Manufacturing

This chapter addresses the vital issue of quality in design and manufacturing. Quality, undoubtedly, has assumed great prominence especially in business and industry. This chapter deals with three areas relating to justify: (i) conventional quality tools and techniques, (ii) Taguchis off-line approach to quality and robust design and, finally, (iii) the contemporary concept of six-sigma quality.

15.1 EVOLUTION OF QUALITY CONCEPTS AND APPLICATIONS

Quality of a product or service is often defined as "fitness for purpose". The success of any industrial enterprise depends upon its ability to supply products of right quality at the lowest cost and with minimum waiting time for the customer. The earliest notion of maintaining quality was centred on inspecting raw material before production and finished goods after production for attaining quality objectives. However, the inspection method had the drawback that it did not forewarn the operator before extraneous causes resulted in the production of a defective piece. Shewhart in 1925 developed the control charts for monitoring the quality of products during the process of manufacture. In 1935, L.H.C. Tippett introduced the concepts of sampling techniques for inspection of goods in bulk with the introduction of sampling plans. As with most of the scientific techniques of management, the US military in 1940 was the first to adopt the statistical tools proposed by Shewhart and Tippett. The statistical quality control movement gathered momentum and found acceptance in industry also. The concept of zero defects (ZD) was started in US in 1970 and adopted widely in Japan through mistake proofing (Poka Yoke) manufacturing system introduced by Shigo Shingeo around 1980s. Apart from control charts and sampling plans which form the classical SQC (Statistical Quality Control), Genichi Taguchi in 1982 introduced the notion of loss to society through quality deviations from ideal targets. According to Taguchi, the loss to a customer is proportional to the square of the deviation of product characteristic from its target value even if this deviation is within the customer's specification limits. Taguchi methods, known as *robust design methods,* use design of experiments and orthogonal arrays to arrive at the best combination of design parameters which maximize or minimize the desired response variable. These methods also strive to deliver products whose performance is not affected by environmental factors such as road conditions for automobiles, reliability of a complex electronic circuit as likely to be affected by ambient temperature or humidity or other factors. The latest addition to the toolkit of quality in design is the concept and practice of six-sigma quality design, introduced by Mikel Harry and Richard Schroder of Motorola. Conventional three-sigma quality resulted in approximately (0.997) proportion of good pieces, with perfect process centring. The C_p value, i.e., relative precision index (for 3σ) quality has a value of 1.

The number of defectives expected in a three-sigma situation is three defectives for every 1000 total pieces production. With six-sigma quality, the C_p value equals 2 and, theoretically, owing to the typical shift in the process centre of ± 1.5 sigma which is inevitable in the long run, the defectives shall be 3.4 parts per million (ppm); ppm quality design is the latest target of quality and design professionals.

The above discussion on various milestones in quality assurance and quality control does not include the contributions of quality "gurus" Deming, Juran, Ishikawa, Philip Crosby and others because their contribution is more focussed in the field of total quality management (TQM) which includes management and motivational aspects in addition to statistical process control. (The reader is advised to study the contributions of these quality "gurus" in texts on TQM, for example, the book by Logothetis [1].)

15.2 QUALITY AND DESIGN SPIRAL

Figure 15.1 shows a modified quality-design spiral originally conceived by Juran and Gryna [2], which indicates the main issues pertaining to product quality and design.

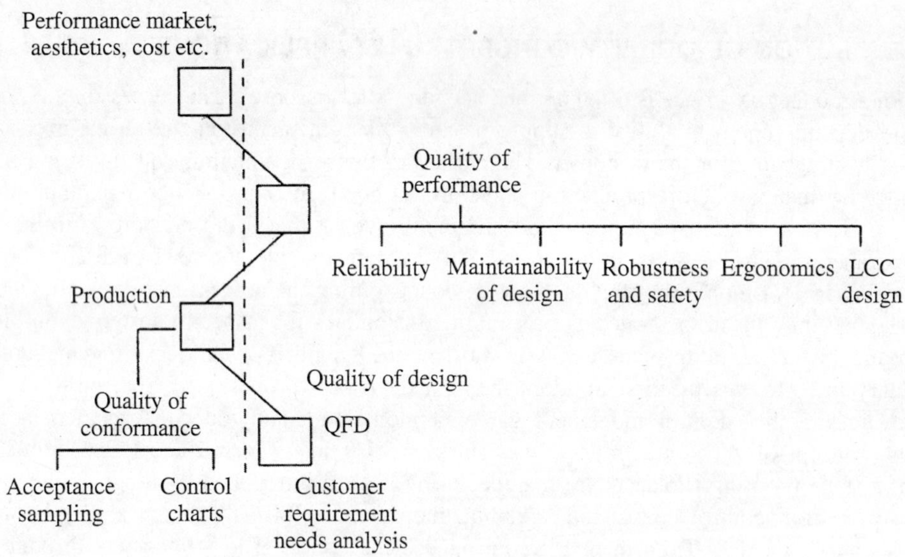

FIGURE 15.1 Quality and design spiral.

The main aspects of quality are quality of design, quality of conformance, and quality of performance which are now briefly discussed.

Quality of design. Quality of design refers to designing product based on deriving specifications so as to meet the customers' needs. This aspect of design is functional and termed *Junctional design.* The quality function deployment discussed in Chapter 14 describes the approach to achieve critical specifications.

Quality of conformance. How well a product meets the specifications derived in stage one determines its quality of conformance. In order that a product has the quality of conformance, it is essential to control the quality of incoming raw material as also to monitor product quality during processing. Sampling plans are the tools used for controlling the quality of incoming raw material.

Control charts are the tools for monitoring the product quality for in-process control. Both these tools of quality control are discussed in some detail in the discussion that follows.

Quality of performance. How well a product performs in tough environmental conditions is determined by the following metrics of product quality:

(a) *Reliability.* It is the probability that a product shall perform the assigned function for a time termed *mission time.*

(b) *Maintainability.* It is the probability that a product can be maintained and brought back to working condition in the shortest service time. The Japanese take another view of maintainability: they address design as maintenance prevention (or MP) design. An MP design is one in which modularity is incorporated so that, if a certain module of the design system fails, instead of repairing, it is substituted by a stand-by module.

(c) *Availability.* Availability of a design is the mutiple of reliability and maintainability. This view has been taken by some authorities such as L.S. Srinath, B.S. Dhillon and others. The formula for availability is

$$A = \frac{\text{Available time of equipment}}{\text{Run time}} = \frac{\text{MTBF}}{\text{MTBF} + \text{MTTR}}$$

where MTBF is the mean time between failures and MTTR the mean time to repair.

15.3 THEORY OF SAMPLING INSPECTION

Sampling inspection is carried out for assessing quality of incoming raw materials and quality of finished goods in stores.

15.3.1 Single Sampling Plans

Sampling plans are used for checking the quality of the material before and after production.

A single random sample of a predetermined size (n) is taken, each of the units in the sample is inspected, and at the end of the inspection, the number of defective (x) found is noted. If this is less than or equal to a stated (acceptance) number (c), then the lot is accepted; otherwise (i.e., if there are more than c defectives in the sample), the lot is rejected. Note that the decision to accept or reject refers to the lot and *not* to the sample. The sample is only an aid to make the decision.

15.3.2 The Operating Characteristic Curve

If a particular specified lot quality (p) is submitted, we work out its probability of acceptance (p_a) by the sampling plan. For various values of p, we can get the corresponding values of p_a. On the x-axis, we mark the quality p, and on the y-axis, the corresponding probability p_a of the acceptance. As will be shown, p_a is a function of lot proportion defective p.

The curve giving the locus of (p, p_a) is defined as the operating characteristic (OC) curve (refer to Figure 15.2); plotting of points on the OC curve can be done by the use of probability theory. Either hypergeometric, Binomial or Poisson distribution may be assumed for the calculation of p_a.

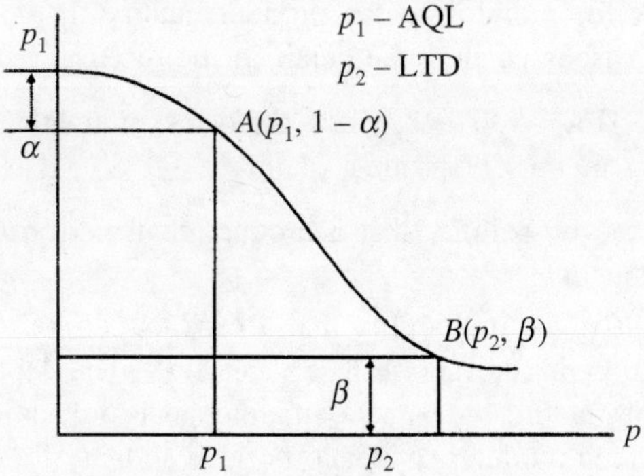

FIGURE 15.2 Typical OC curve.

where α = probability of rejecting good lots. The usual value of α is adopted by the supplier and consumer with mutual consent. Usually, 0.05 is a typical value of α.

β = It is the probability of acceptance of bad lots. Its typical value is 0.1.

Prior probability: An *a priori* assumption of the probability by guess work. In the context of sampling, p is the lot proportion defective which is a parameter. The Binomial formula is

$$p_a = \sum_{0}^{c} {}^{n}C_x p^x (1-p)^{n-x} \tag{15.1}$$

For several n and c values, several OC curves can be generated. The various feasible values of n, C corresponds to various OC curves. We will select the curve having lower value of n, because this will reduce the number of pieces of sampling.

The shape of the ideal OC curve is rectangular (refer to Figure 15.3). The ideal OC curve has a strong ability to discriminate between good and bad lots. Till the submitted lots have proportion defective less than or equal to acceptable quality level AQL, the probability of acceptance is 1. Once p is greater than AQL, the value of p_a drops to zero.

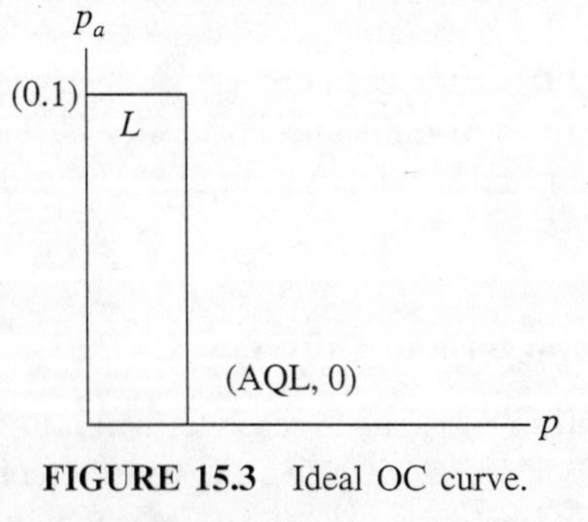

FIGURE 15.3 Ideal OC curve.

15.3.3 The AQL (Acceptable Quality Level) and LTPD (Lot Tolerance Proportion Defective)

Though the OC curve specifies the plan in the entire range of variation of the lot quality p from 0 to 1, it is customary in practical problems to be interested in some selected points. The producer would like to know how the acceptance plan affects him, when he is maintaining the standard of quality at a specified level agreed to by the consumer. This level is referred to as the acceptance quality level (AQL). The AQL is usually given as a proportion or a percentage. If AQL is given by $p = p_1$, we can work out the probability of its acceptance. Even when this AQL is maintained, we have seen above in our analysis of the OC curve that there is a risk α (however small) of its rejection. The probability of the rejection of lots of AQL is referred to as the *producer's risk* and is usually denoted by α. Here, a good producer supplying AQL lots faces the risk or rejection with a probability α, and $(1 - \alpha)$ is the probability of acceptance. $A(p_1, 1 - \alpha)$ is one important point on the OC curve.

Similarly, the consumer may have to take some risk of acceptance; even lots beyond the limits up to which he is willing to be tolerant. He may specify a proportion defective $p - p_2$. He is not willing to accept lots having p_2 or greater proportion defective (LTPD); the probability acceptance of lots of LTPD quality is referred to as the *consumer's risk* β. $B(p_2, \beta)$ is another important point on the OC curve. The producer submitting lots of quality p_1 does not want to be penalised; the consumer, on his part, would not like to accept lots of LTPD (p_2) quality and he would like to keep to a minimum the risk of acceptance of such lots. A sampling plan is selected from several standard available curves so that the OC passes through the two points $A(p_1, 1 - \alpha)$ and $B(p_2, \beta)$. Such plans are known as *AQL-LTPD plans.*

Typical values of parameters representing this two-way protection are:

$$\alpha = 0.05, \qquad \text{AQL } (p_1) = 0.01$$

$$\beta = 0.1, \qquad \text{LTPD } (p_2) = 0.025$$

15.3.4 The AOQ Curve and the AOQL

Another concept, which is useful in assessing the assurance of quality offered by an inspection plan, is the AOQL. This concept is particularly useful where the rejected lots are rectified. That is, the rejected lots are inspected 100 per cent and defectives replaced by good ones. Such a procedure is referred to as *screening* or *detailing* the rejected lots. The sampling plan is then said to operate on an acceptance/rectification scheme. The quality of the submitted lot before inspection is referred to as the *incoming quality*. The quality of the lot after inspection is referred to as the *outgoing quality*. If we have an acceptance scheme for a sampling plan, in the long run, the average proportion defective found in lots that have passed through this inspection plan is referred to as the *average outgoing quality* or as AOQ. This AOQ for each of the incoming lot quality can be worked out. The upper limit of AOQ, termed AOQL, gives an idea to the executive about what is the maximum average proportion defective that may come into the raw material store (or finished goods stores) after passing the inspection with the rectification of the rejected lots. The readers familiar with algebraic notations will easily see that if p is the proportion defective in submitted lots and p_a is the probability of its acceptance, then AOQ = $(p \times p_a)$. For acceptance/rectification scheme,

$$\text{AOQ} = \left(\frac{N - n}{N}\right) p \times p_a$$

Example. (Single sampling). Construct a single plan for attributes from the following data: lot size = N = 1,000, Sample size n = 100, Acceptance number c = 2

Solution. The OC curve is the plot of lot proportion defective vs. probability of acceptance. Either binomial formula or Poisson formula can be used for probability calculations. We shall use the Poisson formula:

$$pX = \frac{e^{-\lambda} \lambda X}{X!} \tag{15.2}$$

where λ (= np) is the parameter of the Poisson distribution. The probability of acceptance is:

$$p_a = \sum_{X=0}^{X=2} \frac{e^{-\lambda} \lambda^X}{X!}$$

The value of n is assumed as 100, and the lot fraction defective is changed between 0.01 and 0.1 in six steps. The tabulated results are as follows:

p	$\lambda = np$	p_a
0.00	0	1.00
0.01	1	0.92
0.03	3	0.42
0.05	5	0.12
0.08	8	0.014
0.1	10	0.003

Sample calculation. Let us see how one point on the OC curve is obtained.
Taking p = 0.05 and n = 100, we have:

$$\lambda = np = (0.05)(100) = 5$$

For λ = 5, to find various values of p_X (i.e. p_0, p_1, p_2), we have:

$$p_0 = \frac{e^{-5} \cdot 5^0}{0!} = e^{-5}$$

$$p_1 = \frac{e^{-5} \cdot 5^1}{1!} = 5e^{-5}$$

$$p_2 = e^{-5} \cdot \frac{5^2}{2!} = 12.5e^{-5}$$

Now with acceptance number c = 2, we have:

$$p_a = p_0 + p_1 + p_2 = e^{-5}(1 + 5 + 12.5) = 0.12$$

Thus,

$$P_a = 0.12 \quad \text{for} \quad p = 0.05,$$

Other values in the table have been worked out in a similar manner. Figure 15.4 shows the OC curve.

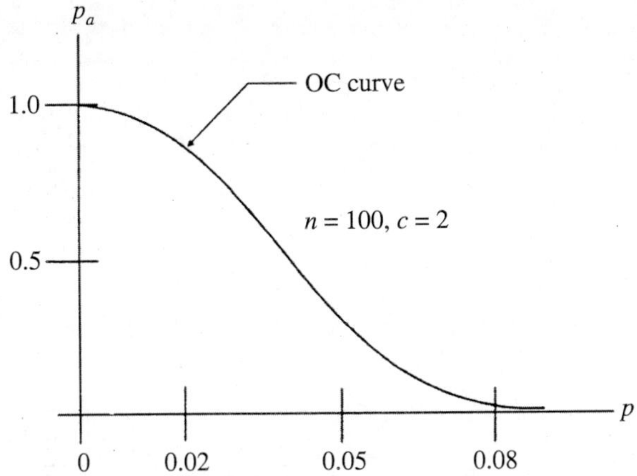

FIGURE 15.4 OC curve.

15.3.5 Average Total Inspection (ATI)

If an acceptance/rectification scheme is adopted, the ATI for a single sampling plan is given by:

$$\text{ATI} = np_a + N(1 - p_a) \tag{15.3}$$

ATI is an important metric for single sampling plans using acceptance/rectification scheme.

15.3.6 Double Sampling Plan

A sampling of n_1 items is drawn from a lot; the lot is accepted if there are no more than c defective items. The lot is rejected if the number of defectives is greater than or equal to r. If there are between $c + 1$ and $r - 1$ defective items, a second sample of size n_2 is drawn. The lot is accepted if there are no more than c defectives in the combined sample of $n_1 + n_2$, the lot is rejected if there are $r = c + 1$ or more defective items in the combined sample of $n_1 + n_2$.

A lot will be accepted on the first sample if the incoming quality is very good. Similarly, a lot will be rejected on the first sample if the incoming quality is very bad. If the lot is of intermediate quality, a second sample may have to be taken. Double sampling plans have the psychological advantage of giving a second chance to doubtful lots. Furthermore, they can have an additional advantage of requiring fewer total inspections, on the average, than single sample plans for any given protection. However, double sampling plans can have the following disadvantages:

1. More complex administrative duties.
2. Inspectors will have variable inspection loads depending upon whether one or two samples are taken.
3. The maximum amount of inspection exceeds that for single sampling plans (which is constant).

Typical double sampling plan

		Combined sample		
Sample	*Sample size*	*Size*	*Acceptance no.*	*Rejected no.*
1	20	20	0(c)	3(r)
2	20	40	3(c)	4(r)

In the above example,

p_a = Probability of getting zero defectives on first sample (p_0)
+ [probability (p) of getting one or equal to two defectives on the first sample × Probability of getting two or less defectives on the second sample]

So that the sum of defectives on the second and the third sample equals 3 or less. The formula for calculating p_a in the above situation is

$$p_a = p_0 + p_1(p_0 + p_1 + p_2) + p_2(p_0 + p_1)$$

The calculation of the first term is straightforward. The second term can be explained with reference to a tree diagram as shown in Figure 15.5.

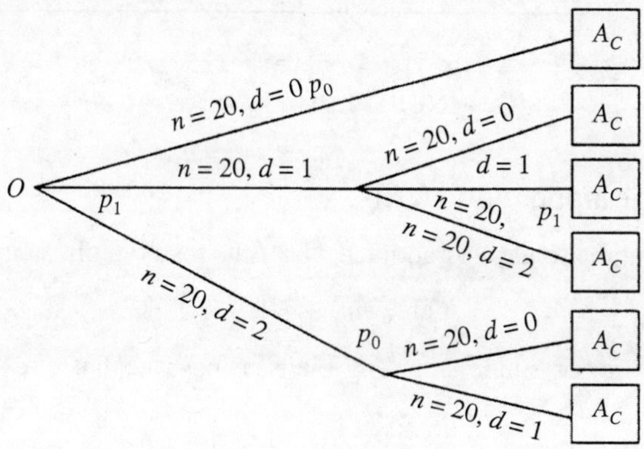

FIGURE 15.5 Tree diagram.

In the theory of acceptance sampling, a plot between p_a and p is very important. It is termed the *operating characteristic curve*. A typical OC curve is shown in Figure 15.6(a).

The calculation of probability by using the tree diagram (Figure 15.5) is:

$$p_a = p_0 + p_1p_0 + p_1p_1 + p_1p_2 + p_2p_0 + p_2p_1 \tag{15.4}$$

The calculation of average sample number (ASN) using the tree diagram:

$$\text{ASN} = 20 + (p_1 + p_2)(20)$$

Figure 15.6(b) shows the plot of average sample number (ASN) for a double sampling plan.

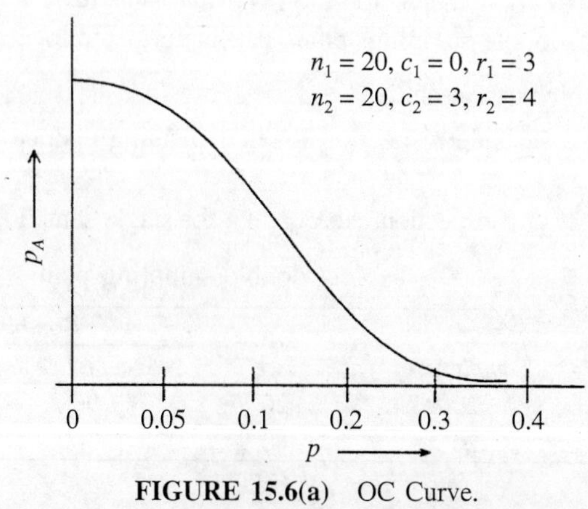

FIGURE 15.6(a) OC Curve.

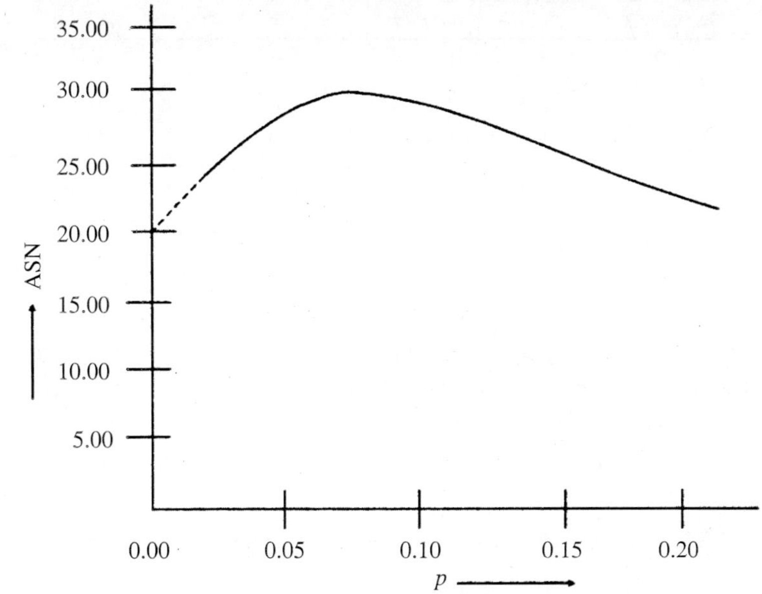

FIGURE 15.6(b) ASN curve.

15.3.7 Multiple Sample Plans

A multiple sampling procedure can be represented through a table. A first sample of n_1 is drawn, the lot is accepted if there are not more than n_1 defectives, the lot is rejected if there are more than $(r_1 - 1)$ defectives. Otherwise a second sample of n_2 is drawn. The lot is accepted if there are no more than c_2 defectives in the combined sample of $n_1 + n_2$. The lot is rejected if there are more than $(r_2 - 1)$ defectives in combined sample of $n_1 + n_2$. The procedure is continued in accordance with the table shown below. If by the end of the sixth sample the lot is neither accepted nor rejected, a sample of n_7 is drawn. The lot is accepted if the number of defectives in the combined sample of $(n_1 + n_2 + n_3 + n_4 + n_5 + n_6 + n_7)$ does not exceed c_7. Otherwise, the lot is rejected.

Multiple sampling plan

Sample	*Sample size*	*Size (combined)*	*Acceptance No.*	*Rejection No.*
First	n_1	n_1	c_1	r_1
Second	n_2	$n_1 + n_2$	c_2	r_2
Third	n_3	$n_1 + n_2 + n_3$	c_3	r_3
Fourth	n_4	$n_1 + n_2 + n_3 + n_4$	c_4	r_4
Fifth	n_5	$n_1 + n_2 + n_3 + n_4 + n_5$	c_5	r_5
Sixth	n_6	$n_1 + n_2 + n_3 + n_4 + n_5 + n_6$	c_6	r_6
Seventh	n_7	$n_1 + n_2 + n_3 + n_4 + n_5 + n_6 + n_6$	c_7	r_7

A specific example of a multiple sampling plan is as follows:

Sample size	*Size (combined)*	*c*	*r*
20	20	0	3
20	40	2	4
20	60	3	5
20	80	4	6
20	100	5	7
20	120	6	8
20	140	7	8

A tree diagram for seven-stage multiple sampling plan is indicated in Figure 15.7. Node [A] indicates acceptance node while node [C] indicates continue sampling.

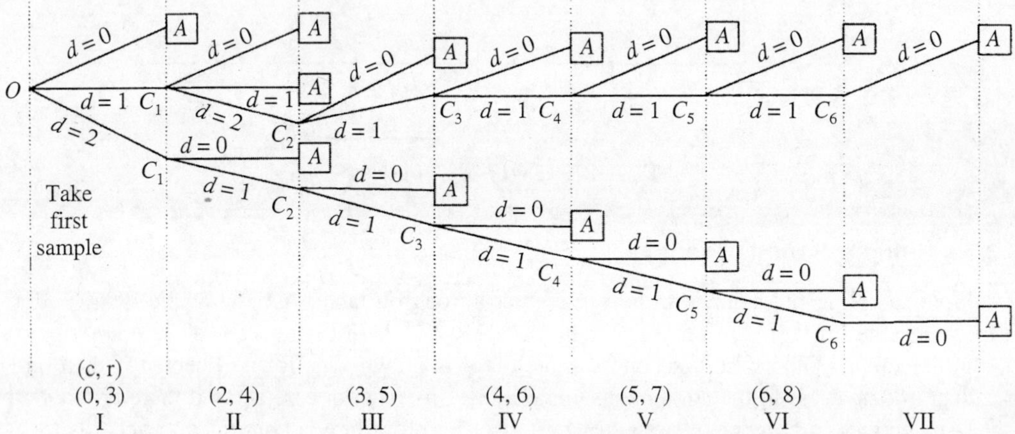

FIGURE 15.7 Tree diagram for a multiple sampling plan $n = 20$ at each stage.

In the tree diagram, *O* indicates the point of origin of sampling, *A* indicates a node denoting acceptance of the lot on the basis of the sample, and *C* indicates a live node from which various arcs lead to success nodes *A*. Keeping in mind the laws of addition and multiplication of probabilities, we have developed the equation for calculating probability of acceptance p_a to any lot.

Note from the sampling plan that $c_1 < c_i + 1$ and $c_2 + 1 < r_i - 1$ for all *i*. Of course, plans can be devised which permit any number of samples before a decision is reached. A multiple sampling plan will generally involve less inspection, on the average, than the corresponding single or double sampling plan guaranteed the same protection (Figure 15.8a). The advantage is considerable since inspection costs are directly related to sample sizes. The disadvantages of multiple sampling are:

1. They usually need higher administrative cost than single or double sampling plans.
2. The variability of inspection load introduces difficulties in scheduling inspection time.
3. Higher caliber inspection personnel may be necessary to guarantee proper use of the plans.
4. Adequate storage facilities must be provided for the lot while multiple sampling is being carried out.

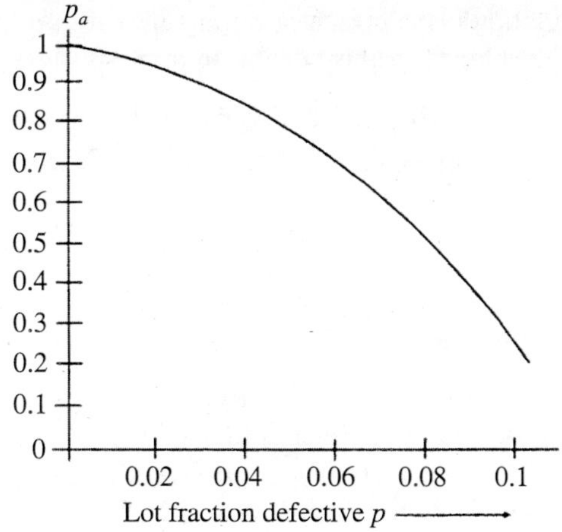

(a) OC curve

FIGURE 15.8(a) Multiple sampling plan (*cont.*).

The probability of acceptance p_a can be calculated by using the tree diagram:

$$
\begin{aligned}
p_a = p_0 &+ (p_1p_0 + p_1p_1 + p_2p_0) + (p_1p_2p_0 + p_2p_1p_0) + (p_1p_2p_1p_0 + p_2p_1p_1p_0) \\
&+ (p_1p_2p_1p_1p_0 + p_2p_1p_1p_1p_0) + (p_1p_2p_1p_1p_1p_0 + p_2p_1p_1p_1p_1p_0) \\
&+ (p_1p_2p_1p_1p_1p_1p_0 + p_2p_1p_1p_1p_1p_1p_0) \qquad (15.5)
\end{aligned}
$$

Equation (15.5) is arrived at by tracing along the branches methodically till the last *A* node in a desired stage is reached. The tracing process is applied to the branches indicated as thick lines of the tree.

ASN equation is arrived at, by tracing along the branches avoiding *A* node, and passing through *C* nodes which indicate continue sampling (Figure 15.8b).

$$
\begin{aligned}
\text{ASN} = 20 &+ 20(p_1 + p_2) + 20(p_1p_2 + p_2p_1) + 20(p_1p_2p_1, + p_2p_1p_1) \\
&+ 20(p_1p_2p_1p_1 + p_2p_1p_1p_1) + 20(p_1p_2p_1p_1p_1 + p_2p_1p_1p_1p_1) \\
&+ 20(p_1p_2p_1p_1p_1 + p_2p_1p_1p_1p_1p_1) \qquad (15.6)
\end{aligned}
$$

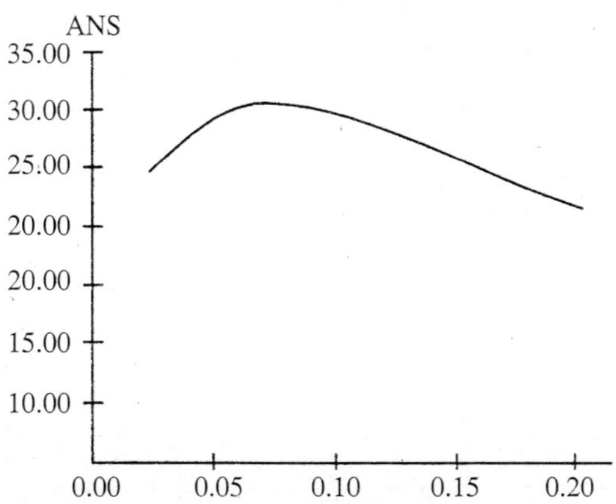

(b) ASN curve

FIGURE 15.8(b) Multiple sampling plan.

Double and multiple sampling plans present a certain amount of difficulty in conceptualization. The utility of tree approach developed in this section improves:

1. ease of understanding the double and multiple sampling inspection plans;
2. facility in calculating probability of acceptance p_a as a function of lot proportion defective p; and
3. ease of calculation of average sample number for double and multiple sampling plans.

15.3.8 Sequential Sampling Plans

Likelihood ratio is the ratio of probability of X defectives in a sample of size n with the lot fraction defective p_2 to the probability when the lot fraction defective is p_1.

If the ratio ever reaches some predetermined high level A, it is concluded that the lot fraction defective is p_2 or more and the lot is rejected. If the ratio falls to some low level B, the lot is acceptable with fraction defective equal to p_1 or less (Figure 15.9).

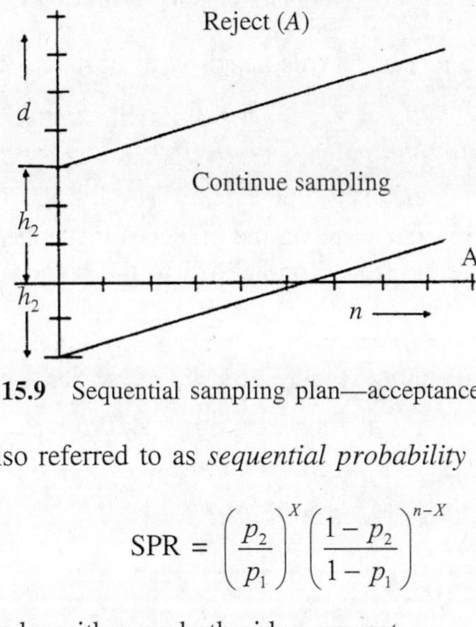

FIGURE 15.9 Sequential sampling plan—acceptance and rejection lines.

The likelihood ratio is also referred to as *sequential probability ratio* (SPR), which is defined as:

$$\text{SPR} = \left(\frac{p_2}{p_1}\right)^X \left(\frac{1-p_2}{1-p_1}\right)^{n-X}$$

See Figure 15.10. Taking logarithm on both sides, we get

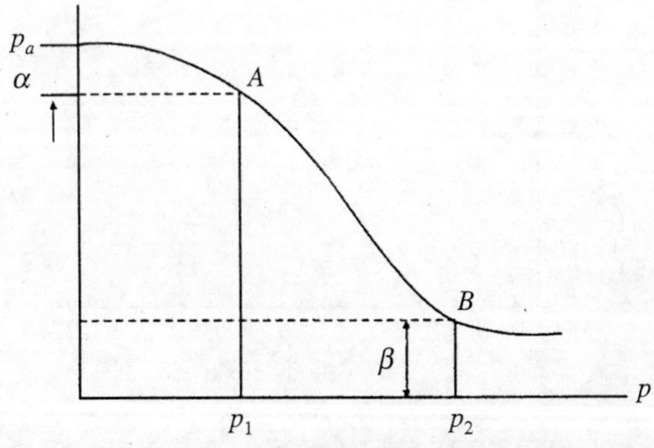

FIGURE 15.10 Explaining sequential probability ratio (SPR).

$$\ln \text{SPR} = X \ln \frac{p_2}{p_1} + (n - X) \ln \frac{1 - p_2}{1 - p_1}$$

$$= X \ln \left[\frac{p_2(1 - p_1)}{p_1(1 - p_2)}\right] + n \left(\ln \frac{1 - p_2}{1 - p_1}\right) \quad (15.7)$$

Since $p_2 > p_1$, SPR increases with X and decreases with n. From the definition of likelihood ratio,

$$\frac{p_2(1 - p_2)^{n-X}}{p_1(1 - p_1)^{n-X}} = A = \frac{1 - \beta}{\alpha}$$

or

$$\frac{p_2(1 - p_2)^{n-X}}{p_1(1 - p_1)^{n-X}} = B = \frac{\beta}{1 - \alpha}$$

Referring to the point A on the OC curve and referring to the point B on the OC curve, we have:

$$\ln \frac{\beta}{1 - \alpha} = X \ln \frac{p_2(1 - p_1)}{p_1(1 - p_2)} + n \ln \frac{1 - p_2}{1 - p_1}$$

or

$$-\ln \frac{1 - \alpha}{\beta} = X \ln \frac{p_2(1 - p_1)}{p_1(1 - p_2)} - n \ln \frac{1 - p_1}{1 - p_2} \quad (15.8)$$

or

$$X = -h_1 + Sn$$

Similarly, for A,

$$\ln \frac{1 - \beta}{\alpha} = X \ln \frac{p_2(1 - p_1)}{p_1(1 - p_2)} + n \ln \left(\frac{1 - p_2}{1 - p_1}\right)$$

or

$$\ln \frac{1 - \beta}{\alpha} = X \ln \frac{p_2(1 - p_1)}{p_1(1 - p_2)} - n \ln \left(\frac{1 - p_1}{1 - p_2}\right) \quad (15.9)$$

or

$$X = h_2 + Sn$$

where

$$h_1 = \frac{\ln [(1 - \alpha)/\beta]}{\ln [p_2(1 - p_1)/p_1(1 - p_2)]}, \quad h_2 = \frac{\ln [(1 - \beta)/a]}{\ln [p_2(1 - p_1)/p_1(1 - p_2)]}, \quad S = \frac{\ln (1 - p_1)/(1 - p_2)}{\ln [p_2(1 - p_1)/p_1(1 - p_2)]}$$

Example. The use of the above formulae is illustrated through the following example:

If $p_1 = 0.04$, $p_2 = 0.08$

$\alpha = 0.15$, $\beta = 0.25$

On solving, we get:

$$x = r = 2.26 + 0.059n \text{ and } x = a = -1.76 + 0.059n$$

Now, we can draw acceptance and rejection lines as in Figure 15.11.

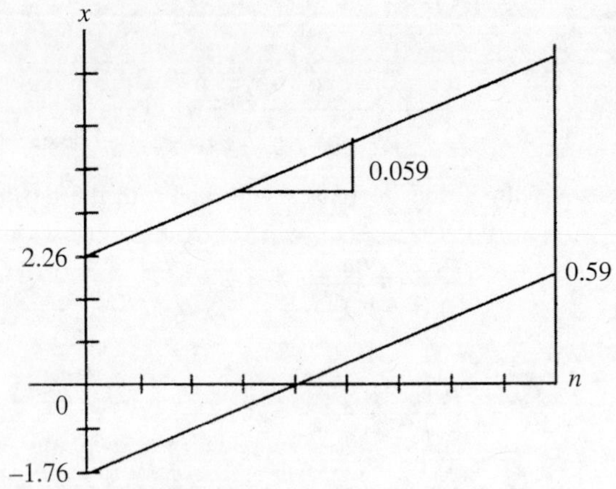

FIGURE 15.11 Acceptance and rejection lines.

15.3.9 Practical Method of Selecting a Sampling Plan

Determination of n and c from Standard MIL/STD tables: The procedure in using MIL-STD-105D for single sampling is first to find the sample size code letter corresponding to the lot size and the desired inspection level and type. Then using the sample size code letter thus obtained and the appropriate AQL, one finds the sample size and the acceptance number from the master table. A portion of the table for finding sample size code letters is given in Table 15.1.

TABLE 15.1 Sample size code letters MIL-STD-105D

	General inspection levels		
Lot or batch size	I	II	III
2–8	A	A	B
9–15	A	B	C
16–25	B	C	D
26–50	C	D	E
51–90	C	E	F
91–150	D	F	G
151–280	E	G	H
281–500	F	H	J
501–1200	G	J	K
1201–3200	H	K	L
3201–10,000	J	L	M
10,001–35,000	K	M	N
35,001–150,000	L	N	P
150,001–500,000	M	P	Q
500,001–to and over	N	Q	R

To illustrate the use of MIL-STD-105D, suppose that incoming lots contain 2000 items, and inspection level II is to be used in conjunction with normal inspection and an AQL of 0.025, or 2.5 per cent. From Table 15.1, we find that the sample size code letter is K. Then, entering Table 15.2 the row labelled K, we find that the sample size to be used is 125. Using the column labelled 2.5, we find that the acceptance number is 7 and the rejection number is 8. Thus, if a single sample of size 125, selected at random from a lot of 2000 items, contains 7 or fewer defectives, the lot is to be accepted; if the sample contains 8 or more defectives, the lot is to be rejected.

Procedure for selecting a sample plan:

1. Given the lot size and the level of inspection (II for "normal", I for "less discrimination", and III for "more discrimination", select the sample size code letter from Table 15.1 for lot size 1500, the code letter is K.
2. Refer to Table 15.2 to determine A_c and R_c when AQL is given. Thus n and c are known.

Example. For code letter K and AQL = 1%, A_c = 3 and R_c = 4.

15.3.10 Sampling Plan for Variables

Variables plans entail measurement, on a continuous scale, of how closely a given variable conforms to a specified characteristic. It is often reasonable to assume that these measurements follow a normal distribution, but even if they do not, the distribution of the means of samples of the measurements does approach normality, especially if they contain 30 or more observations. The theory of sampling plan for variables was develeped by L.H.C. Tippett. The procedure of designing the sampling plan is explained with the help of the following example.

Example. (Given α and β risk: solve for n and c). A ceramic firm produces special bricks whose weights are normally distributed with a standard deviation of $\sigma = 8.0$. Bricks shipments averaging 200 lb are of good quality and those averaging 196 lb are of poor quality. Design a sampling plan, so that:

(a) The probability of rejecting a lot with an average weight of 200 lb is 0.05.

(b) The probability of accepting a lot with an average weight of 196 lb is 0.10.

Solution. The problem situation is described schematically in Fig 15.12. The solution procedure is to first set up simultaneous equations defining the reject limit c in terms of z standard errors, then solve for n and substitute it back into either one of the equations to find c. The two equations locating c are (see Figure 15.12):

$$\text{(i)}\quad c = \mu_1 - z_\alpha \frac{\sigma}{\sqrt{n}} \tag{15.10}$$

$$\text{(ii)}\quad c = \mu_2 - z_\beta \frac{\sigma}{\sqrt{n}} \tag{15.11}$$

Setting the two equations for c equal to each other, we get

$$200 - 1.645\frac{(8)}{\sqrt{n}} = 196 + 1.28\frac{(8)}{\sqrt{n}} \quad \text{or} \quad n = 34$$

TABLE 15.2 MIL-STD 105D AQL

No. of defects values of A_c and R_c

nT	0.01	0.05	0.03	0.04	0.02	0.10	0.15	0.25	0.40	0.65	1.0	1.5	2.5	4.0	6.5	10.0	15.0	25.0	40.0	65.0	100	150	250	400
A 2															0 1			1 2	2 3	3 4	5 6	7 8	10 11	14 15
B 3														0 1			1 2	2 3	3 4	5 6	7 8	10 11	14 15	21 22
C 5													0 1			1 2	2 3	3 4	5 6	7 8	10 11	14 15	21 22	
D 8												0 1			1 2	2 3	3 4	5 6	7 8	10 11	14 15	21 22		
E 13											0 1			1 2	2 3	3 4	5 6	7 8	10 11	14 15	21 22			
F 20										0 1			1 2	2 3	3 4	5 6	7 8	10 11	14 15	21 22				
G 32									0 1			1 2	2 3	3 4	5 6	7 8	10 11	14 15	21 22					
H 50								0 1			1 2	2 3	3 4	5 6	7 8	10 11	14 15	21 22						
J 80							0 1			1 2	2 3	3 4	5 6	7 8	10 10	14 15	21 22							
K 125						0 1			1 2	2 3	3 4	5 6	7 8	10 11	14 15	21 22								
L 200					0 1			1 2	2 3	3 4	5 6	7 8	10 11	14 15	21 22									
M 315				0 1			1 2	2 3	3 4	5 6	7 8	10 11	14 15	21 22										
N 500			0 1			1 2	2 3	3 4	5 6	7 8	10 11	14 15	21 22											
P 800		0 1			1 2	2 3	3 4	5 6	7 8	10 11	14 15	21 22												
Q 1250	0 1			1 2	2 3	3 4	5 6	7 8	10 11	14 15	21 22													
R 2000			1 2	2 3	3 4	5 6	7 8	10 11	14 15	21 22														

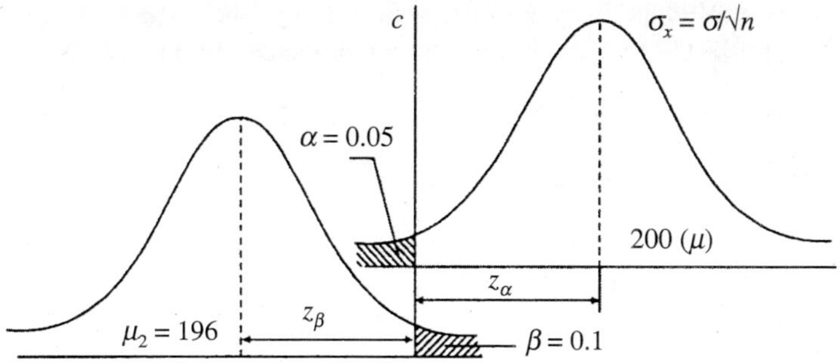

FIGURE 15.12 Sampling distribution where *a* and *b* are specified.

$$c = 200 - 1.645\frac{(8)}{\sqrt{34}} = 197.7\,\text{lb}$$

Plan: Take a random sample of n = 34 ingots and determine the mean weight. If $x > 197.7$ lb, accept the shipment; otherwise reject it.

15.4 CONTROL CHARTS AND IN-PROCESS MONITORING OF QUALITY

15.4.1 Introduction

However, perfect a process of production may be, no two products are completely identical in respect of specifications of the product. The length, diameter, strength, etc. may be preassigned specification of a particular product, e.g., the diameter of a ball-bearing, the length of a bolt, the strength of a fibre, the number of imperfections in a metal produced by a chemical process, etc. In fact, any manufacturing process, however perfect, is characterized by a certain amount of variability of random nature, which cannot be totally eliminated. There is always a small variation, which is caused by large number of uncontrollable factors. It has to be regarded as a chance variation. The monitoring of some measurable or countable property of a product during the process of production of the product is known as *quality control.*

Variability in manufacture. When the variability present in a production process is limited to chance variation, the process is said to be in a state of "statistical control". The state of statistical control is attained by avoiding of another type of variation, called *assignable variation.* An assignable variation may be due to extraneous causes like defective maneuvering of the machine, poor quality raw materials, man-made error, and so on. Since assignable variation may contribute substantially to the deviations from the state of statistical control, a systematic method of detecting and eliminating deviations before or during the course of a manufacturing process is desirable. Thus, the act of getting a process in statistical control involves the identification and elimination of assignable variation. A production process is said to be in a state of statistical control if it is governed by chance variations alone and assignable variations are totally absent in the process.

The main objective in any production process is to control the quality of the finished product so that it conforms to specifications. In other words, this ensures the absence of a large number of defective items in the manufactured product. Shewhart's control charts provide a powerful tool of detecting and rectifying the assignable variations outside the stable pattern of chance variation.

The development of control chart by Shewhart of Bell Telephone Laboratory in 1924 has enabled one to control and stabilize the process at desired performance level and thus to bring the process under statistical control.

15.4.2 Control Charts

A control chart consists of a central line corresponding to the desired standard of the level at which the process is to be performed and lines corresponding to the upper and lower control limits (Figure 15.13).

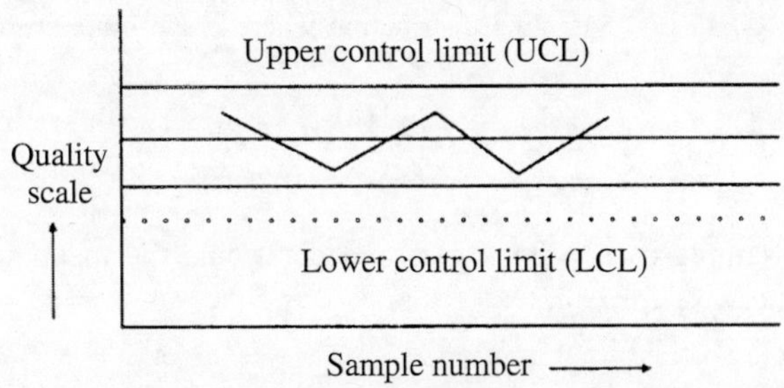

FIGURE 15.13 Outline of a control chart.

These limits are chosen so that values falling between them can be attributed to chance variation while values falling beyond them are attributed to lack of statistical control. By plotting the results obtained from samples taken periodically and at frequent intervals, it is possible to check by means of such control chart whether the process is under control or not. When the sample point falls beyond the control limits, the process is not under control. Even when the sample point lies between the control limits, it is subjected to close scrutiny for possible action to avoid serious trouble; a trend or pattern of the sample points may be a good indication in this case.

There are two types of control charts corresponding to measurements (observations are measured quantities) and count-data (the count of the number of defectives in a sample of given size). The former is called *control charts for measurements* and the latter is termed as *control charts for attributes.*

Control charts for measurements. Two type of quantities, viz., the average quality of a process and its variability should be controlled while dealing with measurements. To control the average quality, the means of the periodic samples chosen should be plotted on the control chart for means, denoted by X-chart. Variability is controlled by plotting the standard deviation or the sample range, on σ-chart or an R-chart, corresponding to the particular statistical parameter used to estimate the population standard deviation.

Assuming the measurements to be sample taken from a normal population, the probability that the mean μ of a random sample of size n will lie between:

$$\left(\mu - 3\frac{\sigma}{(n)^{1/2}}\right) \text{ and } \left(\mu + 3\frac{\sigma}{(n)^{1/2}}\right)$$

is 0.997. Since $E(x) = \mu$, the central line of the x-chart gives the population mean. For convenience of calculation, $\mu \pm 3\sigma/\sqrt{n}$ is replaced by $\mu + A_2R$. Since $\overline{R}$ is an estimator of σ, $\sigma = \overline{R}/d_2$.

To summarize, if μ and σ are estimated from previous observations, the 3–σ control limits for $\bar{x}$ -chart are:

$$\text{Upper control limit (UCL)} = \bar{\bar{x}} + A_2 \bar{R} \tag{15.12}$$

$$\text{Lower control limit (LCL)} = \bar{\bar{x}} - A_2 \bar{R} \tag{15.13}$$

The R-chart based on sample range provides an estimation of process variability. The control chart values are given below:

$$\text{Central line} = \bar{R}$$

$$\text{UCL} = D_4 \bar{R} \tag{15.14}$$

$$\text{LCL} = D_3 \bar{R} \tag{15.15}$$

TABLE 15.3 Table of constants

n	A_2	D_3	D_4
2	1.99	0	3.268
3	1.023	0	2.574
4	0.729	0	2.282
5	0.577	0	2.184

15.4.3 Discussion on Variability in a Constant Cause System

As stated earlier, chance variations and assignable variations form the basic components of variability in mass production. Variability is the basis with which the concept of control charts has been developed. An illustration of variability in the production of pins on a lathe machine should make the notions clearer. The patterns of chance variation and assignable variation are also illustrated.

Variability in manufacture. As stated in the earlier sections, pieces produced from a mass production machine are never exactly alike, but there are always slight variations in dimensions even for the same setting. The following causes can be attributed:

(a) *Chance causes* that are characteristics of the process (Figure 15.14)

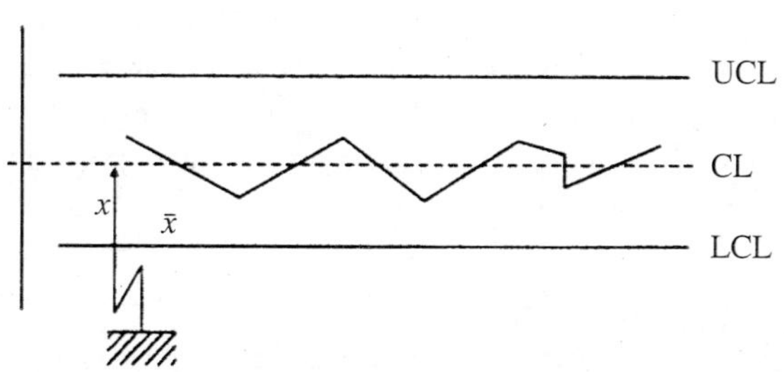

FIGURE 15.14 Chance variations (process in control).

For example, when a capstan lathe is turned on, in which the tooling is present by a skilled tool setter, there is little scope for variation from target value since the tooling is rigidly and usually accurately set. However, due to slight change in material property, vibration, temperature, amount of coolant supplied, pieces with dimension on both the sides of the desired value are obtained due to chance causes. These are not in the operator's control and slight variations on either side of target value do occur even for a fixed setting.

(b) Assignable-causes during turning are tool setting and tool wear (Figure 15.15(a)). These tend to produce pieces whose dimensions are on a particular side of the desired or aimed-at-value. These are in the operator's control.

(c) Other assignable causes are *extreme variations* (Figure 15.16a) and *cyclic variations* (Figure 15.16b).

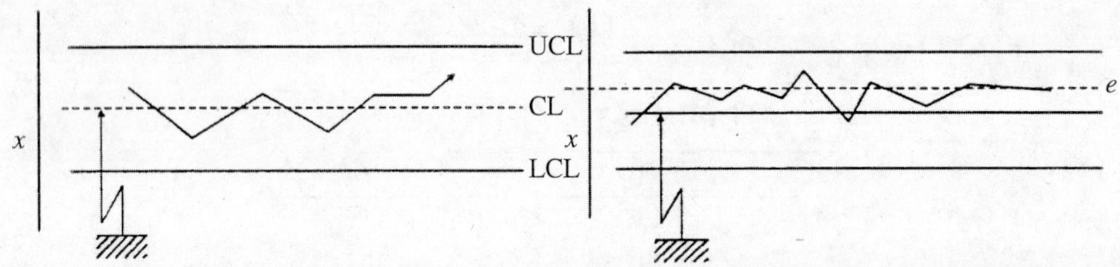

(a) Tool wear (Trend). (b) Tool setting error (*e*) shift.

FIGURE 15.15

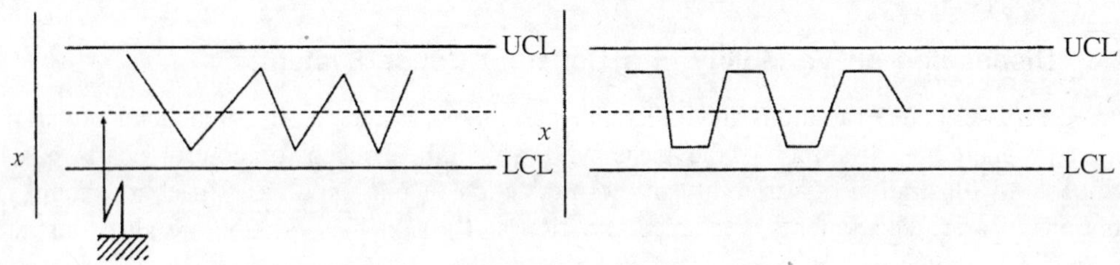

(a) Extreme variation (b) Cyclic variation

FIGURE 15.16

Extreme variations are due to machine incapability (Figure 15.16(a)) and cyclic variation (Figure 15.16(b)) is due to effects such as Monday morning blues. Machine operators are usually not at their best after spending holidays on Saturdays and Sundays. Their performance on Mondays shows, in typical cases, poor quality work. Extreme variation can be caused by errors in machine such as worn-out bearings or excessive vibrations causing dimensional variation on either side of the target value but in much larger magnitude than in the case of slight variation due to chance causes. Extreme variation might need total machine overhaul or just a bearing change.

15.4.4 Procedure in Quality Control

The procedure in quality control consists of two stages, viz., planning stage and control stage.

(i) **Planning stage.** This involves the determination of the higher and lower limits of chance variation inherent in the process to be controlled. These limits are represented on control chart by an upper control limit (UCL) and a lower control limit (LCL). A control chart is constructed after carrying out a trial run or capability test of the process to be controlled. This is pilot test to determine UCL and LCL.

(ii) **Control stage.** The second step in quality control consists of pinpointing the presence of assignable causes such as faulty tool setting or gradual tool wear during the actual production run. Thus, defective pieces are prevented if the operator is warned in good time regarding the intervention of assignable causes.

The operator will, then, readjust the tool, etc.

15.4.5 Theory of Control Charts

We now describe the population distribution (Figure 15.17a) and sampling distribution curves (Figure 15.17b).

Consider a population of 2000 pins. If these are measured on the diameter, they will be found to vary on either side of a mean size. For every manufacturing process, it is accepted that such variations in quality will occur and tolerances are generally introduced into the specification in order to define the acceptable amount of variation.

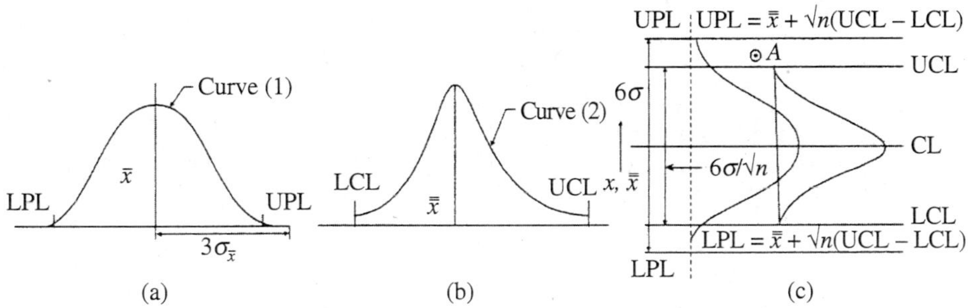

FIGURE 15.17 (a) Distribution of population (x); (b) Distribution of means $(\bar{x})$; (c) Process limits and control limits superimposed.

If the individual reading x obtained is plotted vs. the frequency of occurrence, we have a frequency distribution curve. So long as the process is in a state of control, a symmetrical bell-shaped curve is obtained. The tails of this curve represent the process capability limits (Figure 15.17a). In practice, it is not possible to measure all the pieces in large populations because the resulting time and cost of inspection are high. Therefore, in statistical quality control, samples are drawn from the population and inference is drawn about the lot from the sample observations. If the sample average $\bar{x}$ is plotted vs. the frequency, the resulting curve is also a bell-shaped curve but its tails represent the Control limits (ref. Figure 15.17b). If a sample average x denoted by point A falls outside the control limits, the inference is that it belongs to a sample drawn from a population which is different from the population represented by curve 1.

The various types of process parameters to be controlled fall in the following categories:

1. Measurable quantities such as diameter of a shaft (denoted by x)
2. Number of defectives d in a sample of size n; $d = np$.
3. Number of defects c per unit, where each unit offers infinite opportunities for a defect to be uncovered.

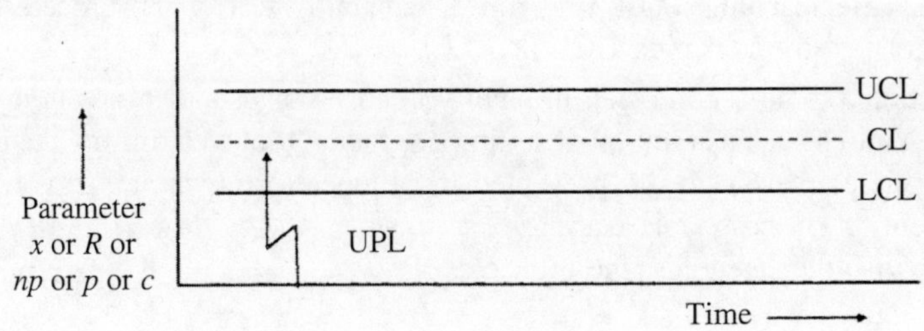

FIGURE 15.18 A typical control chart.

Range or *R* chart. The range value R equals the difference between the smallest and the largest value of sample. The control chart for range will help to detect any change in the process, which causes the spread of the curve of normal distribution to increase. Range R indicates the spread of the curve of normal distribution. Similarly, the range itself has its own variability and frequency distribution. The upper control limit for R is $D_4 \bar{R}$ and the lower control is $D_3 \bar{R}$.

The values of A_2, D_3 and D_4 are given in Table 15.4.

TABLE 15.4 Table of constants for use in quality control charts

n	A_2	D_3	D_4	$1/d_2$
2	1.880	0	3.267	0.8865
3	1.023	0	2.575	0.5905
4	0.729	0	2.282	0.4857
5	0.577	0	2.115	0.4299

The stable limits are obtained by eliminating any points that lie outside the trial limits and by recalculating the new limits. Any points outside trial limits indicate the presence of assignable causes during the capability test.

Application of stable limits for controlling production. After the stable control limits are obtained, the production begins. Samples are taken at periodic intervals from the lots. The trend of variation of critical to quality dimension is monitored. If any assignable causes are present, corrective action is taken and the process is brought back in control. If there is no indication of deterioration of quality due to assignable causes, a warning is issued to the operator even before the stable control limit is crossed. Thus, inferior quality is prevented. Control charts are used in process control, i.e., control during production.

Example. $\bar{x}$ control chart. Samples of five items each are taken from a process at regular intervals during a capability test, $\bar{x}$ and R are calculated particular for each sample for a quality characteristic x. The sums of the $\bar{x}$ and R values for the first 25 samples are determined as:

$$\Sigma\bar{x} = 358.50, \qquad \Sigma R = 9.80$$

(a) Determine the UCL for $\bar{x}$.

(b) If the specification limits are 14.40 + 0.45, what conclusion do you draw about the ability of the process to produce items within these specifications?

Solution.

$$\text{CL}\,\bar{x} = \frac{358.5}{25} = 14.34$$

$$UCL\,\bar{x} = 14.34 + A_2\bar{R} = 14.34 + 0.577 \times \frac{98}{25}$$

$$= 14.34 + 0.226 = 14.566$$

$$\text{UCL}\,\bar{x} = 14.566$$

$$\text{LCL}\,\bar{x} = 14.34 - 0.226 = 14.114$$

$$\text{UPL}\,\bar{x} = 14.34 + \frac{14.566 - 14.114}{2}\sqrt{5}$$

$$= 14.34 + 0.226\sqrt{5} = 14.845$$

$$\text{LPL}\,\bar{x} = 14.34 - 0.505 = 13.835$$

The LPL is crossing the lower specification limit (LSL) to produce scrap, whereas UPL does not exceed USL since USL > UPL, and no oversize scrap is produced.

Determination of scrap per cent (Figure 15.19). The process at the existing level will not be able to produce all the jobs of correct dimensions. A certain percentage of undersize jobs will be produced. How to calculate per cent defective?

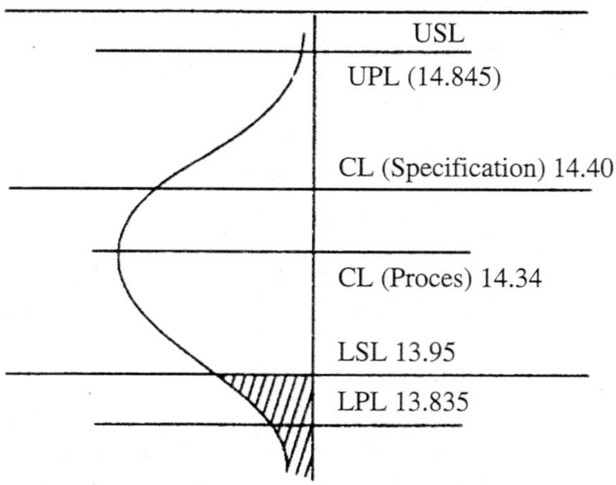

FIGURE 15.19 Determination of scrap percentage.

$$Z = \text{standard normal variate} = (X - \bar{X})/\sigma \qquad (15.16)$$

$$Z = \frac{14.34 - 13.95}{0.168} = 2.3$$

$$\sigma = \bar{R}\frac{1}{d_2} = 0.168$$

For $Z = 2.3$, area under normal curve = 0.489

Scrap per cent = $(0.5 - 0.489) \times 100 = 1.10\%$

15.4.6 Significance of $\bar{X}$ and *R* Charts

The control chart for $\bar{X}$ detects any shifting of arithmetic mean which may be caused by tool wear, changed machine adjustments, or similar causes.

Application of the range chart is called for if, after using a control chart for sample averages for some time, it is found that it frequently or occasionally fails to indicate trouble promptly. The range chart does not replace the sample average chart, but supplements it with additional information about the production process.

To illustrate, let us assume that variability on an automatic lathe machine operation has suddenly increased because of a loose cam. The individual parts vary so much that some of them begin to fall outside the specification limits. The control chart for sample average may not yet indicate any trouble, but the range chart will, because it is specially designed to detect unusual variability.

The field of usefulness of range chart is not limited; it is occasional control of old and worn equipment. High precision processes, whose variability must be carefully held within prescribed limits, are best controlled by keeping a range chart in addition to the regular sample average chart.

15.4.7 Control Chart for Defective: *np* Chart: Comparison with $\bar{X}$ and *R* Charts

The $\bar{X}$ and R charts are for variables, i.e., for quality characteristics that can be measured and expressed in numbers. However, many quality characteristics can be observed only as properties, i.e., classifying the item into one of two classes, usually defective or non-defective. Furthermore, with the existing techniques, $\bar{X}$ and R charts can be used for only one measurable characteristic at a time. For example, if an item consists of 1000 measurable characteristics, each characteristic is a candidate for an $\bar{X}$ and R chart. As a substitute, when characteristics are measured by attribute, a control chart based on the fraction defective can be used. This is known as an *np chart.* An *np* chart can be applied to quality characteristics that are actually observed as attributes even though they may have been measured as variables as in the case of GO-NOT GO gauging. The cost of obtained attribute data is usually less than that for obtaining variables data. The cost of computing and charting may also be less since one *np* chart can apply to any number of characteristics. The *np* chart is based on the binomial distribution of statistics. According to the binomial distribution, if a sample of n pieces is taken from a population having a fraction defective, $\bar{p}$, the expected number of defective equals np and the standard deviation $\sigma n\bar{p}$ equals $[n\bar{p}\ (1 - \bar{p})]^{1/2}$.

Thus, the CL of the number of defectives charts is $n\bar{p}$, and

$$\text{UCL} = n\bar{p} + 3\sigma_{n\bar{p}} = n\bar{p} + 3\sqrt{n\bar{p}(1-\bar{p})}$$

$$\text{LCL} = n\bar{p} - 3\sigma_{n\bar{p}} = n\bar{p} - 3\sqrt{n\bar{p}(1-\bar{p})}$$

Example. Construct a control chart for number of defectives from the following data:

Sample No.	*Sample size n*	*No. of defectives np*
1	400	32
2	400	20
3	400	16
4	400	20
5	400	24
6	400	42
7	400	30
8	400	36
9	400	26
10	400	52
11	400	28
12	400	24
Total		350

$$\text{CL} = n\bar{p} = \frac{350}{12} = 29.16 = 29$$

$$\text{UCL} = n\bar{p} + 3\sqrt{n\bar{p}(1-\bar{p})} = 29 + 3\sqrt{29(1-0.072)} = 44.56$$

$$\text{LCL} = n\bar{p} - 3\sqrt{n\bar{p}(1-\bar{p})} = 29 - 3\sqrt{29(1-0.072)} = 13.44$$

15.4.8 Control Chart for Number of Defectives *c* per Unit: Areas of Application

This control chart is based on the poisson distribution which can be treated as a special case of the binomial distribution. The conditions are:

$$n \to \infty$$
$$p \to 0$$
$$np = c, \text{ a constant; } (1 - p) \to 1; \quad p \to 0$$

The area of application of these charts is when there is a piece on which there can be imperfection at any spot. Thus, the sample size offered by one piece is n tending to infinity, but the probability of finding the imperfection at any specific spot p tends to 0. Examples of the above situation occur in the following cases:

1. Imperfections in a piece of cloth
2. Small air bubbles in a glass bottle
3. Surface defects in the point on an auto
4. Pinholes on an enamelled surface
5. Defective rivets in an aircraft wing
6. Welding defects in a welded assembly
7. Holes in a piece of paper

Using the concept that c chart is a particular case of np chart, we have

$$\text{CL} = n\bar{p} = c$$

$$\text{UCL} = n\bar{p} + 3\sqrt{n\bar{p}(1-\bar{p})} = \bar{c} + 3\sqrt{\bar{c}} \quad (15.17)$$

$$\text{LCL} = n\bar{p} - 3\sqrt{n\bar{p}(1-\bar{p})} = c - 3\sqrt{\bar{c}} \quad (15.18)$$

Example. To construct a c chart from the following data: surface defects observed in machine cabinet (25 in no.) = No. of sub-groups.

7, 6, 6, 7, 4, 7, 8, 12, 9, 9, 8, 5, 3, 9, 8, 15, 6, 4, 13, 7, 8, 15, 6, 6, 10

Solution

$$\text{CL} = \bar{c} = 7.92$$

$$\text{UCL} = \bar{c} + 3\sqrt{\bar{c}} = 7.92 + 3\sqrt{7.92} = 16.36$$

$$\text{LCL} = \bar{c} - 3\sqrt{\bar{c}} = 7.92 - 3\sqrt{7.92} = -0.52 = 0$$

15.4.9 Control Chart for *p* (a special case of *np* chart when *n* varies)

The sub-groups size is usually large as compared with that used for $\bar{X}$ and R charts. The main reason is that if p is very small, and n is small, then the expected number of defectives in a sub-group will be very close to zero.

For each sub-group, compute p given by:

$$\bar{p} = \frac{\text{No. of defectives in the sub-group}}{\text{No. inspected in the sub-group}} = \frac{np}{n}$$

Whenever practicable, no fewer than 25 sub-groups should be used to compute trial control limits. These limits are computed by a two-step approach finding the average fraction defective p given by:

$$\bar{p} = \frac{\text{No. of defectives in the sub-group}}{\text{No. inspected in the sub-group}} = \frac{np}{n}$$

Dividing by n the expressions for UCL and LCL for np in section 15.4.7, we get:

$$\text{UCL} = \bar{p} + \frac{3\sqrt{\bar{p}(1-\bar{p})}}{\sqrt{n}}, \quad \text{LCL} = \bar{p} - \frac{3\sqrt{\bar{p}(1-\bar{p})}}{\sqrt{n}}$$

It will be recognised that UCL and LCL have been obtained by dividing the UCL and LCL of np chart by n. Inference about the existence of control or lack of control can be drawn in a manner similar to that described for X and R charts. The p chart finds application when due to variation in daily production, n varies and the CL which is np no longer remains a straight line. It will be appreciated that for monitoring any process, at least the centre line has to be fixed.

The above formula for UCL and LCL for p indicates that the control limits come closer when the sample size is kept larger. This closeness is inversely proportional to $\sqrt{n}$.

Numerical example. p chart. *Problem:* The number of defectives for 20 samples is indicated in the following table. Sample size $n = 50$, calculate trial control limits and stable control limits.

S. No	1	2	3	4	5	6	7	8	9	10	11	12	13	14	15	16	17	18	19	20
d	2	3	4	1	0	2	4	1	1	3	0	1	2	1	0	3	7	2	1	2
p	.04	.06	.08	.02	00	.04	.08	.02	.02	.06	0	.02	.04	.02	0	.06	.14	.04	.02	.04

Solution

$$\text{UCL}_p = \bar{p} + 3\sigma_p$$

$$\bar{p} = \frac{\text{No. of defectives}}{\text{Total No. of items}} = \frac{40}{50 \times 20}$$

$$\sigma_p = \sqrt{\bar{p}\,\bar{q}/n} = \sqrt{(0.04)(0.096)/50} = 0.028$$

$$\text{UCL}_p = 0.040 + 3(.028) = 0.124$$

$$\text{LCL}_p = \bar{p} - 3\sigma_p = 0.040 - 3(0.028) = 000$$

Point No. 17 is falling outside trial limits. For stable control limits, we discard point no. 17 and recalculate the limits.

Stable limits: Omitting observation no. 17, we get:

$$\bar{p} = 33/50 \times 19 = 0.0347$$

$$\sigma_p = \sqrt{(0.0347)(0.9653)/50} = 0.0259$$

$$\text{UCL}_p = 0.112, \qquad \text{LCL}_p = 000$$

15.4.10 Cusum Chart (Figure 15.20)

The control chart for X provides a criterion by which to judge whether a specified target value is being attained within random variation or not. An important special case of failing to meet a specification is where the X value is drifting either up or down according to a slow trend. In such a situation, a cumulative sum chart becomes essential. In this chart, the cumulative deviation from mean $\Sigma(x_i - \mu)$ is plotted vs. the sample number. If the measured value of x keeps near to target value, the graph of $\Sigma(x_i - \mu)$ vs. sample number will not deviate much from the horizontal. For detecting any deviations, a moving V notch control boundary can be used.

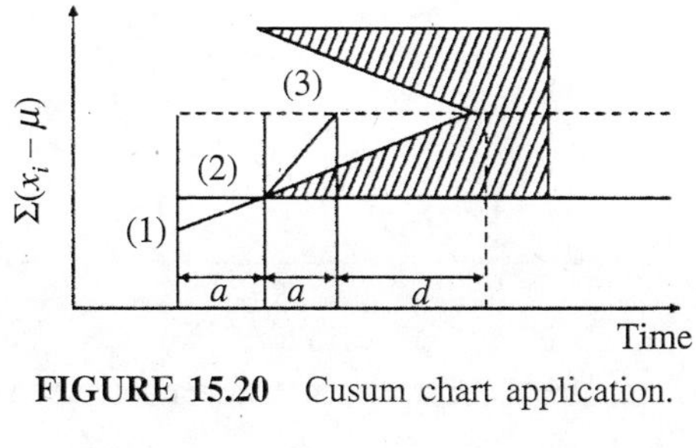

FIGURE 15.20 Cusum chart application.

Any excessive deviation such as h can be detected owing to the point (2) being covered by the V mask, thus between 2 and 3, there has been an excessive jump. If the value of h is fixed from engineering judgement, the value of θ, the semi-angle of the V mark (for a given value of d) can be calculated from simple formula:

$$\tan\theta = \frac{h}{a+d} \tag{15.19}$$

It is essential to convert h, a and d to actual values by use of the scale factor, for vertical and horizontal axes.

Example. A cusum chart for a process mean is plotted with a vertical scale of 0.3 cm/micron and a horizontal scale of 5 sample points per cm. Calculate the angle of aperture of the V mask for detecting a jump in the process mean of 0.5 microns or more if the vertex of the notch is placed 2 sample points ahead.

In this example, $h = 0.5\mu$ represented as (0.5×0.3) cm on the y-axis.

$(a + d) = 3$ sample points along the x-axis as $d = 2a$ (given): $(3 \times 1/5)$ cm = $(3 \times 0.2$ cm)

$$\tan\,\theta = \frac{0.5\times 0.3}{3\times 2}, \quad 2\theta = 28°4'$$

15.5 QUALITY OF PERFORMANCE: RELIABILITY AND ALLIED TOPICS

15.5.1 Failure Pattern of Equipment

A complex piece of equipment contains many components. Referring to Figure 15.21, in the initial troubleshooting stage, time t_1 is instantaneous; failure rate λ is much higher than in the middle portion of the graph when it is λ after the equipment due to failure in the components occurs at random over time. When a component fails, it is immediately replaced by another and the equipment continues to run as before. For a long period of time during the life of the equipment, say from time t_1 and t_2, these failures, called accidental failures, occur at a constant rate. After a period t_2 when the equipment gets old and workout, the failure rate again moves to higher levels. The graph shown in Figure 15.21, which is plotted with time on the x-axis and instantaneous failure rate on the y-axis, is called *bath tub curve* owing to it shape.

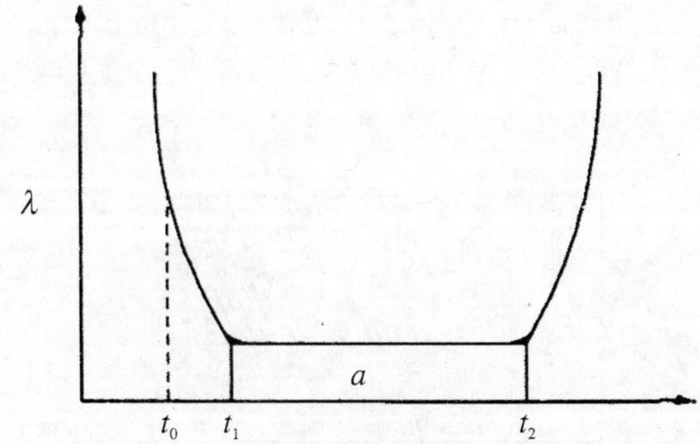

FIGURE 15.21 Instantaneous failure rate vs. time.

15.5.2 Reliability

Reliability of an equipment to the probability of survival through its mission time t in a given environment. Figure 15.22 indicates the decrease of reliability R with time. Figure 15.23 is a plot of density function that the equipment shall fail after a time t, i.e., between time t and $(t + \delta t)$. The term $f(t)$ is very important in statistical analysis of reliability.

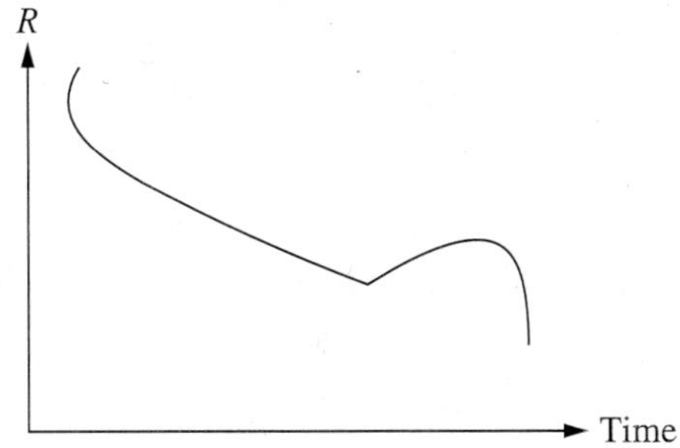

FIGURE 15.22 Reliability vs. time.

From the theorem of conditional probability, the failure density function $f(t)$ = probability of the equipment surviving till a period $t \times$ instaneous failure rate, λ during t and $(t + \delta t)$. Mathematically, $f(t) = \lambda \times R$.

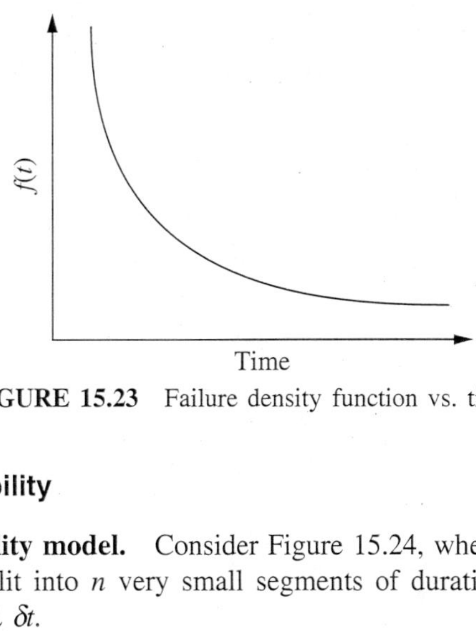

FIGURE 15.23 Failure density function vs. time.

15.5.3 Models of Reliability

1. **Exponential reliability model.** Consider Figure 15.24, where the line segment indicating mission time t is split into n very small segments of duration t. Now, the probability of failure in time $t = \lambda\ \delta t$.

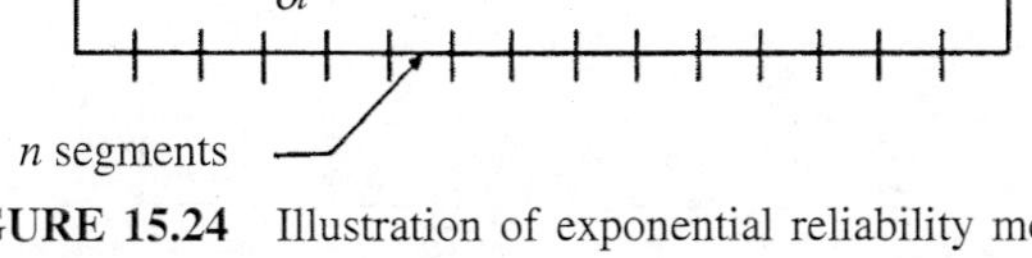

FIGURE 15.24 Illustration of exponential reliability model.

$$\text{Probability of survival during time } t = (1 - \lambda\, \delta t)$$

$$\text{Probability of survival during mission time } t = (1 - \lambda\, \delta t)^n$$

or

$$R = (1 - \lambda\, \delta t)^n = (1 - \lambda n \delta t) = (1 - \lambda \delta t)$$

Thus,

$$R = e^{-\lambda t} \tag{15.20}$$

Now, since λ is the failure rate in pieces failed per unit of time, its reciprocal should be time between failures (for this model). Putting $\lambda = 1/\theta$ in Eq. (15.20), we have: $R = e^{-t/\theta}$, where θ is called characteristic life. The exponential model is applicable for period t_1 to t_2 of the *Bath tub curve* where the failures are random.

2. **General reliability model.** Wallodi Weibull, a Swedish engineer, proposed a general reliability model. The two-parameter Weibull model is:

$$R = e^{-(t/\theta)^\beta} \tag{15.21}$$

The values of β and θ are estimated through life testing of the equipment. In this test, a random sample is drawn and the failure number and the corresponding time are recorded. We have:

$$R = e^{-(t/\theta)^\beta} \tag{15.22}$$

$$1 - F = e^{-(t/\theta)^\beta} \tag{15.23}$$

or

$$\frac{1}{1-F} = e^{(t/\theta)^\beta} \tag{15.24}$$

$$\ln \frac{1}{1-F} = \beta \ln t - \beta \ln \theta \tag{15.25}$$

Equation (15.25) is a linear equation with slope β.

Graphical Estimation of Parameters (Figure 15.25)

The results of the life test, i.e., $F\%$ (percentage of components failing during test) versus time t are plotted on a special graph paper called *Weibull probability paper.* The slope of the line of best fit gives us β. For estimating θ, we use the following concept:

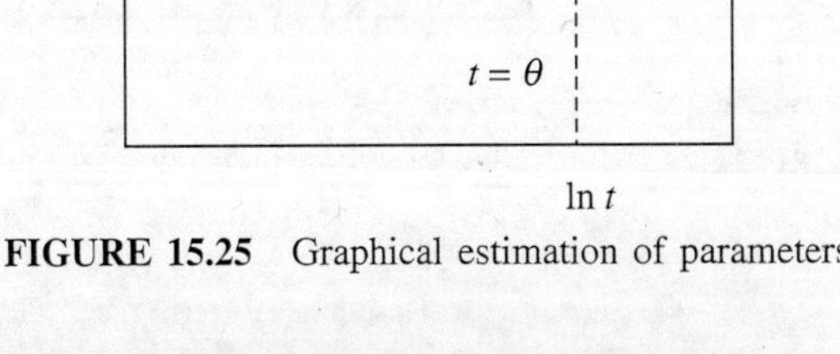

FIGURE 15.25 Graphical estimation of parameters.

Since $R = e^{-(t/\theta)}$, if we put $t = \theta$, $R = e^{-1} = 1/e = 0.368$ and $F = (1 - R) = 0.632$. Thus, at $F = 63.2\%$ $t = \theta$. In other words, the time taken for 63.2% of the samples to fail is the characteristic life θ.

Statistical Properties of the Weibull Model

$$F(t) = \left(1 - e^{(t/\theta)}\right)^{\beta} \qquad f(t) = \frac{\delta F(t)}{\delta t} = \left(\frac{\beta}{\theta}\right)\left(\frac{t}{\theta}\right)^{\beta-1} e^{-(t/\theta)^{\beta}}$$

$$\lambda = \frac{f(t)}{R} = \left(\frac{\beta}{\theta}\right)\left(\frac{t}{\theta}\right)^{\beta-1} \tag{15.26}$$

Equation (15.26) helps us to analyse the *Bath tub curve.* When $\beta = 1$

$$\lambda = \left(\frac{\beta}{\theta}\right) = \frac{1}{\theta}$$

When $\beta > (1)$, the value of (λ) increases with increase in t because the exponent of (t/θ) in Eq. (15.26) is positive. When β is less than 1, the value of λ decreases with increase in t.

Mean and standard deviation We have the Kth moment

$$\mu_K = E(t^K) \int_0^{\infty} t^K f(t) = \int_0^{\infty} t^K \frac{\beta}{\theta}\left(\frac{t}{\theta}\right)^{\beta-1} e^{-(t/\theta)} dt$$

using the transformation

$$u = \left(\frac{t}{\theta}\right)^{\beta}, \qquad \mu_k = \theta^k \int_0^{\infty} y^{k/\beta} e^{-\mu} du$$

$$\mu_k = \theta^k \Gamma\left(1 + K/\beta\right) \qquad \text{where } \Gamma \text{ is gamma function} \tag{15.27}$$

Again,

$$K = 1, \quad \mu_1 = \theta \Gamma(1 + 1/\beta) \quad \mu_2 = \theta_2 \Gamma(1 + 2/\beta)$$

using the transformation

$$\sigma^2 = (\mu_2 - \mu_1)^2 = \theta^2 \left[\Gamma(1 + 2/\beta) - \Gamma(1 + 1/\beta)^2\right] \tag{15.28}$$

The values of (μ_1/θ) and (σ^2/θ^2) are tabulated below along with β in Table 15.5 to facilitate the determination of μ_1 (expected life) and σ (standard deviation).

TABLE 15.5 Values of shape parameter β, (μ/θ) and $(\sigma/\theta)^2$ for Weibull model

	(1)	(2)	(3)	(4)	(5)	(6)	(7)	(8)	(9)
β	0.5	1	2	3	3.5	4	5	6	10
μ/θ	2.0	1	0.886	0.889	0.906	0.916	0.918	0.927	0.951
σ^2/θ^2	20	1	0.215	0.105	0.081	0.065	0.044	0.033	0.013

15.5.4 Numerical Example

Estimate the reliability equation for a certain equipment from the following data. The sample taken for test consisted of 10 pieces though the data below is for 8 failures.

Failure No. (i)	1	2	3	4	5	6	7	8
Time (t)	2,400	5,400	10,400	13,400	15,400	32,400	43,400	84,400

Solution In the above problem, time t is given directly. To convert failure number to $F\%$, the naive method would be to call first failure from 10 pieces since $F\% = 12.5$ for second failure can be assigned $F\% = 25$; for third failure, $F\% = 37$ can be assigned.

However, statisticians prefer to use Median ranking for calculating a statically more sound estimate of $F\%$. The formula using Median ranking concept is $F\% = (1.2i - 4/n) \times 100$. Thus, we have the following table of $F\%$ and (t). Taking, say $i = 3$, $n = 10$, $F\% = 32$. Here, i is the rank of failure. For example, for $i = 1$, $F\% = 8$ and $t = 2400$.

$F\%$	8	20	32	45	55	70	80	92
Time (t)	2,400	5,400	10,400	13,400	15,400	32,400	43,400	84,400

The values so obtained are plotted on the Weibull probability paper in Figure 15.26. We get $\beta = 0.84$, $\theta = 24{,}500$ and the required reliability equation is:

$$R = e^{-(t/24,500).84}$$

Table 15.5 can be utilized to estimate μ and σ for the life of the equipment.

The value of β for this equipment is 0.84 (Figure 15.26). Referring to row 1 of Table 15.5, 0.84 lies between 0.5 and 1. The value of (μ_1/θ) and $(\sigma/\theta)^2$ will have to be taken from rows 2 and 3, somewhere midway between values of columns (1) and (2).

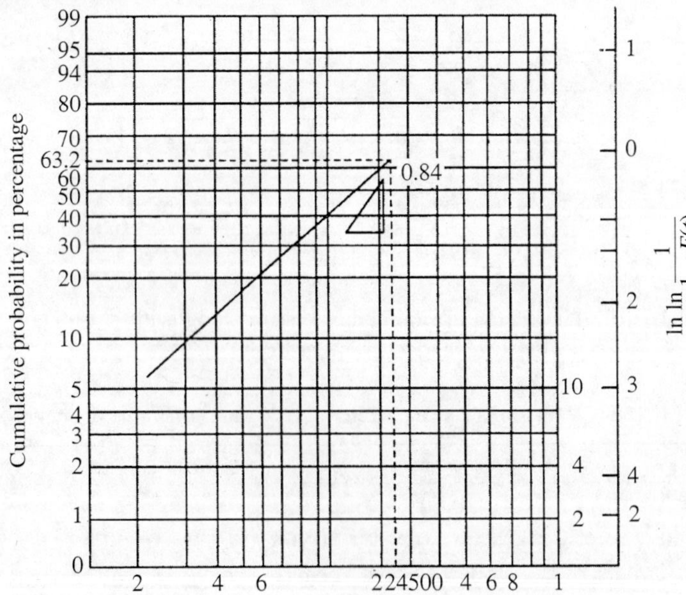

FIGURE 15.26 Use of Weibull plot for estimating β and θ.

As on approximation, $(\mu_1/\theta) = 1.3$ so that $\mu = (1.3 \times 24{,}500) = 318{,}500$.

$$(\sigma/\theta)^2 = 4, \text{ i.e., } \sigma/\theta = 2.00 \text{ and } \sigma = (2.00 \times 24{,}500) = 49{,}000.$$

Thus the mean time between failures (MTBF) = 318,500 and 1 σ limit is

$$\mu_1 \pm \frac{\sigma}{\sqrt{n}} = 318{,}500 \pm \frac{49{,}000}{3.16}$$
$$= 318{,}500 \pm 15{,}500$$

15.5.5 Determination of System Reliability from Subsystem or Component Reliability

1. **Series system** (Figure 15.27). In a series system, the probability of survival depends on the survival of both the components. From the theorem of multiplication of probabilities, $R_s = R_1 * R_2$

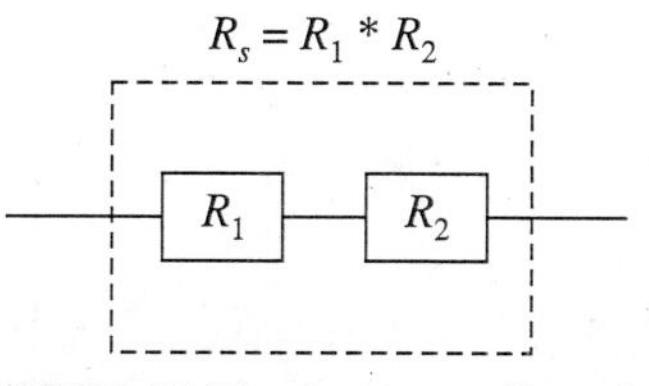

FIGURE 15.27 Series configuration.

In this case, it can be shown that MTBF for exponential model is $\frac{1}{(\lambda_1 + \lambda_2)}$ where λ_1 and λ_2 are failure rates of elements 1 and 2, respectively.

2. **Parallel system** (Figure 15.28). The probability of failure of component 1 = $(1 - R_1)$. The probability of failure of component 2 = $(1 - R_2)$.

$$\text{Probability of failure of both components} = (1 - R_1)(1 - R_2) \qquad (15.29)$$

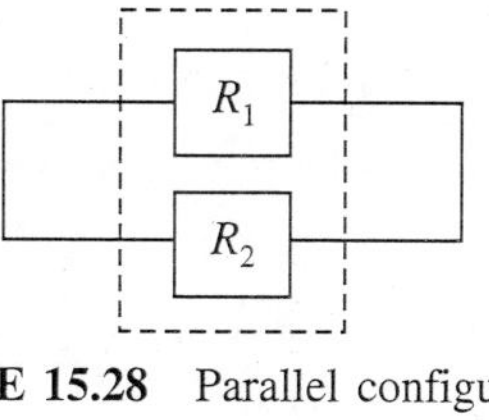

FIGURE 15.28 Parallel configuration.

Hence, the probability of survival of both the components = system reliability. Since $(1 - R_1)$, $(1 - R_2)$ is the probability of failure of both units in parallel, the probability of survival of both the units is $R_p = [1 - (1 - R_1)(1 - R_2)]$. If $R_1 = R_2$, then $R_p = [1 - (1 - R_1)^2]$. Thus,

$$\text{MTBF} = \left(\frac{1}{\lambda} + \frac{1}{2\lambda}\right) \qquad (15.30)$$

3. **Standby system** (Figure 15.29). Assuming Poisson's law to apply for failures, a two-unit standby system will survive if 0 or 1 unit fails. If 2 units fail, it cannot survive. Thus,

$$R_{SB} = \sum_{k=0}^{k=1} \frac{e^{-\lambda t}(\lambda t)^k}{\underline{|K}}$$

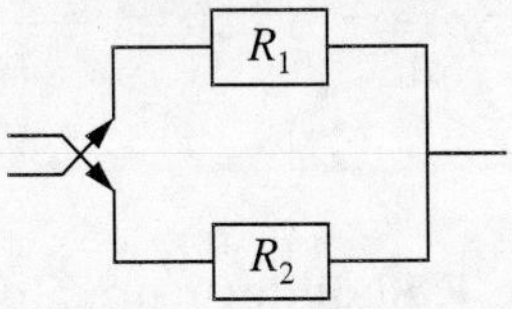

FIGURE 15.29 Standby system configuration.

Opening the Σ notation, we have:

$$R_{SB} = e^{-\lambda t} + (\lambda t)\, e^{-\lambda t}$$

$$R_{SB} = e^{-\lambda t}\,(1 + \lambda t)$$

Mean time to failure:

$$(\text{MTTF}) = \int_0^{\infty} R_{SB}\, dt = \frac{1}{\lambda} + \frac{\lambda}{\lambda^2} = \frac{2}{\lambda} \tag{15.31}$$

MTTF defined. The logic of adopting MTTF = $\int R\, dt$ is explained now.

$$\text{MTTF} = tf(t)\, dt = \int t \cdot \frac{dR}{dt} dt = \int t \cdot R + \int R\, dt$$

When $t = 0,\ R \to \infty$

When $t = \infty,\ R \to 0$

(These two conditions can be imposed from logic.) Therefore, the first term above vanishes. Hence, MTTF = $\int R\, dt$ has been taken in the calculations of mean time to failure of the standby system.

We now give an example of a system containing elements in series as well as parallel: A braking system of bicycle is a well-known and popular example of reliability enhancement through installation of two brakes each on rear as well as front wheel. Referring to Figure 15.30 and considering the reliability of lever, cable and brake shoe we find:

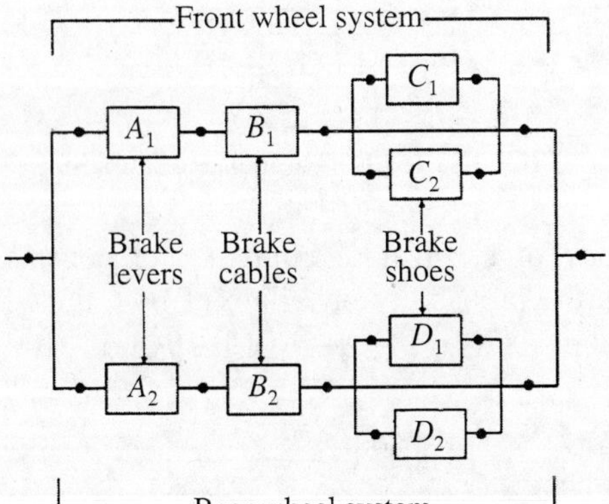

FIGURE 15.30 Model for braking system for a bicycle.

Reliability $R_F = R_{A1} \cdot R_{B1} \cdot [1 - (1 - R_{c1})(1 - R_{c2})]$ (by Analysing the front wheel system) (15.32)

Reliability $R_R = R_{A2} \cdot R_{B2}\ [1 - (1 - R_{D1})(1 - R_{D2})]$ (by Analysing the rear wheel system) (15.33)

Thus, the reliability of the overall braking system comprising the front wheel and rear wheel is:

$$R_B = 1 - [(1 - R_F)(1 - R_R)]$$

Illustrative Examples of reliability.

Example 1. Failure times of five identical bulbs are 2000, 1800, 2100, 2200, 1900 hours, respectively. Estimate means life.

Solution $\mu = 1/5[(2{,}000 + 1{,}800 + 2{,}100 + 2{,}200 + 1{,}900)]$

Reliability allocation. A series system has four independent subsystems with estimated failure rates: 0.0001, 0.0002, 0.0003 and 0.0004 failures/hour. The desired failure rate is $f = 0.002$ failures/hour. Calculate the values of failure rates to be allocated to each of the subsystems.

Solution $f_{sys} = 0.0001 + 0.0002 + 0.0003 + 0.0004$

Note that the failure rates are added up because when the reliability gets multiplied, the exponents get added up to:

$$R_{\text{sys}} = e^{-flq} = (R_1 \cdot R_2 \cdot R_3 \cdot R_4) = \exp\ [-(f_1 + f_2 + f_3 + f_4)]$$

$$f_{\text{sys}} = 0.001 \text{ failures/hour}$$

Weightage factors of subsystems:

$$p_x = 0.0001/0.001 = 0.1, \quad p_2 = 0.0002/0.001 = 0.2$$

$$p_y = 0.0003/0.001 = 0.3, \quad p_4 = 0.0004/0.001 = 0.4$$

Thus the allocations of subsystem reliabilities are:

For subsystem 1, $R_1 = 0.1 \times 0.002 = 0.0002$

For subsystem 2, $R_2 = 0.2 \times 0.002 = 0.0004$

For subsystem 3, $R_3 = 0.3 \times 0.002 = 0.0006$

For subsystem 4, $R_4 = 0.4 \times 0.002 = 0.0008$

15.5.6 Repairable System Reliability Analysis

If f is the failure rate and μ is repair rate, then Availability = MTBF/(MTBF + MTTR)

$$\text{Availability } A = \frac{1/f}{1/f + 1/\mu} = \frac{\mu}{f + \mu} \tag{15.34}$$

Example 2. The A-value and m-value per component of a series system with 7 independent units are 0.98 and 0.25, respectively. Calculate the value of failure rate f.

Solution:

$$A_7 = (0.98)^{1/7} \text{ or } A_7 = 0.99712$$

$$(A_7) = \mu(f + \mu) = 0.25/(f + 0.25) = 0.99712$$

$$A = 0.000722 \text{ failure/hour}$$

Logic gates calculations. In fault-tree analysis, logic gates are used. Illustrative examples are taken up to explain the calculations for logic gates.

Example 3. In the OR logic gate (Figure 15.31), the "fault" event occurrence probability is given. To determine the output probability of occurrence of fault, we must have:

$$P(E_0) = 1 - [1 - E_1)(1 - E_2)(1 - E_3)]$$

$$= 1 - [(1 - 0.01)(1 - 0.02)(1 - 0.03)]$$

$$= 0.058906$$

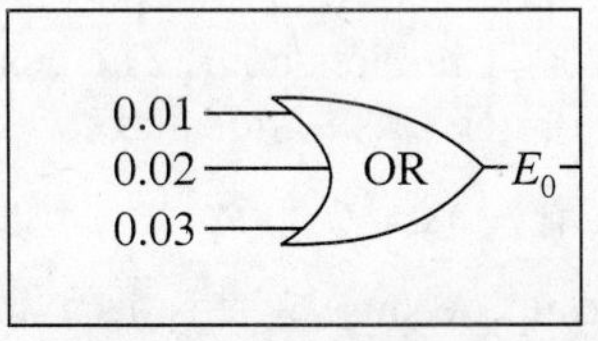

FIGURE 15.31 OR logic gate.

Example 4. Determine the unavailability of the AND logic gate (Figure 15.32) from given data.

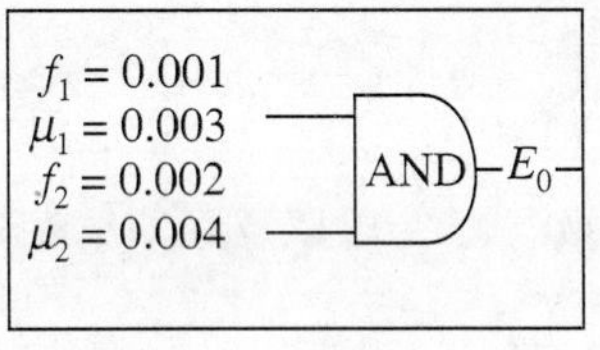

FIGURE 15.32 AND logic gate.

Solution:

$$U_1 = \frac{f_1}{f_1 + \mu_1} = \frac{0.001}{0.001 + 0.003} = 0.25$$

$$U_2 = \frac{f_2}{f_2 + \mu_2} = \frac{0.002}{0.002 + 0.004} = 0.33$$

$$P(E_0) = (0.25)(0.33) = 0.0825$$

Note: The analogy of OR gate with parallel configuration and AND gate with series configuration formula should be noted.

15.5.7 Failure Modes and Effects Analysis and Fault Tree Analysis

Failure modes and effects analysis. Failure modes and effects analysis (FMEA) is a thorough analysis of the malfunctions that can be produced in the components of an engineering system. The thrust is on how to redesign the components to improve system reliability.

To carry out an FMEA, the system is broken into assemblies. Engineering design data is appraised for each subassembly. This is done by making block diagrams of system, subsystem and components to enable analysis. A complete list of the components of each assembly and the function of each component are prepared. From an analysis of the operating and environmental conditions, the failure mechanisms that could affect each component are identified. Then the failure modes of all components are researched. Some components may have more than one failure mode. Each failure mode is analyzed as to ascertain whether it has an effect on the next higher item in the assembly and whether it has an effect on the entire system or product. The preventive measures or corrective actions that have been taken to control or eliminate the hazard are listed. The probability of failure of each component, based on published data or company experience, is listed, and the probabilities of failure of the subassemblies, assemblies, and the complete system are calculated from reliability theory. Often, FMEA is used in conjunction with fault tree analysis which pinpoints the areas in a complex system where FMEA is needed.

15.5.8 Failure Modes and Effects Criticality Analysis (FMECA)

In an extension of FMEA, the criticality of each assembly is examined and the components and assemblies to which special attention should be given are identified. A component that can give rise to a unique failure is one example. A unique point failure is one in which an accident could result from the failure of a single component, a single human error, or any other single undesirable event. This extended version of FMEA is known as *failure modes and effects criticality analysis (FMECA).*

The cause and effect diagram, called *Ishikawa diagram,* is often used for pictorial understanding of failure modes. Referring to Figure 15.33(a), it will be seen that the malfunction is represented by the large Fish bone whereas likely causes are listed on small side bones and their branches.

If a Pareto diagram [Figure 15.33(b)] is used in conjunction with a Fishbone diagram (Figure 15.33a) it reveals defects in terms of criticality in a more effective way. A combination of the two tools mentioned above is highly effective in FMEA.

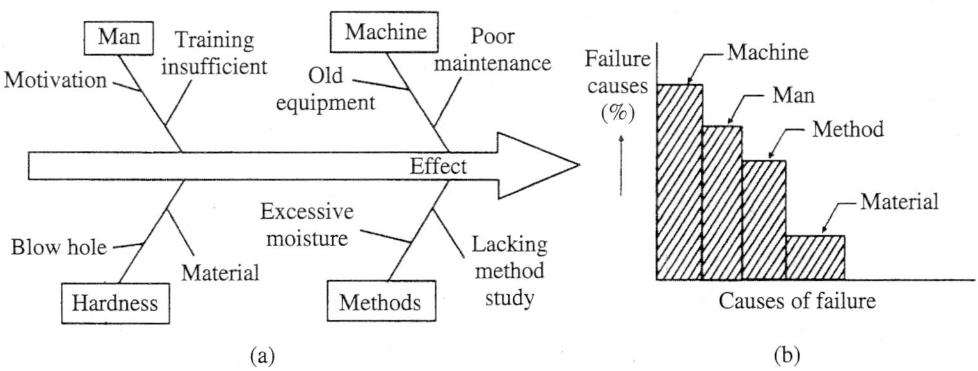

FIGURE 15.33 (a) Fishbone diagram, (b) Pareto diagram.

Fault tree analysis. Fault trees are diagrams that show how the data developed by FMEA should be interlinked to lead to a specific event. FMEA is very effective when applied to a single unit or single failure. When it is applied to a complex system, its effectiveness decreases to a large extent.

Fault tree analysis (FTA) provides a graphic description of the possible combinations in a system that can result in failure or accidents. In FTA, the emphasis is on "how things can fail to work" rather than on "design performance". Basically, fault tree is a logic diagram in which logic gates are used to determine the relations between input events and output events. A full quantitative FTA uses probabilities of failure computed for each event. The present discussion of FTA will be restricted to qualitative level.

Each fault tree deals with a specific event, e.g., failure to start an engine. FTA is a "top-down approach" that starts with the top event and then determines the contributory events that would lead to the failure event. Failures can be either component failures or ergonomic failures. Figure 15.34 shows a *fault tree diagram* which depicts inability of an engine to start.

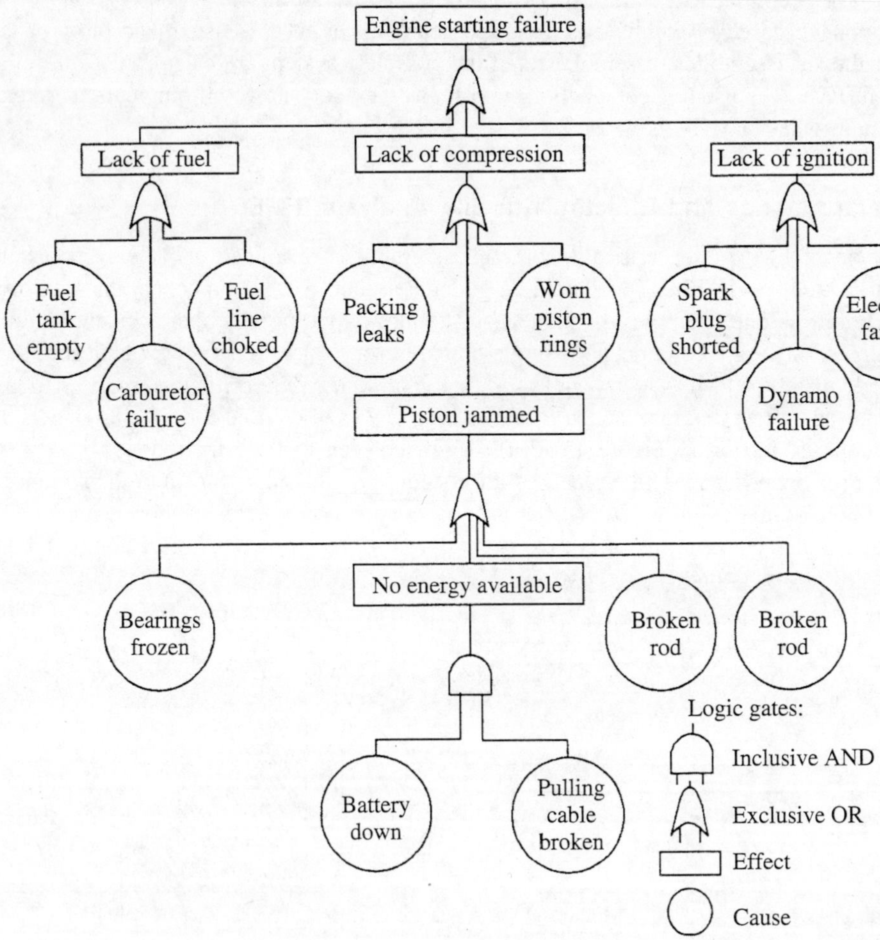

FIGURE 15.34 Failure of an engine – Fault tree diagram.

15.6 TAGUCHI METHOD OF ROBUST DESIGN OF PRODUCTS

Taguchi methods were developed by Dr. Genichi Taguchi after World War II. Statistical Quality Control (SQC) attempts to control the factors that adversely affect the quality of a product. Taguchi off-line methods focus on design and attempt to determine the best combination of design parameters which result in superior performance of the product. In larger-the-better type performance measure, the attempt is to achieve that combination or design parameters which, acting jointly, maximize the objective function. Taguchi calls this approach *parametric design approach.* He classified design from three points of view, which are now briefly described.

1. *System design or functional design.* This step uses the technical knowledge to reach the initial feasible design to fulfill the functional requirements of the product. Use of electronics, stress and strength analysis, fluid mechanics, and so on is helpful in arriving at a basic feasible design.
2. *Parametric design.* In this step, which is the original contribution of Taguchi, the optimum value of each process or design parameter is obtained by using orthogonal arrays and factorial design matrix. The procedure is to alter each design parameter to its highest selected value coded as 2 and its lowest selected value coded as 1, In this way, if there are, say, 4 factors of design affecting the final function of the product, there can be 2^4, i.e., 16 feasible combinations of the four design factors which are altered between two levels. The response or desirable objective function is examined at the end of the experiment and the optimum combination of design factors is selected for the final design. Fortunately, Taguchi has given standard orthogonal arrays for use in factorial experiments. The designer has just to choose the matrix which suits his problem. Table below shows the simplest type of orthogonal design matrix.

   The following table shows two factors *A* and *B* at two levels—level 1 and 2, yielding $2^2 = 4$ possible treatment combinations.

Trial	*Factor level*		*Test result*
	A	*B*	
1	2	2	R_1
2	1	1	R_2
3	1	2	R_3
4	2	1	R_4

   We shall give an example later to clarify the concept further.
3. *Minimization of societal loss:* According to Taguchi, the US concept of treating a product acceptable if it is within specification even if the parameter deviates from target value is not logical. Taguchi calls it the *Goal post model* (see Figure 15.35a).

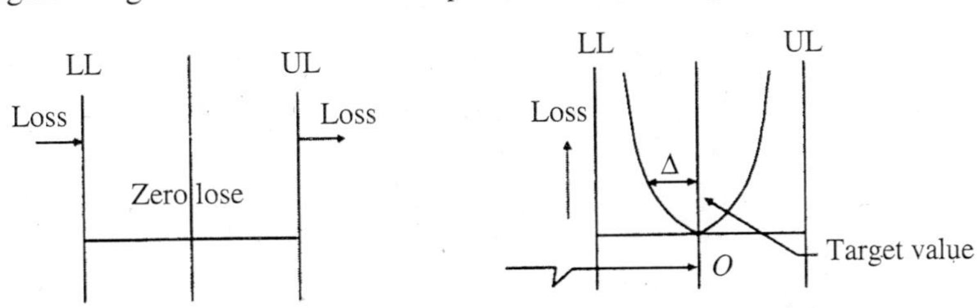

(a) Goal post model (b) Parabolic loss functions

FIGURE 15.35 Loss functions.

Taguchi has proved that the loss to the customer is proportional to the square of the deviation of the parameter from its target value (see Figure 15.36).

Loss function (Figure 15.35b)

$$L(y) = L(m + y - m)$$

Applying Taylor's series expansion, we get:

$$L(y) = L(m) + L'(m)(y - m) + \frac{L''(m)}{2}(y - m)^2$$

In the above equation for $L(y)$,

$$L(m) = 0 \text{ at point } 0$$

$L'(m) = 0$ at point 0 because the slope at point 0 is zero. Thus,

$$L(y) = \frac{L''(m)}{2}(y - m)^2$$

or

$$L(y) = k\delta^2$$

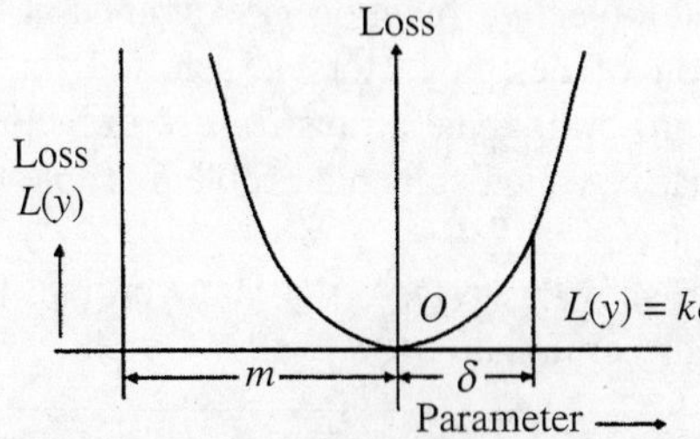

FIGURE 15.36 Taguchi's loss function.

Application of the concept of loss function to tolerance design. It is found that a transformer does not perform well when the voltage deviates by ± 25 volts. The loss incurred is ₹ 300 if the manufacturer can make adjustment at a cost of ₹ 1. Determine manufacturer's tolerance.

Solution. $L = k\delta^2$, Substituting $L =$ ₹ 300 for a deviation,

$$\delta = 25 \text{ volts}, \qquad L = 300,\ k = \frac{L}{\delta^2}$$

Then

$$k = \frac{300}{(25)^2} = 0.48$$

Applying the equation $L = k\delta^2$ again, we get:

$$L = 1 = (0.48)\,\delta_{opt}^2$$

or

$$\delta_{opt} = \text{tolerance} = \sqrt{\left(\frac{1}{0.48}\right)} = 1.4 \text{ volts}$$

Parametric design using factorial experiments. The strategy in parameter design is to understand and recognize control factors and noise factors acting upon any process or product. Control factors are those factors that can be changed without much difficulty and are easy to adjust. Noise factors are, either internal or external, factors which are beyond the designers' control. Noise factors cannot be modified or can be modified with large investment of money. For carrying out Taguchi experiments, the noise factors, as we shall see, are modified to understand their effect on the product property or signal to noise ratio (to be defined).

Signal to noise (S/N) ratio. The *S/N* ratio is a concurrent statistic—a special metric which measures the robustness of a design. The larger the signal to noise ratio or *S/N* ratio, the more robust is the design.

Suppose that μ is an average quality characteristic and σ the standard deviation, caused by noise factors. If μ_0 is a desired target value and μ is the current value, it is possible to convert μ to μ_0 by multiplying the control factor by (μ_0/μ). However, this adjustment also affects the standard deviation which becomes $[(\mu_0/\mu)\sigma]$. Thus the loss due to adjustment is:

$$L = K[(\mu_0/\mu)\sigma]^2 = (K\mu_0^2)\frac{\sigma^2}{\mu^2} = \frac{\text{Constant}}{\mu^2/\sigma^2}$$

Maximizing μ^2/σ^2 amounts to maximizing *S/N* ratio. It is preferable to express *S/N* ratio in decibels so that we have the final mathematical formula for *S/N* as:

$$S/N = \log(\mu^2/\sigma^2) = 10 \log_{10}(\mu^2/\sigma^2) \tag{15.35}$$

Rewriting the above equation and substituting $\mu = y$ and $\sigma = s$, we have $S/N = 10 \log_{10}(\mu^2/\sigma^2)$ $= 10 \log (y^2/s^2)$. For a robust design, the effect of s on *S/N* should vanish since s represents the variation of a reading from target value y. Thus, $S/N = 10 \log (y^2/s^2) = 10 [\log y^2 - \log s^2]$. For nominal, the better, formula for (*S/N*) for robust design should be $S/N = 10 (\log y^2)$ since the effect of s should not affect the result. If the situation is such that the response variable y should become least, a minus sign should be set in the formula and $S/N = -10 \log (y^2)$. On the other hand, if the situation is such that y should be larger, the better, it is and the reciprocal y should be used. Thus,

$$S/N = -10 \log (1/y^2) = -10 \log \left[\frac{1}{n}\left(\frac{1}{y1^2} + \frac{1}{y2^2} + \frac{1}{y3^2} + \cdots + \frac{1}{yn^2}\right)\right] \tag{15.36}$$

Equation (15.36) has been used in the illustrative example on pull-off force in the subsequent section.

Example on parametric design. An automotive part comprises the assembly of a polymer sleeve onto a nylon tube by the glueing process. The objective is to maximize the pull-off force by manipulating for key factors *A*, interference *B*; sleeve wall thickness *C*; insertion depth, *D*, per cent adhesive glue. The different control factors *A*, *B*, *C*, *D* and noise factors, viz., drying time, temperature and humidity, along with their levels are shown in the Table 15.6; these represent step I.

Step I

TABLE 15.6 Factors and levels

Factor		*Levels*		
Control *A*	Interference	(1) Low	(2) Medium	(3) High
B	Interference	(1) Thin	(2) Medium	(3) Thick
C	Interference	(1) Shallow	(2) Medium	(3) Deep
D	Interference	(1) Low	(2) Medium	(3) High
Noise	Drying time	(1) 24 hr	(2) 120 hr	
	Temperature	(1) 72°F	(2) 150°F	
	Relative humidity	(1) 25%	(2) 75%	

Step II

TABLE 15.7 The Factorial Design Matrix and Experimental Results of Pull-off-force Using L_9 (array for control factors)

Experiment L_9 (inner array)					*Outer array for noise factors*								
Treatment A	Interference A	Sleeve wall thickness (B)	Insert depth (C)	Per cent Adhesive (D)	120 150 75%	120 150 25%	120 72 75%	120 72 25%	24 150 75%	24 150 25%	24 72 75%	24 72 25%	*Drying time, hr* *Temperature, °F* *Relative humidity* *S/N ratio (dB)*
1	Low(l)	Thin (1)	Shallow (1)	Low (1)	19	20	20	20	20	17	10	16	24
2	Low(l)	Med. (2)	Med. (2)	Med. (2)	22	24	20	20	20	19	16	15	26
3	Low (1)	Thick (3)	Deep (3)	High (3)	20	23	18	23	16	19	17	16	25
4	Medium (2)	Thin (1)	Med. (2)	High (3)	25	23	19	21	19	19	17	18	26
5	Medium (2)	Med. (2)	Deep (3)	Low (1)	25	28	21	26	25	19	19	20	27
6	Medium(2)	Thick (3)	Shallow (1)	Med. (2)	25	23	20	15	19	20	16	16	25
7	High (3)	Med. (2)	Deep (3)	Med. (2)	22	24	19	17	24	18	19	16	26
8	High (3)	Med. (2)	Shallow (1)	High (3)	24	23	20	15	16	15	16	14	25
9	High(3)	Thick (3)	Med. (2)	Low (1)	29	23	23	23	17	19	20	16	26

Description of Table 15.7: The L_9 orthogonal array is chosen for control factors because it is the most efficient orthogonal design to accommodate four factors at three levels. The L_9 array specifies nine experimental runs but the intention is to find the best of the theoretical $3^4 = 81$ combinations that exist. Fortunately, Taguchi has given standard arrays for use in such applications. Table L_9 array shows the one utilized in the assembled Table 15.7.

TABLE L_9 Array

No.	*A*	*B*	*C*	*D*
1	1	1	1	1
2	1	2	2	2
3	1	3	3	3
4	2	1	2	3
5	2	2	3	1
6	2	3	1	2
7	3	1	3	2
8	3	2	1	3
9	3	3	2	1

For noise factors which are three in number and taken at two levels result in 2^3, that is, 8 combinations which are laid in the assembled matrix of Table 15.7. The pull-off strengths are shown in 8 columns and 9 rows. Corresponding to each experiment, one specific (*S*/*N*) ratio is calculated. For example, for experiment 1, the pull-off strength is, 19, 20, 20, 20, 20, 17, 10, 16, and the *S*/*N* ratio is 24 (approx.).

The formula used for larger the better (*S*/*N*) ratio is,

$$S/N = -10\log(1/y^2) = -10\log\left[\frac{1}{n}\left(\frac{1}{y1^2}+\frac{1}{y2^2}+\frac{1}{y3^2}+\cdots+\frac{1}{yn^2}\right)\right]$$

decibels dB, where $n = 8$

The largest value of *S*/*N* ratio of approximately 27 dB occurs for experiment 5, which indicates that *A*, *B*, *C*, *D* should be held at levels 2, 2, 3, 1. Taguchi recommends plotting *S*/*N* ratio and pull-off strength as functions of the four control factors to have a pictorial representation of the results and to carry out design modifications if needed. It will be seen in the final analysis that a combination of *A*, *B*, *C*, *D* at levels 2, 2, 3, 1 gives not only the largest *S*/*N* ratio but also maximum pull-off force for the glued assembly.

Sometimes, the levels are to be adjusted for slightly sub-optimal results. An example would be to use a sleeve with lesser thickness for economy.

15.7 SIX SIGMA QUALITY CONCEPTS

Introduction

Six Sigma quality (Figure 15.38) is a business strategy first conceptualized by Motorola company in the early 1990s. Mikel Harry and Schröder were the pioneers in the spread of the Six-sigma movement. The success stories of US corporates like General Electric, Sony, Allied Signal and Motorola have generated interest in the corporate world. Even in India, Sunderam Group, Aditya Birla Group, Ranbaxy, and others are attracted to this unique concept and strategy. In this section, we highlight some of the key statistical concepts, potential benefits, and implementation plan of this unique quality concept.

15.7.1 Statistical Background

It is well known that if the specifications of a process have a tolerance band width *T* equal to the process capability *P*, the process is said to operate at three-sigma level. In such a case, the area under the normal curve chopped off by the specification limits is 0.997 (Figure 15.37) of unity.

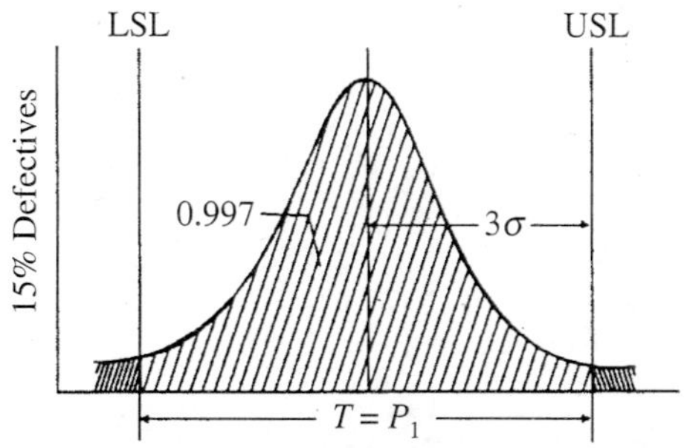

FIGURE 15.37 Three-sigma quality.

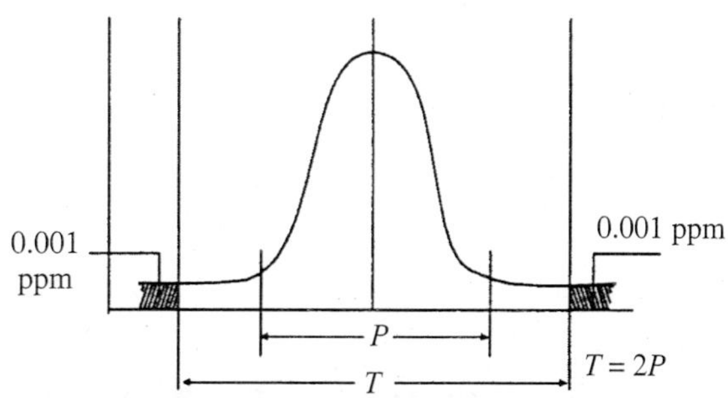

FIGURE 15.38 Six-sigma quality.

In other words, in the long run, 997 nondefectives and 3 defectives shall be produced. Three Sigma quality is achieved when the ratio of Tolerance *T* and Process Capability *P* equals one while Six Sigma Quality is achieved when this ratio is 2. With three sigma quality, 3 defectives per 1000 are obtained while in Six Sigma, 0.002 defectives per million are expected theoretically. This situation is shown in Figures 15.37 and 15.38. Theoretical analysis and practical observations by Harry and Schröder [5] have proved that a process centring does not coincide with design centre during a practical process. Due to this shift and drift in the process which has been found to equal 1.5 sigma, the number of defectives increases from 0.002 ppm to 3.4 ppm. This is shown in Figure 15.39.

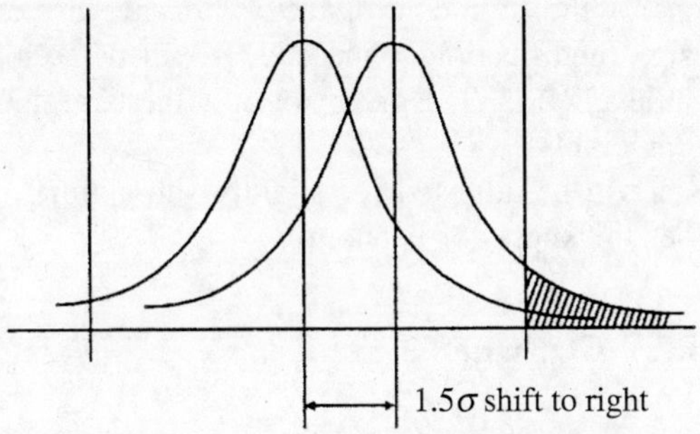

FIGURE 15.39 Effect of shift and drift.

It should be noted that a 3 sigma quality with perfect centring shall produce three parts per 1000 which is equivalent to 3000 parts per million, which is an unacceptable number of defects.

15.7.2 Six Sigma Relationships

Important formulae used in Six Sigma quality are:

Calculations:

$$\text{Defects per unit (DPU)} = \frac{\text{Total No. of defects}}{\text{Total No. of units produced}} = \frac{D}{U}$$

$$\text{Yield } Y = (1 - \text{defects per unit}) = \left(1 - \frac{D}{U}\right)$$

$$\text{Defect per opportunity (DPO)} = \left(\frac{D}{U \times 0}\right)$$

$$\text{Defects per million or ppm value (DPMO)} = \left(\frac{D}{U \times 0}\right) \times 10^6$$

15.7.3 Procedure to Work Out Operating Sigma Level of a Process

Let us assume that the process is giving an output of 1283 pieces/day. Of these, 1138 pieces are acceptable. Then,

$$\text{Yield } Y = \left(\frac{1138}{1283}\right) = 0.887.$$

Defect rate = (1 – 0.887) = 0.113. If the critical to quality factors per piece (O) = 24, the defect rate per opportunity (DPO) is:

$$\text{DPO} = \left(\frac{\text{DPU}}{O}\right) = \frac{0.113}{24} = 0.0047$$

Defects per million opportunities (DPMO) is obtained as:

$$\text{DPMO} = \text{DPO} \times 10^6 = 0.0047 \times 10^6$$

$$= 4709$$

A formula for converting the DPMO value to Sigma quality level with the process centre shift of 1.5 Sigma has been developed by Schmidt and Launsby (1997) as:

$$Z = 0.8406 + \sqrt{29.37 - 2.221 \ln (\text{DPMO})}$$

Thus,

$$Z = 0.8406 + \sqrt{29.37 - 2.221 \ln 4709}$$

$$= 4.1$$

Therefore, the firm is operating at 4.1 Sigma quality.

The value of $Z = 4.1$ can also be directly read from Table 15.8 of Z values shown in its column of 1.5σ. Shifted distribution with the corresponding ppm values being developed by Harry and Schröder [5].

Yield. Yield Y is also estimated from the assumption that the probability of detecting a defect is governed by Poisson's law of statistics as:

$$p(x) = \frac{e^{-\lambda}\lambda^x}{x!}$$

where x is the number of defects and λ is the average number of defects so that λ equals DPU. If we wish to estimate probability p_0 of zero defects, substituting $x = 0$ in the above equation, we get:

$$p_0 = \frac{e^{-\lambda}\lambda^0}{0!} = e^{-\lambda} = e^{-\text{DPU}}$$

The probability of zero defects will give yield Y so that:

$$Y = e^{-\text{DPU}}$$

Figure 15.40 illustrates the physical concept of the above equation. The Z-value so obtained is termed $Z_{\text{equivalent}}$ or $Z_{\text{long term}}$.

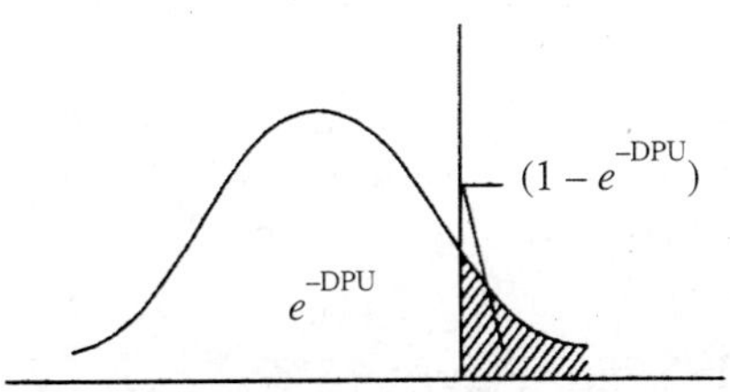

FIGURE 15.40 Effect of Z on yield Y.

It is related with short-term performance value of Z, designated by $Z_s \cdot Z_s$ is related with long-term σ-value Z_L by the equation:

$$Z_S = Z_L + 1.5$$

Any firm claiming a long-term yield corresponding to Z_L is operating at the short-term performance yield Z_s owing to detectable sporadic jumps of target value μ by (1.5σ). Thus, a firm claiming to operate at, say, 5.5σ quality is, in fact, operating at $(5.5 - 1.5)\sigma = 4\sigma$.

Example. Five defects are observed in 467 units produced. To calculate the short-term and long-term Z_{sT} and Z_{LT}, respectively. Also estimate the ppm value.

$$Y = e^{-\text{DPU}}$$

Solution

$$\text{DPU} = 5/467 = 0.0107$$

$$Y = e^{-0.0107} = 0.98935$$

From Standard normal tables: $Z_{LT} = 2.3$; referring to Table 15.9 for area, $a = 0.0107$ (Figure 15.41). Therefore,

$$Z_{sT} = Z_{LT} + 1.5 = 2.30 + 1.5 = 3.8$$

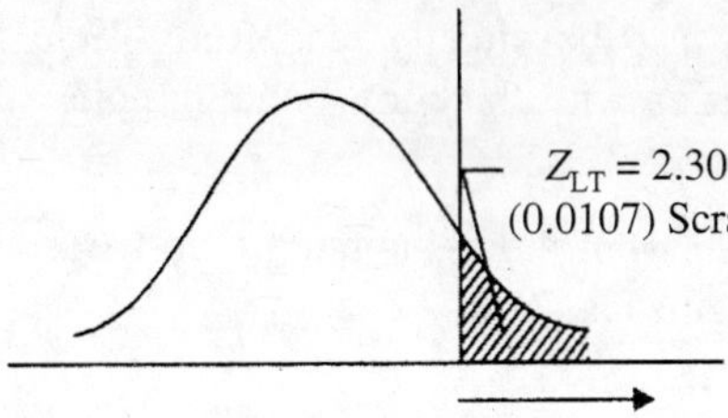

FIGURE 15.41 Determination of scrap.

Substituting $Z = 3.8$ in the Schmidt–Launsby [4] formula, we get:

$$Z = 0.8406 + \sqrt{29.37 - 2.221 \ln \text{DPMO}}$$

the value of defects per million opportunities = 10,724

Defects per million opportunities: An example is now taken up in which a printed circuit board has defects of types I, II and III. It is possible to find the most potent defect.

Characteristic	*D*	*U*	*O*	*U.O.*	*DPU*	*DPO*	*DPMO = DPO × 10⁶*
I	21	327	92	30,084	0.064	0.0007	698
II	10	350	85	29,750	0.029	0.0003	336
III	8	37	43	1,591	0.216	0.0050	5028

On inspection of DPMO values, it is seen that defect type III are most potent, followed by defects type I and type II. Thus, type III defects should be controlled on a top priority basis.

15.7.4 Rolled Throughput Yield (Figure 15.42)

If a fabrication line has n stations, the rolled throughput yield can be calculated by multiplying the throughput yields at each station:

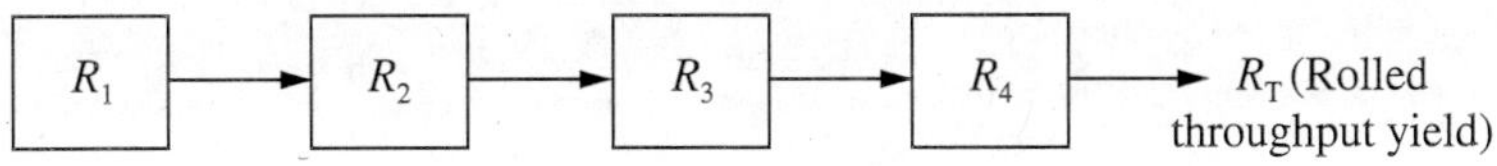

FIGURE 15.42 Calculating rolled throughput yield.

Thus, $R_T = R_1 \cdot R_2 \cdot R_3 \cdot R_4$. Assuming $R_1 = 0.92$, $R_2 = 0.82$, $R_3 = 0.95$ $R_4 = 0.82$, we have

$$R_T = (0.92)\ (0.82)\ (0.95)\ (0.82) = 0.59$$

15.7.5 Advantage of Yield and Allied Calculations

Calculations of rolled throughput yield enable the calculation of material input to account for losses.

Thus, in the example above, it is observed that (1 – 0.59) = 0.41 nonconforming units are produced. Therefore, a raw material input to account for a fraction loss (0.41) should be implemented. Thus the raw material input equals 1 + 0.41 = 1.41. For producing 100 conforming units, the raw material equivalent of (1.41 × 100) = 141 units is essential.

15.7.6 Normalized Yield and *Z*-Value for Benchmarking

Normalized yield assumes that the yield at each step is equal. In the example cited earlier, the rolled throughput yield = 0.59. In this case the normalized yield shall work out to $(0.59)^{1/4}$ per station. For benchmarking purposes, when one is interested in comparing his company with the best-in-the-class:

$$Z_{\text{benchmarking}} = (Z_{\text{normalized}} + 1.5_{\text{shift}})$$

15.7.7 Design for Six Sigma (DFSS)

Firms which have achieved near to Five Sigma quality try to achieve Six Sigma only by one approach—design for Six Sigma (DFSS).

According to Harry and Schröder, [5] the founders of Six Sigma quality:

Product design approach in DFSS is planned to create designs which have the following characteristics:

1. *Resource efficient.* Powerful use of tools such as value analysis may help.
2. *Capable of high yields irrespective of complexity.* Design for manufacture, discussed elsewhere in this book, should be suitably employed.
3. *Can create designs based on parametric design or robust design.* This should enable one to make the design process given minimum variability under most rigorous environmental factors. Thus, value analysis, DFM and Taguchi methods provide with a three-pronged attack to reach the Six Sigma level.

15.7.8 Cost Benefits and Leveraging through Better Design

Referring to Figure 15.43, it will be noted that with better quality, the cost of appraisal or inspection, cost of repairs and cost due to claims on account of defective quality are minimized with (6σ) products as against (4σ) products. Cost of prevention is more for fewer defects and is also shown in the figure. Optimum cost of quality occurs at point P_1 for (4σ) and point P_2 for (6σ) as shown.

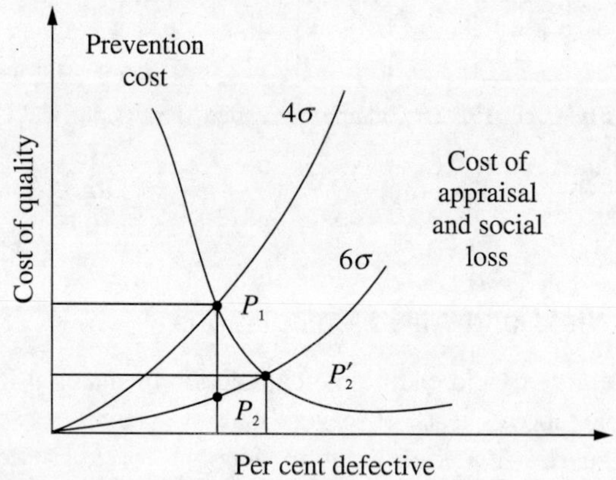

FIGURE 15.43 Economics of six sigma vs. four sigma.

Harry and Schröder [5] claim that the influence of good design on total cost reduction is maximum, i.e., of the tune of 70%. The weightage factors quoted by them is 0.7 for design, 0.2 for material, 0.05 for labour, and 0.05 for overhead as far as their influence on total cost is concerned.

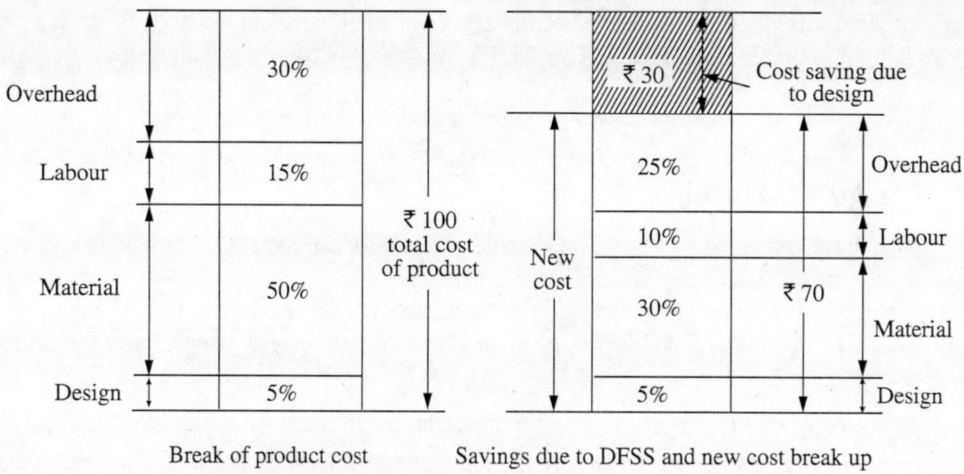

FIGURE 15.44 Cost breakup and savings due to DFSS.

If the initial cost of product was ₹ 100, the cost savings due to design for six sigma would be given by the following equation:

$$C_s = \text{per cent cut in each cost } (W_1 + W_2 + W_3 + W_4)$$

where C_s is cost saving and W_1, W_2, W_3, W_4 are weightages assigned to Design simplification, material modification, labour cost and overhead cost.

Thus, assuming a 30 per cent reduction in cost due to design efforts like simplification and standardization and equal reduction in material, labour and overhead costs, the cost saving (assigning $W_1 = 0.7$, $W_2 = 0.2$, $W_3 = 0.05$, $W_4 = 0.05$) is:

$$\text{Cost saving} = C_s = 30(0.7 + 0.2 + 0.05 + 0.05) = ₹\ 30$$

15.7.9 Relationship between C_P and C_{PK} Values (Figure 15.45)

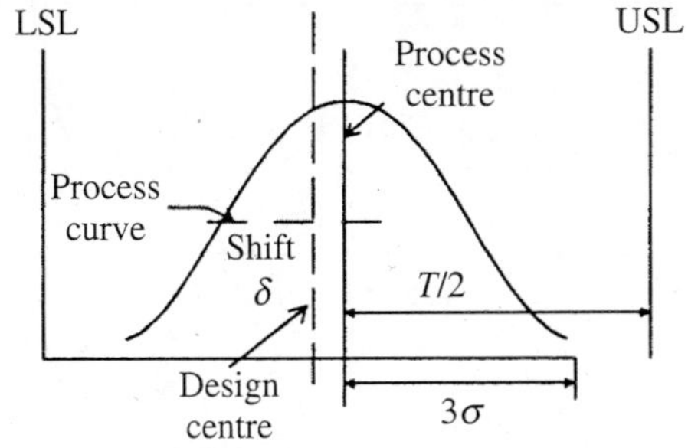

FIGURE 15.45 Relation between C_P and C_{PK} values.

From the definition of C_P value, we have:

$$C_P = \frac{T/2}{3\sigma} \tag{15.37}$$

$$C_{PK} = \frac{(T/2) - \delta}{3\sigma} \tag{15.38}$$

Dividing (15.38) by (15.37), we get:

$$\frac{C_{PK}}{C_P} = \frac{(T/2) - \delta}{T/2}$$

Thus,

$$C_{PK} = C_P\left(1 - \frac{\delta}{T/2}\right) \tag{15.39}$$

Equation (15.39) is important because it tells how a process is performing in the light of shift (δ) and design tolerance T.

15.7.10 Implementation of Six Sigma

The typical hierarchical structure for Six Sigma implementation can be visualized as shown in Figure 15.46.

The expectations from each of the above hierarchical members can be outlined in the following manner.

Top management. A total commitment by top management is a *must* for the success of the six sigma project. The vision, mission statement, and objectives should be clear to the top management.

A CEO should give the employees freedom and flexibility and permit them to generate ideas and stimulate creativity.

Champions. Champions are typically strategic business unit leaders and could be of the level of a vice-president. Harry and Schröder recommend that a champion should be adept at handling cross-functional teams and should have a solid financial and business background to enable effective

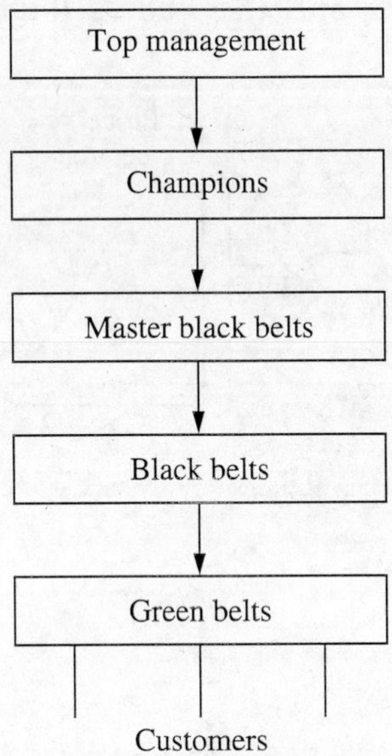

FIGURE 15.46 Typical hierarchical structure for Six Sigma.

deployment of Six Sigma projects. Project champions are in constant touch with senior black belts and enable them to successfully carry out their mission. The champions need not be statisticians but should have a good acquaintance with design of experiments. Understand the motion of throughput yield and its impact on the success of the project.

Master black belts. These persons are experts at spreading the breakthrough strategy across the organization. Master black belts devote all their time to six sigma. They train and coach black belts. Master black belts should be aces in solving statistical problems.

Black belts. Black belts work on specific projects. While CEOs and champions decide what is to be done, Black belts with the help of master black belts work out how it will be done. Though black belts are expected to train about 100 green belts every year, their expertise is more on hands on statistics and problem solving than on human resource management.

Green belts. They are new recruits who are expected to do leg work and data collection. Green belts have training under black belts as a part of their job. Their major job could be different from a full time six sigma project. Many hourly workers are trained on the basics of six sigma project such as measure, analyse, improve and control.

15.7.11 The Twelve MAIC Objectives

Under the Four Point Plan for Six Sigma, there are 12 objectives.

1. *Measure:* Measure the frequency of defects. This comprises: Selection of CTQ characteristics. Define standards of performance. Validate measurement systems.
2. *Analyse: When and where defects occur.* Fix product capability; define performance objectives; identify causes and sources of variation. Classify causes into chronic causes and sporadic causes.

3. *Improve the process.* Screen potential causes. Carry out design of experiments to discover nature of relationship between parameter and response. Establish working tolerances.
4. *Control and fix the process at a satisfactory level.* Validate and calibrate measurement system. Determine process capability. Implement process controls.

15.7.12 Future Avenues

Six-Sigma quality is the most current topic amongst the various approaches in industry to reach perfection and zero-defect situation. The plus point of Six Sigma is that even skeptics of "management fads" take this subject seriously. The main reason for its acceptability is that everything is expressed in "metrics" or numerical values, making Six-Sigma approach above board.

It may be noted that we have taken up the concept for robust quality and design of experiments before opening the topic of Six-Sigma quality. The reason for this choice of sequence is best explained in the words of K.R. Bhote [6], one of the pioneers of world class quality concepts. Even the Japanese concluded that 4σ to 5σ quality was not enough and application of quality during process control at $\pm 3\sigma$ was "too little" and "too late". The Japanese recommended the use of off-line Taguchi methods to bring variation to a minimum before controlling quality during SPC (Statistical Process Control).

Bhote [6] writes. The secret weapon of Japan's quality is that Japanese industries' widespread use of design of experiments. The objective here is to discover key variables in product and process design well ahead of production; to drastically reduce the variations they cause and to open up the tolerances on the large number of unimportant variables so as to reduce costs. DOE can also be used as a tool on old products that were not subjected to the preventive disciplines of DOE before production.

Figure 15.47 indicates the power of DOE in increasing the C_P value. Bhote [6] says: The parts used in production and assembly in *Ford* were within specifications but showed piece to piece variation. On the other hand, *Mazda* parts, made to same drawing, did not show variability and were almost alike. As a result, *Mazda* achieved greater customer satisfaction than *Ford.*

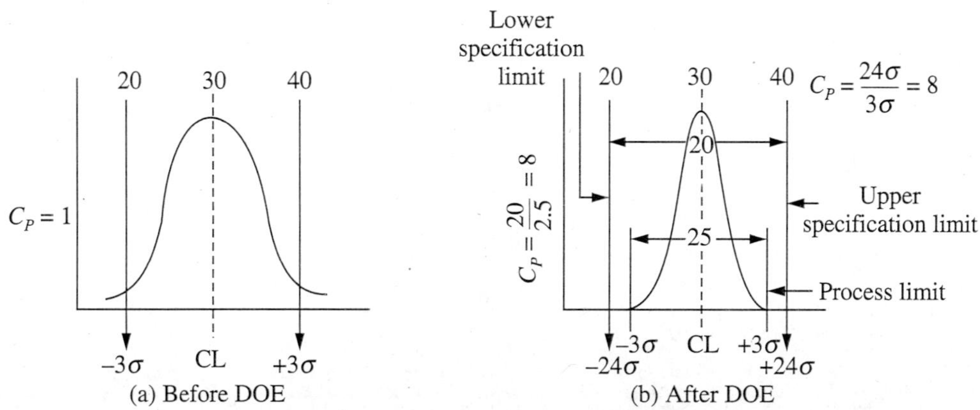

FIGURE 15.47 Effect of DOE on C_P Value.

TABLE 15.8 Conversion between ppm and Sigma

+/– Sigma level at specification limit(Z)*	*Defective ppm centred distribution*	*Defective ppm: 1.5 Sigma shifted distribution*
1	317,310.520	697,672.15
1.1	271,332.203	660,082.92
1.2	230,139.463	621,378.38
1.3	193,604.099	581,814.88
1.4	161,513.423	541,693.78
1.5	133,614.458	501,349.97
1.6	109,598.579	461,139.78
1.7	89,130.864	421,427.51
1.8	71,860.531	382,572.13
1.9	57,432.986	344,915.28
2	45,500.124	308,770.21
2.1	35,728.715	274,412.21
2.2	27,806.798	242,071.41
2.3	21,448.162	211,927.71
2.4	16,395.058	184,108.21
2.5	12,419.360	158,686.95
2.6	9,322.444	135,686.77
2.7	6,934.048	115,083.09
2.8	5,110.381	96,809.10
2.9	3,731.760	80,762.13
3	2,699.934	66,810.63
3.1	1,935.342	54,801.40
3.2	1,374.404	44,566.73
3.3	966.965	35,931.06
3.4	673.962	28,716.97
3.5	465.347	22,750.35
3.6	318.291	17,864.53
3.7	215.660	13,903.50
3.8	144.745	10,724.14
3.9	96.231	8197.56
4	63.372	6,209.70
4.1	41.337	4,661.23
4.2	26.708	3,467.03
4.3	17.092	2,555.19
4.4	10.834	1865.88
4.5	6.802	1,349.97
4.6	4.229	967.67
4.7	2.605	687.20
4.8	1.589	483.48
4.9	0.960	336.98
5	0.574	232.67
5.1	0.340	159.15
5.2	0.200	107.83
5.3	0.116	72.37
5.4	0.067	48.12
5.5	0.038	31.69
5.6	0.21	20.67
5.7	0.012	13.35
5.8	0.007	8.55
5.9	0.004	5.42
6	0.002	3.40

*Sometimes referred to as Sigma level or Sigma quality level when considering process shift.

TABLE 15.9 Area under the standardized normal curve

Z_a	0.00	0.01	0.02	0.03	0.04	0.05	0.06	0.07	0.08	0.09
0.0	0.5000	0.4960	0.4920	0.4880	0.4840	0.4801	0.4761	0.4721	0.4681	0.4641
0.1	0.4602	0.4562	0.4522	0.4483	0.4443	0.4404	0.4364	0.4325	0.4286	0.4247
0.2	0.4207	0.4168	0.4129	0.4090	0.4052	0.4013	0.3974	0.3936	0.3897	0.3859
0.3	0.3821	0.3783	0.3745	0.3707	0.3669	0.3632	0.3694	0.3557	0.3520	0.3483
0.4	0.3446	0.3409	0.3372	0.3336	0.3300	0.3264	0.3228	0.3192	0.3156	0.3121
0.5	0.3085	0.3050	0.3015	0.2981	0.2946	0.2912	0.2877	0.2843	0.2810	0.2776
0.6	0.2743	0.2709	0.2676	0.2643	0.2611	0.2578	0.2546	0.2514	0.2483	0.2451
0.7	0.2420	0.2389	0.2358	0.2327	0.2296	0.2266	0.2236	0.2206	0.2177	0.2146
0.8	0.2119	0.2090	0.2061	0.2033	0.2005	0.1977	0.1949	0.1922	0.1894	0.1867
0.9	0.1841	0.1814	0.1788	0.1762	0.1736	0.1711	0.1685	0.1660	0.1635	0.1611
1.0	0.1587	0.1562	0.1539	0.1515	0.1492	0.1469	0.1446	0.1243	0.1401	0.1379
1.1	0.1357	0.1335	0.1314	0.1292	0.1271	0.1251	0.1230	0.1210	0.1190	0.1170
1.2	0.1151	0.1131	0.1112	0.1093	0.1075	0.1056	0.1038	0.1020	0.1003	0.0985
1.3	0.0968	0.0951	0.0934	0.0918	0.0901	0.0885	0.0869	0.0853	0.0838	0.0823
1.4	0.0808	0.0793	0.0778	0.0764	0.0749	0.0735	0.0721	0.0708	0.0694	0.0681
1.5	0.0668	0.0655	0.0643	0.0630	0.0618	0.0606	0.0594	0.0582	0.0571	0.0559
1.6	0.0548	0.0537	0.0526	0.0516	0.0505	0.0495	0.0485	0.0475	0.0465	0.0455
1.7	0.0446	0.0436	0.0427	0.0418	0.0409	0.0401	0.0392	0.0384	0.0375	0.0367
1.8	0.0359	0.0351	0.0344	0.0336	0.0329	0.0322	0.0314	0.0307	0.0301	0.0294
1.9	0.0287	0.0281	0.0274	0.0268	0.0262	0.0256	0.0250	0.0244	0.0239	0.0233
2.0	0.0228	0.0222	0.0217	0.0212	0.0207	0.0202	0.0197	0.0192	0.0188	0.0183
2.1	0.0179	0.0174	0.0170	0.0160	0.0162	0.0158	0.0154	0.0150	0.0146	0.0143
2.2	0.0139	0.0136	0.0132	0.0129	0.0125	0.0122	0.0119	0.0116	0.0113	0.0110
2.3	0.0107	0.0104	0.0102	0.00990	0.00964	0.00939	0.00914	0.00889	0.00866	0.00842
2.4	0.00820	0.00798	0.00776	0.00755	0.00734	0.00714	0.00695	0.00676	0.00657	0.00639
2.5	0.00621	0.00604	0.00587	0.00570	0.00554	0.00539	0.00523	0.00508	0.00494	0.00480
2.6	0.00466	0.00453	0.00440	0.00427	0.00415	0.00402	0.00391	0.00379	0.00368	0.00357
2.7	0.00347	0.00336	0.00326	0.00317	0.00307	0.00298	0.00289	0.00280	0.00272	0.00264
2.8	0.00256	0.00248	0.00240	0.00233	0.00226	0.00219	0.00212	0.00205	0.00199	0.00193
2.9	0.00187	0.00181	0.00175	0.00169	0.00164	0.00159	0.00154	0.00149	0.00144	0.00139
3	0.00135	0.03988	0.03687	0.03483	0.03337	0.03233	0.03159	0.03108	0.04723	0.04481
4	0.04317	0.04207	0.04133	0.05854	0.05541	0.05340	0.05211	0.05130	0.06793	0.06479
5	0.06287	0.06170	0.07996	0.07579	0.07333	0.07190	0.07107	0.08599	0.08332	0.08182
6	0.09987	0.09530	0.09282	0.09149	0.010777	0.010402	0.010206	0.010104	0.011523	0.011260

“05541 means .00000541. In this text, the tabular value corresponds to Z_a, where a is the value of probability associated with the distribution area pictorially represented as:

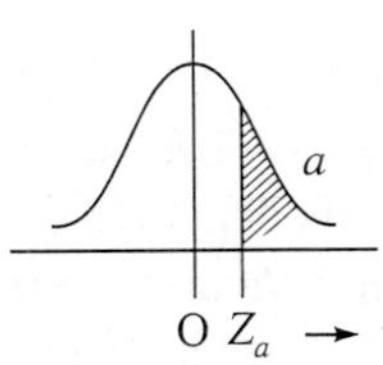

REVIEW QUESTIONS

1. Define quality of design, quality of conformance and quality of performance. Sec. 15.2; P 408, 409
2. Which tool of quality control is applied for monitoring a process? Sec. 15.4
3. What are centre line (CL), upper control limit (UCL), and lower control limit (LCL)? How UCL, CL and LCL are related to upper specification limit and lower specification limit? Sec. 15.4.2
4. What are chance causes of variation and assignable causes of variation in a process? What are trial control limits and stable control limits of a process? Sec. 15.4.3
5. How does population distribution of *X* differ from sampling distribution of $\overline{X}$? What is their relationship? Sec. 15.4.5
6. Which of the following are chance causes and which are assignable causes of variation from the following causes:

   Ans: (ii), (iv), (v), and (vi): Chance Causes

   (i), (iii), and (vii): Assignable Causes

   (i) A faculty batch of castings due to excessive hardness, (ii) slight variation in material property, (iii) quality problem due to change in supplier, (iv) ambient temperature variation during 3 shifts, (v) vibration in the cutting process (vi) variation in coolant supply during cutting, (vii) change in the cutting tool from carbide to HSS, and (viii) change in the operator.
7. What are the areas of application of $\overline{X}$ and *R* charts, *np* chart, *p* chart, *c* chart and CU-SUM chart?

   Ans: X and R chart help to reduce scrap CUSUM. Sec. 15.4.10; Sec.15.4.7 and 15.4.8
8. What is the appropriate sample size for $\overline{X}$ and *R* charts, *np* chart, *p* chart and *c* chart. What type of sampling is done: random or biased. When is random sample recommended?
9. What are single, double, multiple and continuous sampling plans for attributes? Sec. 15.3.1, 15.3.6, 15.3.7, and 15.3.8
10. What is sampling plan for variables? Explain the method of finding sample size when α and β errors as well as mean and standard deviation of good and bad lots are given. Sec. 15.3.10
11. What is OC curve? What is ideal OC curve? What is AOQ curve and AOQL? Explain with graphical plots. Sec. 15.3.2
12. How is US-MIL-STD-105D used in selecting a sampling plan? Assume data on lot size and AQL with "Normal" level of inspection. Sec. 15.3.9; Table 15.2
13. Develop expression for reliability of systems in series and parallel. Sec. 15.5.5
14. What is Weibull model for reliability? How does it help in estimating of reliability estimation if data on %units failing and time of testing to failure is given? P 436–439
15. Differentiate between static and dynamic models of reliability.

    [*Hint:* Static models reliability of individual components of the product is fixed and independent of time. Dynamic models regard reliability as a function of time. Exponential model $R = e^{-\lambda t}$ and Weibull model $R = e^{-(t/\theta)^\beta}$ are dynamic models because the element of time *t* is included in the model.]

16. An aeroplane has four independent engines. The reliability of each engine is 0.98. What is the reliability of the aeroplane?

[***Solution*** In this case, we have four engines and to fly successfully all the four engines should operate efficiently. Thus, it is a case of components in series

$$R = R_1 \cdot R_2 \cdot R_3 \cdot R_4 = (0.98)^4 = 0.9224]$$

17. The reliability of components in parallel is 0.64. But it is desired that the final reliability should be 0.97. How many components in parallel are needed arrive at system probability of 0.97.

[***Solution*** For a parallel system, the reliability of system $R = 1 - [(1 - R)^n]$, where n is the number of components in parallel.

$$\therefore \qquad n = \frac{\ln(1 - R_{sys})}{\ln(1 - R)} = \frac{\ln(1 - 0.97)}{\ln(1 - 0.64)} = 3.43$$

Thus, at least four components should be arranged in parallel.]

18. What is X out of n system? A system has three components. It has been found that at least two out of three subsystems should be operative to make the system work successfully. The reliability of subsystem is 0.9. Calculate the reliability of the system.

[**Ans:** In x out of n system, the binomial formula of statistics is used where:

$$P_{x/n} = R_{xn} = \sum_{x=2}^{x=3} \binom{n}{x} R^x (1 - R)^{n-x}$$

Substituting the values of $n = 3$ and $x = 2$, and $x = 3$ after opening Σ notation.

Thus, $$R_{2/3} = \left[\frac{3!}{2!1!}\right] R^2 (1 - R)^{3-2} + \frac{3!}{3!0!} R^{3-3}$$

Simplify, $R_{2/3} = 3R^2 - 2R^3$

Since $R = 0.9$, we have

$$R_{2/3} = 3(0.9)^2 - 2(0.9)^3 = 0.9720\ (\approx 97.20\%)$$

19. A computer has to CPUs working in parallel. The failure rate of a single CPU is 0.005 failures per hour. Calculate MTTF.

[***Solution*** Apply the formula: $\text{MTTF} = \dfrac{1}{\lambda} + \dfrac{1}{2\lambda}$

$$= \frac{1}{0.005} + \frac{1}{2(0.005)} = 300 \text{ hours }]$$

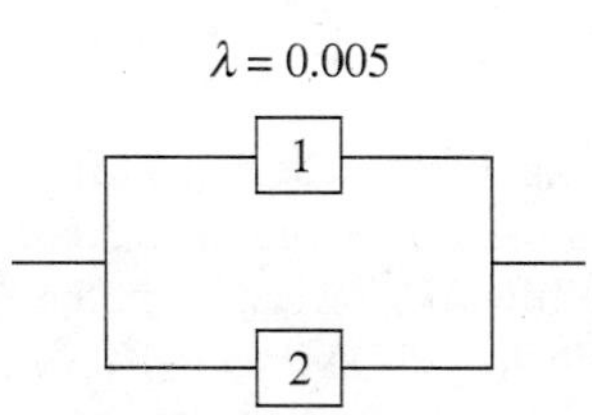

FIGURE 15.48 Units in parallel.

20. In a standby arrangement, two machines are used. Only one machine operates while the other is a standby machine. The mission time is 10 h and the failure rate $\lambda = 0.004$ per hour. Calculate the MTTF and R_{SB} of the standby arrangement.

[***Solution*** The formula for a standby arrangement is

$$MTTF = \frac{2}{\lambda}.$$ Substituting $\lambda = 0.004$, we have,

$$MTTF = \frac{2}{0.004} = 500 \text{ h}, R_{SB} = e^{-\lambda t}(1 + \lambda t) = e^{-(0.004)10}[1+(0.004)(10)] = 0.9992\ (\approx 99.92\%)]$$

21. What is meant by future-modes-effects analysis? How do the three automobile joints of US go about FMEA? What do their vendors do as a part of FMEA programme?

[**Ans:** The risk priority number method is used in the FMEA programme. Risk priority of any component is the product of three probability rankings on a 10-point scale.

(1) Probability of occurrence of a fault

(2) Probability of detection of the fault

(3) Severity of the fault-customer involvement

The above three probabilities are ranked in Tables (1), (2) and (3) and shown below:

Description	*Probability*	*Rank*	*Description*	*Rank*	*Customer*		
Very high	1/2 to 1/8	9–10	Non detection	10	Description	Customer focus	Rank
High	1/20 to 1/40	7–8	Very low	9	Very high	Unsafe customer	9–10
Moderate	1/80 to 1/1000	4–6	Low	7–8	High	Dissatisfaction	7–8
Lower	1/4000 to 1/10000	2–3	Moderate	5–6	Moderate	Dissatisfaction	4,5,6
Remote	Less than $(1/10^6)$	1	High	3,4	Low	Customer annoyance	2,3
			Very high	1,2	Minor	Customer unaware	1
Table (1) Ranking of occurrence			Table (2) Ranking of detection		Table (3) Ranking of severity		

The formula for a RPN or risk priority number is:

$$RPN = (OR)\ (DR)(SR)$$

where OR is *occurrence ranking* on a 10-point scale.

DR is *detection ranking* on a 10-point scale. It is based upon difficulty of detection.

SR is *severity ranking* on a 10-point scale.

Taking an example, if OR is 7, DR is 3 and SR is 8, the risk priority number (RPN) = (7) × (3) × (8) = 168. Since the high limit of RPN is (10)(10)(10) = 1000, management can decide whether a RPN of 168 is acceptable. The effort should be to maintain RPN below 100.

The RPN strategy is applied for design FMEA as well as process FMEA. In design FMEA, components in an assembled product are assigned RPN to various components critical to successful operation/performance of the product. High-risk RPN components are redesigned to reduce their RPN. Likewise, processes which are critical to quality are improved to minimize process-induced defects.]

22. What is fault tree analysis? Make a logic diagram for inability of an engine to start. Sec. 15.5.7, 15.5.8; Figure 15.34

23. What is Taguchi's method for robust design of a process? What is the difference between one-factors at-a-time experiment and Taguchi's experimental design? What is signal-to-noise ratio? Should it be high or low? Sec. 15.6; P 444 to 449

24. What is meant by Six Sigma quality? How does it differ from 3σ quality practice in conventional Shewhart Control Charts? Sec. 15.7; P 449–457

25. What is the procedure for calculating defects-per-million-opportunities for a Taguchi approach? Sec. 15.7.2, 15.7.3; P 450–452

26. One of the objections raised about Six Sigma, calculations is the assumption of a lack of centring by $\pm 1.5\sigma$ in the long run. Do you agree with this objection? Explain.

[*Hint:* The shift varies from industry to industry. Determine actual shift by experiment.]

27. The second objection is concerned with the misuse of the formula: $DPO = \dfrac{D}{U \times O}$. If during the implementation of Six Sigma, the value of number of opportunities (O) by manipulation, the value of DPO reduces and the corresponding value of z, in the Six Sigma table increases. This gives a "false" high value of z and hyped quality of the process. How will you avoid such a situation?

[*Hint:* Attempt to keep value of O down by grouping similar opportunities in one single group and reduce O. For example: cracking, bending, warping, and denting of a moulded plastic cup represent one opportunity instead of four opportunities.]

28. How does Six Sigma quality result in cost reduction of a product? Explain.

[*Hint:* Six Sigma initiative results in saving of material due to elimination of scrap. In conjunction with improved design for manufacturing, Six Sigma initiative results in reduction of material cost to the tune of 20%, reduction of labour by 5% and overheads by 5%. Suppose initial cost breakup before Six Sigma was: design cost: 5%, material cost: 50%, labour cost: 15%, overhead cost: 30%, totaling ₹ 100. After Six Sigma, the new costs will be Design cost: 5% , material cost: 30%, labour cost: 10%, overhead cost: 25%, totaling to 70%. On comparison of total costs before and after Six Sigma, we observe a saving of (100 – 70), i.e., ₹ 30 per ₹ 100. If a product costs ₹ 400, its cost after Six Sigma initiative is ₹ (400 × 0.7), i.e., ₹ 280].

REFERENCES

[1] Logothetis, N., *Managing for Total Quality—From Denting to Taguchi*, Prentice-Hall of India, New Delhi, 1996.

[2] Juran, J.M. and Gryna, *Quality Planning and Analysis*, Tata McGraw-Hill, New Delhi, 1996.

[3] Dieter G.E., *Engineering Design: A material processing approach*, McGraw-Hill International edition, New York, 1985.

[4] Schmidt S. and Launsby, *ppm Quality*, Quality Progress, 1997.

[5] Harry, Mikel and Richard Schröder, *Six Sigma*, Doubleday, New York, 2000.

[6] Bhote K.R., *World Class Quality*, Amacom, New York, 1988.

[7] Chitale, A.K., Shahane A.P., and Thakar G.D., *Modem Quality Management*, Ajanta Books International, New Delhi, 1994.

[8] Bagchi, Tapan, *Taguchi Methods Explained,* Prentice-Hall of India, New Delhi, 1994.

Chapter 16

New Product Development and Product Management

16.1 WHAT IS A PRODUCT?

Basically, a product is the object of the exchange process, the thing which the producer or supplier offers to a potential customer in exchange for something which the supplier thinks as equivalent or of greater value. Conventionally, this "something" is money which is freely exchangeable as a store of value. In the absence of money, we must resort to barter where the two parties agree with each other about how many pounds of wheat are worth a yard of cloth or how many barrels of oil are worth a ton of grain. It follows that for an exchange to occur there must be a demand for the object in question and the willingness to exchange other assets or objects possessing value. Where this demand exists, it represents an opportunity for producers to create supplies of the object in question and for markets to develop where buyers can meet suppliers and negotiate a mutually satisfying exchange relationship, which defines marketing.

It is not practically possible for buyers and producers to come into direct physical contact, therefore, elaborate channels of distribution are required to facilitate the exchange of goods. This is less true of services and especially personal services where the essence of the exchange is an act performed by a seller specifically for the purchaser.

Irrespective of the degree of contact between the producer and the consumer, the product possesses value only to the extent that consumers are willing to exchange. It is for this reason that supply always depends on demand. In times of scarcity, it may appear to be the other way round. Thus the "rediscovery" of marketing in the second half of the twentieth century reflects the potential for excess supply in most markets for goods and services in the more affluent industrialized economies where population growth has stabilized and technological advances result in continuing productivity gains. Because of this potential to create an excess supply, which will probably lead to a reduction in the perceived value of the total supply and to what cannot be consumed becoming worthless, producers have become far less certain about the demand for their products.

16.2 DEFINING PRODUCT BY NATURE OF DEMAND

Products may also be defined from a market perspective. This perspective is based on the premise that all products begin from a core benefit and that products can be represented as building on the core benefit product, which can be portrayed as a group of concentric circles building on the issues of the inner circles, as shown in Figure 16.1.

The essential theme of any product is the *core benefit*. Core benefit represents the fundamental service or benefits and is derived from the consumers' need or want. The benefit must be put into some form or given some features through which it can be offered. Based on this framework, decisions regarding products/services must begin with the core benefit. The second level of a product is the *generic product*. The generic product is the basic version of the product and is typically a *rudimentary* product. 'Rudimentary' means that the product does not have features or forms that classify the given product. It is unbranded, e.g., usually available tea in loose form, atta, milk, etc.

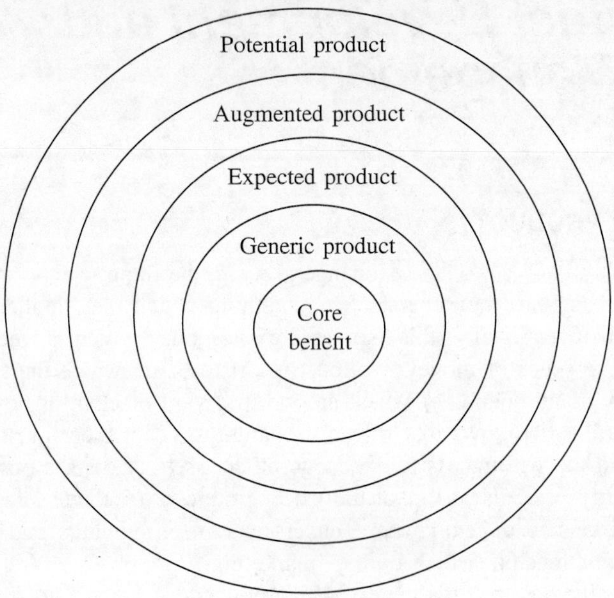

FIGURE 16.1 Product model.

The features and/or forms given to the product or service allow consumers to receive the benefit that they want.

The third level is the *expected product*. It includes a set of attributes and conditions that buyers normally expect and agree to when they purchase such a product.

Augmented product forms the fourth level. It is one that includes additional services and benefits that distinguish the company's offering from competitors' offerings. They are made to meet customer demand from market survey, e.g., Titan watch, Apple iPhone, Aristocrat luggage, etc.

At the fifth and top level is the *potential product*, which includes all the augmentations and transformations that the product might undergo in due course of time. The potential product represents a product that attempts to satisfy all consumers' needs and wants related to the product and thereby make the customer "delighted". It could mean product of future like a robot to help housewife in kitchen.

16.3 NEW PRODUCT STRATEGY

A common misconception is that new products correspond to major changes. In fact, new product strategy can mean different types of new products, depending on how the company classifies the type of market to be served (current or new) and type of technology (existing or new technology). Rather, current customers are those within or associated with the target market or market segment, who may be immediate customers, or competitor's customers. Similarly, current technology means the company has the technology, whereas new technology indicates a technology that needs to be created or acquired from somewhere else through payment of a royalty amount.

Based on this framework, which is called the *Product-Market Matrix*, four general strategies for product planning are identified: market penetration, product development, market development, and diversification (see Figure 16.2).

Market ↑ / Product →	Current	New
current	**Market penetration** (Product improvements, backward integration and cost reductions)	**Product development** (Line extensions or modifications in present product)
New	**Market development** (New uses, new markets)	**Diversification** (e.g., new product and new market, both)

FIGURE 16.2 Product–market matrix.

Market penetration strategy is based on an objective to increase market share. The current customer base is pursued with no major changes to the existing product and technology. Cost reduction and product improvements are characteristic of a market penetration strategy. Naturally these two types of strategies help to attract customers through a lower price, more features, or improved features.

Product development strategy is derived from an objective to capitalize on new product technology and offers more options to the customers. In this way, the company with a more diverse product line can ward off competitors. Line extensions are the result of product development strategy.

Market development strategy stems from a desire to expand sales volume of existing products through new markets. This would include expanding geographically, for example, to international markets, and targeting new market segments. The company is not interested in pursuing any product technology changes; the main interest is to take the product "as is" and find new markets. Market extensions are characteristics of a market development strategy.

Diversification is pursued when the company wishes to expand it into related businesses and unrelated businesses. Thus, new product coupled with new market is a risky but highly beneficial strategy. For instance, Tata Engineering and Locomotive Company (TELCO), now renamed Tata Motors, has gone for passenger cars and new market by launching its cars *Indica* and *Indigo*.

16.4 PRODUCT CLASSIFICATION

As a first step towards refining our consideration of demand, it will be helpful to develop some kind of classification for products as this should enable useful generalizations about particular categories or kinds of products. In fact, a possible classification system exists in consumer goods and consumer durable goods and in distinguishing these from producer goods. This dichotomy between producer and consumer goods is reflected in industrial marketing and consumer marketing, a distinction, which has proved very useful in developing specific recommendations for marketing strategy and marketing decisions.

As we have seen, the demand for industrial goods is derived from that for consumer goods. This being so, we should establish first how consumer goods are perceived, bought and consumed, before explaining how this affects the demand for industrial goods. One of the earliest and most influential contributions to the classifications of consumer goods was made by Melvin T. Copeland in 1923. He proposed that consumer goods could be classified as convenience goods, shopping goods, and speciality goods. These were defined formally by the American Marketing Association's Committee on Definitions (1948) as follows:

(i) **Convenience goods.** Those consumer goods which the customer purchases frequently, immediately, and with minimum effort. For example, chocolate, pens, tea, coffee, etc.

(ii) **Shopping goods.** Those consumer goods which the customer in the process of selection and purchase characteristically compares in terms of suitability, quality, price, and style. For example, cosmetics, TVs, PCs, hairstyle, etc.

(iii) **Specialty goods.** Those consumer goods, on which a significant group of buyers are habitually willing to make a special purchasing effort. For example, house, car, holiday, etc.

Industrial Goods: Industrial goods are classified depending upon their entry in the production system. They are classified into the following categories:

(A) Material and parts
(B) Capital items
(C) Supplies

(A) Materials can be divided into two categories:

1. Raw materials
2. Manufactured materials and parts

1. Raw materials can be divided into—(a) farm products such as wheat, rice, fruits, vegetables, and even livestock, and (b) natural products such as fish, iron ore, lumber, and petroleum.
2. Manufactured materials and parts:
   (a) Component materials have examples such as galvanized steel, yarn, cement, and wires which have a primary operation performed upon them to add value to them. These can be fabricated and further to be used in manufacture of further products such as garments, buildings, and construction work.
   (b) Component parts have examples of motors, shafts, bearings, and tires, which can be directly used in any design or assembly. These are sold directly to industries and price and service are major considerations.

(B) Capital items: These are typically high-priced items such as installations such as office buildings, workshops, elevators and lifts, and EOT cranes, equipment such as portable factory equipment, lift trucks used in material handling, and welding sets which do not become a part of any final product.

(C) Supplies include short-term items which help in running the system maintenance such as paints, nails, brooms, hand tools, and office supplies such as paper, pencil, and lubricating oils.

16.5 PRODUCT DEVELOPMENT AND PRODUCT MANAGEMENT

Firms represent themselves in the marketplace and make product offerings. These offerings may be in the form of products or services. Profitability is the main objective while company's image, customer satisfaction, and market share are essential for its long-term viability. Product planning is formally defined as the process of visioning, conceptualizing, developing, producing, testing, commercializing, sustaining and disposal of products. Product planning can be thought of as comprising two processes:

- Product development
- Product management

While product development represents the process where the product is conceived, developed, produced and tested, product management includes the launch effort and all other activities that take place after the launch. Thus, product development occurs during the pre-market phase of extended product life cycle. Product management essentially occurs in the post launch or marketing phase of the product life cycle. This is shown in Figure 16.4. In contrast, Figure 16.3 shows the product life cycle in the conventional way. In this chapter, the new product development model proposed by the famous US consultancy firm, Booz, Allen, and Hamilton is discussed in detail.

Product Life Cycle Management (PLM): In recent years, a new concept in product life cycle management has been introduced. Product life cycle management is the process of managing the entire life cycle of a product from its conception through design and manufacturing to service and disposal. PLM integrates people, data, processes, and business systems and provides information backbone for companies and their extended enterprises. Interested readers should refer to a book by John Stark titled Product Life Cycle Management published by Springer in 2011. It is according to Figure 16.4 which represents total or expanded life cycle. Product life cycle (PLC) covers all the 12 phases of expanded life cycle.

16.5.1 The Product Life Cycle

Designers and marketing people find great utility in a study of product life cycle (PLC). Every product goes through a cycle from birth, into an initial growth stage, to a relatively stable period, and finally to a declining stage that eventfully ends in the death of the product as shown in Figure 16.3.

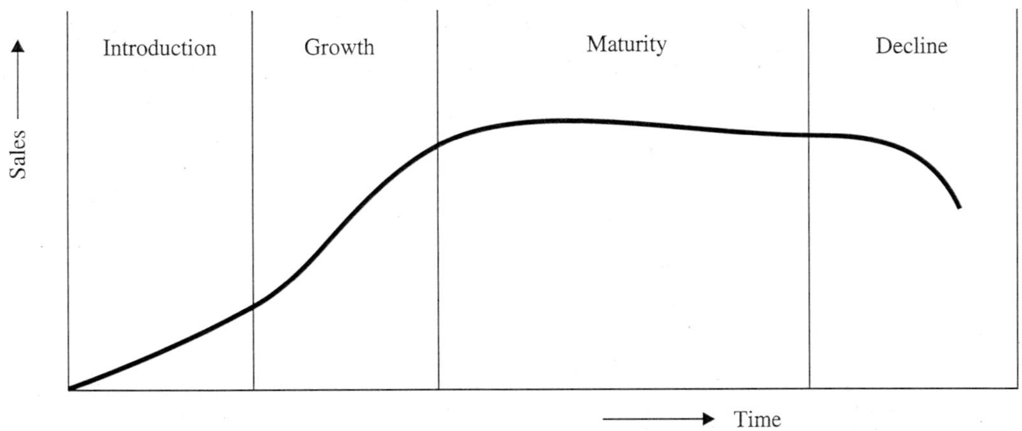

FIGURE 16.3 Product life cycle.

In the introductory stage, the product is new and consumer acceptance is low, so sales are low. In this early stage of the product life cycle, the rate of product change is rapid as management tries to maximize performance or product uniqueness in an attempt to enhance customer acceptance. When the product has entered the growth stage, knowledge of the product and its capabilities are known to a large number of customers. There may be emphasis on custom designing the product for slightly different customer needs. At the maturity stage, the product is widely accepted, sales are stable and are growing at the same rate as the economy as a whole. When the product reaches this stage, attempts should be made to rejuvenate it by incremental innovation or the development of still new applications. Products in the maturity stage usually experience considerable competition. Thus, there is great emphasis on reducing the cost of a mature product. At some point, the product enters the decline stage and sales decrease because a new and better product has entered the market to fulfill the same societal need. A closer look at the product life cycle in Figure 16.4 will indicate that the cycle is made up of many individual processes. In this case, the cycle has been divided into the pre-market and market phases. The former extends back to the idea generation, concept, development and includes the research, development and marketing studies needed to bring the product to the market phase. The investment (negative profits) needed to create the product is shown along with the profit. The numbers along the profit versus time curve correspond to the following process in the product life cycle. This introduction emphasizes that innovation leading to a new product is a complex, costly, and time-consuming process.

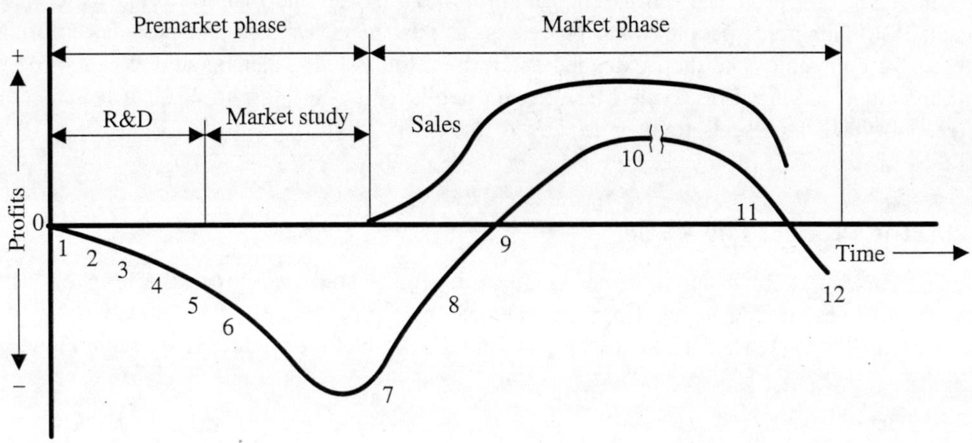

S. No.	*Pre-market phase or new product development phases*	S. No.	*Market phase or post-launch product life cycle phases*
1.	Idea generation	8.	Product introduction
2.	Idea screening	9.	Product growth
3.	Concept development	10.	Product maturity
4.	Business analysis	11.	Product decline
5.	Prototype development	12.	Product abandonment
6.	Test marketing		
7.	Marketing launch		

FIGURE 16.4 Expanded product life cycle.

16.5.2 Booz, Allen, Hamilton New Product Development Process

The process of developing a new product is inherently risky, with uncertainty at every stage. Along the various stages, the uncertainty is reduced—whether it is technology, marketability, or potential customer response. Table 16.1 analyzes the BAH process model to clarify its implications for information search, source and use.

TABLE 16.1 Analysis of the NPD process based on Booz, Allen and Hamilton (1982) model

Stage of development	*Information needed for stage; nature of information*	*Sources of information*	*Likely output of stage in light of information*
Explicit statement of new product strategy, budget allocation	Preliminary market and technical analysis; company objectives	Generated as part of continuous MIS and corporate planning	Identification of market opportunities to be exploited by new products
1. Idea generation (or gathering)	Customer needs and technical developments in previously identified markets	Inside company; salespeople technical functions, outside company; customers, competitors, inventors, etc	Body of initially acceptable ideas
2. Screening ideas: finding those with most potential	Assessment of whether there is a market for this type of product, and whether the company can make it. Assessment of financial implications: market potential and costs. Knowledge of company goals and its assessment	Main internal functions: — R&D — Sales — Marketing finance — Production	Ideas which are acceptable for further development
3. Concept development: turning an idea into a recognizable product concept with attributes and market position identified	Explicit assessment of customer needs to appraise market potential. Explicit assessment of technical requirements	Initial research with customer(s). Input from marketing and technical functions	Identification of key attributes that need to be incorporated in the product, major technical costs, target markets, and potential
4. Business analysis: full analysis of the proposal in terms of its business potential	Fullest information thus far: — detailed market analysis — explicit technical feasibility and costs — production implications — corporate objectives	Main internal functions are customers	Major go–no go decision: company needs to be sure the venture is worthwhile as expenditure dramatically increases after this stage. Initial marketing plan. Development plan and budget specification
5. Product development: crystallizing the product into semi-finalized shape	Customer research with product. Production information to check	Customer production	Explicit marketing plans
6. Test marketing: small-scale tests with customers	Profile of new product performance in light of competition, promotion and marketing mix variables	Market research: production, sales, marketing, technical people	Final go–no go for launch
7. Commercialization	Test market results and report	As for test market	Increment changes to test launch, full-scale launch

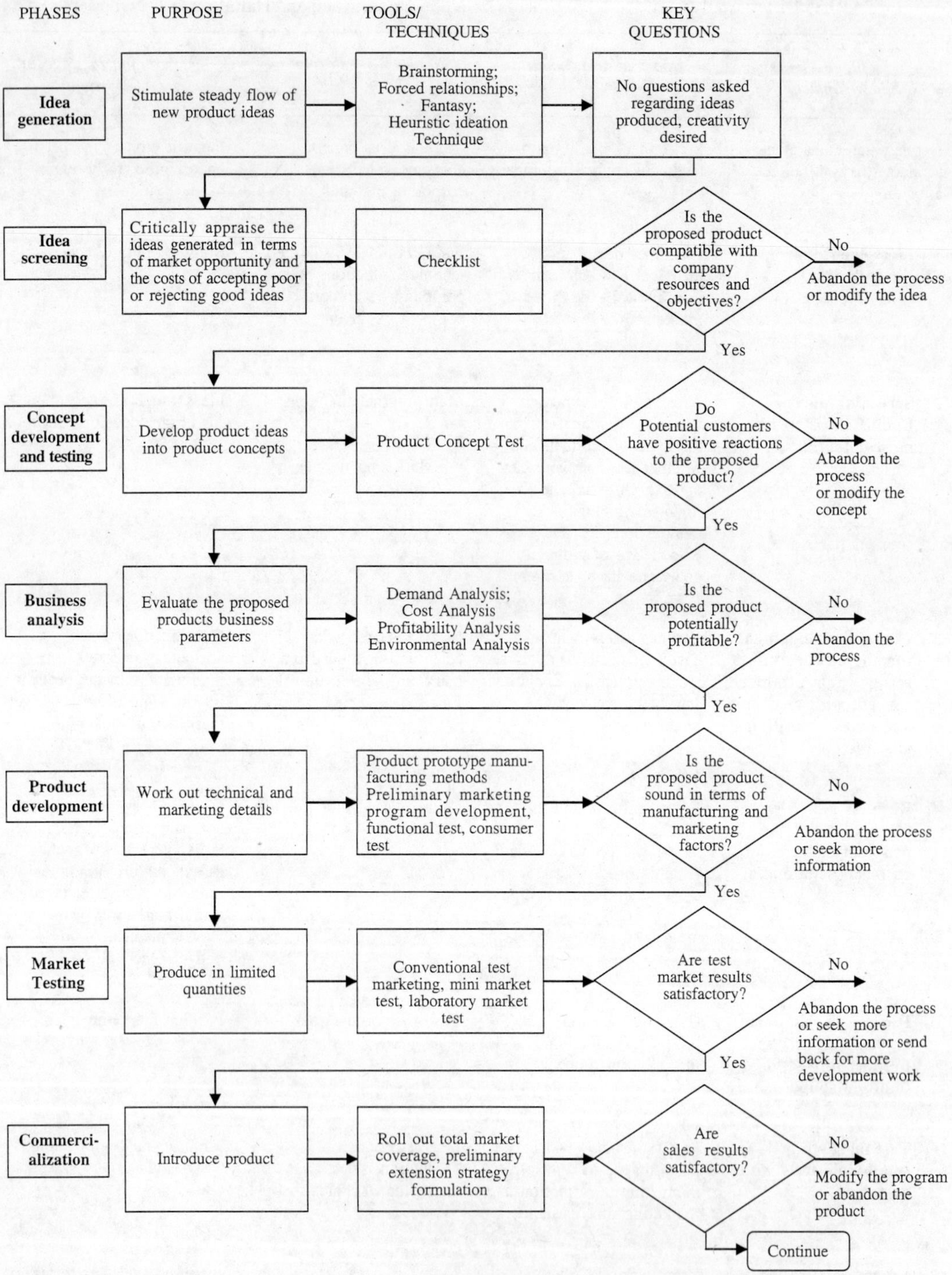

FIGURE 16.5 An overview of new product development process (flow chart for new product development). (*Source:* Willam F. Schoell and Joseph P. Guiltinan, *Marketing,* 5th ed., Allyn & Bacon, Needham Heights, Mass. (1992), p. 323.)

16.6 NEW PRODUCT DEVELOPMENT

What is "new" product—new brand of automobile in the market, a new model of television, the relaunch of a product, reduced price version of brand, or a totally new concept like educational multimedia LCD? Let us try to understand this. Marketing experts have classified the following categories of new products:

1. Product that is new to the company but not new to the market. Part of an existing, growing market can be captured with an imitation product.
2. Products that are significantly different from the existing ones and are good replacements. For example, compact disc replacing a floppy as a storage medium in computers; Laser printer as against inkjet printer.

The need for a balanced portfolio of products and shortened life cycle are the two reasons that motivate marketers to develop new products. According to Philip Kotler, the "marketing Guru", progressive industries focus on two major activities: new product innovation and aggressive selling.

16.6.1 New Product Development Process

The flowchart for new product development is shown in Figure 16.5. In this section, we discuss the various phases of new product development in detail.

(1) **Idea generation.** The term "idea generation" is actually a misnomer. This is because in many companies, ideas do not have to be "generated". They do, however, need to be managed. This involves identifying sources of ideas and developing means by which these sources can be activated. The aim of this stage in the process is to develop a bank of ideas that fall within the parameters set by "new product strategy". Sources of new product ideas exist both within and outside the firms.

Inside the company, technical departments such as research and development (R&D), and design and engineering work on developing applications and technologies are translated into new product ideas. Equally, commercial functions such as sales and marketing are exposed to ideas from customers and competitors. Otherwise, many company employees may have useful ideas: service mechanics, customer relations, manufacturing and warehouse employees are continually exposed to "product problems" which can be translated into new product ideas. Outside the company, competitors, customers, distributors, inventors and universities are fertile repository of information from which new product ideas come. Both sources, however, may have to be organized in such a way as to extract ideas. In short, the sources have to be activated. A large number of techniques may be used to activate sources of new ideas.

This stage decides the fate of a company in the process of its commitment to new product development. In-house development or using acquisitions is a route to new product development. The sources of new product ideas are many and varied. Table 16.2 lists the new product idea generation possibilities:

TABLE 16.2 Sources of new product ideas

Internal sources	*External sources*
Research and development	Customer
Sales marketing	Contract research companies

(*Contd.*)

Internal sources	*External sources*
Production	Consultant
Other executives and board of directors	Technical publications
	Competitors
	Universities
	Inventors
	Advertising agency
	Suppliers
	Government agencies

Companies have to identify the idea generating groups and give them a clear concept of the company's interest fields. It is important that the creative personnel are exposed to idea generating facts. These people are kept away from the distractions from day-to-day problems the company might face. Some companies designate an idea collection point. Many companies in India in the manufacturing sector have a suggestion box or idea box in the factory/office premises. Some companies even provide incentives/bonuses for the employees whose suggestions have been carried forward to the next stage.

To find and nurture novel ideas, an organization should resort to the following plan:

1. Start with a clear strategic vision on product development.
2. Add a culture conducive to cross-functional creativity.
3. Feed in forecast from trends, technology mapping, and outside learning.
4. Invite customer wisdom, intuition, understanding, and input.

In addition, a company's scientists and technicians often make discoveries that lead to new products. At Titan, for example, ideas originate with the marketing brief on the shop floor as an outcome from a new material or process, in a laboratory. An R&D idea, no matter where it comes from is acceptable. Eicher Motors, in the first week of the month, begins with a meeting headed by the CEO and attended by functional heads of manufacturing, sales, R&D and marketing purely for the purpose of product development and brainstorming. They have the policy to set the standards and creativity follows as a natural outcome. The most common methods of idea generation in companies are:

(i) **Brainstorming.** This method, developed by Alex Osborn, uses the recognition that the really new ideas often mix several ideas to produce something that is non-obvious and exciting. Group discussions are held to generate as many new ideas as possible. The group generally consists of six to ten people. The group members are encouraged to be as wild as they want in suggesting solutions. No idea is criticized and hence no ideas are held back. As ideas start to flow, one leads to another. Within a short time, hundreds of ideas can be on the table. Only after ideas are generated freely, the group looks forward to critically evaluate them for the purpose of practicability. A specific problem or goal is set at the beginning of the meeting, by the facilitator.

(ii) **Market analysis.** Companies have to identify the needs of the customers through the use of market research. Most of the companies rely on this method since the customer analysis is the best way of offering a product to fulfill their need. Nowadays, in the field of market research, many consultants and agencies provide the necessary support to companies.

(iii) **Futuristic studies.** Often a long-term forecasting by companies can yield the required results. The customer lifestyle changes over the years, the changing societal trend, etc. can be forecasted and products brought accordingly. Dishwashers, aquaguard, and microwave ovens are some examples to this category of research.

(iv) **Need heedology or gap analysis.** Gap analysis is a technique which plans maps of the market and is used to determine how various products are perceived by users and positioned on the market map. This method helps in understanding the flaws in the existing products and the need for a new product.

A product map is a very useful tool to identify gaps which exist in a market. An example of a market map is given in the section on "concept development".

(v) **Management think tank.** Top managers form the think tank of the companies and act as the source of new product ideas by identifying the consumer needs and changing society?

(vi) **Lifestyle watching.** This technique is used by companies in ascertaining the usage of a product. For example, Maruti Omni was intended as a cargo vehicle but however, the usage of the product showed that it was more used as a passenger vehicle. Hence the positioning and the product itself were changed to the requirement. Similarly, P&G studied the washing habits of 3000 customers in the target segment of its middle market laundry brand, Ariel Gain Super Soaker, to identify the one critical need of removing grease stains that the brand addresses.

(vii) **Global study.** Sometimes, many multinational companies translate their experiences from another country. Some Indian companies search various products, which are not available in India and offer this product after obtaining the necessary agreements. Many times, a product successful in one country fails in other. Soya milk which has not succeeded in India is highly successful in USA.

(viii) **Morphology approach.** This method analyzes the structural dimensions of the product, which helps in getting to their relationships between them. When a writing instrument is analyzed, the extent of its length, clarity, and convenience become the relationship factors from where a new product can be found out. Research on the old Ford Escort indicated that a three-box design was favoured than a hatchback. Apart from more space for luggage, consumers felt the boot also provided more safety than a hatch. Indian customers also told Ford that rear seats were used for 70% of the time. In other markets, the rear seat is used for less than 10% of the time, whereas in India, it is used extensively to cram in people. So, the Ikon was to have a roomier rear seat with full roll-down windows, reading lights and comfortable centre seating as well. The rear door openings are claimed to be the largest in the industry while the height of the chassis is such that it will be easy to get in and out. Ford Ikon has also considered one of the factors as poor road conditions during monsoons in India.

(2) **Idea screening.** The next stage in the product development process involves an initial assessment of the extent of demand for the ideas generated and of the capability the company that has to make the product. As this is the first of several evaluative stages, only a rough assessment can be made of an idea at this stage, which will not yet be expressed in terms of design, materials, features, or price. Internal company opinion can be canvassed from R&D, sales, marketing, finance, and production to assess whether the idea has potential, is practical, would fit a market demand, and could be produced by the existing plant. It is also helpful

in estimating the payback period. The net result of this stage is a body of ideas which are acceptable for further development. Several checklists and forms have been devised to facilitate this process.

During the screening process, a company evaluates the commercial potential of a new product. The commercial potential of a product includes such criteria as profitability, marketability, and costs of production. Screening also calls for the participation of other departments in the development of new ideas within the company. The ideas and advice of people at different levels of production aid the product in areas such as its eventual, ease of production, and production costs. Allowing all levels of employees to be involved in the process increases the empowerment within the company.

After the necessary ideas are generated, the next stage is to reduce their number to a manageable size. It is important to expand each idea into a full product concept. New product ideas should fit into the company's overall strategy. They should also build on the company's resources and skills. They have to collect facts and opinions which are quickly available, bearing on the product ideas as business propositions. This stage should translate the ideas into business terms. At this stage, it is important to identify the best sources of facts and qualified opinions.

Product profiles quantified data. Product profiling method as shown in Table 16.3 is a useful screening tool. It assumes the following:

1. The ratings are averages of response by number of respondents on a five-point scale.
2. Each criterion is given a weightage depending upon its importance.
3. Scores and weights are multiplied and the total weighted score is worked out.
4. The overall rating $R = \Sigma W_i S_i$, while the scores range from 1 to 5.

Table 16.3 shows the calculated results for a particular product idea.

TABLE 16.3 Calculations for a product idea

			← Score (S_i) →					
	Criterion	*Weight* W_i	*Very good* (5)	*Good* (4)	*Average* (3)	*Poor* (2)	*Very poor* (1)	W_iS_i
(1)	Newness	0.15			×			0.45
(2)	Feasibility	0.13		×				0.52
(3)	Saleability	0.12	×					0.60
(4)	Profit	0.11	×					0.55
(5)	Life	0.10			×			0.30
(6)	Perishability	0.10					×	0.10
(7)	Labour	0.09		×				0.36
(8)	Logistics	0.09		×				0.36
(9)	Compatibility	0.08			×			0.24
(10)	Aesthetics	0.03	×					0.15
	Total	$\Sigma W_i = 1.00$						$\Sigma W_i S_i = 3.53$

(3) **Concept development and testing.** Once screened, an idea is turned into a more clearly specified concept and testing this concept begins for its fit with company capability and its fulfillment of customer expectations. Developing the concept from the idea requires that a decision be made on the content and form of the idea. For example, a food company which has generated the idea of a low-calorie spread as a sandwich filler will decide on the type of spread—whether it has to be a low calorie peanut butter, fish or mincemeat, or a mayonnaise based concoction. All these concept variations may be specified and then subjected to concept tests. Internally, the development team needs to know which varieties are most compatible with current production plant, which require plant acquisition, and which require new supplies. This needs to be matched externally, in relation to which versions are more attractive to customers. The latter involves direct customer research to identify the appeal of the product concept, or alternative concepts to the customer. Concept testing is worth spending time and effort on collecting sufficient data to provide/acquire information upon which the full business analysis is made.

A perceptual map can be used as a tool to estimate customer reaction to various types of spread. One such map is shown in Figure 16.6.

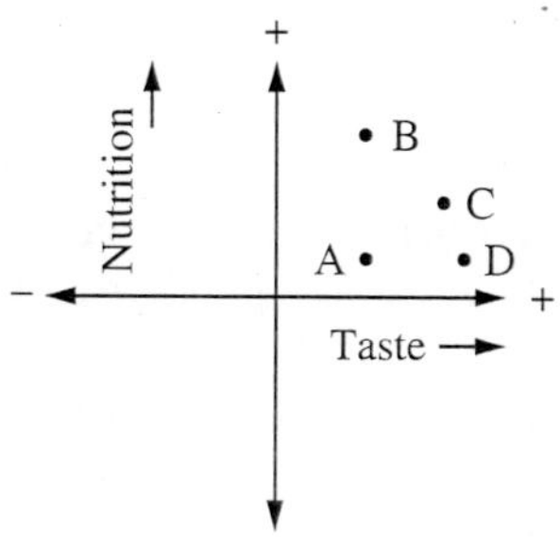

FIGURE 16.6 Perceptual map for concept testing.

The product map in Figure 16.6 indicates that spread A is low on nutrition and low on taste; B is high on nutrition but low on taste; C is high on nutrition as well as taste. Finally, D is high on taste and low on nutrition. Such maps could be useful in conceptualization of ideas.

(4) **Business analysis.** At this stage, the major "go–no go" decision is made. The company needs to be sure that the venture is potentially worthwhile, as expenditure will increase dramatically in prototype development after this stage. The analysis is based on the fullest information available to the company so far. It encompasses:

- A market analysis detailing potential total market, estimated market share within specific time horizon, competing products, likely price, break-even volume, identification of early adopters, and specific market segments.
- Explicit statement of technical aspects, costs, production implications, supplier management and further R&D.
- Explanation of how the project fits with corporate objectives.

The sources of information for this stage are both internal and external, incorporating any market or technical research carried out so far. The output of this stage is a development plan with budget and an initial marketing plan.

In business analysis, the company decides whether the new product fits well within the company's product line distribution methods and promotion methods. Also marketers further test the potential for sales, profits, market growth, and competitiveness. Human welfare is also considered in the operation of the company. The ideas are made more specific in this stage. This is the stage where the concept has to be further refined and made into business terms. The aspects that need to be formulated for making an idea into a concept are:

1. Target audience of the new product
2. The primary benefit of the new product
3. The usage pattern of the new product

Based on these, once the concept has been developed, it has to be tested. Consumer reactions are obtained by using a verbal description or a picture of the product and asking for unbiased opinions. In major manufacturing industries, products are brought to business or industrial consumers at designated test sites, and developers work closely with these consumers to spot the problems and refine the designs. After this, the company has to project costs, profits, and returns on investment and cash flow if the product is placed on the market. Projections of potential sales at various prices need to be made, as well as detailed cost projections for different volumes of production. Start-up and continuing costs, fixed and variable costs, and the impact of economies of scale need to be determined. Tentative marketing plans need to be set, along with the costs associated with them. Lastly, a set of full-blown budgets is required to estimate the potential return on the product. Thus business analysis must include an assessment of the amount of risk the company will face if the new product is introduced. If the new product can be produced using existing production and marketing capabilities, the risk is lower. Less investment in new plant and equipment will be needed, and the marketer can benefit from already acquired knowledge of the market. TVS Suzuki and Bajaj Auto use the technique of target costing to determine the price of the product and working backwards to fix the maximum acceptable cost to develop new products. ATAR and other financial tools are also used for financial feasibility check.

(5) **Product development and testing.** This is the stage in which prototypes are physically made. Several tasks are related to this development. First, the finished product will be assessed regarding its level of functional performance. Until now, the product has only existed in theoretical form or mock-up. It is only when components are brought together in a functional form that the validity of the theoretical product can be definitively established. Second, it is the first physical step in the manufacturing chain. Whilst manufacturing considerations have entered into previous deliberations, it is not until the prototype is developed that alterations to the specification or to manufacturing configurations can be designed and put into place. Third, the product has to be tested with potential customers to assess the overall impression of the test product. Some categories of product are more amenable to customer testing than others. Capital equipment, for example, is difficult to be assessed by potential customers in the same way as a chocolate bar can be taste-tested, or a dishwasher evaluated by an in-house trial. One evolving technique in industrial marketing, however, is called *beta-testing*, practised informally by many industrial product developers. Beta-testing is carried out at the potential customer's site as compared with alpha-testing, which is carried out in-house.

Once a company reaches prototype process development, the fourth stage of new product development, it is committing to spend a lot of money on the initial production of a still unproven product. Product development is aimed at better serving through a disciplined process, with clearly defined targets for every stage, continuous interaction with other functions and more than one eye on costs, delays, and the extent of manufacturability. During this stage, many companies implement computer-aided production programs. Not only do these reduce overall costs in production, but also should a flaw be found with either the product or the production process, computer-aided production systems can easily correct the problem. This saves valuable time in redesign and production restructuring. By getting the product to the market more quickly, a company can convert potential profit into realized profit. In a typical sequence, production engineers and R&D specialists construct a model; the marketing department develops a brand name to match the idea or concept; packaging is designed; and the major elements of the marketing mix are put together. The positioning strategy is also identified. At this stage, many different functional areas of the company are called upon to cooperate in the creation of prototypes and development of production or delivery processes, marketing plans and other elements required to make the idea a reality.

At Bajaj Auto, product development is carried out concurrently, involving activities like product definition and design, manufacturing process development, marketing, planning, and tooling. This involves different departments in different application areas, industrial design on styling, engineering on machine tool design and systems on system configuration. Maruti Udyog has introduced Maruti *Alto* to provide the customer with a city car which is more roomy than Maruti 800 and has an engine which is more powerful than Maruti 800. Maruti *Alto* is positioned in between Maruti 800 and Maruti *Zen*, and is priced in between the prices of these two cars.

(6) **Test marketing.** The penultimate phase in the development cycle called *test marketing*, consists of small-scale tests with customers. Until now, the idea, the concept, and the product have been "tested" or "evaluated" in a somewhat artificial context. Although several of these evaluations may well have compared the new product to competitive offering, other elements of the marketing mix have not been tested, nor has the likely marketing reaction by competitors. At this stage, the appeal of the product is tested amidst the mix of activities comprising the market launch: salesmanship, advertising, sales promotion, distributor incentives and public relations.

Test marketing is not always feasible or desirable. Management must decide whether the costs of test marketing can be justified by the additional information that will be gathered. Further, not all products are suitable of a small-scale launch. Passenger cars, for example, have market testing complete before the launch, while other product, once launched on a small scale, cannot be withdrawn, as with personal insurance. Finally, the delay involved in getting a new product to market may be advantageous to the competition, who can use the opportunity to be "first-to-market". Competitors may also wait until a company's test market results are known and use the information to help their own launch, or can distort the test results using their own tactics.

Practical problems like these have encouraged the development and use of computer-based market simulation models, which use basic models of consumer buying as inputs. Information on consumer awareness, trail and repeat purchases is collected via limited surveys or store data, and is used to predict adoption of the new product.

Information mangers can also decide if they have the right target market, the right-price, and the right level of advertising.

In this stage, the new product and relevant marketing programme are tried out for the first time in well-selected market segments under representative marketing environments. Hence, test marketing is the process of introducing a new product or service to a small "test market", i.e., considered to be representative of the large target market. Test marketing has many alternatives like advertisement with coupons and samples. Launching a new product in the market is risky because the product development responds to changing customer needs and test-new technology, shortening of product life cycle, and increased domestic and foreign competition.

Test marketing is done mainly to identify the following:

- Potential sales volume generation
- Identification of innovative buyers
- Comparison of target and actual number/type of buyers
- Recognition of strong points of product by buyers
- Ability of advertising message to transmit products strong points
- Competence to attain planned distribution
- Potentials for repeat purchases

Rationale for test marketing

1. Test marketing should be conducted when the potential financial loss to the company through new product failure, or through the failure of market plan or approach is significantly greater than the cost of the proposed test marketing procedure.
2. Where the cost and risk of product failure are high relative to the profit and probability of success test marketing is recommended.
3. Where the difference in the scale of investment involved in the test versus national launch route has an important bearing on deciding whether to test or not. If the company investment for a national launch is far greater than the test launch, testing should be preferred.
4. When the possibilities of and the speed with which copying of the test product by competitors are great, testing may be avoided. This is particularly relevant in soft technology industries.

Objectives of test marketing. Test marketing is undertaken in order to:

- Find out the consumer needs of buying
- Evaluate impact of local advertising and promotion during the test
- Evaluate the market potential for other competing product
- Find out the area coverage for sales
- Find the consumers ability to buy the product based on price

Process of test marketing. The process of test marketing includes:

- City selection
- Selection of the sales representatives
- Duration of the test
- Selecting suitable data
- Implementation

The test market area to be selected should be a restricted geographical area, which represents the national market. In India, cites like Bangalore, Mumbai, Chandigarh, Delhi, and Kolkata are usually selected by companies to test market their products. However, where the purpose of the test is to estimate the sales potential of a product to be nationally marketed, markets in at least four geographic areas should be used. According to reports of national survey, Pepsodent failed in the first test marketing mainly because it was test marketed only at Kolkata. As the significance of the variables to be tested decreases, the number of markets necessary to reflect the effect of these variables increases. Marketing achievements in the test-market should be recorded and then projected nation-wide. For example, if monthly volume in 2 per cent of the country is ₹ 2000, at national launch the sales could be 2000/0.02 = ₹ 100,000.

All available data should be carefully reviewed to make sure that the test-market is by and large representative of the whole market in terms of social class, caste, age, and other demographic variables. Also all available data should be reviewed to make sure that the test-market is representative in terms of consumption of similar or substitute products. It is also advisable to be assured that competitive strength in the test-market is approximately to that equal in the whole market. After having considered the above factors in test marketing, it is also advisable to check up different components of the marketing-mix to be employed in the test marketing and their probable future relationships. It is important because distortion in any one component at the commercialization stage would bring about distortion in the test results and the actual product performance. For example, if testing is accompanied by an aggressive sales promotion campaign but not so in commercialization stage then subsequent results would be different. Based on the response in the test marketing, a company can follow any of the following three options:

1. Abandonment of the product
2. Additional testing
3. Commercialization

The test marketing needs to incorporate the following as the tools:

- Sales personal demonstrations
- Free samples
- Coupons
- Local advertisement
- Door-to-door distributions

Controlling the test market. Controlled test marketing allows the company to the insure factors, i.e., alpha testing which means the testing from within the company and limited advertising on buying behaviour. A sample of consumers can be tested or interviewed later to find their impression of the product. However, controlled test marketing provides no information on how to sell the new product. This technique also exposes the product and product features to competition. Even the company does not have to use its own sales force, give trade allowances or buying distributions to agents.

Simulated test marketing. In this testing, 30–40 qualified shoppers have to be selected and questioned about brand familiarity and preferences in specified consumption of product. This testing involves interview with the shoppers about the product that is moving fast and about placing the new product in the market. Consumers receive a small amount of money and are invited into a store where they may buy the product. Some weeks later, they are interviewed over phone to determine product attribute, usage, satisfaction and repurchase frequency and are offered an opportunity for repurchasing of the product. Results are incorporated in forecasting the sales levels.

(7) **Commercialization or launch.** This is the final stage of the initial development process and is very costly. It involves decision making on issues such as when to launch the product, where to launch it, how and to whom to launch. It is based on information collected throughout the development process. With regard to timing, important considerations include:

1. Seasonality of the product
2. Whether the launch should fit any trade or commercial event
3. Whether the new product is a replacement for the old one.

Location for large companies describes the number of countries in which the product will be launched and whether national launches need be simultaneous or they need to roll out from one country to another. For smaller companies, the decision is restricted to a narrower geographical region. The factors upon which such decisions are based depend upon the required lead-times for product to reach all the distributive outlets and the relative power and influence of channel members.

Launch strategy encompasses any advertising and trade promotions necessary. Space must be booked, copy and visual material prepared, both for the launch proper and for the pre-sales into the distribution pipeline. The sales force may require extra training in order to sell the new product effectively.

The final target segment should not at this stage, be a major decision for companies who have developed a product with the market in mind and who have executed the various testing stages. Attention should be more focused on identifying the likely early adopters of the product and on focusing communications on them. In industrial markets, early adopters tend to be innovators in their own markets. The major concern of the launch should be the development of a strong, unified message to promote to the market. Once accepted by the market, the company obtains feedback to continue the improvement and redevelopment of the product.

Methods of launching:

(i) *Immediate national launch:* This is one way to overcome the competition and to save on the cost of launch. The risk of national launch is that it leaves the company with many problems, which were not contemplated during the test marketing. Production routines that work well in theory may not result as expected. Early problems of supply may create problems during actual launch.

(ii) *Rolling launch:* This is an alternative to the full national launch. It involves building towards full national coverage by starting with one or two recognized distribution areas, then gradually adding new regions to those already served as experience and success of the product further increases. This helps the company to concentrate on getting the logistics and production schedules in tune with the requirements. Coca Cola, Kellogg's, and several other major players including HLL use this strategy effectively.

The launch cycle. Once test marketing gives a "go ahead" the launch cycle begins. The launch of a product proceeds in four phases: (i) prelaunch preparation, (ii) announcement, (iii) beachhead, and (iv) early growth. Figure 16.7 depicts the product launch cycle.

(i) *Prelaunch preparation.* It consists of the activities before the point at which the product is officially offered for sale. These activities typically include marking pre-announcements, building marketing capability, establishing service capability, promoting the new product via public relations, and filling the distribution pipeline. Together, these activities have the purpose of building enthusiasm and ensuring that the company is ready to meet market demand.

(ii) *Announcement.* Announcement is the second phase when the product is officially offered to the complete market. With the announcement, all decisions are finalized.

(iii) *Beachhead.* In this third phase, efforts focus on achieving market awareness and generating an initial flow of sales. Expenditures in beachhead stage tend to exceed sales revenue.

(iv) *Early growth.* This is the fourth phase of launch when usually, sales grow as customer interest in the new product grows. If sales are not growing, a decision needs to be made urgently. In general, there are five decision options:

1. Increase spending
2. Revise the launch/marketing strategy
3. Revise the product (a costly, time-consuming, and potentially risky alternative)
4. Pull the product temporarily from the marketplace which is a risky option, and often does not to lead to success the second time around
5. Abandon the product.

Option 5 is to be considered last. Note that options 1 and 2 should be considered initially. If these two options do not work, then options 3, 4, and 5 should be considered in that order.

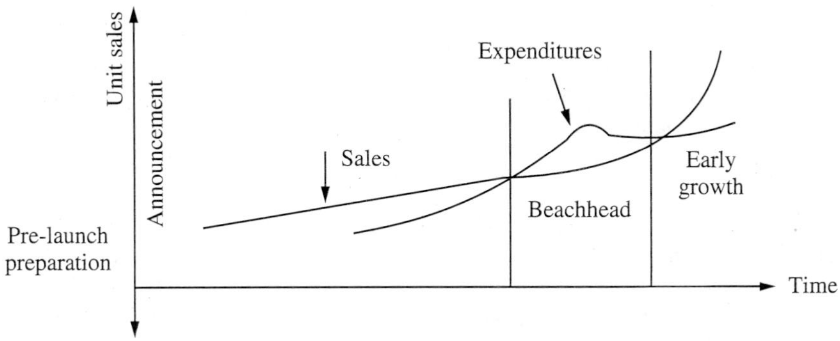

FIGURE 16.7 Product launch cycle.

Launch control protocol. One tool that is useful during prelaunch preparation is the launch control protocol. The launch protocol is used to monitor and control activities during the launch cycle. The launch control protocol identifies key success measures during product launch. Such measures correspond to sales volume, profitability, market awareness etc.

A launch control protocol is undertaken in four steps:

***Step* 1.** Potential problems that might occur during a particular product's launch are identified. Ways to identify such problems include reviewing the situation from the marketing plan to outline potential threat, and looking at the company's product launch history to indicate problems from previous product launches. Simulations and role play, in which employees represent various channel members and competitors, are especially powerful for revealing problems. A company can find out, after several iterations of a rolè-playing exercise, a list of foreseeable problems and remedies can be established for these problems. As it turned out in one case, the company was able to stay one step ahead of competitors because they had foreseen competitor responses and potential market problems through role play.

***Step* 2.** The second step in a launch control protocol is to select the problems that should be monitored and controlled. Selection should be based on the potential impact of the problem on the commercial success of the product. Problems that could severely hamper success should be selected.

***Step* 3.** The third step in a launch control protocol is to design a system for monitoring and controlling each of the selected problems. To do this, it is necessary, first, to identify a measurable variable that corresponds to the problem. For example, if a selected problem is "sales lower than expected" what would represent a situation of lower than expected: A possible quantification is unit sales less than 100,000 units? Revenue sales less than ₹ 1 million? The boundary of a problem which exists should be specified. The limits of expected outcomes should be specified.

***Step* 4.** The fourth step in a launch control protocol is to develop remedies or contingency plans which set out a course of action that the company can undertake in the event that the problem arises. Let us take up an example where 16 activities are listed. These activities are classified as:

(a) *Production and distribution related activities:* 1. Acquire production machine, 2. Inspect product, 3. Further production, 4. Transport

(b) *Materials related activities:* 5. Locate suppliers, 6. Get raw materials

(c) *Sales and distribution related activities:* 7. Appointment of sales manager, 8. Select salesman, 9. Negotiate with distributors

(d) *Promotional activities:* 10. Plan sampling campaign, 11. Coupon tie-up

(e) *Advertising related activities:* 12. Contact with ad agency, 13. Finalize advertising copy, 14. Select media plan, 15. Synchronize advertising and promotion, 16. Initial advertising, sampling, and couponing.

These activities are shown as a CPM network in Figure 16.8.

Critical path analysis. One method of managing the issue of launch timing and coordination is called critical path analysis. This method structures the sequence of activities and identifies those that are most critical to the success of the timing.

When a launch is planned, a wide range of supporting activities are carried out in the marketing and production areas. Some activities are independent and can proceed simultaneously. For example, the development of advertising copy does not depend upon the negotiations with raw material suppliers. But some activities are sequential. For example, advertising copy must be stocked before production begins.

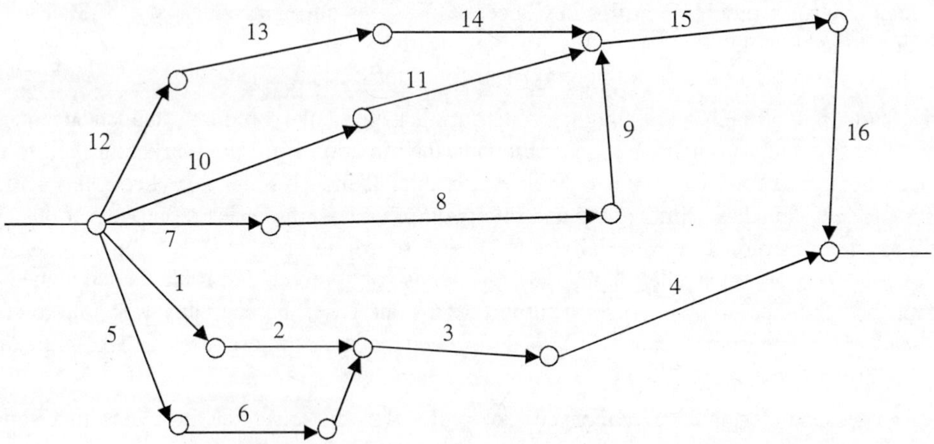

FIGURE 16.8 Simple critical path analysis (example).

Techniques of critical path analysis help in structuring the various sequential and parallel activities in the form of a network. For example, Figure 16.8 shows a simple critical path network for a new product launch. That is, it provides information to:

- Show the interrelationship between tasks
- Evaluate alternative strategies and approaches
- Pinpoint responsibilities of various task forces

- Check progress at interim points against original plans and objectives
- Forecast bottlenecks
- Replan and redesign a project with revised data.

Management of launch. As the product moves towards launch, there is a shift in the management responsibility. The design and testing phases are handled by a product team comprising of specialists who are essentially experts in converting voice of customer into technical product. They know every detail about the product. For planning a launch, a different set of skills is needed such as marketing mix optimization and sales skills. In the launch team, a product development specialist is added along with marketing experts to achieve success. It is a good strategy to have hand holding between product development people, project management people, and sales persons for the first few months of the launch. Later on, there can be a transfer of control to the sales group.

It should be recalled that there are certain changes which are likely to occur between test marketing and actual launch. Firstly, economic changes may occur which affect the price. Secondly, distribution channels may have to be modified. Thirdly, competitors might become more aggressive and care has to be taken to ward them off.

Control system and tracking. A control system comprises the following steps: (i) plans are made depending upon forecasts, (ii) forecasts are compared with actual results in market to initial diagnosing of the difference. Modification of marketing mix and production is done in an attempt to reduce the difference between forecast and actual results, and (iii) until a full diagnosis is done, production has to be tuned with demand to avoid overproduction or underproduction.

This systematic comparison between forecast and actual sales is termed as *tracking*.

16.7 MODELS UTILIZED IN VARIOUS PHASES OF NEW PRODUCT DEVELOPMENT

16.7.1 Similarity/Dissimilarity Analysis Applied to Comparison of Product Concepts

In new product development, it becomes essential to convert an idea into a concept. If there are several concepts, it becomes essential to choose the best feasible amongst them. Similarity analysis is often resorted to. Let us consider three types of tiers: (i) Steel belted radial, (ii) Side reinforced, and (iii) Heavy duty. To find out the best option, these need to be compared for their characteristics. Tables 16.4 and 16.5 help in carrying out the similarly/dissimilarity analysis.

TABLE 16.4 Y–N classification

		Criteria			
	Product	*Warranty > 60,000 km*	*Steel belted radial*	*Side reinforced*	*Heavy duty*
Product	A	Y	Y	Y	Y
↓	B	Y	Y	N	Y
	C	N	Y	Y	N
	D	N	N	N	N
	E	Y	N	N	N

TABLE 16.5 Similarity matrix

	A	*B*	*C*	*D*	*E*
A	–				
B	3/4	–			
C	1/2	1/4	–		
D	0	1/4	1/2	–	
E	1/4	1/2	1/4	3/4	–

Result of paired comparison: Group 1 (A, B); Group 2: (D, E) Group 3: (C).

16.7.2 A-T-A-R Model Applied to Financial Analysis in Business Worthiness Phase

Crawford developed this approach where A, T, A, R stand for awareness, trial, availability, and repeat purchase respectively. Advertising and promotion are expected to be 90% effective; Tier percent is 30%; 50% retailers make it available to the customer; market research suggests 25% shall repurchase the tablets. If one bottle contains one month requirement of 30 tablets, the monthly bottle consumption shall be: If market size is 1,000,000: Monthly consumption = (1000,000 × 0.9 × 0.3 × 0.5 × 0.25). Annual consumption = 33750 × 12 = 405,000 per year. If the profit margin is ₹2 per bottle, the annual profit shall be ₹810,000.

16.7:3 Expected Commercial Value Approach

This approach was developed by Cooper, et al. It uses a decision tree methodology. Referring to the Figure 16.9,

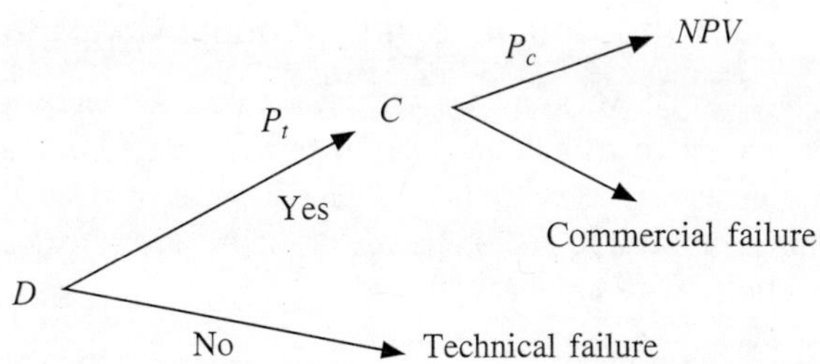

Key
D : Development costs (₹)
P_t : Probability of technical success
C : Commercialization cost
P_c : Probability of commercial (Launch) success

FIGURE 16.9 Tree diagram.

The formula used is:

$$\text{Expected Commercial Value } (ECV) = (NPV \times P_c - C)P_t - D$$

Here, *NPV* is the net present value of product concepts future earnings discounted to the present. An example of the *ECV* approach is indicated in Table 16.6 as follows:

TABLE 16.6 Sample calculation for *ECV*

Product concept	*NPV*	P_t	P_c	*D* ₹	*C* ₹	*ECV*
A	30	0.8	0.5	3	4	5.8
B	45	0.5	0.4	5	4	2

It is observed that even though concept B has a higher *NPV* as compared to A, its *ECV* is lower than concept A owing to lower probabilities of technological and commercial success and higher development cost *D*.

16.7.4 House of Quality for Converting Voice of Customer to Technical Specifications

This technique has already been discussed in Section 14.2. However, due to the importance of quality function deployment (QFD), we consider an illustration of developing technical specifications of lead pencils to enable the product to compete effectively with competitors X and Y as shown in Figure 16.10 which also indicates the results of calculations done in QFD stage one. The various steps of calculation are: (i) Calculate absolute weight (*AW*) of each customer need by using the formula: AW = Rate of importance on 5 points scale × Ratio of improvement × Sales point. For a customer need recognized as 'point lasts' $AW = (5 \times 1.25 \times 1.5) = 9.4$, which is 44% on percent scale.

The cell entry for the cell is product of 'point lasts' (customer need) and 'time between sharpening' (engineering parameter) and derived as

$$\text{Cell value} = \text{Percent weightage } 44 \times \text{Correlation value } 9 \text{ as shown by}$$
$$= 44 \times 9 = 396 \text{ in the matrix}$$

Engineering parameters

A–1 Pencil (Customer Needs)	Length ▲	Time between sharpening ▲	Lead dust generated ▼	Hexagonality ▲		Rate of importance	Company now	Competitor X	Competitor Y	Plan	Ratio of improvement	Sales points	Absolute wt.	Demanded wt.
Easy to hold	○ 42			○ 42		3	4	3	3	4	1	1	3.0	14%
Does not Smear		○ 42	◎ 207			4	5	4	5	5	1	1.2	4.8	23%
Point lasts	△ 44	◎ 396	○ 132			5	4	5	3	5	1.25	1.5	9.4	44%
Does not roll	△ 19			◎ 171		3	3	3	3	4	1.33	1	4.0	19%
Total	105	465	339	213	1122						Total		21.2	100%
%	9%	41%	30%	19%	100%									
company now	5″	3pgs	3g	70%										
competitor x	5″	5pgs	2g	80%										
competitor y	4″	2.5pgs	4g	60%										
plan	5.5″	6pgs	2g	80%										

Main Correlations
◎ 9 = strong correlation
○ 3 = some correlation
△ 1 = possible correlation
Sales Points = 1.5, 1.2, or 1

FIGURE 16.10 The "house of quality for QFD process".

The cell values of 69 and 396 are added to yield 465 which is 41% marking time between sharpening as the most important technical specification. Likewise, targets of length of pencil of 5.5" are derived by comparison with competitor X.

Time between sharpening expressed by number of pages equals 6 pages, lead dust generated equals 2 grams, and hexagonality is 80%; these are the requisites for pencils to beat the competition. These values are chosen so that they are greater than those of competitors X and Y.

16.8 MANAGING PRODUCT LIFE CYCLE

The concept of a product life cycle has occupied a prominent place in the marketing literature, both as a forecasting tool and a guideline for corporate marketing strategy. In its simplest form, it serves as a descriptive model of the stages of market acceptance of a product. It can thus be considered the "supply" view of the diffusion model which conceives a product reaching the customer through a "diffusion" process. The concept is borrowed from biology and sees the life of product as analogous to the life of an organism, in that it progresses through the stages of birth, growth, maturity, decline, and death. In view of its importance, the diffusion process has been discussed including intensive mathematical analysis.

Biological studies have established the S-shaped logistic curve as the best representation of the process of life. This representation has been widely accepted in the study of product life cycle, with the result that PLCs are said to have four identifiable stages, namely introduction phase, growth phase, the maturity and saturation phase, and a decline phase. Figure 16.11 illustrates a typical PLC.

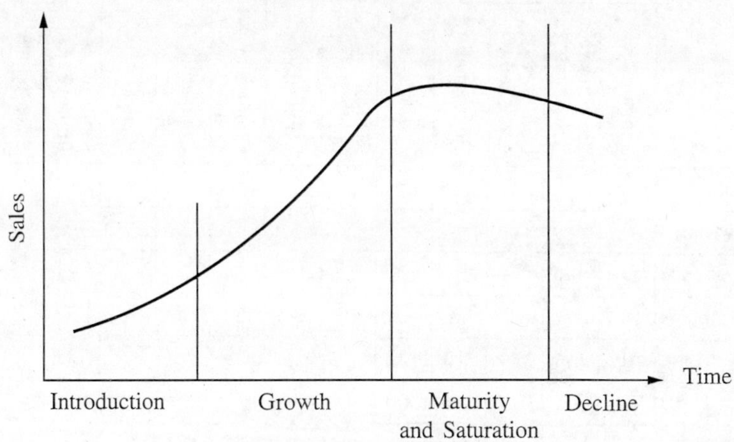

FIGURE 16.11 Product life cycle.

The general pattern of product life cycle was found in a number of empirical investigations. The sales histories of consumer products indicated that 52 per cent of the products (non-food grocery products, food products, and durables) followed the general pattern of the PLC model.

A number of studies were conducted on the product life cycle of industrial products. It was found that the United Kingdom sales trend of automobile components, chemicals, and general engineering products is represented fairly accurately by the general PLC model. In many of these and other PLC studies, the life cycle has been found to be either a modified S-shape function PLC or some alternative function. New food products do pass through a period of slow growth, followed by a stage of rapid growth. Sales of "mature" products, on the other hand, did not necessarily follow the predicted stable pattern. Three patterns were observed: (1) the expected stable maturity, (2) a growth maturity due to some changes in market conditions, and (3) innovative maturity, which is due to some innovation by the processors. Concerning the decline stage, the empirical evidence shows that some products ultimately reach a stage of decline.

However, this empirical support for the S-shaped product life cycle is not universal. Polli and Cook (1969),[1] who tested the life cycle model against sales behaviour for 140 consumer non-durable products, found the sales behaviour to be consistent with the PLC model for less than half the products studied. Their conclusion, therefore, was:

"After completing the initial test of the life cycle expressed as a verifiable model of sales behaviour, we must register strong reservations about its general validity, even stated in its weakest, most flexible form (*ibid*)."

An examination of the PLC of the product forms of cigarettes, make-up bases, and cereals suggests that "no PLC rule (indicting the movement of the product from one stage to another) can be developed". The lack of any conclusive evidence concerning the validity of the concept requires that it should be examined carefully.

16.8.1 Various Stages of Product Life Cycle

Whether one accepts the S-shaped curve as a "typical" product sales pattern or only as a pattern which holds for some products (but not for others), it is useful to briefly review the conclusions which are frequently stated concerning the relationship between the various PLC stages and the various marketing forces. These generalizations should be viewed, however, only as hypotheses and not as facts. Only an examination of the sales pattern of a given product in a given marketing environment can lead to the acceptance or rejection of such hypotheses.

Introduction stage. The introductory sales of a product are believed to be relatively slow, even after its technical problems have been ironed out, due to a number of marketing forces and consumer behaviour factors. The major marketing obstacle to rapid introduction of a product is often distribution. Retail outlets are often reluctant to introduce new products, and many prefer to wait until a track record has been established before including them in their stock. Imagine, for example, that you are the marketing manager of a super market with an average inventory of 10,000 items. How likely would you be to buy, stock, and devote precious shelf space to a new and untested cereal?

Sequential regional introduction of a new product again leads to a slow and lengthy introductory period (when the product life cycle is developed for the entire national market) and often reflects logistical problems with physical distribution.

Consumer acceptance of new products tends to be relatively slow. The new-product diffusion models discussed later have highlighted the fact that only 2.5 per cent of consumers tend to be "innovators." The newer the product, the greater the marketing effort required to create the demand for it. The length of the introductory period depends on the product's complexity, its degree of newness, its fit into consumer needs, the presence of competitive substitutes of one form or another, and the nature, magnitude and effectiveness of the introductory marketing effort.

At this stage, it is usually assumed that there are no competitors, and some even define the market structure at this stage as virtual monopoly. Yet, although there are a very few really radical innovations with no existing substitutes, most new products face considerable competition from existing products.

In addition to competition from existing products, many new products face severe competitive pressure from other new products. There have been a notable number of cases in which two firms introduce similar products almost at the same time, an occurrence quite possible if the two companies are working on similar technological developments. In other cases, one company goes through a test market, which is noticed by a competitor who decides after observing the first company's test market results, to introduce a similar product. Whatever the reasons leading to do it, if two or more firms introduce products at about the same time, the result is likely to be a shorter introductory period.

The length of the introductory period is one of the most crucial aspects of the product life cycle. From a managerial point of view, the shorter the introductory period, the better it is. The marketing strategy of subsequent stages is often based on the assumption that those who buy the product in the introductory stages are the innovators, and those who buy it in subsequent stages are the late adapters or laggards who respond differently to the firm's marketing strategy. The classification of a buyer as an innovator or laggard depending on the time that elapses between his purchase and the introduction of the product may be misleading. Consider, for example, a buyer who hears about the product for the first time two years after its introduction.

In general, a study of new product adoption process has indicated that buyers can be classified in 5 categories: (i) innovators 2.5%, (ii) early adopters 13.5%, (iii) early majority 34%, (iv) late majority 34%, and (v) laggards 16%. This is depicted in Figure 16.12.

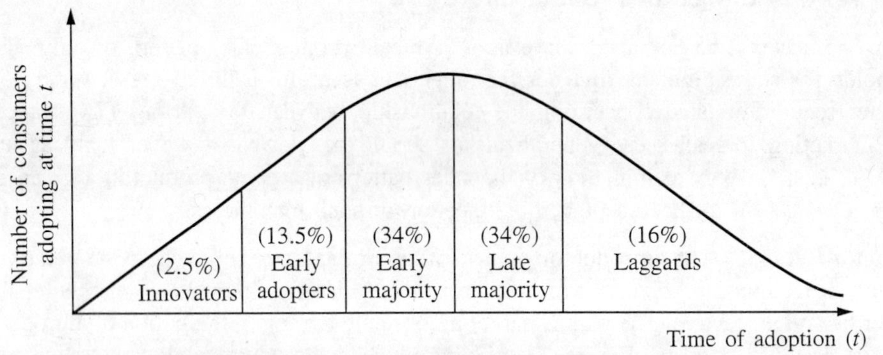

FIGURE 16.12 New product adoption categories.

Growth stage. The growth stage begins when demand for the new product starts increasing rapidly. In the case of frequently-purchased products, innovators move from the trial to repeat purchase if they are satisfied with the product though innovators may influence others by word-of-mouth, which is often considered the most effective mode of communication.

Of greatest importance at this stage is the entry of competitors who, through their advertising and promotional efforts, increase the total demand for the product. When Kodak entered the instant photography market, for example, Polaroid sales increased significantly from 3.5 million cameras shopped to U.S. distributors and dealers to 4.5 million units, while Kodak sold during that period over 2 million units.

Maturity stage. The maturity or saturation stage occurs when distribution has reached its planned or unplanned peak, and the percentage of total population that is ever going to buy the product has been reached. Volume reflecting the number of customers, quantity purchased, and frequency of purchase is stable in the maturity stage.

This is the stage in which it becomes difficult to maintain effective distribution, and price competition is quite common.

Decline stage. Changes in competitive activities, consumer preferences, product technology, and other environmental forces tend to lead to the decline of most mature products. If the decline is for a product (as distinct from a brand), producers may discontinue some brands and even withdraw from the given product category. The typical reason for a product decline is the entry of new products, coupled with decreased consumer interest in the specific product. Under these conditions, one of the few options left for keeping a brand alive is price reduction and other drastic means that depress the profit margin and lead the company to consider the product's withdrawal.

A somewhat different case of product decline occurs when most customers no longer buy the product, but a small, loyal customer base remains. These customers continue to buy the product even if it receives no advertising or other promotional support. If this is the case the company may decide to follow a "milking" strategy, i.e., retain the product with no marketing support as long as it generates some sales. The problem with this strategy is that it requires to maintain the distribution of the product, which becomes less and less profitable compared to other investment opportunities, as the volume of sales and margins decrease.

These and some of the other marketing implications, which are often suggested for the various PLC stages, are summarized in Table 16.7.

TABLE 16.7 Marketing implications of PLC stages

Product Life Cycle Stages

	Introduction	*Growth*	*Maturity*	*Decline*
Market characteristics				
Sales	Low sales	Rapidly rising sales	Peak sales	Declining sales
Costs	High cost per customer	Average cost per customer	Low cost per customer	Low cost per customer
Profits	Negative	Rising profits	High profits	Declining profits
Customers	Innovators	Early adopters	Middle majority	Laggards
Competitors	Few	Growing number	Stable number beginning to decline	Declining number
Strategic considerations				
Marketing objectives	Create product awareness and trail	Maximize market share	Maximize profits while defending market share	Reduce expenditures and milk the brand
Product strategies	Offer a basic product	Offer product extensions, service, Warranty	Diversify brand and models	Phase out weak items
Distribution strategies	Build selective distribution	Build intensive	Build more intensive	Go selective and phase out unprofitable lets
Promotion strategies	Build product awareness among early adopters and dealers; use heavy sales promotions to entice trial	Build awareness and interest in mass market; reduce sales promotion to take advantage of heavy consumer demand	Stress brand differences and benefits; increase sales promotions to encourage brand switching	Reduce promotion activity to the level needed to retain hard core loyal customers
Price strategies	Charge cost-plus	Price to penetrate market	Price to match or beat competitors	Cut price

Source: Philip Kotler[2]

16.8.2 Utilizing the Product Life Cycle Concept: Yoram Wind's[11] Analysis

The utilization of the product life cycle concept, that is, answering the question of how one can determine the exact product life cycle position of a product, is necessary before the product life cycle concept can be used as a forecasting or diagnostic tool. Yoram Wind, famous product management expert has analysed PLC, as outlined below.

Utilizing the product life cycle concept requires six major conceptual and measurement decisions. These are briefly discussed in this section.

(i) **Unit of analysis.** Let us try to find out whether the product life cycle analysis be undertaken for a product class, product form, product line, an individual product, or a brand. A product life cycle analysis can be undertaken for each of these product levels at both the firm and industry levels. It is surprising, therefore, that little attention has been given to the identification of the most appropriate units of analysis, and to the nature of the relationships among the life cycles of these various product levels. In an attempt to validate the product life cycle model, it is essential that the fit of the life cycle model should have clear definition of product used and the relevance of product class partitioning. Attention, therefore, should be given to explicit definition of the unit of analysis.

The importance of developing an explicit definition of the unit of analysis is evident when one considers, for example, the PLC of television sets. Should one focus on all TV sets? On black and white or colour? On battery-operated or electricity-powered? On size of screen? With respect to size, should certain sizes be grouped together? It is essential that "correct" unit of analysis should be specified. Management should select the unit(s) of analysis based on their needs and how they intend to use the PLC information.

(ii) **Relevant market.** Traditional approaches ignore the possibility of sequential entry into distinctly different market segments, each of which can be further segmented according to customers' degree of innovativeness. Such sequential entry to various market segments may result in the type of a product life cycle presented in Figure 16.13.

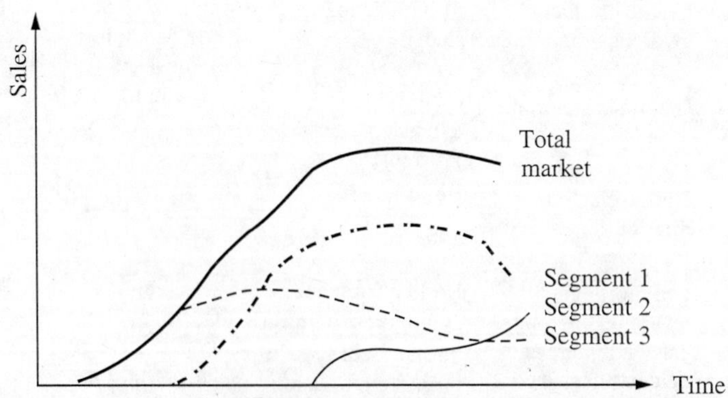

FIGURE 16.13 Product life cycle with sequential entry to three market segments. (*Source:* Wind[11])

Whereas most PLC studies have focused on product sales at the total market level, there are occasions in which it would be important to consider the PLC by type of market. For example, domestic versus multinational distribution outlet; discount stores versus departmental stores or market segment; and large versus small industrial buyers.

(iii) **Life cycle pattern and number of stages.** The most common product life cycle pattern is the S-shaped logistic function with four major stages—introduction, growth, maturity and decline. The typical logistic function or the growth function is presented in Figure 16.14. This function was developed to describe population growth over time. Detailed analysis of this pattern is given in a later section.

The equation of the logistic curve is:

$$S = \frac{1}{1 + e^{-(a+bt)}}$$

Since a is merely a location parameter, one can consider the simplified logistic function to be

$$S = \frac{1}{1 + e^{-bt}}$$

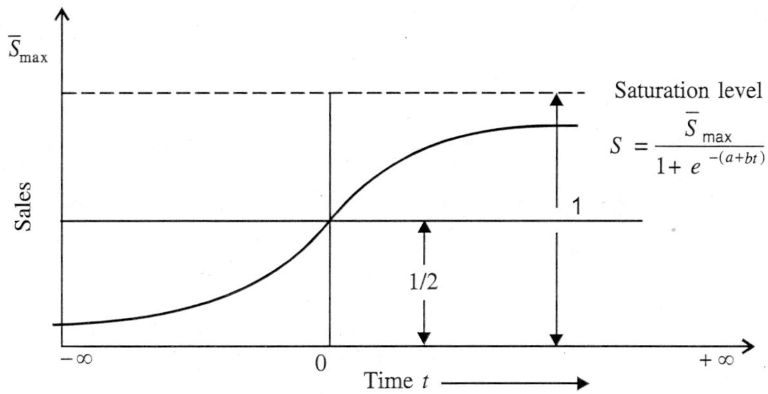

FIGURE 16.14 The S-curve logistic function.

where

$$S = 1/2 \quad \text{when } t = 0,$$
$$S = 0 \quad \text{when } t = -\infty, \text{ and}$$
$$S = 1 \quad \text{when } t = +\infty.$$

Thus, $S = 0$ and $S = 1$ are asymptotes, and the curve is skew-symmetric about the line $t = 0$, $S = 1/2$.

The slope of the curve is

$$\frac{dS}{dt} = bS(1 - S)$$

This differential equation suggests that the rate of change of sales with respect to time is proportional to the sales multiplied by a factor which decreases as sales increase.

Graphical estimation of b: Rewriting,

$$S = \left(\frac{\overline{S}_{max}}{1 + e^{-bt}}\right) \tag{16.1}$$

Sales fraction ($S/\bar{S}_{max}$) is denoted by f which is given by

$$f = S/\bar{S}_{max} = \left(\frac{e^{-bt}}{1+e^{-bt}}\right) \tag{16.2}$$

$$(1-f) = \left(\frac{e^{-bt}}{1+e^{-bt}}\right)$$

$$\frac{f}{1-f} = \frac{1}{e^{-bt}} = e^{bt}$$

This gives

$$\ln\left(\frac{f}{1-f}\right) = bt$$

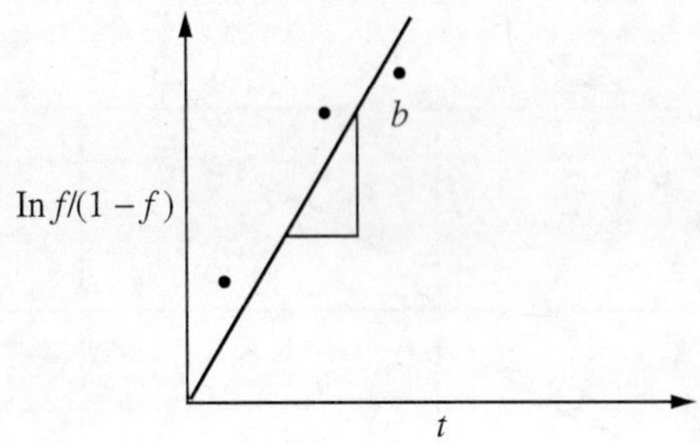

FIGURE 16.15 Graph for estimation of parameter b.

Plotting a graph between time t on arithmetic scale and $[(f/(1-f)]$ on a logarithmic scale as shown in Figure 16.15, we can estimate b from sales–time data.

(iv) **Identifying product's stage in the PLC model.** Two key questions facing those who attempt to use the product life cycle concept are: (a) how to determine the PLC stage in which a product is, and (b) how to determine when a product moves from one PLC stage to another. Given that the time–series sales data rarely obey the theoretical pattern of a smooth curve and that the S-shaped curve is only one of a number of possible life cycle patterns, it is not at all clear whether a product's position in its life cycle pattern and its shift from one stage to another can be identified simply by observing the historical sales pattern of the product.

One of the possible operational approaches to the identification of a product's position in its life cycle pattern was proposed by Polli and Cook (1969), based on the percentage change in real sales from one year to the next. Plotting these changes as a normal distribution with mean zero, they determined that if a product has percentage changes less than -0.5σ, it is to be classified in the decline stage. Products with percentage change greater than 0.5σ were classified as being in the growth stage, and products in the range of 0.5σ were considered to be stable, corresponding to the maturity stage. This latter stage was further divided into decaying maturity and sustained maturity. The distribution in Figure 16.16 is a Standard Normal Curve with Mean = 0 and Standard Deviation of 1.

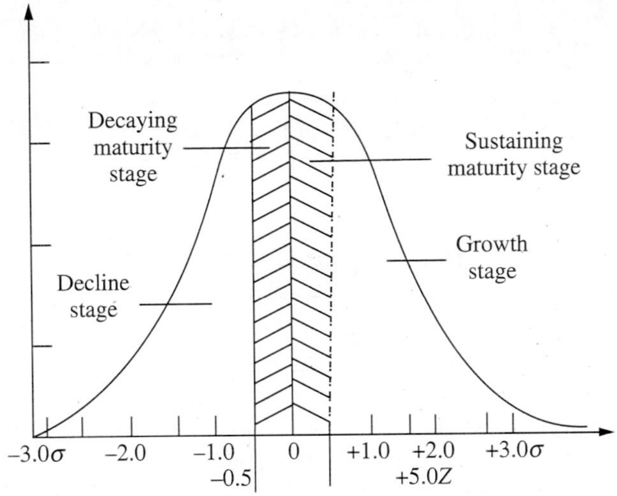

FIGURE 16.16 Percentage change in sales to estimate product position on PLC. (*Source:* Wind [11])

Identifying the length of time of each PLC stage and the exact point at which a product shifts from one PLC stage to another is closely related to the use of the PLC model for forecasting sales. No generalized pattern can be identified, since the length of each PLC stage depends on a large number of factors such as the product's characteristics, market acceptance, and competitive actions.

Example (a) If sales in year 1 is 400 units and in year 2 it is 430 units and standard derivation is 40 units, calculate in which stage the product is:

$$Z = \Delta s/\sigma = \left(\frac{430 - 400}{40}\right) = 0.75$$

Therefore,

$Z = +0.75$ the product is in growth stage because value of Z is greater than 0.5.

(b) If sales in year 2 are 410 units, predict the stage of the product. Then,

$$Z = \left(\frac{410 - 400}{40}\right) = 0.25$$

Thus, the product is in sustained maturity stage.

(v) **The unit of measurement.** Whereas most product life cycle analyses are based on actual sales, there still are a number of unresolved issues. The first is whether one should use unit sales or money value. Second, should the analysis be based on actual sales or adjusted sales? For example, should they be adjusted to per capita sales? Corrected for strike periods, or other supply shortages? Adjusted for general economic conditions (current versus real prices), and the like? Furthermore, should sales be the sole yardstick, or should market share figures or profits be used as well?

(vi) **The relevant time unit.** Most published product life cycle analyses are based on annual data. Yet, it is not clear why the analysis should be limited to this unit of time. In many instances, one may want to develop a product life cycle based on quarterly, monthly, or even weekly data. Given that the shorter the time period, the higher the likelihood of seasonal and other fluctuations, one may use some form of moving average. Given that most new products seem to have shorter life cycles—A.C. Nielsen (The Nielsen Researcher 1968), for example, has estimated that about 50% of food products have a PLC of less than two years and thus it becomes important to use a shorter unit of measurement than the traditional annual database.

16.8.3 Product Life Cycle and Marketing Strategy

In considering the possible relationship between marketing strategy and the product life cycle, it will be desirable to consider whether the product life cycle is an inevitable independent force that decides about the marketing efforts of companies or whether the firms marketing strategy can change the course of the product life cycle.

Most of the product life cycle literature tends to accept the first option. Only a few PLC studies have investigated empirically the marketing strategy determinants of a product's life cycle. It has been found that seven factors which triggered the take off of colour TV are price, volume of network colour programming, public exposure to colour, obsolescence of black and white sets, colour quality, clarity of black and white pictures, and attitude of major set makers.

Whether one colour accepts the independency or dependency of PLC, knowledge of the product's stage in its life cycle provides useful input for the design of the product's marketing strategy.

Recommendations have frequently been made concerning the type and level of advertising. Pricing, distribution, and other product/marketing activities required at each stage of the product life cycle. One such typical recommendation is the following illustrative statement from a marketing text by Buzzel:

The introductory period is characterized by heavy promotion aimed at building up primary demand; price is relatively unimportant. During the growth phase, more competition appears and there is an increasing pressure on price. Promotional expenditures decline in relation to sales; there is a shift to competition on the basis of brands and specific features. As the product enters maturity, there is increasing product brand competition, promotional expenditures and prices tend to stabilize, manufacturers begin efforts to extend life cycles, and new brands may appear. Finally, in the decline phase, further declines in price and promotional expenditures can be expected.

These recommendations are typical of those presented in many leading marketing texts. Some authors have provided specific recommendations for marketing strategies at various stages of the product life cycle.

Some of the more common recommendations are discussed below but should be viewed only as hypotheses, and not as facts or recommendations for taking actions.

(i) **Advertising.** The changing nature of advertising at each stage of the product life cycle was studied by Forrester (1961). According to him, in the introductory stage, advertising informs customers about the existence, advantages, and uses of new products. During the growth stage, advertising stresses the merits of the products compared to competing products. In the maturity phase, advertising attempts to create impressions of product differentiation. Massive advertising campaigns attempt to attract attention. And in the decline stage, the percentage of sales is going into advertising decrease.

(ii) **Product changes.** Changes in the features, performance, design, and so forth of a product were explored by Schewing (1974), who suggested the following product changes at each stage of the product life cycle—introduction of new product; growth—product modification; maturity–product modification and differentiating; saturation–product modification, differentiating, and diversification; and decline–product diversification.

Another view of product decisions at various stages of the PLC is presented by those who feel that a product is usually introduced in a single version and accompanied by various product problems and "bugs". At the growth stage, the product is improved, while at the maturity stage, new versions are introduced. At the decline stage, stripped-down versions are introduced.

(iii) **Pricing.** Price is usually believed to be high at the introductory period and to decline with the product life cycle stages as price becomes an increasingly important competitive weapon, especially at the late stages of growth and throughout the maturity and decline.

In determining the product's price strategy, not only the introductory price should be considered, but also what the next move might be, being alternative competitive actions. In this context, a relatively low introductory price which is contrary to the strategy suggested by many life cycle writers should not be related out automatically but should be fully examined.

(iv) **Distribution.** Initial distribution is believed to be selecting and learn, and to reach its full coverage at the growth stage, when retail outlets are seeking the product. At the maturity stage, retail outlets are the first to suffer from changes in consumer purchase patterns, hence a manufacturer may start losing outlets. At the same time, efforts are made by manufacturers to establish new methods of distribution (bypassing the wholesaler, for instance) and new outlets (direct mail, for example).

There are similar attempts to prescribe a marketing strategy and guide the allocation of marketing resources over the stages of a product's life cycle, to a large extent unsupported by empirical evidence. These are based on the erroneous assumption that the important determinant of a product's marketing strategy is the product's stage in its life cycle. Further, it is implied in such an assumption that, at any one stage of the product life cycle, the firm has only single "reasonable" marketing strategy it can follow. This implicit assumption is not only misleading but also dangerous, since it can constrain management's creativity in generating new marketing strategies.

The correct question, therefore, is not what specific strategy the firm should follow at each stage of the product life cycle, but rather how input of the product stage in its life cycle curve can be utilized in generating, developing, and evolving of better marketing strategies. It is to be noted that accepting this view means that the preceding speculative discussion on the "typical" marketing strategies at the various stages of the product life cycle should be viewed only as a possible hypothesis.

(v) **Life extension.** This strategy is based on the basic premise of the life cycle concept that all products do follow the life cycle of introduction, growth, maturity, and decline. According to Levitt (1965)[4], life extension or market stretching is based on the important proposition that:

"When a company develops a new product or service, it should try to plan at the very outset a series of actions to be employed at various subsequent stages in the product's existence so that its sales and profit curves are constantly sustained rather than following their usual declining slope."

The key question now is obviously: What are the marketing strategies that can lead to life extensions. Levitt suggests four possible strategies as follows:

(i) *Promoting more frequent use of the product among current users.* DuPont, for example, emphasized the necessity of wearing nylon stockings at all times, while General Food increased the number of available flavours, and 3M developed a variety of tape dispensers that made the product easier to use.

(ii) *Developing more diverse use of the product among current users.* DuPont achieved this objective by offering tinted, patterned, and highly textured hosiery. General Food (GF) achieved this objective by emphasizing the use of Jello not only as a dessert but also as base for salads. 3M developed a range coloured, patterned, waterproof, invisible, and write-on-Scotch tapes.

(iii) *Creating new users for the product by expanding the market.* To achieve this objective, according to Levitt, DuPont tried to legitimize the wearing of hosiery among early teenagers. GF presented Jello as a fashion-oriented weight-control product, and 3M developed a line of commercial cellophane tapes of various widths, length, and strengths.

(iv) *Finding new users for the basic material.* The case of nylon is quite familiar, with nylon used in rugs, tires, and numerous other products. General Foods were less fortunate in discovering new uses for Jello, however, flavourless gelatin was promoted as a means of strengthening fingernails. 3M also developed new uses for the basic product, such as the double-coated tape that competes with liquid adhesives and the marker strips that compete with paint.

These strategies and examples suggest some of the ways a firm can extend the life cycle of its product or brand.

16.8.4 Product Life Cycle Extensions

As noted earlier, the product life cycle alone cannot and should not be used as the sole guideline for designing the marketing strategy. Any PLC-based normative strategy guidelines are likely to be misleading. The concept of life cycle is, however, intriguing. It recognizes the fact that any product is subject to change. It focuses on the need to assess empirically the correct long-term pattern of sales and other key variables. It is the dynamic longitudinal focus of the concept of life cycle that can turn it into one of the major building blocks of marketing strategy. To achieve this potential, the life cycle concept must, however be extended to at least two other areas—profitability and competitive position. The relations between profit and product life cycles are discussed next and are followed by a brief discussion of the new concept of competitive life cycle.

16.8.5 Product Life Cycle and Profitability

Most life cycle models propose a parallel profit curve, such as the one illustrated in Figure 16.17. This profit curve assumes very low profit margins (and negative unit profit) at the introductory stages. The profits rise substantially as volume increases until a stage in the growth phase where the profit levels start declining.

In evaluating the profitability of a product at various stages in its life cycle, it is important to remember that profits are a function of not only the sales volume and price but also the cost associated with the product. The marketing costs are assumed to be the highest at the introductory stages of product, given the need to develop the market. Similarly, the production costs are also assumed to be the highest at the introductory phase, since production is still at the beginning stages of the production learning curve.

A crucial factor in this respect is the allocation of costs to a product. This allocation is affected by the firm's accounting practices. It is particularly complicated by such problems as how to allocate the R&D costs and other pre-introduction development and marketing costs when the marketing effort involves more than a single brand (such as in the case of advertising more than a single product in one commercial or distribution efforts that involve an entire product line).

Given these complexities in determining the cost of a product at a given time period, it is difficult to determine conclusively the profitability of product at various stages of its life cycle.

The pattern suggested in Figure 16.17 is probably a good approximation for it but has to be examined explicitly in each case after determination of the accounting practices required to portray a realistic picture of product performance.

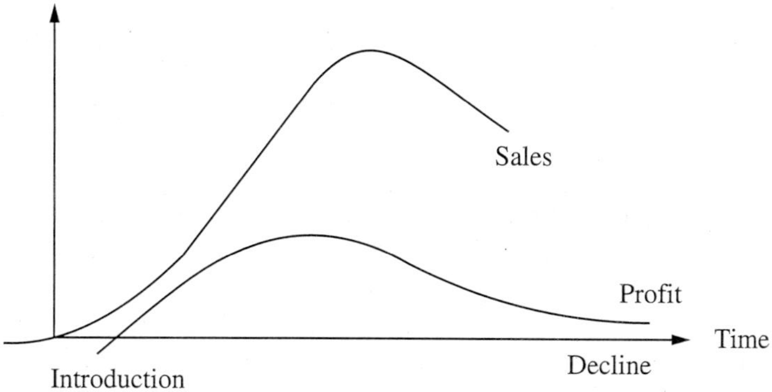

FIGURE 16.17 A typical PLC and its associated profit curve.

16.9 DIFFUSION MODELS: MODELS OF FIRST PURCHASE

The task of a diffusion model is to produce a life cycle sales curve based on (usually) a small number of parameters, which may or may not have behavioural content. The pre-supposition is that these parameters may be estimated either by analogy to the histories of similar new products introduced in the past, by consumer pretests, or by early sales returns as the new product enters the market. In the past three decades, a great deal of work on diffusion modelling has been done, initially based on the earlier, well developed theory of contagious diseases or the spread of epidemics.

Prior to 1969, most diffusion models in marketing could be classified as pure innovative or pure imitative types. A pure innovative model assumes that only innovative or advertising are operative in the diffusion process while a pure imitative model assumes that the only effects on the process are driven by imitation or word of mouth. Let us discuss these two models.

(i) **Pure innovative model.** [Fourt and Woodlock (1960)[5]] One of the earliest market-penetration models was an exponential model proposed by Fourt and Woodlock (1960), which was tested against several new products. Their retrospective observation of many market-penetration curves showed that (a) the cumulative curve approaches a limiting penetration level of less than 100% of all households and frequently far less, and (b) the successive increments of gain decline. They found that an adequate approximation to these observations was provided by a curve of the following form:

$$S_t = ps(1-p)^{t-1} \tag{16.3}$$

where,

S_t = increment in cumulative sales (i.e., sales at time t) as fraction potential sales
p = rate of penetration of untapped potential (a constant)
s = total potential sales as fraction of all buyers
t = time period

The formula is completely specified by the two parameters p and s.

To illustrate how it works, let us assume that a new product is to be introduced. Assume that 40% of all households will eventually try the new product ($s = 0.4$) and that in each period 30% of the remaining new buyer potential buys ($p = 0.3$). Therefore, the first period increment in new buyer penetration of this market is

$$S_1 = ps(1 - p)^{t-1} = ps = (0.3 \times 0.4) = 0.12 \tag{16.4}$$

and the second period increment in new buyer penetration of this market is

$$S_2 = ps(1 - p)^{2-1} = ps(1 - p) = 0.3(0.4 - 0.3)0.4 = 0.084 \tag{16.5}$$

Note that Eq. (16.3) produces and (exponentially) declining curve of new-buyer sales over time. Figure 16.18 displays the shape of this curve. To use the model, we need an estimate of the ultimate penetrations, usually derived from market research studies. The second parameter p can be derived from the cumulative decline in the penetration rate observed in several periods of sales data.

(ii) **Fisher and Pry model.** One of the well-known models is the logistic model or S-curve model. This model is well known due to its application in diffusion of technology in the field of technology management. It is also used by marketing analysts in the context of operationalizing the product life cycle curve.

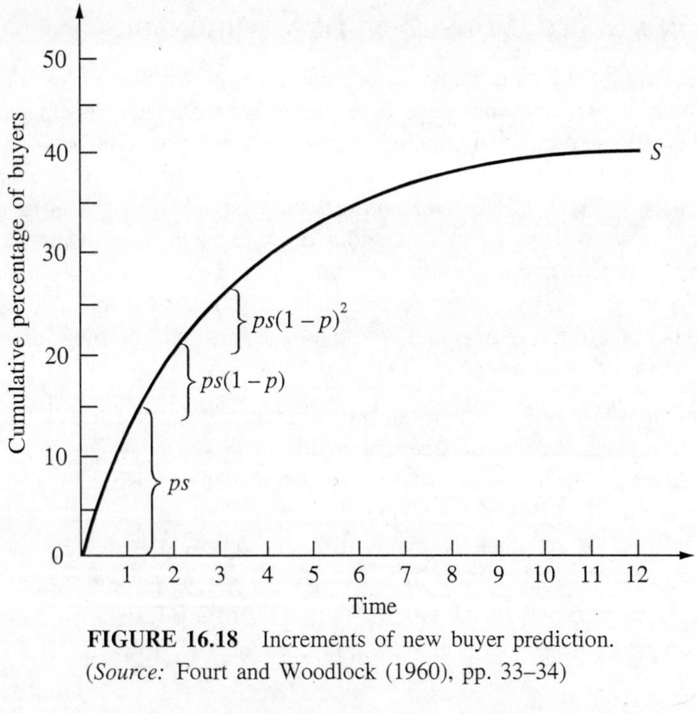

FIGURE 16.18 Increments of new buyer prediction.
(*Source:* Fourt and Woodlock (1960), pp. 33–34)

To start, let us assume an equation giving, say the rate of increase or sales with time t as follows:

$$\frac{dS}{dt} = KS - bS^2 \tag{16.6}$$

Thus,

$$\frac{dS}{KS - bS^2} = dt$$

$$\int \frac{1}{S(K - bS)} dS = t + \text{constant}$$

Using the method of partial fractions, we get

$$\int \frac{1}{K}\left(\frac{1}{S} + \frac{b}{K - bS}\right) dS = t + C$$

or

$$\frac{1}{K}\left[\ln(S) - \ln(K - bS)\right] = t + C \tag{16.7}$$

To evaluate C, at $t = 0$, $S = S_0$,

$$\frac{1}{K}\left[\ln(S_0) - \ln(K - bS_0)\right] = C$$

Equation (16.7) now becomes

$$\frac{1}{K}\left[\ln(S) - \ln(K - bS)\right] = t + \frac{1}{K}\left[\ln(S_0) - \ln(K - bS_0)\right]$$

Solving for S, after some algebraic manipulation, yields

$$S = \frac{K}{b + \left(\frac{K}{S_0} - b\right)e^{-kt}} \tag{16.8}$$

In the above equation,

$$S = S_{max} = K/b \quad \text{for } t \to \infty,$$
$$S = S_{min} = 0 \quad \text{for } t \to -\infty,$$
$$S = \frac{K}{2b} \quad \text{for } t \to 0,$$

Using the value of $S = K/2b$ at $t = 0$, Eq. (16.7) can be further expressed in a more useful form.

Rewriting Eq. (16.7), we obtain

$$\frac{1}{K}\left[\ln(S) - \ln(K - bS)\right] = t + C$$

At $t = 0$, we have

$$S = \frac{K}{2b}$$

Then,

$$\frac{1}{K}\left[\ln\left(\frac{K}{2b}\right) - \ln\left(K - \frac{bK}{2b}\right)\right] = 0 + C$$

$$C = \frac{1}{K}\ln\left(\frac{1}{b}\right)$$

$$\frac{1}{K}\ln\left(\frac{S}{K - bS}\right) = t + \frac{1}{K}\ln\left(\frac{1}{b}\right) \tag{16.9}$$

or

$$\frac{1}{K}\left[\ln\left(\frac{S}{K - bS}\right) - \ln\left(\frac{1}{b}\right)\right] = t$$

or

$$\ln\left(\frac{S}{K - bS}\right)b = Kt$$

or

$$\frac{bS}{K - bS} = e^{kt}$$

$$S = \frac{K/b}{1 + e^{-kt}} \tag{16.10}$$

Exponential model. In exponential model, the basic equation is:

$$\frac{dS}{dt} = KS$$

Since $b = 0$ in this model, substituting $b = 0$ in Eq. (16.8), we get the value of $b = 0$. Thus,

$$S = S_0 e^{kt} \tag{16.11}$$

(iii) **The Bass model**[7]**.** Fourt and Woodlock developed a model on the process of pure innovation. In the innovation model, the purchase decision is taken by the buyer based on his own motivation. On the other hand, Fisher and Pry model is based on a slow diffusion based on word of mouth publicity and imitation effect. According to Bass, in any buying situation both the innovative and imitative components are present. This model has the following notations:

S_t = adopters at time t
m = ultimate number of adopters
Y_t = cumulative number of adopters to date
p = coefficient of innovation
q = coefficient of imitation

The values of p and q have been reported to be 0.03 and 0.38, respectively. However, p and q depend upon the product type.

The basic equation of Bass can be developed on the assumption that initially a small number Y_t did the purchase. Seeing this, the imitators were motivated and the probability of purchase by imitators is proportional to the ratio of initial buyers as a fraction of total population. Thus, probability of buying by imitators is proportional to (Y_t/m). Out of the $(m - Y_t)$ left, the number of imitative buyers shall be proportional to $(Y_t/m)(m - Y_t)$. Adding the two categories of buyers, Bass concluded that number of buyers S_t at time t shall be:

$$S_t = p(m - Y_t) + q(Y_t/m)(m - Y_t) \tag{16.12}$$

Equation (16.12) can be rewritten as:

$$S_t = pm + (q - p)Y_t - q/m(Y_t)^2 \tag{16.13}$$

Setting $a = pm$, $(q - p) = b$ and $c = -q/m$, Eq. (16.13) can be rewritten as:

$$S_t = a + bY_t + cY_t^2 \tag{16.14}$$

To calculate the maxima for S_t, it is necessary that $\frac{dS_t}{dY_t} = 0$, or $0 = b + 2cY_t = 0$ or $Y_t = \frac{-b}{2c}$

Substituting $Y_t = \frac{-b}{2c}$ in Eq. (16.14) for S_t:

$$S_t^* = a - b(b/2c) + c(b^2/4c^2) = \left(a + \frac{b^2}{4c}\right) \tag{16.15}$$

Substituting $a = pm$; $b = (q - p)$; $c = -q/m$, Eq. (16.15) reduces to

$$S_t^* = \frac{m(p+q)^2}{4q} \tag{16.16}$$

The time for the sales rate S_t to become maximum was derived by Bass and found to be:

$$T_0 \text{ opt} = \frac{1}{p+q} \ln\left(\frac{q}{p}\right) \tag{16.17}$$

Bass tested his model by comparing forecasted sales with actual sales for room air conditioners. The result is shown in Figure 16.19. The Bass model and its extensions have become a topic of interesting research in the field of sales forecast analysis, product management, and technology management.

16.10 CONCLUDING REMARKS

The product life cycle has long been considered one of the fundamental concepts of product policy. Yet, in recent years the concept has been under attack. Dhalla and Yuspeh (1976), for example, suggested that "in numerous cases a brand is discounted, not because of irreversible changes in consumer values or tastes, but because management, on the basis of the PLC theory, believes that the brand has entered a dying stage." Hence, the recommendation: *forget the product life cycle concept.*

Should management accept this conclusion? Can the product life cycle concept offer any useful insight into product management? Can it be operationally in a way that would provide useful input to the design of marketing strategies? To answer these and similar questions, it would be useful for the reader to select a product, attempt to develop its PLC, and answer the question of "what can be done with the PLC information once it has been collected?" and how can product life cycle of typical product help in better management of products of similar type?

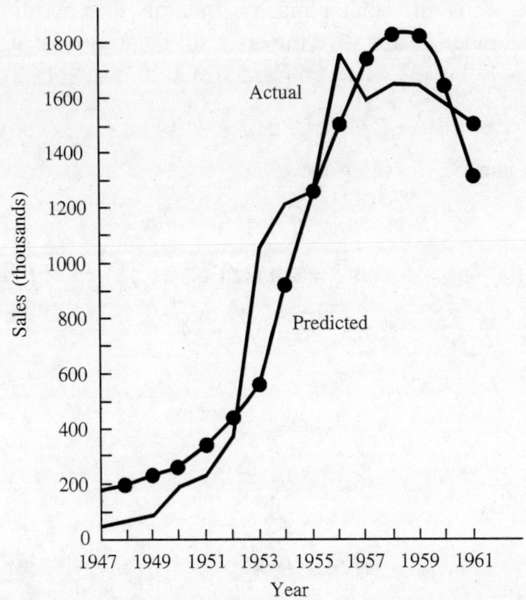

FIGURE 16.19 Actual sales and predicted sales for room air conditioners (Bass models). (*Source:* Bass, 1969a, p. 219)

REVIEW QUESTIONS

1. Define the word 'product'. Sec. 16.1; P 465
2. How is a product defined by concentric circles?
   Explain: (i) Core benefit, (ii) generic product, (iii) expected product, (iv) augmented product, and (v) potential product. Sec. 16.2; P 465, 466
3. What are the outcomes of product–market interaction as proposed by H. Igor Ansoff? Sec. 16.3; P 466, 467
4. Classify products according to Melvin Copeland's theory. What are the benefits of such classification to the marketing personnel? Sec. 16.4; P 467, 468
5. What is meant by new product development and product management? In an expanded product life cycle, what are premarket phase and marketing phase? Sec. 16.5 and 16.5.1
6. Explain the new product development process according to Booz, Allen and Hamilton in your own words. Sec. 16.5.2
7. Make a flowchart on new product development process proposed by Schoell and Guiltinan? What is the missing aspect in the flowchart? Explain critically. Sec. 16.6.1, 16.6; P 470
8. What are the sources of new product ideas? How are product ideas quantified? What is the difference between idea and concept? Illustrate with an example. Table 16.3
9. Which tool is used to evaluate a concept? P 476; Figure 16.6
10. What is the aim of business analysis? How is economic commercial value (ECV) determined? P 477–486; Figure 16.9
11. How is a prototype tested? What is the difference between α and β testing? P 478
12. What is test marketing? What is the advantage of test marketing and what are its risk factors? P 478

13. What is the rationale of test marketing? What is pretest marketing? Why does it become essential? P 479

14. What is meant by commercialization? What is a launch cycle? What are the four phases of launch cycle? P 481

15. What is a launch control protocol? P 482

16. What is the role of critical path analysis in a launch project? P 483, 484; Figure 16.8

17. What are the different strategies available to a firm during the four stages of a product life cycle? Sec. 16.8.3; P 495–497

18. How is a products stage determined in a product life cycle if the sales data in year 1 and year 2 is known and the standard deviation σ of the sales is known?

If the sales of a product in year 1 is 400 and in year 2 it is 370, predict the stage where the product is of standard deviation 40 units.

[*Hint:* Calculate $z = \dfrac{370 - 400}{40} = -0.75$]

[*Hint:* Since $z = -0.75$ is less than –0.5, the product is in decaying maturity stage.]

19. How sales forecasting is done for grocery goods in a limited marketing area under pure innovation? Sec. 169 (i); P 499

[*Hint:* Use Fourt and Woodlock model]

20. How sales forecast for industrial goods is made over a span of 10 years?

[*Hint:* Use Bass model] Sec. 16.9 (iii); P 502

The ultimate number of buyers is m;

Coefficient of innovation $p= 0.008$

Coefficient of imitation $q = 0.392$

REFERENCES

[1] Polli, R. and Cook, V., Validity of the product life cycle, *The Journal of Business,* Vol.42, No. 4, October, pp. 385–400, 1969.

[2] Kotler, Philip, *Marketing Management,* 11th ed., Prentice Hall of India, New Delhi, 2004.

[3] Forrester, *World Dynamics,* Prentice Hall, Englewood Cliffs, New Jersey, 1978.

[4] Theodore, Levitt, Exploit the Product Life Cycle, *Harvard Business Review,* Vol. 43, Nov./Dec., pp. 81–94, 1965.

[5] Fourt, L. and Woodlock J., Early Prediction of Market Success for New Grocery Products, *Journal of Marketing,* Vol. 24, October, pp. 31–38, 1960.

[6] Fisher, J.C. and Pry, R.H., A simple substitution model of technological change, *Technology Forecast and Social Change,* Vol. 3, pp. 75–78, 1971.

[7] Bass, F., A new product growth model for consumer durables, *Management Science,* Vol. 15, pp. 215–27 (1969a).

[8] Mahajan, Muller and Bass, F., New product diffusion models in marketing, *Journal of Marketing,* Vol. 54, pp. 1–26, 1960.

[9] Kahn, K.B., *New Product Planning,* Sage Publications, New Delhi, 2001, p. 124.

[10] Chaturvedi, M., *New Product Development,* Wheeler Publishing, New Delhi, 1998.

[11] Wind, Yoram, *Product Policy Management,* Wiley, New York, 1989.

Chapter 17

Design for Environment

Design for environment (DfE) is a design approach to reduce the impact of a product or process or service on human health. These impacts are considered across its life cycle of the product. Figure 17.1 shows the total life cycle of any product. Different software tools have been developed to assist designers in assessing what design would result in minimum impact on human beings. This would help designers in finding optimized products or process/service. DfE is also the original name of a United States Environmental Protection Agency (EPA), created in 1992, that works to prevent pollution and the risk pollution presents to humans and the environment. The program provides information regarding safer chemical formulations for cleaning and other products. EPA renamed its program as Safer Choice in 2015.

Papanek in 1971 pointed out that designers should be aware of their social responsibility and should carry out their designs keeping in mind environmental responsibility instead of focusing on just the commercial aspect. Brandt head report in 1989 said that while we go about designing, we should think of the next generation whom we should hand over a legacy of good environment. Fiskel in 1976 used the phrase design for environment and lifecycle thinking into new product development. Brezel and Von Hemel introduced the word eco-design in 1990. Technical University of Delft and Philips Electronics along with Danish Government cooperated to develop a software to assess life cycle assessment (LCA). Today, eco-design, green design, and design for environment have been used as synonymous initiatives. Initial guidelines for a DfE approach were written by Anneke van Waesberghe with her "East meets West not for profit" became a Global movement targeting design initiatives and incorporating environmental motives to improve product design in order to minimize health and environmental impacts by incorporating it from design stage all the way to the manufacturing process and distribution and use by customer. By incorporating eco-efficiency into design tactics, DfE takes into consideration the entire life cycle of a product. Care is taken to minimize resources such as material and energy used for the design process. The key focus of DfE is the environmental and economic cost to consumers, by balancing both customer needs and environmental and social impact. DfE aims to improve the product use experience both for consumers and for producers while minimally impacting the environment.

17.1 VARIOUS STAGES OF TOTAL LIFE CYCLE MATERIALS

(1) *Earth*: Derive materials from earth by mining, drilling, or harvesting resulting in raw materials such as ore, coal, sand, oil, and rock; (2) extraction or refining processes resulting in bulk materials such as metals, chemicals, cement, paper, and fibres; (3) *processing of bulk materials* to give engineering materials of same nomenclature; (4) *design and manufacture* to give products, machines, structures; (5) *use of products and service* by mankind; (6) *generation of waste* dumped in earth as landfill or recycled to give bulk materials in stage 3 or stage 4.

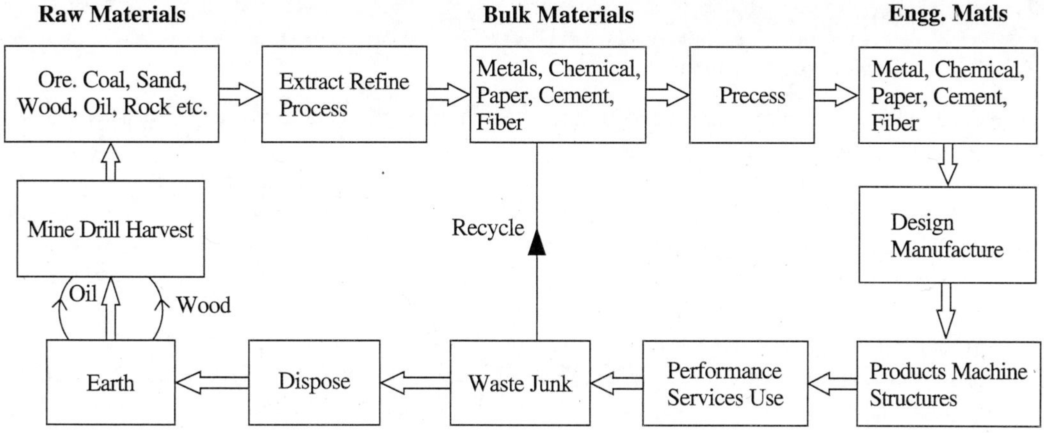

Total Life Cycle–Materials Cycle

FIGURE 17.1 Various stages of total life cycle materials.

Four major initiatives under the DfE umbrella are:

1. *Design for environmental processing and manufacturing*: Raw material extraction such as mining and drilling, processing reusable materials and processes which are not dangerous to environment and people working there. This includes minimization of waste and hazardous byproducts, air pollution, energy expenditure, etc.
2. *Design for environmental packaging*: The packaging should be of material which is biodegradable or could be recycled to original state.
3. *Design for disposal or reuse*: The end of life of a product is very important because some products emit dangerous chemicals into air, ground, and water after they are disposed in a landfill. Planning for reuse or refurbishing of a product will change the type of materials that will be used, how they could be disassembled and reused.
4. Design for energy efficiency aims to reduce the overall energy consumption throughout the products life.

17.1.1 Life Cycle Assessment

Life cycle assessment is employed to forecast the impacts of different alternatives of making the product in question. This enables to choose the most environmental friendly alternative for manufacture. A life cycle analysis can serve as a tool to determine the environmental impact of a product or process. Several different products can be compared for assessing the impact .The categories under which the impact is evaluated are energy use, toxicity, acidification, CO_2 emissions, ozone depletion, resource depletion, and many others. By studying different products, the designer can make decisions about which environmental hazard to focus on in order to make the product more eco-friendly.

17.2 ECO-INDICATOR 95

17.2.1 Eco-Indicator 95 Method

Eco-indicator 95 is a method developed before eco-Indicator 99 used at present. The two methods share same principle of implementation.

Instead of a full life cycle assessment, one might instead inventory the parts used in a product and weight them by "average" impact weightings. One might break the product down into quantities of materials in the parts of the product by weight. Then establish environmental impact of different materials by weight and sum this score. This process approximates the life cycle stages of the product an "average" typical use for each material.

One such approach was developed in Europe on the initiative of the Ministry of Housing, Spatial Planning and the Environment in the Netherlands, called the Eco-indicator 95 (Goedkoop, Demmers, and Collignon, 1996). The eco-indicator system provides weightings by mass for materials, treatment processes, transport processes, energy generation processes, and disposal scenarios. As shown in Figure 17.2, the weightings themselves are based on a valuation of damage to public health and to the ecosystem through contribution to several effects, such as ozone layer depletion, smog, and so forth. The actual effects are shown in Figure 17.2.

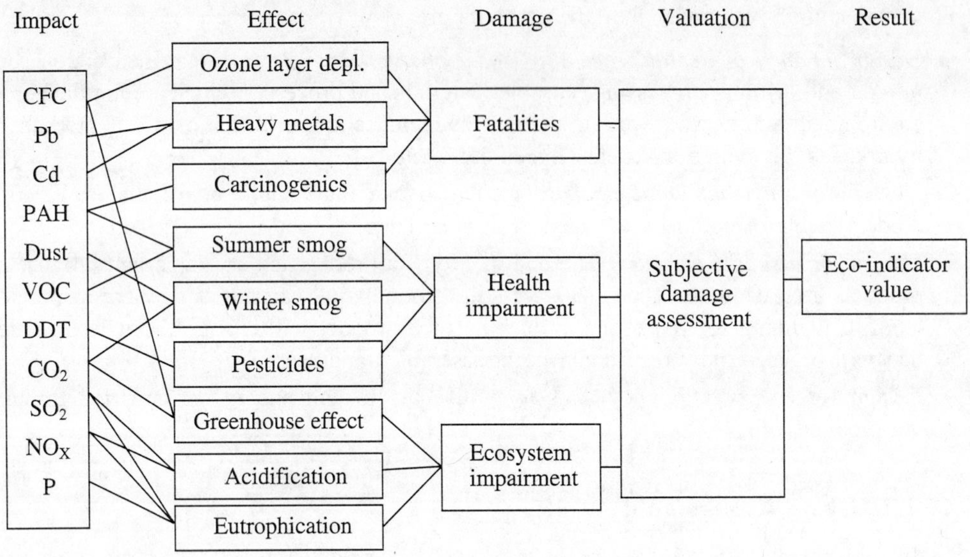

FIGURE 17.2 Eco-indicator flowchart 95.

The eco-indicator system operates by first establishing the mass of component materials in the product, their means of production, and the means of disposal. A worksheet to evaluate the product is then used, as shown in Figure 17.3.

Environmental effect	Weighing factor	Criteria
Greenhouse effect	2.5	01YC rise every 10 years, 5% ecosystem degradation
Ozone layer depletion	100	Probability of 1 fatality per year million inhabitants
Acidification	10	5% ecosystem degradation
Eutrophication	5	Rivers and lakes, degradation of an unknown number of aquatic ecosystems (5% degradation)
Summer smog	2.5	Occurrence of smog periods, health complaints, particularly amongst asthma patients and the elderly, prevention of agricultural damage
Winter smog	5	Occurrence of smog periods, health complaints, particularly amongst asthma patients and the elderly
Pesticides	25	5% ecosystem degradation
Airborne heavy metals	5	Lead content in children's blood, reduced life expectancy and learning performance in an unknown number of people
Waterborne heavy metals	5	Cadmium content in rivers, ultimately also impacts on people (see airborne)
Carcinogenic substances	10	Probability of 1 fatality per year per million people

FIGURE 17.3 Development of weightings for the Eco-indicator 95.

For impact weighting values, the data of Figure 17.4 are used.

Transport (in millipoints)

	Indicator	*Description and explanation of score*
Truck (28 ton)	0.340	Per ton kilometer, 60% loading, and European average
Truck ($75m^3$)	0.130	Per m^3 km, 60% loading, and European average
Train	0.43	Per ton kilometer, European average for diesel and electric traction
Container ship	0.056	Per ton kilometer, fast ship, with relatively high fuel consumption
Aircraft	10.00	Per kg, with continental flights the distance is not relevant

Production of energy (in millipoints)

	Indicator	*Description and explanation of score*
Electricity high voltage	0.57	Per kWh, for industrial use
Electricity low voltage	0.67	Per kWh, for consumer use (230 V)
Heat from (MJ)	0.063	Per MJ heat
Heat from oil (MJ)	0.15	Per MJ heat
Mechanical (diesel, MJ)	0.17	Per MJ mechanical energy from a diesel engine

Production of metals (in millipoints)

	Indicator	*Description and explanation of score*
Secondary aluminium	0	Made completely of secondary material
Aluminium	18	Containing average 20% secondary material
Copper, primary	85	Primary electrolytic copper from relatively American factories
Copper, 60% primary	60	Normal proportion secondary and primary copper
Secondary copper	23	100% secondary copper, relatively high score through heavy metal emissions
Other non-ferrous metals	100	Estimate for zinc, brass, chromium, nickel, etc.; lack of data
Stainless steel	17	Sheet material, grade 18–8
Secondary steel	13	Block material made of 100% scrap
Steel	4.1	Block material made of 100% scrap
Sheet steel	4.3	Cold-rolled sheet with average 20% scrap

FIGURE 17.4 Eco-indicator 95 weightings.

Other life cycle data must be estimated to complete the numerical analysis. In particular, how long the product is used, how it is delivered to the consumer, and how it is disposed must be estimated. Table 17.1 provides a list of typical product life spans that can be used as a first approximation of the actual useful life for different products. Delivery can be estimated based on the source—domestic or international. Disposal should simply be approximated as landfill, unless either the material is very hazardous and laws apply to its disposal or the material is very valuable.

TABLE 17.1 Common product life cycles without recycling

Product type	*Useful life (years)*
Novelties	1
Photographic film	1
Disposable dinnerware and hospital goods	1
Packaging	1–2
Construction film	2
Footwear	2
Apparel	4
Household goods	5
Toys	5
Jewellery	5
Saucepans	5
Sporting goods	7
Domestic applications	7–10
Luggage	10
Cameras	10
Furniture	10
Motor vehicles	10
Electrical goods	10–15
Hardware	15

Product type	*Useful life (years)*
Aircraft	15
Wire and cable	15–30
Construction	25–40
Machinery	30

17.3 ECO-INDICATOR 95 WORKSHEET

Example: Kitchen Mixer

Define the life cycle. We first define the product life cycle for the Kitchen Mixer. That is, we determine exactly what inputs and outputs during a product's life cycle should be considered in the analysis of the product. Figure 17.5 shows the life cycle determined for the Kitchen Mixer. The shaded areas are the sections that are not being considered in the analysis. The preparations of kitchen mixer potatoes are not considered because the design of the kitchen mixer has no impact on this process. Likewise, the assumption is made that the kitchen mixer is disposed of in regular municipal waste to be recycled, another fraction to be incinerated, and the remainder to end up in a landfill. Although recycling every unit could reduce the product's impact on the environment, the assumption is made that as the product is a consumer product, it would be disposed of with the rest of the household trash. Several inputs (such as felt) are not considered in the process tree because they are not mentioned in the eco-indicator 95 model.

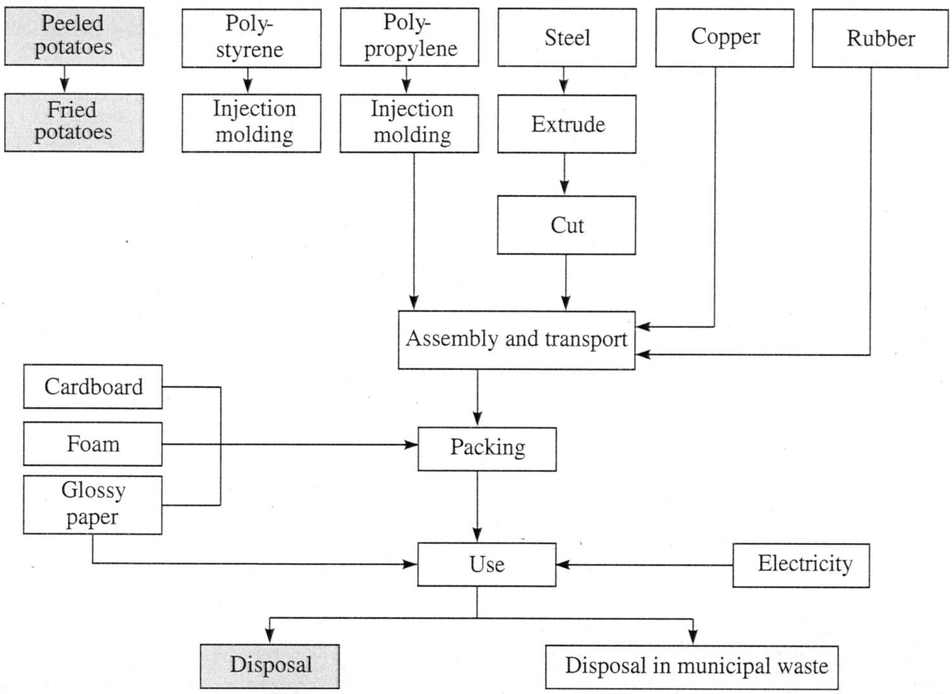

FIGURE 17.5 Process tree for kitchen mixer.

Comparisons to other materials of the excluded inputs are made to determine if their absence would affect the overall result of the model. Felt, for example, is compared with paper, cardboard, and polyethylene terephthalate (PET) plastic. The results confirm the assumption that the excluded inputs are negligible.

The next step in the analysis is to quantify the materials and processes used in the production, use, and disposal of the kitchen mixer. The application of eco-indicator 95 to the kitchen mixer is quite simple once the list of materials is obtained. The materials and processes are summed, and then their impact is calculated by using the weights from the eco-indicator data given in Figure 17.4.

Production and processing. The production matrix for the kitchen mixer is the most complex of the three matrices to expand. The motor for the kitchen mixer is examined separately because the motor comprises the majority of the weight of the kitchen mixer, and a large quantity of the environmental impact of the kitchen mixer results from the motor.

A number of assumptions are needed to allow the actual materials and processes to fit within the categories of the impact weightings that are part of eco-indicator 95, as shown in Table 17.4. For the purposes of the study, brass is assumed to be equivalent to 60% primary copper, the foam used in packaging is assumed to be PUR rigid foam, the cord is assumed to contain 50% natural rubber product and 50% copper. The assumption is also made that the kitchen mixer is shipped at an average of 2,000 miles by a 28-ton truck, although the environmental impact of the shipping appears to be inconsequential. The assumptions with the most potential impact and, therefore, uncertainty are the material percentages present in the motor.

Use. An effective determination of the environmental impact of the use of the kitchen mixer is dependent on the frequency and duration of use. These data points must be determined by a survey of the customers. The assumptions used are an average product life of 10 years, a 10-second daily usage, and power consumption of the motor around 125 W, as shown in Table 17.5. This estimated impact would probably be greater than the actual impact of the kitchen mixer due to the generous usage assumptions.

Tables 17.2, 17.3, and 17.4 are most important for understanding the accounting procedure.

TABLE 17.2 Eco-indicator 95 results for production of the kitchen mixer.

Production and processes			
Material, processing, transport, and extra energy			
Material or process	*Amount*	*Indicator*	*Result in micropoints*
Polystyrene(g)	38.5	5.8	223.3
Polypropylene	138.6	3.3	457.6
Injection moulding of plastic	177	0.53	93
Steel	28.6	4.1	117.7
Brass	0	60	1.1
Copper	30.25	60	181.5
Natural rubber product	30.25	4.3	129.8
Cardboard	78.1	1.4	107.8
Foam	1.1	8.4	8.8
Paper	22	3.3	72.6

Production and processes			
Material, processing, transport, and extra energy			
Material or process	*Amount*	*Indicator*	*Result in micropoints*
Subtotal			**3,027.2**
Motor			
Paper (1%)	4.23	3.3	14.3
Steel/Iron (65%)	275.25	4.1	1,128.6
Copper (15%)	63.52	60	14,991
Ceramics (19%)	80.46	0.47	37.4
Motor Total	423.5		**4,991.8**
Transport by truck	3.168	0.34	**1.1**
Grand Total			**8,020**

TABLE 17.3 Eco-indicator 95 results for use of the kitchen mixer

Use			
Material, processing, transport, and extra energy			
Process	*Amount*	*Indicator*	*Result in micropoints*
Electricity, low-voltage (kWh)	1672	0.67	1,119.8

Disposal. There are a number of methods by which a product can be disposed. However, as mentioned above, consumers utilize their household trashcans and most consumer waste ends up being processed as municipal waste. A certain fraction of the municipal waste is incinerated, while the rest is disposed of in a landfill. Certain metals are reclaimed and recycled from the incinerator slag. Consequently, the indicator for the disposal of these metals is negative. The negative number represents an environment gain because the recovered metals are used in place of newly processed metals and because electricity is also generated. The results for the kitchen mixer are shown in Table 17.4.

TABLE 17.4 Eco-indicator 95 results for disposal.

Production and processes			
Material, processing, transport, and extra energy			
Material and type of processing	*Amount*	*Indicator*	*Result in micropoints*
Plastics and rubbers	207.35	0.69	143
Steel	303.87	1.2	365.2
Paper and cardboard	99	0.33	33
Copper	93.77	–2.6	–244.2
Total			297

Interpretation of the results. The eco-indicator model provides some significant insight into the fundamental environmental stress of the kitchen mixer. Table 17.5 provides a summary of some of the relevant data from the above analysis. One of the most notable observations that result from the analysis is that 85% of the environmental damage occurs during the production of the kitchen mixer. And, even more notable, only 1% of that damage occurs during the production of the materials before they arrive on the factory floor. The design team will thus have to assign the greatest priority to examine the production phase of the product.

TABLE 17.5 Summary of relevant ECO-indicator data.

	Category	*Score in micropoints*	*Percentage of total damage*
Life cycle phase	Production and process	8,020	85%
	Use	1,119.8	12%
	Disposal	297	3%
	Total score	9,437	100%
Impact by material	Copper (whole product)	5,382	57%
	Plastics	917.4	10%
	Non-copper metals	1,610.4	17%
	Other materials	352	4%
	Sub-total	8,263.2	88%
Impact by phase	Motor	4,991.8	53%
	Power: use of motor	1,119.8	12%
	Cord	1,944.8	21%
	Base and housing	857	9%
	Packaging	222.2	2%
	Others	275	3%
	Total impact	9,437	100%

The eco-indicator 95 model of the kitchen mixer leads to the suggestion that improved material selection could greatly reduce the damage that the product impacts on the environment. The most damaging of the materials in the product, copper, accounts for 57% of the total environmental damage of the product. Potential improvements could involve using aluminum wiring instead of the copper wiring that is used in both the motor and the cord. Although the reduced conductivity of the aluminum wiring will result in significantly hotter wires, the short operating time of the motor may prevent the unit from heating up noticeably. Even if the replacement of all copper wiring is not feasible, portions of the wiring, such as the power cord, could integrate both copper and aluminium or be all aluminium. A significant effort would be required to fully examine this option.

Life cycle assessment method. A life cycle assessment is a more complete numerical analysis of environmental impact. Rather than using average values for regional impact, actual environmental impact is inventoried, considering the actual production system, operation, and disposal system used. An inventory of all emissions that occur from all processes during the life cycle of a product is summarized into a list of all emissions released, all raw materials used, and all waste generated.

For each of these steps, energy and raw material requirements are determined for the actual product as well as emission levels produced. The values for each stage of the product's life cycle are then summed with appropriate units.

A life cycle assessment result is complete, comprehensive, accurate, and expensive. The analysis is currently reserved for special products that have high impact materials, such as cleansers, chemical film products, and medical products. Nonetheless, LCA technology is developing, and costs of analysis are decreasing. In the near future, it will be a standard tool for product development.

Key areas for eco-design according to McDowan and Kagert are:

1. **Material chemistry:** What chemicals are used? Are they safe for humans?
2. **Disassembly:** At the end of a products life, is it easy to disassemble the various parts? Thus, the parts which are to be discarded could be sent for incineration and landfill. The reusable parts would be used again.
3. **Does the design contain parts** which have been used after disassembly and are giving good service life?

Factors of environmental impact

1. **Global warming.** Accumulation of greenhouse gases and water vapour in the upper atmosphere, CO_2 emission, methane, CFC, black carbon particles, nitrogen oxides, created by industrial processes and products in use.
2. Depletion of resources such as iron ore, gas, oil, and coal, which are non-recoverable resources. They are in a limited supply, the shortage of which could create problems of less power generation.
3. **Solid waste.** Generation during life cycle, incineration of waste materials generates undesirable air pollution. Landfill creates toxic ash and results in ground water pollution.
4. **Water pollution.** Discharge from industrial processes pollutes water if not treated for effluent treatment. Heavy metals, fertilizers, solvents, oils acids, and suspended solids these affect ground water and drinking water.
5. **Air pollution.** Emissions from factories, power plants, and incinerators create air pollution. Motor vehicles are responsible for doing air pollution by emitting CO_2, NO_x, SO_2, Ozone, etc.
6. Land degradation is due to mining, deforestation, and soil degradation due to inorganic farming.
7. Biodiversity is affected due to land clearing for urban development, mining, etc. Thus, flora and fauna are affected to a great extent.
8. Ozone depletion results due to use of chemicals which rupture the ozone layer in the atmosphere. This permits sun rays and UV rays to reach the earth which is harmful to human beings.

DfE agenda

Step One: 1—drivers, 2—goals, 3—team

1. **Drivers:**
   - **Internal drivers.** The DfE gets motivation due to internal drivers.
     List of internal drivers is as under:
     1 Product quality, (2) Public image, (3) Cost cutting, (4) Innovation, (5) Safety, (6) Early motivation, (7) Ethical responsibility, and (8) Consumer behaviour
   - **External drivers.** (1) Environmental factors, (2) Market pressures, (3) Competition, (4) Other trade organizations which want to join and offer help, (5) Suppliers, and (6) Social pressures

2. **Goals.** (1) Zero landfill, (2) Zero hazardous waste generation, (3) Zero hazardous emissions, (4) Zero water use, (5) All green environment use, (5) Buildings certified for soundness
3. **Teams.** The DfE team should have a leader who has a rich experience of having installed DfE initiative in a number of industries

Life cycle strategies and questions asked in each strategy

(1) Material, (2) Production, (3) Distribution, (4) Use, (5) Recovery

Identification of Potential Environmental Impact

1. **Materials.** Questions: What plastics and additives are used? What metals are used? Whether glass or ceramics are used?
2. **Production**. Questions: Which process is used? Any secondary materials are used? Is water generated? Is waste generated?
3. **Distribution.** Questions: Which transport mode is used? How packaging is done?
4. **Use:** Questions: Life of product, aesthetic life of product
5. **Recovery.** Questions: Is disassembly easy? Are disassembly tools OK? Is reuse of components possible?

Companies and products

Starbucks. This company is decreasing its carbon footprint by building more energy-efficient stores and facilities, conserving energy and water, and purchasing renewable energy credits. Starbucks has achieved LEED certificates in 116 stores in 12 countries. Starbucks has even created a portable LSSD certified store in Denver. It was their goal to reduce energy consumption by 25% and to cover 100% of its electricity with renewable energy by 2015.

Hewlett Packard. HP is working towards reducing energy used in manufacturing, developing, materials that have less environmental impact, and designing easily recyclable equipment.

IBM. Their goal is to extend product life beyond just production and to use recyclable and reusable products that can be safely disposed of at the end of product life. They are also reducing consumption of energy and minimize their carbon footprint.

Philips. For almost 20 years, non-sustainable development has been a crucial part of Philips decision making and manufacturing process. The goal of Philips is to produce products with their environmental responsibility in mind. Not only are they working on reducing energy during manufacture, they are also participating in a unique project, philanthropy through design. Since 2005, Philips has been working on philanthropy but also collaborating with other organizations to use their expertise and innovation to help the more fragile sections of society.

Besides these large brand names, there are several other consumer products companies in the DfE program including:

- Atlantic Chemical and Equipment Co.
- American Cleaning Solutions
- BCD Supply
- Beta Technology
- Brighton USA

REVIEW QUESTIONS

1. Explain various stages of Total Life Cycle–Materials. P 516
2. Explain Eco-indicator Method 95 for determining environmental impact in case of a kitchen mixer. P 508
3. How Eco-indicator 95 worksheet is developed for assessment of environmental impact in case of a Kitchen Mixer. Draw a process Tree in this case. Figure 17.5
4. What are the various factors of environmental impact? Discuss in detail. P 515
5. What are the different tenets of DfE agenda? Describe what is meant by Drivers, Goals and Teams. P 515–516
6. What are different life cycle strategies and Questions asked in each stage? P 516
7. List the names of some prominent companies that have contributed towards DfE drive and achieved LEED and other certificates. Also mention some other companies which have contributed in DfE drive. P 516

REFERENCES

[1] Goekoop M.J., The Eco indicator 95 Final report NOH report 9523 Pre Associates: Amerfoot Netherlands 1995.

[2] Otto, Kevin and K. Wood, Product Design and Technology the reverse engineering and New Product development, 2004, Pearson Education Singapore.

Question Bank

1. What is meant by engineering design process?

Ans: According to ABET (Accreditation Board for Engineering and Technology), engineering design is the process of devising a system, component, or process to meet the desired needs.

2. What is the relationship between science, technology, and engineering?

Ans: Science is systematized knowledge, technology is conversion of knowledge into something useful for mankind, and engineering is conversion of technology into something of use to society.

3. How is a designer different from an engineer?

Ans: A designer develops designs by converting concepts into reality while an engineer through his expertise in manufacturing converts it into physical form for use by society.

4. What is the role of an artist in solving a design problem?

Ans: An artist has knowledge of aesthetics which involves rendering, good looks to the product which would bring success to the product at the marketplace.

5. What are the various steps involved in engineering design process?

Ans: Refer to Figure 1. The ten steps involved in engineering design process are:

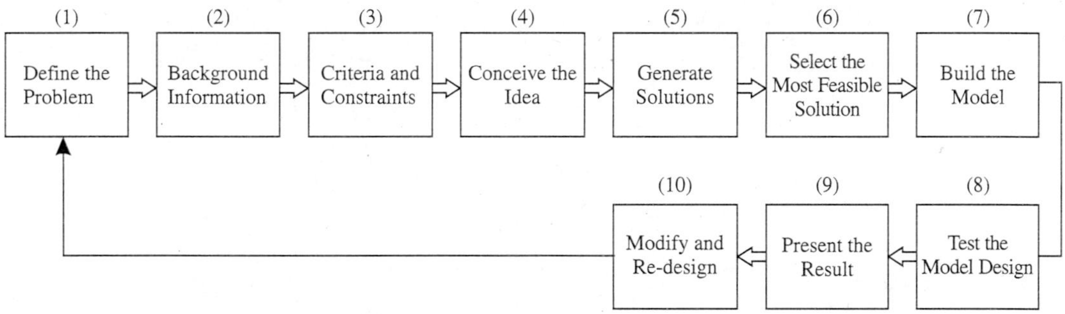

FIGURE 1 Phases of design process.

1. **Problem definition:** This step involves the following steps: problem statement involves a primitive need statement which makes a general requirement from the product. For example, a primitive need statement for designing a fire alarm could be a gadget which would sense rise in temperature in the room above 70°C and warn the inhabitant about it.

2. **Information gathering:** Internet, patents, technical papers, and journals
3. Statement of criteria and constraints for the design
4. **Concept generation**: Creativity and brainstorming

   Evaluation of concepts: Analytic hierarchy. Process AHP is a technique to develop ranking of various factors affecting a process
5. Generate alternative solutions
6. Selection of the best solution
7. Build the model with knowledge of size of parts, material, and process
8. Test the model design
9. Presentation of the results to authorities for acceptance or revision and feedback
10. Modify and redesign

6. Compare engineering design method with scientific method.

Ans: Refer to Figure 2.

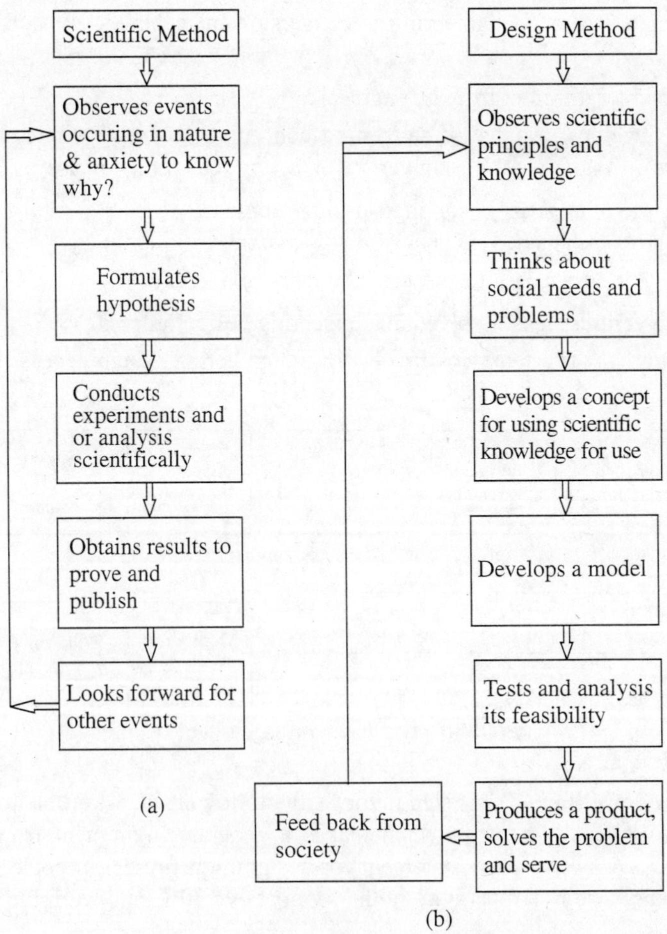

FIGURE 2 Scientific method vs. design method.

Steps of engineering design method are:

1. Need identification
2. Conceptualization
3. Feasibility analysis
4. Production

Steps of scientific method are:

1. Scientific curiosity
2. Hypothesis
3. Logical analysis
4. Proof through experiment
5. Presentation

7. If a product has economic worth, does it mean that it is financially feasible at the project level?

Ans: Economic worth means whether a customer will be ready to pay for the price tagged on a single piece of the product. Financially feasible product on the other hand means that society will be able to purchase the product in quantities large enough in the marketing phase of the product during its lifetime to justify the amount of money invested in the product development and premarket phase, during which the earning is negative being an investment.

Example: The initial investment cost for a product project is ₹ 10,000; return on investment per year is ₹ 4,500 for the first 3 years. Check the financial feasibility of the product project if the cost of capital is 10%.

Solution: I = ₹10,000, return = 4,500/(1+0.1) + 4,500/(1+0.10) 2 + 4,500/(1 + 0.1) 2 = ₹ 11,192, which is greater than the initial investment. Thus, the product project is financially feasible.

8. Differentiate between the following:

- Scientist, designer, and engineer

Ans: A scientist has the motive of discovery of truth. A designer is interested in converting concept into producible form while engineer is responsible to convert the designers output into concrete product using production processes and create products for use by people.

9. In design process, which steps are concept steps and which are embodiment steps?

Ans: The first 4 steps are called concept steps while the steps 5–8 are called embodiment steps.

10. What are the characteristics of engineering design?

Ans:

1. Goal oriented, i.e., problem identification
2. Constrained by physical laws of science, economic constraint, human consideration, i.e., aesthetics, cultural, environmental, legal, and production facility constraint
3. Evolutionary
4. Probabilistic due to difficulty in precise estimation of material property hazards
5. Value competitive
6. Compromise due to opposing functional requirements for the product
7. Variform meaning a large number of feasible solutions to the same problem of which the best could be selected

11. What are the desirable characteristics of designer?

Ans: 1. Ability to quickly identify problem before others
2. *Imaginative and farsighted*: Foresee the conditions in which the product would be operating in various environments
3. Inventive
4. Sense of urgency without panicking
5. Ability to simplify the problem without oversimplifying
6. Numerical ability and skill in software development
7. Decisive in regard identifying the best amongst several feasible solutions
8. Open minded without being dogmatic, open to suggestions and constructive criticism

12. What is the difference between product design and product development?

Ans: Product design as stated before comprises conversion of ideas into reality. Product development, on the other hand, includes set of activities which cover the expanded product life cycle which covers the premarket phase of new product development as well as the marketing phase of the product which involves the various marketing activities during the sale of the product.

13. What is meant by the term product?

Ans: A product is a good, a service or an idea consisting of a bundle of tangible and intangible attributes, received in exchange for money targeted to satisfy customers. It can be considered the output of a firm. A definition given by Philip Kotler is as follows:

- A product is anything that can be offered to a market for attention, acquisition, use, or consumption that might satisfy a want or a need.
- Refer to Figure 3 for a broad classification of products based upon various criteria like durability which include consumer durable products, consumer products depending on buying habits of shoppers, and industrial products, which are in a class by themselves.

14. Give a classification of products based upon the criteria of durability.

Ans: 1. *Non-durable goods:* These are tangible goods consumed in one or few uses such as ice cream, chocolates, etc. These are purchased frequently and need to be advertised for positioning them in the minds of the customers.
2. *Durable goods*: These are tangible goods that survive in long run use. They are also called consumer durable goods.

Examples of this category are shoes, clothing, machine tools, and air conditioners. These products need personal selling effort and more seller warrantees. They yield higher profits to the firm.

15. What are industrial goods? Classify industrial goods and give their examples.

Ans: Refer to Figure 3. Industrial goods are classified depending upon their entry in the production system. They are classified into the following categories:

(A) Material and parts, (B) Capital Items, and (C) Supplies

(A) Materials can be divided into two categories:

1. **Raw materials:** It can be divided into—(a) farm products such as wheat, rice, fruits, vegetables, and even livestock, and (b) natural products such as fish, iron ore, lumber, and petroleum

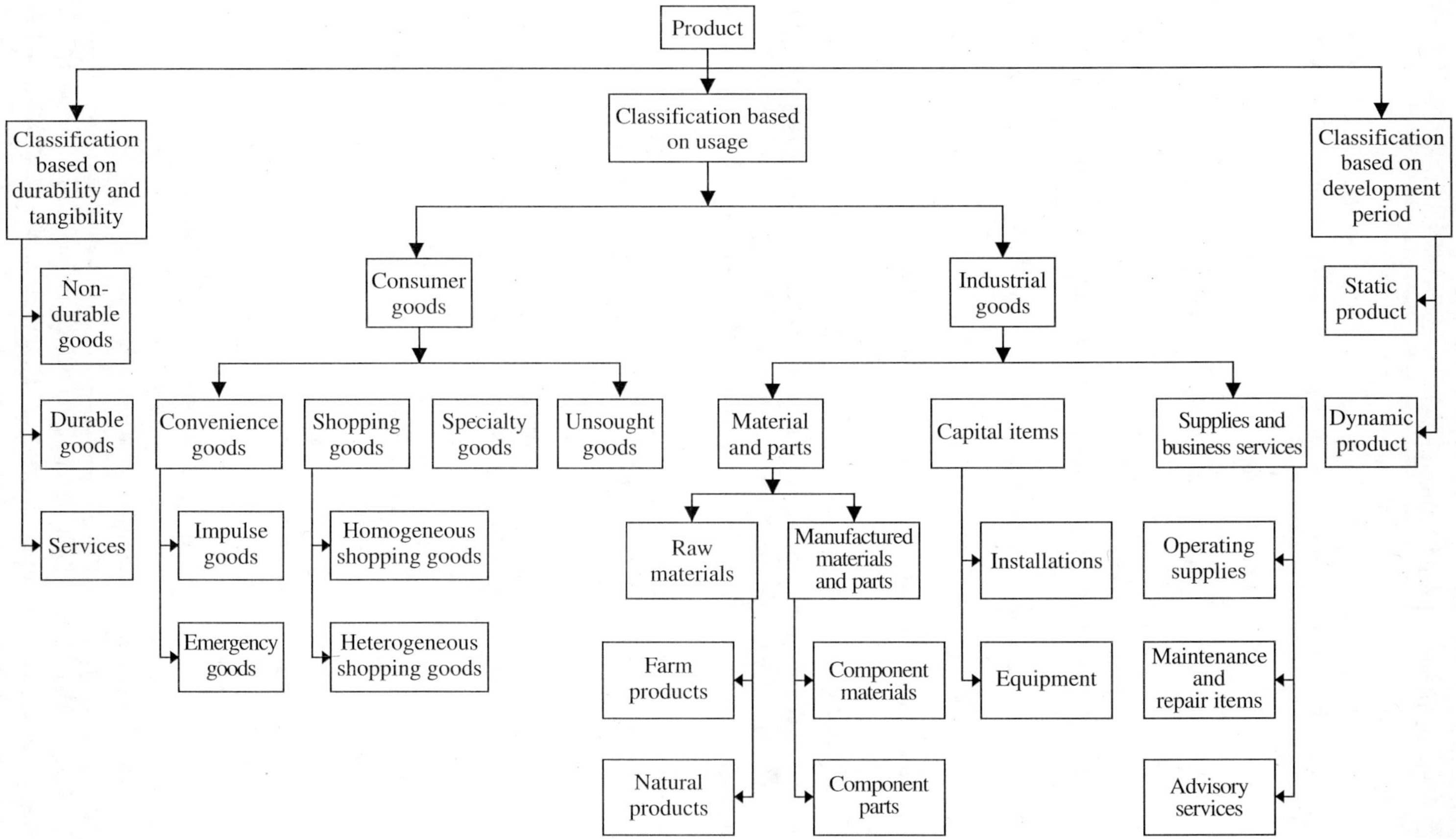

FIGURE 3 Broad classification of products from three major perspectives.

2. **Manufactured materials and parts:**
   (a) Component materials have examples such as galvanized steel, yarn, cement, wires which have a primary operation performed upon them to add value to them. These can be fabricated further to be used in manufacture of further products such as garments, buildings, and construction work.
   (b) Component parts have examples of motors, shafts, bearings, and tires which can be directly used in any design or assembly. These are sold directly to industries and price and service are major considerations.

(B) *Capital items*: These are typically high-priced items such as:
- Installations such as office buildings, workshops, elevators and lifts, and EOT cranes
- Equipment such as portable factory equipment, lift trucks used in material handling, and welding sets which do not become a part of any final product.

(C) Supplies include short-term items which help in running the system maintenance such as paints, nails, brooms, and hand tools, and office supplies such as paper, pencil, lubricating and oils

16. Give a classification of products based on development time.
Refer to Figure 3.

Ans: These are classified as:

(1) *Static products*: In these products, the deign takes place over a long period of time through incremental changes in subsystem and component levels. Examples in this category include automobile parts, and common consumer appliances such as air conditioners and dishwashers.

(2) *Dynamic products*: In this case, the features depend on a specific technology and a change takes place as soon as the technology changes, for example, mobile phones and software.

17. What is meant by intangible goods/products?

Ans: Intangible products do not have physical nature as opposite of physical goods. Digital goods such as downloadable music and mobile Apps are virtual goods. Services also belong to the class of intangible goods. Examples are barber's shop, beautician's parlours.

18. What are the different patterns of the product life cycle curve (PLC) which deviate from standard life cycle curve? Explain the implications of various PLC patterns?

Ans: Refer to Figure 4. There are three patterns of life cycle curves, which deviate from standard life cycle curve:

(1) *Growth–slump–maturity pattern*: Found with small kitchen appliances such as microwave ovens and toasters. With such products, sales grow rapidly due to early adopters when the product is first introduced. Then, the sales fall to a lower level and are sustained by late adopters buying the product for the first time.

(2) *Cycle–recycle pattern* is observed in case of new drugs. Later when the sales start declining, the company gives the drug another promotional push. So, another wave of growth is generated which is lower than the first wave.

(3) *Scalloped pattern* is observed in case the sales go through a succession of life cycles due to development of new applications of the same produce. An example is nylon, which has found application in parachutes, hosiery, shirts, carpets, boat sails, and automobile tires—that continue to be discovered over time.

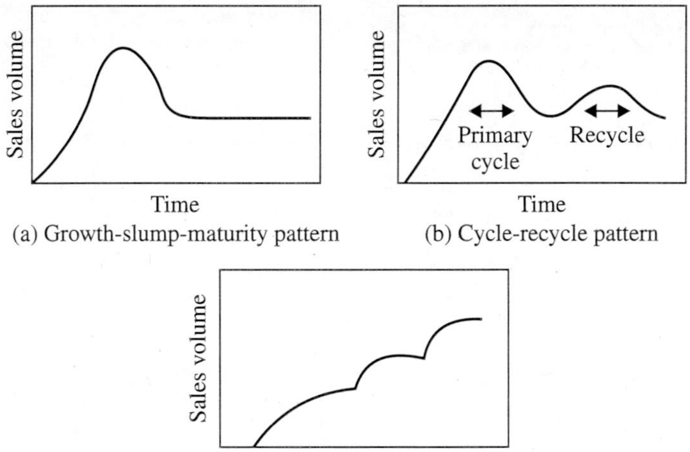

(a) Growth-slump-maturity pattern

(b) Cycle-recycle pattern

(c) Scalloped pattern

Patterns of PLC

FIGURE 4 Various shapes of PLC other than normal.

19. What is Maslow's theory of need hierarchy?

Ans: The general theory of needs developed by Abraham Maslow is:

1. Men are wanting beings
2. Fresh needs can motivate persons to work
3. Man's needs have a hierarchy of importance

20. Give a list of Maslow's hierarchy of needs.

Ans: Refer to Figure 5. The list is as follows:

FIGURE 5 Maslow's heirarchy of needs.

- **Level I.** Physiological needs
- **Level II.** Safety and security needs

- **Level III.** Social needs
- **Level IV.** Psychological needs
- **Level V.** Self-fulfilment needs

21. Classify different types of product attributes which result in satisfying customer needs.

Ans: Refer to Figure 6, which is known as Kano Model. There are four types of product attributes, which result fulfilling customer needs.

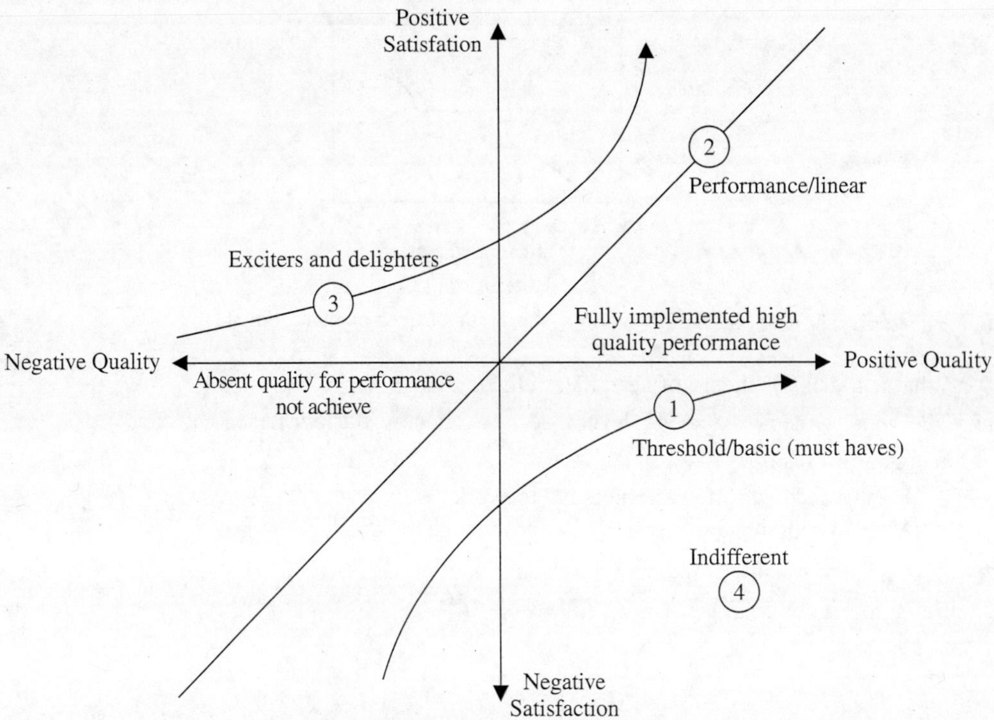

FIGURE 6 Kano model of product types.

1. Expected features or expecters, which a customer normally expects from a product. The customer takes them for granted as standard features.
2. Spoken features are those which the customer wants in any case because these are provided by the designer on priority under his specifications.
3. Unspoken features are those which the customer forgets to mention though it is deeply embedded in his psyche.
4. Exciters or delighters result in customer delight because of the element of surprise. Sometimes even though the quality is not high, there is another factor in the product which delights the customer. For example, in case of Tata's Nano car, the sheer beauty of the shape of this car delights the customer though its performance is questionable.

22. What is meant by market research? What are the 3 stages of market research?

Ans: Market research consists of 3 stages usually called STP—(1) segmentation of a big markets into valid market segments on segmentation criteria, (2) targeting the product to the correct market segments, (3) positioning the product in the selected market segment to maximize marketing effectiveness.

23. What constitutes a valid market segment?

Ans: Valid market segment has the following criteria: (1) The size of the market should be adequate; (2) It must be capable of being described; (3) It should be accessible; (4) Different segments should respond differently to marketing initiatives; (5) Coherence should respond consistently to similar initiatives; (6) *Stability*: The segments should be stable.

24. What are the various criteria for segmenting the market?

Ans: The various criteria are as follows:

1. *Demographic*: The considerations are gender, marital status, location, age, and education.
2. *Psychographic*: Lifestyle, personality, and culture.
3. *Geographic*: For example in India, it is North, South, East, and West parts of the country.
4. Benefit segmentation
5. *User-based segmentation*: Value system of a company as customer. For example, two companies buying staple pins one going for steel staple pins while the other company going for plastic staple pins which are less injurious than the steel staple pins. The former is not safety conscious while the latter is safety conscious.

25. How companies carry out market research? What are the various techniques?

Ans: The following techniques are used for market research process:

Sales visits to gather information: In this method, the following 7 steps have been recommended—

1. The information to be collected is decided first.
2. Types of customer to be visited should be decided.
3. The team members should be from various departments.
4. Generate topics and questions in advance.
5. Interview buyer's representative
6. Discuss outcomes of the interviews with members
7. Analyze reports and store in a database

26. What are secondary sources of information? How do they differ from primary sources of information.

Ans: While primary source of information is based on actual interview of customer by market research personnel of the company, the secondary sources are as under:

Secondary sources of information are:

1. Use of experts
2. Publications
3. Use of specialist market research companies
4. Observation through spy camera to watch eye and finger movements giving clues
5. Roleplay by team members
6. Customer suggestion box
7. Key user analysis

27. What is meant by technology assessment? State the outcomes of technology–product interaction.

Ans: There are two types of technology: old technology and new technology. Likewise, there are two types of products: old products and new products. An example of old technology comprises heating of food on gas burner with use of cooking gas. While heating of food in microwave oven is new technology. This is the result of a scientific discovery of using infrared heat source for the heating of food. A study of interaction of technology and products results in outcomes which are called assessment of technology. This serves as a guideline regarding the best course of action beneficial to firms.

Outcomes:

1. Old product with old technology will not succeed unless a cost reduction strategy is adopted.
2. New product and old technology could succeed only if aesthetics and ergonomics are improved in the product.
3. Old product with new technology could be possible if better positioning of the product in the market is done.
4. New product in a new market would result in the product becoming a market leader.

28. What is market assessment and how it is done?

Ans: Market assessment is done by determining the following factors related with the market under consideration:

1. *Market size*: It is measured by units of currency.
2. Market growth is measured by number of units sold in a certain time frame.
3. Return on sales (ROS), return on investment (ROI), return on capital (ROC), contribution which is sales–cost
4. Buyers decision where there is straight buy or through an intermediary
5. *Financial market structure*: Whether there is pure competition, oligopoly with 3–4 manufacturers and several buyers, monopoly where there is only one manufacturer with several buyers, or perfect competition with many manufacturers and many buyers.

29. State the requirements from a good product.

Ans:
1. Optimal performance of the main function
2. Easy to repair and maintain
3. Reliability in use
4. Aesthetic
5. Durable
6. Producible in large numbers
7. Simple to use and handle
8. Compact and not heavy and bulky

30. What are the various stages of thought process which go on in the minds of born designers? Could other persons become made designers?

Ans: Stages in the thought process of born designers are: (1) defining need, (2) period of incubation, (3) conception of solution, (4) weighing the solutions, and (5) decision on the best solution. There is a school of thought, which believes that even persons who have not gone through any creative experience in the past can be made into designers through regimentation called design thinking.

31. Explain the idea-generating methods due to Linsey.

Ans: Refer to Figure 7. Linsey gave 4 idea-generating methods:

1. *Brainstorming*: It is also called Osborn technique. A group of persons exchange ideas based on the following rules: (1) Criticism not allowed, (2) Wild ideas welcomed, (3) Building on each other's ideas, (4) Large number of ideas welcomed—150 in 30–45 minutes, (5) Stay focused on the topic. Tangency not allowed, (6) One person should be allowed to make presentation at a time so that a brilliant shy person will not be eliminated, (7) Be visual. Sketch ideas to help others

2. *Brainsketching*: Members exchange sketches made by one another.
3. *Gallery method*: Sketches are made on large sheets of paper and mounted on a wall. Participants move about the room and each other's ideas.
4. *6–3–5 method*: 6 participants seat around a table with each participant generating 3 ideas in 5 minutes, i.e., 90 ideas in 5 minutes.

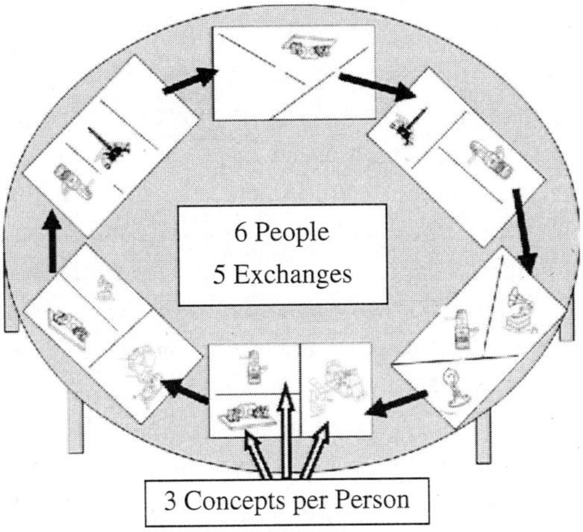

6–3–5 M Method of idea generation

FIGURE 7 Some methods of idea generation.

32. Give an example of specifications development based on ergonomic considerations.

Ans: Refer to Figure 8. A popular example based on human body dimensions or ergonomic considerations is in the determination of blackboard dimensions to suit all populations of professors. (1) The height of the blackboard is fixed from knowledge of comfortable highest reach of a shortest professor. Likewise, the lowest comfortable reach of a tallest professor will fix the lowest height of the blackboard. Thus, the height of the blackboard is determined. (2) The width of the blackboard can be derived from the width of the auditorium or classroom.

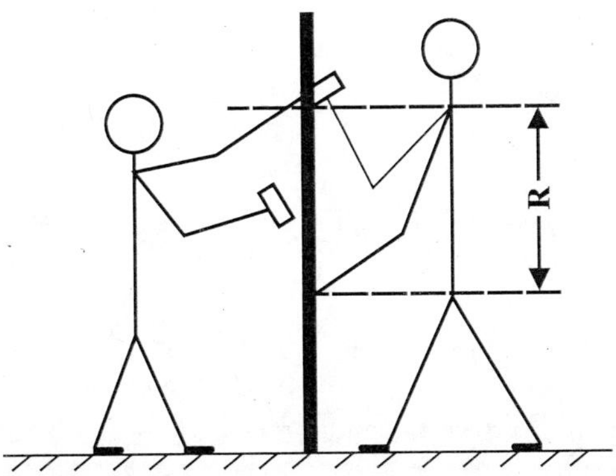

FIGURE 8 Specification development for blackboard from human dimensions.

33. List the various types of design with brief explanation of each.

Ans: Various types of design are: (1) *Original design:* Based on innovation and new technology, it needs to be pushed in the market. Examples are ballpoint pen, electric bulb, locomotive, and drone plane. (2) *Adaptive design:* Modifying existing design to fulfil new requirement, e.g., simple lathe to retrofitted lathe to make it semiautomatic or numerically controlled lathe. (3) *Selection design:* Design selected from manufacturers catalogues to be fitted in larger design, e.g., ball bearing, pumps, and motors. (4) *Industrial design:* Industrial design emphasizes on aesthetics and ergonomics, examples are torch, dentist's chair, and mosquito net. (5) *Production design:* Designs which assist in production such as jigs and fixtures, gauges, cutting tools, and material handling equipment. (6) *Configuration design:* Represented as assembly drawings to show how parts fit. Possible configuration developed like possible arrangements for computer system showing alternative configurations of computer table screen, CPU, and keyboard. (7) *Parametric design:* The various dimensions, tolerances, etc. are decided after configurations are decided. For example, the diameter, wall thickness, and length of a cylinder are finalized to give maximum strength or minimum space. An automobile engine is fixed for size to fit in the space available. (8) *Optimum design* falls in 4 categories—(a) Design by evolution, (b) Innovation, (c) By trial and error, (d) Numerical algorithm in case of optimization subject to constraints. (9) *Redesign* is done to improve initial design to improve cost, efficiency, and producibility. Example is development of LED bulb instead of filament bulb. (10) Design for environment consists in designing for minimum environmental impact also called green design. (11) *User-centric design:* It involves users and a clear understand between user and designer. In this kind of design, the design will be based upon customer's continuous involvement. User will even do early testing and evaluation. The design shall progress iteratively to achieve final successful design.

34. What is meant by creativity? Why it is an essential attribute for a designer?

Ans: Creativity is the ability of a few individuals to create something new. It is an important attribute in designers because design demands conversion of an idea into concrete reality. So, the starting point in design is creation of idea which demands creativity.

35. What are the characteristics of a good design?

Ans: The following characteristics are to be satisfied by good design:

1. *Functional requirements:* It should satisfy the requirements of force, strength, energy, power, and deflection. These requirements should be fulfilled with reliability, safety, economy, and easily operable.
2. *Physical properties:* It includes shape, size, weight, and surface finish. Use can be made of CADD, i.e., Computer aided drafting and design.
3. *Environment:* Should be able to perform in extreme conditions of dirt, noise, vibration, and humidity. Perform in a safe way as laid down by governmental laws.
4. Aesthetics or good looks to please the eye of customer.
5. *Manufacturing:* The materials and processes of manufacture should be selected to minimize the cost.
6. *Cost:* Product development cost, initial product cost and life cycle cost should be reasonable.

QUESTIONS ON STANDARDS AND REGULATORY NORMS

36. What are the regulatory bodies and standards to be followed by business organizations to control the performance parameters of a product or service?

Ans: Examples of regulatory bodies and standards are:

1. ISO 9000, which provides guidelines for good and efficient business operations
2. The big three of automobile line Ford, Chrysler, and General Motors subscribe standards for suppliers of components and parts
3. ISO 14000 is environmental management standards for protection of environmental balance during manufacture and service
4. OHSAS 18000 is for operational heal and safety services

37. How are various standards developed by BIS? Mention the steps.

Ans: The steps are: (1) Submission of papers to BIS, (2) Formulation of standard, (3) Circulation of standards to interested parties, and (4) Finalization of standards.

38. What are the human factors issues involved during design of a product?

Ans: The human factors are: (1) Anatomy, (2) physiology, and (3) psychology of the human operator who is regarded as: (a) Occupant of space provided by the chair, (b) Reader of display of the machine, (c) Operator of controls on the machine, and (d) Decision maker of operations of the machine.

Planogram on Wall of Retail Stores

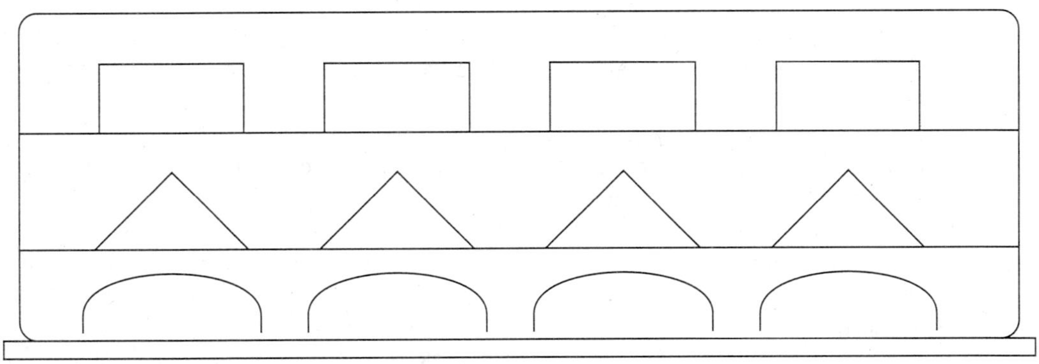

FIGURE 9 Planogram on a wall in retail stores.

VISUAL MERCHANDISING QUESTIONS

39. Define the term visual merchandising.

Ans: Visual merchandising is defined as the presentation of all goods and merchandise in a retail shop setting at its best. It should be colour coordinated, accessorised, and self-explanatory. Visual merchandising denotes everything a shopper/customer views at the venue of business or point of sale in a retail outlet. It should create a positive image of the goods and result in AIDA, i.e., attention, interest, desire, and action on the part of the shopper/customer.

40. What are the objectives of visual merchandising?

Ans: *Objectives of visual merchandising*: To attract shoppers/customers to the place of business and the retail shop, show the goods in better light and generate sales. The details are as follows:

1. To educate the shopper/customer regarding goods/products features and qualities in an effective way
2. Presentation of the product in environment similar to real-life application creating a strong impact
3. To create a suitable background in the retail stores for selling the goods or product or merchandise
4. New customers should be attracted by the merchandising process
5. To enable the customers to test the product on the spot and build their confidence regarding the product

41. What are the trends and techniques in visual merchandising?

Ans: The contemporary trends in visual merchandizing are listed below:

1. *Hi-tech showcasing*: Industries provide customers with IT-based tablets which enable customers to browse and select the product of their choice in the stores without their having to move about in the stores.
2. *Pop-up stores*: It is referred to as flash retailing which began in Europe and US in 2003, initially occupying vacant mall spaces and abandoned storefronts. Examples are: (1) online retailer bluefly.com opened a brick and mortar stores in New York, clearing old stock in a temporary boutique, (2) gap incorporated furnished a school bus with apparel and accessories, utilizing the bus as a temporary pop-up stores.
3. *Use of natural materials*: Many industries make eco-friendliness and sustainability as their key concept in store retailing. They use natural materials and textures in the stores.
4. *Futuristic displays*: In order to make a trendy store design, luxury brands, curvy and streamlined shapes of fixtures are resorted to achieve projection into future.
5. *Materials mix*: Use of unconventional and eccentric mix of materials to distinguish the stores from other conventional stores.
6. *Local design elements*: Local should be made vocal. Support should be provided for the local goods. Homeliness is created by using local elements in the clothing, crockery, and use of local musical sounds creates a homely atmosphere for local customer audience.
7. *Warm colour palettes*: When majority of customers are ladies, a suitable atmosphere should be created to win the customer through use of warm colours, soft furnishings, and textures.
8. *Use of copper*: Use of copper in store design with clothing, fixtures, and lamps display tables gives the stores a rich, aristocratic look. White backdrop with copper frontage is also desirable.
9. *Marble effect*: Marble effect created by painting to create a marble pattern is a good strategy. Even use of real marble lends a store dignity and charm.
10. *Industrial style*: Industrial background is created by using cement floor, big windows, and open steel bins which give the stores industrial look.

42. What are the principal materials used in visual merchandising? List them.

Ans: The following materials are used in visual merchandising in retail stores:

(1) *Acrylics*: Acrylic sheets of thickness 1 mm to 12 mm can be used for displaying prices, donation boxes, mobile recharging units, etc. (2) Vinyl stickers are used for sticking on walls or Sunboard. Vinyl is PVC, i.e., polyvinyl chloride. It is World's most versatile plastic used for foodwrap to automobile body parts. (3) *Digital prints*: These are digital images reproduced on a physical surface like paper, film, cloth, and plastic. Digital prints have glue coating on their backside so that they can be applied on any surface. (4) *Translights*: Any transparency lit from behind and used as a background picture for feature films and TV products. (5) *Sunboards*: These are light, strong, easily cut sheet material used for mounting of vinyl prints. These are also used as backing for paintings. It has three layers, inner layer of polystyrene foam and a white clay coated paper on outside.

43. What are miscellaneous materials used to develop visual merchandising?

Ans: Along list of miscellaneous materials which shows the materials needed to guide aspiring retailing enthusiasts to develop visual merchandising stores on their own is as under:

(1) Stands for items, (2) Cloth to cover display tables, (3) Artificial flowers, (4) Digital camera, (5) Display tables, (6) Scotch tape, (7) Glass cleaner and mop, (8) Glitters to make displays twinkle, (9) Hammers, screw drivers and pliers, (10) Glue guns and glue sticks, (11) Laminating plastics, (12) Various types of lights, tubes, and LED strips, (13) Nails and screws, (14) Paint and paint brushes, (15) Notepads, pens and markers, (16) Personal computer, printer and paper, (17) Rubber bands, (18) Scissors and utility knife, (19) Staple gun and staples, (20) Steel rule, (21) White glue, spray adhesive, and adhesive remover, (22) Electrical wires.

44. What are the tools of visual merchandising for a good retail stores? List them.

Ans: The various visual merchandising tools needed for a good retail stores are:

1. *External signage*: (a) Marquees—to display the name of merchandising venue, (b) Banners: Eye catching means of promotion to be hung from flagpoles or building tops, (c) Awning provides protection from weather while watching window display.
2. *Walks and displays*: Required for effective watching of visual merchandise. Planogram shown in Figure 9 is a device to display on the wall and informs the shopper about what are the items in the particular section of the stores.
3. Window display acts as information link to potential customer. It promotes stores image.
4. *Colour*: Blue colour is cool, relaxes excited people; green colour is easy on the eye; red excites and stimulates; yellow is cheerful colour; orange is friendly, warm, and vibrant; violate indicates elegance; brown is relaxing and warm grey is depressing and cool.
5. *Lightings*: Lighting is used to draw attention to a part of display area.
6. *Props, fixtures, and signage*: A prop clarifies the function of the merchandise on display.

45. What are the techniques of visual merchandising? Explain.

Ans:
1. *Creating themes*: A story of the product is painted on wall and create a theme
2. Co-ordination
3. *Blocking*—into small sections
4. Colour contrasting
5. Symmetry and balance

6. Repetition of the items is done to attract the attention of the customer.
7. Triangular grouping consists of using three cubes for differentiation. For example, amongst three products, two products are placed at lower height on either side of the most costly and valuable product which is placed highest.

TRANSPORTATION QUESTIONS INVOLVING AEROPLANE, LOCOMOTIVE, SHIP, AND AUTOMOBILE

While the Bullock cart remains the eternal land transport in India, this section will examine other means of transport such as aeroplane, locomotive, ship, and automobile.

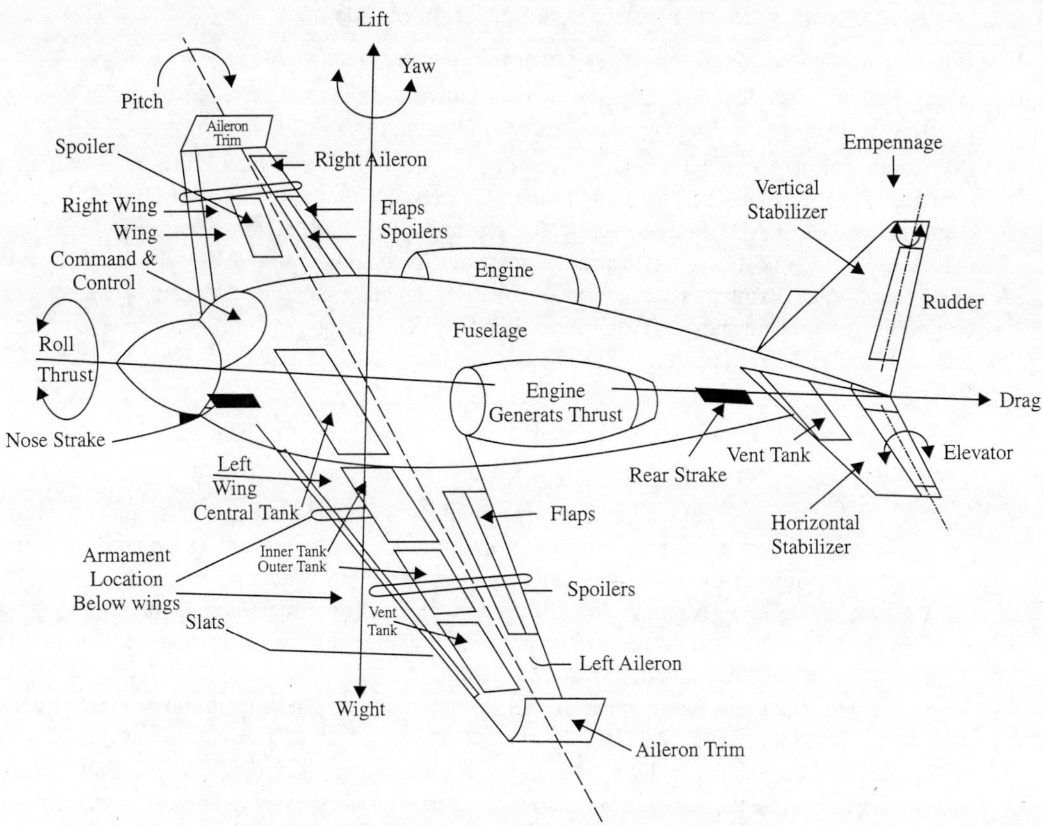

FIGURE 10 Details of various important parts and surfaces of an aircraft.

46. Describe the various parts of an aeroplane with their functions.

Ans: Referring to Figure 10, the main parts of an aeroplane are:

1. Wing extends from the outside from each side of the aeroplane. Streamlined shape of the wing helps to generate the leverage which lifts it from the ground and keeps it in the air. Ailerons are in the wing.
2. *Body or fuselage*: Body extends from forefront to the tail. The body has a tubular shape covered with a light aluminium cover, contains the control devices, crew, passengers, cargo.

3. *Tail section or empennage*: It consists of the tail cone, fixed aerodynamic surfaces of vertical and horizontal type which help in stabilizing the plane, movable surfaces including rudder, located at back edge, and elevator located at the rear edge of the horizontal stabilizer. Movable surfaces in the tail help in directing the aircraft during the flight
4. *Landing gear:* It contains wheels to help its motion on ground or water.
5. Display panel for use by pilot to have information on different parameters during flight. Also, there are control devices for the pilot.
6. Propeller or Chopper blades mounted on hub, which get power from engine. When propeller blades rotate, they produce thrust which has components lift and drag as shown in Figure 11.

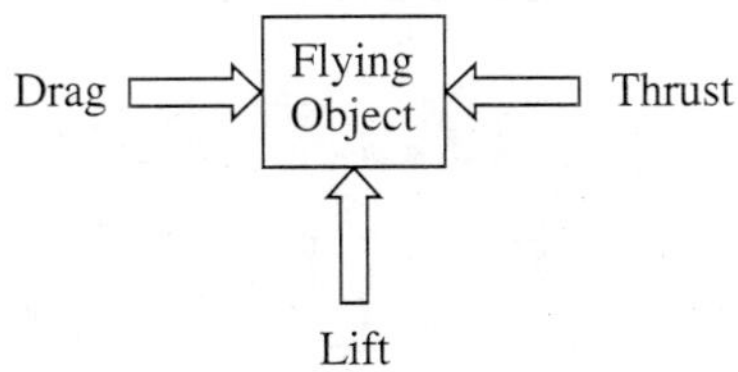

FIGURE 11 Lift and drag on aircraft.

47. What is meant by pitch, roll, and yaw as applied to aeroplane during its flight? How are they effected?

Ans: Refer to Figure 12. Pitch refers to rotation about a transverse horizontal axis, roll is the rotation about a longitudinal axis along the body of the plane, and yaw is the rotation about the vertical axis. Ailerons in the wing control the roll, rudder in the tail controls yaw, and elevators in the tail control the pitch.

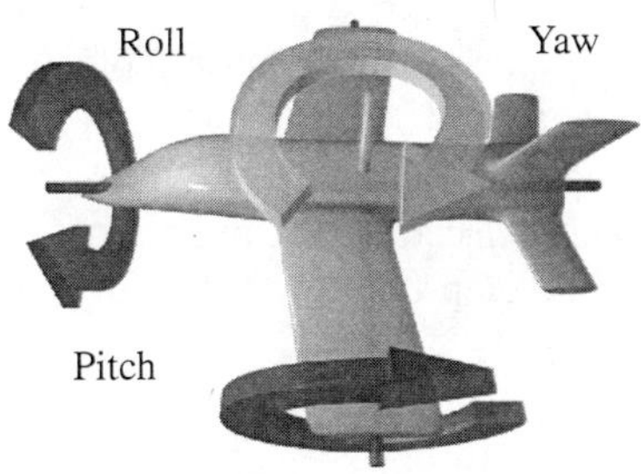

FIGURE 12 Three degrees of rotational freedom of aircraft.

48. Describe the working of modern electric locomotive? Highlight its important parts and their function.

Ans: Refer to Figure 13. In electric locomotive, the transmission of power takes place by means of an overhead wire. A hinged steel framework called pantograph connects the overhead wires to the locomotive. They receive the power at extremely high voltage and are equipped with a transformer which reduces the voltage to a level at which it can be used. The power is then fed through main inverter to four 3-Phase AC Traction motors which give the drive to the wheels. The contact is made through Axle Brush.

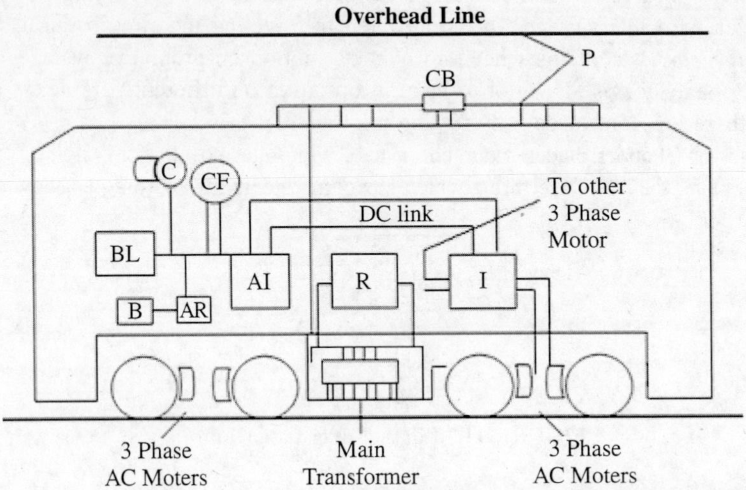

FIGURE 13 Block diagram showing parts of electric locomotive.

Principal parts:

1. Main transformer
2. Main rectifier AC to DC
3. Main inverter DC to AC
4. Auxiliary inverter is a part of cooling system
5. Compressor consists of pump driven by electric motor
6. Motor blowers keep temperature of traction motors to reasonable levels
7. Battery is used to supply starting current
8. Axle brush supplies current to the four AC motors
9. Cooling fans are provided to keep the power systems cool

49. Describe the various parts of a ship.

Ans: Refer to Figure 14. The various parts of a ship are:

1. *Bow*: It is the front section of the ship.
2. Desk is the permanent top covering over a compartment.
3. *Superstructure*: It is the extension above the baseline
4. *Smokestack*: It is a device used to expel boiler steam and smoke or engine exhaust
5. Stern is the back end of the ship
6. Propeller and rudder propeller is a fan that transmits power by converting rotational motion into thrust. Rudder is a primary control surface used to steer the ship.
7. Anchor is a heavy metallic object which links the ship to the bed of water and prevents its drift due to wind or other effects.
8. *Bulbous bow*: Protruding bulb at the front of a ship just below the waterline and enables the ship move effortlessly.

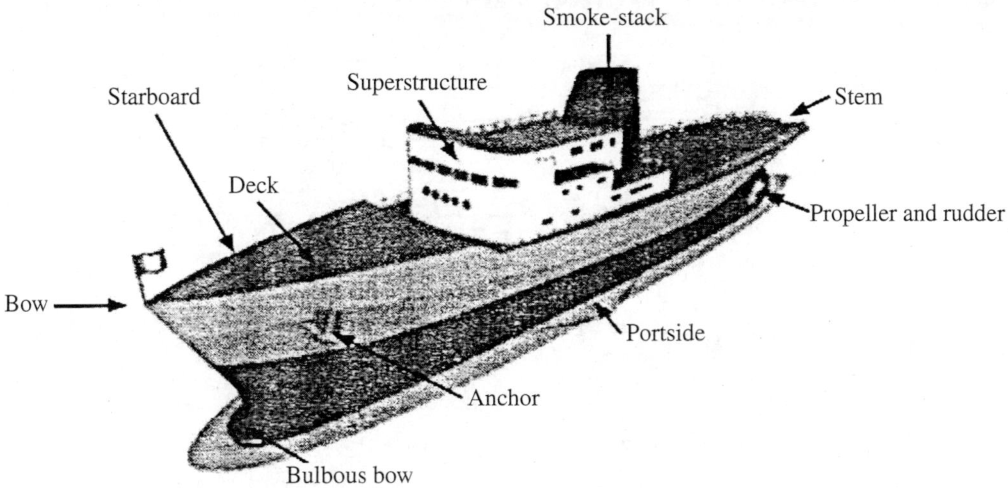

FIGURE 14 Main parts of a ship

50. Classify different types of vessels used in marine transport.

Ans: The various types of water transport facilities are:

1. *Boat*: For small-scale water activities
2. *High-speed craft*: For civilian use
3. *Offshore oil vessel*: Transportation of personnel and goods to offshore
4. *Fishing vessel*: Commercial fishing purposes
5. *Harbour work craft*: General-purpose vessel
6. *Dry cargo ship*: Transportation of solid raw materials
7. *Liquid cargo ship*: For transportation of liquids and gases
8. *Passenger vessel*: To carry passengers
9. *Recreational boat*: For recreation and sporting activities
10. *Special purpose vessel*: To perform unique activities such as marine weather forecasting, heavy machinery transport, and planes.
11. *Submersible*: For underwater activities
12. *Submarine*: For naval activities
13. *Yacht*: For cruising or racing

AUTOMOBILES, TRUCK, AND THEIR PART DETAILS

51. Describe the various parts of an automobile stating their function in brief.

Ans: The two figures shown in Figure 15 have been selected to highlight the various parts of—(1) automobile top view, and (2) truck side view.

AUTOMOBILE CHASSIS

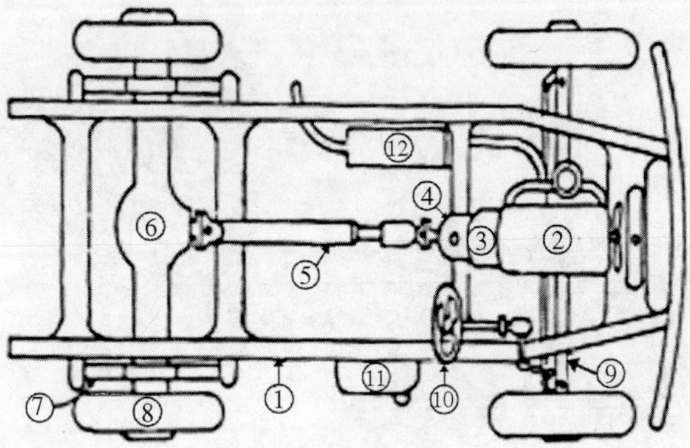

(1) Frame (2) Engine (3) Clutch (4) Gear box (5) Propeller shaft (6) Rear axle (7) Road spring (8) Wheel (9) Front axle (10) Steering (11) Fuel tank (12) Silencer

SIDE VIEW OF A TRUCK

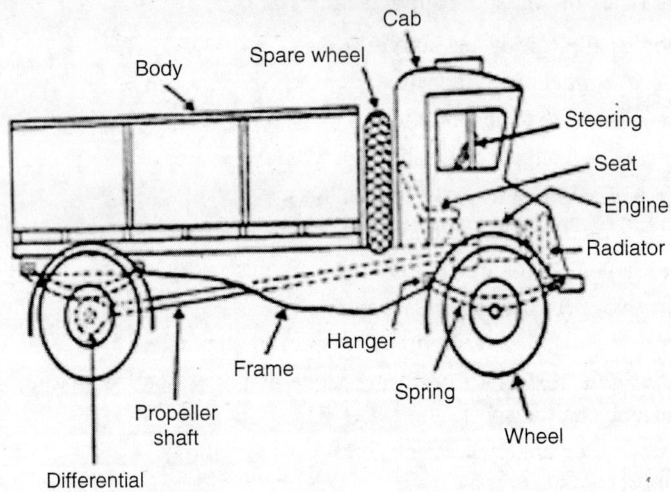

FIGURE 15 Plan view of automotive chassis and side view of a truck showing all the details.

The automobile top view shows the following parts of automobile:

1. Frame
2. *Engine:* Develops the power through combustion of fuel through spark ignition or compression ignition
3. *Clutch*: Transmits power from engine to rear axle
4. Gearbox
5. Propeller shaft

6. Rear axle
7. Road spring
8. Wheel
9. *Front axle*: It enables the turning of the vehicle through the steering mechanism
10 *Steering wheel*: It enables the operation of the steering mechanism to enable the car to turn where needed.
11. *Fuel tank*: For the storage of petrol or diesel
12. *Silencer*: Dampens the noise which could be created by the exhaust gases

Truck side view:

1. Steering
2. Seat
3. Engine
4. Radiator
5. Spring
6. Wheel
7. Spare wheel
8. Frame
9. Propeller shaft

Components of chassis with brief description:

1. *Frame*: It is made up of two long members and riveted with the help of number of cross members
2. Clutch transfers power from engine to transmission system
3. Gear box enables various speeds transmitted to the propeller shaft through universal joint
4. U joint exists at both the ends of the propeller shaft in floating condition
5. Transmits power from engine to rear wheel in a floating condition through crown wheel and pinion and a Propeller shaft held on universal joints at either end.
6. Crown wheel and pinion are housed in Banjo in the rear axle
7. Elliptical spring supports the weight of chassis and the passengers

Appendix **A**

Limits, Fits and Tolerances

Appendix A deals with the various aspects of limits, fits and tolerances with which a design or manufacturing engineer should be well conversant. This aspect was touched upon in brief in the chapters. The appendix aims at giving more details of this essential area of precision engineering with which any reader should be acquainted. For a detailed study, textbooks by R.K. Jain, R.L. Murthy should be referred.

A.1 METHOD OF CALCULATION OF TOLERANCE GRADES IT AND FUNDAMENTAL DEVIATION IN ASSEMBLIES

The standards for limits and fits are given in IS: 919–1963 in which 16 grades of tolerances and 27 fundamental deviations are provided. In this section, the formulae for calculating the tolerances are presented to enable the calculation of tolerances and fundamental deviations are explained in brief. For grades 5–16, the tolerance values are determined in terms of unit tolerance i:

$$i(\text{microns}) = 0.45\sqrt[3]{D} + 0.001D$$

where D is the nominal diameter of an assembly.

The magnitudes of each grade are then derived from Table A.1.

TABLE A.1 Tolerance magnitudes corresponding to tolerance grades

IT5	IT6	IT7	IT8	IT9	IT10	IT11	IT12	IT13	IT14	IT15	IT16
$7i$	$10i$	$16i$	$25i$	$40i$	$64i$	$100i$	$160i$	$250i$	$400i$	$640i$	$1000i$

A.1.1 Fundamental Deviations

Capital letters A–Z except the letters I, L, O, Q are used for designating FD values for holes and lowercase letters a–z for shafts as shown below. They indicate how the tolerance zone is placed with respect to the zero line on the conventional diagram of fits.

For holes: A B C D E F G H J K M N P R S T U V W X Y Z etc.

For shafts: a b c d e f g h j k m n p r s t u v w x y z

For rules of calculating the FD magnitudes, the IS Standards should be referred because they are standardized and complex. Formula FD = $5.5D^{0.41}$ is used for calculating FD values representing f, F ÷ f is negative and F is positive. For shaft with FD g, it is $-2.5D^{0.34}$, for m and for M, FD IT7-IT6, where m is for shaft and M is for hole.

Example 1. Calculate the tolerance for a shaft g6 82 mm. This lies in the range 80–120. Thus, $D = \sqrt{120 \times 80} = \sqrt{9600} = 98\,\text{mm}$ and $i = 0.45\sqrt[3]{98} + 0.001 \times 98 = 2.173$ microns. The tolerance from Table A.1 shows that the tolerance for IT6 is $10i$ = 21.73 microns.

Example 2. Calculate FD for shaft g if nominal size is 32 mm. Assume that FD for g = IT6-IT7 and IT6 = 0.016 and IT7 = 0.025. On using the given data, we have g = 0.016 – 0.025 = – 0.009 mm. The value of FD for g can also be found from the formula FD = $-2.5D^{0.34}$.

A.2 TOLERANCE BUILD UP IN ASSEMBLIES

Example 1. If four components are stacked in an assembly of which the final tolerance is to be 0.42, determine the individual tolerances on each of the four components if the tolerance on each of them is assumed to be equal (1) working on an algebraic basis and (2) working on a statistical basis assuming that the dimensions of the pieces are distributed according to a normal distribution.

Solution.

(1) On the algebraic basis, the tolerance on each component will be divided equally among the four components. Thus, the tolerance on each component will be 0.42/4 = 0.105 mm.

(2) On the statistical basis, assume the tolerances to be analogous to the standard deviations and normally distributed. To find out the tolerance of an assembly, square of an assembly tolerance shall equal the sum of the squares of tolerances of individual components (from a theorem in statistics on normal populations). Therefore $t_a^2 = 4t_c^2$, where t_a is the tolerance on the assembly and t_c is the tolerance on the component. Substituting the values in $t_c = t_a/2$ = 0.42/4 = 0.21 mm which is more than if algebraic addition is done.

Example 2. Utility of conventional diagram of fits for tolerances—algebraic approach and statistical approach: The theory of fits is explained through an illustrative example. An assembly of a hole and shaft is to be made by picking up components from a large number of shafts and broached holes. The nominal diameter is 30 mm, the minimum clearances 0.015 mm and the maximum clearance 0.05. The production processes for the shaft and holes are such that the tolerance on the size of hole is 1.5 times the tolerance on the shaft which is prepared by grinding to a specification IT6. Analyze the situations when (1) an ideal situation of guaranteed clearance is assumed and (2) a risk of 1 in 1000 is permitted. Explain the calculations for both the cases and use conventional diagram of fits.

Solution. Case (1) The conventional diagram of fits is given in Figure A.1 which shows all labeled dimensions:

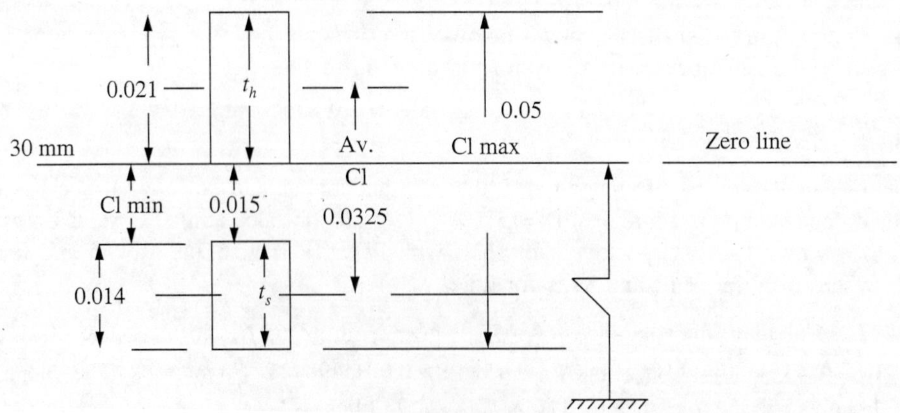

FIGURE A.1 Conventional diagram of fits.

Calculation for **Case (1):**

$$\text{LH: Largest hole size} = 30 + t_h = 30 + 1.5t \tag{A.1}$$

$$\text{SS: Smallest shaft size} = 30 - (0.015 + t_s) \tag{A.2}$$

It is given that the largest clearance is 0.05:

$$\text{LH} - \text{SS} = 30 + 1.5t_s - [30 - (0.015 + t_s)] = 0.05 \tag{A.3}$$

Solving for t_s, we get $t_s = 0.014$ mm. Thus, $t_h = 1.5 \times t_s = 0.021$ mm. Hence, with 100% correct assemblies:

Hole size = 30.021/30.00; average clearance = 0.0325 mm.

Case (2): For this case, statistical approach should be used. $P_a = P_s \times P_h = 0.001$ is the probability that there will be no clearance. Assuming probabilities for shaft and hole to create a mismatch in the assembly to be equal, $P_s \times P_h = P_a^2 = 0.001$.

$$P_s = P_h = 0.0316$$

(For the assemblies to be perfect as in case (1), we assume $Z = \pm 3.09$.)

Using the property of standard normal curve, the value of Z for risk 0.0316 is $Z = \pm 2.2$.

Now for this case, the tolerances on the shaft and the hole will need to be increased in the ratio

$$\frac{3.09}{2.2} = 1.4$$

Thus, keeping the mean or average clearance to be same, i.e., 0.0325 mm,

$$t_h = 1.4 \times 0.021 = 0.03 \text{ mm}$$
$$t_s = 1.4 \times 0.014 = 0.02 \text{ mm}$$

Using the same nominal size of 30 mm, we can now represent the conventional diagram of fits as shown in Figure A.2.

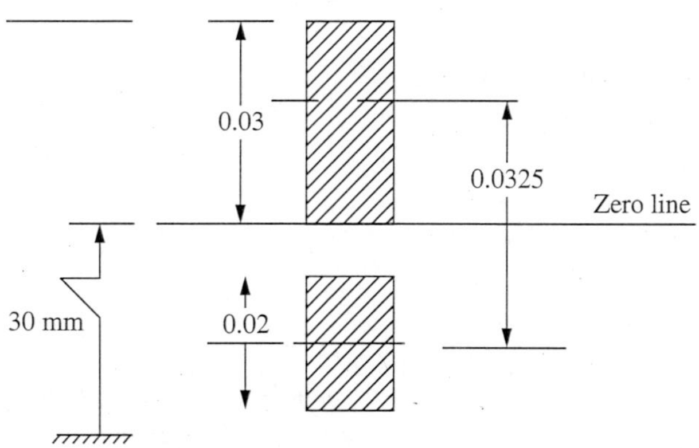

FIGURE A.2 Conventional diagram of fits with 99.9% good assemblies.

The size of hole in this case is 30.03/30 and the size of shaft in this case is (30 – 0.02)/30 – 0.04 = 29.98/29.96. It will be noted that while in case (1) the minimum clearance was 0.015 mm, the statistical tolerance results in a minimum clearance of 0.0075 mm, which is half that of case one (reader to verify this from the above geometry).

A.3 USE OF CONVENTIONAL DIAGRAM OF FITS IN TOLERANCES FOR ASSESSING THE CHROMIUM PLATING PROCESS PARAMETERS

An application of conventional diagram of fits is illustrated through an example where a inspection plug manufacturer has to work out different dimensions including final grinding allowance to arrive at the final plug design. In the illustrative example, the nominal diameter is 30 mm. for a IT6 grade is = 0.009 and the value of IT6 for a nominal size of 30 mm is 0.016. The minimum chrome plating thickness desired on the plug should be t_p = 0.05 mm. The chrome plating process has a tolerance of minimum value 0.25 on diameter and the maximum value of 0.3 mm on diameter. The problem is to calculate the maximum possible grinding allowance on diameter in the final grinding operation after plating (Figure A.3).

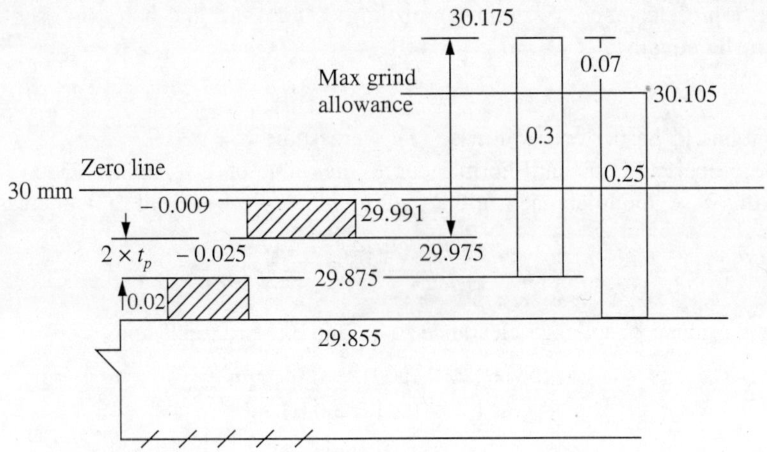

FIGURE A.3 Various dimensions for production of plug gauge.

Steps:

(i) Start with zero line at 30 mm.

(ii) Calculate high limit for plug gauge

$$= 30.00 - 0.009 = 29.991 \text{ mm}$$

Low limit for plug gauge

$$= 30.000 - 0.025 = 29.975 \text{ mm}$$

(iii) Diameter of bar stock, high limit

$$= \text{low limit of plug} - 2 \times \text{desired plating thickness}$$
$$= 29.975 - 2 \times 0.05 = 29.875 \text{ mm}$$

Diameter of bar stock, low limit

$$= 29.875 - 0.02 = 29.855 \text{ mm}$$

(iv) Thus maximum diameter after plating

$$= 29.875 + \text{high limit of plating thickness } (0.3)$$
$$= 30.175$$

(v) Minimum diameter after adding low limit of plating thickness 0.25 to low limit of initial bar stock

$$= 29.855 + 0.250 = 30.105$$

(vi) Maximum grinding allowance

= maximum diameter after adding high limit of plating – low limit of plug gauge size
= 30.175 – 29.975
= 0.20 mm

It is also worthwhile to find if any grinding allowance is available after considering that the lower limit of plating thickness is added to the lower limit of the initial plug and subtracting lower limit of plug.

$$= 30.105 - 29.975 = 0.13 \text{ mm}$$

The excessively low value of minimum grinding allowance in the final operation should be avoided.

One alternative is to enhance the process capability of the plating process with, say, the lower value of plating thickness as 0.35 and higher value as 0.4. This will result in maximum grinding allowance as 0.20 + 0.10 = 0.30 mm and minimum grinding allowance as 0.13 + 0.10 = 0.23 mm.

The advantage of tolerance diagram to visualize the plating process becomes much better, which would otherwise be quite difficult intuitively.

A.4 SPECIFICATION OF FITS ON ENGINEERING DRAWINGS AND CALCULATION OF DIMENSIONS

It is very helpful to production personnel to be able to visualize the type of fit by merely having a look at the specification of a fit. As is well known, there are three kinds of fits:

1. **Clearance fit**. A fit which guarantees clearance between a shaft and a hole. For example, 40.H7 d8 denotes that the nominal size indicated by a zero line is at 40 mm; H7 indicates a fundamental deviation of zero which corresponds to a hole H having a IT7 tolerance grade IT7 of 25 microns. As such, this hole with grade IT7 can be achieved by reaming or broaching operation. d8 indicates a shaft with upper dimension below the zero line with a fundamental deviation (calculated from standard formula) of 80 microns and a tolerance corresponding to IT8 grade which equals 40 microns. From the above information, a drawing showing conventional diagram of fits for a specification 40H7 d8 can be readily made as shown in Figure A.4.

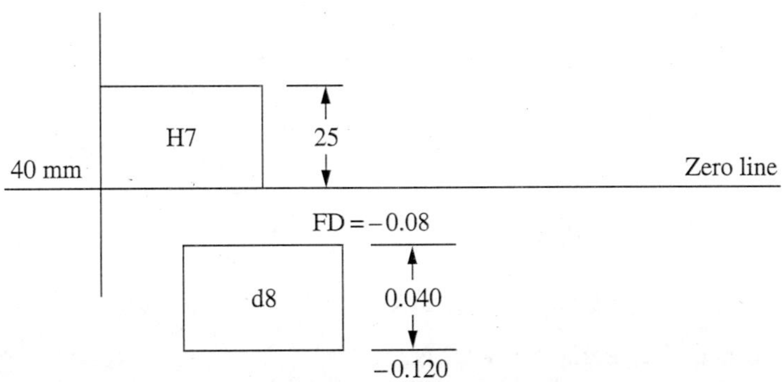

FIGURE A.4 Clearance fit.

The hole is represented by 40.25/40, showing its high and low limits.

The shaft is represented by 39.92/39.88 as its high and low limits. The grade IT8 can be produced by turning operation and the fit can be useful for bearing application. There is a minimum guaranteed clearance of 0.80 mm in such a fit.

2. **Transition fit**. A type of fit indicated by the designation 40 H7k6 can be deciphered by the production person as a transition type fit. This is because the letter k appears after the letter H in the alphabets. As before 40.H7 can be interpreted as a reamed or broached hole of minimum size 40 mm and maximum size of 40+ tolerance grade IT7, i.e., 40.025 as in the first case. As far as the designation k6 is concerned, the fundamental deviation corresponding to letter k is 2 microns, i.e., 002 mm and the tolerance grade corresponding to IT6 for nominal size of 40 is 0.016 mm. Based on the above information, a tolerance diagram as drawn (Figure A.5). A transition fit can result in a clearance or interference and it is applied for keying and location fits.

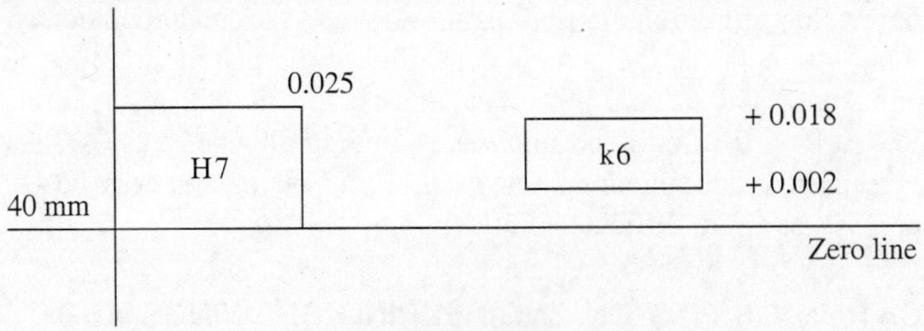

FIGURE A.5 Transition fit.

In this case, the hole can be described as 40.025/40.00 and the shaft can be described as 40.018/40.002. The maximum clearance is calculated as 40.025 – 40.002 = 0.023 mm. The maximum interference is calculated as the difference between largest shaft and smallest hole, i.e., 40.018 – 40.00 = 0.018. As stated before, the hole is made by reaming or broaching and the shaft is made by grinding because of IT6 grade on the shaft.

3. **Interference fit**. The third designation 40 H7/p6 indicates a guaranteed interference fit. As before, the hole H7 can be deciphered. As far as the designation p is concerned, the fundamental deviation for letter p is 25 microns and the tolerance grade for IT6 is 17 microns. Thus, the conventional diagram of fits can be drawn as shown in Figure A.6.

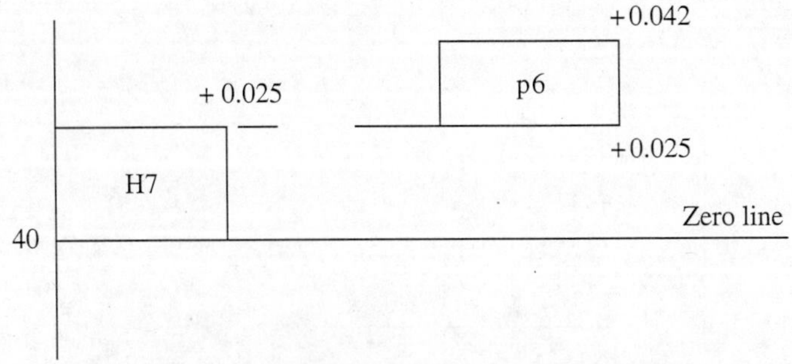

FIGURE A.6 Conventional diagram for interference fit.

In the above fit, which is a guaranteed interference,

$$\text{The maximum interference} = 40.042 - 40.00 = 0.042 \text{ mm}$$
$$\text{The minimum interference} = 40.025 - 40.025 = 0$$

An interference fit is created by

1. Heating the member so as to increase the size of the hole and the shaft is pushed into the hole
2. On cooling, the compressive stresses are developed on the mating surfaces and the shafts and the part with hole become integral.

A.5 ANALYSIS OF A TRANSITION FIT USING STATISTICAL APPROACH

In the previous examples, focus was only on the high and low limits of tolerance. It is known that parts produced on a machine follow a bell-shaped 'normal curve', whether it be a hole for a bush or a shaft. It was found in the example taken up earlier that in case of a fit of the type H7/k6, a transition fit resulted. In a transitional fit, there is neither a guaranteed clearance fit nor a guaranteed interference fit. Several research workers interested in statistical methods have worked out the probability of interference fit or a clearance fit, assuming a normal distribution of the shaft and the hole. An example is now taken up to explain the procedure to calculate these probabilities.

The fit considered for analysis is a 40 H7/n6 type transition fit in which a fundamental deviation for the shaft is arbitrarily assumed to be 0.0144 mm. The conventional diagram of fits is shown in Figure A.7 along with the normal distribution curves associated with the tolerances.

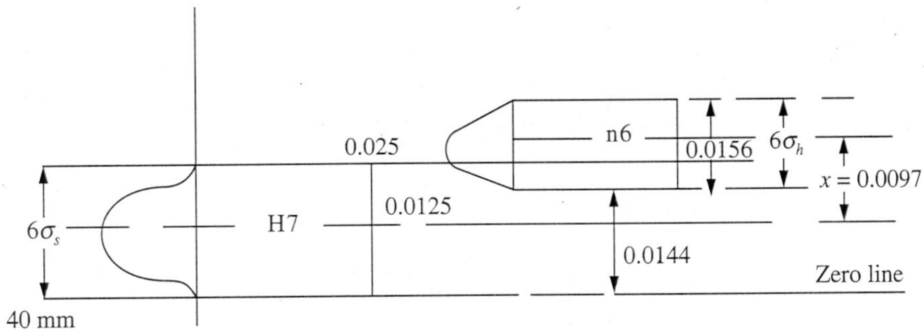

FIGURE A.7 Conventional diagram of fits (with normal distribution curves superimposed).

Figure A.8 shows the two normal distribution curves, one for hole tolerance and the other for shaft tolerance.

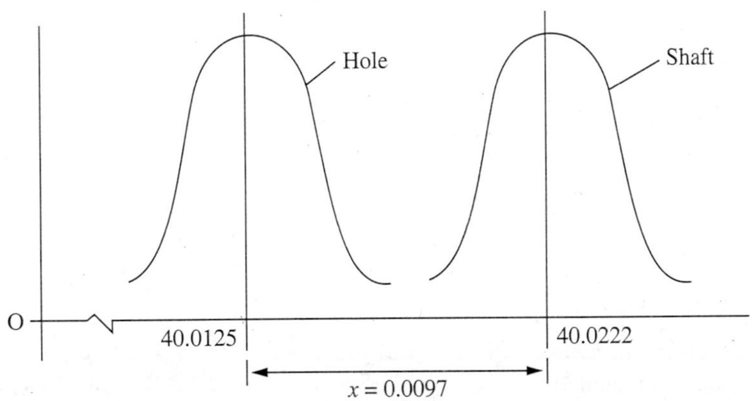

FIGURE A.8 Interaction of two normal populations.

Calculation of standard deviation σ for the fit (referring to Figure A.7):

$$6\sigma_h = 0.25 \text{ mm}, \qquad \sigma_h = \frac{0.025}{6} \text{ mm}$$

$$6\sigma_s = 0.0156 \text{ mm}, \quad \sigma_s = \frac{0.0156}{6} \text{ mm}$$

Since the holes and shafts are combined as two 'normal' populations, the resulting standard deviation of the 'fit' is given by

$$\sigma = \sqrt{\sigma_h^2 + \sigma_s^2} = \sqrt{\left(\frac{0.025}{6}\right)^2 + \left(\frac{0.0156}{6}\right)^2}$$

Thus, $\sigma = 0.0049$ mm

Using the equation $x = z\sigma$, we get

$$z = \frac{x}{\sigma}$$

Substituting the values of x and σ, we get

$$\frac{0.0097}{0.0049} = 1.97$$

A.5.1 PROBABILITY VALUES

Referring to Figure A.9 and using the properties of the standard normal curve, we get

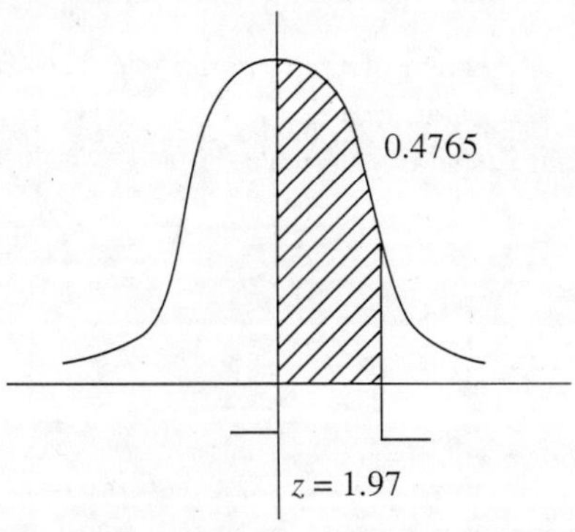

FIGURE A.9 Area under standard normal curve.

Area under standard normal curve 0.5 + 0.4765 = 0.9765

Probability of interference = 0.9765

97.65% parts result in interference fit and (100 – 97.65) = 2.35% parts result in clearance fit in the above situation. It amounts to saying that 23.5 assemblies in 1000 result in clearance while the remaining 976.5 assemblies result in interference.

A.6 TOLERANCES AND SURFACE FINISH ATTAINABLE IN MANUFATURING PROCESSES

In this section, the tolerances and surface finish that can be attained by any manufacturing process are discussed. It is a useful guideline to a process engineer to select the correct manufacturing process when a designer gives the specifications on the drawing (Table A.2).

TABLE A.2 Tolerance and surface finish attainable in manufacturing processes

Manufacturing process/size (mm)	*Tolerances Magnitudes* (mm)	*Tolerance grade*	*Surface finish CLA microns*
Primary processes			
Sand casting: small–large	0.3–1.6	IT16	12.5–25
Forging: small–large	0.05–0.2	IT15–IT16	12.5–32.2
Precision die casting: small–large	0.1–1.4	IT10–IT12	0.8–1.6
Secondary processes			
Shaping/Planning	0.1–0.3	IT10–IT11	1.6–12.5
Drilling 6–20	0.10–0.18	IT11–IT12	1.6–6.3
Reaming	0.02–0.035	IT7–IT8	0.8–3.2
Broaching 6–50	0.02–0.04	IT7–IT8	0.8–3.2
Milling	0.08–0.12	IT8–IT10	0.8–6.3
Turning 25–50 over 50	0.1–0.12	IT8–IT10	0.4–6.3
Micro finishing processes			
Honing 50 mm	0.01–0.016	IT6	0.1–0.8
Grinding up to 25 25–50	0.007–0.016	IT5–IT6	0.1–1.6
Machine lapping	0.002–0.01	IT4–IT5	0.05–0.4
Super finishing	Below 0.002	IT01–IT3	0.05–0.2

REFERENCES

[1] Jain, R.K., *Engineering Metrology*, Khanna Publishers, New Delhi, 2006.

[2] Murty, R.L., *Precision Engineering in Manufacturing*, New Age, New Delhi, 2007.

Appendix B

Introduction to Part Programming in G and M Codes

Part programme is an important task of the CNC system. The shape of the finished parts depends upon the correctness of the part programme. Part programme consists of instructions which control the machine tool about the processing steps to be taken for the production of a component. The part programme is next passed on to one of the available input media, which is used to control the NC machine.

B.1 NC WORDS CONVENTION

A NC word is a collection of characters used to form an instruction in binary digits. Typical NC words specify X-coordinate, Y-coordinate, feed rate, etc. A collection of NC words is termed a block and a set of blocks forms a complete NC instruction. The various sets of words are as follows:

(i) *N word or sequence number.* The first word in every block is the sequence number. It identifies the block. The sequence number begins with N and is written as N0001, N0002, N999, etc. It is customary to start with block number 0001 or 0010.

(ii) *G word or preparatory number.* The preparatory number drives the control unit to execute the instructions to be followed. This function has two digits preceded by G, i.e., G00,..., G99. The preparatory function enables the controller to interpret the data which follow and it precedes the coordinate words. For example, G01 is used for linear interpolation. Some of the preparatory functions are given in Table B.1. The table gives standard G codes. Table B.2 gives standard M codes.

TABLE B.1 Preparatory function (G codes)

Code	*Function*
G00	Rapid traverse
G01	Linear interpolation
G02	Circular interpolation (clockwise)
G03	Circular interpolation (counterclockwise)
G04	Dwell
G05	Hold/delay
G17	XY plane designation
G18	ZX plane designation
G19	YZ plane designation
G33	Thread cutting
G40	Cutter compensation—cancel
G41	Cutter compensation—left
G42	Cutter compensation—right

(*Contd.*)

Code	*Function*
G63	Thread cutting cycle
G70	Dimensioning in inch units
G71	Dimensioning in metric units
G80	Canned cycle—cancel
G81–G89	Canned cycles
G90	Absolute dimensioning
G91	Incremental dimensioning
G92	Zero preset
G94	Feed rate (mm/min)
G95	Feed rate (mm/rev)

TABLE B.2 Miscellaneous functions (M codes)

Code	*Function*
M00	Program Stop
M01	Optional Stop
M02	Program End
M03	Spindle Forward
M04	Spindle Reverse
M05	Spindle Stop
M06	Tool Change
M08	Coolant On
M09	Coolant Off
M10	Vice Open
M11	Vice Close
M12	Spindle Forward and Coolant On
M13	Spindle Reverse and Coolant On
M14	Drill Extend
M25	Drill Extend
M26	Drill Retract
M30	Program Rest and Reward
M38	Door Open
M39	Door Close
M62	Output 1 On
M63	Output 2 On
M64	Output 1 Off
M65	Output 2 Off
M66	Wait for Input 1 On
M67	Wait for Input 2 On
M76	Wait for Input 1 On
M77	Wait for Input 2 On
M98	Subprogram Call
M99	Subprogram Exit

(iii) *Coordinates (X-, Y- and Z-words).* These words give final coordinate positions for XYZ motions. In two-axis CNC system, only two-coordinate words would be used.

The instruction block with G00 will move the cutting tool at the rapid feed rate. Because of the rapid feed rate, it has to be ascertained that before the beginning of rapid movement, the cutting tool should avoid accidental hitting of the work piece during these rapid movements. G00 is a modal function, i.e., it is written in first block only and it remains active in the subsequent blocks in most of the programs.

B.1.1 Linear Interpolation Function (G01)

Any machining along a straight line is done using the linear interpolation function G01. The general format for writing an instruction block using G01 is

N – G01 X – Y – Z – F – EOB

The above instruction block will move the cutting tool to a position specified by the X, Y and Z values in this block. The feed rate is specified while using G01. The use of G00 in writing the instructional blocks is discussed with reference to Figure B.1. Illustrative example modified from Pabla et al. is now taken up with explanation.

B.1.2 Pocket Milling in a Rectangular Block Using an End Mill

Figurere B.1 shows top view and sectional elevation AA of a block in which a pocket is to be milled by an end mill along the path N3, N4, N5, N6, N7.

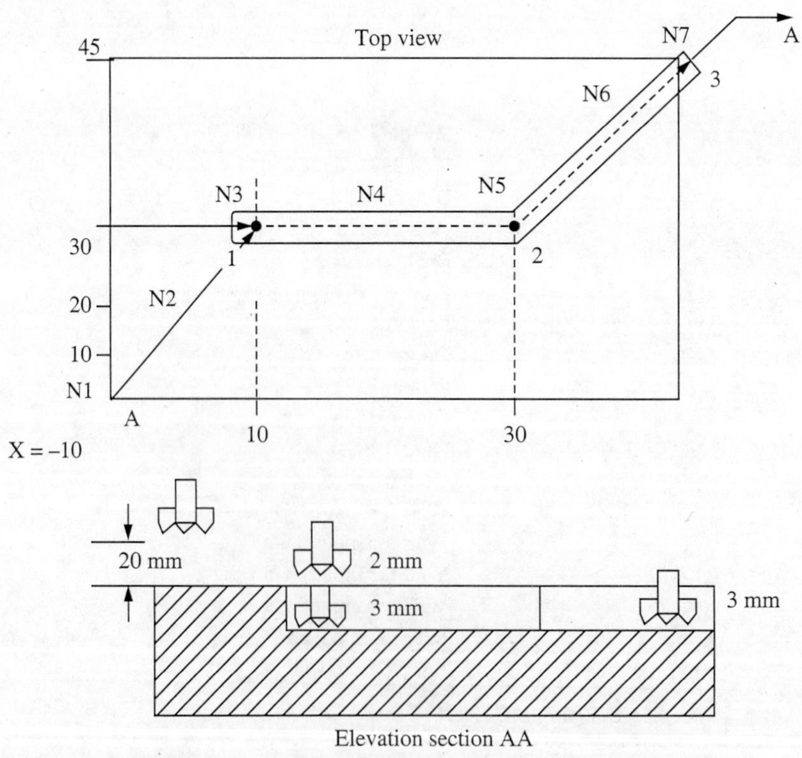

FIGURE B.1 Pocket milling operation in a rectangular block.

1. Starting point is (0, 0) and tool is 20 mm above the job surface.
2. Machining is to be done along 1-2-3 as shown in top view.
3. Z = 0 is at the surface of work piece.
4. Depth of groove is 3 mm.

N1 G90 G71 G94 M03 S800 EOB	Absolute mode, metric mode, feed in mm/min and spindle start at 800 rpm CW
N2 G00 X 10.00 Y 30.00 EOB	The cutting tool from starting point 0, 0 and moving at a rapid feed rate to point 1 with no change in Z coordinate
N3 G00 Z 2.00 EOB	The cutting tool moves to a point 2 mm above the job surface at a rapid feed rate
N4 G01 Z 5.00 F 200 EOB	The cutting tool moves in linear interpolation to a depth 3 mm inside the work piece at the feed rate of 200 mm/min (shown in section AA)
N5 G01 X 30.00 EOB	In linear interpolation, the cutting tool moves to point 2 (writing G01 is optional)
N6 G01 X 50.00 Y 45.00 EOB	The cutting tool moves in linear interpolation to point3 (see top view)
N7 G00 Z 20.00 EOB	Tool moves to a point 20 mm above the job surface at a rapid feed rate
N8 G00 X – 10.00 Y 0.00 EOB	To clear the job for loading/unloading, move the point to X – 10
N9 M02 EOB	Programme ends

B.1.3 Turning Operation Involving Facing and Turning Outside Diameter

In case of CNC cylindrical turning, only two axes (X-axis and Z-axis) are involved. The Y-axis is the axis of the spindle and X-axis is the direction of transverse motion of the tool post. CNC part programme for lathe operations is achieved by the following procedure:

(i) Moving the cutting tool in the rapid mode (G00) near the job
(ii) Set linear interpolation (G01) and move to the needed depth of cut in X-direction
(iii) Move along Z-axis to the correct length of the job as per specification
(iv) Set rapid mode (G00) and retract the tool along X-axis
(v) Move to start point in G00 mode

To illustrate the procedure, consider the CNC part programme for the component shown in Figure B.2(a) and (b) the operations to be done are:

(i) Facing operation
(ii) Reduction in the diameter of bar from 40 mm to 36 mm

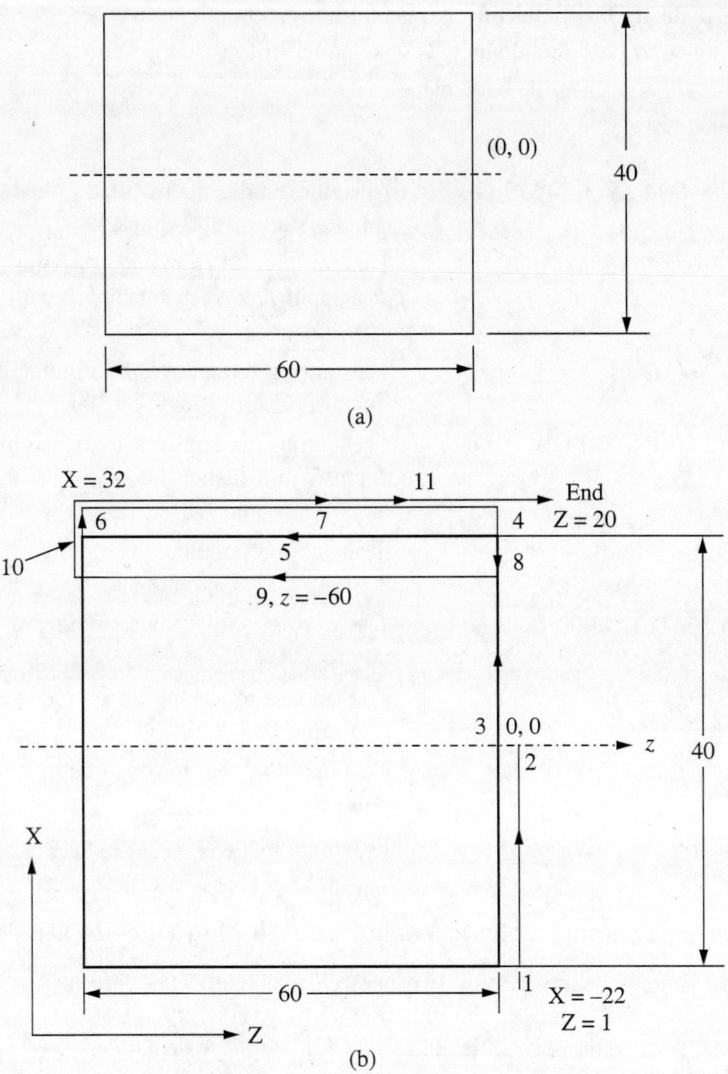

FIGURE B.2 (a) Part drawing and (b) part drawing showing tool movement 1 to 11.

N0010 P02 G71 G90 G94 EOB	Tool 1, feed rate 20 mm/min and speed
N0020 T01 F 200 M03 S 800 EOB	800 rpm
N0030 G00 X22.00 Z 1.00 EOB	Move to point X = 22, Z-1 in rapid mode
N0040 G00X0 EOB	Z remaining constant, move to X = 0.
N0050 G01 Z0 EOB	In G01 mode, move to Z = 0
N0060 X 40.00 EOB	For facing operation, move to X = 40 in G01 mode
N0070 Z 60.00 EOB	For a dummy, cut parallel to the axis of the job, move to Z = −60 in GO1 mode

N0080 G00 X 42.00 EOB	Withdraw the tool by 1 mm, i.e., to X = 42 so that when the tool is taken back to Z = 0, it does not leave a scratch mark on the job
N0090 G00 Z0 EOB	Move in rapid mode to Z = 0
N00100 G01 X 36.00 EOB	Move to X = 36 in G01 mode. It gives a depth of cut of 2 mm
N0110 G01 Z –60.00 EOB	Move to Z = –60 to turn the job
N0120 G00 X 42.00 EOB	Withdraw the tool to X = 42 in rapid movement
N0130 Z 20.00 EOB	Go to Z = 20
N0140 M 02 EOB	End of programme

For enhanced knowledge of advanced part programming the authors recommend the text by Pabla and Adithan.

REFERENCE

[1] Pabla, B.S. and Adithan, M., *Numerical Control of Machine Tools*, New age, New Delhi 1994.

Appendix C

Aesthetics in Industrial Design

Industrial design is an important activity of engineers and technologists. It is concerned with creating products and equipment for use by the society. The products should be ergonomic, i.e., easy to use, which is made possible by application of principles of ergonomics for equipment and product design. The second aspect which is concerned with appealing to the aesthetic senses is taken care of by imparting beauty to the product and it is covered by a branch of study called aesthetics. Aesthetics is the focus of the section. Apart from functional requirement of a product, the appearance of a product is also of importance for generating appeal in the perception of the user. Unfortunately, Indian products have yet to reach the aesthetic level attained by the products designed and manufactured by countries such as Japan, USA and Europe. Design training and education is available in India only in a few national institutes, such as NID Ahmadabad, IIT Bombay, and to some extent IIT Delhi. The subject of industrial design is now gaining importance and more and more professionals are attracted to it. This section highlights certain fundamental concepts of product aesthetes and form design.

C.1 ROLE OF AESTHETICS

There are two schools of thought on aesthetics in design. The Germans believe that primarily attention should be focused on the functional aspect. Once a product fulfils the functional requirement, there is not much need to pay attention to the frills in a conscious effort to enhance the beauty of the product. There is a well-known saying 'form follows function', which is of German origin. The other school of thought is the one believed and practiced by the Italians who strongly believe in the appearance of a product. In Italy, even machine tools, engines and engineering equipment are made as much aesthetic as possible.

In any case, once the functional design is over, the attention of the designer is consciously focused on aesthetics. This is true for products such as machine tools, electric equipments and engines. In case of consumer durables, such as domestic appliances, radios, TVs and tape recorders, aesthetics has to be given equal priority with functional design right at the concept stage. In case of consumer durables, the customer appeal is of great importance for obtaining fair market share.

C.2 FUNDAMENTAL CONCEPTS ON APPEARANCE OF A PRODUCT

The appearance of a product is the consequence of the following factors:

(i) Structure
(ii) Form
(iii) Rhythm
(iv) Proportion

(v) Run of lines and planes
(vi) Colour
(vii) Product message

Some of these aspects have been explained next.

Structure. The structure, i.e., the elements of the product and their relationship, is a characteristic of the product assembly as a whole. to produce a holistic group effect.

Unity of the structure is the quality which makes the product appear as one complete unit. The details bring about a group effect in a logical and harmonious way. Nowhere something should appear missing or an extra projection or protuberance encroach which should offend the eye. Order of structure in the most rigid and dogmatic sense is the repetition of a pattern. But in design it should be more free and should not result in a boring and monotonous repetition.

Form. Most industrial products are built up of a number of relatively simple geometrical forms such as the sphere, ellipsoid, cylinder and cone. Choice of basic forms is decided by the fact that the human eye is used vertically and horizontally as the main visual directions. Further, the simple forms are easy to manufacture on available machines such as the lathe, press machine and molding machine with greater ease, thereby fulfilling the producibility requirement of the component.

Combining form elements. This can be done to achieve the balance with asymmetry or balance without asymmetry. Even a slight imbalance gives the product an ugly appearance or offends the aesthetic sense unless the designer has deliberately introduced imbalance to break monotony.

Rhythm. Rhythm in a product can be produced by creating order within a variation. For example, in the automobiles shown in Figure C.1.

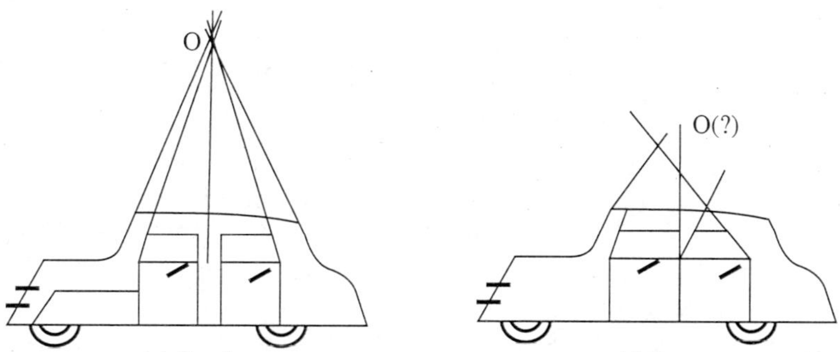

(a) Good (a) Poor

FIGURE C.1 Single point (O) perspective projection for new and old automobiles.

the shapes of the windows and doors are emphasized by the lines they form. The arrangement, shape and angle of the lines together form a rhythm by utilizing the concept of single point projection as shown in Figure C.1.

Proportions. From historic times, design philosophers have been occupied with the concept of proportion and beauty. A square has sides in the ratio 1:1. It is too static and uninteresting. In exceptional cases, a square shape is used to convey a message of stability or to give a product a distinctive identity.

A rectangle with width at least equal to the diagonal of a basic square is acceptable. The ratio (A/B) for such a shape is 1.4. The divine section invented by Pythagoras and Euclid has the following geometrical property: "A rectangle with this ratio between its sides is characterized by being divisible into a square and another rectangle with the same ratio between its sides" (Figure C.2).

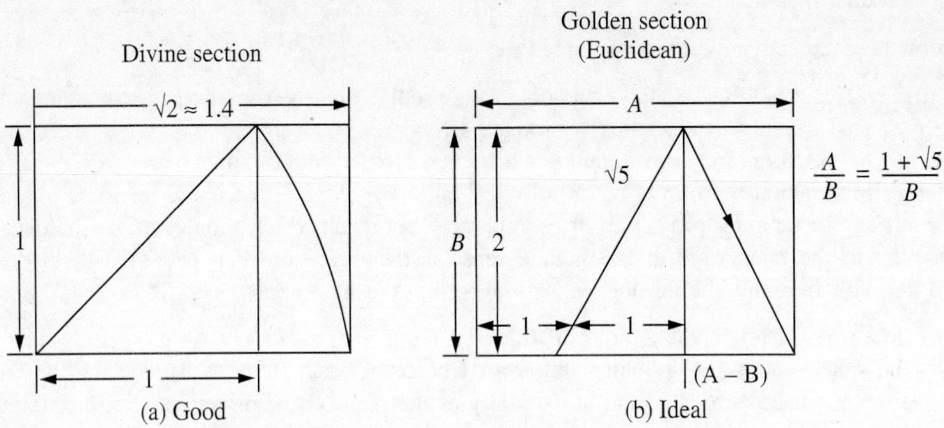

FIGURE C.2 Good section and golden section.

$$\frac{A}{B}=\frac{B}{A-B} \quad \text{or} \quad \frac{A}{B}=\frac{1+\sqrt{5}}{2}=1.618$$

Lines and planes. The qualities of unity and order depend on the run of the lines and planes. A designer usually tries to give the prominent lines in the product the same character, e.g. straight lines, curves and lines, at a certain angle.

C.3 PRODUCT MESSAGE: MEANS OF EXPRESSION

Lightness. A machine with a box-like shape and smooth joints produces the impression of heavy and ungainly mass of metal. The machine assumes a much lighter and well proportional appearance if the alternating horizontal components are made slightly different in length with flanges along the contour of the joints. The contours of the flanges have a practical purpose also. They can be machined to correct casting dimensions to match the contours of the contacting surfaces which can be bolted accurately and securely.

'Carve out design' is a usual practice with designers who can visualize carving out material where it is not needed. A good designer can see through a part and visualize the flow of the forces. He can reduce the section and slim down the part where there is lesser flow of force and fill up material where there is more flow of force. A balanced design is the one in which at any point in the design the strength is proportional to the stress.

Weight and Stability. To express weight and stability through the forms such as in machine tool beds, the aim should be as low as possible. Products which as a result of their functions are needed to be heavy and solid can be shaped so that this feature is expressed in their form.

Movement. An impression of movement and speed can be achieved by using sloping lines which meet at a point to give their association with an arrowhead. Speed stripes on cars or railway carriages serve the same purpose.

C.4 APPLICATION OF CONCEPTS

Development of a grill design from divine section concept. A simple geometrical construction has been developed for arriving at interesting designs. Figure C.3(a) shows a grill for an air conditioner where the squares have progression in geometric series. Figure C.3(b) shows the consequences of choosing an arithmetic progression. Figure C.3(c) shows the effect produced when the progression is greater than AP. The geometrical construction for arriving at a pleasing design of the grill with progression in GP is also shown at the top.

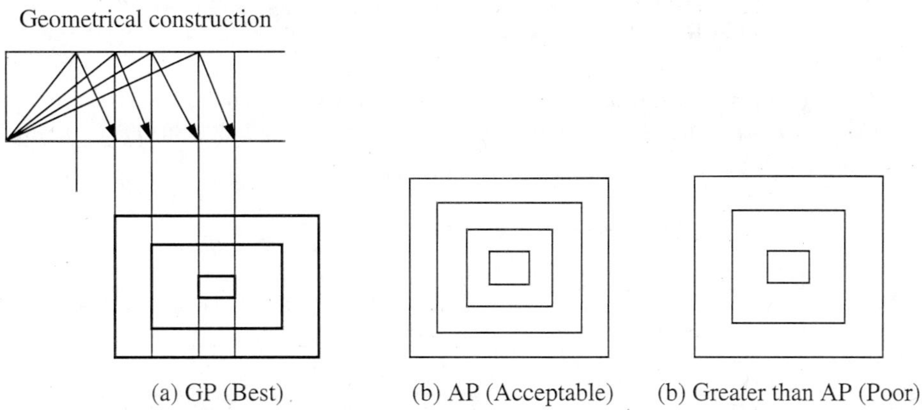

FIGURE C.3 Design possibilities for air conditioner front view.

Subtleties and peculiarities of solids. Industrial design basics consider certain peculiarities of basic solids. They are as follows:

(a) **Sphere.** A sphere is a solid having a property that every point on its surface is equidistant from its centre. Due to this, from the standpoint of design, a slightest variation such as cutting off a sphere disturbs the spherical shape. To restore the spherical shape, it becomes essential to use two different radii in case of a sphere to give it spherical shape. Figure C.4 shows the design of a kettle. Here, the radius r_2 is lesser than radius r_1 of the sphere.

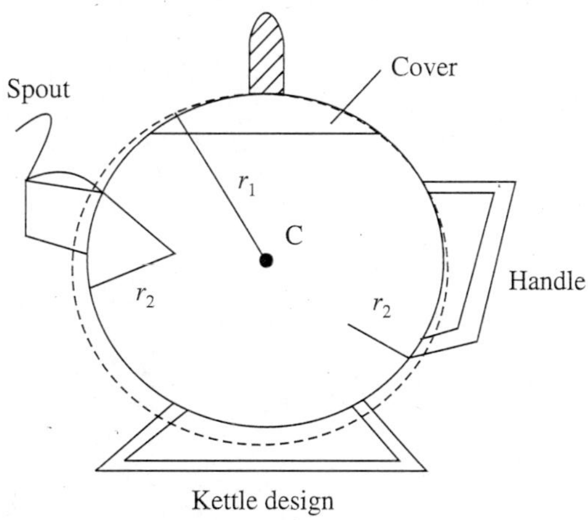

FIGURE C.4 Kettle design.

(b) **Cone.** The frustum of a cone in Figure C.5(a) and (b) is shown with straight line generators. A drinking glass with shape of perfect frustum of a cone has a **knock-kneed** appearance. On the other hand, a barreled cone with curved generators gives the 'goblet' an aesthetic and non-monotonous appearance.

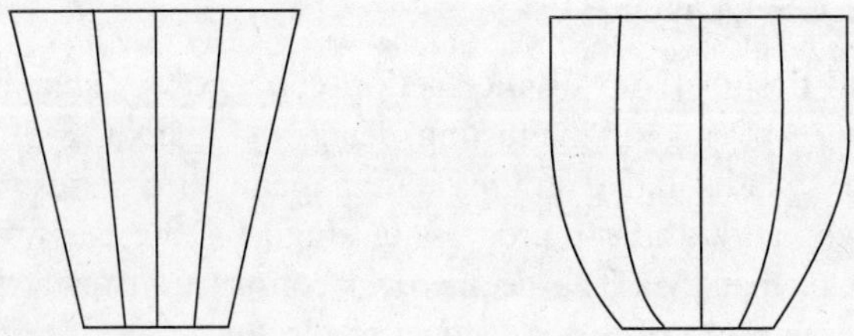

(a) Knock-kneed glass (poor) (b) Goblet (desirable)

FIGURE C.5 Poor and desirable shapes of conical objects.

(c) **Ellipsoid.** An ellipsoid has all the plus points of a sphere and is not prone to 'distortion effect' because it has two foci (Figure C.6). Designers use this shape for cosmetic and decorative boxes.

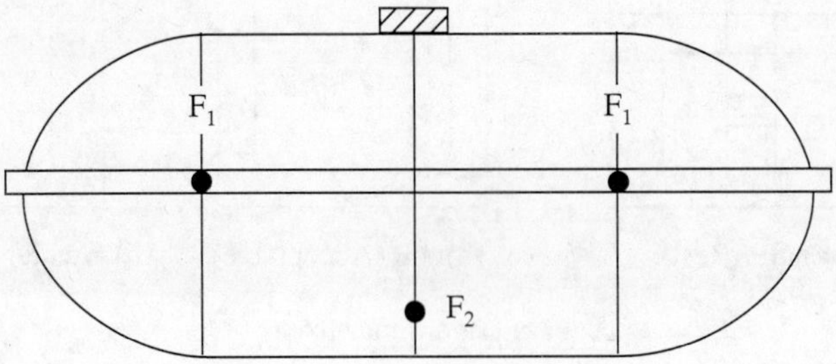

Ellipse of revolution (powder box)

FIGURE C.6 Desirable shape of an ellipsoid.

(d) **Cylinder.** A cylinder with a hemispherical dome is often used for high pressure vessels. The sphere should be modified to a flatter dome with two radii r_1 and r_2 as shown in Figure C.7(a) and (b). Dieter and Chow have done strength analysis of such pressure vessels.

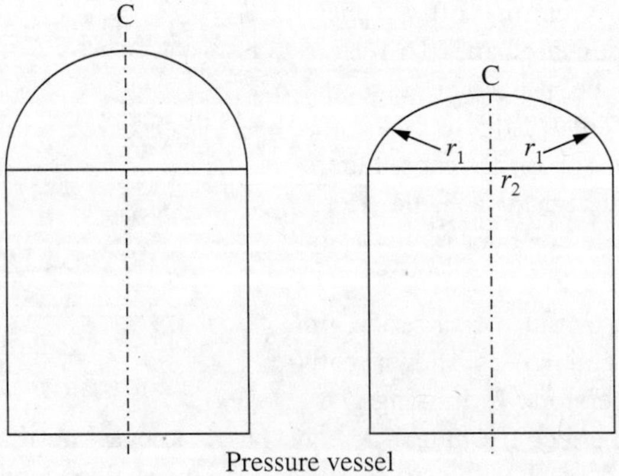

Pressure vessel

(a) Poor (b) Good

FIGURE C.7 Poor and good shapes of cylindrical pressure vessels.

C.5 TOOLS USED BY DESIGNERS TO ENHANCE AESTHETICS IN DESIGN

- **Use of special materials.** They are used either as parts of housings or as an additional decoration. Also, use of chromium strips, plastics, wood, glass and fabrics.
- **Use of colour.** Either natural colour of the material is used or paints, electroplating, spraying or even lighting and illumination are employed. Composition of colour and contrast of colours are of great importance to the industrial designer in facilitating convenient operation and attractive appearance.
- **Texture.** Texture such as matt finish, bright finish or directional texture as in wood can be taken advantage of. Final finishing operation will depend upon the surface texture desired.
- **Compact design.** The success of styling of some popular small cars, such as Maruti, Datsun or Tata Nano, may be partly due to designers' talent in creating feeling of completeness equivalent to the full size version. Compact designs conserve material, reduce transportation costs and reduce storage costs. Modern TV sets have large picture tubes but small overall dimensions. Modern pocket calculators and cassette tape recorders show what miniaturization can do. Microfilms help to store huge volumes of data and documents.
- Foldable, stackable and assembled goods have been developed by designers for ease of transportation, storage and good looks.
- Providing packing, especially for small items. With this, novelty and attractiveness are generated in the minds of the consumers. Today, packaging has attained great importance. Design of economic cartoons to have the maximum volume for a minimum use of sheet material is a problem of importance in package design.
- Development of aesthetic ideas at a conceptual phase by emulation of a number of existing designs of the proposed product from the market. This mode of idea generation technique termed **design space** is quite different from matrix approach or visualization through synectics. It is akin to brainstorming.

C.6 CONCLUSION

To be able to compete globally, engineers and technologists of our country can direct their talent towards aesthetic aspect of the product. Aesthetics often go hand in hand with functional design and advantage can be taken of this fact to produce low cost aesthetic designs.

REFERENCES

[1] Chitale, A.K., *Product Design and Role of Aesthetics*, Industrial Products Finder, May 1994: pp. 239

[2] Dieter, G.E., *Engineering Design—A Material Processing Approach*, McGraw-Hill, 1986.

[3] Chow, W., *Cost Reduction in Product Design*, Van Nostrand Reinhold, 1978.

Appendix D

Application of Bernoulli's Laws to Casting System

D.1 CASTING SYSTEM

Fundamentals of tool design (ed F.W. Wilson)[1]
ASTME discusses casting process as a system which is also known as *tooling for casting*. The authors intend to follow a similar approach regarding the assemblage, as a casting system comprising 7 elements forming the system.

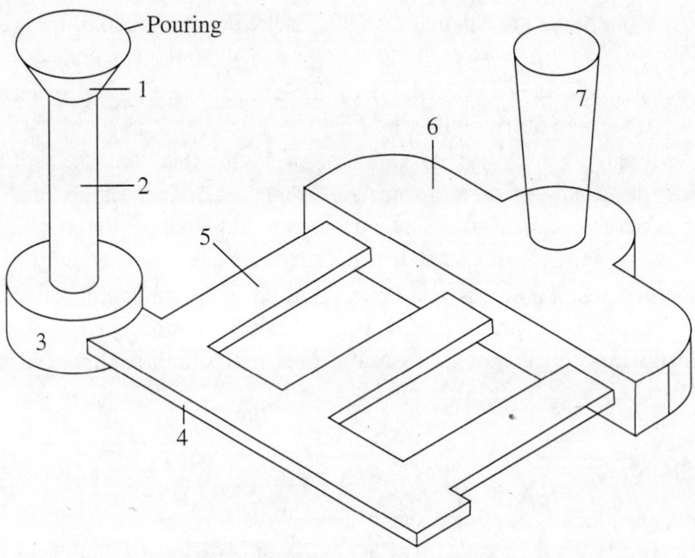

FIGURE D.1 Casting system.

As shown in Figure D.1 there are seven elements which form the casting system. They are:

1. **Pouring basin:** This is where the molten metal employed to manufacture the parts enters the mould.
2. **Sprue:** It is essential, as its function is to filter the filter the molten metal which to be poured and pour it at the correct pouring rate. Too slow a pouring rate results in incomplete filling of the casting. On the other hand excessively high pouring rate results in turbulence in the molten metal which flows under acceleration due to gravity through the sprue, thereby resulting in the poured metal leaving the contact with sprue walls. It is essential to design a sprue wall in a taper design to avoid aspiration or sucking in of air in metal flowing down the sprue.
3. **Well:** The well accommodates the molten metal and permits it to flow freely through the runner.
4. **Runner:** The function of the runner is to permit flow through the gates.

5. **Gate:** To fill up the mold cavity so as to form the casting.
6. **Casting:** This indicates the main body of the casting.
7. **Riser:** After filling the mold cavity, the molten metal flows up the riser.

The design of a good casting system should see to it that the riser is the last to solidify in a system. Its function is to fill up the mould cavity and supply molten metal to heavy sections in the end thereby solidifying metal in the mould .and the riser

D.2 DESIGN CONSIDERATIONS

D.2.1 Gating Ratio

There are two types of gating system: *unpressurized* and *pressurized*, Figure D.2 and Figure D.3 shows two kinds of gating systems. In the free flow system the gate is placed in a higher position with respect to runner. This results in free sever like trickle of molten metal in the gate. On in the other hand, a gate located in a lower position is termed *pressurized gate*.

The gating ratio for unpressurised gating system is indicated in Figure D.2 is 1:3:3. The gating ratio for pressurized gate in the Figure D.3 is 1:0.75:0.5. The design plan for this kind of gating system is to achieve increasing pressure on the molten metal flowing through the gates to the mould cavity.

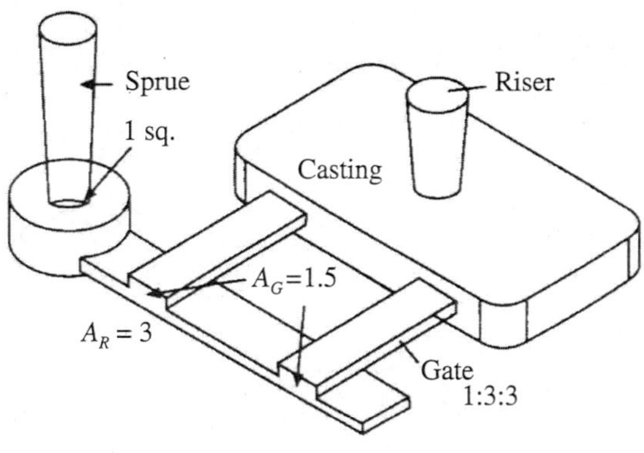

FIGURE D.2 Unpressurized gating system (Gating Ratio-1:3:3).

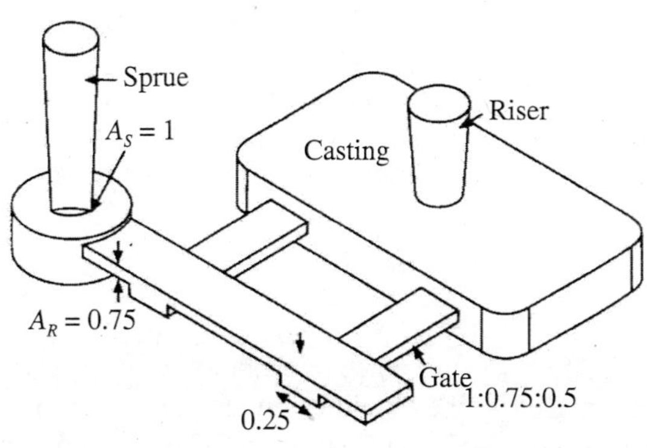

FIGURE D.3 Pressurized gating system (Gating Ratio-1:0.75:0.5).

D.2.2 Pouring of the Metal

The pouring of molten metal to mould first takes place in pouring basin. The objective of designing the pouring basin is to reduce (i) turbulence of the molten metal, and (ii) filter impurities by placing a tin sheet with pours to permit pure metal to flow down the sprue. Figure D.4 shown a pouring basin with labelling of proportions.

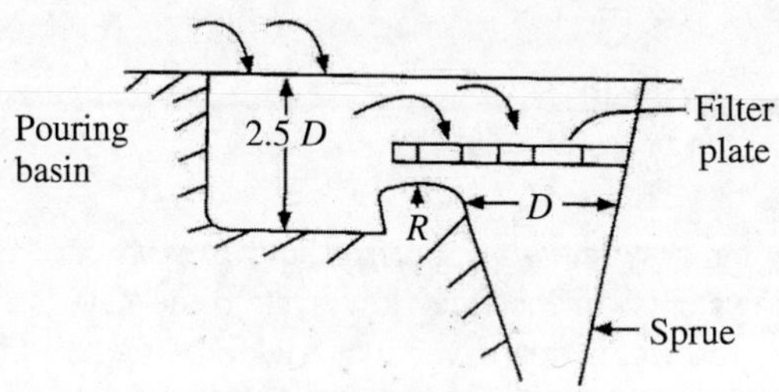

FIGURE D.4 Pouring basin.

D.3 SPRUE BASE WELL PROPORTIONING

Figure D.5 shows commonly adopted sprue base well proportioning. In the Figure the notations are

w: width of runner

d: Sprue chock diameter

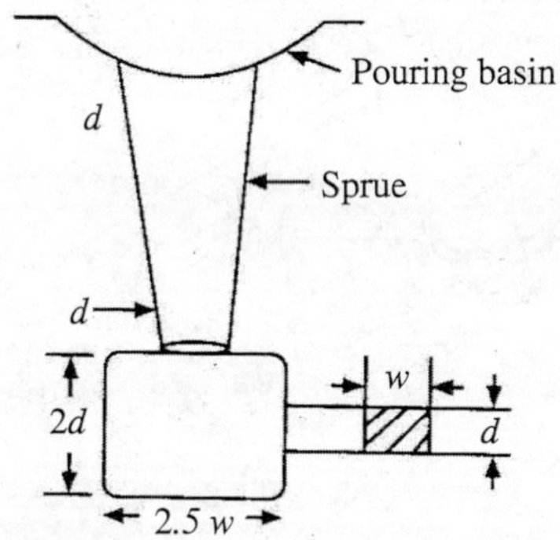

FIGURE D.5 Sprue base well.

A rough guideline is that the well base area should be five times chock area. It should be seen that the molten metal is swirled before it enters the gate by making provision of a swirl chamber of circular cross section which permits only pure molten metal in the gates while the light impurities remains at the center.

D.4 POURING TIME [2], [3]

From the point of view of efficiency the objective should be to have least pouring time. Pouring time can be defined as time to fill up the mould cavity completely. More pouring time requires the molten metal to be at higher temperatures which is undesirable. Too small a pouring time results in turbulent flow of molten metal and entrapment of air, formation of oxides and slag. The casting becomes defective in such a case. Pouring time has to be optimized. Foundrymen have successfully developed formulae of empirical nature. No well grounded theory has been developed so far as far as pouring time is concerned. The factors which appear to affect pouring time should be considered (1) surface to volume ratio of casting, and (2) size/mass of casting.

The following working rules have been used by foundrymen to calculate the poring time:

(1) Grey cast iron (C.I.), mass less than 450 kg:

Pouring time

$$\theta = K\left[1.41 + \frac{t}{14.59}\right]\sqrt{W} \text{ sec}$$

where, $K = \dfrac{\text{Fluidity of iron}}{40}$

t : average section thickness (mm)

W : Mass of casting (kg)

(2) Grey cast iron, mass exceeding 450 kg:

$$\theta = K\left[1.236 + \frac{t}{16.65}\right]W^{1/3}$$

Easily remembered values for C.I

TABLE D.1 Pouring time

Mass (Kg)	*Time* (Sec)
20	6–10
100	15–30
>100	60–180

(3) Steel castings:

$$\theta = (2.4335 - 0.3953 \log W)\sqrt{W}$$

(4) Copper alloys:

$$\theta = K_2 W^{1/3}$$

Where K_2 is a constant

TABLE D.2 Pouring time for top gating

Top Gating	1.30
Bottom Gating	1.80
Brass	1.90
Tin Bronze	2.80

Generalized Rules:

TABLE D.3 Pouring time for different metals

Grey C.I	40 sec
Steel	20 sec
Brass	15–45 sec

Pouring time calculation through empirical formula due to Lange:

Example 1. Calculate pouring time for a casting of mass 20 kg with mean cross-sectional thickness t = 15 mm. The material of casting is grey iron. Assume fluidity of iron as 28 inches.

Solution. For C.I., pouring time = $\theta = K[1.41 + t/14.59]\ \sqrt{W}$ sec

$$\theta = \frac{28}{40} 1.41 + 15/14.59]\ \sqrt{20}\ \text{sec} = 7.63\ \text{sec}$$

For steel, pouring time = $\theta = (2.4335 - 0.3953\ \log w)\ \sqrt{W}$

$$\theta = (2.4335 - 0.3953\ \log \sqrt{20}\ )\ 8.5825\ \text{sec}$$

The formulae for pouring time could be taken from foundry handbooks. The student has to memorize the formulae if the handbook is not provided.

D.5 DESIGN OF RISER

The design of riser is done by resorting to 3 approaches:

D.5.1 Caines Method[4]

The most basic model governing the solidification time of casting t_s is given by Chvorinov's[5]equation:

$$t_s = K\left[\frac{S}{V}\right]^2$$

where K is a constant called *mould constant* which depends upon poring temperature, casting and mold thermal characteristic Caines[4] was able to show as an extension of Chovoroniov's rule that $X = \dfrac{a}{\gamma - b} + C$ where, X is the freezing ratio or (Surface/Volume) relationship of casting: Riser which can be written as $(S_{Casting}/V_{Casting})$.

The values of a, b and c for various metals were tabulated by Caines[1].

TABLE D.4 Values of a, b and c for various metals

	a	b	c
Steel	0.1	0.03	1
Aluminum	0.1	0.06	1
Grey Cast Iron	0.33	0.03	1
Bronze	0.24	0.017	1

Caines equation for freezing ratio:

$$X = \frac{a}{\gamma - b} + C$$

Figure D.6 displays Caine's equation as a hyperbolic curves dividing the sound casting zone from shrinkage zone.

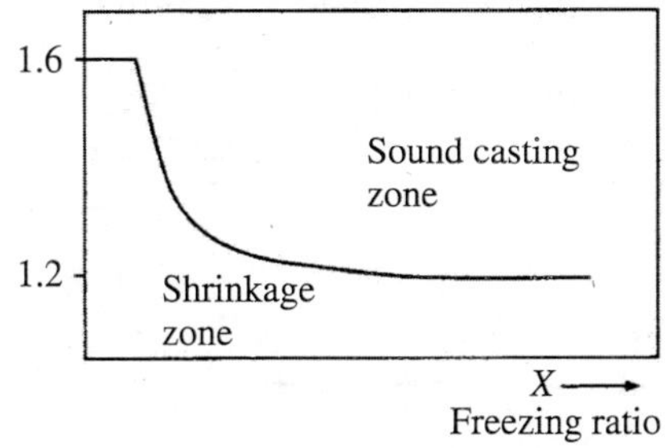

FIGURE D.6 Caine's hyperbolic curve

D.5.2 Modulus Method

Wiawdower[6] and Bishop[7] proposed an easy method to decide riser dimensions. The modulus is reverse of cooling characteristic *S/V* i.e. Modulus $M_C = (V/S)$. The basic premise of modulus method is that if the modulus M_r of riser exceeds the modulus M_C of the casting by a ratio 1.2 it can be regarded as satisfactory.

As an example, in steel castings a riser of height: diameter can be adopted as 1.2. The modulus of such a riser can be calculated as:

$$M_C = \frac{Vc}{Sc} = \frac{\frac{\pi}{4}D^2 H}{\pi DH + 2.\frac{\pi}{4}D^2} = \frac{\frac{\pi}{4}D^3}{\pi D^2 + \frac{\pi}{4}D^2} = \frac{D}{6}$$

According to Wiadower,

$$M_r = 1.2\ M_c$$

$$M_r = 1.2 \times \frac{D}{6} = \frac{D}{5}$$

Thus it is possible to determine the size of a riser if the modulus of casting is known

Table D.5 shows modulus of simple geometric shapes from which the corresponding riser dimensions can be calculated on multiplying by 1.2.

In actual practice, most of casting designs rarely have simple geometric shapes. For such complex shapes it becomes difficult to calculate modulus M_c.

D.5.3 Author's Approach

The authors propose the use of a practical approach to obtain the value of $M_c = [V_c/V_s]$

(1) To obtain V_c, a scale model of the casting shape made of some easily workable material should be immersed in a trough filled with water. Then the volume of water displaced after immersion can directly give value of V_c.

(2) The surface S_c can be calculated after sticking adhesive tape on the heat transfer surface of the model. Next, peel of the adhesive tape to yield S_c. The ratio of $[V_c/S_c] \times$ scale factor of the model should be accurate estimate of modulus M_c of casting.

TABLE D.5 Moduli of Simple Geometric Shapes of Castings

S.No.		*Shapes*	*Modulus M_c*
1.	Plate	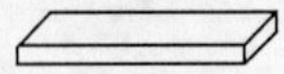	$0.5t$
2.	Disc		$0.5t$
3.	Long bar	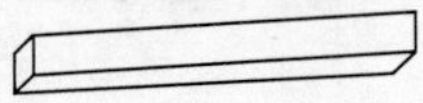	$a, b/2(2 + b)$
4.	Cube	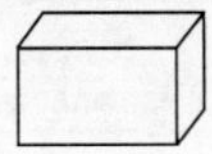	$D/6$
	Cylinder	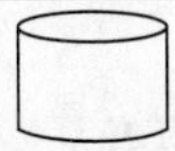	$D/6$
	Sphere		$D/6$
5.	Rod		$DH/2(D + 2H)$
6.	Annular cylinder	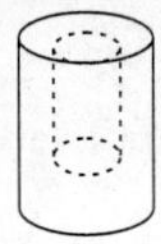	$th/2(t + h)$

D.5.4 Naval Research Laboratory System

Because of the problem faced in the modulus method regarding the need to work out the modulus M_c of the casting an easier method is followed in recent years. This method is popularized by the U.S. Navy. In this method, the X axis of the Caines curve[4] used a shape factor $\left(\frac{\text{Lenth + Width}}{\text{Thickness}}\right)$ instead of the freeze ratio. This is shown in Figure D.7 which shows one such curve for a rectangular steel casting.

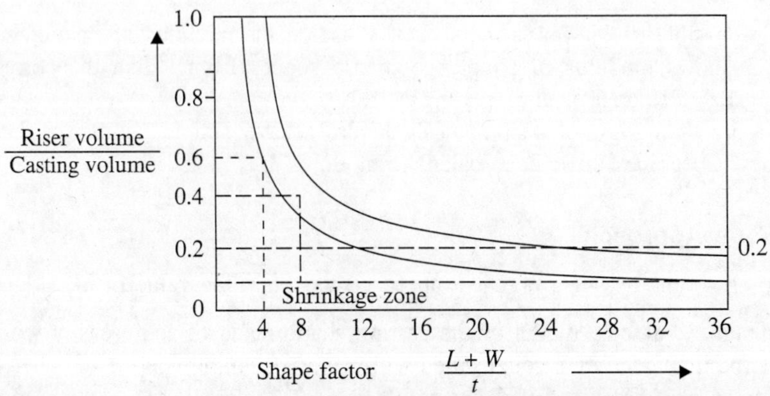

FIGURE D.7 Graph Between Shape factor and volume ratio (Ref 7: Myskovsky)

Illustrative example on design of riser

Example 2. Determine the modulus $\left(\frac{V}{S}\right)$ of a riser to effectively feed a component of spherical shape and of diameter D = 100 mm. Use modulus method.

Solution. Referring to table D.4 it is seen that the riser of modulus $\frac{D}{6} = \frac{100}{6}$ = 16.67 mm should be sufficient.

Example 3. For determining the modulus of the riser by the **Chitale–Gupta** method an experiment is conducted. The observations are as follows:

(i) Increase in the water level in a trough of diameter 200 mm, the height of water displaced is 100 mm.

(ii) The area of the adhesive grid paper used to cover a model. Area of adhesive paper is 20930 sq.cm. Assume a scale factor of 2.

Calculate the volume to surface ratio of the model.

Solution.

Volume of the liquid displaced = $\pi/4 \times 200^2 \times 100$ = 3140000

Area of the adhesive paper = 20930 sq.mm

Modulus of the model

$$= \frac{3140000}{20930} = 150 \text{ mm}$$

Modulus of the casting = Scale factor × Mode. of model

$$= 2 \times 150 = 300 \text{ mm}$$

$$= 30 \text{ cm}$$

Example 4. Use Caine's method to determine the dimensions of a cylindrical riser with $d = h$, from the given data.

Casting is 50 × 50 × 10 made of steel.

Solution. Caines equation is as under.

$X = \frac{a}{\gamma - b} + C$, where X is freeze ratio which reflects $\left(\frac{S}{V}\right)$ ratio of casting to $\left(\frac{S}{V}\right)$ ratio of riser.

Referring to table D.4 a = 0.1, b = contraction fraction = 0.03.

Surface area of casting = (50 × 50) × 2 + (10 × 15) × 4

$$= 5000 + 2000$$

$$= 7000 \text{ cm}^2$$

Volume of casting = 50 × 50 × 10 = 25000 cm^3

Riser Surface: $\left[\frac{\pi}{4}D^2 \times 2 + \frac{\pi D^2}{4}\right] = 1.5\ \pi D^2$

Volume of riser: $\frac{\pi}{4} D^2 \times D = \frac{\pi}{4} D^3$

$$Y = \frac{\text{Volume of riser}}{\text{Volume of casting}}$$

$X = 0.056\ D$

Substituting in Caine's equation.

$$X = \frac{a}{\gamma - b} + C$$

$$X = 0.056\ D = \frac{a}{\frac{0.25\pi\ D^3}{25000} - 0.03} + 1$$

Solving by trial,

$D \approx 16.2$ mm

Example 5. Use Naval research lab method[6] to calculate riser dimension for which $D = H$ when the steel plate to be cast has $l = 25$, $w = 10$, $t = 5$.

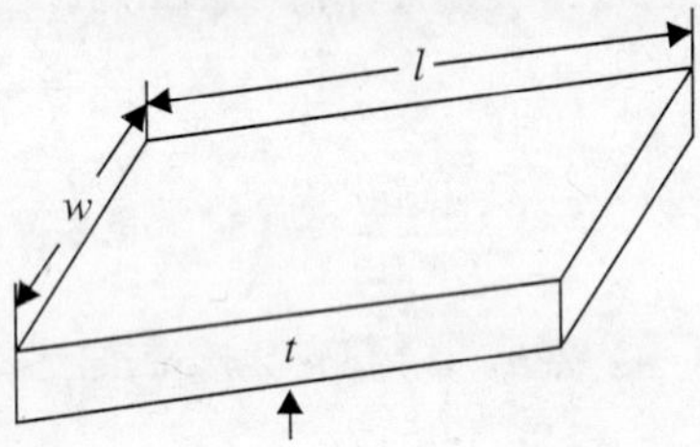

FIGURE D.8 Notation for rectangular block.

Solution. In Naval research lab method the shape factor is given by: $\left\{\frac{l + w}{h}\right\} = \frac{25 + 10}{5} = 7.$

This is plotted along X axis instead of freeze ratio used in Caine's method. Y axis has same meaning as in Caine's method.

The logic of this approach is that plate like casting with small h compared with the area, the freezing occurs faster. The curve is hyperbolic. Referring to the graph shown in Figure D.9, for a shape factor of 7.

$$\frac{V_r}{V_c} = 6.2,\ V_r = 6.2\ V_c = 6.2 \times 25 \times 10 \times 5 = 775\ \text{cm}^3$$

$$\frac{\pi}{4} D^2 \times D = \frac{\pi}{4} D^3 = 775$$

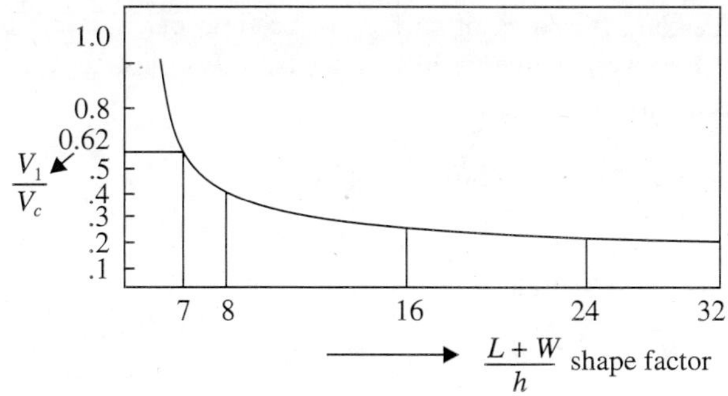

FIGURE D.9 Shape Factor v/s volume ratio.

$D^3 = 987 \text{ cm}^3$
$D = 987^{1/3} \approx 10 \text{ cm}$
$H \approx 10 \text{ cm}.$
If the volume shrinkage is assumed to be 10%, determine additional material for riser.
$V_r = 0.1 \times 25 \times 10 \times 5$
$= 125 \text{ cm}^3$
Total material = 775 + 125 = 900
$D = 1147^{1/3} \approx 10.4$
Thus, when shrinkage is accounted with the riser $D = H = 10.4$

D.6 DISTANCE OF RISERS FOR PLATE LIKE CASTINGS WITHOUT AND WITH CHILLS

It has been found experimentally that risers should be located at a distance $4.5t$ from the end. Figures D.10 (a), (b), and (c) shows such schemes of riser locations with effect of chills which add up 50 mm at end.

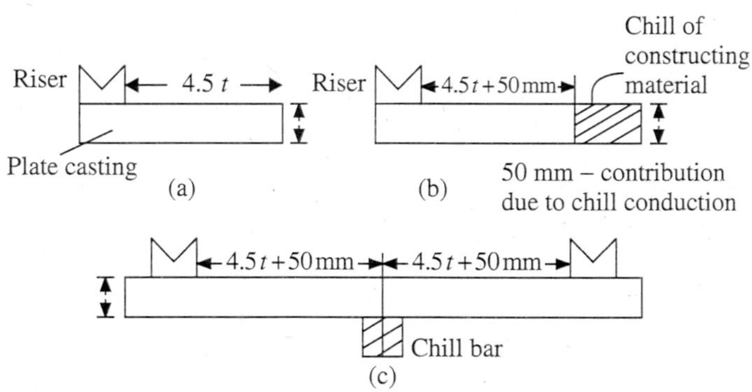

FIGURE D.10 Schemes of riser locations.

D.7 APPLICATION OF CHIVIRNOV'S FORMULA TO DETERMINE BEST SHAPE FOR A RISER

Chivirnov showed that the time θ_f for complete solidification of a cast shape is given by the formulae:

$$\theta_f = K(V/A)^2$$

Where V = volume of casting, A = area of surface of casting and K is mold constant. Obviously, since the foundrymen is interested in riser being the last to solidify, V/A riser should be greater than V/A casting.

Example 6. There are three solids as shown in Figure D.11

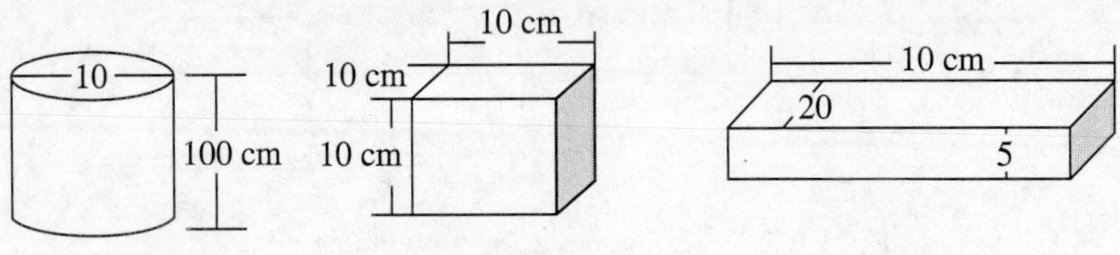

(a) Cylinder (b) Cube (c) Plate

FIGURE D.11 Three solids.

All the shapes have equal volume of 1000 cm^3, assume mold constant K = 2.19.
Time of solidification:

(1) Cube: $\theta_f = 2.19\ (1000/600)^2 = 2.19 \times 2.766 = 6$ mins

(2) Cylinder: $\theta_f = 2.19\left(\dfrac{\pi \times 5^2 \times 10}{\pi \times 10 \times 10}\right)^2 = 13.6$ mins.

(3) Plate: $\theta_f = 2.19\left(\dfrac{1000}{5 \times 10 \times 2 + 10 \times 20 \times 2 + 5 \times 20 \times 2}\right)^2 = 4.467$ mins.

The inference of the above calculations:

(i) Cylindrical shaped riser with solidification time of 13.6 min takes maximum time. It should be the preferred shape for riser.

(ii) Cubical and plate type risers should be avoided.

Practically, risers are joined to castings as shown in Figure D.12.

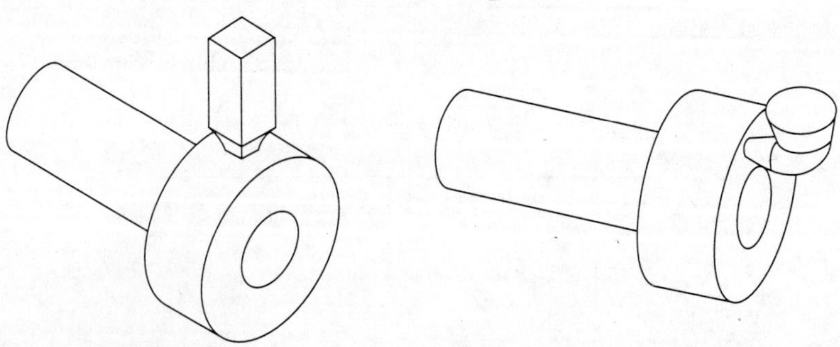

Cubical riser Cylindrical riser

FIGURE D.12 Attachment of riser of cubic and cylindrical risers.

D.8 ILLUSTRATIVE EXAMPLES ON USE OF BERNOULLI'S EQUATION AND CONTINUITY EQUATION

The above two equations are often used in fluid mechanics. They can be effectively applied for calculation in foundry practice.

Top gate with mold directly below

Referring to Figure D.13, it can be seen that liquid poured from top flows through sprue inside the mould. Because of porosity of the sand, the air is free to enter the mould and pressure at points 1,2,3 due to atmosphere is constant.

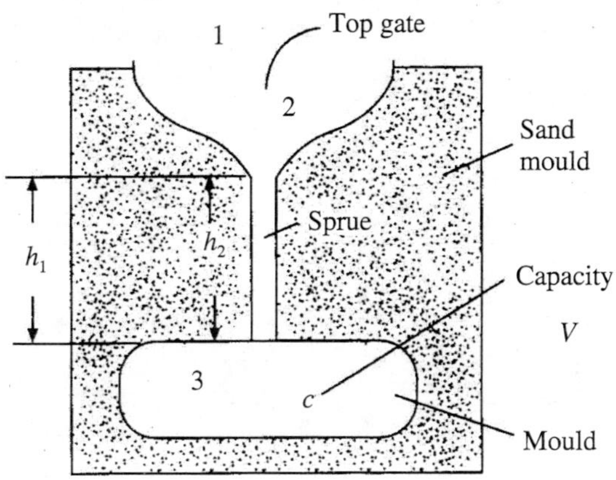

FIGURE D.13 Design of pouring basin.

From Bernoulli's theorem, the sum total of three energies

(a) Gage pressure energy, P
(b) Potential energy, h
(c) Kinetic energy

is equal if friction loss in the sprue is neglected.
Thus, writing total energy at point 1 and point 3

$$P_1 + \rho g h_1 + \frac{1}{2}\rho v_1^2 = P_3 + \rho g h_3 + \frac{1}{2}\rho v_2^3$$

Since $P_1 = P_3$ = Atmospheric pressure
ρ = density, $v_1 = 0$ being at entrance to pouring basin, v_3 = velocity of liquid at entrance to mould, V = mould volume, $h_3 = 0$. being at the datum line. Thus, finally we have:

$$\frac{1}{2}\rho v_3^2 = \rho g h_1$$

$$= v_3^2 = 2gh^1$$

or, $$v_3 = \sqrt{2gh^1} \quad (1)$$

If V is the mold capacity or volume we get time t of filling the mould cavity with volume V

As, $$t = \frac{V}{v_3} \tag{2}$$

Thus in a top gating case, if mould volume V and height of static head h_1 are known, the mould filling time can be easily calculated.

Case with bottom gate

In this case the liquid has to take a U turn. The liquid first flows down the sprue with acceleration due to gravity to attain a velocity v_3 as in case (1). Then it traverses horizontally. Then it fills up the mould by moving vertically. The liquid fills up the mould of height h_m while moving up against gravity. At any instant of time t the height is h and increases incrementally by dh in a time dt. Due to such a filling up process, application of integral calculus becomes necessary.

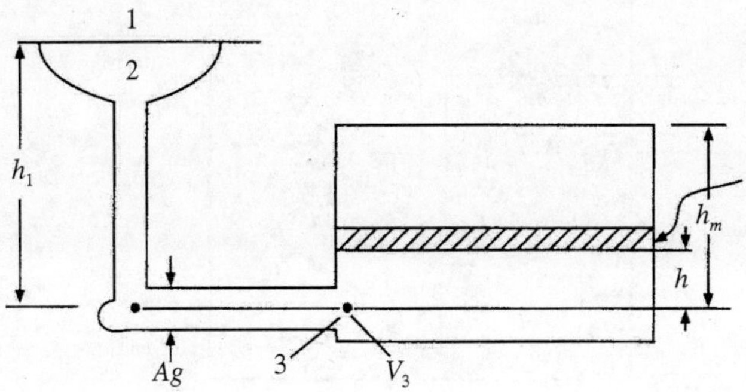

FIGURE D.14 Path of fluid flowing in a casting.

The various steps are as follows:
The notations are:

θ = Mass density of molten metal.
P_3 = Pressure at point 3.
h_1 = Sprue height.
h = Instant height in mould
h_m = Height of mould.

The flow takes place with the velocity v_3 governed by differential head $(h_1 - h)$. this is the effective head to calculate v_3. v_3 is also the velocity v_g at the entrance to the gate. Thus, the potential energy is converted to kinetic energy as under:

$$v_g = v_3 = \sqrt{2g(h_1 - h)}$$

From equating volume at gate and mould

$$a_m dh = a_g v_g dt$$

$$\frac{a_m}{a_g} dt = \frac{1}{\sqrt{2g}} \cdot \frac{dh}{\sqrt{h_1 - h}}$$

At, $t = 0$, $h = 0$ and at, $t = t_f$, $h = h_m$

$$\frac{1}{\sqrt{2g}}\int_0^{h_m}\frac{dh}{(h_1 - h)} = \frac{A_g}{A_m}\int_0^{t_f} dt$$

The final result for filling time

$$t_f = \frac{A_m}{A_g}\cdot\frac{1}{\sqrt{2g}}\cdot 2(\sqrt{h_1} - \sqrt{h_1 - h_m})$$

Numerical on mould filling time

Example 7. A mould has dimensions of 25 cm × 25 cm × 15 cm, the area of cross section of gate is 5 sq.cm. Calculate the time of filling of the mould if height of sprue and pouring basin is 20 cm. Calculate filling time for (a) Top gate, and (b) Bottom gate.

Solution. Calculations: (i) Applying formula for velocity of filling top gating:

$$v = \sqrt{2gh_1} = \sqrt{2\times 981\times 20} = 198 \text{ cm/sec}$$

Mould volume $V = 25 \times 25 \times 15 = 9375$ cm^3
Average gate $a_g = 5$ sq.cm, if $t_f =$ time of filling,
Now, $t_f \times a_g \times v = V$

$$t_f = \frac{9375}{5\times 198} = 9.469 \text{ sec.}$$

(ii) Case with bottom gate

$$h_1 = 20 \text{ cm},\ h_m = 20 \text{ cm},\ a_g = 5 \text{ cm}^2\ A_m = 25 \times 25$$

$$t_f = \frac{a_m}{a_g} = \frac{1}{\sqrt{2g}}2\left[\sqrt{h_1} - \sqrt{h_1 - h_m}\right]$$

$$= \frac{25\times 25}{5}\cdot\frac{\sqrt{2}}{\sqrt{2\times 981}}\cdot\sqrt{20}$$

$$= 17.84 \text{ sec}$$

Example 8. For a down gate casting, the following data is available $a_1 = 600$ mm^2, flow rate $Q = 6.5 \times 10^5$ mm^3/sec. Assume $g = 981$ mm/sec^2. Calculate area of down sprue a_2.

Solution. Refer to Figure D.15: $Q = a_1 v_1 = 6.5 \times 10^5$

$$V_1 = \frac{6.5\times 10^5}{600} = 1083 \text{ mm/sec.}$$

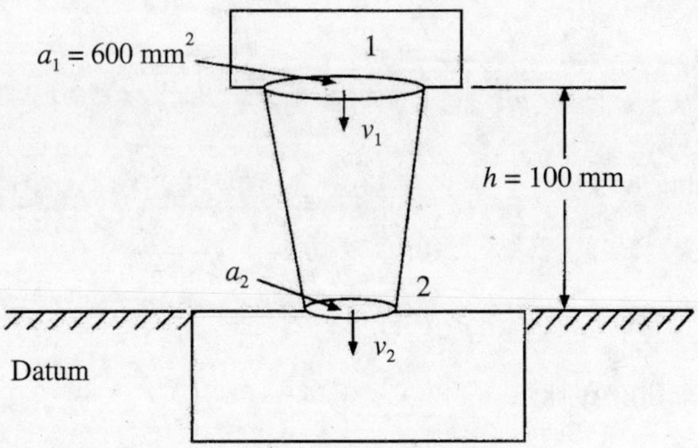

FIGURE D.15 Down gate casting.

From Bernoulli's theorem: Static head + dynamic head = constant at points 1 and 2.

$$h + \frac{v_1^2}{2g} = 0 + \frac{v_2^2}{2g}$$

$$100 + \frac{(1083)^2}{2 \times 981} = \frac{v_2^2}{2 \times 981}$$

$$v_2^2 = 1369476$$

$$v_2 = 1170 \text{ mm/sec.}$$

$$a_2 = \frac{Q}{v_2} = \frac{6.5 \times 10^5}{1170} = 555.5$$

$$a_2 = 555.5 \text{ mm}^2$$

REFERENCES

[1] Wilson F.W., "Fundamentals of Tool Design", *ASTME,* 1972.

[2] Lange, E.A., *Pouring Time for Steel Castings,* US Naval Research Lab Report, Washington DC, 1958.

[3] Dietert, H.W., "How Fast Should a Metal be Poured?" *Foundry*, vol. 81, August 1953.

[4] Caine, J.B., "Risering Castings", *Transactions of AFS,* vol. 57, 1949, page 66.

[5] Chvorinov, N., "Theory of Solidification of Castings", *Geissereb*, vol. 27, 1940, page 177–225.

[6] Wlowder, R., The *Directional Solidification of Steel*, Pergamon Press, Oxford 1966.

[7] Myskovsky, E.T., and W.S. Pellini, A Simplified Method for Determining Riser Dimensions, *Transaction of AFS,* vol. 63, 1955, page 61–80.

Appendix **E**

Some Physical Metallurgical Aspects of Ferrous and Non-ferrous Metals

E.1 FERROUS METALS: ALLOTROPY

Iron exhibits allotropy which has been profitably exploited by engineers in the 20th as well as present century Allotropy of an element is the property. By virtue of which the atoms in a perfect crystal are arranged in more than one possible arrangement. The physical properties of any two or more of these allotropic forms are different. In case of iron as an allotropic element these physical properties such as strength, ductility ,shock absorbing ability is very much influenced by the presence of carbon percentage. This particular phenomenon is of great benefit to engineers. Iron forms solid solutions with carbon which are mixtures. At the same time iron also forms compound Fe-3-C called cementite.

A Cooling curve of molten iron shows the formation of various allotropic forms stated earlier.

Figure E.1 shows that melting point of iron = 1539°C. The Figure also shows that essentially 2 allotropic forms of iron exist.

(i) Iron at 3 temperatures

Iron between 910°C and 1401°C. Between 768 and 1539°C iron is weakly magnetic.

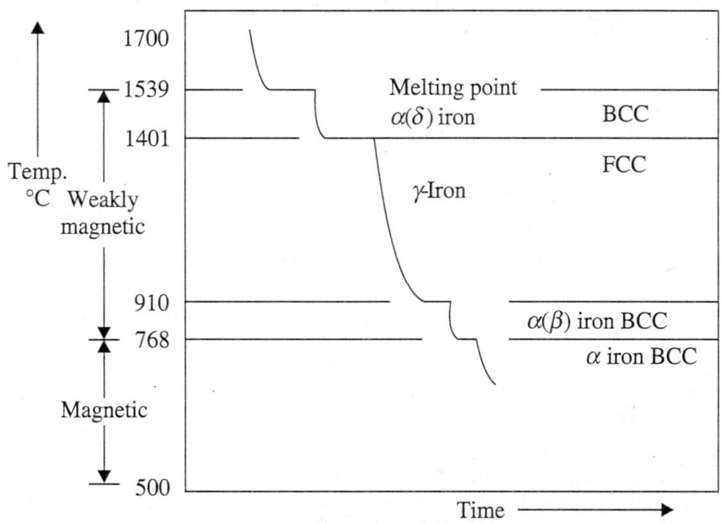

FIGURE E.1 Cooling curve for pure iron showing allotropic change points

Figure E.2 shows the allotropic forms of iron:

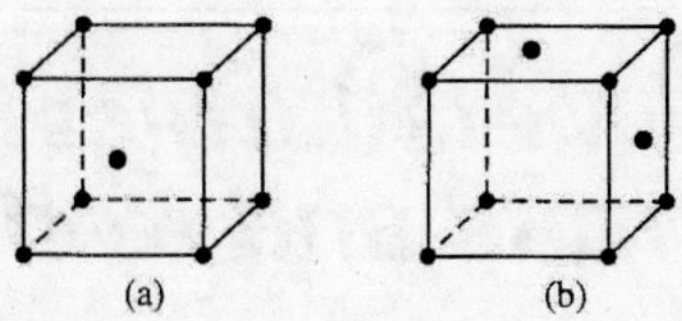

FIGURE E.2 (a) Body centred cubic lattice (b) Face centred cubic lattice—Allotropic (8 and 12 atomic sites) forms of iron.

E.2 EQUILLIBRIUM DIAGRAMS IN FERROUS METALS

In general, solidification of metals and alloys is very clearly understood by seeing the equillibrium diagram. It is a pictorial representation which shown 'change in phase' due to change in concentration of an important element like carbon and temperature in case of Iron–Carbon equilibrium diagram. Due to this, it is also called *phase diagram*. The binary iron–carbon equillibrium diagram is the basis for transformation of phases from pure iron to the compound called *cementite Fe_3C*. Actually, there are two types of iron–carbon equillibrium diagrams.

1. Iron–cementite system
2. Iron–graphite system.

Rapid cooling results in the Fe-Fe_3C system. It is unstable and is rarely used for analysis. On the other hand the Fe-Graphite system is stable. It is often used for analysis. However, the temperatures of transformation for both systems differ very little.

Figure E.3 shows a **simplified** Iron-Carbon equillibrium diagram including liquid phase also.

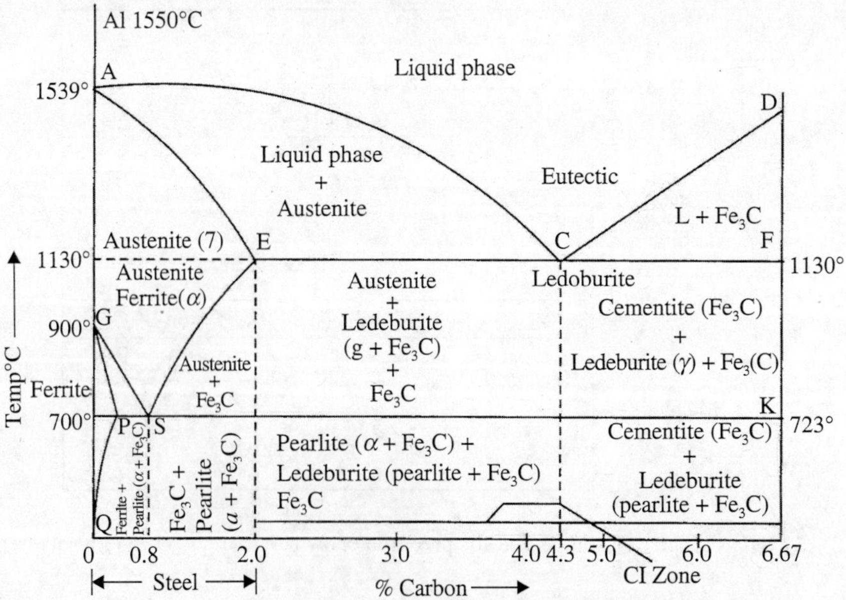

FIGURE E.3 Simplified iron-carbon equilibrium diagram.

Figure E.3 With the various phases labelled on the diagram.

A_1 : Melting point of cementite
A : Melting point of pure iron (1539°C)
E : Solubility limit of carbon in (1130°C) iron

Eutectic: Figure E.3 shows eutectic point C in which the components of the mixture solidity simultaneously at a constant temperature, being thrown out of the mixture at the same time. These are called *eutectic alloys*.

Eutectoid: This occurs in case when the critical phase is solid. A solid solution of ferrite and cementite is formed when carbon percentage is 0.8 percent. It is shown at point S in Figure E.3 and the mixture of crystals is called *ferrite*.

In Ferrous metallurgy, the reader should be conversant with the following nomenclatures shown on the equillibrium diagram.

Ferrite: Solid solution of carbon in α iron.

Austenite: Solid solution of carbon in iron. The solubility of carbon in iron is 2% at 1130°C.
Cementite or Fe_3C: It is not a solid solution of iron with carbon. It has carbon content of 6.67% and melts at 1550°C.

Pearlite: It is the eutectoid of ferrite and cementite. It forms at 0.8% carbon and shines like pearl under the microscope.

E.3 TIME TEMPERATURE TANSFORMATION CURVES

It should be noted that Austenite is formed due to allotropic change when carbon steel is heated to about 724°C. ON rapid cooling, austenite, changes to Martensite where is has a needle like structure. Martensite was first discovered by Hans Martens in Germany. Being too hard, it has to be tempered to its less hard constituents like Bainite, Troostite, Sorbite, etc. to be of any practical utility. It is usual to obtain these less hard constituents in closed bath type Furnaces having optical pyrometers and at constant temperatures to yield the various constituents.

Theoretically speaking it is possible to cool at infinite cooling rate i.e. Instantaneous cooling. In that case a Time–temperature–Transformation (T–T–T) from austenite to its different relatively less harder constituents are achieved as shown in Figure E.4.

Time–Temperature–Transformation–diagrams in theory and practice: Lakhtin, Nayak and others have displayed these T–T–T diagrams. Figure E.4 shows one such curve. To fulfill the requirement of instantaneous cooling at various temperatures, time has to be plotted on a logarithmic scale.

Defining the constituents

- Sorbite is a fine mixture of ferrite + cementite.
- Troostite is a more dispersed mixture of ferrite + cementite
- Bainite is a very intimate mixture ferrite + cementite.

It is formed at a temperature below the nose of the curve.

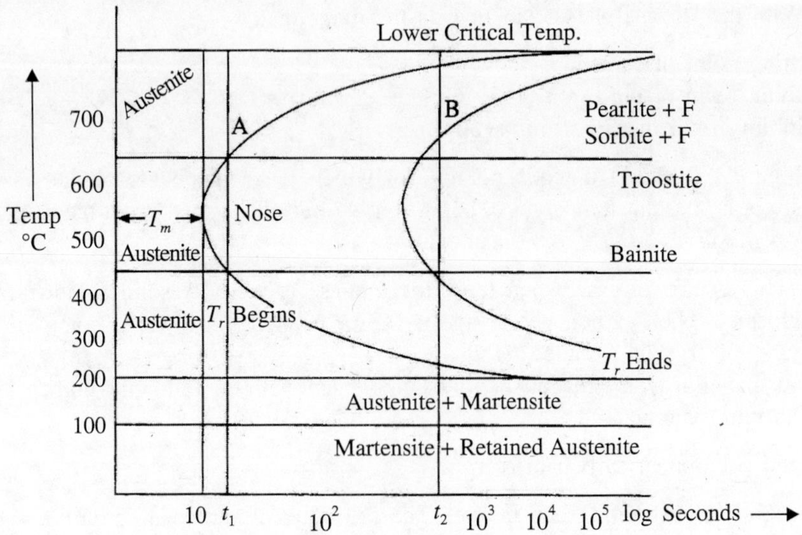

FIGURE E.4 T–T–T diagram for austentic steel.

Practical case when continuous cooling takes place

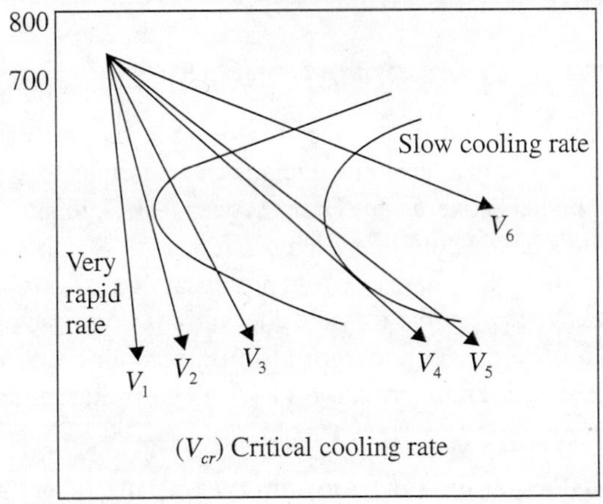

FIGURE E.5 Transformation of supercooled austentic when cooling rate is not infinite.

Referring to Figure E.5, V_6 indicates very slow cooling when pearlite is formed; V_5 is the case of air quenching when sorbite is formed V_4 refers to oil quenching when Troostile. Is formed; V_5 refers to quenching in water when acicular troostite is formed, V_2 and V_1 indicte very fast cooling. V_2 is called *critical cooling rate*. V_1 results in almost total martensite transformation.

E.4 EFFECT OF ALLOYING ELEMENTS ON THE PROPERTIES OF STEEL

Steel is obtained from pig iron due to the reduction of impurities like sulphur, phosphorus, etc. Carbon is the most important element which affects the strength and other properties of steel. It has been shown in Figure E.3 that below 8% carbon, steel is termed as *medium carbon steel.* Below 2%

it is termed as low *carbon steel* and above 1.2% carbon, steel is designated as *high carbon steel.* At and beyond 2%, carbon, iron has saturation with carbon. Carbon is dissolved in iron as graphite. These percentages should be observed in Figure E.3 which is termed *iron-carbon equillibrium diagram.* It is well known that the hardness of steel increases with increase in percentage of carbon. Steel is classified as: (1) Low carbon steel, (2) Medium carbon steel, and (3) High carbon steel depending upon its carbon percentage. Some alloying elements in steel are (Manganese: 1.65% which forms MnS and neutralizes effect of sulphur by forming FeS at grain boundaries which is harmful), (2) Phosphorus 0.4% forms MnP within the grains, (3) Silicon 6%, (4) Sulphur 0.3%.

E.4.1 Alloy Steels

The main objective of this section is to discuss the effect of **other alloying elements**, on the properties of the so called 'Alloy Steels'.

Chromium increases the hardenability of steel. FW Taylor discovered that High speed steel which contains 18% tungsten, 4% chromium and 1% vanadium. Taylor found that chromium in iron increases the depth of case of hardened layer in of steel as shown in Figure E.6.

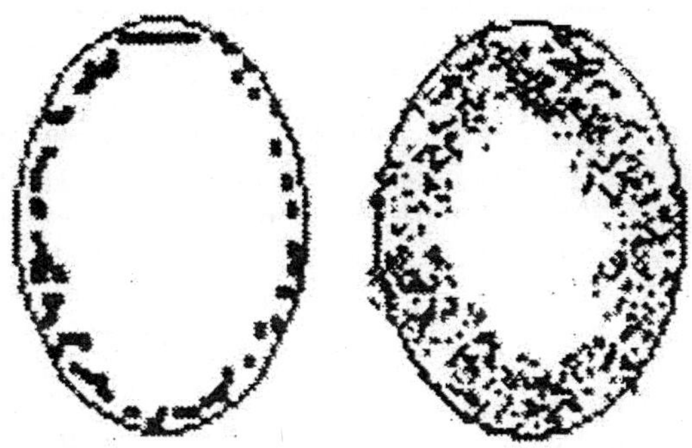

FIGURE E.6 Effect of chromium on depth of case in steel

Figure E.6 showing increased depth of hard layer in steel. Nickel has a unique property of steel in austenitic form at room temperature .Under cutting stresses there forms martensic structure. Molybdenum as discussed by Taylor ascribed it to the formation of fine hard grains of molybdenum carbide. It is a good substitute for Tungsten owing to its low cost. Tungsten is present as tungsten carbide in 18:4:1. HSS is responsible for hard particles of Tungsten Carbide.

Hot hardness: Vanadium does not permit grain growth in HSS, thereby imparting it hot hardness.

E.5 HEAT TREATMENT OF METALS

E.5.1 Quenching

Quenching of steel castings is the first treatment given to achieve martensite from austenite Subsequent tempering treatment is given primarly to give it ductility. Figure E.7 shown the various temperatures and the transforming structures.

Practical application of silicon is acting as a graphitizer when present in steel. It increases the propensity of formation graphite from cast iron. An emperical formula is: carbon equivalent CE% = C% + (Si% + P%)/3.

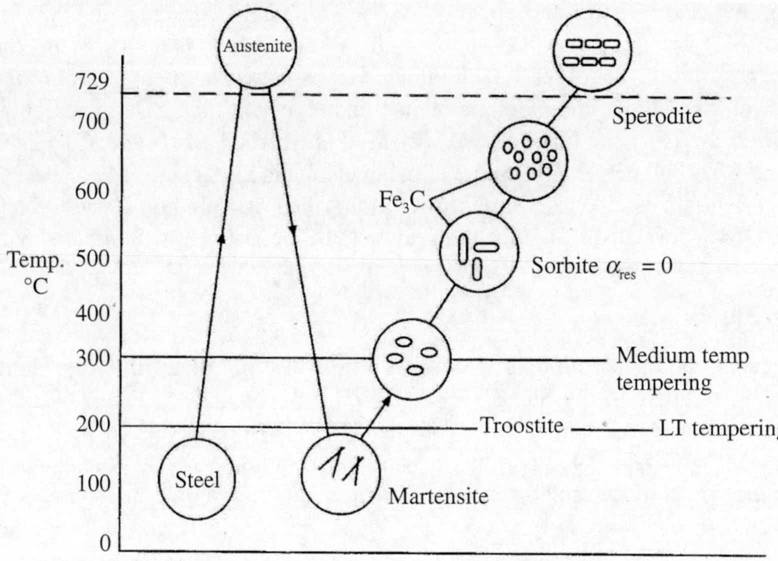

FIGURE E.7 Practical application of tempered martensite.

Table E.1 shows which temperature is suitable for producing which product:

TABLE E.1 Suitable temperature for producing different products.

Temperature °C	*Applications*
228	Screw drivers wtc.
260	Cold chisels, axels
266	Twistdrills, shears
300	Springs
221	Surgical instruments
233	Rolling dies

E.5.2 Annealing and Normalizing

Full annealing is a heat treatment for steel castings which homogenizes the structures and does grain refining. It is known that the grain size increases where, $T_{recrystallization} = (.5\ T_m)$°C. Where T_m is the melting point of steel. Alloying elements like vanadium and chromium need a temperature = .8 T_m for achieving grain growth.

Full annealing consists in heating to the austenite region and holding long enough to allow homogenization of austienite grains.

The casting is then subjected to furnance cooling to allow formation of coarse pearlite. Homogenity temperature is around **85–110°C above upper** critical temperature.

Normalizing consists of homogenizing followed by air cooling. It results in better tensile, yield and inpact properties as compared with annealing. (As shown in Figure E.8 the zone of normalizing is termed comprising *hypoeutectoid composition.* The resulting micro-structure is composed of pearlite and some ferrite. In highly alloyed steels some bainite and martensite is present).

Figure E.8 shows various heat treatment temperatures and carbon percentage zones to enable students to be able to easily distinguish one type of process from other.

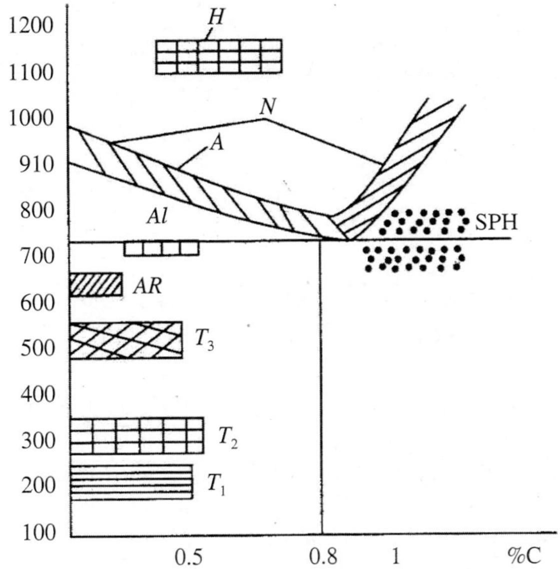

FIGURE E.8 Various heat treatment processes superimposed on Fe-C equilibrium diagram.

Legend:

T_1 : Low temperature tempering
T_2 : Medium temperature tempering
T_3 : High temperature tempering
AR : Annealing for recrystallization
AI : Isothermal annealing
N : Normalizing
A : Annealing
SPH : Spheroidizing
H : Homogenizing

E.5.3 Hardening of Steel

It is a heat treatment process in which steel is heated to a temperature above the critical point and then quenched (rapidly coaled) in water, oil or salt bath. Hypoeutectoid steels are heated 30–50°C above AC_3 while hypereuctoid steels are heated above AG (refer to Figure E.9)

E.5.4 Martempering

After heating steel to the hardening temperature it is quenched in a medium slightly above and below M (150°C to 300°C).

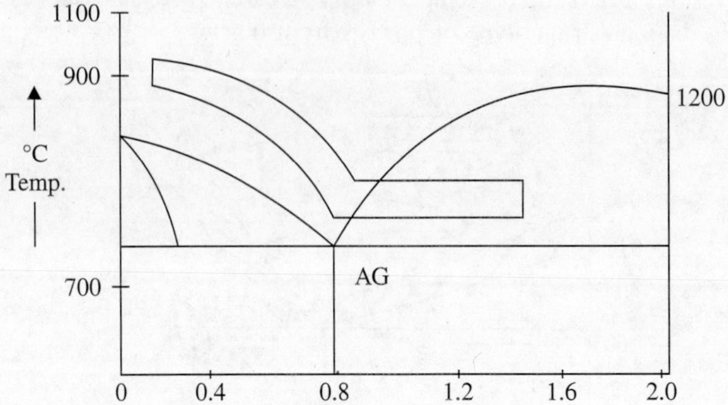

FIGURE E.9. Hardening of steel.

The pieces held until it reaches the temperature of the medium and cooled further to room temperature. Austenite gets transformed to martensite Austempening is a high temperature process in which the piece is heated in a salt bath to about 815°C until there is complete conversion to austenite. The quenching temperature is 200°C–450°C for sometime until there is conversion to Bainite. Austempering cycle is shown in Figure E.10.

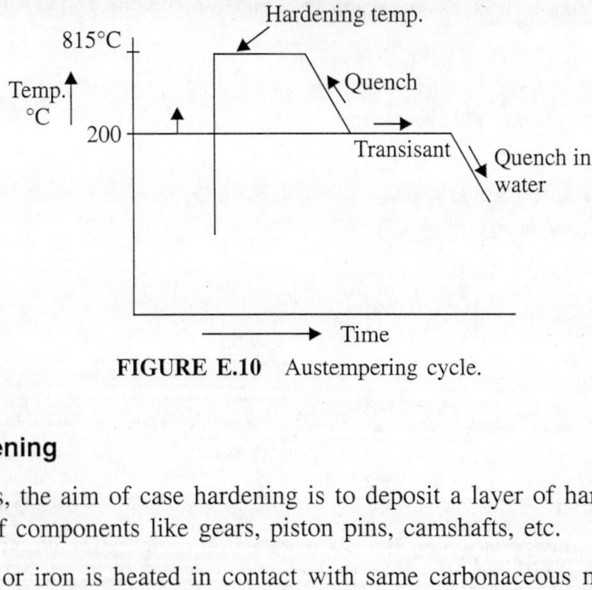

FIGURE E.10 Austempering cycle.

E.5.5 Case Hardening

As the name suggests, the aim of case hardening is to deposit a layer of hard material to improve the wear resistance of components like gears, piston pins, camshafts, etc.

Carburising: Steel or iron is heated in contact with same carbonaceous material like $BaCO_3$ to its critical temperature. The carbon forms a layer of solid solution with iron and results in a hard layer on the surface. Finally heat treating is done to yield hard skin by case hardening. Carburizing develops a layer of high carbon steel with .9–1.2%.

(i) Pack carburizing: In this process, as the same suggests the parts are packed in a metal box and sealed with day after covering with compounds as shown:

Carburizing	% C
Charcoal	80–85%
$BaCO_3$	10–12%
$CaCO_3$	1–30%
Na_2CO_3	1%

Chemical Reaction:

$BaCO_3 \rightarrow BaO + CO_2$

$C + CO_2 \rightarrow 2CO$; $2CO + 3Fe \rightarrow Fe_3C + CO_2$

The compounds on RHS penetrate into surface of the article during heating. The depth of penetration depends upon the time for which the box remains in the furnace. 1.00 mm layer needs 10 hours heating.

After carburizing, the article is subjected to temperature of about 850°C and then quenched in oil for toughening the core and hardening the case.

(ii) Liquid carburizing: A molten salt (850–900) is used. After taking out the article it is quenched immediately.

The salt contains Na_2CO_3 and SiC.

Chemical Reaction:

$$Na_2CO_3 + SiC \rightarrow Na_2SiC + Na_2O + 2CO + C$$

Depth of case is .3 mm in 1 hour.

Gas carburizing makes use of some gas like CH_4, butane, propane, etc., which is circulated in the furnace while the article is heated up. The product of combustion contains diffused carbon and results in carburized layer.

(iii) Nitriding: Ammonia (NH_3) saturates the surface of steel with Nitrogen

$$2NH_3 \rightarrow 2N + 6H$$

Nitrogen diffuses in α iron and then the article is cooled to 200°C. Nitriding is effective for alloys of iron and renders a BHN of 730 = 1100.

(iv) Cyaniding: The articles are immersed in a pot containing sodium cyanide (850°C). The CYN group helps absorption of carbon and nitrogen.

(v) Flame hardening: It makes the use of oxy-acetylene flame for local hardening of articles.

(vi) Induction hardening: High frequency current which flows through a coil heats up the skin of the article. In very few seconds, the article is healed up, removed a sprayed with water to lend a hard layer.

(vii) Precipitation hardening: The example frequency taken up to illustrate precipitation hardening is alloy of copper in aluminum.

The resulting product being lightweight and strong is eminently suited for aircraft manufacture. Figure E.8 explains the 2 important stages (1) In the first stage, a supersaturated solid solution of Cu and Al of the alloy is prepared. This condition shown at (b) in centre is unstable except at high temperature. This is because when quenching is done, (2) In stage two the solubility of copper in aluminium decreases sharply. Very fine particles of copper are distributed throughout aluminium. This is shown on left side in the Figure E.11 at (a) Slow cooling, shown at (c) results in globules of copper in aluminium. The ultimate tensile strength of material at (b) is 16 at (1) is 24 and at (c) it is lesser at 12.

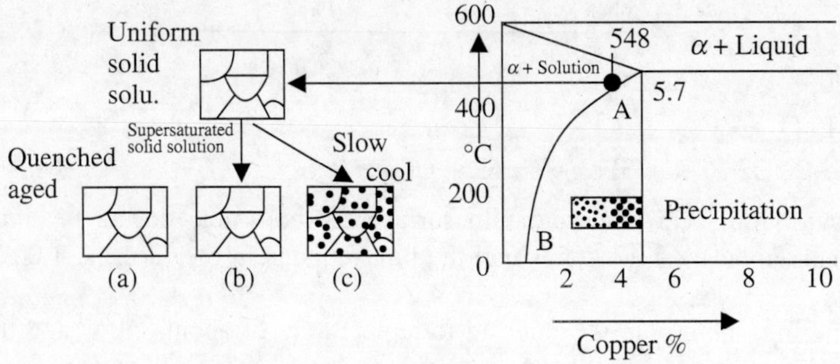

FIGURE E.11 Age hardening process.

E.5.6 Age Hardening of Steel

In case of age hardening of steel, i.e., carbon in kept at 80°C its maximum hardness is reached in 10 hours. If it is kept for 20°C it takes 500 hours. In case of age hardening of steel, both *time* and *temperature* are important for precipitation of carbon.

E6 CAST IRON (C.I.)

Cast iron (C.I.) is derived from pig iron by adding limestone, steel scrap and rejected castings in cupola furnace. Carbon in exists in two forms:

(1) A compound form, cementite Fe_3C. It is known as *white cast iron.*

(2) As free carbon, usually in the form of graphite and is termed *gray cast iron*; mixed C.I contains both the above forms. Cast iron used for engineering application are classified as:

(i) Grey C.I., (ii) White C.I., (iii) Malleable CI., (iv) S.G. C.I., (v) Chilled C.I., (vi) Alloyed C.I., (vii) Meehanite C.I.

E.6.1 Grey C.I.

It is obtained by slow cooling of Iron in which carbon is dissolved. With carbon percentage of more than 2%. It is readily thrown out of solution, being the saturation % of C in iron. Usually other elements like sulphur, phosphorus, silicon and mangnese are also present in Grey C.I in small quantities. Any engineer working on machine tools and cutting grey cast iron will find in a short time that this white shirt will become greyish. The UTS of Grey iron, i.e., 12–13 kgf/mm^2

But it is strong in compression and its compressive strength is 60–75 kg/mm^2. Grey C.I has a melting point 1150°C to 1200°C. It has high degree of fluidity in molten states; it has high machinability and is used where low coefficient of friction and shock absorbing capacity is the demand by designer.

E.6.2 White (Fe_3C)

It is hard, brittle and as the name suggests, gives a white fracture appearance. Rapid cooling rate, presence of manganese and low percentage of silica encourage the formation of white cast iron, technically called *cementite*. It is used in cheap sheet metal working dies as die material.

E.6.3 Malleable C.I.

The so called malleable C.I. is produced from white C.I. There are two methods of producing malleable CI. In the **white heart process**, the white cast iron is decarburised by packing the article in closed, at 950°C for 5 days . Next, it is followed by slow cooling for several more days. The resulting article is a casting which is tough. This process is suitable for small articles, maximum being 150–200 kg. The **black heart process,** on the other hand consists in heating the casting 1000°C for a shorter time, i.e. 2–3 days in a neutral atmosphere. As a result, Fe_3C is converted to a fine blackish structure. Black heart castings are needed where a lot of machining is needed. In recent years spheroidal cast iron has been preferred over malleable cast iron.

E.6.4 S.G. Iron

Spheroidal graphite iron is superior to malleable iron, because of precipitation of graphite in the form of modulus instead of flakes. This is made possible by addition of elements like magnesium, bismith, zinc, boron, etc. SG iron can be made in heavier sections, has much more fluidity. Castings of this type are presently used widely where sealing joint, like cylinder head cover, pipes and fittings are manufactured. S.G. iron has strength 33 kg/mm^2.

E.6.5 Chilled Cast Iron

During solidification of cast iron, the liquid naturally comes in contact with sand and is 'chilled' at its usual pace. But some portions of the castings our surface is intentionally chilled much quicker due to functional requirement of those outer surfaces by employing" chills" made of cast iron. Such chilled surfaces contain Fe_3C, while other parts of the casting are grey cast iron.

E.6.6 Alloy C.I.

Particularly, with Nickel has been found even at small percentage to improve wear resistance to it. Research has shown that nickel keeps austenite form intact ever at room temperature. Chromium is another effective alloying element which increases wear resistance of C.I. nickel added to the tune of 25% makes C.I. corrosion resistant.

E.6.7 Meehanite or Semi Steel

It is formed by adding calcium silicide in the furnace while C.I. is made. The percentage of carbon in meehanite is 2.5% to 3%. 'Meehanite' or semi-steel fills the gap between C.I. and steel and exists in several forms. Each form is suitable for specific application like heat resistance, wear resistance, corrosion resistance, special nodular type, etc. Meehanite responds to heat treatment. Machine tool structures are always made from meehanite. It is a patented form of C.I. and its BHN is about 200.

E.7 NON-FERROUS METALS

In the present section, the most important cast nonferrous alloy groups are taken up in the order of increasing melting point, which also implies increasing cost and difficulty of melting them.

E.7.1 Tin-based Alloys

These are the most widely used metals because tin has the lowest melting point (232°C). It is highly corrosion resistant and nonpoisonous unlike lead. However, its low strength eliminates its use as a construction material.

It is widely used in bearings where its low shear strength and low adhesion to other metals ensures low friction even when conventional oil based lubrication fails. It is widely used in bimetallic bearings where it must be backed by a stronger material. Alternatively, if the bearing layer is to be thicker, it must be strengthened by creating a composite structure developed in which a hard compound is dispersed in the soft tin matrix. This is achieved by adding Sb (antimony) to form the inter-metallic compound SbSn. It is in the shape of small, hard, cubic crystals. Some copper is also added to form a copper-tin alloy which appears as a network of needles and embeds the cuboids as shown in Figure E.12.

FIGURE E.12 Micro structure of tin, antimony and copper

E.7.2 Lead-based Alloys

Lead also has a low melting point (327°C) and good corrosion resistance, but it is poisonous and its use is confined to where human contact is to be avoided. Large lead castings are used as x-ray and γ-ray shields in laboratories and hospitals.

The low strength of lead and its low solubility in other metals makes it useful as a bearing material, of lower quality than tin. Strengthening is again obtained by alloying, so that the SbSn cuboids are dispersed in a matrix of Sn-Pb-Sb eutectic. These ternary alloys are not only hard but also possess a high fluidity due to tin.

Antimony-based lead is very widely used for cast lead-acid battery grids. Great economy is ensured by recycling the majority of all lead used in the metallic form.

E.7.3 Zinc-based Alloys

Zinc is the only low-melting (419°C) metal, widely used as a structural design casting material. Its major weakness is low creep strength. Also, its corrosion resistance is low . However, its high fluidity and low melting point make it very suitable for casting into steel dies. Strengthening is done by solid-solution alloying with approximately 4% A1 and 1–2% Cu. By the use of 99.99% pure zinc and careful control of contaminants, good corrosion resistance is secured, making these alloys highly competent with plastics like trifloro-tetra-ethyelene for thin-walled parts of intricate shape, such as instrument housings and automotive components. Alloy with 11% aluminum offer high strength combines with good fluidity.

E.7.4 Magnesium-based Alloys

The melting point of magnesium is much higher (649°C) but allows casting by using other mould materials, like graphite or plaster of paris. Its low density (1.74 g/cm) and reasonable strength, and corrosion resistance make it suited for structural applications including automobile engine blocks and wheels. The major problem is cost. Casting alloys are solid-solution strengthened, and some precipitation hardening may be obtained by adding Mn, Zr, or Zn. Fluidity is quite adequate because MgO is not dense and does not hinder flow. The Mg-Zn-Zr, rare earth alloys are suitable for service up to 260°C. Grains are refined by adding zirconium.

E.7.5 Aluminium-based Alloys

Melting at an only slightly higher temperature (660°C), almost as light and considerably cheaper than magnesium, aluminium and its alloys represent barring nodular iron the fastest-growing segment of the casting industry. The corrosion resistance of aluminum is excellent to acids and its strength is readily improved through solid-solution and precipitation-hardening mechanisms. In precipitation hardening aluminum is combined with excess of copper and the mixture is rapidly cooled. Later on with ageing the extra copper partly segregates and is dispersed in the matrix to give it added strength. Increased recycling of secondary scrap has reduced the total energy consumed in making aluminum parts.

Pure aluminium is used for domestic utensils. High-conductivity, 99.6% pure aluminum is pressure die cast for applications like electrical motors, etc.

The Al_2O_3 film on the melt is dense and tough and reduces fluidity. The ease of casting is greatly affected by the influence alloying elements on this oxide film. Silicon is most beneficial, making silicon alloys the most cast able aluminum alloys. The eutectic composition (around 12% Si, with a melting point of 577°C) is, of course, the most favourable. Its properties are greatly improved by refining (modifying) the eutectic structure through rapid cooling or, more frequently, by the addition of a small quantity of sodium or strontium to the melt just prior to pouring, after which the eutectic silicon is modified and separates in the form of fine rods or fibers instead of corse flakes. Hypereutectic alloys contain the very hard and brittle silicon is a pro-eutectic form and is thus, extremely wear-resistant. The structure is refined by the addition of 0.01% phosphorus to form aluminum-phosphide nuclei. The hard and brittle silicon of the eutectic limits the ductility of the alloy. Therefore, in the most popular casting alloys some Si is replaced with Cu which increases strength by solid-solution strengthening and also promotes precipitation or age hardening. Castability is still high, especially in die casting where the dendrites are broken by the applied pressure. Hydrogen leads to porosity and scavenging with argon or chlorine just prior to pouring is essential. Grain refinement is achieved by adding TiB alloy nucleating agents.

The use of aluminum alloy castings is very wide ranging and is always worth considering, especially when high strength-to-weight ratio and corrosion resistance are desired. Typical applications include automotive transmission cases, pistons, engine blocks, and some aircraft components. Four important aluminum alloys are (1) **Duralumin** which contains the following alloying elements: copper 3.5–4.5%, manganese 4–7%, magnisum 4–7%. This alloy has a strength of 400 N/mm^2 after heat treatment and precipitation hardening. (2) **Y-alloy** has copper 3.5–4.5%, manganese 1,2–1.7%, nickel 1.8–2.3%, silicon, magnesium, iron 6% each, and is in a cast form. Both the above alloys are eminently suited for aircraft applications. (3) **Magnalium** has 2 to 10% magnesium and 1.75% copper and is used in automotive industry. (4) **Hindalium** is a trademark of Hindalco and contains small percentages of alumonium, chromium and copper. It is used mainly for making utensils.

E.7.6 Copper-based Alloys

The melting point of copper (1083°C) is too high for steel dies unless protected by heavy coatings, but other casting methods are practiced because the metal has attractive color, good corrosion resistance, and high electrical conductivity. There are few copper alloy systems with useful eutectic; therefore, most casting alloys are hardened by adding solid-solution elements, up to the limit of solubility for maximum strength without undue embrittlement by excessive inter-metallic particle content. Whenever the solidification range is wide, fluidity suffers.

Bronzes are essentially copper-tin alloys. (Cu-Sn alloys) have a very long freezing range, and fluidity is increased by added phosphorus which forms a low-melting ternary eutectic. It is as popular as phosphor bronze and also deoxidizes the melt. Hydrogen porosity is prevented by purging with nitrogen. The addition of zinc with its low boiling point also increases fluidity. An 88Cu-10Sn-2Zn alloy has high strength making it suitable for gears, bearings, and pump parts. Lead is often added, primarily to improve machinability. The 85Cu-5Sn-5Pb-5Zn alloy is the most castable of all and is extensively used for fixtures, pump bodies, and general castings. The high lead content in the 80Cu-10Sn-10Pb alloy is suitable for bearing applications.

Phosphor bronze contains Phosphorus and produces sound castings. Normally its tensile strength is 215–280 N/mm^2 but increases to 2300 if rolled or drawn. Its typical percentage is: copper: 87.9%, tin = 9.1% and phosphorus = 0.1 to 0.3%. It is especially suited for protection against salt water.

Aluminum bronzes have a short freezing range and Al_2O_3 reduces fluidity. However, they impart high strength, especially in the heat-treated condition and with iron and other precipitation-hardening additions. Their excellent corrosion resistance makes them favorites for marine applications.

Brasses are Cu-Zn alloys with approximately 50% of each of the above elements Their properties can be controlled by varying the percentage of other alloying elements. They have a short freezing range and are especially suitable for fitting, plumbing fixtures, and other smaller parts. Many casting alloys also contain lead, which improves fluidity.

E.7.7 Beryllium-based Alloys

Only slightly more dense (1.85 g/mm) than Mg but of a much higher melting point (1277°C), Be offers very high stiffness (E = 280 Gpa). Newly developed alloys (30Al-3Ag with Co, Ge, Si additions) allow investment casting of thin-walled parts for aerospace applications.

E.7.8 Nickel and Cobalt-based Alloys

The high melting points of nickel (1435°C) and cobalt (1495°C) and their corrosion resistance make them eminently suitable for many critical applications. Their strength and, particularly, hot strength can be greatly increased with solid-solution and precipitation-hardening alloying elements. Some of these super alloys have such high second-phase content that they are not deformable, and these cast super-alloys can totally replace other materials in high-temperature application, particularly as in case of gas turbine parts.

E.7.9 High-temperature Materials

Some of the higher-melting alloys are used in only specific cases to produce castings.

Titanium (melting point 1670°C) can be alloyed to give high elevated-temperature strength combined with low weight and corrosion resistance. These alloys are thus, used in chemical plants and even in supersonic aircraft construction. The great affinity of Ti to oxygen, the high melting point, and the low fluidity are challenges to the foundry men. Properties of such castings can be greatly improved by High temperature iso-static pressing which is a three-dimensional hot pressing of a casting at a very high temperature.

Refractory metals are resistant to heat and are difficult to melt. The most important ones are: molybdenum, Mo (melting point: 2610°C); columbium, Cb, 2470°C; and tungsten, W (3410°C). They oxidize extremely rapidly. Due to this, special techniques like vacuum arc or electron beam melting and casting techniques are needed. They are indispensable in some very high temperature applications.

REFERENCES

[1] Lakhtin P; *Engineering Physical Metallurgy*, Mir Publications Moscow 1998.

[2] Nayak S.P., *Physical Metallurgy for Engineers*, Charottar publishers 1995.

[3] Lindberg, Roy, *Processes and Materials of Manufacture*, 4th ed., Prentice Hall of India, 1990

[4] Taylor H, M.C. Flemings and John Wulf, *Foundry Engineering*, Wiley Eastern Ltd., New York, 1993.

Appendix F

Example of Applying Autodesk AutoCAD for Solid Modeling an Object Given the Orthographic Views

F.1 SOLID MODELING WITH AUTODESK AUTOCAD

AutoCAD is a Computer modelling software from Autodesk that can be used to create 2D and 3D geometric models of products. It is the most popular CAD software in the market across the World. CAD is an acronym that may be called Computer Aided Drawing or Computer aided Design. In 1963 Ivan Sutherland formulated the theoretical basis for CAD graphics in his PhD Thesis titled "Sketchpad". He demonstrated that graphic entities could be interactively picked on the Computer screen using a light pen. This was the beginning of interactive graphics on computer. This gave rise to the development of techniques for representing images in digital form. In due course of time, advances in computer hardware made larger memory and greater computational capacities possible micro computers and personal computers.

Thus 3D Modeling could be done even on personal computers instead of Large mainframe computers. Solid models are the most accurate and realistic descriptions of any Solid in question. It could be as good as real physical model which would be very costly. Solid models accurately communicate design intent and could be used for Finite Element Method. Fits and tolerances can be visualized in assemblies and misfit can be checked and eliminated. Manufacturing codes for computer numerical control (CNC) can be generated from solid models in Computer Aided Manufacture (CAM). Physical models can be generated from solid models easily and with least effort in Rapid Prototyping and 3D printing. Solid Models can be utilized by other departments, such as marketing, purchasing, etc. For detailed Engineering analysis information is required on material properties and geometric properties like centroid, cross-sectional area and physical properties like mass, weight, CG, moment of inertia, etc. Solid models are useful for such applications. Historically speaking Autodesk was formed by John Walker and his team of programmers in April 1982. AutoCAD was first released by the company in December 1982. By March 1986 it had become the most widely used software in the World. In March 2014, AutoCAD 2015 was released making it 29th Major release by Autodesk for Windows. Presently 2015, 2017 and 2022 versions of Autodesk are widely used across the World.

F.2 DIGITAL SOLID MODELS IN AUTOCAD

A digital solid is a 3D model consists of vertices, edges, faces and partially filled or totally filled interior. AutoCAD uses Constructive Solid Geometry CSG to create complex solids from a combination of simple and Compound solid forms. Simple solid forms are called as "Primitives" and examples could be spheres, boxes, cones, pyramids, torus, etc. Solid forms could be generated from 2D profiles by extrusion or by revolution. Popular commands by Autodesk AutoCAD are extrusion, union, subtract, fillet, intersect, etc. The authors have utilized these commands in the Example taken in this Appendix F.

Example of applying Autodesk AutoCAD for solid modeling an object given the orthographic views

Figure F.1 shows orthographic views of a solid for which solid modeling with Autodesk AutoCAD software has been carried out.

Is also shows elevation and top view of the solid with complete dimensions in both the views.

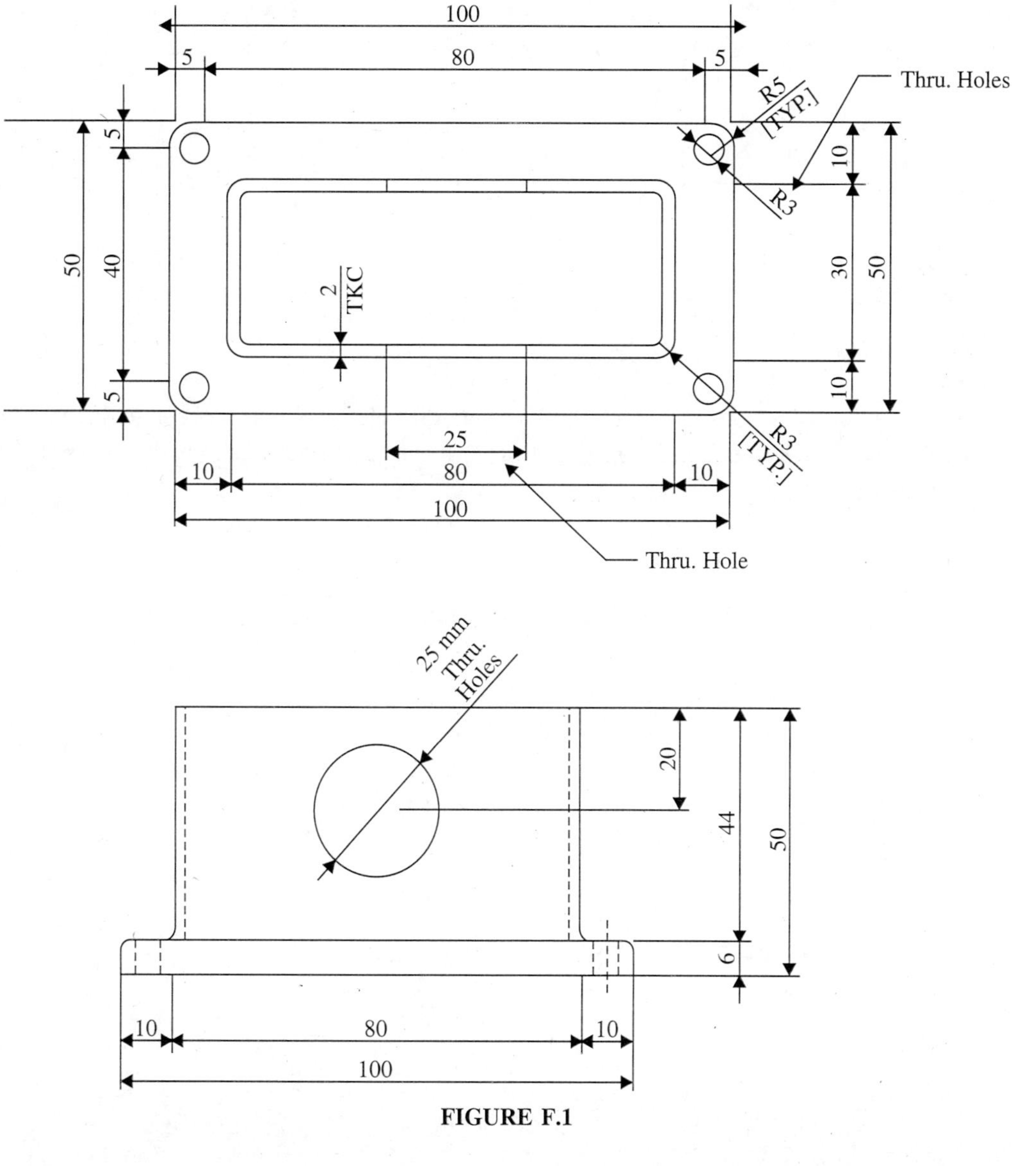

FIGURE F.1

Figure F.2 shows Step 1 and Step 2.

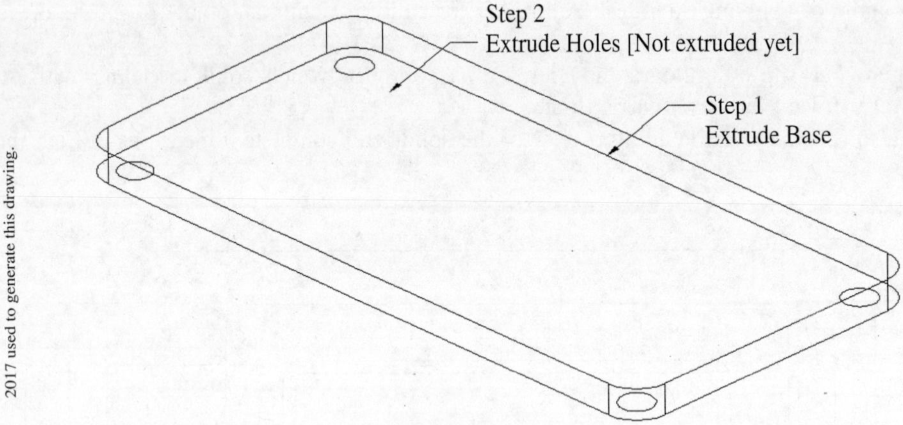

FIGURE F.2

Step 1 shows how a solid rectangular object is extruded from a rectangular base of 100 mm × 50 mm.

Step 2 indicates positions where 4 holes of 5 mm diameter of R5 are to be extruded in a later step. These holes are 90 mm apart along length and 40 mm apart across the width of base of the solid as shown in top view in Figure F.1.

Figure F.3 shows Step 3 "Extrude" holes of diameter 5 mm and extrude base size of 100 mm × 50 mm to yield a rectangular solid.

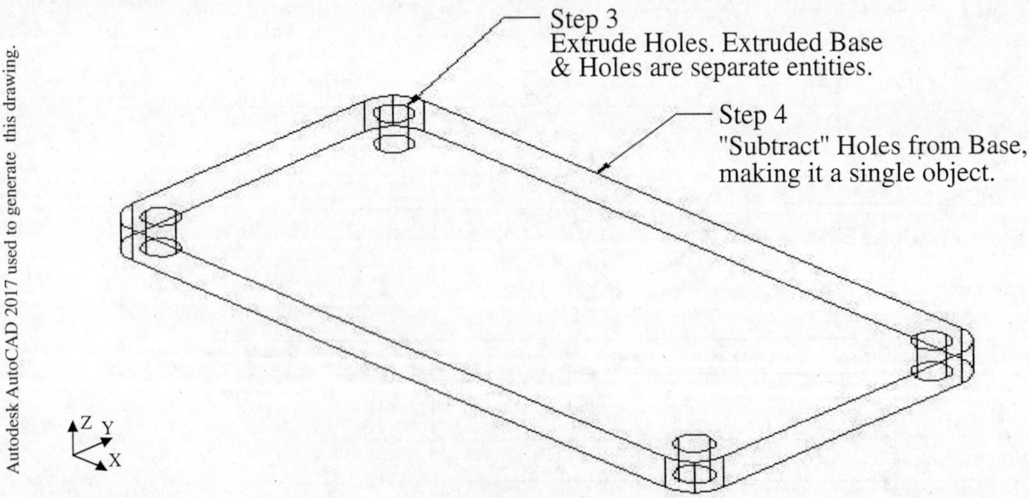

FIGURE F.3

Step 4 "Subtract" 4 holes diameter 5 mm and height 6 mm from rectangular solid base. Now, we have a rectangular base as object 4 holes.

Figure F.4 shows Step 5 "Extrude" exterior body 80 mm in length and 30 mm in width and 44 mm in height.

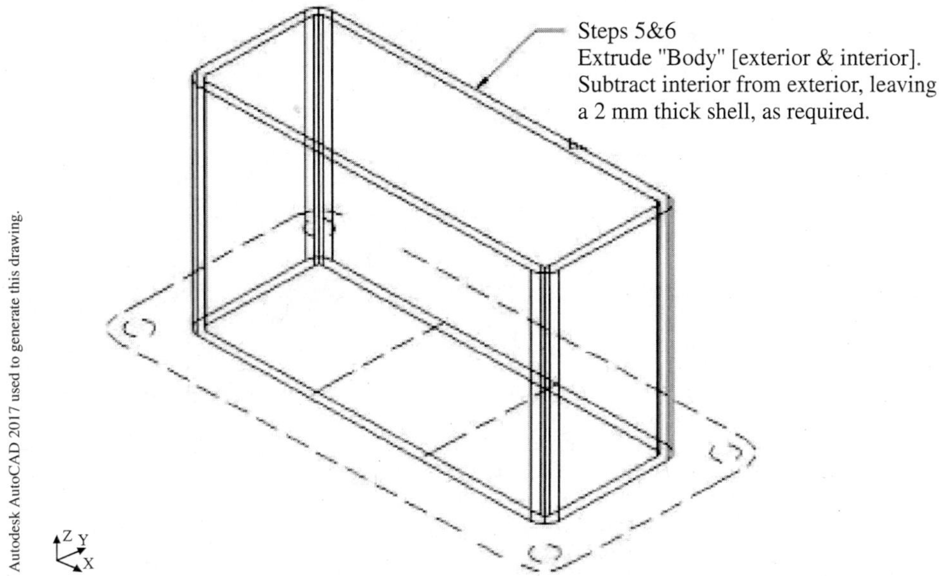

FIGURE F.4

Step 6 "Subtract" interior body 76 mm long, 26 mm wide, and 44 mm in height. This leaves a shell 2 mm thick as required in the drawing. This shell is shown as located on an imaginary base 100 mm × 50 mm.

Figure F.5 shows Step 7 in which body and base are placed together and "Union" command is used to fuse the two together.

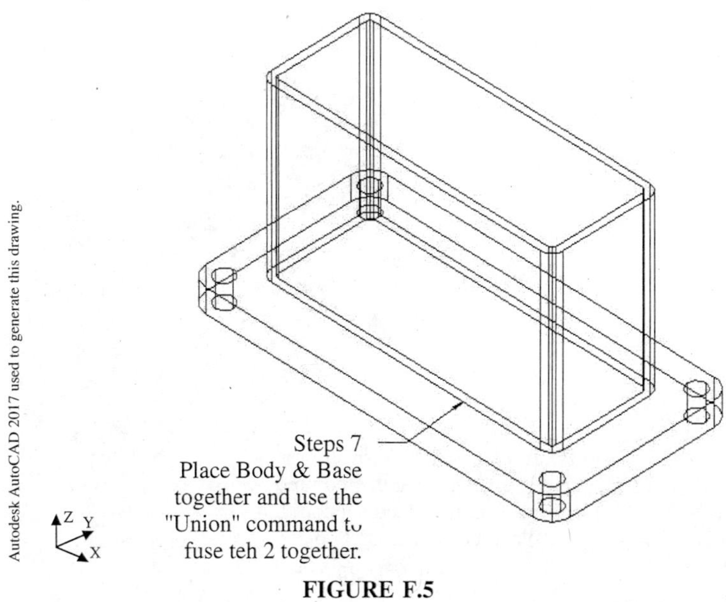

FIGURE F.5

Figure F.6 shows Steps 8 and 9.

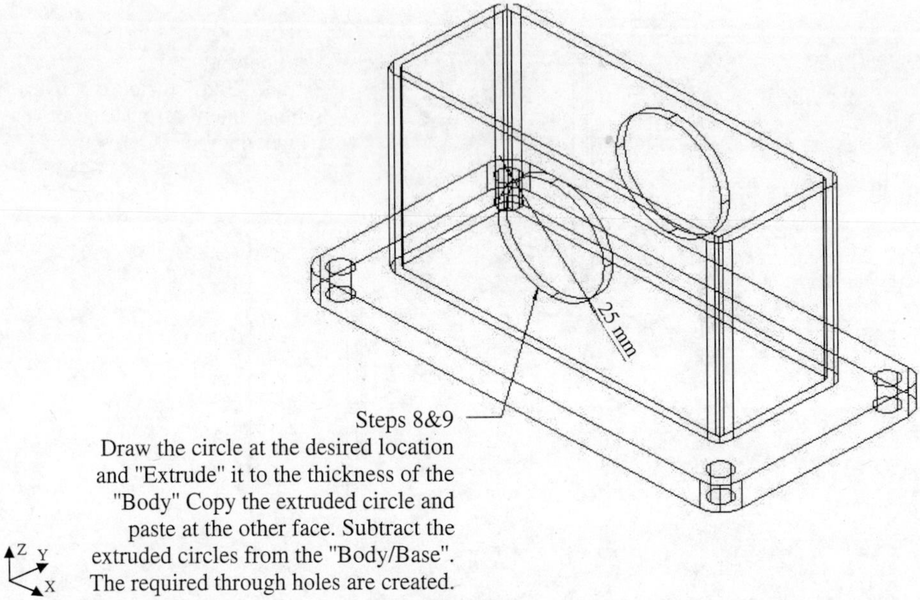

Autodesk AutoCAD 2017 used to generate this drawing.

FIGURE F.6

In Step 8, a circle of 25 mm diameter is drawn at a height of 30 mm from base. A hole of 25 mm is extruded to a thickness of 2 mm of the body. Next, “Copy” the extruded hole of 25 mm diameter in the other face of the wall at 30 mm from the initial face of the wall.

Step 9 “Subtract” extruded circles from body and base. This would create required through holes in the base and the body to complete all the essential features of the object.

Figure F.7 shows Step 10: Make use of “Fillet” command to convert straight edges into curved edges of 3 mm radius (shown as R3 in orthographic view). This view shows shaded version to illustrate the finished solid.

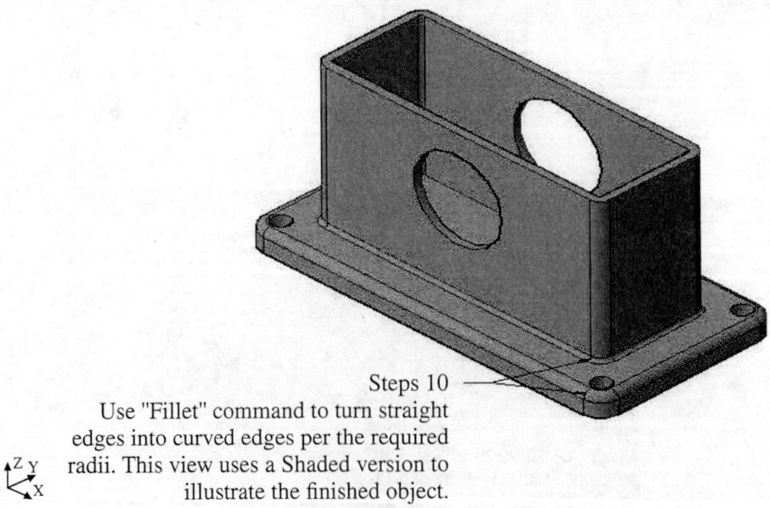

Autodesk AutoCAD 2017 used to generate this drawing.

FIGURE F.7

***Euler's equation applied to the object*:**

$$V - E + F - H + P - 2S = 0 \qquad \text{Eq. (1)}$$

where,

V—Number of vertices or corners in combined solid;
E—Number of edges;
F—Number of faces;
H—Number of holes;
P—Number of passages;
S—Number of shells.

Study of the object in Figure F.7 shows that it is a combination of 2 cubical objects namely, the base and the body. The values of various features are found to be as under from observations:

$$V = 12,\ E = 12,\ F = 10,\ H = 6,\ P = 0,\ 2S = 4$$

Inserting values in Eq. (1) yields 12 – 12 = 10 – 6 = 0 – 4 = 0 which verifies the solidity of the object as per Euler's rule.

REFERENCES

[1] Vijay, History of CAD. http://www.artinlesbase.com/software-articles/history-of-cad.

[2] CAD Software History,http://cadazz.com/cad-software-history.com.

Index

Abrasive, 158
Abrasive jet machining (AJM), 158
Absolute weight, 394
Accelerators or hardeners, 190
Adaptive design, 59
Adhesiveness, 196
Aesthetic aspect (of product), 34
Aesthetics, role of, 47
Agrawal, H.N., 86
Air conditioning, 303
Air movement, 302
Air pressure moulding, 204
Allowance, 18
Allowance *A* for drill, 177
Alloyed cast iron, 109
Alting, Leo, 148, 161
Aluminium, impact extrusions, 121
Analysis
  break even, 32, 264, 276
  of grinding process, 276
  of metal cutting process, 144, 149
  of metal forming mechanics, 115
  of product aesthetics, 47
  of the product, 32
  of turning operation, 147
Anthropometric data, 243, 287
Anthropometry, 243
AOQ, 411
AOQL, 411
Appearance significance of, 38, 282, 335
Arc welding, 116, 128, 132
Arch bridge supports, 74
Arithmetic mean (AM), 257
Arkles, B., 187, 205, 227
Artifical intelligence, 361
Asimow, M., 1, 4, 12, 22
ASRS system, 385
Assembly, 18
  atmospheric surfaces, 20
  attribute listing technique, 316
  auditory and kinesthetic sensory channels, 296
  designer, 323, 392
  line, 273
Automated drafting, 347
Automated guided vehicle, 383
Automation, 273

Balance, 49
  of strength, 70
Balanced design, 65
  for gear and pinion teeth, 68
Barrier of indifference, 43
Basic form elements, 48
Bath tub curve, 434
Beams, elastic and plastic behaviour, 83
Bedworth, David, 288, 392
Bending, 119
  of a curved beam, 67
Benefits
  of CAD/CAM, 348
  of CAPP, 360
  of CIM, 351
  from concurrent design approach, 392
Benzene, 191
Bhattacharya, Amitabh, 133, 148
Biasing, 54
Biodiversity, 515
Body size and posture, 289
Bolted assembly, 65
Bond strength, 150
Boothroyd. R.J., 392
Bouey, 255, 284, 308
Brainstorming technique, 315
Bralla, James, 184, 199, 205, 225, 239
Brazing, 129
Break-even chart, 229, 233, 273, 276
Break-even point, 228, 232, 272, 275
Breathing (a mould), 197
Brittle (materials), 70
Buckling
  and instability, 77
  local, 77

Budynas, S., 65
Buna, N., 208
Buna, S., 208
Bush cut from extrusion, 234
Business analysis, 477
Business process reengineering (BPR), 395
Butyl rubber, 208

CAAP, types of, 360
Campbee, J.A., 169, 170, 183
Cantilever beams, 65
Carbon dioxide process for moulding, 102
Cardboard models, 85
Cascading, 55
Cast copper alloys, 111
Casting
- of plastic, 201
- process, 101
- resins, 196

C-clamp, 63
Ceiling heaters, 303
Cellular manufacturing, 382
Cement bonded sand moulds, 102
Centrifugal casting, 114
Ceramic moulds, 103
Ceramics, 215
Ceramics and glass parts, design of, 238
Ceramics and glass, properties of, 238
Chain polymerization, 191
Checklisting technique, 315
Chemistry of plastics, 190
China clay, 215
Chip formation mechanism, 143
Chow, W.W., 74, 75, 92, 225
Chrysler corporation, 47
CIM, information flow of, 350
Classification and coding of parts, 357
- of casting, 113
- of plastics, 196
- of resins, 197

Clay-based ceramics, 215
Clay studies, 46
Closed-die forging design, 122
Cloud, P.J., 227, 248
Coatings, 220
Co, N, laser, 161
Cochran, W.G., 17, 29
Columns
- design of, 81
- failure of hollow, 81
- hollow, 81
- length formula for, 82
- one end fixed and one lateral support, 79
- one end fixed and two lateral supports, 79
- Rankine-Gordon's formula, 96

Commercialization (or launch), 481
Communication network, 352
Compact design, 273
Compacted graphite cast iron, 108
Compatibility, 335
- analysis, 15
- and matching, 56

Competitiveness (of the product), 274
Complementary product planning, 273
Component with bosses, 168
Composite materials, 72
- FRC, 221
- particulate, 221

Composite part, 358
Compression
- bucking, 201
- moulding, 197

Computer aided design (CAD), 340
Computer aided manufacturing (CAM), 340
Computer control (in FMS), 367
Computer integrated manufacturing (CIM), 294, 296, 349, 351
Computer, role of, 340
Concave and plate, 64, 65, 74
Concave spherical surfaces, 178
Concept development and testing, 477
Concept formulation, 332
Concurrent design, 377, 400
Condensation reaction, 192
Conical springs with plastics, 226
Contact lay-up method, 202
Control, 291
- positions, 292
- stereotypes, 293
- types of, 292

Control charts, 423
- for averages, 424
- for number of defectives, 430
- for number of defects, 431
- for range, 424

Controls, identification of, 293
Conventional extrusions, 121
Convex end plate, 74
Cooling curves, 211
Co-polymerization, 190
Core, 101
- sand moulding, 102

Cored holes, 179
Corner radii, 127

Costs, 336
  fixed, 272
  fixed and variable, 272
Cox, D.L., 17, 29
Crawford slip writing techniques, 318
Creative
  design, 60, 337
  phase, 325
  process, 313
  techniques, 315
Creativity, 313
  blocks to, 314
  factors conducive to, 314
  step, 312
Creativity evaluation, the comparison checklist, 317
Creep, 225
Critical path analysis, 484
Cultural blocks, 314
Cusum charts, 433
Cutting coolents, 155

Davies, O.L., 17, 29
Deep drawing, 119
Defect free or fail safe design, 266
Degree of difficulty, 256
Design
  approaches, 249
  of brazed joints, 131
  of components, 16
  consideration for casting, 111
  consideration for metal forming, 120
  consideration for weldings, 129
  of controls, 291
  creativity with hinges, 228
  criteria and objective of, 70
  criterion, 3, 23
  detailer, 392
  of displays, 294
  for ergonomics, 59
  by evolution, 1
  factors for ceramic parts, 239
  of grooves, 241
  group, 60
  for holes in rubber, 232
  ideas with wood joints, 246
  innovation, 2
  for machining, 176
  for maintainability, 58
  organisation, 60
  phases and flowcharting, 11
  of plastic parts, 205
  with plastics, 229
  preliminary, 8, 14
  problem identification and formulation, 12
  process, 4
  for production, 57, 167
  recommendations for ceramics, 239
  for reliability, 269
  of rubber parts, 231
  for safety, 265, 266
  for stability, 62
  of studs, 72
  of subsystems, 16
  tests, 26
  for transportation, 58
  tree, 5
  types of, 59
Designer, role of, 42
Designing for uniform strength, 72
Detailed design, 8, 16
  of parts, 17
DfE agenda—drivers, goals and team, 515
Dhillon, B.S., 409
Diagonal ribs, 91
Die casting, 113
Die design for compression moulding, 198
Diffusion models
  Bass model, 502
  exponential model, 502
  Fisher and Pry model, 500
  Fourt and Woodlock model, 499, 500
Dimensions
  of modelling, 345
  of models, 345
  for ribs in ceramics, 242, 243
Disc in torsion, 77
Display, 295
  design of, 295
  digital, 296
  fixed pointer moving scale, 296
  moving pointer fixed scale, 296
  pictorial, 295
  qualitative, 295
  quantitative, 296
Distortion in rubber, 236
Draft, 125
  in ceramics, 241
  on rubber parts, 234
Drawing, 119
Drilling, 142
Drilling torque and thrust, 146
Dry sand moulding, 102
Ductile cast iron, 108
Dynamic similarity, 25

Earthenwares, 216
Eco-indicator 95, 508
Economic
    analysis, 274
    factors, 264
    feasibility, 22
    of FMs, 368
    of a new product, 281
    worthwhileness, 369
Eilon, S., 30, 36, 62, 279, 283
El Wakil, S.D., 122, 166
Elastic bucking, 82
Elastomers, 190
Electric discharge machining (EDM), 160
Electric lamps, 304
Electrochemical machining (ECM), 159
Electron beam machining (EBM), 160
Elegance and rhythm, 50
Emotional blocks, 314
End plates (of steel and cast iron), 74
Engineering design, 337
Environment, 335
Environmental impact factor, 515
Equalizing radius *R*, 182
Equilibrium condition, 116
Ergonomics, 284
Essential factors of product design, 2
Ethylene monomer, 189
Euler, L., 29
Euler's model for buckling, 80
Evaluation phase, 313
Evolution compression techniques, 317
Expanded metal products, 185
Expanded plastic, 204
Expanded product life cycle, 470
Experimental construction, 17
Expert systems, 362
Extrusion, 119
    of plastics, 201

Factor of safety, 267
Failure modes and effects analysis, 443
Fasteners (in plastic), 228
Feasibility ranking matrix, 325
Feasibility study, 7
Feldspar, 215
Ferrous metal, 107
Fibre reinforce plastics (see FRP)
Fillers, 190
Fillet radii, 127
Financial feasibility, 3, 14
Finite element analysis, 346
Fits
    clearance, 19
    types of, 19
Fitting trials, 291
Fixed and variable costs, 272
Flames, 139
Flash (in rubber), 235
Flask, 101
Flexible manufacturing cell, 366, 368
Flexible manufacturing systems, 362, 364
Floor heaters, 303
Flow and value addition, 6
Fluid flow analogy, 65
FMEA, 462
Foldable stackable design, 273
Ford Motor Company, 47
Forged and forged cum welds, 171
Forging, 119
    design, 168
Formal optimization, 15
Forming
    of plastic sheets, 204
    practical details, 118
    process, 115
Fracture, 70
French, M., 62, 76, 99
Friction
    angle, 144
    coefficients of plastics, 225
FRP, 202, 217
    contact lay-up method, 202
    design rules, 218
    filament winding, 217
    hand lay-up process, 217
    matched SMC moulding, 217
    rubber bag method, 202
Function, 311, 331
    analysis phase, 325
    analysis, 309
    cost worth analysis, 325
    glass making oxides, 213
    of the product, 377
Functional
    aspect, 34
    constraints, 248
    design practice, 54, 57
    requirements, 265
Fused deposition modelling (FDM), 404
Fusion (liquid state) welding, 128

Gas
turbines, 57
welding, 128, 139
Gear
with curved arms, 77
in plastic, 227
produced by P/M, 184
train, 69
Generalized yielding, 82
Generative type, 360
Geometric mean (GM), 257
Geometric modelling, 342
Geometric programming, 256
Geometry, 334
Ghosh, Amitabh, 148, 166
Glare, 305
Glass, 210
type materials, 210
Glass making oxide, 211
Glassy state, 210
Goods
convenience, 468
industrial, 468
shopping, 468
speciality, 468
Goals, 516
Gordon technique, 315
Graphite moulds, 106
Gravity die casting, 113
Green sand mould, 101
Grill, 186
Grinding, 143
on ceramics, 243
as micromilling, 149
ternery diagram, 223
vitrified bond, 223
wheel specification, 150, 223
Grit size (Mesh No.), 150
Group technology, 273

Habitual blocks, 314
Hall, Robert, 395
Harry, M., 449
Heat transfer, 162
Heat treatment cycle, 109
Heating, 301
of thermoplastic, 192
Hendersen, M., 349, 392
High frequency resistance welding, 138
High impact styrene, 71
High pressure laminates, 201
Hollow and solid noncircular sections, 88
Honing, 157
House of quality for QFD process, 487
Human engineering considerations, 284
Human factors engineering, 284
Human motor systems, 284
Humidity, 302

IDC, 42
Idea generation, 473
Idea screening, 475
Ideation, 314
Identity matrix, 256
Impact based design, 71
Impact extrusion, 121
Inclined planes and lines, 52
Incubation, 314
Industrial designer, 392
problems faced by, 45
procedure adopted by, 45
Inequality constraints, 253
Information, 7
step, 311
system phase, 324
Initial stresses, 69
Injection moulding, 199
Instrument design, 71
Interference fit, 19
Interlocks, 267
Intermediate glass formers, 212
Islands of automation, 350
Isometric application (of forces), 287
Isotonic action, 287

Johnson, R.C., 15, 115, 166, 263
Johnson's method of optimum design, 260
Johnson's parabolic formula, 81
Joining processes, 128
Joint design, 130
Joints, 53
Just in Time (JIT)
manufacturing, 372
and product design, 370

Kanban or visible card system, 370, 392
Kaolinite, 215
Kinesthetic feedback, 287
Kinetic energy, 71
Kovan, V., 167, 188

Lagrange expression, 251
Lagrange multipliers, 251
Laminations, 220

Laminated object modelling (LOM), 404
Landfills, 568
Lapping, 157
Laser beam machining (LBM), 162
Latent existence, 7
Layer(s)
  datalink, 353
  internetwork, 353
  physical, 353
  presentation, 354
  session, 354
  transport, 354
Lead time (LT), 361
Lever design, 171
Life cycle strategies and questions, 516, 517
Lifting and carrying, 285
Lighting, 303
  level, 304
Linear programming, 252
Liquid core binders, 196
Loam moulds, 103
Local
  bucking, 78
  yielding, 81
Locked up stresses, 225
Long columns, theory of, 78
Lost wax process, 105
Lot sizing concept, 361
Louver design, 186
Low polymer, 189

Machinability, 150
  index or rating, 151
Machine cells using PFA, 359
Machine tool
  design, 71
  in FMs, 364
Machining process, 140
  forming, 166
  generating, 165
  principles, 164
Magnesium alloys, 111
Mallik, A.K., 148
Malleable cast iron, 108
Malleabilizing cost, 109
Man/machine information exchange, 296
Man/machine interface, 296
Manufacture of glass, 213
Manufacturing automation protocol (MAP), 353
Margin of safety, 277
Market research, 32
Marketing manager, 392
Marketing strategy, 275
Matched metal moulding method, 203
Material
  handling systems in FMS, 366
  requirements, 334
  saving, 91
  saving in design, 85
  toughness, 71
Material requirement planning (MRP), 361
Material selection, 334
  parameters, 335
Materials engineer, 392
Mathematical models, formulation of, 15
Maximum value, 310
McCormick, E.J., 284, 307
Measurement
  techniques, 308
  of value, 309
Membrance
  analogy, 87
  structures, 89, 95
Merchant constant *C* values of, 146
Merchant, M.E., 144, 146
Merchant's circle diagram, 144
Merchants analysis, utility of, 145
Metal cutting, 151
  economics, 151
Metal inert gas welding (MIG), 138
Metal parts, 167
Michael Hammer and James Champy, 393
Michell strain fields, 77
Microfinishing operations, 157
Micrometer, 70
Miles, L.D., 308, 339
Milling, 143
MIL-STD (US) 105D, 420, 421
Mistake proofing, 266
  devices, 368
Mock-ups, 46
Models, types of, 24, 46
  analogue, 24
  clay, 24
  mathematical, 25
  scale, 24, 62
Modelling, 24
Modifiers, 190
Modular design gear, 228
Moh scale, 150
Mohr, J. Gilbert, 240
Momentum, 286
Monomeric ethylene, 189
Morphological analysis, 315
Morphological approach, 316

for machine element, material and process, 323
Morphology, 4
of design (the seven phases), 7
Motor mount, 186
Moulded bush, 234
Moulding, 163
permanent, 163
plaster, 163
Mudge, A.E., 309, 339
Multiproduct, profit volume chart, 280
Multivariable chart, 336
Muscle contraction and energy release, 287

Natural rubber, 206
NC part programming, 340
Neoprene, 209
Network
architectures, 353
formers, 211
modifiers, 212
structure, 353
New product adoption categories, 490
New product strategy, 466
NID, 42
Noise, 300
Nonferrous metals, 110
Nontraditional machining processes, 158
Normal working area, 298
NPD (new product development), 465, 470
flow/chart, 472
models, 485
sources of, 473
Nylon, formation of, 76

OC curve, 409
Objective function, 248
Ohno Taichi, 368, 392
Operational
aspect, 35
overheads ratio, 271
point, 56
Optimality, 3
Optimization, 248
by calculus approach, 250
by evolution, 249
by intuition, 249
by numerical algorithm, 250
Optiz product classification, 372
Order, 48
Orientation, 314
Ozone layer, 508, 509

Packaging, 37
Paint strips, 384
Pallet pool and rotary buffer, 365
Paraffin (aliphatic), 191
Parallel system, 268
Parker, D.E., 319, 339
Parting line, 122
Pattern, 101
Perceptual blocks, 314
Permanent moulds, 106
Phenol formaldehyde, 196
Phillips 66 Buzz Session techniques, 318
Physical reliability, 2, 14
Planning
computer added process, 359
for consumptions, 10
for distribution, 10
the production process, 9
for retirement, 10
Plaster moulds, 103
Plastic(s), 189
bearing, 226
bush bearing, 226
deformation, 83
design, 83
advantages of, 84
disadvantages of, 84
properties of, 195
Plasticity, condition of, 116
Plasticizers, 190
Pockets and recesses, 128
Point of inflexion, 251
Polybutadiene styrene copolymer, 194
Polycode classification, 357
Polymer PE (polyethylene), 191
Polymer, thermal behaviour of, 193
Polymeric ethylene, 189
Polymerization, 182
Polymers, molecular structures of, 190
Polynomial, 256
Polypropylene (PP), 191
Polystyrene, 191
Polytetrafluoethylene, (PTFE), 191
Polyurethane, structure of, 194
Polyvinyl chloride (PVC), 191
Polyvinyl fluoride, 191
Polyvinylidene chloride, 191
Poplietal height, 286
Population stereotypes, 294
Porcelain, 215

Post forming, 204
Prandtl, L., 87
Prandtl's analogy for noncircular prisms, 87
Precision moulding, 103
Preparation, 260
  of assembly drawings, 17
  for design, 16
Pressed components design, 171
Pressure welding, 128
Price structure, 271
Pricing strategy, 274
Primary processes, 101
Principal stress trajectories, 63
Process analysis of Booz, Allen and Hamilton model, 471
Process planning, 380
Process selection, 333
  parameters, 334
Producibility, 336
Product, 309
  augmented, 466
  characteristics, 34
  classification, 467
  cycle with computer, 342
  definition, 465
  design engineer, 393
  design practice and industry, 30
  development, 468
  development and testing, 478
  development life cycle, 469
  diffusion model, 499
  expected, 466
  generic, 466
  idea calculations, 476
  launch cycle, 482
  management, 468
  marketing manager, 394
  and market, 32
  market matrix, 467
  message, 53
  parameters, 333
  potential, 466
  profiles, 476
  test programme, 17
  value, 220
Product design, essential factors of, 2
Production
  consumption cycle, 5
  cycle and CAD/CAM, 340
  design, 57
  engineer, 394
  flow analysis (PFA), 358
  by masses, 1
  process for rubber, 230
  processes, 100
  scheduling, 340
  systems as decided by variety and schematic layout, 363
  volume, 334
Product life cycle (PLC)
  concept utilization (Yoram Wind), 492
  extensions, 498
  and marketing strategy, 496
  and profitability, 498
  stages in, 488, 491, 494
Profit volume chart, 279
Programmable logic controller, 387
Properties
  of ceramics and glass, 238
  of plastics, 195
Proportion (of the object), 50
Prototypes, 46
Pull system, 369
Punching and blanking, 120
Punchout holes, 127
Pure columns, 76
Pure struts, 76

Quality
  assurance, 266
  of conformance of performance, 409
  control, 266
  control specialist, 394
  of design, 408
  six sigma, 449
  table, 397
Quality function deployment (QFD), 395, 401

Radial wear (cm/hr), 227
Rake angle, 144
Range of body size, importance in design, 289
Rao, P.N., 115, 166
Rapid prototyping, 402
Reaction injection moulding, 217
Reamed holes, 177
Recycling, 510, 511
Redesign, 17, 520
Reduction
  of in-house production cost, 275
  of variety, 41
Regeneration, 55
Regional constraints, 248
Reinforcement, achieving balance through, 85
Reinforced plastic moulding, 202